Elizabeth Gaskell

WIVES AND DAUGHTERS:
An Every-day Story

Edited and introduced by
GRAHAM HANDLEY

EVERYMAN
J. M. DENT · LONDON
CHARLES E. TUTTLE
VERMONT

Series Editor for the Everyman Elizabeth Gaskell
Graham Handley

Introduction and other critical material
© J. M. Dent 2000

This edition first published by Everyman Paperbacks
in 2000

J. M. Dent
Orion Publishing Group
Orion House
5 Upper St Martin's Lane
London WC2H 9EA
and
Tuttle Publishing
Airport Industrial Park
364 Innovation Drive
North Clarendon, VT 05759-9436

Typeset by SetSystems Ltd, Saffron Walden
Printed in Great Britain by
The Guernsey Press Co. Ltd, Guernsey C.I.

British Library Cataloguing-in-Publication Data
is available upon request

ISBN 0 460 87651 1

For Joan Leach, with warm regard

CONTENTS

NOTE ON THE AUTHOR AND EDITOR

ELIZABETH GASKELL was born Elizabeth Cleghorn Stevenson in Chelsea, London, on 29 September 1810. Her father, William Stevenson, who had been a Unitarian preacher, was a clerk and also a journalist at this time. After the death of her mother, when Elizabeth was a year old, she was sent to Knutsford in Cheshire (the town upon which Cranford is modelled) where she was brought up by her aunt, Hannah Lumb. She attended the Misses Byerleys' school in Warwickshire 1821–6. In 1832 she married William Gaskell, a minister at Cross Street Unitarian Chapel, Manchester. The Gaskells had six children, two sons dying in infancy. To alleviate her grief Mrs Gaskell began writing fiction: her first stories appeared in Howitt's Journal in 1847, and Mary Barton, her novel about industrial life in Manchester, in 1848. Despite these being published anonymously, her name became known. She contributed stories and then Cranford to Charles Dickens's magazine Household Words from 1850 onwards. Ruth (1853) boldly dealt with the controversial subject of the unmarried mother, while North and South was serialized in Household Words in 1854–5. Her next major undertaking, at the suggestion of Patrick Brontë, was The Life of Charlotte Brontë (1857). Mrs Gaskell was an untiring worker in support of her husband in Manchester, but she also found time for much travel in Europe. She produced a remarkable number of stories which reflect her talent. Sylvia's Lovers (1863) is a major historical novel, while her masterpiece, Wives and Daughters (1864–5), was unfinished at her death from a heart attack at Alton, Hampshire, on 12 November 1865.

GRAHAM HANDLEY is series editor for the Everyman Elizabeth Gaskell, for which he has edited Cranford and Mr Harrison's Confessions. He has written widely on nineteenth-century literature and has edited works by George Eliot and Anthony Trollope, and Emily Brontë's *Wuthering Heights*. His books include *George Eliot: The State of the Art* (1990), *George Eliot's Midlands: Passion in Exile* (1991), *Criticism in Focus: Jane Austen* (1992) and *Trollope the Traveller* (1993).

ACKNOWLEDGEMENTS

The editor and publishers wish to thank the following for permission to use copyright material: Faber and Faber Ltd for material from Jenny Uglow, *Elizabeth Gaskell: Her Life and Works* (1993); Manchester University Press for material from Arthur Pollard, *Mrs Gaskell: Novelist and Biographer* (1965); Open Gate Press for material from JG Sharp, *Mrs Gaskell's Observation and Invention*, Linden Press (1970) pp. 483–5; Oxford University Press for material from Winifred Gerin, *Elizabeth Gaskell* (1976); Routledge for material from Angus Easson, *Elizabeth Gaskell*, Routledge & Kegan Paul (1979). Every effort has been made to trace the copyright holders but if any have been inadvertently overlooked the publishers will be pleased to make the necessary arrangement at the first opportunity.

CHRONOLOGY OF ELIZABETH GASKELL'S LIFE

Year	Age	Life
1810		Born 29 September, second surviving child of William and Elizabeth Stevenson, in Chelsea, London. (An older brother, John)
1811	1	October. Her mother dies. In November Elizabeth is taken to Knutsford, Cheshire, where she will be brought up by her aunt, Hannah Lumb
1821	10	Goes to the Misses Byerleys' school at Barford, Warwickshire

CHRONOLOGY OF HER TIMES

Year	Literary Context	Historical Events
1812	Birth of Charles Dickens Crabbe, *Tales* Byron, *Childe Harold's Pilgrimage*	
1813	Jane Austen, *Pride and Prejudice*	Wellington defeats French at Vittoria, Spain
1814	Scott, *Waverley* Wordsworth, *Excursion*	
1815		Battle of Waterloo, Napoleon banished to St Helena
1816	Birth of Charlotte Brontë	
1817	Death of Jane Austen Ricardo, *Principles of Political Economy and Taxation*	
1818	Mary Shelley, *Frankenstein* Scott, *Heart of Midlothian*	Frontier between USA and Canada agreed
1819	Birth of George Eliot (Mary Ann Evans) Byron, *Don Juan*	'Peterloo massacre': troops fire on workers in Manchester
1820		George III dies; succeeded by George IV
1821	Death of Keats	Napoleon dies on St Helena

Year	Age	Life
1824	14	The school moves to 'Avonbank', Stratford-upon-Avon
1826	16	June. Leaves school
1827	17	Knutsford, holiday in Wales
1828	18	Her brother John disappears on a voyage to India. Elizabeth goes to Chelsea to live with her father and stepmother
1829	19	March. William Stevenson dies. Elizabeth goes to stay with Rev. William Turner, Newcastle upon Tyne
1830	20	Spent in Knutsford and Newcastle
1831	21	Visits Edinburgh with Anne Turner. Summer in Liverpool then Knutsford. In Manchester meets Rev. William Gaskell, junior minister at Cross Street Unitarian Chapel
1832	22	30 August. Marries William Gaskell, moves to Manchester
1833	23	Birth of a still-born daughter
1834	24	12 September. Her daughter Marianne is born
1837	27	January. 'Sketches among the Poor' (with William), in *Blackwood's Edinburgh Magazine* 5 February. Margaret Emily (Meta) born May. Aunt Lumb dies

Year	Literary Context	Historical Events
1822	Shelley drowns at Lerici Beethoven, *Missa Solemnis*	
1823	Lamb, *Essays of Elia*	
1824	Death of Byron at Missolonghi	
1826	Fenimore Cooper, *Last of the Mohicans*	
1827	Keble, *Christian Year* Manzoni, *I promessi sposi*	Treaty between Britain, Russia and France to assure independence of Greece (confirmed 1830)
1830	Tennyson, *Poems, Chiefly Lyrical* Charles Lyell, *Principles of Geology*	George IV dies; succeeded by William IV Revolutionary uprisings in Germany, Poland, Belgium, France (abdication of Charles IX; election of Louis Philippe as King)
1831	Ebenezer Elliot, *Corn Law Rhymes*	Russell introduces first Reform Bill
1832	Deaths of Sir Walter Scott and Goethe	First Reform Act passed
1833	Carlyle, *Sartor Resartus*	Factory inspection introduced in England
1834		Slavery ended in British possessions
1836	Dickens, *Pickwick Papers*	
1837	Dickens, *Oliver Twist*	William IV dies; succeeded by Queen Victoria

Year	Age	Life
1839	29	Infant son dies
1840	30	'Copton Hall' included in William Howitt, *Visits to Remarkable Places*
1841	31	Visits Germany with William
1842	32	7 October. Florence Elizabeth (Flossy) born
1844	34	23 October. Birth of her son, William
1845	34	10 August. William dies, aged ten months, in North Wales
1846	36	3 September. Fourth daughter, Julia Margaret Bradford, born
1847–8	37	'Libbie Marsh's Three Eras', 'The Sexton's Hero', 'Christmas Storms and Sunshine', in *Howitt's Journal*

Year	Literary Context	Historical Events
1838		Anti-Corn-Law League founded in Manchester
1839	Carlyle, *Chartism*	Chartist petition presented to Parliament Opium War with China: Hong Kong taken New Zealand declared a British colony
1840	Browning, *Sordello*	Marriage of Queen Victoria to Prince Albert of Saxe-Coburg-Gotha
1841		Peel succeeds Melbourne as British Prime Minister
1842	Comte, *Cours de la philosophie positive* Macaulay, *Lays of Ancient Rome*	Hong Kong ceded to Britain Widespread Chartist riots
1843	Carlyle, *Past and Present* Ruskin, *Modern Painters*, I	
1844	Disraeli, *Coningsby*	
1845	Disraeli, *Sybil*	Texas made USA state; Mexico loses Arizona; California, New Mexico join USA in 1847 Beginning of potato famine in Ireland
1846	Edward Lear, *Book of Nonsense*	Pius IX elected Pope Repeal of Corn Laws in Britain
1847	Tennyson, *The Princess* Charlotte Brontë, *Jane Eyre* Emily Brontë, *Wuthering Heights*	Poland made a Russian province

Year	Age	Life
1848	38	November. *Mary Barton*
1849	39	Visits London: meets Dickens, Carlyle, Forster
1850	40–41	Begins to write for Dickens's *Household Words*: 'Lizzie Leigh', 'The Well of Pen Morfa', 'The Heart of John Middleton' The Gaskells move to 84 Plymouth Grove, Manchester August. First meeting with Charlotte Brontë December. *The Moorland Cottage*
1851	41	July. Visits Great Exhibition December–May 1853. *Cranford* in *Household Words*
1852	42	'The Old Nurse's Story'
1853	42	January. *Ruth* May. Visit to Paris July. Holiday in Normandy 19–23 September. Visit to Haworth
1854	43–4	February. Visits Paris September–January 1855. *North and South* in *Household Words*
1855	44	February. Visits Paris 31 March. Death of Charlotte Brontë June. Patrick Brontë asks her to write Charlotte's *Life*

Year	Literary Context	Historical Events
1848	Thackeray, *Vanity Fair* J. S. Mill, *Principles of Political Economy*	Revolutions in Sicily, Austria (Emperor Ferdinand abdicates in favour of nephew, Francis Joseph), and France (Republic proclaimed: Louis Napoleon elected President). Uprisings against Austria in Italy Lord Dalhousie appointed Governor-General of India First Women's Rights Convention, Seneca Falls, USA Pre-Raphaelite Brotherhood formed
1849	Charlotte Brontë, *Shirley*	Garibaldi enters Rome Britain annexes Punjab
1850	Dickens *David Copperfield* *Household Words* founded Tennyson, *In Memoriam* Death of Wordsworth; Tennyson becomes Poet Laureate	Australian Constitution Act
1851	Ruskin, *The Stones of Venice* Melville, *Moby-Dick*	Great Exhibition in London Gold found in New South Wales and Victoria First women's suffrage petition presented to House of Commons
1852	Harriet Beecher Stowe, *Uncle Tom's Cabin*	South African Republic established at Sand River Convention
1853	Charlotte Brontë, *Villette* Dickens, *Bleak House*	France: Napoleon III proclaimed Emperor Russian army enters Turkey: Turkey declares war
1854	Thoreau, *Walden*	France and Britain declare war on Russia: armies land in Crimea
1855	Death of Charlotte Brontë Browning, *Men and Women*	Paris World Exhibition

Year	Age	Life
1856	45	'The Poor Clare'
1857	46	February. The *Life* completed; holiday in Italy. Meets Charles Eliot Norton March. *The Life of Charlotte Brontë*; libel cases and revisions
1858	48	June–September. *My Lady Ludlow* in *Household Words* September. Holiday in Germany
1859	49	'Lois the Witch'
1861	51	'The Grey Woman'
1862	52	Spring. Visits France, planning the memoir of Mme de Sévigné Autumn. Intense relief work in the Manchester 'cotton famine' due to the American Civil War
1863	53	February. *Sylvia's Lovers* March–June. Trip to France and Italy September. Florence Gaskell marries
1864	53	*Cousin Phillis* concluded in the *Cornhill Magazine*

Year	Literary Context	Historical Events
1856		Paris Peace Congress ends Crimean War
1857	Dickens, *Little Dorrit* Trollope, *Barchester Towers* George Eliot, *Scenes of Clerical Life* Elizabeth Barrett Browning, *Aurora Leigh* Flaubert, *Madame Bovary* Baudelaire, *Les Fleurs du mal*	'Indian Mutiny': Massacre of Cawnpore, loss of Delhi
1858	Tennyson, *Idylls of the King*	Ottawa declared capital of Canada
1859	Darwin, *The Origin of Species* J. S. Mill, *On Liberty* George Eliot, *Adam Bede* Dickens, *A Tale of Two Cities*	Revolutions against Austrian rule in Parma, Modena and Tuscany USA: John Brown's raid on Harper's Ferry De Lesseps begins Suez Canal
1860	George Eliot, *The Mill on the Floss*	Plebiscites in favour of Italian unification, Garibaldi enters Naples Abraham Lincoln elected President of USA
1861	George Eliot, *Silas Marner* Dickens, *Great Expectations*	Confederation of Southern States proclaimed: American Civil War Victor Emanuel King of Italy Prince Consort dies
1862		Bismarck appointed Prussian Premier
1863	Death of Thackeray Tolstoy begins *War and Peace* (published 1868–9)	
1864	Browning, *Dramatis Personae* J. H. Newman, *Apologia pro Vita Sua*	

Year	Age	Life
1865	54–5	August. *Wives and Daughters* begins in the *Cornhill Magazine* (concluded January 1866) 12 November. Elizabeth dies of a heart attack at her newly bought house, 'The Lawn', Holybourne, Hampshire

Year	Literary Context	Historical Events
1865	Lewis Carroll, *Alice's Adventures in Wonderland* Dickens, *Our Mutual Friend*	Lincoln assassinated: Confederate army surrender Palmerston dies: Russell Prime Minister; Gladstone Leader of the House

INTRODUCTION

Wives and Daughters is generally regarded as the pinnacle of Elizabeth Gaskell's literary achievement, despite the fact that it is sadly, though not seriously, incomplete. Its author died suddenly on 12 November 1865, and it was left to her friend Frederick Greenwood, editor of the *Cornhill Magazine* in which the novel was being serialized, to summarize her intentions and pay his own tribute in commentary as a fitting conclusion. *Wives and Daughters* is the first of a fictional line exemplifying new departures and vital power in their parts which would never be a complete whole: one thinks of Dickens's *The Mystery of Edwin Drood*, of R. L. Stevenson's *Weir of Hermiston*, of F. Scott Fitzgerald's *The Last Tycoon*. These have their expectations and vivid particularities, but they lack the overall surety that distinguishes Gaskell's novel in its perspectives, its ironies, its sure sense of structure, its radiant wisdom and its compelling and tremulous humanity. *Wives and Daughters* (1864–6) began publication seven years before *Middlemarch* appeared in its serial form. This novel of provincial life – placed historically close in time to George Eliot's forthcoming masterpiece – anticipates much of its matter and more of its moment with delightful ease and insistent charm. George Eliot's combination of head and heart in *Middlemarch* is unsurpassed; Gaskell's heart, always to the fore, is finely complemented by her head in *Wives and Daughters*, a work of consummate maturity.

The title and the sub-title are appropriately modest, and one might even question the first as being inappropriately misleading, since the wives – the second Mrs Gibson, Mrs Hamley, Lady Cumnor, Aimée – have a balance of daughters and sons, and the fathers – Mr Gibson and Squire Hamley, for example – are as important as their wives. But this is a quibble or passing glance, and the sub-title, 'An Every-day Story', is art revealing art, since the balance of intimate feeling and social behaviour and suggestion (often misleading) is maintained throughout. The immediacy of Molly's childhood is succeeded by the immediacy of her adolescence through selective and revealing incident: the casually insidious power of suggestion and fortuitous opportunity pushes Mr Gibson to ill-considered matrimony and an aftermath of uneven acceptance as 'Clare' gets what she wants (or what a woman needs economically) – an establishment, a position desirable from the outside though perhaps somewhat less comfortable once within. There are also literary derivations in this novel, an Austenesque flair about some of the Gaskellian figures, with Lady Cumnor descended from Lady Catherine de Bourgh but having a greater fullness, a more complete humanity than her ancestor, while the Misses Browning would have been natural commentators in Cranford and gossip cousins to the garrulous Miss Bates of *Emma*.

But *Wives and Daughters* needs no gloss of comparison, no analogies to boost its effects. The tracing of Molly's development from childhood (she is both the central focus and the narrative lens) to the edge of maturity is sure, partial and for the most part uncloying because we feel her vulnerability both in single-parent dependence and in two-parent adjustment. She is the moral pivot of the novel, seeing the inherent goodness and warmth of Roger despite her early prejudice, and rescuing Cynthia from Preston by obtaining the letters, sacrificing her social pride and putting her reputation at risk. She bears her new mamma stoically though with a certain repressed sadness, accepting a less frequent closeness with her father yet always striving to do the right thing in her family and social contexts. She is seen with warm identification and stringent clarity, and is anxious to befriend Cynthia, with whom she forms a natural contrast which enhances them both. This contrast – and the word defines so much of Gaskell's method and aesthetic achievement in the novel – is remarkable for its literal truthfulness and also as evidence of the mature grasp and perspective of the author. Cynthia the beauty, made more than a touch selfish by a selfish mother, responds to difference and to genuineness with a fineness of feeling which reflects how carefully her author has conceived her. Growth in character is fundamental in a Gaskell novel, with adaptation, change, discovery and self-discovery, recognitions and acceptance as parts of the ongoing development. Mr Gibson, as we shall see below, adjusts to marital compromise, conscious of his own frailty almost as soon as he has committed himself, so clear is the mirror of Hyacinth's superficiality; Squire Hamley is elevated (in character) to a genuine pride in Roger which supplants his previously misplaced worship of primogeniture in Osborne, though he hardly adjusts his anti-French stance despite Aimée and his grandchild. Mrs Gibson learns a little tact, though less wisdom, in dealing with her husband's integrity, and even a somewhat stereotypic womanizer such as Mr Preston recognizes his put-down by Lady Harriet, and the courage of Molly, as chastening life experience. The interactions throughout are convincing, and if Lady Cumnor is somewhat larger than life, Lady Harriet perhaps a little too radical in her social attitudes, Osborne rather too indolently vapid (though remember his illness) and Aimée a creature of sad romance rather than positive fictional reality, they never dip or slip into caricature. Gaskell's eye is sure and her ear tuned to the natural dialogue of an everyday story which, like all our everyday stories, sometimes takes on an unusual or climactic stress. *Wives and Daughters* is true to life in the sense that its life is true: nothing jars, nothing is improbable or strained.

There is a perfect sense of period, of a society which has its fixed inheritances but is also on the edge of change. Set back half a lifetime ago, it yet partakes of contemporary time as well, its innuendoes not dissimilar from those of *Vanity Fair*, where Thackeray marches to Waterloo and soaks us in its aftermath but keeps his satire flowing with contemporary events in mind, giving his readers a taste of their own lives as well as of those caught in the past tides of history. Lord Hollingford's scientific bent, which embraces the active encouragement of Roger's, shows Gaskell's awareness of social as well as intellectual and practical advance and, as I have indicated above, if Lord and Lady Cumnor represent the old county aristocracy, then Lady Harriet signals a shift in the social scale. The Misses Browning represent the past, Mr Preston as efficient land agent the future: his confrontation with Squire Hamley shows Gaskell at her best, since there is a suggestion that progress may carry with it a diminishing of humanity. The Squire, humiliated and angry, still represents one of the positives of the feudal tradition he upholds, visiting his dying tenant (to the latter's comfort) despite his own frustrations. Hollingford is an extended Cranford in the sense that we get a wider sense of community and social interaction, a sense of educational progress in the fullest sense of the term, with the old order gradually adjusting to the new, sometimes painfully. There is a feeling of space, physical, mental, emotional: Hollingford is both place and symbol, its past building its present and signalling the future.

Another aspect of *Wives and Daughters* reflective of its high art is its style. I use the term in the full sense of expression, atmosphere, tone, the overall consonance which gives it its major appeal. From that first eventful visit to Cumnor Towers (certainly not everyday, and traumatic for the vulnerable Molly) the ironic mode is superbly compassionate, warm, enthralled, light or a little acid, depending on personality and situation. When Mr Gibson puts down Mr Coxe with his reflexive Latin wit, we deplore the sternness and understand the motive. When Cynthia almost casually engages herself (with an emphasis on outside-the-family secrecy) to the importunate (but defenceless) Roger, we again understand the motive and anticipate the consequences. Here there is cunning narrative expectation. Cynthia, subjected from time to time to the Kirkpatrick London influence (and the domestic Kirkpatrick influence in the shape of her mother), may succumb to the socially desirable blandishments of the much-talked-of but little-seen Mr Henderson. If this happens – eventually it does – Roger will suffer at a distance or on his return, Molly will be indignant on his behalf, there will be ramifications for the Squire, Mrs Gibson will be triumphant, Mr Gibson perhaps sardonic. The irony here encompasses the reader, who is being scrupulously given the alternatives, led into plot possibilities, stimulated into speculation. For an everyday story must have a happy ending, and just as Emma comes to recognize her covert feelings for Mr Knightley by contemplating his supposed feelings for Harriet Smith or Jane Fairfax, so Molly comes to a full appreciation of the fact that her love for Roger, revealed at every turn of the later narrative, is returned in full by his own recognition of her worth and by his own feelings, which are rooted in the actuality of sympathy and understanding as distinct from his febrile fascination with Cynthia. This is in no sense to diminish Cynthia or her behaviour. In engaging herself to a 'good' man Cynthia is appreciative of Roger's worth and is acting against her own tendencies. But the uncertainty about her own feelings – is it fair to Roger? – brings her to truth and integrity in personal dealing, a development in her own moral responsibility. It would be incomplete to stop our appraisal there: although she has come to greater self-recognition, the Gaskellian irony emphasizes that she has, as might have been expected, chosen a socially desirable partner. And that irony, consummate in its own range, includes silence on her future as part of its effect.

If Gaskell's mode here in plot handling is distinctive in its innuendo and associations, it is seen to even greater advantage in the ironic exchanges that shape the everyday story into something more intimate for reader and character alike. Mr Gibson's fears for Molly in the wake of the discovery of Mr Coxe's calf-love, his casual conversation with the Misses Browning which shows him that he was expected to marry again after his wife's death, and the beautifully inserted sigh which has him going back to his own first love (who was not his wife) culminates in the following when Mrs Kirkpatrick says:

> 'You are thinking of your own daughter. It was careless of me to say what I did. Dear child! how well I remember her sweet little face, as she lay sleeping on my bed! I suppose she is nearly grown-up now. She must be near my Cynthia's age. How I should like to see her!'
>
> 'I hope you will. I should like you to see her. I should like you to love my poor little Molly – to love her as your own' – He swallowed down something that rose in his throat, and was nearly choking him.
>
> 'Is he going to offer? *Is* he?' she wondered; and she began to tremble in the suspense before he next spoke.
>
> 'Could you love her as your daughter? Will you try? Will you give me the right of introducing you to her as her future mother; as my wife?'
>
> There! he had done it – whether it was wise or foolish – he had done it! but he was aware that the question as to its wisdom came into his mind the instant that the words were said past recall.
>
> She hid her face in her hands.
>
> 'Oh! Mr Gibson,' she said; and then, a little to his surprise, and a great deal to her own, she burst into hysterical tears: it was such a wonderful relief to feel that she need not struggle any more for a livelihood.
>
> (Chapter 10)

This dextrous blend of consciousness and commentary, the dialogue at once revelatory of character and situation, moves the everyday story into a new gear of experience. The irony is expressive of division at the moment of consummation, and Mr Gibson is still to learn from the irrepressible Lady Cumnor of

Lord Cumnor's speculation – which Clare, now Hyacinth, has seen – about the desirability of his marrying just her. For her the relief is immediate, for him the salutary nature of what he has just committed himself to is both immediate and prolonged. The dialogue is richly ironic, since Mrs Kirkpatrick acts out the lies which she believes are truth: she is glib with the realization of opportunity, her remembrance of Molly as child, and her wish to see Molly now, the convenient hypocrisies of hope. Yet even while we recognize this, we see the pathos beneath the part, the woman's lot circumscribed by petty economy (elegant economy would have been Gaskell's phrase earlier), the dependence that kills integrity, the consciousness of momentous change causing her to tremble. Gibson's words are the natural foil to her silence: simple and direct as ever, he is yet conscious at once that what he has done may cost him dear in terms of his own independence. It is a triumph of immediacy, the marriage thought convenient by each which has no substance of feeling to irradiate it. While the words produce the situation, there is an unverbalized corollary to it: each knows so little of the other that the posture of closeness is the prelude to distance. When Lady Cumnor reveals her husband's speculation, that distance has begun or, as the author puts it, 'there was nothing for it but for them to return to the library; Mrs Kirkpatrick pouting a little, and Mr Gibson feeling more like his own cool, sarcastic self, by many degrees, than he had done when last in that room' (Chapter 10). And immediately, though in low key, the lack of common ground between them is seen in her affectation about her late husband and in his ironic response, which is only a little softened. Naturally, he has patients to visit and does not stop longer.

I give this extract and some evaluation of it to indicate in brief compass the stringent nature of Gaskell's art, the insightful levels on which she writes, her superb control of text and sub-text. And this extract is typical in its impact: we are aware of the literal, the superficial, the layering of words *and* the expressive potency of what is not said. Two lives – and more – are changed because of this scene. Every everyday story contains incidents like this, and we recognize the realism that informs it. The greatest novels have this quality: we appreciate, we respond under the compulsion of timeless truth.

Wives and Daughters is leisurely in its unfolding but insistent in its interest. As Jenny Uglow makes clear in the subtitle to her critical biography of Elizabeth Gaskell, the latter had 'a habit of stories'. She is never in the grip of a literary or philosophical theory, and this final novel registers the ultimate progression from her earlier and all of her slighter work. No thematic obtrusion of Christian reconciliation or duty mars the unforced tenor of the narrative and the natural evolution of her plot. The communal voice of Cranford has become the communal voices of Hollingford, with a range from the Towers through the Misses Browning to Mrs Goodenough. The interior atmospheres are complemented by the exterior descriptions, from the Gibson house to Hamley Hall, from Molly's view of Cynthia importuned by Mr Preston to Roger's discovery of Molly after she feels rejected by her father, and the discriminating sympathy he displays on that occasion. It is part of Gaskell's superb control of her material that in the same chapter in which we have just seen Gibson's proposal, the immediate emotional effects are felt by his daughter. The ironic climax that we have just looked at is enhanced by the poignant aftermath which Roger witnesses:

> His steps led him in the direction of the ash-tree seat, much less screened from observation on this side than on the terrace. He stopped; he saw a light-coloured dress on the ground – somebody half-lying on the seat, so still just then, that he wondered if the person, whoever it was, had fallen ill or fainted. He paused to watch. In a minute or two the sobs broke out again – the words. It was Miss Gibson crying in a broken voice –
>
> 'Oh, papa, papa! if you would but come back!'
>
> (Chapter 10)

The very simplicity of this carries its own appeal. Roger's perspective (Molly is still 'Miss Gibson', not 'Molly' as yet) is direct, unconscious of eavesdropping; the language – 'light-coloured', 'half-lying', 'fallen' and 'fainted', for example – has an evocative and sensual quality, encompassing a moment in time. And the rising curve of interest and involvement, the impetus of the scene which half-tells a story, stimulates expectation: it is conscious art, narrative skill, human understanding, and these qualities are what make *Wives and Daughters* one of the greatest, and certainly one of the most rewarding and wise, of nineteenth-century novels.

GRAHAM HANDLEY

NOTE ON THE TEXT

Wives and Daughters first appeared in the *Cornhill Magazine* as a monthly serial from August 1864 to January 1866. It was reprinted in two volumes in 1866 with eighteen illustrations by George du Maurier. The text used here is that of the Knutsford Edition of 1906, edited by A. W. Ward, and issued by the original publishers, Smith, Elder & Co. Misprints or obvious errors have been silently corrected.

WIVES AND DAUGHTERS
An Every-day Story

CHAPTER I

The Dawn of a Gala Day

To begin with the old rigmarole of childhood.* In a country there was a shire, and in that shire there was a town, and in that town there was a house, and in that house there was a room, and in that room there was a bed, and in that bed there lay a little girl; wide awake and longing to get up, but not daring to do so for fear of the unseen power in the next room – a certain Betty, whose slumbers must not be disturbed until six o'clock struck, when she wakened of herself 'as sure as clock-work', and left the household very little peace afterwards. It was a June morning, and, early as it was, the room was full of sunny warmth and light.

On the drawers opposite to the little white dimity bed in which Molly Gibson lay, was a primitive kind of bonnet-stand, on which was hung a bonnet, carefully covered over from any chance of dust, with a large cotton-handkerchief, of so heavy and serviceable a texture that, if the thing underneath it had been a flimsy fabric of gauze and lace and flowers, it would have been altogether 'scomfished'* (again to quote from Betty's vocabulary). But the bonnet was made of solid straw, and its only trimming was a plain white ribbon put over the crown, and forming the strings. Still, there was a neat little quilling* inside, every plait of which Molly knew; for had she not made it herself the evening before, with infinite pains? and was there not a little blue bow in this quilling, the very first bit of such finery Molly had ever had the prospect of wearing?

Six o'clock now! the pleasant, brisk ringing of the church bells told that; calling every one to their daily work, as they had done for hundreds of years. Up jumped Molly, and ran with her bare little feet across the room, and lifted off the handkerchief and saw once again the bonnet – the pledge of the gay bright day to come. Then to the window; and, after some tugging, she opened the casement and let in the sweet morning air. The dew was already off the flowers in the garden below, but still rising from the long hay-grass in the meadows directly beyond. At one side lay the little town of Hollingford,* into a street of which Mr Gibson's front door opened; and delicate columns and little puffs of smoke were already beginning to rise from many a cottage chimney, where some housewife was already up, and preparing breakfast for the bread-winner of the family.

Molly Gibson saw all this; but all she thought about it was, 'Oh! it will be a fine day! I was afraid it never, never would come; or that, if it ever came, it would be a rainy day!' Five-and-forty years ago,* children's pleasures in a country town were very simple, and Molly had lived for twelve long years without the occurrence of any event so great as that which was now impending. Poor child! it is true that she had lost her mother, which was a jar to the whole tenour of her life; but that was hardly an event in the sense referred to; and, besides, she had been too young to be conscious of it at the time. The pleasure she was looking forward to today was her first share in a kind of annual festival in Hollingford.

The little straggling town faded away into country on one side, close to the entrance-lodge of a great park, where lived my Lord and Lady Cumnor:* 'the earl' and 'the countess', as they were always called by the inhabitants of the town; where a very pretty amount of feudal feeling still lingered, and showed itself in a number of simple ways, droll enough to look back upon, but serious matters of importance at the time. It was before the passing of the Reform Bill;* but a good deal of liberal talk took place occasionally between two or three of the more enlightened free-holders living in Hollingford; and there was a great Tory family in the county who, from time to time, came forward and contested the election with the rival Whig family of Cumnor.* One would have thought that the above-mentioned liberal-talking inhabitants would have, at least, admitted the possibility of their voting for the Hely-Harrison, and thus trying to vindicate their independence. But no such thing! 'The earl' was lord of the manor, and owner of much of the land on which Hollingford was built; he and his household were fed, and doctored, and, to a certain measure, clothed by the good people of the town; their fathers' grandfathers had always voted for the eldest son of Cumnor Towers, and, following in the ancestral track, every man-jack in the place gave his vote to the liege-lord, totally irrespective of such chimeras as political opinions.

This was no unusual instance of the influence of the great landowners over humbler neighbours in those days before railways,* and it was well for a place where the powerful family, who thus overshadowed it, were of so respectable a character as the Cumnors. They expected to be submitted to, and obeyed; the simple worship of the townspeople was accepted by the earl and countess as a right; and they would have stood still in amazement, and with a horrid memory of the French *sansculottes** who were the bugbears of their youth, had any inhabitant of Hollingford ventured to set his will or opinions in opposition to those of the earl. But, yielded all that obeisance, they did a good deal for the town, and were generally condescending, and often thoughtful and kind in their treatment of their vassals. Lord Cumnor was a forbearing landlord; putting his steward a little on one side sometimes, and taking the reins into his own hands now and then, much to the annoyance of the agent, who was, in fact, too rich and independent to care greatly for preserving a post where his decisions might any day be overturned by my lord's taking a fancy to go 'pottering' (as the agent irreverently expressed it in the sanctuary of his own home); which, being interpreted, meant that occasionally the earl asked his own questions of his own tenants, and used his own eyes and ears in the management of the smaller details of his property. But his tenants liked my lord all the better for this habit of his. Lord Cumnor had certainly a little time for gossip, which he contrived to combine with the failing of personal intervention between the old land-steward and the tenantry. But, then, the countess made up by her unapproachable dignity for this weakness of the earl's. Once a year she was condescending. She and the ladies, her daughters, had set up a school; not a school after the manner of schools now-a-days, where far better intellectual teaching is given to the boys and girls of labourers and workpeople than often falls to the lot of their betters in worldly estate; but a school of the kind we should call 'industrial',* where girls are taught to sew beautifully, to be capital housemaids, and pretty fair cooks, and, above all, to dress neatly in a kind of charity-uniform devised by the ladies of Cumnor Towers – white caps, white tippets, check aprons, blue gowns, and ready curtseys, and 'please, ma'ams', being *de rigueur.**

Now, as the countess was absent from the Towers for a considerable part of the year, she was glad to enlist the sympathy of the Hollingford ladies in this school, with a view to obtaining their aid as visitors during the many months that she and her daughters were away. And the various unoccupied gentlewomen of the town responded to the call of their liege lady, and gave her their service as required; and, along with it, a great deal of whispered and fussy admiration. 'How good of the countess! So like the dear countess – always thinking of others!' and so on; while it was always supposed that no strangers had seen Hollingford properly, unless they had been taken to the countess's school, and been duly impressed by the neat little pupils, and the still neater needlework, there to be inspected. In return, there was a day of honour set apart every summer, when, with much gracious and stately hospitality, Lady Cumnor and her daughters received all the school visitors at the Towers, the great family mansion standing in aristocratic seclusion in the centre of the large park, of which one of the lodges was close to the little town. The order of this annual festivity was this. About ten o'clock, one of the Towers carriages rolled through the lodge, and drove to different houses, wherein dwelt a woman to be honoured; picking them up by ones or twos, till the loaded carriage drove back again through the ready portals, bowled along the smooth, tree-shaded road, and deposited its covey* of smartly-dressed ladies on the great flight of steps leading to the ponderous doors of Cumnor Towers. Back again to the town; another picking-up of womenkind in their best clothes, and another return, and so on, till the whole party were assembled either in the house or in the really beautiful gardens. After the proper amount of exhibition on the one part, and admiration on the other, had been done, there was a collation for the visitors, and some more display and admiration of the treasures inside the house. Towards four o'clock, coffee was brought round; and this was a signal of the approaching carriage that was to take them back to their own homes; whither they returned with the happy consciousness of a well-spent day, but with some fatigue at the long-continued exertion of behaving their best, and talking on stilts for so many hours. Nor were Lady Cumnor and her daughters free from something of the same self-approbation, and something, too, of the same fatigue – the fatigue that always follows on conscious efforts to behave as will best please the society you are in.

For the first time in her life, Molly Gibson was to be included among the guests at the Towers. She was much too young to be a visitor at the school, so it was not on that account that she was to go; but it had so happened that, one day when Lord Cumnor was on a 'pottering' expedition, he had met Mr Gibson, *the* doctor of the neighbourhood,* coming out of the farm-house my lord was entering; and, having some small question to ask the surgeon (Lord Cumnor seldom passed any one of his acquaintance without asking a question of some sort – not always attending to the answer; it was his mode of conversation), he accompanied Mr Gibson to the out-building, to a ring in the wall of which the surgeon's horse was fastened. Molly was there too, sitting square and quiet on her rough little pony, waiting for her father. Her grave eyes opened large and wide at the close neighbourhood and evident advance of 'the earl'; for to her little imagination the grey-haired, red-faced, somewhat clumsy man, was a cross between an archangel and a king.

'Your daughter, eh, Gibson? – nice little girl; how old? Pony wants grooming, though,' patting it as he talked. 'What's your name, my dear? He's sadly behindhand with his rent, as I was saying; but, if he's really ill, I must see after Sheepshanks, who is a hardish man of business. What's his complaint? You'll come to our school-scrimmage* on Thursday, little girl – what's-your-name? Mind you send her, or bring her, Gibson; and just give a word to your groom, for I'm sure that pony wasn't singed* last year; now, was he? Don't forget Thursday, little girl – what's-your-name? – it's a promise between us, is it not?' And off the earl trotted, attracted by the sight of the farmer's eldest son on the other side of the yard.

Mr Gibson mounted, and he and Molly rode off. They did not speak for some time. Then she said, 'May I go, papa?' in rather an anxious little tone of voice.

'Where, my dear?' said he, wakening up out of his own professional thoughts.

'To the Towers – on Thursday, you know. That gentleman' (she was shy of calling him by his title) 'asked me.'

'Would you like it, my dear? It has always seemed to me rather a tiresome piece of gaiety – rather a tiring day, I mean – beginning so early – and the heat, and all that.'

'Oh, papa!' said Molly reproachfully.

'You'd like to go then, would you?'

'Yes; if I may! – He asked me, you know. Don't you think I may? – he asked me twice over.'

'Well! we'll see – yes! I think we can manage it, if you wish it so much, Molly.'

Then they were silent again. By-and-by, Molly said –

'Please, papa – I do wish to go – but I don't care about it.'

'That's rather a puzzling speech. But I suppose you mean you don't care to go, if it will be any trouble to get you there. I can easily manage it, however; so you may consider it settled. You'll want a white frock, remember; you'd better tell Betty you're going, and she'll see after making you tidy.'

Now, there were two or three things to be done by Mr Gibson, before he could feel quite comfortable about Molly's going to the festival at the Towers, and each of them involved a little trouble on his part. But he was very willing to gratify his little girl; so, the next day, he rode over to the Towers, ostensibly to visit some sick housemaid, but, in reality, to throw himself in my lady's way, and get her to ratify Lord Cumnor's invitation to Molly. He chose his time, with a little natural diplomacy; which, indeed, he had often to exercise in his intercourse with the great family. He rode into the stable-yard about twelve o'clock, a little before luncheon-time, and yet after the worry of opening the post-bag and discussing its contents was over. After he had put up his horse, he went in by the back-way to the house; the 'House' on this side, the 'Towers' at the front. He saw his patient, gave his directions to the housekeeper, and then went out, with a rare wild-flower in his hand, to find one of the ladies Tranmere in the garden, where, according to his hope and calculation, he came upon Lady Cumnor too – now talking to her daughter about the contents of an open letter which she held in her hand, now directing a gardener about certain bedding-out plants.

'I was calling to see Nanny, and I took the opportunity of bringing Lady Agnes the plant I was telling her about as growing on Cumnor Moss.'

'Thank you so much, Mr Gibson! Mamma, look! this is the *Drosera rotundifolia** I have been wanting so long.'

'Ah! yes; very pretty, I daresay, only I am no botanist. Nanny is better, I hope? We can't have any one laid up next week, for the house will be quite full of people – and here are the Danbys writing to offer themselves as well. One comes down for a fortnight of quiet, at Whitsuntide, and leaves half one's establishment in town;* and, as soon as people know of our being here, we get letters without end, longing for a breath of country-air, or saying how lovely the Towers must look in spring; and, I must own, Lord Cumnor is a great deal to blame for it all, for, as soon as ever we are down here, he rides about to all the neighbours, and invites them to come over and spend a few days.'

'We shall go back to town on Friday the 18th,' said Lady Agnes, in a consolatory tone.

'Ah, yes! as soon as we have got over the school visitors' affair. But it is a week to that happy day.'

'By the way!' said Mr Gibson, availing himself of the good opening thus presented, 'I met my lord at the Crosstrees Farm yesterday, and he was kind enough to ask my little daughter, who was with me, to be one of the party here on Thursday; it would give the lassie great pleasure, I believe.' He paused for Lady Cumnor to speak.

'Oh, well! if my lord asked her, I suppose she must come; but I wish he was not so amazingly hospitable! Not but what the little girl will be quite welcome; only, you see, he met a younger Miss Browning the other day, of whose existence I had never heard.'

'She visits at the school, mamma,' said Lady Agnes.

'Well, perhaps she does; I never said she did not. I knew there was one visitor of the name of Browning; I never knew there were two, but, of course, as soon as Lord Cumnor heard there was another, he must needs ask her; so the carriage will have to go backwards and forwards four times now to fetch them all. So your daughter can come quite easily, Mr Gibson, and I shall be very glad to see her for your sake. She can sit bodkin* with the Brownings, I suppose? You'll arrange it all with them; and mind you get Nanny well up to her work next week!'

Just as Mr Gibson was going away, Lady Cumnor called after him, 'Oh! by-the-bye, Clare is here; you remember Clare, don't you? She was a patient of yours, long ago.'

'Clare!' he repeated, in a bewildered tone.

'Don't you recollect her? Miss Clare, our old governess,' said Lady Agnes. 'About twelve or fourteen years ago, before Lady Cuxhaven was married.'

'Oh, yes!' said he. 'Miss Clare, who had the scarlet fever here; a very pretty, delicate girl. But I thought she was married!'

'Yes!' said Lady Cumnor. 'She was a silly little thing, and did not know when she was well off; we were all very fond of her, I'm sure. She went and married a poor curate, and became a stupid Mrs Kirkpatrick; but we always kept on calling her "Clare". And now he's dead, and left her a widow, and she is staying here; and we are racking our brains to find out some way of helping her to a livelihood, without parting her from her child. She's somewhere about the grounds, if you like to renew your acquaintance with her.'

'Thank you, my lady. I'm afraid I cannot stop today; I have a long round to go. I've stayed here too long as it is, I'm afraid.'

Long as his ride had been that day, he called on the Miss Brownings in the evening, to arrange about Molly's accompanying them to the Towers. They were tall, handsome women, past their first youth, and inclined to be extremely complaisant to the widowed doctor.

'Eh, dear! Mr Gibson, but we shall be delighted to have her with us. You should never have thought of *asking* us such a thing,' said Miss Browning the elder.

'I'm sure I'm hardly sleeping at nights, for thinking of it,' said Miss Phoebe. 'You know I've never been there before. Sister has, many a time; but, somehow, though my name has been down on the visitors' list these three years, the countess has never named me in her note; and you know I could not push myself into notice, and go to such a grand place without being asked; now, could I?'

'I told Phoebe last year,' said her sister, 'that I was sure it was only inadvertence, as one may call it, on the part of the countess, and that her ladyship would be as hurt as any one when she didn't see Phoebe among the school visitors; but Phoebe has got a delicate mind, you see, Mr Gibson, and, for all I could say, she wouldn't go, but stopped here at home; and it spoilt all my pleasure all that day, I do assure you, to think of Phoebe's face, as I saw it over the window-blinds, as I rode away; her eyes were full of tears, if you'll believe me.'

'I had a good cry after you was gone, Sally,' said Miss Phoebe; 'but for all that, I think I was right in stopping away from where I was not asked. Don't you, Mr Gibson?'

'Certainly,' said he. 'And you see you are going this year; and last year it rained.'

'Yes! I remember! I set myself to tidy my drawers, to string myself up,* as it were; and I was so taken up with what I was about that I was quite startled when I heard the rain beating against the window-panes. "Goodness me!" said I to myself, "whatever will become of sister's white satin shoes, if she has to walk about on soppy grass after such rain as this?" for, you see, I thought a deal about her having a pair of smart shoes; and this year she has gone and got me a white satin pair, just as smart as hers, for a surprise.'

'Molly will know she's to put on her best clothes,' said Miss Browning. 'We could perhaps lend her a few beads, or artificials,* if she wants them.'

'Molly must go in a clean white frock,' said Mr Gibson, rather hastily; for he did not admire the Miss Brownings' taste in dress, and was unwilling to have his child decked up according to their fancy; he esteemed his old servant Betty's as the more correct, because the more simple. Miss Browning had just a shade of annoyance in her tone as she drew herself up, and said, 'Oh! very well. It's quite right, I'm sure.' But Miss Phoebe said, 'Molly will look very nice in whatever she puts on, that's certain.'

CHAPTER 2

A Novice amongst the Great Folk

At ten o'clock on the eventful Thursday, the Towers carriage began its work. Molly was ready long before it made its first appearance, although it had been settled that she and the Miss Brownings were not to go until the last, or fourth, time of its coming. Her face had been soaped, scrubbed, and shone brilliantly clean; her frills, her frock, her ribbons were all snow-white. She had on a black mode cloak* that had been her mother's; it was trimmed round with rich lace, and looked quaint and old-fashioned on the child. For the first time in her life she wore kid gloves; hitherto she had only had cotton ones. Her gloves were far too large for the little dimpled fingers, but, as Betty had told her they were to last her for years, it was all very well. She trembled many a time, and almost turned faint once with the long expectation of the morning. Betty might say what she liked about a watched pot never boiling;* Molly never ceased to watch the approach through the winding street, and after two hours the carriage came for her at last. She had to sit very forward to avoid crushing the Miss Brownings' new dresses; and yet not too forward, for fear of incommoding* fat Mrs Goodenough and her niece, who occupied the front seat of the carriage: so that, although the fact of sitting down at all was rather doubtful, to add to her discomfort, Molly felt herself to be very conspicuously placed in the centre of the carriage, a mark for all the observation of Hollingford. It was far too much of a gala day for the work of the little town to go forward with its usual regularity. Maid-servants gazed out of upper windows; shop-keepers' wives stood on the door-steps; cottagers ran out, with babies in their arms; and little children, too young to know how to behave respectfully at the sight of an earl's carriage, huzza-ed merrily as it bowled along. The woman at the lodge held the gate open, and dropped a low curtsey to the liveries. And now they were in the Park; and now they were in sight of the Towers, and silence fell upon the carriageful of ladies, only broken by one faint remark from Mrs Goodenough's niece, a stranger to the town, as they drew up before the double semicircular flight of steps which led to the door of the mansion.

'They call that a *perron*,* I believe, don't they?' she asked. But the only answer she obtained was a simultaneous 'hush'. It was very awful, as Molly thought, and she half wished herself at home again. But she lost all consciousness of herself, by-and-by, when the party strolled out into the beautiful grounds, the like of which she had never even imagined. Green velvet lawns, bathed in sunshine, stretched away on every side into the finely-wooded park; if there were divisions and ha-has between the soft sunny sweeps of grass, and the dark gloom of the forest-trees beyond, Molly did not see them; and the melting away of exquisite cultivation into the wilderness had an inexplicable charm for her. Near the house there were walls and fences; but they were covered with climbing roses, and rare honeysuckles and other creepers just bursting into bloom. There were flower-beds, too, scarlet, crimson, blue, orange; masses of blossom lying on the greensward. Molly held Miss Browning's hand very tight, as they loitered about in company with several other ladies, marshalled by a daughter of the Towers, who seemed half amused at the voluble admiration showered down upon every possible thing and place. Molly said nothing, as became her age and position; but every now and then she relieved her full heart by drawing a deep breath, almost like a sigh. Presently, they came to the long glittering range of greenhouses and hothouses, and an attendant gardener was there to admit the party. Molly did not care for this half so much as for the flowers in the open air; but Lady Agnes had a more scientific taste; she expatiated on the rarity of this plant, and the mode of cultivation required by that, till Molly began to feel very tired, and then very faint. She was too shy to speak for some time; but at length, afraid of making a greater sensation, if she began to cry, or if she fell against the stands of precious flowers, she caught at Miss Browning's hand, and gasped out –

'May I go back, out into the garden? I can't breathe here!'

'Oh, yes, to be sure, love! I daresay it's hard understanding for you, love; but it's very fine and instructive, and a deal of Latin in it too.'

She turned hastily round, not to lose another word of Lady Agnes's lecture on orchids; and Molly turned back and passed out of the heated atmosphere. She felt better in the fresh air; and, unobserved and at liberty, went from one lovely spot to another, now in the open park, now in some shut-in flower-garden, where the song of the birds and the drip of the central fountain were the only sounds, and the tree-tops made an enclosing circle in the blue June sky; she went along without more thought as to her where-abouts than a butterfly has, as it skims from flower to flower, till at length she grew very weary, and wished to return to the house, but did not know how, and felt afraid of encountering all the strangers who would be there, unprotected by either of the Miss Brownings. The hot sun told upon her head, and it began to ache. She saw a great wide-spreading cedar-tree upon a burst of lawn towards which she was advancing, and the black repose beneath its branches lured her thither. There was a rustic seat in the shadow; and weary Molly sate down there, and presently fell asleep.

She was startled from her slumbers after a time, and jumped to her feet. Two ladies were standing by her, talking about her. They were perfect strangers to her, and, with a vague conviction that she had done something wrong, and also because she was worn-out with hunger, fatigue, and the morning's excitement, she began to cry.

'Poor little woman! She has lost herself; she belongs to some of the people from Hollingford, I have no doubt,' said the oldest-looking of the two ladies; she who appeared to be about forty, though she did not really number more than thirty years. She was plain-featured, and had rather a severe expression on her face; her dress was as rich as any morning dress could be; her voice deep and unmodulated – what in a lower rank of life would have been called gruff; but that was not a word to apply to Lady Cuxhaven, the eldest daughter of the earl and countess. The other lady looked much younger, but she was in fact some years the elder; at first sight Molly thought she was the most beautiful person she had ever seen, and she was certainly a very lovely woman. Her voice, too, was soft and plaintive, as she replied to Lady Cuxhaven –

'Poor little darling! she is overcome by the heat, I have no doubt – such a heavy straw-bonnet, too. Let me untie it for you, my dear!'

Molly now found voice to say – 'I am Molly Gibson, please. I came here with Miss Brownings;' for her great fear was that she should be taken for an unauthorised intruder.

'Miss Brownings?' said Lady Cuxhaven to her companion, as if inquiringly.

'I think they were the two tall, large young women that Lady Agnes was talking about.'

'Oh, I daresay. I saw she had a number of people in tow;' then, looking again at Molly, she said, 'Have you had anything to eat, child, since you came? You look a very white little thing; or is it the heat?'

'I have had nothing to eat,' said Molly, rather piteously; for, indeed, before she fell asleep she had been very hungry.

The two ladies spoke to each other in a low voice; then the elder said in a voice of authority, which, indeed, she had always used in speaking to the other, 'Sit still here, my dear; we are going to the house, and Clare shall bring you something to eat before you try to walk back; it must be a quarter of a mile at least.' So they went away, and Molly sat upright, waiting for the promised messenger. She did not know who Clare might be, and she did not care much for food now; but she felt as if she could not walk without some help. At length she saw the pretty lady coming back, followed by a footman with a small tray.

'Look how kind Lady Cuxhaven is,' said she who was called Clare. 'She chose you out this little lunch herself; and now you must try and eat it, and you'll be quite right when you've had some food, darling. – You need not stop, Edwards; I will bring the tray back with me.'

There was some bread, and some cold chicken, and some jelly, and a glass of wine, and a bottle of sparkling water, and a bunch of grapes. Molly put out her trembling little hand for the water; but she was too faint to hold it. Clare put it to her mouth, and she took a long draught and was refreshed. But she could not eat;

she tried, but she could not; her headache was too bad. Clare looked bewildered. 'Take some grapes, they will be the best for you; you must try and eat something, or I don't know how I shall get you to the house.'

'My head aches so,' said Molly, lifting her heavy eyes wistfully.

'Oh, dear, how tiresome!' said Clare, still in her sweet gentle voice, not at all as if she were angry, only expressing an obvious truth. Molly felt very guilty and very unhappy. Clare went on, with a shade of asperity in her tone: 'You see, I don't know what to do with you here, if you don't eat enough to enable you to walk home. And I've been out for these three hours, trapesing about the grounds till I'm as tired as can be, and I've missed my lunch and all.' Then, as if a new idea had struck her, she said – 'You lie back in that seat for a few minutes, and try to eat the bunch of grapes; and I'll wait for you, and just be eating a mouthful meanwhile. You are sure you don't want this chicken?'

Molly did as she was bid, and leant back, picking languidly at the grapes, and watching the good appetite with which the lady ate up the chicken and jelly, and drank the glass of wine. She was so pretty and so graceful in her deep mourning, that even her hurry in eating, as if she was afraid of some one coming to surprise her in the act, did not keep her little observer from admiring her in all she did.

'And now, darling, are you ready to go?' said she, when she had eaten up everything on the tray. 'Oh, come; you have nearly finished your grapes; that's a good girl. Now, if you will come with me to the side-entrance, I will take you up to my own room, and you shall lie down on the bed for an hour or two; and, if you have a good nap, your headache will be gone.'

So they set off, Clare carrying the empty tray, rather to Molly's shame; but the child had enough work to drag herself along, and was afraid of offering to do anything more. The 'side-entrance' was a flight of steps leading up from a private flower-garden into a private matted hall, or ante-room, out of which many doors opened, and in which were deposited the light garden-tools and the bows and arrows* of the young ladies of the house. Lady Cuxhaven must have seen their approach, for she met them in this hall as soon as they came in.

'How is she now?' she asked; then glancing at the plates and glasses, she added, 'Come, I think there can't be much amiss! You're a good old Clare, but you should have let one of the men fetch that tray in; life in such weather as this is trouble enough of itself.'

Molly could not help wishing that her pretty companion would have told Lady Cuxhaven that she herself had helped to finish up the ample luncheon; but no such idea seemed to come into her mind. She only said – 'Poor dear! she is not quite the thing* yet; has got a headache, she says. I am going to put her down on my bed, to see if she can get a little sleep.'

Molly saw Lady Cuxhaven say something in a half-laughing manner to 'Clare', as she passed her; and the child could not keep from tormenting herself by fancying that the words spoken sounded wonderfully like 'Overeaten herself, I suspect.' However, she felt too poorly to worry herself long; the little white bed in the cool and pretty room had too many attractions for her aching head. The muslin curtains flapped softly, from time to time, in the scented air that came through the open windows. Clare covered her up with a light shawl, and darkened the room. As she was going away, Molly roused herself to say, 'Please, ma'am, don't let them go away without me! Please ask somebody to waken me if I go to sleep! I am to go back with Miss Brownings.'

'Don't trouble yourself about it, dear; I'll take care,' said Clare, turning round at the door, and kissing her hand to little anxious Molly. And then she went away, and thought no more about it. The carriages came round at half-past four, hurried a little by Lady Cumnor, who had suddenly become tired of the business of entertaining, and annoyed at the repetition of indiscriminating admiration.

'Why not have both carriages out, mamma, and get rid of them all at once?' said Lady Cuxhaven. 'This going by instalments is the most tiresome thing that could be imagined.' So, at last, there had been a great hurry and an unmethodical way of packing off every one at once. Miss Browning had gone in the chariot (or 'chawyot', as Lady Cumnor called it; – it rhymed to her daughter, Lady Hawyot – or Harriet, as the name was spelt in the *Peerage**), and Miss Phoebe had been speeded, along with several other guests, away in a great roomy family conveyance, of the kind which we should now call an 'omnibus'. Each thought that Molly Gibson was with the other; and the truth was, that she lay fast asleep on Mrs Kirkpatrick's bed – Mrs Kirkpatrick, *née* Clare.

The housemaids came in to arrange the room. Their talking aroused Molly, who sat up on the bed, and tried to push back the hair from her hot forehead, and to remember where she was. She dropped down on her feet by the side of the bed, to the astonishment of the women, and said – 'Please, how soon are we going away?'

'Bless us and save us! who'd ha' thought of any one being in the bed? Are you one of the Hollingford ladies, my dear? They are all gone this hour or more!'

'Oh, dear, what shall I do? That lady they call Clare promised to waken me in time. Papa will so wonder where I am, and I don't know what Betty will say.'

The child began to cry, and the housemaids looked at each other in some dismay and much sympathy. Just then, they heard Mrs Kirkpatrick's step along the passages, approaching. She was singing some little Italian air in a low musical voice, coming to her bedroom to dress for dinner. One housemaid said to the other, with a knowing look, 'Best leave it to her;' and they passed on to their work in the other rooms.

Mrs Kirkpatrick opened the door, and stood aghast at the sight of Molly.

'Why, I quite forgot you!' she said at length. 'Nay, don't cry; you'll make yourself not fit to be seen. Of course, I must take the consequences of your over-sleeping yourself; and, if I can't manage to get you back to Hollingford tonight, you shall sleep with me, and we'll do our best to send you home tomorrow morning.'

'But papa!' sobbed out Molly. 'He always wants me to make tea for him; and I have no night-things.'

'Well, don't go and make a piece of work* about what can't be helped now! I'll lend you night-things, and your papa must do without your making tea for him tonight. And, another time, don't over-sleep yourself in a strange house; you may not always find yourself among such hospitable people as they are here. Why now, if you don't cry and make a figure of yourself, I'll ask if you may come in to dessert with Master Smythe and the little ladies. You shall go into the nursery, and have some tea with them; and then you must come back here and brush your hair and make yourself tidy. I think it is a very fine thing for you to be stopping in such a grand house as this; many a little girl would like nothing better.'

During this speech she was arranging her toilette for dinner – taking off her black morning-gown; putting on her dressing-gown; shaking her long soft auburn hair over her shoulders, and glancing about the room in search of various articles of her dress – a running flow of easy talk babbling out all the time.

'I have a little girl of my own, dear! I don't know what she would not give to be staying here at Lord Cumnor's with me; but, instead of that, she has to spend her holidays at school; and yet you are looking as miserable as can be at the thought of stopping for just one night. I really have been as busy as can be with those tiresome – those good ladies, I mean, from Hollingford – and one can't think of everything at a time.'

Molly – only child as she was – had stopped her tears at the mention of that little girl of Mrs Kirkpatrick's; and now she ventured to say –

'Are you married, ma'am; I thought she called you Clare?'

In high good-humour, Mrs Kirkpatrick made reply – 'I don't look as if I was married, do I? Every one is surprised. And yet I have been a widow for seven months now; and not a grey hair on my head, though Lady Cuxhaven, who is younger than I, has ever so many.'

'Why do they call you "Clare"?' continued Molly, finding her so affable and communicative.

'Because I lived with them when I was Miss Clare. It is a pretty name, isn't it? I married a Mr Kirkpatrick; he was only a curate, poor fellow; but he was of a very good family; and, if three of his relations had died without children, I should have been a baronet's wife. But Providence did not see fit to permit it; and we must always resign ourselves to what is decreed. Two of his cousins married, and had large families; and poor dear Kirkpatrick died, leaving me a widow.'

'You have a little girl?' asked Molly.

'Yes: darling Cynthia! I wish you could see her; she is my only comfort now. If I have time, I will show you her picture when we come up to bed; but I must go now. It does not do to keep Lady Cumnor waiting a moment; and she asked me to be down early, to help with some of the people in the house. Now I shall ring this bell; and, when the housemaid comes, ask her to take you into the nursery, and to tell Lady Cuxhaven's nurse who you are. And then you'll have tea with the little ladies, and come in with them to dessert. There! I'm sorry you've overslept yourself, and are left here; but give me a kiss, and don't cry – you really are rather a pretty child, though you've not got Cynthia's colouring! Oh, Nanny, would you be so very kind as to take this young lady –

(what's your name, my dear? Gibson?) – Miss Gibson, to Mrs
Dyson, in the nursery, and ask her to allow her to drink tea with
the young ladies there; and to send her in with them to dessert?
I'll explain it all to my lady.'

Nanny's face brightened out of its gloom when she heard the
name Gibson; and, having ascertained from Molly that she was
'the doctor's' child, she showed more willingness to comply with
Mrs Kirkpatrick's request than was usual with her.

Molly was an obliging girl, and fond of children; so, as long as
she was in the nursery, she got on pretty well, being obedient to
the wishes of the supreme power, and even very useful to Mrs
Dyson, by playing at tricks, and thus keeping a little one quiet,
while its brothers and sisters were being arrayed in gay attire –
lace and muslin, and velvet, and brilliant broad ribbons.

'Now, miss,' said Mrs Dyson, when her own especial charges
were all ready, 'what can I do for you? You have not got another
frock here, have you?' No, indeed, she had not; nor, if she had
had one, could it have been of a smarter nature than her present
thick white dimity. So she could only wash her face and hands,
and submit to the nurse's brushing and perfuming her hair. She
thought she would rather have stayed in the park all night long,
and slept under the beautiful quiet cedar, than have had to
undergo the unknown ordeal of 'going down to dessert', which
was evidently regarded both by children and nurses as the event
of the day. At length there was a summons from a footman; and
Mrs Dyson, in a rustling silk gown, marshalled her convoy, and
set sail for the dining-room door.

There was a large party of gentlemen and ladies sitting round
the decked table, in the brilliantly-lighted room. Each dainty little
child ran up to its mother, or aunt, or particular friend; but Molly
had no one to go to.

'Who is that tall girl in the thick white frock? Not one of the
children in the house, I think?'

The lady addressed put up her glass, gazed at Molly, and
dropped it in an instant. 'A French girl, I should imagine. I know
Lady Cuxhaven was inquiring for one to bring up with her little
girls, that they might get a good accent early. Poor little woman,
she looks wild and strange!' And the speaker, who sate next to
Lord Cumnor, made a little sign to Molly to come to her; Molly
crept up to her as to the first shelter; but, when the lady began

talking to her in French, she blushed violently, and said in a very low voice –

'I don't understand French. I'm only Molly Gibson, ma'am.'

'Molly Gibson!' said the lady, out loud; as if that was not much of an explanation.

Lord Cumnor caught the words and the tone.

'Oh, ho!' said he. 'Are you the little girl who has been sleeping in my bed?'

He imitated the deep voice of the fabulous bear, who asks this question of the little child in the story; but Molly had never read the 'Three Bears',* and fancied that his anger was real; she trembled a little, and drew nearer to the kind lady who had beckoned her as to a refuge. Lord Cumnor was very fond of getting hold of what he fancied was a joke, and working his idea threadbare; so, all the time the ladies were in the room, he kept on his running fire at Molly, alluding to the Sleeping Beauty, the Seven Sleepers,* and any other famous sleeper that came into his head. He had no idea of the misery his jokes were to the sensitive girl, who already thought herself a miserable sinner, for having slept on, when she ought to have been awake. If Molly had been in the habit of putting two and two together, she might have found an excuse for herself, by remembering that Mrs Kirkpatrick had promised faithfully to awaken her in time; but all the girl thought of was, how little they wanted her in this grand house; how she must seem like a careless intruder who had no business there. Once or twice she wondered where her father was, and whether he was missing her; but the thought of the familiar happiness of home brought such a choking in her throat, that she felt she must not give way to it, for fear of bursting out crying; and she had instinct enough to feel that, as she was left at the Towers, the less trouble she gave, the more she kept herself out of observation, the better.

She followed the ladies out of the dining-room, almost hoping that no one would see her. But that was impossible, and she immediately became the subject of conversation between the awful Lady Cumnor and her kind neighbour at dinner.

'Do you know, I thought this young lady was French when I first saw her? she has got the black hair and eye-lashes, and grey eyes, and colourless complexion which one meets with in some parts of France, and I knew Lady Cuxhaven was trying to find a well-educated girl who would be a pleasant companion to her children.'

'No!' said Lady Cumnor, looking very stern, as Molly thought. 'She is the daughter of our medical man at Hollingford; she came with the school visitors this morning, and she was overcome by the heat and fell asleep in Clare's room, and somehow managed to over-sleep herself, and did not waken up till all the carriages were gone. We will send her home tomorrow morning; but for tonight she must stay here, and Clare is kind enough to say she may sleep with her.'

There was an implied blame running through this speech, that Molly felt like needle-points all over her. Lady Cuxhaven came up at this moment. Her tone was as deep, her manner of speaking as abrupt and authoritative, as her mother's, but Molly felt the kinder nature underneath.

'How are you now, my dear? You look better than you did under the cedar-tree. So you're to stop here tonight? Clare, don't you think we could find some of those books of engravings that would interest Miss Gibson?'

Mrs Kirkpatrick came gliding up to the place where Molly stood; and began petting her with pretty words and actions, while Lady Cuxhaven turned over heavy volumes in search of one that might interest the girl.

'Poor darling! I saw you come into the dining-room, looking so shy; and I wanted you to come near me, but I could not make a sign to you, because Lord Cuxhaven was speaking to me at the time, telling me about his travels. Ah, here is a nice book – *Lodge's Portraits;** now I'll sit by you and tell you who they all are, and all about them. Don't trouble yourself any more, dear Lady Cuxhaven; I'll take charge of her; pray leave her to me!'

Molly grew hotter and hotter as these last words met her ear. If they would only leave her alone, and not labour at being kind to her; would 'not trouble themselves' about her! These words of Mrs Kirkpatrick's seemed to quench the gratitude she was feeling to Lady Cuxhaven for looking for something to amuse her. But, of course, it was a trouble; and she ought never to have been there.

By-and-by, Mrs Kirkpatrick was called away to accompany Lady Agnes's song, and then Molly really had a few minutes' enjoyment. She could look round the room, unobserved, and, sure, never was any place out of a king's house so grand and magnificent! Large mirrors, velvet curtains, pictures in their gilded frames, a multitude of dazzling lights decorated the vast saloon; and the floor was studded with groups of ladies and gentlemen, all dressed in gorgeous attire. Suddenly, Molly bethought her of the children whom she had accompanied into the dining-room, and to whose ranks she had appeared to belong – where were they? Gone to bed an hour before, at some quiet signal from their mother. Molly wondered if she might go, too – if she could ever find her way back to the haven of Mrs Kirkpatrick's bedroom. But she was at some distance from the door; a long way from Mrs Kirkpatrick, to whom she felt herself to belong more than to any one else. Far, too, from Lady Cuxhaven, and the terrible Lady Cumnor, and her jocose and good-natured lord. So Molly sate on, turning over pictures which she did not see; her heart growing heavier and heavier in the desolation of all this grandeur. Presently a footman entered the room, and, after a moment's looking about him, he went up to Mrs Kirkpatrick, where she sate at the piano, the centre of the musical portion of the company, ready to accompany any singer, and smiling pleasantly as she willingly acceded to all requests. She came now towards Molly, in her corner, and said to her –

'Do you know, darling, your papa has come for you, and brought your pony for you to ride home; so I shall lose my little bedfellow, for I suppose you must go?'

Go! was there a question of it in Molly's mind, as she stood up quivering, sparkling, almost crying out loud? She was brought to her senses, though, by Mrs Kirkpatrick's next words.

'You must go and wish Lady Cumnor good-night, you know, my dear, and thank her ladyship for her kindness to you. She is there, near that statue, talking to Mr Courtenay.'

Yes! she was there – forty feet away – a hundred miles away! All that blank space had to be crossed; and then a speech to be made!

'Must I go?' asked Molly, in the most pitiful and pleading voice possible.

'Yes; make haste about it; there is nothing so formidable in it, is there?' replied Mrs Kirkpatrick, in a sharper voice than before, aware that they were wanting her at the piano, and anxious to get the business in hand done as soon as possible.

Molly stood still for a minute, then, looking up, she said softly –

'Would you mind coming with me, please?'

'No! not I!' said Mrs Kirkpatrick, seeing that her compliance was likely to be the most speedy way of getting through the affair; so she took Molly's hand, and, on the way, in passing the group at the piano, she said, smiling, in her pretty genteel manner –

'Our little friend here is shy and modest, and wants me to accompany her to Lady Cumnor to wish good-night; her father has come for her, and she is going away.'

Molly did not know how it was, afterwards; but she pulled her hand out of Mrs Kirkpatrick's on hearing these words, and, going a step or two in advance, came up to Lady Cumnor, grand in purple velvet, and dropping a curtsey, almost after the fashion of the school-children, she said –

'My lady, papa is come, and I am going away; and, my lady, I wish you good-night, and thank you for your kindness. Your ladyship's kindness, I mean,' she said, correcting herself as she remembered Miss Browning's particular instructions as to the etiquette to be observed to earls and countesses, and their honourable progeny, as they were given that morning on the road to the Towers.

She got out of the saloon somehow; she believed afterwards, on thinking about it, that she had never bidden good-bye to Lady Cuxhaven, or Mrs Kirkpatrick, or 'all the rest of them', as she irreverently styled them in her thoughts.

Mr Gibson was in the housekeeper's room, when Molly ran in, rather to the stately Mrs Brown's discomfiture. She threw her arms round her father's neck. 'Oh, papa, papa, papa! I am so glad you have come!' and then she burst out crying, stroking his face almost hysterically as if to make sure he was there.

'Why, what a noodle you are, Molly! Did you think I was going to give up my little girl to live at the Towers all the rest of her life? You make as much work about my coming for you, as if you thought I had. Make haste, now, and get on your bonnet! Mrs Brown, may I ask you for a shawl, or a plaid, or a wrap of some kind, to pin about her for a petticoat?'

He did not mention that he had come home from a long round not half-an-hour before, a round from which he had returned dinnerless and hungry; but, on finding that Molly had not come back from the Towers, he had ridden his tired horse round by Miss Brownings', and found them in self-reproachful, helpless dismay. He would not wait to listen to their tearful apologies; he galloped home, had a fresh horse and Molly's pony saddled; and, though Betty called after him with a riding-skirt for the child, when he was not ten yards from his own stable-door, he refused to turn back for it, but went off, as Dick the stableman said, 'muttering to himself awful.'

Mrs Brown had her bottle of wine out, and her plate of cake, before Molly came back from her long expedition to Mrs Kirkpatrick's room, 'pretty nigh on to a quarter of a mile off,' as the housekeeper informed the impatient father, as he waited for his child to come down, arrayed in her morning's finery, with the gloss of newness worn off. Mr Gibson was a favourite in all the Towers household, as family doctors generally are; bringing hopes of relief at times of anxiety and distress; and Mrs Brown, who was subject to gout, especially delighted in petting him whenever he would allow her. She even went out into the stable-yard to pin Molly up in the shawl, as she sate upon the rough-coated pony, and hazarded the somewhat safe conjecture –

'I daresay she'll be happier at home, Mr Gibson,' as they rode away.

Once out into the park, Molly struck her pony, and urged him on as hard as he would go. Mr Gibson called out at last –

'Molly! we're coming to the rabbit-holes; it's not safe to go at such a pace. Stop!' And, as she drew rein, he rode up alongside of her.

'We're getting into the shadow of the trees, and it's not safe riding fast here.'

'Oh! papa, I never was so glad in all my life. I felt like a lighted candle when they're putting the extinguisher on it.'

'Did you? How d'ye know what the candle feels?'

'Oh, I don't know, but I did.' And again, after a pause, she said – 'Oh, I am so glad to be here! It is so pleasant riding here in the open, free, fresh air, crushing out such a good smell from the dewy grass. Papa! are you there? I can't see you.'

He rode close up alongside of her: he was not sure but what she might be afraid of riding in the dark shadows, so he laid his hand upon hers.

'Oh! I am so glad to feel you,' squeezing his hand hard. 'Papa, I should like to get a chain like Ponto's,* just as long as your longest round, and then I could fasten us two to each end of it, and when I wanted you I could pull; and, if you didn't want to come, you could pull back again; but I should know you knew I wanted you, and we could never lose each other.'

'I'm rather lost in that plan of yours; the details, as you state them, are a little puzzling; but, if I make them out rightly, I am to go about the country, like the donkeys on the common, with a clog fastened to my hind leg.'

'I shouldn't mind your calling me a clog, if only we were fastened together.'

'But I do mind you calling me a donkey,' he replied.

'I never did. At least I didn't mean to. But it is such a comfort to know that I may be as rude as I like.'

'Is that what you've learnt from the grand company you've been keeping today? I expected to find you so polite and ceremonious, that I read a few chapters of *Sir Charles Grandison*,* in order to bring myself up to concert pitch.'*

'Oh, I do hope I shall never be a lord or a lady.'

'Well, to comfort you, I'll tell you this: I'm sure you'll never be a lord; and I think the chances are a thousand to one against your ever being the other, in the sense in which you mean.'

'I should lose myself every time I had to fetch my bonnet, or else get tired of long passages and great staircases long before I could go out walking.'

'But you'd have your lady's-maid, you know.'

'Do you know, papa, I think lady's-maids are worse than ladies. I should not mind being a housekeeper so much.'

'No! the jam-cupboards and dessert would lie very conveniently to one's hand,' replied her father meditatively. 'But Mrs Brown tells me that the thought of the dinners often keeps her from sleeping; there's that anxiety to be taken into consideration. Still, in every condition of life, there are heavy cares and responsibilities.'

'Well! I suppose so,' said Molly gravely. 'I know Betty says I wear her life out with the green stains I get in my frocks from sitting in the cherry-tree.'

'And Miss Browning said she had fretted herself into a headache, with thinking how they had left you behind. I'm afraid you'll be as bad as a bill of fare to them tonight. How did it all happen, goosey?'

'Oh, I went by myself to see the gardens; they are so beautiful! and I lost myself, and sat down to rest under a great tree; and Lady Cuxhaven and that Mrs Kirkpatrick came; and Mrs Kirkpatrick brought me some lunch, and then put me to sleep on her bed – and I thought she would waken me in time; and she didn't; and so they'd all gone away; and, when they planned for me to stop till tomorrow, I didn't like saying how very, very much I wanted to go home – but I kept thinking how you would wonder where I was.'

'Then it was rather a dismal day of pleasure, goosey, eh?'

'Not in the morning. I shall never forget the morning in that garden. But I was never so unhappy in all my life, as I have been all this long afternoon.'

Mr Gibson thought it his duty to ride round by the Towers, and pay a visit of apology and thanks to the family, before they left for London. He found them all on the wing; and no one was sufficiently at liberty to listen to his grateful civilities but Mrs Kirkpatrick, who, although she was to accompany Lady Cuxhaven, and pay a visit to her former pupil, made leisure enough to receive Mr Gibson, on behalf of the family, and assured him of her faithful remembrance of his great professional attention to her in former days in the most winning manner.

CHAPTER 3

Molly Gibson's Childhood

Sixteen years before this time, all Hollingford had been disturbed to its foundations by the intelligence* that Mr Hall, the skilful doctor, who had attended them all their days, was going to take a partner. It was no use reasoning with them on the subject; so Mr Browning the vicar, Mr Sheepshanks (Lord Cumnor's agent), and Mr Hall himself, the masculine reasoners of the little society, left off the attempt, feeling that the *Che sarà sarà** would prove more silencing to the murmurs than many arguments. Mr Hall had told his faithful patients that, even with the strongest spectacles, his sight was not to be depended upon; and they might have found out for themselves that his hearing was very defective, although, on this point, he obstinately adhered to his own opinion, and was frequently heard to regret the carelessness of people's communication nowadays, 'like writing on blotting-paper, all the words running into each other,' he would say. And, more than once, Mr

Hall had had attacks of a suspicious nature – 'rheumatism' he used to call them, but he prescribed for himself as if they had been gout – which had prevented his immediate attention to imperative summonses. But, blind and deaf, and rheumatic as he might be, he was still Mr Hall the doctor who could heal all their ailments – unless they died meanwhile – and he had no right to speak of growing old, and taking a partner.

He went very steadily to work, all the same; advertising in medical journals, reading testimonials, sifting character and qualifications; and, just when the elderly maiden ladies of Hollingford thought that they had convinced their contemporary that he was as young as ever, he startled them by bringing his new partner, Mr Gibson, to call upon them, and began, 'slyly', as these ladies said, to introduce him into practice. And 'Who was this Mr Gibson?' they asked, and echo might answer the question, if she liked, for no one else did. No one ever in all his life knew anything more of his antecedents than the Hollingford people might have found out the first day they saw him: that he was tall, grave, rather handsome than otherwise; thin enough to be called 'a very genteel figure', in those days, before muscular Christianity* had come into vogue; speaking with a slight Scotch accent;* and, as one good lady observed, 'so very trite in his conversation', by which she meant sarcastic. As to his birth, parentage, and education – the favourite conjecture of Hollingford society was, that he was the illegitimate son of a Scotch Duke by a Frenchwoman; and the grounds for this conjecture were these: – He spoke with a Scotch accent; therefore, he must be Scotch. He had a very genteel appearance, an elegant figure, and was apt – so his ill-wishers said – to give himself airs; therefore, his father must have been some person of quality; and, that granted, nothing was easier than to run this supposition up all the notes of the scale of the peerage – baron, viscount, earl, marquis, duke. Higher they dared not go, though one old lady, acquainted with English history, hazarded the remark, that 'she believed that one or two of the Stuarts* – ahem – had not always been – ahem – quite correct in their – conduct; and she fancied such – ahem – things ran in families.' But, in popular opinion, Mr Gibson's father always remained a duke; nothing more.

Then his mother must have been a Frenchwoman, because his hair was so black; and he was so sallow; and because he had been in Paris. All this might be true, or might not; nobody ever knew, or found out anything more about him than what Mr Hall told them, namely, that his professional qualifications were as high as his moral character, and that both were far above the average, as Mr Hall had taken pains to ascertain before introducing him to his patients. The popularity of this world is as transient as its glory, as Mr Hall found out before the first year of his partnership was over. He had plenty of leisure left him now to nurse his gout and cherish his eyesight. The younger doctor had carried the day; nearly every one sent for Mr Gibson. Even at the great houses – even at the Towers, that greatest of all, where Mr Hall had introduced his new partner with fear and trembling, with untold anxiety as to his behaviour and the impression he might make on my lord the Earl, and my lady the Countess – Mr Gibson was received, at the end of a twelvemonth, with as much welcome respect for his professional skill as Mr Hall himself had ever been. Nay – and this was a little too much for even the kind old doctor's good temper – Mr Gibson had even been invited once to dinner at the Towers; to dine with the great Sir Astley,* the head of the profession! To be sure. Mr Hall had been asked as well; but he was laid up just then with his gout (since he had had a partner, the rheumatism had been allowed to develop itself), and he had not been able to go. Poor Mr Hall never quite got over this mortification; after it he allowed himself to become dim of sight and hard of hearing, and kept pretty closely to the house during the two winters that remained of his life. He sent for an orphan grand-niece, to keep him company in his old age; he, the woman-contemning old bachelor, became thankful for the cheerful presence of the pretty, bonny Mary Pearson, who was good and sensible, and nothing more. She formed a close friendship with the daughters of the vicar, Mr Browning; and Mr Gibson found time to become very intimate with all three. Hollingford speculated much on which young lady would become Mrs Gibson, and was rather sorry when the talk about possibilities, and the gossip about probabilities, with regard to the handsome young surgeon's marriage, ended in the most natural manner in the world, by his marrying his predecessor's niece. The two Miss Brownings showed no signs of going into a consumption* on the occasion, although their looks and manners were carefully watched. On the contrary, they were rather boisterously merry at the wedding; and poor Mrs Gibson it was that died of consumption, four or five years after her marriage – three years after the death of her great-uncle, and when her only child, Molly, was just three years old.

Mr Gibson did not speak much about the grief at the loss of his wife which it was supposed that he felt. Indeed, he avoided all demonstrations of sympathy, and got up hastily and left the room, when Miss Phoebe Browning first saw him after his loss, and burst into an uncontrollable flood of tears, which threatened to end in hysterics. Miss Browning declared she never could forgive him for his hard-heartedness on that occasion; but, a fortnight afterwards, she came to very high words with old Mrs Goodenough for gasping out her doubts whether Mr Gibson was a man of deep feeling; judging by the narrowness of his crape hat-band,* which ought to have covered his hat, whereas there was at least three inches of beaver to be seen. And, in spite of it all, Miss Browning and Miss Phoebe considered themselves as Mr Gibson's most intimate friends, in right of their regard for his dead wife; and they would fain have taken a quasi-motherly interest in his little girl, had she not been guarded by a watchful dragon in the shape of Betty, her nurse, who was jealous of any interference between her and her charge, and especially resentful and disagreeable towards all those ladies whom, by suitable age, rank, or propinquity, she thought capable of 'casting sheeps' eyes at Master.'

Several years before the opening of this story, Mr Gibson's position seemed settled for life, both socially and professionally. He was a widower, and likely to remain so; his domestic affections were centred on little Molly, but even to her, in their most private moments, he did not give way to much expression of his feelings; his most caressing appellation for her was 'Goosey', and he took a pleasure in bewildering her infant mind with his badinage. He had rather a contempt for demonstrative people, arising from his medical insight into the consequences to health of uncontrolled feeling. He deceived himself into believing that still his reason was lord of all, because he had never fallen into the habit of expression on any other than purely intellectual subjects. Molly, however, had her own intuitions to guide her. Though her papa laughed at her, quizzed her,* joked at her, in a way which the Miss Brownings called 'really cruel' to each other when they were quite alone, Molly took her little griefs and pleasures and poured them into her papa's ears sooner even than into Betty's, that kind-hearted termagant. The child grew to understand her father well, and the two had the most delightful intercourse together – half banter, half seriousness, but altogether confidential friendship. Mr Gibson kept three servants: Betty, a cook, and a girl who was supposed to be housemaid, but who was under both the elder two, and had a pretty life of it in consequence. Three servants would not have been required if it had not been Mr Gibson's habit, as it had been Mr Hall's before him, to take two 'pupils', as they were called in the genteel language of Hollingford – 'apprentices' as they were in fact, being bound by indentures, and paying a handsome premium to learn their business. They lived in the house, and occupied an uncomfortable, ambiguous, or, as Miss Browning called it with some truth, 'amphibious', position. They had their meals with Mr Gibson and Molly, and were felt to be terribly in the way; Mr Gibson not being a man who could make conversation, and hating the duty of talking under restraint. Yet something within him made him wince, as if his duties were not rightly performed, when, as the cloth was drawn, the two awkward lads rose up with joyful alacrity; gave him a nod, which was to be interpreted as a bow; knocked against each other in their endeavours to get out of the dining-room quickly; and then might be heard dashing along a passage which led to the surgery, choking with half-suppressed laughter. Yet the annoyance he felt at this dull sense of imper-fectly-fulfilled duties only made his sarcasms on their inefficiency, or stupidity, or ill-manners, more bitter than before.

Beyond direct professional instruction, he did not know what to do with the succession of pairs of young men, whose mission seemed to be to be plagued by their master consciously, and to plague him unconsciously. Once or twice Mr Gibson had declined taking a fresh pupil, in the hopes of shaking himself free from the incubus; but his reputation as a clever surgeon had spread so rapidly that his fees, which he had thought prohibitory, were willingly paid, in order that the young man might make a start in life, with the prestige of having been a pupil of Gibson of Hollingford. But, as Molly grew to be a little girl instead of a child, when she was about eight years old, her father perceived the awkwardness of her having her breakfasts and dinners so often alone with the pupils, without his uncertain presence. To do away with this evil, more than for the actual instruction she could give, he engaged a respectable woman, the daughter of a shop-keeper in the town, who had left a destitute family, to come every morning before breakfast, and stay with Molly till he came home at night; or, if he was detained, until the child's bed-time.

'Now, Miss Eyre,'* said he, summing up his instructions the day before she entered on her office, 'remember this: you are to make good tea for the young men, and see that they have their meals comfortably; and – you are five-and-thirty, I think you said? – try and make them talk – rationally, I am afraid is beyond your or anybody's power; but make them talk without stammering or giggling. Don't teach Molly too much: she must sew, and read, and write, and do her sums; but I want to keep her a child; and, if I find more learning desirable for her, I'll see about giving it to her myself. After all, I'm not sure that reading or writing is necessary. Many a good woman gets married with only a cross* instead of her name; it's rather a diluting of mother-wit, to my fancy; but, however, we must yield to the prejudices of society, Miss Eyre, and so you may teach the child to read.'

Miss Eyre listened in silence, perplexed but determined to be obedient to the directions of the doctor, whose kindness she and her family had good cause to know. She made strong tea; she helped the young men liberally in Mr Gibson's absence, as well as in his presence, and she found the way to unloosen their tongues, whenever their master was away, by talking to them on trivial subjects in her pleasant homely way. She taught Molly to read and write, but tried honestly to keep her back in every other branch of education. It was only by fighting and struggling hard, that, bit by bit, Molly persuaded her father to let her have French and drawing-lessons. He was always afraid of her becoming too much educated, though he need not have been alarmed; the masters who visited such small country towns as Hollingford forty years ago, were no such great proficients in their arts. Once a week she joined a dancing-class in the assembly-room at the principal inn in the town, the 'Cumnor Arms'; and, being daunted by her father in every intellectual attempt, she read every book that came in her way, almost with as much delight as if it had been forbidden. For his station in life, Mr Gibson had an unusually good library; the medical portion of it was inaccessible to Molly, being kept in the surgery, but every other book she had either read, or tried to read. Her summer place of study was that seat in the cherry-tree, where she got the green stains on her frock, that have already been mentioned as likely to wear Betty's life out. In spite of this 'hidden worm i' th' bud',* Betty was to all appearance strong, alert, and flourishing. She was the one crook* in Miss Eyre's lot, who was otherwise so happy in having met with a suitable well-paid employment, just when she needed it most. But Betty, though agreeing in theory with her master when he told her of the necessity of having a governess for his little daughter, was vehemently opposed to any division of her authority and influence over the child who had been her charge, her plague, and her delight ever since Mrs Gibson's death. She took up her position as censor of all Miss Eyre's sayings and doings from the very first, and did not for one moment condescend to conceal her disapprobation in her heart. She could not help respecting the patience and pains-taking of the good lady – for a 'lady' Miss Eyre was in the best sense of the word, though in Hollingford she only took rank as a shop-keeper's daughter. Yet Betty buzzed about her with the teasing pertinacity of a gnat, always ready to find fault, if not to bite. Miss Eyre's only defence came from the quarter whence it might least have been expected – from her pupil; on whose fancied behalf, as an oppressed little personage, Betty always based her attacks. But, very early in the day, Molly perceived their injustice; and soon afterwards she began to respect Miss Eyre for her silent endurance of what evidently gave her far more pain than Betty imagined. Mr Gibson had been a friend in need to her family; so Miss Eyre restrained her complaints, sooner than annoy him. And she had her reward. Betty would offer Molly all sorts of small temptations to neglect Miss Eyre's wishes; Molly steadily resisted, and plodded away at her task of sewing or her difficult sum. Betty made cumbrous jokes at Miss Eyre's expense; Molly looked up with the utmost gravity, as if requesting the explanation of an unintelligible speech; and there is nothing so quenching to a wag as to be asked to translate his jest into plain matter-of-fact English, and to show wherein the point lies. Occasionally Betty lost her temper entirely, and spoke impertinently to Miss Eyre; but, when this had been done in Molly's defence, the girl flew out in such a violent passion of words in defence of her silent trembling governess, that even Betty herself was daunted, though she chose to take the child's anger as a good joke, and tried to persuade Miss Eyre herself to join in her amusement.

'Bless the child! one 'ud think I was a hungry pussycat, and she a hen-sparrow, with her wings all fluttering, and her little eyes aflame, and her beak ready to peck me, just because I happened to look near her nest. Nay, child! if thou lik'st to be stifled in a nasty close room, learning things as is of no earthly good when

they is learnt, instead o' riding on Job Donkin's hay-cart, it's thy
look-out, not mine. She's a little vixen, isn't she?' smiling at Miss
Eyre, as she finished her speech. But the poor governess saw no
humour in the affair; the comparison of Molly to a hen-sparrow
was lost upon her. She was sensitive and conscientious, and knew,
from home experience, the evils of an ungovernable temper. So
she began to reprove Molly for giving way to her passion, and the
child thought it hard to be blamed for what she considered her
just anger against Betty. But, after all, these were the small
grievances of a very happy childhood.

CHAPTER 4

Mr Gibson's Neighbours

Molly grew up among these quiet people in calm monotony of
life, without any greater event than that which has been recorded
– the being left behind at the Towers – until she was nearly
seventeen. She had become a visitor at the school, but she had
never gone again to the annual festival at the great house; it was
easy to find some excuse for keeping away, and the recollection of
that day was not a pleasant one on the whole, though she often
thought how much she should like to see the gardens again.

Lady Agnes was married; there was only Lady Harriet remaining at home; Lord Hollingford, the eldest son, had lost his wife,
and was a good deal more at the Towers since he had become a
widower. He was a tall, ungainly man, considered to be as proud
as his mother, the countess; but, in fact, he was only shy, and
slow at making commonplace speeches. He did not know what to
say to people whose daily habits and interests were not the same
as his; he would have been very thankful for a hand-book of
small-talk, and would have learnt off his sentences with good-
humoured diligence. He often envied the fluency of his garrulous
father, who delighted in talking to everybody, and was perfectly
unconscious of the incoherence of his conversation. But, owing to
his constitutional reserve and shyness, Lord Hollingford was not
a popular man, although his kindness of heart was very great, his
simplicity of character extreme, and his scientific acquirements
considerable enough to entitle him to much reputation in the

European republic of learned men. In this respect Hollingford was proud of him. The inhabitants knew that the great, grave, clumsy heir to its fealty was highly esteemed for his wisdom; and that he had made one or two discoveries, though in what direction they were not quite sure. But it was safe to point him out to strangers visiting the little town, as 'That's Lord Hollingford – the famous Lord Hollingford, you know; you must have heard of him, he is so scientific.' If the strangers knew his name, they also knew his claims to fame; if they did not, ten to one but they would appear as if they did, and so conceal not only their own ignorance, but that of their companions, as to the exact nature of the sources of his reputation.

He was left a widower with two or three boys. They were at a public school; so that their companionship could make the house in which he had passed his married life but little of a home to him, and he consequently spent much of his time at the Towers; where his mother was proud of him, and his father very fond, but ever so little afraid of him. His friends were always welcomed by Lord and Lady Cumnor; the former, indeed, was in the habit of welcoming everybody everywhere; but it was a proof of Lady Cumnor's real affection for her distinguished son, that she allowed him to ask what she called 'all sorts of people' to the Towers. 'All sorts of people' meant really those who were distinguished for science and learning, without regard to rank; and, it must be confessed, without much regard to polished manners likewise.

Mr Hall, Mr Gibson's predecessor, had always been received with friendly condescension by my lady, who had found him established as the family medical man, when first she came to the Towers on her marriage; but she never thought of interfering with his custom of taking his meals, if he needed refreshment, in the housekeeper's room, not *with* the housekeeper, *bien entendu*.* The comfortable, clever, stout, and red-faced doctor would very much have preferred this, even if he had had the choice given him (which he never had) of taking his 'snack', as he called it, with my lord and my lady, in the grand dining-room. Of course, if some great surgical gun (like Sir Astley) was brought down from London to bear on the family's health, it was due to him, as well as to the local medical attendant, to ask Mr Hall to dinner, in a formal ceremonious manner; on which occasion Mr Hall buried his chin in voluminous folds of white muslin, put on his knee-breeches, with bunches of ribbon at the sides, his silk stockings and buckled shoes, and otherwise made himself excessively uncomfortable in his attire, and went forth in state in a post-chaise from the 'Cumnor Arms', consoling himself in the private corner of his heart for the discomfort he was enduring with the idea of how well it would sound the next day in the ears of the squires whom he was in the habit of attending: 'Yesterday at dinner the earl said,' or 'the countess remarked,' or 'I was surprised to hear when I was dining at the Towers yesterday.' But somehow things had changed since Mr Gibson had become 'the doctor' *par excellence* at Hollingford. Miss Brownings thought that it was because he had such an elegant figure, and 'such a distinguished manner'; Mrs Goodenough, 'because of his aristo-cratic connections' – 'the son of a Scotch duke, my dear, never mind on which side of the blanket.'* But the fact was certain; although he might frequently ask Mrs Brown to give him some-thing to eat in the housekeeper's room – he had no time for all the fuss and ceremony of luncheon with my lady – he was always welcome to the grandest circle of visitors in the house. He might lunch with a duke any day that he chose; given that a duke was forthcoming at the Towers. His accent was Scotch, not provincial. He had not an ounce of superfluous flesh on his bones; and leanness goes a great way to gentility. His complexion was sallow, and his hair black; in those days, the decade after the conclusion of the great continental war,* to be sallow and black-a-vised* was of itself a distinction; he was not jovial (as my lord remarked with a sigh, but it was my lady who endorsed the invitations), sparing of his words, intelligent, and slightly sarcastic. Therefore he was perfectly presentable.

His Scotch blood (for that he was of Scottish descent there could be no manner of doubt) gave him just the kind of thistly dignity* which made every one feel that they must treat him with respect; so that on that head he was assured. The grandeur of being from time to time an invited guest to dinner at the Towers gave him but little pleasure for many years; but it was a form to be gone through in the way of his profession, without any idea of social gratification.

But, when Lord Hollingford returned to make the Towers his home, affairs were altered. Mr Gibson really heard and learnt things that interested him seriously, and that gave fresh flavour to his reading. From time to time he met the leaders of the scientific world; odd-looking, simple-hearted men, very much in earnest about their own particular subjects, and not having much to say on any other. Mr Gibson found himself capable of appreciating such persons, and also perceived that they valued his appreciation, as it was honestly and intelligently given. Indeed, by-and-by, he began to send contributions of his own to the more scientific of the medical journals, and thus, partly in receiving, partly in giving out, information and accurate thought, a new zest was added to his life. There was not much intercourse between Lord Hollingford and himself; the one was too silent and shy, the other too busy, to seek each other's society with the perseverance required to do away with the social distinction of rank that prevented their frequent meetings. But each was thoroughly pleased to come into contact with the other. Each could rely on the other's respect and sympathy with a security unknown to many who call themselves friends, and this was a source of happiness to both; to Mr Gibson the most so, of course; for his range of intelligent and cultivated society was the smaller. Indeed, there was no one equal to himself among the men with whom he associated, and this he had felt as a depressing influence, although he never recognised the cause of his depression. There was Mr Ashton, the vicar, who had succeeded Mr Browning, a thoroughly good and kind-hearted man, but one without an original thought in him; whose habitual courtesy and indolent mind led him to agree to every opinion not palpably heterodox, and to utter platitudes in the most gentlemanly manner. Mr Gibson had once or twice amused himself by leading the vicar on in his agreeable admissions of arguments 'as perfectly convincing', and of statements as 'curious but undoubted', till he had planted the poor clergyman in a bog of heretical bewilderment. But then Mr Ashton's pain and suffering at suddenly finding out into what a theological predicament he had been brought, his real self-reproach at his previous admissions, were so great that Mr Gibson lost all sense of fun, and hastened back to the Thirty-nine Articles* with all the good-will in life, as the only means of soothing the vicar's conscience. On any other subject, except that of orthodoxy, Mr Gibson could lead him any lengths; but then his ignorance on most of them prevented bland acquiescence from arriving at any results which could startle him. He had some private fortune, and was not married, and lived the life of an indolent and refined bachelor; but, though he himself was no very active visitor among his poorer parishioners, he was always willing to relieve their wants in the most liberal, and, considering his habits, occasionally in the most self-denying, manner, whenever Mr Gibson, or any one else, made them clearly known to him. 'Use my purse as freely as if it was your own, Gibson,' he was wont to say. 'I'm such a bad one at going about and making talk to poor folk – I daresay I don't do enough in that way – but I am most willing to give you anything for any one you may consider in want.'

'Thank you; I come upon you pretty often, I believe, and make very little scruple about it; but, if you'll allow me to suggest, it is that you shouldn't try to make talk when you go into the cottages, but just talk.'

'I don't see the difference,' said the vicar, a little querulously; 'but I daresay there is a difference, and I have no doubt what you say is quite true. I shouldn't make talk, but talk; and as both are equally difficult to me, you must let me purchase the privilege of silence by this ten-pound note.'

'Thank you. It's not so satisfactory to me; and, I should think, not to yourself. But probably the Joneses and Greens will prefer it.'

Mr Ashton would look with plaintive inquiry into Mr Gibson's face after some such speech, as if asking if a sarcasm was intended. On the whole, they went on in the most amiable way; only, beyond the gregarious feeling common to most men, they had very little actual pleasure in each other's society. Perhaps the man of all others to whom Mr Gibson took the most kindly – at least, until Lord Hollingford came into the neighbourhood – was a certain Squire Hamley.* He and his ancestors had been called squire as long back as local tradition extended. But there was many a greater landowner in the county, for Squire Hamley's estate was not more than eight hundred acres or so. But his family had been in possession of it, long before the Earls of Cumnor had been heard of; before the Hely-Harrisons had bought Coldstone Park; no one in Hollingford knew the time when the Hamleys had not lived at Hamley. 'Ever since the Heptarchy,'* said the vicar. 'Nay,' said Miss Browning, 'I have heard that there were Hamleys of Hamley before the Romans.' The vicar was preparing a polite assent, when Mrs Goodenough came in with a still more startling assertion. 'I have always heerd,' said she, with all the slow authority of an oldest inhabitant, 'that there was Hamleys of Hamley afore the time of the pagans.' Mr Ashton could only bow, and say, 'Possibly; very possibly, madam.' But he said it in so courteous a manner that Mrs Goodenough looked round in a gratified way, as much as to say, 'The Church confirms my words; who now will dare dispute them?' At any rate, the Hamleys were a very old family, if not aborigines. They had not increased their estate for centuries; they had held their own, if even with an effort, and had not sold a rood of it for the last hundred years or so. But they were not an adventurous race. They never traded, or speculated, or tried agricultural improvements of any kind. They had no capital in any bank; nor, what perhaps would have been more in character, hoards of gold in any stocking. Their mode of life was simple, and more like that of yeomen than squires. Indeed, Squire Hamley, by continuing the primitive manners and customs of his forefathers, the squires of the eighteenth century, did live more as a yeoman, when such a class existed, than as a squire of this generation. There was a dignity in this quiet conservatism that gained him an immense amount of respect both from high and low; and he might have visited at every house in the county, had he so chosen. But he was very indifferent to the charms of society; and perhaps this was owing to the fact that the squire, Roger Hamley, who at present lived and reigned at Hamley, had not received so good an education as he ought to have done. His father, Squire Stephen, had been plucked* at Oxford, and, with stubborn pride, he had refused to go up again. Nay more: he had sworn a great oath, as men did in those days, that none of his children to come should ever know either university* by becoming a member of it. He had only one child, the present Squire, and he was brought up according to his father's word; he was sent to a petty provincial school, where he saw much that he hated, and then turned loose upon the estate as its heir. Such a bringing-up did not do him all the harm that might have been anticipated. He was imperfectly educated, and ignorant on many points; but he was aware of his deficiency, and regretted it in theory. He was awkward and ungainly in society, and so kept out of it as much as possible; and he was obstinate, violent-tempered, and dictatorial in his own immediate circle. On the other side, he was generous, and true as steel; the very soul of honour, in fact. He had so much natural shrewdness, that his conversation was always worth listening to, although he was apt to start by assuming entirely false premises, which he considered as incontrovertible as if they had been mathematically proved; but, given the correctness of his premises, nobody could bring more natural wit and sense to bear upon the arguments based upon them. He had married a delicate fine London lady; it was one of those perplexing marriages of which one cannot understand the reasons. Yet they were very happy, though possibly Mrs Hamley would not have sunk into the condition of a chronic invalid, if her husband had cared a little more for her various tastes, or allowed her the companionship of those who did. After his marriage, he was wont to say he had got all that was worth having out of the crowd of houses they called London. It was a compliment to his wife which he repeated until the year of her death; it charmed her at first, it pleased her up to the last time of her hearing it; but, for all that, she used sometimes to wish that he would recognise the fact that there might still be something worth hearing and seeing in the great city. But he never went there again; and, though he did not prohibit her going; yet he showed so little sympathy with her, when she came back full of what she had done on her visit, that she ceased caring to go. Not but what he was kind and willing in giving his consent, and in furnishing her amply with money. 'There, there, my little woman, take that! Dress yourself up as fine as any on 'em, and buy what you like, for the credit of Hamley of Hamley; and go to the park and the play, and show off with the best on 'em! I shall be glad to see thee back again, I know; but have thy fling while thou'rt about it.' Then, when she came back, it was, 'Well, well, it has pleased thee, I suppose, so that's all right. But the very talking about it tires me, I know, and I can't think how you have stood it all. Come out and see how pretty the flowers are looking in the south garden. I've made them sow all the seeds you like; and I went over to Hollingford nursery to buy the cuttings of the plants you admired last year. A breath of fresh air will clear my brain after listening to all this talk about the whirl of London, which is liked to have turned me giddy.'

Mrs Hamley was a great reader, and had considerable literary taste. She was gentle and sentimental; tender and good. She gave up her visits to London; she gave up her sociable pleasure in the company of her fellows in education and position. Her husband, owing to the deficiencies of his early years, disliked associating with those to whom he ought to have been an equal; he was too proud to mingle with his inferiors. He loved his wife all the more dearly for her sacrifices for him; but, deprived of all her strong interests, she sank into ill-health; nothing definite; only she never was well. Perhaps, if she had had a daughter, it would have been better for her; but her two children were boys, and their father, anxious to give them the advantages of which he himself had suffered the deprivation, sent the lads very early to a preparatory school. They were to go on to Rugby* and Cambridge; the idea of Oxford was hereditarily distasteful in the Hamley family. Osborne, the eldest – so called after his mother's maiden name – was full of taste, and had some talent. His appearance had all the grace and refinement of his mother's. He was sweet-tempered and affectionate, almost as demonstrative as a girl. He did well at school, carrying away many prizes, and was, in a word, the pride and delight of both father and mother; the confidential friend of the latter, in default of any other. Roger was two years younger than Osborne; clumsy and heavily built, like his father; his face was square, and the expression grave, and rather immobile. He was good, but dull, his schoolmasters said. He won no prizes, but brought home a favourable report of his conduct. When he caressed his mother, she used laughingly to allude to the fable of the lap-dog and the donkey;* so thereafter he left off all personal demonstration of affection. It was a great question as to whether he was to follow his brother to college after he left Rugby. Mrs Hamley thought it would be rather a throwing away of money, as he was so little likely to distinguish himself in intellectual pursuits; anything practical – such as a civil engineer – would be more the kind of life for him. She thought that it would be too mortifying for him to go to the same college and university as his brother, who was sure to distinguish himself – and to be repeatedly plucked, and to come away with a bare degree at last. But his father persevered doggedly, as was his wont, in his intention of giving both his sons the same education; they should both have the advantages of which he had been deprived. If Roger did not do well at Cambridge, it would be his own fault. If his father did not send him thither, some day or other he might be regretting the omission, as the Squire had done himself for many a year. So Roger followed his brother Osborne to Trinity, and Mrs Hamley was again left alone, after the year of indecision as to Roger's destination, which had been brought on by her urgency. She had not been able for many years to walk beyond her garden; the greater part of her life was spent on a sofa, wheeled to the window in summer, to the fireside in winter. The room which she inhabited was large and pleasant; four tall windows looked out upon a lawn dotted over with flower-beds, and melting away into a small wood, in the centre of which there was a pond, filled with water-lilies. About this unseen pond in the deep shade Mrs Hamley had written many a pretty four-versed poem since she lay on her sofa, alternately reading and composing verse. She had a small table by her side on which there were the newest works of poetry and fiction; a pencil and blotting-book, with loose sheets of blank paper; a vase of flowers always of her husband's gathering; winter and summer, she had a sweet fresh nosegay every day. Her maid brought her a draught of medicine every three hours, with a glass of clear water and a biscuit; her husband came to her as often as his love for the open air and his labours out-of-doors permitted; but the event of her day, when her boys were absent, was Mr Gibson's frequent professional visit.

He knew there was real secret harm going on, all this time that people spoke of her as a merely fanciful invalid, and that one or two accused him of humouring her fancies. But he only smiled at such accusations. He felt that his visits were a real pleasure and lightening of her growing and indescribable discomfort; he knew that Squire Hamley would have been only too glad, if he had come every day; and he was conscious that by careful watching of her symptoms he might mitigate her bodily pain. Besides all these reasons, he took great pleasure in the Squire's society. Mr Gibson enjoyed the other's unreasonableness; his quaintness; his strong conservatism in religion, politics, and morals. Mrs Hamley tried sometimes to apologise for, or to soften away, opinions which she fancied were offensive to the doctor, or contradictions which she thought too abrupt; but at such times her husband would lay his great hand almost caressingly on Mr Gibson's shoulder, and soothe his wife's anxiety by saying, 'Let us alone, little woman. We understand each other, don't we, doctor? Why, bless your life, he gives me better than he gets many a time; only, you see, he sugars it over, and says a sharp thing, and pretends it's all civility and humility; but I can tell when he's giving me a pill.'

One of Mrs Hamley's often-expressed wishes had been, that Molly might come and pay her a visit. Mr Gibson always refused this request of hers, though he could hardly have given his reasons for these refusals. He did not want to lose the companionship of his child, in fact; but he put it to himself in quite a different way. He thought her lessons and her regular course of employment would be interrupted. The life in Mrs Hamley's heated and scented room would not be good for the girl; Osborne and Roger Hamley would be at home, and he did not wish Molly to be thrown too exclusively upon them for young society; or they would not be at home, and it would be rather dull and depressing for his girl to be all the day long with a nervous invalid.

But at length the day came when Mr Gibson rode over, and volunteered a visit from Molly; an offer which Mrs Hamley received with the 'open arms of her heart', as she expressed it, and of which the duration was unspecified.

CHAPTER 5

Calf-Love

The cause for the change in Mr Gibson's wishes just referred to was as follows. It has been mentioned that he took pupils – rather against his inclination, it is true; but there they were, a Mr Wynne and a Mr Coxe, 'the young gentlemen', as they were called in the household; 'Mr Gibson's young gentlemen', as they were termed in the town. Mr Wynne was the elder, the more experienced one, who could occasionally take his master's place, and who gained experience by visiting the poor and the 'chronic cases'. Mr Gibson used to talk over his practice with Mr Wynne, and try and elicit his opinions in the vain hope that, some day or another, Mr Wynne might start an original thought. The young man was cautious and slow; he would never do any harm by his rashness, but at the same time he would always be a little behind his day.* Still Mr Gibson remembered that he had had far worse 'young gentlemen' to deal with; and was content with, if not thankful for, such an elder pupil as Mr Wynne. Mr Coxe was a boy of nineteen or so, with brilliant red hair, and a tolerably red face, of both of which he was very conscious and much ashamed. He was the son of an Indian officer, an old acquaintance of Mr Gibson's. Major Coxe was at some unpronounceable station in the Punjaub, at the present time; but the year before he had been in England, and had repeatedly expressed his great satisfaction at having placed his only child as a pupil with his old friend, and had in fact almost charged Mr Gibson with the guardianship as well as the instruction of his boy, giving him many injunctions which he thought were special in this case; but which Mr Gibson, with a touch of annoyance, assured the major were always attended to in every case, with every pupil. But, when the poor major ventured to beg that his boy might be considered as one of the family, and that he might spend his evenings in the drawing-room instead of the surgery, Mr Gibson turned upon him with a direct refusal.

'He must live like the others. I can't have the pestle and mortar carried into the drawing-room, and the place smelling of aloes.'*

'Must my boy make pills himself, then?' asked the major ruefully.

'To be sure. The youngest apprentice always does. It's not hard work. He'll have the comfort of thinking he won't have to swallow them himself. And he'll have the run of the pomfret cakes,* and the conserve of hips, and on Sundays he shall have a taste of tamarinds to reward him for his weekly labour at pill-making.'

Major Coxe was not quite sure whether Mr Gibson was not laughing at him in his sleeve;* but things were so far arranged, and the real advantages were so great, that he thought it was best to take no notice, but even to submit to the indignity of pill-making. He was consoled for all these rubs by Mr Gibson's manner at last when the supreme moment of final parting arrived. The doctor did not say much; but there was something of real sympathy in his manner that spoke straight to the father's heart, and an implied 'You have trusted me with your boy, and I have accepted the trust in full,' in each of the few last words.

Mr Gibson knew his business and human nature too well to distinguish young Coxe by any overt marks of favouritism; but he could not help showing the lad occasionally that he regarded him with especial interest as the son of a friend. Besides this claim upon his regard, there was something about the young man himself that pleased Mr Gibson. He was rash and impulsive, apt to speak, hitting the nail on the head sometimes with unconscious cleverness, at other times making gross and startling blunders. Mr Gibson used to tell him that his motto would always be 'kill or cure', and to this Mr Coxe once made answer that he thought it was the best motto a doctor could have; for if he could not cure the patient, it was surely best to get him out of his misery quietly, and at once. Mr Wynne looked up in surprise, and observed that he should be afraid that such putting out of misery might be looked upon as homicide by some people. Mr Gibson said, in a dry tone, that for his part he should not mind the imputation of homicide, but that it would not do to make away with profitable patients in so speedy a manner; and that he thought that, as long as they were willing and able to pay two-and-sixpence* for the doctor's visit, it was his duty to keep them alive; of course, when they became paupers the case was different. Mr Wynne pondered over this speech; Mr Coxe only laughed. At last Mr Wynne said –

'But you go every morning, sir, before breakfast to see old Nancy Grant; and you've ordered her this medicine, sir, which is about the most costly in Corbyn's bill?'*

'Have you not found out how difficult it is for men to live up to their precepts? You've a great deal to learn yet, Mr Wynne!' said Mr Gibson, leaving the surgery as he spoke.

'I never can make the governor out,' said Mr Wynne, in a tone of utter despair. 'What are you laughing at, Coxey?'

'Oh! I'm thinking how blest you are in having parents who have instilled moral principles into your youthful bosom. You'd go and be poisoning all the paupers off, if you hadn't been told that murder was a crime by your mother; you'd be thinking you were doing as you were bid, and quote old Gibson's words when you came to be tried. "Please, my lord judge, they were not able to pay for my visits; and so I followed the rules of the profession as taught me by Mr Gibson, the great surgeon at Hollingford, and poisoned the paupers."'

'I can't bear that scoffing way of his.'

'And I like it. If it wasn't for the governor's fun, and the tamarinds, and something else that I know of, I would run off to India. I hate stifling towns, and sick people, and the smell of drugs, and the stink of pills on my hands; – faugh!'

One day, for some reason or other, Mr Gibson came home unexpectedly. He was crossing the hall, having come in by the garden-door – the garden communicated with the stable-yard, where he had left his horse – when the kitchen door opened, and the girl who was underling in the establishment, came quickly into the hall with a note in her hand, and made as if she was taking it upstairs; but on seeing her master she gave a little start, and turned back as if to hide herself in the kitchen. If she had not made this movement, so conscious of guilt, Mr Gibson, who was anything but suspicious, would never have taken any notice of her. As it was, he stepped quickly forwards, opened the kitchen door, and called out 'Bethia' so sharply that she could not delay coming forwards.

'Give me that note,' he said. She hesitated a little.

'It's for Miss Molly,' she stammered out.

'Give it to me!' he repeated more quickly than before. She looked as if she would cry; but still she kept the note tight held behind her back.

'He said as I was to give it into her own hands; and I promised as I would, faithful.'

'Cook, go and find Miss Molly. Tell her to come here at once.'

He fixed Bethia with his eyes. It was of no use trying to escape: she might have thrown it into the fire, but she had not presence of mind enough. She stood immovable; only her eyes looked any way rather than encounter her master's steady gaze.

'Molly, my dear!'

'Papa! I did not know you were at home,' said innocent, wondering Molly.

'Bethia, keep your word. Here is Miss Molly; give her the note.'

'Indeed, miss, I couldn't help it!'

Molly took the note, but, before she could open it, her father said – 'That's all, my dear; you needn't read it. Give it to me. Tell those who sent you, Bethia, that all letters for Miss Molly must pass through my hands. Now be off with you, goosey, and go back to where you came from.'

'Papa, I shall make you tell me who my correspondent is.'

'We'll see about that, by-and-by.'

She went a little reluctantly, with ungratified curiosity, upstairs to Miss Eyre, who was still her daily companion, if not her governess. He turned into the empty dining-room, shut the door, broke the seal of the note, and began to read it. It was a flaming love-letter from Mr Coxe; who professed himself unable to go on seeing her day after day without speaking to her of the passion she had inspired – an 'eternal passion', he called it; on reading which Mr Gibson laughed a little. Would she not look kindly at him? would she not think of him whose only thought was of her? and so on, with a very proper admixture of violent compliments to her beauty. She was fair, not pale; her eyes were loadstars, her dimples marks of Cupid's finger,* etc.

Mr Gibson finished reading it; and began to think about it in his own mind. 'Who would have thought the lad had been so poetical? but, to be sure, there's a "Shakespeare" in the surgery-library: I'll take it away and put "Johnson's Dictionary"* instead. One comfort is the conviction of her perfect innocence – ignorance, I should rather say – for it's easy to see it's the first

"confession of his love", as he calls it. But it's an awful worry –
to begin with lovers so early. Why, she's only just seventeen – not
seventeen, indeed, till July; not for six weeks yet. Sixteen and
three-quarters! Why, she's quite a baby. To be sure – poor Jeanie
was not so old, and how I did love her!' (Mrs Gibson's name was
Mary; so he must have been referring to some one else.) Then his
thoughts wandered back to other days, though he still held the
open note in his hand. By-and-by his eyes fell upon it again, and
his mind came back to bear upon the present time. 'I'll not be
hard upon him. I'll give him a hint; he's quite sharp enough to
take it. Poor laddie! if I send him away, which would be the wisest
course, I do believe he's got no home to go to.'

After a little more consideration in the same strain, Mr Gibson
went and sat down at the writing-table and wrote the following
formula: –

Master Coxe.

('That "master" will touch him to the quick,' said Mr Gibson
to himself as he wrote the word.)

> R. Verecundiae ʒi.
> Fidelitatis Domesticae ʒi.
> Reticentiae gr. iij.
> M. Capiat hanc dosim ter die in aquâ purâ.
>   R.GIBSON, *Ch.**

Mr Gibson smiled a little sadly as he re-read his words. 'Poor
Jeanie,' he said aloud. And then he chose out an envelope,
enclosed the fervid love-letter, and the above prescription; sealed
it with his own sharply-cut seal-ring, 'R. G.', in old English letters,
and then paused over the address.

'He'll not like *Master* Coxe outside; no need to put him to
unnecessary shame.' So the direction on the envelope was –

Edward Coxe, Esq.

Then Mr Gibson applied himself to the professional business
which had brought him home so opportunely and unexpectedly,
and afterwards he went back through the garden to the stables;
and just as he had mounted his horse, he said to the stable-man –
'Oh! by the way, here's a letter for Mr Coxe. Don't send it
through the women; take it round yourself to the surgery-door,
and do it at once.'

The slight smile upon his face, as he rode out of the gates, died away as soon as he found himself in the solitude of the lanes. He slackened his speed, and began to think. It was very awkward, he considered, to have a motherless girl growing up into womanhood in the same house with two young men, even if she only met them at meal-times, and all the intercourse they had with each other was merely the utterance of such words as 'May I help you to potatoes?' or, as Mr Wynne would persevere in saying, 'May I assist you to potatoes?' – a form of speech which grated daily more and more upon Mr Gibson's ears. Yet Mr Coxe, the offender in this affair which had just occurred, had to remain for three years more as a pupil in Mr Gibson's family. He should be the very last of the race. Still there were three years to be got over; and, if this stupid passionate calf-love of his lasted, what was to be done? Sooner or later Molly would become aware of it. The contingencies of the affair were so excessively disagreeable to contemplate, that Mr Gibson determined to dismiss the subject from his mind by a good strong effort. He put his horse to a gallop, and found that the violent shaking over the lanes – paved as they were with round stones, which had been dislocated by the wear and tear of a hundred years – was the very best thing for the spirits, if not for the bones. He made a long round that afternoon, and came back to his home imagining that the worst was over, and that Mr Coxe would have taken the hint conveyed in the prescription. All that would be needed was to find a safe place for the unfortunate Bethia, who had displayed such a daring aptitude for intrigue. But Mr Gibson reckoned without his host.* It was the habit of the young men to come in to tea with the family in the dining-room, to swallow two cups, munch their bread and toast, and then disappear. This night Mr Gibson watched their countenances furtively from under his long eyelashes, while he tried against his wont to keep up a *dégagé** manner, and a brisk conversation on general subjects. He saw that Mr Wynne was on the point of breaking out into laughter, and that red-haired, red-faced Mr Coxe was redder and fiercer than ever, while his whole aspect and ways betrayed indignation and anger.

'He will have it, will he?' thought Mr Gibson to himself; and he girded up his loins for the battle.* He did not follow Molly and Miss Eyre into the drawing-room as he usually did. He remained where he was, pretending to read the newspaper, while Bethia, her face swelled up with crying, and with an aggrieved and offended aspect, removed the tea-things. Not five minutes after the room was cleared, came the expected tap at the door. 'May I speak to you, sir?' said the invisible Mr Coxe, from outside.

'To be sure. Come in, Mr Coxe. I was rather wanting to talk to you about that bill of Corbyn's. Pray sit down.'

'It is about nothing of that kind, sir, that I wanted – that I wished – No, thank you, I would rather not sit down.' He, accordingly, stood in offended dignity. 'It is about that letter, sir – that letter with the insulting prescription, sir.'

'Insulting prescription! I am surprised at such a word being applied to any prescription of mine – though, to be sure, patients are sometimes offended at being told the nature of their illnesses; and, I daresay, they may take offence at the medicines which their cases require.'

'I did not ask you to prescribe for me.'

'Oh, no! Then you were the Master Coxe who sent the note through Bethia! Let me tell you it has cost her her place, and was a very silly letter into the bargain.'

'It was not the conduct of a gentleman, sir, to intercept it, and to open it, and to read words never addressed to you, sir.'

'No!' said Mr Gibson, with a slight twinkle in his eye and a curl on his lips, but unnoticed by the indignant Mr Coxe. 'I believe I was once considered tolerably good-looking, and I daresay I was as great a coxcomb as any one at twenty; but I don't think that even then I should quite have believed that all those pretty compliments were addressed to myself.'

'It was not the conduct of a gentleman, sir,' repeated Mr Coxe, stammering over his words – he was going on to say something more, when Mr Gibson broke in –

'And let me tell you, young man,' replied Mr Gibson, with a sudden sternness in his voice, 'that what you have done is only excusable in consideration of your youth and extreme ignorance of what are considered the laws of domestic honour. I receive you into my house as a member of the family – you induced one of my servants – corrupting her with a bribe, I have no doubt'—

'Indeed, sir! I never gave her a penny.'

'Then you ought to have done. You should always pay those who do your dirty work.'

'Just now, sir, you called it corrupting with a bribe,' muttered Mr Coxe.

Mr Gibson took no notice of this speech, but went on –

'Inducing one of my servants to risk her place, without offering her the slightest equivalent, by begging her to convey a letter clandestinely to my daughter – a mere child.'

'Miss Gibson, sir, is nearly seventeen! I heard you say so only the other day,' said Mr Coxe, aged twenty. Again Mr Gibson ignored the remark.

'A letter which you were unwilling to have seen by her father, who had tacitly trusted to your honour, by receiving you as an inmate of his house. Your father's son – I know Major Coxe well – ought to have come to me, and have said out openly, "Mr Gibson, I love – or I fancy that I love – your daughter; I do not think it right to conceal this from you, although unable to earn a penny; and with no prospect of an unassisted livelihood, even for myself, for several years, I shall not say a word about my feelings – or fancied feelings – to the very young lady herself." That is what your father's son ought to have said; if, indeed, a couple of grains of reticent silence wouldn't have been better still.'

'And if I had said it, sir – perhaps I ought to have said it,' said Mr Coxe, in a hurry of anxiety, 'what would have been your answer? Would you have sanctioned my passion, sir?'

'I would have said, most probably – I will not be certain of my exact words in a suppositional case – that you were a young fool, but not a dishonourable young fool; and I should have told you not to let your thoughts run upon a calf-love until you had magnified it into a passion. And I daresay, to make up for the mortification I should have given you, I might have prescribed your joining the Hollingford Cricket Club,* and set you at liberty, as often as I could, on the Saturday afternoons. As it is, I must write to your father's agent in London, and ask him to remove you out of my household, repaying the premium, of course, which will enable you to start afresh in some other doctor's surgery.'

'It will so grieve my father,' said Mr Coxe, startled into dismay, if not repentance.

'I see no other course open. It will give Major Coxe some trouble (I shall take care that he is at no extra expense); but what I think will grieve him the most is the betrayal of confidence; for I trusted you, Edward, like a son of my own!' There was something in Mr Gibson's voice when he spoke seriously, especially when he referred to any feeling of his own – he who so rarely betrayed what was passing in his heart – that was irresistible to most people: the change from joking and sarcasm to tender gravity.

Mr Coxe hung his head a little, and meditated.

'I do love Miss Gibson,' said he, at length. 'Who could help it?'

'Mr Wynne, I hope!' said Mr Gibson.

'His heart is pre-engaged,' replied Mr Coxe. 'Mine was free as air till I saw her.'

'Would it tend to cure your – well! passion, we'll say – if she wore blue spectacles at meal-times? I observe you dwell much on the beauty of her eyes.'

'You are ridiculing my feelings, Mr Gibson. Do you forget that you yourself were young once?'

'Poor Jeanie' rose before Mr Gibson's eyes; and he felt a little rebuked.

'Come, Mr Coxe, let us see if we can't make a bargain,' said he, after a minute or so of silence. 'You have done a really wrong thing; and I hope you are convinced of it in your heart, or that you will be, when the heat of this discussion is over, and you come to think a little about it. But I won't lose all respect for your father's son. If you will give me your word that, as long as you remain a member of my family – pupil, apprentice, what you will – you won't again try to disclose your passion – you see I am careful to take your view of what I should call a mere fancy – by word or writing, looks or acts, in any manner whatever, to my daughter, or to talk about your feelings to any one else, you shall remain here. If you cannot give me your word, I must follow out the course I named, and write to your father's agent.'

Mr Coxe stood irresolute.

'Mr Wynne knows all I feel for Miss Gibson, sir. He and I have no secrets from each other.'

'Well, I suppose he must represent the reeds. You know the story of King Midas's barber,* who found out that his royal master had the ears of an ass beneath his hyacinthine curls. So the barber, in default of a Mr Wynne, went to the reeds that grew on the shores of a neighbouring lake, and whispered to them, "King Midas has the ears of an ass." But he repeated it so often that the reeds learnt the words, and kept on saying them all day long, till at last the secret was no secret at all. If you keep on telling your tale to Mr Wynne, are you sure he won't repeat it in his turn?'

'If I pledge my word as a gentleman, sir, I pledge it for Mr Wynne as well.'

'I suppose I must run the risk. But remember how soon a young girl's name may be breathed upon, and sullied. Molly has no mother, and for that very reason she ought to move among you all, as unharmed as Una* herself.'

'Mr Gibson, if you wish it, I'll swear it on the Bible', cried the excitable young man.

'Nonsense. As if your word, if it's worth anything, wasn't enough! We'll shake hands upon it, if you like.'

Mr Coxe came forward eagerly, and almost squeezed Mr Gibson's ring into his finger.

As he was leaving the room, he said, a little uneasily, 'May I give Bethia a crown-piece?'

'No, indeed! Leave Bethia to me. I hope you won't say another word to her, while she's here. I shall see that she gets a respectable place, when she goes away.'

Then Mr Gibson rang for his horse, and went out on the last visits of the day. He used to reckon that he rode the world around in the course of the year. There were not many surgeons in the county who had so wide a range of practice as he; he went to lonely cottages on the borders of great commons; to farmhouses at the end of narrow country lanes that led to nowhere else, and were overshadowed by the elms and beeches overhead. He attended all the gentry within a circle of fifteen miles round Hollingford, and was the appointed doctor to the still greater families who went up to London every February – as the fashion then was – and returned to their acres in the early weeks of July. He was, of necessity, a great deal from home, and on this soft and pleasant summer evening he felt the absence as a great evil. He was startled at discovering that his little one was growing fast into a woman, and already the passive object of some of the strong interests that affect a woman's life; and he – her mother as well as her father – so much away that he could not guard her as he would have wished. The end of his cogitations was that ride to Hamley the next morning, when he proposed to allow his daughter to accept Mrs Hamley's last invitation – an invitation that had been declined at the time.

'You may quote against me the proverb, "He that will not when he may, when he will he shall have nay." And I shall have no reason to complain,' he had said.

But Mrs Hamley was only too much charmed with the prospect of having a young girl for a visitor; one whom it would not be a trouble to entertain; who might be sent out to ramble in the gardens, or told to read when the invalid was too much fatigued for conversation; and yet one whose youth and freshness would bring a charm, like a waft of sweet summer air, into her lonely shut-up life. Nothing could be pleasanter, and so Molly's visit to Hamley was easily settled.

'I only wish Osborne and Roger had been at home,' said Mrs Hamley, in her low soft voice. 'She may find it dull, being with old people, like the Squire and me, from morning till night. When can she come? the darling – I am beginning to love her already.'

Mr Gibson was very glad in his heart that the young men of the house were out of the way; he did not want his little Molly to be passing from Scylla to Charybdis:* and, as he afterwards scoffed at himself for thinking, he had got an idea that all young men were wolves in chase of his one ewe-lamb.*

'She knows nothing of the pleasure in store for her,' he replied; 'and I'm sure I don't know what feminine preparations she may think necessary, or how long they may take. You'll remember she is a little ignoramus, and has had no . . . training in etiquette; our ways at home are rather rough for a girl, I'm afraid. But I know I could not send her into a kinder atmosphere than this.'

When the Squire heard from his wife of Mr Gibson's proposal, he was as much pleased as she at the prospect of their youthful visitor; for he was a man of hearty hospitality, when his pride did not interfere with its gratification; and he was delighted to think of his sick wife's having such an agreeable companion in her hours of loneliness. After a while, he said – 'It's as well the lads are at Cambridge; we might have been having a love-affair if they had been at home.'

'Well – and if we had?' asked his more romantic wife.

'It wouldn't have done,' said the Squire decidedly. 'Osborne will have had a first-rate education – as good as any man in the county – he'll have this property, and he's a Hamley of Hamley; not a family in the shire is as old as we are, or settled on their ground so well. Osborne may marry when he likes. If Lord Hollingford had a daughter, Osborne would have been as good a match as she could have required. It would never do for him to fall in love with Gibson's daughter – I shouldn't allow it. So it's as well he's out of the way.'

'Well! perhaps Osborne had better look higher.'

'Perhaps! I say he must.' The Squire brought his hand down with a thump on the table near him, which made his wife's heart beat hard for some minutes. 'And as for Roger,' he continued, unconscious of the flutter he had put her into, 'he'll have to make his own way, and earn his own bread; and, I'm afraid, he's not getting on very brilliantly at Cambridge. He mustn't think of falling in love for these ten years.'

'Unless he marries a fortune,' said Mrs Hamley, more by way of concealing her palpitation than anything else; for she was unworldly and romantic to a fault.

'No son of mine shall ever marry a wife who is richer than himself, with my good will,' said the Squire again, with emphasis, but without a thump.

'I don't say but what, if Roger is gaining five hundred a year by the time he's thirty, he shall not choose a wife with ten thousand pounds down; but I do say, if a boy of mine, with only two hundred a year – which is all Roger will have from us, and that not for a long time – goes and marries a woman with fifty thousand to her portion, I'll disown him – it would be just disgusting.'

'Not if they loved each other, and their whole happiness depended upon their marrying each other,' put in Mrs Hamley mildly.

'Pooh! away with love! Nay, my dear, we loved each other so dearly we should never have been happy with any one else; but that's a different thing. People aren't like what they were when we were young. All the love now-a-days is just silly fancy, and sentimental romance, as far as I can see.'

Mr Gibson thought that he had settled everything about Molly's going to Hamley before he spoke to her about it, which he did not do, until the morning of the day on which Mrs Hamley expected her. Then he said – 'By the way, Molly! you're to go to Hamley this afternoon; Mrs Hamley wants you to go to her for a week or two, and it suits me capitally that you should accept her invitation just now.'

'Go to Hamley! This afternoon! Papa, you've got some odd reason at the back of your head – some mystery, or something! Please tell me what it is. Go to Hamley for a week or two! Why, I never was from home before this without you in all my life.'

'Perhaps not. I don't think you ever walked before you put your feet to the ground. Everything must have a beginning.'

'It has something to do with that letter that was directed to me, but that you took out of my hands before I could even see the writing of the direction.' She fixed her grey eyes on her father's face, as if she meant to pluck out his secret.

He only smiled and said – 'You're a witch, goosey!'

'Then it had! But if it was a note from Mrs Hamley, why might I not see it? I have been wondering if you had some plan in your head, ever since that day – Thursday, wasn't it? You've gone about in a kind of thoughtful, perplexed way, just like a conspirator. Tell me, papa' – coming up at the time, and putting on a beseeching manner – 'why mightn't I see that note? and why am I to go to Hamley all on a sudden?'

'Don't you like to go? Would you rather not?' If she had said that she did not want to go, he would have been rather pleased than otherwise, although it would have put him into a great perplexity; but he was beginning to dread the parting from her even for a short time. However, she replied directly –

'I don't know – I daresay I shall like it when I have thought a little more about it. Just now I'm so startled by the suddenness of the affair, I haven't considered whether I shall like it or not. I shan't like going away from you, I know. Why am I to go, papa?'

'There are three old ladies sitting somewhere,* and thinking about you just at this very minute; one has a distaff in her hands, and is spinning a thread; she has come to a knot in it, and is puzzled what to do with it. Her sister has a great pair of scissors in her hands, and wants – as she always does, when any difficulty arises in the smoothness of the thread – to cut it off short; but the third, who has the most head of the three, plans how to undo the knot; and she it is who has decided that you are to go to Hamley. The others are quite convinced by her arguments; so, as the Fates have decreed that this visit is to be paid, there is nothing left for you and me but to submit.'

'That's all nonsense, papa, and you're only making me more curious to find out this hidden reason.'

Mr Gibson changed his tone, and spoke gravely now. 'There is a reason, Molly, and one which I do not wish to give. When I tell you this much, I expect you to be an honourable girl, and to try and not even conjecture what the reason may be – much less endeavour to put little discoveries together till very likely you may find out what I want to conceal.'

'Papa, I won't even think about your reason again. But then I shall have to plague you with another question. I've had no new gown this year, and I've outgrown all my last summer frocks. I've only three that I can wear at all. Betty was saying only yesterday that I ought to have some more.'

'That'll do that you have got on, won't it? It's a very pretty colour.'

'Yes; but papa' (holding it out as if she was going to dance), 'it's made of woollen, and so hot and heavy; and every day it will be getting warmer.'

'I wish girls could dress like boys,' said Mr Gibson, with a little impatience. 'How is a man to know when his daughter wants clothes? and how is he to rig her out when he finds it out, just when she needs them most and hasn't got them?'

'Ah, that's the question!' said Molly, in some despair.

'Can't you go to Miss Rose's? Doesn't she keep ready-made frocks for girls of your age?'

'Miss Rose! I never had anything from her in my life,' replied Molly, in some surprise; for Miss Rose was the great dressmaker and milliner of the little town, and hitherto Betty had made the girl's frocks.

'Well, but it seems people consider you as a young woman now; and so I suppose you must run up milliners' bills like the rest of your kind. Not that you're to get anything anywhere that you can't pay for down in ready money. Here's a ten-pound note; go to Miss Rose's, or Miss Anybody's, and get what you want at once. The Hamley carriage is to come for you at two, and anything that isn't quite ready can easily be sent by their cart on Saturday, when some of their people always come to market. Nay, don't thank me! I don't want to have the money spent, and I don't want you to go and leave me. I shall miss you, I know; it's only hard necessity that drives me to send you a-visiting, and to throw away ten pounds on your clothes. There, go away; you're a plague, and I mean to leave off loving you as fast as I can.'

'Papa!' holding up her finger as in warning, 'you're getting mysterious again; and, though my honourableness is very strong, I won't promise that it will not yield to my curiosity, if you go on hinting at untold secrets.'

'Go away, and spend your ten pounds! What did I give it you for but to keep you quiet?'

Miss Rose's ready-made resources and Molly's taste combined did not arrive at a very great success. She bought a lilac print, because it would wash, and would be cool and pleasant for the mornings; and this Betty could make at home before Saturday.

And for high-days and holidays – by which was understood afternoons and Sundays – Miss Rose persuaded her to order a gay-coloured flimsy plaid silk, which she assured her was quite the latest fashion in London, and which Molly thought would please her father's Scotch blood. But, when he saw the scrap which she had brought home as a pattern, he cried out that the plaid belonged to no clan in existence, and that Molly ought to have known this by instinct. It was too late to change it, however; for Miss Rose had promised to cut the dress out as soon as Molly had left her shop.

Mr Gibson had hung about the town all the morning, instead of going away on his usual distant rides. He passed his daughter once or twice in the street, but he did not cross over when he was on the opposite side – only gave her a look or a nod and went on his way, scolding himself for his weakness in feeling so much pain at the thought of her absence for a fortnight or so.

'And, after all,' thought he, 'I'm only where I was when she comes back; at least, if that foolish fellow goes on with his imaginating fancy. She'll have to come back some time; and, if he chooses to imagine himself constant, there's still the devil to pay.' Presently he began to hum the air out of the 'Beggars' Opera'* –

> I wonder any man alive
> Should over rear a daughter!

CHAPTER 6

A Visit to the Hamleys

Of course the news of Miss Gibson's approaching departure had spread through the household before the one o'clock dinner-time came; and Mr Coxe's dismal countenance was a source of much inward irritation to Mr Gibson, who kept giving the youth sharp glances of savage reproof for his melancholy face and want of appetite, which he trotted out, with a good deal of sad ostentation; all of which was lost upon Molly, who was too full of her own personal concerns to have any thought or observation to spare from them; excepting once or twice, when she thought of the many days that must pass over, before she should again sit down to dinner with her father.

When she named this to him after the meal was done, and they were sitting together in the drawing-room, waiting for the sound of the wheels of the Hamley carriage, he laughed and said –

'I'm coming over tomorrow to see Mrs Hamley; and I daresay I shall dine at their lunch; so you won't have to wait long before you've the treat of seeing the wild beast feed.'

Then they heard the approaching carriage.

'Oh, papa,' said Molly, catching at his hand, 'I do so wish I wasn't going, now that the time is come.'

'Nonsense; don't let us have any sentiment! Have you got your keys? that's more to the purpose.'

Yes; she had got her keys, and her purse; and her little box was put up on the seat by the coachman; and her father handed her in; the door was shut, and she drove away in solitary grandeur, looking back and kissing her hand to her father, who stood at the gate, in spite of his dislike of sentiment, as long as the carriage could be seen. Then he turned into the surgery, and found Mr Coxe had had his watching too, and had, indeed, remained at the window gazing, moon-struck, at the empty road up which the young lady had disappeared. Mr Gibson startled him from his reverie by a sharp, almost venomous, speech about some small neglect of duty a day or two before. That night Mr Gibson insisted on passing by the bedside of a poor girl, whose parents were worn-out by many wakeful anxious nights, succeeding to hard-working days.

Molly cried a little, but checked her tears, as soon as she remembered how annoyed her father would have been at the sight of them. It was very pleasant driving quickly along in the luxurious carriage, through the pretty green lanes, with dog-roses and honeysuckles so plentiful and fresh in the hedges, that she once or twice was tempted to ask the coachman to stop till she had gathered a nosegay. She began to dread the end of her little journey of seven miles; the only drawback to which was, that her silk was not a true clan-tartan,* with a little uncertainty as to Miss Rose's punctuality. At length they came to a village; straggling cottages lined the road, an old church stood on a kind of green, with the public-house close by it; there was a great tree, with a bench all round the trunk, midway between the church gates and the little inn. The wooden stocks* were close to the gates. Molly had long passed the limit of her rides, but she knew this must be the village of Hamley, and that they must be very near to the Hall.

They swung in at the gates of the park in a few minutes, and drove up through meadow-grass, ripening for hay – it was no grand aristocratic deer-park this – to the old red-brick hall;* not three hundred yards from the highroad. There had been no footman sent with the carriage, but a respectable servant stood at the door, even before they drew up, ready to receive the expected visitor, and take her into the drawing-room where his mistress lay awaiting her.

Mrs Hamley rose from her sofa to give Molly a gentle welcome; she kept the girl's hand in hers after she had finished speaking, looking into her face, as if studying it, and unconscious of the faint blush she called up on the otherwise colourless cheeks.

'I think we shall be great friends,' said she, at length. 'I like your face, and I am always guided by first impressions. Give me a kiss, dear.'

It was far easier to be active than passive during this process of 'swearing eternal friendship', and Molly willingly kissed the sweet pale face held up to her.

'I meant to have gone and fetched you myself; but the heat oppresses me, and I did not feel up to the exertion. I hope you had a pleasant drive?'

'Very,' said Molly, with shy conciseness.

'And now I'll take you to your room; I have had you put close to me; I thought you would like it better, even though it was a smaller room than the other.'

She rose languidly and, wrapping her light shawl round her yet elegant figure, led the way upstairs. Molly's bed-room opened out of Mrs Hamley's private sitting-room; on the other side of which was her own bed-room. She showed Molly this easy means of communication; and then, telling her visitor she would await her in the sitting-room, she closed the door, and Molly was left at leisure to make acquaintance with her surroundings.

First of all, she went to the window to see what was to be seen. A flower-garden right below; a meadow of ripe grass just beyond, changing colour in long sweeps, as the soft wind blew over it; great old forest-trees a little on one side; and, beyond them again, to be seen only by standing very close to the side of the window-sill, or by putting her head out, if the window was open, the silver shimmer of a mere, about a quarter of a mile off. On the opposite side to the trees and the mere, the look-out was bounded by the old walls and high-peaked roofs of the extensive farm-buildings. The deliciousness of the early summer silence was only broken by the song of the birds, and the nearer hum of bees. Listening to these sounds, which enhanced the exquisite sense of stillness, and puzzling out objects obscured by distance or shadow, Molly forgot herself, and was suddenly startled into a sense of the present by a sound of voices in the next room – some servant or other speaking to Mrs Hamley. Molly hurried to unpack her box, and arrange her few clothes in the pretty old-fashioned chest of drawers, which was to serve her as dressing-table as well. All the furniture in the room was as old-fashioned and as well-preserved as it could be. The chintz curtains were Indian calico of the last century – the colours almost washed out, but the stuff itself exquisitely clean. There was a little strip of bedside carpeting, but the wooden flooring, thus liberally displayed, was of finely-grained oak, so firmly joined, plank to plank, that no grain of dust could make its way into the interstices. There were none of the luxuries of modern days; no writing-table, or sofa, or pier-glass. In one corner of the walls was a bracket, holding an Indian jar filled with pot-pourri; and that and the climbing honey-suckle outside the open window scented the room more exquisitely than any toilette perfumes. Molly laid out her white gown (of last year's date and size) upon the bed, ready for the (to her new) operation of dressing for dinner, and, having arranged her hair and dress, and taken out her company worsted-work, she opened the door softly, and saw Mrs Hamley lying on the sofa.

'Shall we stay up here, dear? I think it is pleasanter than down below; and then I shall not have to come upstairs again at dressing-time.'

'I should like it very much,' replied Molly.

'Ah! you've got your sewing, like a good girl,' said Mrs Hamley. 'Now, I don't sew much. I live alone a great deal. You see, both my boys are at Cambridge, and the Squire is out-of-doors all day long – so I have almost forgotten how to sew. I read a great deal. Do you like reading?'

'It depends upon the kind of book,' said Molly. 'I'm afraid I don't like "steady reading", as papa calls it.'

'But you like poetry!' said Mrs Hamley, almost interrupting

Molly. 'I was sure you did, from your face. Have you read this last poem of Mrs Hemans'?* Shall I read it aloud to you?'

So she began. Molly was not so much absorbed in listening but that she could glance round the room. The character of the furniture was much the same as in her own. Old-fashioned, of handsome material, and faultlessly clean, the age and the foreign appearance of it gave an aspect of comfort and picturesqueness to the whole apartment. On the walls there hung some crayon sketches – portraits. She thought she could make out that one of them was a likeness of Mrs Hamley, in her beautiful youth. And then she became interested in the poem, and dropped her work, and listened in a manner that was after Mrs Hamley's own heart. When the reading of the poem was ended, Mrs Hamley replied to some of Molly's words of admiration, by saying –

'Ah! I think I must read you some of Osborne's poetry some day; under seal of secrecy, remember; but I really fancy it is almost as good as Mrs Hemans'.'

To be nearly as good as Mrs Hemans' was saying as much to the young ladies of that day, as saying that poetry is nearly as good as Tennyson's would be in this.* Molly looked up with eager interest.

'Mr Osborne Hamley? Does your son write poetry?'

'Yes. I really think I may say he is a poet. He is a very brilliant, clever young man, and he quite hopes to get a fellowship at Trinity. He says he is sure to be high up among the wranglers,* and that he expects to get one of the Chancellor's medals.* That is his likeness – the one hanging against the wall behind you.'

Molly turned round, and saw one of the crayon sketches – representing two boys, in the most youthful kind of jackets and trousers, with falling collars. The elder was sitting down, reading intently. The younger was standing by him, and evidently trying to call the attention of the reader off to some object out-of-doors – out of the window of the very room in which they were sitting, as Molly discovered when she began to recognise the articles of furniture faintly indicated in the picture.

'I like their faces!' said Molly. 'I suppose it is so long ago now, that I may speak of their likenesses to you as if they were somebody else; may not I?'

'Certainly,' said Mrs Hamley, as soon as she understood what Molly meant. 'Tell me just what you think of them, dear; it will amuse me to compare your impressions with what they really are.'

'Oh! but I did not mean to guess at their characters. I could not do it; and it would be impertinent, if I could. I can only speak about their faces as I see them in the picture.'

'Well! tell me what you think of them!'

'The eldest – the reading boy – is very beautiful; but I can't quite make out his face yet, because his head is down, and I can't quite see the eyes. That is the Mr Osborne Hamley who writes poetry?'

'Yes. He is not quite so handsome now; but he was a beautiful boy. Roger was never to be compared with him.'

'No; he is not handsome. And yet I like his face. I can see his eyes. They are grave and solemn-looking; but all the rest of his face is rather merry than otherwise. It looks too steady and sober, too good a face, to go tempting his brother to leave his lesson.'

'Ah! but it was not a lesson. I remember the painter, Mr Green, once saw Osborne reading some poetry, while Roger was trying to persuade him to come out and have a ride in the hay-cart – that was the "motive" of the picture, to speak artistically. Roger is not much of a reader; at least, he doesn't care for poetry, and books of romance, or sentiment. He is so fond of natural history; and that takes him, like the Squire, a great deal out-of-doors; and, when he is in, he is always reading scientific books that bear upon his pursuits. He is a good, steady fellow, though, and gives us great satisfaction; but he is not likely to have such a brilliant career as Osborne.'

Molly tried to find out in the picture the characteristics of the two boys, as they were now explained to her by their mother; and in questions and answers about the various drawings hung round the room the time passed away, until the dressing-bell rang for the six o'clock dinner.

Molly was rather dismayed by the offers of the maid whom Mrs Hamley had sent to assist her. 'I am afraid they expect me to be very smart,' she kept thinking to herself. 'If they do, they'll be disappointed; that's all. But I wish my plaid silk gown had been ready.'

She looked at herself in the glass with some anxiety, for the first time in her life. She saw a slight, lean figure, promising to be tall, a complexion browner than cream-coloured, although in a year or two it might have that tint; plentiful curly black hair, tied up in a bunch behind with a rose-coloured ribbon; long, almond-shaped, soft grey eyes, shaded both above and below by curling black eyelashes.

'I don't think I am pretty,' thought Molly, as she turned away from the glass; 'and yet I'm not sure.' She would have been sure, if, instead of inspecting herself with such solemnity, she had smiled her own sweet, merry smile, and called out the gleam of her teeth, and the charm of her dimples.

She found her way downstairs into the drawing-room in good time; she could look about her, and learn how to feel at home in her new quarters. The room was forty feet long or so; fitted up with yellow satin of some distant period; high spindle-legged chairs and pembroke-tables abounded. The carpet was of the same date as the curtains, and was thread-bare in many places, and in others was covered with drugget. Stands of plants, great jars of flowers, old Indian china and cabinets gave the room the pleasant aspect it certainly had. And to add to it there were five high, long windows on one side of the room, all opening to the prettiest bit of flower-garden in the grounds – or what was considered as such – brilliant-coloured, geometrically-shaped beds, converging to a sun-dial in the midst. The Squire came in abruptly, and in his morning dress; he stood at the door, as if surprised at the white-robed stranger in possession of his hearth. Then, suddenly remembering himself, but not before Molly had begun to feel very hot, he said –

'Why, God bless my soul, I'd quite forgotten you; you're Miss Gibson, Gibson's daughter, aren't you? Come to pay us a visit? I'm sure I'm very glad to see you, my dear.'

By this time, they had met in the middle of the room, and he was shaking Molly's hand with vehement friendliness, intended to make up for his not knowing her at first.

'I must go and dress, though,' said he, looking at his soiled gaiters. 'Madam likes it. It's one of her fine London ways, and she's broken me into it at last. Very good plan, though, and quite right to make oneself fit for ladies' society. Does your father dress for dinner, Miss Gibson?' He did not stay to wait for her answer, but hastened away to perform his toilette.

They dined at a small table in a great large room. There were so few articles of furniture in it, and the apartment itself was so vast, that Molly longed for the snugness of the home dining-room; nay, it is to be feared that, before the stately dinner at Hamley Hall came to an end, she even regretted the crowded chairs and tables, the hurry of eating, the quick, informal manner in which everybody seemed to finish their meal as fast as possible, so as to return to the work they had left. She tried to think that at six o'clock all the business of the day was ended, and that people might linger if they chose. She measured the distance from the sideboard to the table with her eye, and made allowances for the men who had to carry things backwards and forwards; but, all the same, this dinner appeared to her a wearisome business, prolonged because the Squire liked it, for Mrs Hamley seemed tired out. She ate even less than Molly, and sent for fan and smelling-bottle to amuse herself with, until at length the tablecloth was cleared away, and the dessert was put upon a mahogany table, polished like a looking-glass.

The Squire had hitherto been too busy to talk, except about the immediate concerns of the table, and one or two of the greatest breaks to the usual monotony of his days; a monotony in which he delighted, but which sometimes became oppressive to his wife. Now, however, peeling his orange, he turned to Molly –

'Tomorrow, you'll have to do this for me, Miss Gibson.'

'Shall I? I'll do it today, if you like, sir.'

'No; today I shall treat you as a visitor, with all proper ceremony. Tomorrow I shall send you errands, and call you by your Christian name.'

'I shall like that,' said Molly.

'I was wanting to call you something less formal than Miss Gibson,' said Mrs Hamley.

'My name's Molly. It is an old-fashioned name, and I was christened Mary. But papa likes Molly.'

'That's right. Keep to the good old fashions, my dear.'

'Well, I must say I think Mary is prettier than Molly, and quite as old a name, too,' said Mrs Hamley.

'I think it was,' said Molly, lowering her voice, and dropping her eyes, 'because mamma was Mary, and I was called Molly while she lived.'

'Ah, poor thing!' said the Squire, not perceiving his wife's signs to change the subject, 'I remember how sorry every one was when she died; no one thought she was delicate, she had such a fresh colour, till all at once she popped off, as one may say.'

'It must have been a terrible blow to your father,' said Mrs Hamley, seeing that Molly did not know what to answer.

'Ay, ay. It came so sudden, so soon after they were married.'

'I thought it was nearly four years,' said Molly.

'And four years is soon – is a short time to a couple who look to spending their lifetime together. Every one thought Gibson would have married again.'

'Hush,' said Mrs Hamley, seeing in Molly's eyes and change of colour how completely this was a new idea to her. But the Squire was not so easily stopped.

'Well – I'd perhaps better not have said it; but it's the truth, they did. He's not likely to marry now; so one may say it out. Why, your father is past forty, isn't he?'

'Forty-three. I don't believe he ever thought of marrying again,' said Molly, recurring to the idea, as one does to that of danger which has passed by, without one's being aware of it.

'No! I don't believe he did, my dear. He looks to me just like a man who would be constant to the memory of his wife. You must not mind what the Squire says.'

'Ah! you'd better go away, if you're going to teach Miss Gibson such treason as that against the master of the house.'

Molly went into the drawing-room with Mrs Hamley; but her thoughts did not change with the room. She could not help dwelling on the danger which she fancied she had escaped, and was astonished at her own stupidity at never having imagined such a possibility as her father's second marriage. She felt that she was answering Mrs Hamley's remarks in a very unsatisfactory manner.

'There is papa, with the Squire!' she suddenly exclaimed. There they were coming across the flower-garden from the stable-yard, her father switching his boots with his riding-whip, in order to make them presentable in Mrs Hamley's drawing-room. He looked so exactly like his usual self, his home-self, that the seeing him in the flesh was the most efficacious way of dispelling the phantom fears of a second wedding, which were beginning to harass his daughter's mind; and the pleasant conviction that he could not rest, till he had come over to see how she was going on in her new home, stole into her heart, although he spoke but little to her, and that little was all in a joking tone. After he had gone away, the Squire undertook to teach her cribbage,* and she was happy enough now to give him all her attention. He kept on prattling while they played; sometimes in relation to the cards; at others telling her of small occurrences which he thought might interest her.

'So you don't know my boys, even by sight! I should have thought you would have done, for they're fond enough of riding into Hollingford; and I know Roger has often enough been to borrow books from your father. Roger is a scientific sort of a fellow. Osborne is clever like his mother. I shouldn't wonder if he published a book some day. You're not counting right, Miss Gibson. Why, I could cheat you as easily as possible.' And so on, till the butler came in with a solemn look, placed a large prayer-book before his master, who huddled the cards away in a hurry, as if caught in an incongruous employment; and then the maids and men trooped in to prayers – the windows were still open, and the sounds of the solitary corncrake, and of the owl hooting in the trees, mingled with the words spoken. Then to bed; and so ended the day.

Molly looked out of her chamber-window – leaning on the sill, and snuffing up the night-odours of the honeysuckle. The soft velvet darkness hid all the things that were at any distance from her; although she was as conscious of their presence as if she had seen them.

'I think I shall be very happy here,' was in Molly's thoughts, as she turned away at length, and began to prepare for bed. Before long the Squire's words, relating to her father's second marriage, came across her, and spoilt the sweet peace of her final thoughts. 'Who could he have married?' she asked herself. 'Miss Eyre? Miss Browning? Miss Phoebe? Miss Goodenough?' One by one, each of these was rejected for sufficient reasons. Yet the unsatisfied question rankled in her mind, and darted out of ambush to disturb her dreams.

Mrs Hamley did not come down to breakfast; and Molly found out, with a little dismay, that the Squire and she were to have it by themselves. On this first morning, he put aside his newspapers – one an old-established Tory journal, with all the local and country news, which was the most interesting to him; the other the *Morning Chronicle*,* which he called his dose of bitters, and which brought out many a strong expression and tolerably pungent oath. Today, however, he 'was on his manners', as he afterwards explained to Molly; and he plunged about, trying to find ground for a conversation. He could talk of his wife and his sons, his estate, and his mode of farming; his tenants, and the mismanagement of the last county election. Molly's interests were her father, Miss Eyre, her garden and pony; in a fainter degree,

Miss Brownings, the Cumnor Charity School,* and the new gown that was to come from Miss Rose's; into the midst of which the one great question, 'Who was it that people thought it was possible papa might marry?' kept popping up into her mouth, like a troublesome Jack-in-the-box. For the present, however, the lid was snapped down upon the intruder as often as he showed his head between her teeth. They were very polite to each other during the meal; and it was not a little tiresome to both. When it was ended, the Squire withdrew into his study, to read the untasted newspapers. It was the custom to call the room in which Squire Hamley kept his coats, boots, and gaiters, his different sticks and favourite spud,* his gun and fishing-rods, 'the study'. There was a bureau in it, and a three-cornered arm-chair, but no books were visible. The greater part of them were kept in a large, musty-smelling room, in an unfrequented part of the house; so unfrequented that the housemaid often neglected to open the window-shutters, which looked into a part of the grounds over-grown with the luxuriant growth of shrubs. Indeed, it was a tradition in the servants' hall that, in the late Squire's time – he who had been plucked at college – the library-windows had been boarded up to avoid paying the window-tax.* But, when the 'young gentlemen' were at home, the housemaid, without a single direction to that effect, was regular in her charge of this room; opened the windows and lighted fires daily, and dusted the handsomely-bound volumes, which were really a very fair collection of the standard literature in the middle of the last century. All the books that had been purchased since that time were held in small book-cases between each two of the drawing-room windows, and in Mrs Hamley's own sitting-room upstairs. Those in the drawing-room were quite enough to employ Molly; indeed, she was so deep in one of Sir Walter Scott's novels* that she jumped as if she had been shot, when, an hour or so after breakfast, the Squire came to the gravel-path outside one of the windows, and called to ask her if she would like to come out-of-doors and go about the garden and home fields with him.

'It must be a little dull for you, my girl, all by yourself, with nothing but books to look at, in the mornings here; but, you see, madam has a fancy for being quiet in the mornings: she told your father about it, and so did I; but I felt sorry for you all the same, when I saw you sitting on the ground all alone in the drawing-room.'

Molly had been in the very middle of the 'Bride of Lammermoor',* and would gladly have stayed indoors to finish it; but she felt the Squire's kindness all the same. They went in and out of old-fashioned green-houses, over trim lawns; the Squire unlocked the great walled kitchen-garden, and went about giving directions to gardeners; and all the time Molly followed him like a little dog, her mind quite full of Ravenswood and Lucy Ashton. Presently, every place near the house had been inspected and regulated, and the Squire was more at liberty to give his attention to his companion, as they passed through the little wood that separated the gardens from the adjoining fields. Molly, too, plucked away her thoughts from the seventeenth century; and, somehow or other, that question, which had so haunted her before, came out of her lips before she was aware – a literal impromptu –

'Who did people think papa would marry? That time – long ago – soon after mamma died?'

She dropped her voice very soft and low, as she spoke the last words. The Squire turned round upon her, and looked at her face, he knew not why. It was very grave, a little pale, but her steady eyes almost commanded some kind of answer.

'Whew,' said he, whistling to gain time; not that he had anything definite to say, for no one had ever had any reason to join Mr Gibson's name with any known lady; it was only a loose conjecture that had been hazarded on the probabilities – a young widower, with a little girl.

'I never heard of any one – his name was never coupled with any lady's – 'twas only in the nature of things that he should marry again; he may do it yet, for aught I know, and I don't think it would be a bad move either. I told him so, the last time but one he was here.'

'And what did he say?' asked breathless Molly.

'Oh: he only smiled and said nothing. You shouldn't take up words so seriously, my dear. Very likely he may never think of marrying again; and, if he did, it would be a very good thing both for him and for you!'

Molly muttered something, as if to herself, but the Squire might have heard it if he had chosen. As it was, he wisely turned the current of the conversation.

'Look at that!' he said, as they suddenly came upon the mere, or large pond. There was a small island in the middle of the glassy water, on which grew tall trees, dark Scotch firs in the centre, silvery shimmering willows close to the water's edge. 'We must get you punted over there, some of these days. I'm not fond of using the boat at this time of the year, because the young birds are still in the nests among the reeds and water-plants; but we'll go. There are coots and grebes.'

'Oh, look, there's a swan!'

'Yes; there are two pair of them here. And in those trees there's both a rookery and a heronry; the herons ought to be here by now, for they're off to the sea in August; but I've not seen one yet. Stay! isn't that one – that fellow on a stone, with his long neck bent down, looking into the water?'

'Yes! I think so. I have never seen a heron, only pictures of them.'

'They and the rooks are always at war, which doesn't do for such near neighbours. If both herons leave the nest they are building, the rooks come and tear it to pieces; and once Roger showed me a long straggling fellow of a heron, with a flight of rooks after him, with no friendly purpose in their minds, I'll be bound. Roger knows a deal of natural history, and finds out queer things sometimes. He'd have been off a dozen times during this walk of ours, if he'd been here: his eyes are always wandering about, and see twenty things where I only see one. Why! I've known him bolt into a copse because he saw something fifteen yards off – some plant, maybe, which he'd tell me was very rare, though I should say I'd seen its marrow* at every turn in the woods; and, if we came upon such a thing as this,' touching a delicate film of cobweb upon a leaf with his stick, as he spoke, 'why, he could tell you what insect or spider made it, and if it lived in rotten fir-wood, or in a cranny of good sound timber, or deep down in the ground, or up in the sky, or anywhere. It's a pity they don't take honours in Natural History at Cambridge.* Roger would be safe enough, if they did.'

'Mr Osborne Hamley is very clever, is he not?' Molly asked timidly.

'Oh, yes. Osborne's a bit of a genius. His mother looks for great things from Osborne. I'm rather proud of him myself. He'll get a Trinity fellowship, if they play him fair. As I was saying at the magistrates' meeting yesterday, "I've got a son who will make a noise at Cambridge, or I'm very much mistaken." Now, isn't it a queer quip of Nature,' continued the Squire, turning his honest face towards Molly, as if he was going to impart a new idea to her, 'that I, a Hamley of Hamley, straight in descent from nobody knows when – the Heptarchy, they say – What's the date of the Heptarchy?'

'I don't know,' said Molly, startled at being thus appealed to.

'Well! it was some time before King Alfred,* because he was the King of all England, you know; but, as I was saying, here am I, of as good and as old a descent as any man in England, and I doubt if a stranger, to look at me, would take me for a gentleman, with my red face, great hands and feet, and thick figure, fourteen stone, and never less than twelve even when I was a young man; and there's Osborne, who takes after his mother, who couldn't tell her great-grandfather from Adam, bless her; and Osborne has a girl's delicate face, and a slight make, and hands and feet as small as a lady's. He takes after madam's side; who, as I said, can't tell who was her grandfather. Now, Roger is like me, a Hamley of Hamley, and no one who sees him in the street will ever think that red-brown, big-boned, clumsy chap is of gentle blood. Yet all those Cumnor people you make such ado of in Hollingford are mere muck of yesterday. I was talking to madam the other day about Osborne's marrying a daughter of Lord Hollingford's – that's to say, if he had a daughter – he's only got boys, as it happens; but I'm not sure if I should consent to it. I really am not sure; for, you see, Osborne will have had a first-rate education, and his family dates from the Heptarchy, while I should be glad to know where the Cumnor folk were in the time of Queen Anne?'* He walked on, pondering the question of whether he could have given his consent to this impossible marriage; and, after some time, and when Molly had quite forgotten the subject to which he alluded, he broke out with – 'No! I'm sure I should have looked higher. So, perhaps, it's as well my Lord Hollingford has only boys.'

After a while, he thanked Molly for her companionship, with old-fashioned courtesy, and told her that he thought, by this time, madam would be up and dressed, and glad to have her young visitor with her. He pointed out the purple-red house, with its stone-facings, as it was seen at some distance between the trees, and watched her protectingly on her way along the field-paths.

'That's a nice girl of Gibson's,' quoth he to himself. 'But what a tight hold the wench got of the notion of his marrying again! One had need be on one's guard as to what one says before her. To think of her never having thought of the chance of a stepmother! To be sure, a stepmother to a girl is a different thing to a second wife to a man!'

CHAPTER 7

Foreshadows of Love Perils

If Squire Hamley had been unable to tell Molly who had ever been thought of as her father's second wife, fate was all this time preparing an answer of a pretty positive kind to her wondering curiosity. But fate is a cunning hussy, and builds up her plans as imperceptibly as a bird builds her nest; and with much the same kind of unconsidered trifles.* The first 'trifle' of an event was the disturbance which Jenny (Mr Gibson's cook) chose to make at Bethia's being dismissed. Bethia was a distant relation and *protègée* of Jenny's, and she chose to say it was Mr Coxe the tempter who ought to have 'been sent packing', not Bethia the tempted, the victim. In this view there was quite enough plausibility to make Mr Gibson feel that he had been rather unjust. He had, however, taken care to provide Bethia with another situation, to the full as good as that which she held in his family. Jenny, nevertheless, chose to give warning; and, though Mr Gibson knew full well from former experience that her warnings were words, not deeds, he hated the discomfort, the uncertainty, the entire disagreeableness, of meeting a woman at any time in his house, who wore a grievance and an injury upon her face as legibly as Jenny took care to do.

Down into the middle of this small domestic trouble came another, and one of greater consequence. Miss Eyre had gone with her old mother, and her orphan nephews and nieces, to the seaside, during Molly's absence, which was only intended at first to last for a fortnight. After about ten days of this time had elapsed, Mr Gibson received a beautifully-written, beautifully-worded, admirably-folded, and most neatly-sealed letter from Miss Eyre. Her eldest nephew had fallen ill of scarlet fever, and there was every probability that the younger children would be attacked by the same complaint. It was distressing enough for poor Miss Eyre – this additional expense, this anxiety – the long detention from home which the illness involved. But she said not a word of any inconvenience to herself; she only apologised with humble sincerity for her inability to return at the appointed time to her charge in Mr Gibson's family; meekly adding, that perhaps it was as well, for Molly had never had the scarlet fever, and, even if Miss Eyre had been able to leave the orphan children to return to her employments, it might not have been a safe or a prudent step.

'To be sure not,' said Mr Gibson, tearing the letter in two, and throwing it into the hearth, where he soon saw it burnt to ashes. 'I wish I'd a five-pound house* and not a woman within ten miles of me! I might have some peace then.' Apparently, he forgot Mr Coxe's powers of making mischief; but indeed he might have traced that evil back to the unconscious Molly. The martyr-cook's entrance to take away the breakfast things, which she announced by a heavy sigh, roused Mr Gibson from thought to action.

'Molly must stay a little longer at Hamley,' he resolved. 'They've often asked for her, and now they'll have enough of her, I think. But I can't have her back here just yet; and so the best I can do for her is to leave her where she is. Mrs Hamley seems very fond of her; and the child is looking happy, and stronger in health. I'll ride round by Hamley today at any rate, and see how the land lies.'

He found Mrs Hamley lying on a sofa placed under the shadow of the great cedar-tree on the lawn. Molly was flitting about her, gardening away under her directions; tying up the long sea-green stalks of bright budded carnations, snipping off dead roses.

'Oh! here's papa!' she cried out joyfully, as he rode up to the white paling which separated the trim lawn and trimmer flower-garden from the rough park-like ground in front of the house.

'Come in – come here – through the drawing-room window,' said Mrs Hamley, raising herself on her elbow. 'We've got a rose-tree to show you that Molly has budded all by herself. We are both so proud of it.'

So Mr Gibson rode round to the stables, left his horse there, and made his way through the house to the open-air summer-parlour under the cedar tree, where there were chairs, table, books, and tangled work. Somehow, he rather disliked asking for Molly to prolong her visit; so he determined to swallow his bitter first, and then take the pleasure of the delicious day, the sweet repose, the murmurous, scented air. Molly stood by him, her hand on his shoulder. He sate opposite to Mrs Hamley.

'I've come here today to ask a favour,' he began.

'Granted before you name it. Am not I a bold woman?'

He smiled and bowed, but went straight on with his speech.

'Miss Eyre, who has been Molly's governess – I suppose I must call her – for many years, writes today to say that one of the little nephews she took with her to Newport while Molly was staying here, has caught the scarlet fever.'

'I guess your request. I make it before you do. I beg for dear little Molly to stay on here. Of course Miss Eyre can't come back to you; and of course Molly must stay here!'

'Thank you; thank you very much! That was my request.'

Molly's hand stole down to his, and nestled in that firm, compact grasp.

'Papa! – Mrs Hamley! – I know you'll both understand me – but mayn't I go home? I am very happy here; but – oh papa! I think I should like to be at home with you best.'

An uncomfortable suspicion flashed across his mind. He pulled her round, and looked straight and piercingly into her innocent face. Her colour came at his unwonted scrutiny, but her sweet eyes were filled with wonder, rather than with any feeling which he dreaded to find. For an instant he had doubted whether young red-headed Mr Coxe's love might not have called out a response in his daughter's breast; but he was quite clear now.

'Molly, you're rude to begin with. I don't know how you're to make your peace with Mrs Hamley, I'm sure. And in the next place, do you think you're wiser than I am; or that I don't want you at home, if all other things were comfortable? Stay where you are, and be thankful!'

Molly knew him well enough to be certain that the prolongation of her visit at Hamley was quite a decided affair in his mind; and then she was smitten with a sense of ingratitude. She left her father, and went to Mrs Hamley, and bent over her and kissed her; but she did not speak. Mrs Hamley took hold of her hand, and made room on the sofa for her.

'I was going to have asked for a longer visit the next time you came, Mr Gibson. We are such happy friends, are not we, Molly? and now that this good little nephew of Miss Eyre's'—

'I wish he was whipped,' said Mr Gibson.

' – has given us such a capital reason, I shall keep Molly for a real long visitation. You must come over and see us very often. There's a room here for you always, you know; and I don't see why you should not start on your rounds from Hamley every morning, just as well as from Hollingford.'

'Thank you. If you hadn't been so kind to my little girl, I might be tempted to say something rude in answer to your last speech.'

'Pray say it. You won't be easy till you have given it out, I know.'

'Mrs Hamley has found out from whom I get my rudeness,' said Molly triumphantly. 'It's an hereditary quality.'

'I was going to say, that proposal of yours that I should sleep at Hamley was just like a woman's idea – all kindness, and no common-sense. How in the world would my patients find me out, seven miles from my accustomed place? They'd be sure to send for some other doctor, and I should be ruined in a month.'

'Couldn't they send on here? A messenger costs very little.'

'Fancy old Goody Henbury struggling up to my surgery, groaning at every step, and then being told to just step on seven miles farther! Or take the other end of society – I don't think my Lady Cumnor's smart groom would thank me for having to ride on to Hamley, every time his mistress wants me.'

'Well, well, I submit. I am a woman. Molly, thou art a woman! Go and order some strawberries and cream for this father of yours. Such humble offices fall within the province of women. Strawberries and cream are all kindness and no common-sense, for they'll give him a horrid fit of indigestion.'

'Please speak for yourself, Mrs Hamley,' said Molly merrily. 'I ate – oh, such a great basketful yesterday, and the Squire went himself to the dairy and brought out a great bowl of cream, when he found me at my busy work. And I'm as well as ever I was, today, and have never had a touch of indigestion near me.'

'She's a good girl,' said her father, when she had danced out of hearing. The words were not quite an inquiry, he was so certain of his answer. There was a mixture of tenderness and trust in his eyes, as he awaited the reply, which came in a moment.

'She's a darling. I cannot tell you how fond the Squire and I are of her; both of us. I am so delighted to think she isn't to go away for a long time. The first thing I thought of this morning when I wakened up, was that she would soon have to return to you, unless I could persuade you into leaving her with me a little longer. And now she must stay – oh, two months at least.'

It was quite true that the Squire had become very fond of Molly. The chance of having a young girl dancing and singing inarticulate ditties about the house and garden, was indescribable in its novelty to him. And then Molly was so willing and so wise; ready both to talk and to listen at the right times. Mrs Hamley was quite right in speaking of her husband's fondness for Molly. But either she herself chose a wrong time for telling him of the prolongation of the girl's visit, or one of the fits of temper to which he was liable, but which he generally strove to check in the presence of his wife, was upon him; at any rate, he received the news in anything but a gracious frame of mind.

'Stay longer! Did Gibson ask for it?'

'Yes! I don't see what else is to become of her; Miss Eyre away and all. It's a very awkward position for a motherless girl like her to be at the head of a household with two young men in it.'

'That's Gibson's look-out; he should have thought of it before taking pupils, or apprentices, or whatever he calls them.'

'My dear Squire! why, I thought you'd be as glad as I was – as I am – to keep Molly. I asked her to stay for an indefinite time; two months at least.'

'And to be in the house with Osborne! Roger, too, will be at home.'

By the cloud in the Squire's eyes, Mrs Hamley read his mind.

'Oh, she's not at all the sort of girl young men of their age would take to. We like her, because we see what she really is; but lads of one and two and twenty want all the accessories of a young woman.'

'Want what?' growled the Squire.

'Such things as becoming dress, style of manner. They would not at their age even see that she is pretty; their ideas of beauty would include colour.'

'I suppose all that's very clever; but I don't understand it. All I know is, that it's a very dangerous thing to shut two young men of one and three and twenty up in a country-house like this with a girl of seventeen – choose what her gowns may be like, or her hair, or her eyes. And I told you particularly I didn't want Osborne, or either of them, indeed, to be falling in love with her. I'm very much annoyed.'

Mrs Hamley's face fell; she became a little pale.

'Shall we make arrangements for their stopping away while she is here; staying up at Cambridge, or reading with some one? going abroad for a month or two?'

'No; you've been reckoning this ever so long on their coming home. I've seen the marks of the weeks on your almanack. I'd sooner speak to Gibson, and tell him he must take his daughter away, for it's not convenient to us'—

'My dear Roger! I beg you will do no such thing. It will be so unkind; it will give the lie to all I said yesterday. Don't, please, do that! For my sake, don't speak to Mr Gibson!'

'Well, well, don't put yourself in a flutter,' for he was afraid of her becoming hysterical; 'I'll speak to Osborne when he comes home, and tell him how much I should dislike anything of the kind.'

'And Roger is always far too full of his natural history and comparative anatomy, and messes of that sort, to be thinking of falling in love with Venus herself.* He has not the sentiment and imagination of Osborne.'

'Ah, you don't know; you never can be sure about a young man! But with Roger it wouldn't so much signify. He would know he couldn't marry for years to come.'

All that afternoon the Squire tried to steer clear of Molly, to whom he felt himself to have been an inhospitable traitor. But she was so perfectly unconscious of his shyness of her, and so merry and sweet in her behaviour as a welcome guest, never distrusting him for a moment, however gruff he might be, that by the next morning she had completely won him round, and they were quite on the old terms again. At breakfast this very morning, a letter was passed from the Squire to his wife, and back again, without a word as to its contents; but –

'Fortunate!'

'Yes! very!'

Little did Molly apply these expressions to the piece of news Mrs Hamley told her in the course of the day; namely, that her son Osborne had received an invitation to stay with a friend in the neighbourhood of Cambridge, and perhaps to make a tour on the Continent with him subsequently; and that, consequently, he would not accompany his brother when Roger came home.

Molly was very sympathetic.

'Oh, dear! I am so sorry!'

Mrs Hamley was thankful her husband was not present, Molly spoke the words so heartily.

'You have been thinking so long of his coming home. I am afraid it is a great disappointment.'

Mrs Hamley smiled – relieved.

'Yes! it is a disappointment certainly, but we must think of Osborne's pleasure. And with his poetical mind, he will write us such delightful letters about his travels. Poor fellow! he must be going into the examination today! Both his father and I feel sure, though, that he will be a high wrangler. Only – I should like to have seen him, my own dear boy. But it is best as it is.'

Molly was a little puzzled by this speech, but soon put it out of her head. It was a disappointment to her, too, that she should not see this beautiful, brilliant young man, his mother's hero. From time to time, her maiden fancy had dwelt upon what he would be like; how the lovely boy of the picture in Mrs Hamley's dressing-room would have changed in the ten years that had elapsed since the likeness was taken; whether he would read poetry aloud; whether he would ever read his own poetry? However, in the never-ending feminine business of the day, she soon forgot her own disappointment; it only came back to her on first wakening the next morning, as a vague something that was not quite so pleasant as she had anticipated, and then was banished as a subject of regret. Her days at Hamley were well filled up with the small duties that would have belonged to a daughter of the house, had there been one. She made breakfast for the lonely Squire, and would willingly have carried up Madam's; but that daily piece of work belonged to the Squire, and was jealously guarded by him. She read the smaller print of the newspapers aloud to him, city-articles, money and corn-markets included. She strolled about the gardens with him, gathering fresh flowers, meanwhile, to deck the drawing-room against Mrs Hamley should come down. She was her companion when she took her drives in the close carriage; they read poetry and mild literature together in Mrs Hamley's sitting-room upstairs. She was quite clever at cribbage now, and could beat the Squire if she took pains. Besides these things, there were her own independent ways of employing herself. She used to try to practise an hour daily on the old grand-piano in the solitary drawing-room, because she had promised Miss Eyre she would do so. And she had found her way into the library, and used to undo the heavy bars of the shutters, if the housemaid had forgotten this duty, and mount the ladder, sitting on the steps for an hour at a time, deep in some book of the old English classics. The summer days were very short to this happy girl of seventeen.

CHAPTER 8

Drifting into Danger

On Thursday, the quiet country-household was stirred through all its fibres with the thought of Roger's coming home. Mrs Hamley had not seemed quite so well, or quite in such good spirits for two or three days before; and the Squire himself had appeared to be put out without any visible cause. They had not chosen to tell Molly that Osborne's name had only appeared very low down in the mathematical tripos. So all that their visitor knew was that something was out of tune, and she hoped that Roger's coming home would set it to rights; for it was beyond the power of her small cares and wiles.

On Thursday, the housemaid apologised to her for some slight negligence in her bedroom, by saying she had been busy scouring Mr Roger's rooms. 'Not but what they were as clean as could be beforehand; but mistress would always have the young gentle-men's rooms cleaned afresh, before they came home. If it had been Mr Osborne, the whole house would have had to be done; but, to be sure, he was the eldest son, so it was but likely.' Molly was amused at this testimony to the rights of heirship; but, somehow, she herself had fallen into the family manner of think-ing that nothing was too great or too good for 'the eldest son'. In his father's eyes, Osborne was the representative of the ancient house of Hamley of Hamley, the future owner of the land which had been theirs for a thousand years. His mother clung to him, because they two were cast in the same mould, both physically and mentally – because he bore her maiden-name. She had indoc-trinated Molly with her faith, and, in spite of her amusement at the housemaid's speech, the girl visitor would have been as anxious as any one to show her feudal loyalty to the heir, if indeed it had been he that was coming. After luncheon, Mrs Hamley went to rest, in preparation for Roger's return; and Molly also retired to her own room, feeling that it would be better for her to remain there until dinner-time, and so to leave the father and mother to receive their boy in privacy. She took a book of MS. poems with her; they were all of Osborne Hamley's composition, and his mother had read some of them aloud to her young visitor more than once. Molly had asked permission to copy one or two of those which were her greatest favourites; and this quiet summer-afternoon she took this copying for her employment, sitting at the pleasant open window, and losing herself in the dreamy outlooks into the gardens and woods, quivering in the noon-tide heat. The house was so still, in its silence it might have been the 'moated grange';* the bomming buzz of the blue flies, in the great staircase window, seemed the loudest noise indoors. And there was scarcely a sound out-of-doors but the humming of bees, in the flower-beds below the window. Distant voices from the far-away fields where they were making hay – the scent of which came in sudden wafts, distinct from that of the nearer roses and honeysuckles – these merry piping voices just made Molly feel the depth of the present silence. She had left off copying, her hand weary with the unusual exertion of so much writing; and she was lazily trying to learn one or two of the poems off by heart.

> I asked of the wind, but answer made it none,
> Save its accustomed sad and solitary moan –

she kept saying to herself, losing her sense of whatever meaning the words had ever had, in the repetition which had become mechanical. Suddenly, there was the snap of a shutting gate; wheels crackling on the dry gravel; horses' feet on the drive; a loud cheerful voice in the house, coming up through the open windows, the hall, the passages, the staircase, with unwonted fulness and roundness of tone. The entrance-hall downstairs was paved with diamonds of black and white marble; the low wide staircase that went in short flights around the hall, till you could look down upon the marble floor from the top storey of the house, was uncarpeted – uncovered. The Squire was too proud of his beautifully-joined oaken flooring to cover this staircase up unnecessarily; not to say a word of the usual state of want of ready money to expend upon the decorations of his house. So, through the undraperied hollow square of the hall and staircase every sound ascended clear and distinct; and Molly heard the Squire's glad 'Hallo! here he is!' and Madam's softer, more plaintive voice; and then the loud, full, strange tone, which she knew must be Roger's. Then there was an opening and shutting of doors, and only a distant buzz of talking. Molly began again –

> I asked of the wind, but answer made it none.

And this time she had nearly finished learning the poem, when she heard Mrs Hamley come hastily into her sitting-room that adjoined Molly's bedroom, and burst out into an irrepressible, half-hysterical fit of sobbing. Molly was too young to have any complication of motives which would prevent her going at once to try and give what comfort she could. In an instant, she was kneeling at Mrs Hamley's feet, holding the poor lady's hands, kissing them, murmuring soft words; which, all unmeaning as they were of aught but sympathy with the untold grief, did Mrs Hamley good. She checked herself, smiling sadly at Molly through the midst of her thick-coming sobs.

'It's only Osborne,' said she, at last. 'Roger has been telling us about him.'

'What about him?' asked Molly eagerly.

'I knew on Monday; we had a letter – he said he had not done so well as we had hoped – as he had hoped himself, poor fellow! He said he had just passed, but was only low down among the *junior optimes*,* and not where he had expected, and had led us to expect. But the Squire has never been at college, and does not understand college terms, and he has been asking Roger all about it; and Roger has been telling him, and it has made him so angry. But the Squire hates college slang – he has never been there, you know; and he thought poor Osborne was taking it too lightly; and he has been asking Roger about it, and Roger' —

There was a fresh fit of the sobbing crying. Molly burst out – 'I don't think Mr Roger should have told; he had no need to begin so soon about his brother's failure. Why, he hasn't been in the house an hour!'

'Hush, hush, love!' said Mrs Hamley. 'Roger is so good. You don't understand. The Squire would begin and ask questions before Roger had tasted food – as soon as ever we had got into the dining-room. And all he said – to me, at any rate – was that Osborne was nervous, and that, if he could only have gone in for the Chancellor's medals, he would have carried all before him. But Roger said that, after failing like this, he is not very likely to get a fellowship, which the Squire had placed his hopes on. Osborne himself seemed so sure of it, that the Squire can't understand it, and is seriously angry, and growing more so the more he talks about it. He has kept it in two or three days, and that never suits him. He is always better when he is angry about a thing at once, and doesn't let it smoulder in his mind. Poor, poor

Osborne! I did wish he had been coming straight home, instead of going to these friends of his; I thought I could have comforted him. But now I'm glad, for it will be better to let his father's anger cool first.'

So, talking out what was in her heart, Mrs Hamley became more composed; and at length she dismissed Molly to dress for dinner, with a kiss, saying –

'You're a real "blessing to mothers", child! You give one such pleasant sympathy, both in one's gladness and in one's sorrow; in one's pride (for I was so proud last week, so confident), and in one's disappointment. And now your being a fourth at dinner will keep us off that sore subject; there are times when a stranger in the household is a wonderful help.'

Molly thought over all that she had heard, as she was dressing and putting on the terrible, over-smart plaid gown in honour of the new arrival. Her unconscious fealty to Osborne was not in the least shaken by his having come to grief at Cambridge. Only she was indignant – with or without reason – against Roger, who seemed to have brought the reality of bad news as an offering of first-fruits on his return home.

She went down into the drawing-room with anything but a welcome to him in her heart. He was standing by his mother; the Squire had not yet made his appearance. Molly thought that the two were hand in hand when she first opened the door, but she could not be quite sure. Mrs Hamley came a little forwards to meet her, and introduced her in so fondly intimate a way to her son, that Molly, innocent and simple, knowing nothing but Hollingford manners, which were anything but formal, half put out her hand to shake hands with one of whom she had heard so much – the son of such kind friends. She could only hope he had not seen the movement, for he made no attempt to respond to it; only bowed.

He was a tall, powerfully-made young man, giving the impression of strength rather than elegance. His face was rather square, ruddy-coloured (as his father had said), hair and eyes brown – the latter rather deep-set beneath his thick eyebrows; and he had a trick of wrinkling up his eyelids when he wanted particularly to observe anything, which made his eyes look even smaller still at such times. He had a large mouth, with excessively mobile lips; and another trick of his was, that when he was amused at anything, he resisted the impulse to laugh, by a droll manner of twitching and puckering up his mouth, till at length the sense of humour had its way, and his features relaxed, and he broke into a broad, sunny smile; his beautiful teeth – his only beautiful feature – breaking out with a white gleam upon the red-brown countenance. These two tricks of his – of crumpling up the eyelids, so as to concentrate the power of sight, which made him look stern and thoughtful; and the odd twitching of the lips that was preliminary to a smile, which made him look intensely merry – gave the varying expressions of his face a greater range 'from grave to gay, from lively to severe',* than is common with most men. To Molly, who was not finely discriminative in her glances at the stranger this first night, he simply appeared 'heavy-looking, clumsy', and 'a person she was sure she should never get on with.' He certainly did not seem to care much what impression he made upon his mother's visitor. He was at that age when young men admire a formed beauty more than a face with any amount of future capability of loveliness, and when they are morbidly conscious of the difficulty of finding subjects of conversation in talking to girls in a state of feminine hobbledehoyhood.* Besides, his thoughts were full of other subjects, which he did not intend to allow to ooze out in words, yet he wanted to prevent any of that heavy silence which he feared might be impending – with an angry and displeased father, and a timorous and distressed mother. He only looked upon Molly as a badly-dressed and rather awkward girl, with black hair and an intelligent face, who might help him in the task he had set himself of keeping up a bright general conversation during the rest of the evening; might help him – if she would, but she would not. She thought him unfeeling in his talkativeness; his constant flow of words upon indifferent subjects was a wonder and a repulsion to her. How could he go on so cheerfully, while his mother sat there, scarcely eating anything and doing her best, with ill success, to swallow down the tears that would keep rising to her eyes; when his father's heavy brow was deeply-clouded, and he evidently cared nothing – at first at least – for all the chatter his son poured forth? Had Mr Roger Hamley no sympathy in him? She would show that she had some, at any rate. So she quite declined the part, which he had hoped she would have taken, of respondent, and possible questioner; and his work became more and more like that of a man walking in a quagmire. Once the Squire roused himself to speak to the butler;

he felt the need of outward stimulus – of a better vintage than usual.

'Bring up a bottle of the Burgundy with the yellow seal.'

He spoke low; he had no spirit to speak in his usual voice. The butler answered in the same tone. Molly sitting near them, and silent herself, heard what they said.

'If you please, sir, there are not above six bottles of that seal left; and it is Mr Osborne's favourite wine.'

The Squire turned round with a growl in his voice.

'Bring up a bottle of the Burgundy with the yellow seal, as I said.'

The butler went away wondering. 'Mr Osborne's' likes and dislikes had been the law of the house in general until now. If he had liked any particular food or drink, any seat or place, any special degree of warmth or coolness, his wishes were to be attended to; for he was the heir, and he was delicate, and he was the clever one of the family. All the out-of-doors men would have said the same. Mr Osborne wished a tree cut down, or kept standing, or had such-and-such a fancy about the game, or desired something unusual about the horses – and they had all to attend to it as if it were law. But today the Burgundy with the yellow seal was to be brought; and it was brought. Molly testified with quiet vehemence of action; she never took wine, so she need not have been afraid of the man's pouring it into her glass; but, as an open mark of fealty to the absent Osborne, however little it might be understood, she placed the palm of her small brown hand over the top of the glass, and held it there, till the wine had gone round, and Roger and his father were in full enjoyment of it.

After dinner, too, the gentlemen lingered long over their dessert, and Molly heard them laughing; and then she saw them loitering about in the twilight out-of-doors; Roger hatless, his hands in his pockets, lounging by his father's side, who was now able to talk in his usual loud and cheerful way, forgetting Osborne. *Vae victis*!*

And so, in mute opposition on Molly's side, in polite indifference, scarcely verging upon kindliness on his, Roger and she steered clear of each other. He had many occupations in which he needed no companionship, even if she had been qualified to give it. The worst was, that she found he was in the habit of occupying the library, her favourite retreat, in the mornings before Mrs Hamley came down. She opened the half-closed door a day or two after his return home, and found him busy among books and papers, with which the large leather-covered table was strewn; and she softly withdrew before he could turn his head and see her, so as to distinguish her from one of the housemaids. He rode out every day, sometimes with his father about the out-lying fields, sometimes far-away for a good gallop. Molly would have enjoyed accompanying him on these occasions, for she was very fond of riding; and there had been some talk of sending for her habit and grey pony when first she came to Hamley; only the Squire, after some consideration, had said he so rarely did more than go slowly from one field to another, where his labourers were at work, that he feared she would find such slow work – ten minutes riding through heavy land, twenty minutes sitting still on horseback, listening to the directions he should have to give to his men – rather dull. Now, when, if she had had her pony here, she might have ridden out with Roger, without giving him any trouble – she would have taken care of that – nobody seemed to think of renewing the proposal.

Altogether it was pleasanter before he came home.

Her father rode over pretty frequently; sometimes there were long unaccountable absences, it was true; when his daughter began to fidget after him, and to wonder what had become of him. But, when he made his appearance, he had always good reasons to give; and the right she felt that she had to his familiar household tenderness, the power she possessed of fully under-standing the exact value of both his words and his silence, made these glimpses of intercourse with him inexpressibly charming. Latterly, her burden had always been, 'When may I come home, papa?' It was not that she was unhappy, or uncomfortable; she was passionately fond of Mrs Hamley; she was a favourite of the Squire's, and could not as yet fully understand why some people were so much afraid of him; and, as for Roger, if he did not add to her pleasure, he scarcely took away from it. But she wanted to be at home once more. The reason why she could not tell; but this she knew full well.* Mr Gibson reasoned with her, till she was weary of being completely convinced that it was right and necess-ary for her to stay where she was. And then, with an effort, she stopped the cry upon her tongue; for she saw that its repetition harassed her father.

During this absence of hers, Mr Gibson was drifting into

matrimony. He was partly aware of whither he was going; and partly it was like the soft, floating movement of a dream. He was more passive than active in the affair; though, if his reason had not fully approved of the step he was tending to – if he had not believed that a second marriage was the very best way of cutting the Gordian knot* of domestic difficulties – he could have made an effort without any great trouble, and extricated himself without pain from the mesh of circumstances. It happened in this manner. Lady Cumnor, having married her two eldest daughters, found her labours as a chaperon to Lady Harriet, the youngest, considerably lightened by co-operation; and, at length, she had leisure to be an invalid. She was, however, too energetic to allow herself this indulgence constantly; only she permitted herself to break down occasionally after a long course of dinners, late hours, and London atmosphere; and then, leaving Lady Harriet with either Lady Cuxhaven or Lady Agnes Manners, she betook herself to the comparative quiet of the Towers, where she found occupation in doing her benevolence, which was sadly neglected in the hurly-burly of London. This particular summer she had broken down earlier than usual, and longed for the repose of the country. She believed that her state of health, too, was more serious than previously; but she did not say a word of this to her husband or daughters, reserving her confidence for Mr Gibson's ears. She did not wish to take Lady Harriet away from the gaieties of town, which she was thoroughly enjoying, by any complaint of hers, which might, after all, be ill-founded; and yet she did not quite like being without a companion in the three weeks or a month that might intervene before her family would join her at the Towers, especially as the annual festivity to the school-visitors was impending, and both the school and the visit of the ladies connected with it had rather lost the zest of novelty.

'Thursday the 19th, Harriet,' said Lady Cumnor meditatively; 'what do you say to coming down to the Towers on the 18th, and helping me over that long day. You could stay in the country till Monday, and have a few days' rest and good air; you would return a great deal fresher to the remainder of your gaieties. Your father would bring you down, I know; indeed, he is coming naturally.'

'Oh, mamma!' said Lady Harriet, the youngest daughter of the house – the prettiest, the most indulged; 'I cannot go; there's the water-party up to Maidenhead on the 20th, I should be so sorry to miss it; and Mrs Duncan's ball, and Grisi's concert;* please, don't want me! Besides, I should do no good. I can't make provincial small-talk; I'm not up in the local politics of Hollingford. I should be making mischief, I know I should.'

'Very well, my dear,' said Lady Cumnor, sighing; 'I had forgotten the Maidenhead water-party, or I would not have asked you.'

'What a pity it isn't the Eton holidays, so that you could have had Hollingford's boys to help you to do the honours, mamma. They are such affable little prigs. It was the greatest fun to watch them last year at Sir Edward's, doing the honours of their grandfather's house to much such a collection of humble admirers as you get together at the Towers. I shall never forget seeing Edgar gravely squiring about an old lady in a portentous black bonnet, and giving her information in the correctest grammar possible.'

'Well, I like those lads,' said Lady Cuxhaven; 'they are on the way to become true gentlemen. But, mamma, why shouldn't you have Clare to stay with you? You like her, and she is just the person to save you the troubles of hospitality to the Hollingford people; and we should all be so much more comfortable if we knew you had her with you.'

'Yes, Clare would do very well,' said Lady Cumnor; 'but isn't it her school-time, or something? We must not interfere with her school so as to injure her, for I am afraid she is not doing too well as it is; and she has been so very unlucky ever since she left us – first her husband died, and then she lost Lady Davies' situation, and then Mrs Maude's, and now Mr Preston told your father it was all she could do to pay her way in Ashcombe, though Lord Cumnor lets her have the house rent-free.'

'I can't think how it is,' said Lady Harriet. 'She's not very wise, certainly; but she's so useful and agreeable, and has such pleasant manners, I should have thought any one who wasn't particular about education would have been charmed to keep her as a governess.'

'What do you mean by not being particular about education? Most people who keep governesses for their children are supposed to be particular,' said Lady Cuxhaven.

'Well, they think themselves so, I've no doubt; but I call you particular, Mary, and I don't think mamma was; but she thought herself so, I'm sure.'

'I can't think what you mean, Harriet,' said Lady Cumnor, a

good deal annoyed at this speech of her clever, heedless, youngest daughter.

'Oh dear, mamma, you did everything you could think of for us; but you see you'd ever so many other engrossing interests, and Mary hardly allows even her love for her husband to interfere with her all-absorbing care for the children. You gave us the best of masters in every department, and Clare to dragonise and keep us up to our preparation for them, as well as ever she could; but then you know, or rather you didn't know, some of the masters admired our very pretty governess, and there was a kind of respectable veiled flirtation going on, which never came to anything, to be sure; and then you were often so overwhelmed with your business as a great lady – fashionable and benevolent, and all that sort of thing – that you used to call Clare away from us at the most critical times of our lessons, to write your notes, or add up your accounts; and the consequence is, that I'm about the most ill-informed girl in London. Only Mary was so capitally trained by good awkward Miss Benson, that she is always full to overflowing with accurate knowledge, and her glory is reflected upon me.'

'Do you think what Harriet says is true, Mary?' asked Lady Cumnor rather anxiously.

'I was so little with Clare in the school-room. I used to read French with her; she had a beautiful accent, I remember. Both Agnes and Harriet were very fond of her. I used to be jealous for Miss Benson's sake, and perhaps' – Lady Cuxhaven paused a minute – 'that made me fancy that she had a way of flattering and indulging them – not quite conscientious, I used to think. But girls are severe judges, and certainly she had had an anxious enough lifetime. I am always so glad when we can have her, and give her a little pleasure. The only thing that makes me uneasy now is the way in which she seems to send her daughter away from her so much; we never can persuade her to bring Cynthia with her when she comes to see us.'

'Now, that I call ill-natured,' said Lady Harriet; 'here's a poor dear woman trying to earn her livelihood, first as a governess, and what could she do with her daughter then, but send her to school? and after that, when Clare is asked to go visiting, and is too modest to bring her girl with her – besides all the expense of the journey, and the rigging out* – Mary finds fault with her for her modesty and economy.'

'Well, after all, we are not discussing Clare and her affairs, but trying to plan for mamma's comfort. I don't see that she can do better than ask Mrs Kirkpatrick to come to the Towers – as soon as her holidays begin, I mean.'

'Here is her last letter,' said Lady Cumnor, who had been searching for it in her escritoire, while her daughters were talking. Holding her glasses before her eyes, she began to read, ' "My wonted misfortunes appear to have followed me to Ashcombe" – um, um, um; that's not it – "Mr Preston is most kind in sending me fruit and flowers from the Manor-house, according to dear Lord Cumnor's kind injunction." Oh, here it is! "The vacation begins on the 11th, according to the usual custom of schools in Ashcombe; and I must then try and obtain some change of air and scene, in order to fit myself for the resumption of my duties on the 10th of August." You see, girls, she would be at liberty, if she has not made any other arrangement for spending her holidays. Today is the fifteenth.'

'I'll write to her at once, mamma,' Lady Harriet said. 'Clare and I are always great friends: I was her confidant in her loves with poor Mr Kirkpatrick, and we've kept up our intimacy ever since. I know of three offers she had besides.'

'I sincerely hope Miss Bowes is not telling her love-affairs to Grace or Lily. Why, Harriet, you could not have been older than Grace, when Clare was married!' said Lady Cuxhaven, in maternal alarm.

'No; but I was well versed in the tender passion, thanks to novels. Now, I daresay you don't admit novels into your schoolroom, Mary; so your daughters wouldn't be able to administer discreet sympathy to their governess, in case she was the heroine of a love-affair.'

'My dear Harriet, don't let me hear you talking of love in that way; it is not pretty. Love is a serious thing.'

'My dear mamma, your exhortations are just eighteen years too late. I've talked all the freshness off love, and that's the reason I'm tired of the subject.'

This last speech referred to a recent refusal of Lady Harriet's, which had displeased Lady Cumnor, and rather annoyed my lord; as they, the parents, could see no objection to the gentleman in question. Lady Cuxhaven did not want to have the subject brought up, so she hastened to say –

'Do ask the poor little daughter to come with her mother to the

Towers; why, she must be seventeen or more; she would really be a companion to you, mamma, if her mother was unable to come.'

'I was not ten when Clare married, and I'm nearly nine-and-twenty,' added Lady Harriet.

'Don't speak of it, Harriet; at any rate you are but eight-and-twenty now, and you look a great deal younger. There is no need to be always bringing up your age on every possible occasion.'

'There was need of it now, though. I wanted to make out how old Cynthia Kirkpatrick was. I think she can't be far from eighteen.'

'She is at school at Boulogne, I know; and so I don't think she can be as old as that. Clare says something about her in this letter: "Under these circumstances" (the ill-success of her school), "I cannot think myself justified in allowing myself the pleasure of having darling Cynthia at home for the holidays; especially as the period when the vacation in French schools commences differs from that common in England; and it might occasion some confusion in my arrangements if darling Cynthia were to come to Ashcombe, and occupy my time and thoughts so immediately before the commencement of my scholastic duties as the 8th of August, on which day her vacation begins, which is but two days before my holidays end." So, you see, Clare would be quite at liberty to come to me, and I daresay it would be a very nice change for her.'

'And Hollingford is busy seeing after his new laboratory at the Towers, and is constantly backwards and forwards. And Agnes wants to go there for change of air, as soon as she is strong enough after her confinement. And even my own dear insatiable "me" will have had enough of gaiety in two or three weeks, if this hot weather lasts.'

'I think I may be able to come down for a few days too, if you will let me, mamma; and I'll bring Grace, who is looking rather pale and weedy; growing too fast, I'm afraid. So I hope you won't be dull.'

'My dear,' said Lady Cumnor, drawing herself up, 'I should be ashamed of feeling dull with my resources, my duties to others and to myself!'

So the plan in its present shape was told to Lord Cumnor, who highly approved of it; as he always did of every project of his wife's. Lady Cumnor's character was perhaps a little too ponderous for him in reality; but he was always full of admiration for all her words and deeds, and used to boast of her wisdom, her benevolence, her power and dignity, in her absence, as if by this means he could buttress up his own more feeble nature.

'Very good – very good, indeed! Clare to join you at the Towers! Capital! I couldn't have planned it better myself! I shall go down with you on Wednesday in time for the jollification on Thursday. I always enjoy that day; they are such nice, friendly people, those good Hollingford ladies. Then I'll have a day with Sheepshanks, and perhaps I may ride over to Ashcombe and see Preston. Brown Jess can do it in a day, eighteen miles – to be sure! But there's back again to the Towers! – how much is twice eighteen – thirty?'

'Thirty-six,' said Lady Cumnor sharply.

'So it is; you're always right, my dear. Preston's a clever, sharp fellow.'

'I don't like him,' said my lady.

'He takes looking after; but he's a sharp fellow. He's such a good-looking man, too, I wonder you don't like him.'

'I never think whether a land-agent is handsome or not. They don't belong to the class of people whose appearance I notice.'

'To be sure not. But he is a handsome fellow; and what should make you like him is the interest he takes in Clare and her prospects. He's constantly suggesting something that can be done to her house, and I know he sends her fruit, and flowers, and game just as regularly as we should ourselves, if we lived at Ashcombe.'

'How old is he?' said Lady Cumnor, with a faint suspicion of motives in her mind.

'About twenty-seven, I think. Ah! I see what is in your lady-ship's head. No! no! he's too young for that. You must look out for some middle-aged man, if you want to get poor Clare married; Preston won't do.'

'I'm not a match-maker, as you might know. I never did it for my own daughters. I'm not likely to do it for Clare,' said she, leaning back languidly.

'Well! you might do a worse thing. I'm beginning to think she'll never get on as a school-mistress, though why she shouldn't, I'm sure I don't know; for she's an uncommonly pretty woman for her age, and her having lived in our family, and your having had her so often with you, ought to go a good way. I say, my lady, what do you think of Gibson? He would be just the right age – widower – lives near the Towers.'

'I told you just now I was no match-maker, my lord. I suppose we had better go by the old road – the people at those inns know us?'

And so they passed on to speaking about other things than Mrs Kirkpatrick and her prospects, scholastic or matrimonial.

CHAPTER 9

The Widower and the Widow

Mrs Kirkpatrick was only too happy to accept Lady Cumnor's invitation. It was what she had been hoping for, but hardly daring to expect, as she believed that the family were settled in London for some time to come. The Towers was a pleasant and luxurious house in which to pass her holidays; and, though she was not one to make deep plans, or to look far ahead, she was quite aware of the prestige which her being able to say she had been staying with 'dear Lady Cumnor' at the Towers was likely to give her and her school in the eyes of a good many people; so she gladly prepared to join her ladyship on the 17th. Her wardrobe did not require much arrangement; if it had done, the poor lady would not have had much money to appropriate to the purpose. She was very pretty and graceful, and that goes a great way towards carrying off shabby clothes; and it was her taste, more than any depth of feeling, that had made her persevere in wearing all the delicate tints – the violets and greys – which, with a certain admixture of black, constitute half-mourning. This style of becoming dress she was supposed to wear in memory of Mr Kirkpatrick; in reality, because it was both lady-like and economical. Her beautiful hair was of that rich auburn that hardly ever turns grey; and, partly out of consciousness of its beauty, and partly because the washing of caps is expensive, she did not wear anything on her head; her complexion had the vivid tints that often accompany the kind of hair which has once been red; and the only injury her skin had received from advancing years was that the colour was rather more brilliant than delicate, and varied less with every passing emotion.* She could no longer blush; at eighteen she had been very proud of her blushes. Her eyes were soft, large, and china-blue in colour; they had not much expression or shadow about them, which was perhaps owing to the flaxen colour of her eyelashes. Her figure was a little fuller than it used to be, but her movements were as soft and sinuous as ever. Altogether, she looked much younger than her age, which was not far short of forty. She had a very pleasant voice, and read aloud well and distinctly, which Lady Cumnor liked. Indeed, for some inexplicable reasons, she was a greater, more positive favourite with Lady Cumnor than with any of the rest of the family, though they all liked her up to a certain point, and found it agreeably useful to have any one in the house who was so well acquainted with their ways and habits; so ready to talk, when a little trickle of conversation was required; so willing to listen, and to listen with tolerable intelligence, if the subjects spoken about did not refer to serious solid literature, or science, or politics, or social economy. About novels and poetry, travels and gossip, personal details, or anecdotes of any kind, she always made exactly the remarks which are expected from an agreeable listener; and she had sense enough to confine herself to those short expressions of wonder, admiration, and astonishment, which may mean anything, when more recondite things were talked about.

It was a very pleasant change to a poor unsuccessful school-mistress to leave her own house, full of battered and shabby furniture (she had taken the good-will* and furniture of her predecessor at a valuation, two or three years before), where the look-out was as gloomy, and the surroundings as squalid, as is often the case in the smaller streets of a country town, and to come bowling through the Towers Park in the luxurious carriage sent to meet her; to alight, and feel secure that the well-trained servants would see after her bags, and umbrella, and parasol, and cloak, without her loading herself with all these portable articles, as she had had to do while following the wheelbarrow containing her luggage, in going to the Ashcombe coach-office that morning; to pass up the deep-piled carpets of the broad shallow stairs into my lady's own room, cool and deliciously fresh, even on this sultry day, and fragrant with great bowls of freshly gathered roses of every shade of colour. There were two or three new novels lying uncut on the table; the daily papers, the magazines. Every chair was an easy-chair of some kind or other; and all covered with French chintz that mimicked the real flowers in the garden below. She was familiar with the bed-room called hers, to which she was soon ushered by Lady Cumnor's maid. It seemed to her far more like home than the dingy place she had left that morning; it was so natural to her to like dainty draperies, and harmonious colouring, and fine linen, and soft raiment. She sate down in the arm-chair by the bed-side, and wondered over her fate something in this fashion –

'One would think it was an easy enough thing to deck a looking-glass like that with muslin and pink ribbons; and yet how hard it is to keep it up! People don't know how hard it is, till they've tried as I have. I made my own glass just as pretty when I first went to Ashcombe; but the muslin got dirty, and the pink ribbons faded, and it is so difficult to earn money to renew them; and, when one has got the money, one hasn't the heart to spend it all at once. One thinks and one thinks how one can get the most good out of it; and a new gown, or a day's pleasure, or some hot-house fruit, or some piece of elegance that can be seen and noticed in one's drawing-room, carries the day – and good-bye to prettily-decked looking-glasses! Now here, money is like the air they breathe. No one even asks or knows how much the washing costs, or what pink ribbon is a yard. Ah! it would be different if they had to earn every penny as I have! They would have to calculate, like me, how to get the most pleasure out of it. I wonder if I am to go on all my life toiling and moiling* for money? It's not natural. Marriage is the natural thing; then the husband has all that kind of dirty work to do, and his wife sits in the drawing-room like a lady. I did, when poor Kirkpatrick was alive. Heigho! it's a sad thing to be a widow.'

Then there was the contrast between the dinners which she had to share with her scholars at Ashcombe – rounds of beef, legs of mutton, great dishes of potatoes, and large batter-puddings – with the tiny meal of exquisitely cooked delicacies, sent up on old Chelsea china,* that was served every day to the earl and countess and herself at the Towers. She dreaded the end of her holidays, as much as the most home-loving of her pupils. But at this time that end was some weeks off; so Clare shut her eyes to the future, and tried to relish the present to its fullest extent. A disturbance to the pleasant, even course of the summer days came in the indisposition of Lady Cumnor. Her husband had gone back to London, and she and Mrs Kirkpatrick had been left to the very even tenor of life, which was according to my lady's wish just now. In spite of her

languor and fatigue, she had gone through the day when the
school-visitors came to the Towers, in full dignity, dictating clearly
all that was to be done, what walks were to be taken, what hothouses to be seen, and when the party were to return to the
'collation'. She herself remained indoors, with one or two ladies
who had ventured to think that the fatigue or the heat might be
too much for them, and who had therefore declined accompanying
the ladies in charge of Mrs Kirkpatrick, or those other favoured
few to whom Lord Cumnor was explaining the new buildings in
his farmyard. 'With the utmost condescension',* as her hearers
afterwards expressed it, Lady Cumnor told them all about her
married daughters' establishments, nurseries, plans for the education of their children, and manner of passing the day. But the
exertion tired her; and, when every one had left, the probability is
that she would have gone to lie down and rest, had not her
husband made an unlucky remark in the kindness of his heart. He
came up to her and put his hand on her shoulder.

'I'm afraid you're sadly tired, my lady?' he said.

She braced her muscles, and drew herself up, saying coldly –

'When I am tired, Lord Cumnor, I will tell you so.' And her
fatigue showed itself during the rest of the evening in her sitting
particularly upright, and declining all offers of easy-chairs or
footstools, and refusing the insult of a suggestion that they should
all go to bed earlier. She went on in something of this kind of
manner, as long as Lord Cumnor remained at the Towers. Mrs
Kirkpatrick was quite deceived by it, and kept assuring Lord
Cumnor that she had never seen dear Lady Cumnor looking
better, or so strong. But he had an affectionate heart, if a
blundering head; and, though he could give no reason for his
belief, he was almost certain his wife was not well. Yet he was too
much afraid of her to send for Mr Gibson without her permission.
His last words to Clare were –

'It's such a comfort to leave my lady with you; only don't you
be deluded by her ways. She'll not show she's ill, till she can't help
it. Consult with Bradley' (Lady Cumnor's 'own woman', – she
disliked the new-fangledness of 'lady's-maid'); 'and, if I were you,
I'd send and ask Gibson to call – you might make any kind of
pretence' – and then the idea he had had in London of the fitness
of a match between the two coming into his head just now, he
could not help adding – 'Get him to come and see you, he's a very
agreeable man; Lord Hollingford says there's no one like him in

these parts; and he might be looking at my lady while he was talking to you, and see if he thinks her really ill. And let me know what he says about her.'

But Clare was just as great a coward about doing anything for Lady Cumnor which she had not expressly ordered, as Lord Cumnor himself. She knew she might fall into such disgrace, if she sent for Mr Gibson without direct permission, that she might never be asked to stay at the Towers again; and the life there, monotonous in its smoothness of luxury as it would be to some, was exactly to her taste. She in her turn tried to put upon Bradley the duty which Lord Cumnor had put upon her.

'Mrs Bradley,' she said one day, 'are you quite comfortable about my lady's health? Lord Cumnor fancied that she was looking worn and ill?'

'Indeed, Mrs Kirkpatrick, I don't think my lady is herself. I can't persuade myself as she is; though if you was to question me till night I couldn't tell you why.'

'Don't you think you could make some errand to Hollingford, and see Mr Gibson, and ask him to come round this way some day, and make a call on Lady Cumnor?'

'It would be as much as my place is worth, Mrs Kirkpatrick. Till my lady's dying-day, if Providence keeps her in her senses, she'll have everything done her own way, or not at all. There's only Lady Harriet that can manage her the least, and she not always.'

'Well, then – we must hope that there is nothing the matter with her; and I daresay there is not. She says there is not, and she ought to know best herself.'

But a day or two after this conversation took place, Lady Cumnor startled Mrs Kirkpatrick, by saying suddenly – 'Clare, I wish you'd write a note to Mr Gibson, saying I should like to see him this afternoon. I thought he would have called of himself before now. He ought to have done so, to pay his respects.'

Mr Gibson had been far too busy in his profession to have time for mere visits of ceremony, though he knew quite well he was neglecting what was expected of him. But the district of which he may be said to have had medical charge was full of a bad kind of low fever, which took up all his time and thought, and often made him very thankful that Molly was out of the way in the quiet shades of Hamley.

His domestic 'rows' had not healed over in the least, though he was obliged to put the perplexities on one side for the time. The last drop – the final straw – had been an impromptu visit of Lord Hollingford's, whom he had met in the town one forenoon. They had had a good deal to say to each other about some new scientific discovery, with the details of which Lord Hollingford was well acquainted, while Mr Gibson was ignorant and deeply interested. At length, Lord Hollingford said suddenly –

'Gibson, I wonder if you'd give me some lunch; I've been a good deal about since my seven-o'clock breakfast, and am getting quite ravenous.'

Now, Mr Gibson was only too much pleased to show hospitality to one whom he liked and respected so much as Lord Hollingford, and he gladly took him home with him to the early family dinner. But it was just at the time when the cook was sulking at Bethia's dismissal – and she chose to be unpunctual and careless. There was no successor to Bethia as yet appointed to wait at the meals. So, though Mr Gibson knew well that bread-and-cheese, cold beef, or the simplest food available, would have been welcome to the hungry lord, he could not get any of these things for luncheon, or even the family dinner, at anything like the proper time, in spite of all his ringing, and as much anger as he liked to show, for fear of making Lord Hollingford uncomfortable. At last, dinner was ready; but the poor host saw the want of nicety – almost the want of cleanliness – in all its accompaniments: dingy plate, dull-looking glass, a table-cloth that, if not absolutely dirty, was anything but fresh in its splashed and rumpled condition, and compared it in his own mind with the dainty delicacy with which even a loaf of brown bread was served up at his guest's home. He did not apologise directly; but, after dinner, just as they were parting, he said – 'You see a man like me – a widower – with a daughter who cannot always be at home – has not a regulated household, which would enable me to command the small portions of time I can spend there.'

He made no allusion to the comfortless meal of which they had both partaken, though it was full in his mind. Nor was it absent from Lord Hollingford's, as he made reply –

'True, true. Yet a man like you ought to be free from any thought of household cares. You ought to have somebody. How old is Miss Gibson?'

'Seventeen. It's a very awkward age for a motherless girl.'

'Yes; very. I have only boys, but it must be very awkward with a girl. Excuse me, Gibson, but we're talking like friends. Have you never thought of marrying again? It wouldn't be like a first marriage, of course; but, if you found a sensible, agreeable woman of thirty or so, I really think you couldn't do better than take her to manage your home, and so save you either discomfort or wrong; and, besides, she would be able to give your daughter that kind of tender supervision which, I fancy, all girls of that age require. It's a delicate subject, but you'll excuse my having spoken frankly.'

Mr Gibson had thought of this advice several times since it was given; but it was a case of 'first catch your hare'.* Where was the 'sensible and agreeable woman of thirty or so?' Not Miss Browning, nor Miss Phoebe, nor Miss Goodenough. Among his country-patients there were two classes pretty distinctly marked: farmers, whose children were unrefined and uneducated; squires, whose daughters would, indeed, think the world was coming to a pretty pass, if they were to marry a country-surgeon.

But, the first day on which Mr Gibson paid his visit to Lady Cumnor, he began to think it possible that Mrs Kirkpatrick was his 'hare'. He rode away with slack rein, thinking over what he knew of her, more than about the prescriptions he should write, or the way he was going. He remembered her as a very pretty Miss Clare: the governess who had the scarlet fever; that was in his wife's days, a long time ago; he could hardly understand Mrs Kirkpatrick's youthfulness of appearance when he thought how long. Then he had heard of her marriage to a curate; and the next day (or so it seemed, he could not recollect the exact duration of the interval), of his death. He knew, in some way, that she had been living ever since as a governess in different families; but that she had always been a great favourite with the family at the Towers, for whom, quite independent of their rank, he had a true respect. A year or two ago he had heard that she had taken the good-will of a school at Ashcombe; a small town close to another property of Lord Cumnor's, in the same county. Ashcombe was a larger estate than that near Hollingford, but the old Manor-house there was not nearly so good a residence as the Towers; so it was given up to Mr Preston, the land-agent for the Ashcombe property, just as Mr Sheepshanks was for that at Hollingford. There were a few rooms at the Manor-house reserved for the occasional visits of the family; otherwise, Mr Preston, a handsome young bachelor, had it all to himself. Mr Gibson knew that Mrs Kirkpatrick had one child, a daughter, who must be much about the same age as Molly. Of course she had very little, if any, property. But he himself had lived carefully, and had a few thousands well invested; besides which, his professional income was good, and increasing rather than diminishing every year. By the time he had arrived at this point in his consideration of the case, he was at the house of the next patient on his round, and he put away all thought of matrimony and Mrs Kirkpatrick for the time. Once again, in the course of the day, he remembered with a certain pleasure that Molly had told him some little details connected with her unlucky detention at the Towers five or six years ago, which had made him feel at the time as if Mrs Kirkpatrick had behaved very kindly to his little girl. So there the matter rested for the present, as far as he was concerned.

Lady Cumnor was out of health; but not so ill as she had been fancying herself during all those days when the people about her dared not send for the doctor. It was a great relief to her to have Mr Gibson to decide for her what she was to do; what to eat, drink, avoid. Such decisions *ab extra*,* are sometimes a wonderful relief to those whose habit it has been to decide, not only for themselves, but for every one else; and, occasionally, the relaxation of the strain which a character for infallible wisdom brings with it does much to restore health. Mrs Kirkpatrick thought in her secret soul that she had never found it so easy to get on with Lady Cumnor; and Bradley and she had never done singing the praises of Mr Gibson, 'who always managed my lady so beautifully.'

Reports were duly sent up to my lord, but he and his daughters were strictly forbidden to come down. Lady Cumnor wished to be weak and languid, and uncertain both in body and mind, without the family observation. It was a condition so different to anything she had ever been in before, that she was unconsciously afraid of losing her prestige if she was seen in it. Sometimes she herself wrote the daily bulletins; at other times she bade Clare do it, but she would always see the letters. Any answers she received from her daughters she used to read herself, occasionally imparting some of their contents to 'that good Clare'. But anybody might read my lord's letters. There was no great fear of family-secrets oozing out in his sprawling lines of affection. But once Mrs Kirkpatrick came upon a sentence in a letter from Lord Cumnor, which she was reading out loud to his wife, that caught her eye before she came to it; and, if she could have skipped it and kept it for private perusal, she would gladly have done so. My lady was too sharp for her, though. In her opinion 'Clare was a good creature, but not clever', the truth being that she was not always quick at resources, though tolerably unscrupulous in the use of them.

'Read on. What are you stopping for? There is no bad news, is there, about Agnes? Give me the letter.'

Lady Cumnor read, half aloud –

'How are Clare and Gibson getting on! You despised my advice to help on that affair; but I really think a little match-making would be a very pleasant amusement now that you are shut up in the house; and I cannot conceive any marriage more suitable.'

'Oh!' said Lady Cumnor, laughing, 'it was awkward for you to come upon that, Clare: I don't wonder you stopped short. You gave me a terrible fright, though.'

'Lord Cumnor is so fond of joking,' said Mrs Kirkpatrick, a little flurried, yet quite recognising the truth of his last words – 'I cannot conceive any marriage more suitable.' She wondered what Lady Cumnor thought of it. Lord Cumnor wrote as if there was really a chance. It was not an unpleasant idea; it brought a faint smile out upon her face, as she sat by Lady Cumnor, while the latter took her afternoon nap.

CHAPTER 10

A Crisis

Mrs Kirkpatrick had been reading aloud till Lady Cumnor fell asleep, the book rested on her knee, just kept from falling by her hold. She was looking out of the window, not seeing the trees in the park, nor the glimpses of the hills beyond, but thinking how pleasant it would be to have a husband once more – some one who would work, while she sate at her elegant ease in a prettily-furnished drawing-room; and she was rapidly investing this imaginary bread-winner with the form and features of the country surgeon, when there was a slight tap at the door, and almost before she could rise, the object of her thoughts came in. She felt herself blush, and she was not displeased at the consciousness. She advanced to meet him, making a sign towards her sleeping ladyship.

'Very good,' said he, in a low voice, casting a professional eye on the slumbering figure; 'can I speak to you for a minute or two in the library?'

'Is he going to offer?' thought she, with a sudden palpitation, and a conviction of her willingness to accept a man whom, an hour before, she had simply looked upon as one of the category of unmarried men with whom matrimony was possible.

He was only going to make one or two medical inquiries; she found that out very speedily, and considered the conversation as rather flat to her, though it might be instructive to him. She was not aware that he finally made up his mind to propose, during the time that she was speaking – answering his questions in many words, but he was accustomed to winnow the chaff from the corn;* and her voice was so soft, her accent so pleasant, that it struck him as particularly agreeable after the broad country accent he was perpetually hearing. Then the harmonious colours of her dress, and her slow and graceful movements, had something of the same soothing effect upon his nerves that a cat's purring has upon some people's. He began to think that he should be fortunate if he could win her, for his own sake. Yesterday he had looked upon her more as a possible step-mother for Molly; today he thought of her more as a wife for himself. The remembrance of Lord Cumnor's letter gave her a very becoming consciousness; she wished to attract, and hoped that she was succeeding. Still they only talked of the countess's state for some time; then a lucky shower came on. Mr Gibson did not care a jot for rain, but just now it gave him an excuse for lingering.

'It's very stormy weather,' said he.

'Yes, very. My daughter writes me word, that for two days last week the packet could not sail from Boulogne.'

'Miss Kirkpatrick is at Boulogne, is she?'

'Yes, poor girl; she is at school there, trying to perfect herself in the French language. But, Mr Gibson, you must not call her Miss Kirkpatrick. Cynthia remembers you with so much – affection, I may say. She was your little patient when she had the measles here four years ago, you know. Pray call her Cynthia; she would be quite hurt at such a formal name as Miss Kirkpatrick from you.'

'Cynthia seems to me such an out-of-the-way name; only fit for poetry, not for daily use.'

'It is mine,' said Mrs Kirkpatrick, in a plaintive tone of reproach. 'I was christened Hyacinth,* and her poor father would have her called after me. I'm sorry you don't like it.'

Mr Gibson did not know what to say. He was not quite prepared to plunge into the directly personal style. While he was hesitating, she went on –

'Hyacinth Clare! Once upon a time I was quite proud of my pretty name; and other people thought it pretty, too.'

'I've no doubt' – Mr Gibson began; and then stopped.

'Perhaps I did wrong in yielding to his wish to have her called by such a romantic name. It may excite prejudice against her in some people; and, poor child! she will have enough to struggle with. A young daughter is a great charge, Mr Gibson, especially when there is only one parent to look after her.'

'You are quite right,' said he, recalled to the remembrance of Molly; 'though I should have thought that a girl who is so fortunate as to have a mother could not feel the loss of her father so acutely as one who is motherless must suffer from her deprivation.'

'You are thinking of your own daughter. It was careless of me to say what I did. Dear child! how well I remember her sweet little face, as she lay sleeping on my bed! I suppose she is nearly grown-up now. She must be near my Cynthia's age. How I should like to see her!'

'I hope you will. I should like you to see her. I should like you to love my poor little Molly – to love her as your own' – He swallowed down something that rose in his throat, and was nearly choking him.

'Is he going to offer? *Is* he?' she wondered; and she began to tremble in the suspense before he next spoke.

'Could you love her as your daughter? Will you try? Will you give me the right of introducing you to her as her future mother; as my wife?'

There! he had done it – whether it was wise or foolish – he had done it! but he was aware that the question as to its wisdom came into his mind the instant that the words were said past recall.

She hid her face in her hands.

'Oh! Mr Gibson,' she said; and then, a little to his surprise, and a great deal to her own, she burst into hysterical tears: it was such a wonderful relief to feel that she need not struggle any more for a livelihood.

'My dear – my dearest,' said he, trying to soothe her with word and caress, but, just at the moment, uncertain what name he ought to use. After her sobbing had abated a little, she said herself, as if understanding his difficulty –

'Call me Hyacinth – your own Hyacinth! I can't bear "Clare", it does so remind me of being a governess; and those days are all past now.'

'Yes; but surely no one can have been more valued, more beloved, than you have been in this family at least.'

'Oh, yes! they have been very good. But still one has always had to remember one's position.'

'We ought to tell Lady Cumnor,' said he; thinking, perhaps, more of the various duties which lay before him in consequence of the step he had just taken, than of what his future bride was saying.

'You'll tell her, won't you?' said she, looking up in his face with beseeching eyes. 'I always like other people to tell her things, and then I can see how she takes them.'

'Certainly! I will do whatever you wish. Shall we go and see if she is awake now?'

'No! I think not. I had better prepare her. You will come tomorrow, won't you? and you will tell her then.'

'Yes; that will be best. I ought to tell Molly first. She has the right to know. I do hope you and she will love each other dearly.'

'Oh, yes! I'm sure we shall. Then you'll come tomorrow and tell Lady Cumnor? And I'll prepare her.'

'I don't see what preparation is necessary; but you know best, my dear. When can we arrange for you and Molly to meet?'

Just then a servant came in, and the pair started apart.

'Her ladyship is awake, and wishes to see Mr Gibson.'

They both followed the man upstairs; Mrs Kirkpatrick trying hard to look as if nothing had happened, for she particularly wished 'to prepare' Lady Cumnor; that is to say, to give her version of Mr Gibson's extreme urgency, and her own coy unwillingness.

But Lady Cumnor had observant eyes, in sickness as well as in health. She had gone to sleep with the recollection of the passage in her husband's letter full in her mind; and, perhaps, it gave a direction to her wakening ideas.

'I'm glad you're not gone, Mr Gibson. I wanted to tell you—What's the matter with you both? What have you been saying to Clare? I'm sure something has happened.'

There was nothing for it, in Mr Gibson's opinion, but to make a clean breast of it, and tell her ladyship all. He turned round, and took hold of Mrs Kirkpatrick's hand, and said out straight, 'I have been asking Mrs Kirkpatrick to be my wife, and to be a mother to my child; and she has consented. I hardly know how to thank her enough in words.'

'Umph! I don't see any objection. I daresay you'll be very happy. I'm very glad of it! Here! shake hands with me, both of you!' Then laughing a little, she added, 'It does not seem to me that any exertion has been required on my part.'

Mr Gibson looked perplexed at these words. Mrs Kirkpatrick reddened.

'Did she not tell you? Oh, then, I must. It's too good a joke to be lost, especially as everything has ended so well. When Lord Cumnor's letter came this morning – this very morning, I gave it to Clare to read aloud to me; and I saw she suddenly came to a full stop, where no full stop could be; and I thought it was something about Agnes, so I took the letter and read – stay! I'll read the sentence to you. Where's the letter, Clare? Oh, don't trouble yourself; here it is. "How are Clare and Gibson getting on? You despised my advice to help on that affair, but I really think a little match-making would be a very pleasant amusement, now that you are shut up in the house; and I cannot conceive any marriage more suitable." You see, you have my lord's full approbation. But I must write, and tell him you have managed your own affairs without any interference of mine. Now we'll just have a little medical talk, Mr Gibson, and then you and Clare shall finish your *tête-à-tête*.'

They were neither of them quite as desirous of further conversation together as they had been before the passage out of Lord Cumnor's letter had been read aloud. Mr Gibson tried not to think about it; for he was aware that if he dwelt upon it, he might get to fancy all sorts of things as to the conversation which had ended in his offer. But Lady Cumnor was imperious now, as always.

'Come, no nonsense! I always made my girls go and have *tête-à-têtes* with the men who were to be their husbands, whether they would or no; there's a great deal to be talked over before every marriage, and you two are certainly old enough to be above affectation. Go away with you!'

So there was nothing for it but for them to return to the library; Mrs Kirkpatrick pouting a little, and Mr Gibson feeling more like his own cool, sarcastic self, by many degrees, than he had done when last in that room.

She began, half crying –

'I cannot tell what poor Kirkpatrick would say, if he knew what I have done. He did so dislike the notion of second marriages, poor fellow!'

'Let us hope that he doesn't know, then; or that, if he does, he is wiser – I mean, that he sees how second marriages may be most desirable and expedient in some cases.'

Altogether, this second *tête-à-tête*, done to command, was not so satisfactory as the first; and Mr Gibson was quite alive to the necessity of proceeding on his round to see his patients, before very much time had elapsed.

'We shall shake down into uniformity before long, I've no doubt,' said he to himself, as he rode away. 'It's hardly to be expected that our thoughts should run in the same groove all at once. Nor should I like it,' he added. 'It would be very flat and stagnant to have only an echo of one's own opinions from one's wife. Heigho! I must tell Molly about it: dear little woman, I wonder how she'll take it? It's done, in a great measure, for her good.' And then he lost himself in recapitulating Mrs Kirkpatrick's good qualities, and the advantages to be gained to his daughter from the step he had taken.

It was too late to go round by Hamley that afternoon. The Towers and the Towers round lay just in the opposite direction to Hamley. So it was the next morning, before Mr Gibson arrived at the Hall, timing his visit as well as he could so as to have half-an-hour's private talk with Molly, before Mrs Hamley came down into the drawing-room. He thought that his daughter would require sympathy after receiving the intelligence he had to communicate; and he knew there was no one more fit to give it than Mrs Hamley.

It was a brilliantly hot summer's morning; men in their shirt-sleeves were in the fields getting in the early harvest of oats; as Mr Gibson rode slowly along, he could see them over the tall hedge-rows, and even hear the soothing, measured sound of the fall of the long swathes; as they were mown. The labourers seemed too hot to talk; the dog, guarding their coats and cans, lay panting loudly on the other side of the elm, under which Mr Gibson stopped for an instant to survey the scene, and gain a little delay before the interview that he wished was well over. In another minute, he had snapped at himself for his weakness, and put spurs to his horse. He came up to the Hall at a good sharp trot; it was earlier than the usual time of his visits, and no one was expecting him; all the stable-men were in the fields, but that signified little to Mr Gibson; he walked his horse about, for five minutes or so, before taking him into the stable, and loosened his girths, examining him with perhaps unnecessary exactitude. He went into the house by a private door, and made his way into the drawing-room, half expecting, however, that Molly would be in the garden. She had been there; but it was too hot and dazzling now for her to remain out-of-doors, and she had come in by the open window of the drawing-room. Oppressed with the heat, she had fallen asleep in an easy-chair, her bonnet and open book upon her knee, one arm hanging listlessly down. She looked very soft, and young, and child-like; and a gush of love* sprang into her father's heart as he gazed at her.

'Molly!' said he gently, taking the little brown hand that was hanging down, and holding it in his own. 'Molly!'

She opened her eyes, that for one moment had no recognition in them. Then the light came brilliantly into them; and she sprang up and threw her arms round his neck, exclaiming –

'Oh, papa, my dear, dear papa! What made you come while I was asleep? I lose the pleasure of watching for you.'

Mr Gibson turned a little paler than he had been before. He still held her hand, and drew her to a seat by him on a sofa, without speaking. There was no need; she was chattering away.

'I was up so early! It is so charming to be out here in the fresh morning air. I think that made me sleepy. But isn't it a gloriously hot day? I wonder if the Italian skies they talk about can be bluer than that – that little bit you see just between the oaks – there!'

She pulled her hand away, and used both it and the other to turn her father's head, so that he should exactly see the very bit she meant. She was rather struck by his unusual silence.

'Have you heard from Miss Eyre, papa? How are they all? And this fever that is about? Do you know, papa, I don't think you are looking well? You want me at home, to take care of you. How soon may I come home?'

'Don't I look well? That must be all your fancy, goosey. I feel uncommonly well; and I ought to look well, for—I have a piece of news for you, little woman.' (He felt that he was doing his business very awkwardly, but he was determined to plunge on.) 'Can you guess it?'

'How should I?' said she; but her tone was changed, and she was evidently uneasy, as with the presage of an instinct.

'Why, you see, my love,' said he, again taking her hand, 'that you are in a very awkward position – a girl growing up in such a family as mine – young men – which was a piece of confounded stupidity on my part. And I am obliged to be away so much.'

'But there is Miss Eyre,' said she, sick with the strengthening indefinite presage of what was to come. 'Dear Miss Eyre, I want nothing but her and you.'

'Still, there are times like the present when Miss Eyre cannot be with you; her home is not with us; she has other duties. I've been in great perplexity for some time; but at last I've taken a step which will, I hope, make us both happier.'

'You're going to be married again,' said she, helping him out with a quiet, dry voice, and gently drawing her hand out of his.

'Yes. To Mrs Kirkpatrick – you remember her? They call her "Clare" at the Towers. You recollect how kind she was to you that day you were left there?'

She did not answer. She could not tell what words to use. She was afraid of saying anything, lest the passion of anger, dislike, indignation – whatever it was that was boiling up in her breast – should find vent in cries and screams, or worse, in raging words that could never be forgotten. It was as if the piece of solid ground on which she stood had broken from the shore, and she was drifting out into the infinite sea alone.

Mr Gibson saw that her silence was unnatural, and half-guessed at the cause of it. But he knew that she must have time to reconcile herself to the idea, and still believed that it would be for her eventual happiness. He had, besides, the relief of feeling that the secret was told, the confidence made, which for the last twenty-four hours he had dreaded making. He went on recapitulating all the advantages of the marriage; he knew them off by heart, now.

'She's a very suitable age for me. I don't know how old she is exactly, but she must be nearly forty. I shouldn't have wished to marry any one younger. She's highly respected by Lord and Lady Cumnor and their family, which is of itself a character. She has very agreeable and polished manners – of course, from the circles she has been thrown into – and you and I, goosey, are apt to be a little brusque, or so; we must brush up our manners now.'

No remark from her on this little bit of playfulness. He went on –

'She has been accustomed to house-keeping – economical house-keeping, too – for of late years she has had a school at Ashcombe, and has had, of course, to arrange all things for a large family. And last, but not least, she has a daughter – about your age, Molly – who, of course, will come and live with us, and be a nice companion – a sister – for you.'

Still she was silent. At length she said –

'So I was sent out of the house that all this might be quietly arranged in my absence?'

Out of the bitterness of her heart she spoke, but she was roused out of her assumed impassiveness by the effect produced. Her father started up, and quickly left the room, saying something to himself – what, she could not hear, though she ran after him, followed him through dark stone-passages, into the glare of the stable-yard, into the stables –

'Oh, papa, papa – I'm not myself – I don't know what to say about this hateful – detestable'—

He led his horse out. She did not know if he heard her words. Just as he mounted, he turned round upon her with a grey, grim face –

'I think it's better, for both of us, for me to go away now. We may say things difficult to forget. We are both much agitated. By tomorrow we shall be more composed; you will have thought it over, and seen that the principal – one great motive, I mean – was your good. You may tell Mrs Hamley – I meant to have told her myself. I will come again tomorrow. Good-bye, Molly.'

For many minutes after he had ridden away – long after the sound of his horse's hoofs on the round stones of the paved lane, beyond the home-meadows, had died away – Molly stood there, shading her eyes, and looking at the empty space of air in which his form had last appeared. Her very breath seemed suspended; only, two or three times, after long intervals, she drew a miserable sigh, which was caught up into a sob. She turned away at last, but could not go into the house, could not tell Mrs Hamley, could not forget how her father had looked and spoken – and left her.

She went out through a side-door – it was the way by which

the gardeners passed when they took the manure into the garden – and the walk to which it led was concealed from sight as much as possible by shrubs and evergreens and over-arching trees. No one would know what became of her – and, with the ingratitude of misery, she added to herself, no one would care. Mrs Hamley had her own husband, her own children, her close home interests – she was very good and kind, but there was a bitter grief in Molly's heart, with which the stranger could not intermeddle. She went quickly on to the bourne which she had fixed for herself – a seat almost surrounded by the drooping leaves of a weeping-ash – a seat on the long broad terrace-walk on the other side of the wood, that overlooked the pleasant slope of the meadows beyond. The walk had probably been made to command this sunny, peaceful landscape, with trees and a church spire, two or three red-tiled roofs of old cottages, and a purple bit of rising ground in the distance; and at some previous date, when there might have been a large family of Hamleys residing at the Hall, ladies in hoops, and gentlemen in bag-wigs* with swords by their sides, might have filled up the breadth of the terrace as they sauntered, smiling, along. But no one ever cared to saunter there now. It was a deserted walk. The Squire or his sons might cross it, in passing to a little gate that led to the meadow beyond; but no one loitered there. Molly almost thought that no one knew of the hidden seat under the ash-tree but herself; for there were not more gardeners employed upon the grounds than were necessary to keep the kitchen-gardens and such of the ornamental part as was frequented by the family, or in sight of the house, in good order.

When she had once got to the seat, she broke out with suppressed passion of grief. She did not care to analyse the sources of her tears and sobs – her father was going to be married again – her father was angry with her; she had done very wrong – he had gone away displeased; she had lost his love; he was going to be married – away from her – away from his child – his little daughter – forgetting her own dear, dear mother. So she thought in a tumultuous kind of way, sobbing till she was wearied out, and had to gain strength by being quiet for a time, to break forth into her passion of tears afresh. She had cast herself on the ground – that natural throne for violent sorrow – and leant up against the old moss-grown seat; sometimes burying her face in her hands; sometimes clasping them together, as if by the tight painful grasp of her fingers she could deaden mental suffering.

She did not see Roger Hamley returning from the meadows, nor hear the click of the little white gate. He had been out dredging in ponds and ditches, and had his wet sling-net,* with its imprisoned treasures of nastiness, over his shoulder. He was coming home to lunch, having always a fine mid-day appetite, though he pretended to despise the meal in theory. But he knew that his mother liked his companionship then; she depended much upon her luncheon, and was seldom downstairs and visible to her family much before the time. So he overcame his theory, for the sake of his mother, and had his reward in the hearty relish with which he kept her company in eating.

He did not see Molly, as he crossed the terrace-walk on his way homewards. He had gone about twenty yards along the small wood-path at right angles to the terrace, when, looking among the grass and wild plants under the trees, he spied out one which was rare, one which he had been long wishing to find in flower, and saw it at last, with those bright keen eyes of his. Down went his net, skilfully twisted so as to retain its contents, while it lay amid the herbage, and he himself went, with light and well-planted footsteps, in search of the treasure. He was so great a lover of nature that, without any thought, but habitually, he always avoided treading unnecessarily on any plant; who knew what long-sought growth or insect might develop itself in that which now appeared but insignificant?

His steps led him in the direction of the ash-tree seat, much less screened from observation on this side than on the terrace. He stopped; he saw a light-coloured dress on the ground – somebody half-lying on the seat, so still just then, that he wondered if the person, whoever it was, had fallen ill or fainted. He paused to watch. In a minute or two the sobs broke out again – the words. It was Miss Gibson crying in a broken voice –

'Oh, papa, papa! if you would but come back!'

For a minute or two, he thought it would be kinder to leave her fancying herself unobserved; he had even made a retrograde step or two, on tip-toe; but then he heard the miserable sobbing again. It was farther than his mother could walk; or else, be the sorrow what it would, she was the natural comforter of this girl, her visitor. However, whether it was right or wrong, delicate or obtrusive, when he heard the sad voice talking again, in such tones of uncomforted, lonely misery, he turned back, and went to the green tent under the ash-tree. She started up, when he came thus close to her; she tried to check her sobs, and instinctively smoothed her wet, tangled hair back with her hands.

He looked down upon her with grave, kind sympathy, but he did not know exactly what to say.

'Is it lunch-time?' said she, trying to believe that he did not see the traces of her tears and the disturbance of her features – that he had not seen her lying, sobbing her heart out there.

'I don't know. I was going home to lunch. But – you must let me say it – I couldn't go on when I saw your distress. Has anything happened? – anything in which I can help you, I mean; for, of course, I've no right to make the inquiry, if it is any private sorrow, in which I can be of no use.'

She had exhausted herself so much with crying, that she felt as if she could neither stand nor walk just yet. She sate down on the seat, and sighed, and turned so pale, that he thought she was going to faint.

'Wait a moment,' said he – quite unnecessarily, for she could not have stirred – and he was off like a shot to some spring of water that he knew of in the wood; and in a minute or two he returned with careful steps, bringing a little in a broad green leaf, turned into an impromptu cup. Little as it was, it did her good.

'Thank you!' she said: 'I can walk back now, in a short time. Don't stop.'

'You must let me,' said he; 'my mother wouldn't like me to leave you to come home alone, while you are so faint.'

So they remained in silence for a little while; he breaking off and examining one or two abnormal leaves of the ash-tree, partly from the custom of his nature, partly to give her time to recover.

'Papa is going to be married again,' said she at length.

She could not have said why she told him this; an instant before she spoke, she had no intention of doing so. He dropped the leaf he held in his hand, turned round, and looked at her. Her poor wistful eyes were filling with tears as they met his, with a dumb appeal for sympathy. Her look was much more eloquent than her words. There was a momentary pause before he replied, and then it was more because he felt that he must say something than that he was in any doubt as to the answer to the question he asked.

'You are sorry for it?'

She did not take her eyes away from his, as her quivering lips formed the word 'Yes', though her voice made no sound. He was silent again now; looking on the ground, kicking softly at a loose pebble with his foot. His thoughts did not come readily to the surface in the shape of words; nor was he apt at giving comfort, till he saw his way clear to the real source from which consolation must come. At last he spoke – almost as if he was reasoning out the matter with himself.

'It seems as if there might be cases where – setting the question of love entirely on one side – it must be almost a duty to find some one to be a substitute for the mother. . . . I can believe,' said he, in a different tone of voice, and looking at Molly afresh, 'that this step may be greatly for your father's happiness – it may relieve him from many cares, and may give him a pleasant companion.'

'He had me. You don't know what we were to each other – at least, what he was to me,' she added humbly.

'Still he must have thought it for the best, or he wouldn't have done it. He may have thought it the best for your sake even more than for his own.'

'That is what he tried to convince me of.'

Roger began kicking the pebble again. He had not got hold of the right end of the clue.* Suddenly he looked up.

'I want to tell you of a girl I know. Her mother died when she was about sixteen – the eldest of a large family. From that time – all through the bloom of her youth – she gave herself up to her father, first as his comforter, afterwards as his companion, friend, secretary – anything you like. He was a man with a great deal of business on hand, and often came home only to set-to afresh to preparations for the next day's work. Harriet was always there, ready to help, to talk, or to be silent. It went on for eight or ten years in this way; and then her father married again – a woman not many years older than Harriet herself. Well – they are just the happiest set of people I know – you wouldn't have thought it likely, would you?'

She was listening, but she had no heart to say anything. Yet she was interested in this little story of Harriet – a girl who had been so much to her father, more than Molly in this early youth of hers could have been to Mr Gibson. 'How was it?' she sighed out at last.

'Harriet thought of her father's happiness before she thought of her own,' Roger answered, with something of severe brevity. Molly needed the bracing. She began to cry again a little.

'If it were for papa's happiness' —

'He must believe that it is. Whatever you fancy, give him a chance. He cannot have much comfort, I should think, if he sees you fretting or pining – you who have been so much to him, as you say. The lady herself, too – if Harriet's stepmother had been a selfish woman, and been always clutching after the gratification of her own wishes – but she was not: she was as anxious for Harriet to be happy as Harriet was for her father – and your father's future wife may be another of the same kind, though such people are rare.'

'I don't think she is, though,' murmured Molly, a waft of recollection bringing to her mind the details of her day at the Towers long ago.

Roger did not want to hear Molly's reasons for this doubting speech. He felt as if he had no right to hear more of Mr Gibson's family life, past, present, or to come, than was absolutely necessary for him, in order that he might comfort and help the crying girl, whom he had come upon so unexpectedly. And, besides, he wanted to go home, and be with his mother at lunch-time. Yet he could not leave her alone.

'It is right to hope for the best about everybody, and not to expect the worst. This sounds like a truism, but it has comforted me before now, and some day you'll find it useful. One has always to try to think more of others than of oneself, and it is best not to prejudge people on the bad side. My sermons aren't long, are they? Have they given you an appetite for lunch? Sermons always make me hungry, I know.'

He appeared to be waiting for her to get up and come along with him, as indeed he was. But he meant her to perceive that he should not leave her; so she rose up languidly, too languid to say how much she should prefer being left alone, if he would only go away without her. She was very weak, and stumbled over the straggling root of a tree that projected across the path. He, watchful though silent, saw this stumble, and, putting out his hand, held her up from falling. He still held her hand when the occasion was past; this little physical failure impressed on his heart how young and helpless she was, and he yearned to her, remembering the passion of sorrow in which he had found her, and longing to be of some little tender bit of comfort to her, before they parted – before their *tête-à-tête* walk was merged in the general familiarity of the household life. Yet he did not know what to say.

'You will have thought me hard,' he burst out at length, as they were nearing the drawing-room windows and the garden door. 'I never can manage to express what I feel – somehow I always fall to philosophising – but I am sorry for you. Yes, I am; it's beyond my power to help you, as far as altering facts goes; but I can feel for you, in a way which it's best not to talk about, for it can do no good. Remember how sorry I am for you! I shall often be thinking of you, though I daresay it's best not to talk about it again.'

She said, 'I know you are sorry,' under her breath; and then she broke away, and ran indoors, and upstairs to the solitude of her own room. He went straight to his mother, who was sitting before the untasted luncheon, as much annoyed by the mysterious unpunctuality of her visitor as she was capable of being with anything; for she had heard that Mr Gibson had been, and was gone, and she could not discover if he had left any message for her; and her anxiety about her own health, which some people esteemed hypochondriacal, always made her particularly craving for the wisdom which might fall from her doctor's lips.

'Where have you been, Roger? Where is Molly? – Miss Gibson, I mean,' for she was careful to keep up a barrier of forms between the young man and the young woman who were thrown together in the same household.

'I've been out dredging. (By the way, I left my net on the terrace walk.) I found Miss Gibson sitting there, crying as if her heart would break. Her father is going to be married again.'

'Married again! You don't say so!'

'Yes, he is; and she takes it very hardly, poor girl. Mother, I think if you could send some one to her with a glass of wine, a cup of tea, or something of that sort – she was very nearly fainting' —

'I'll go to her myself, poor child,' said Mrs Hamley, rising.

'Indeed you must not,' said he, laying his hand upon her arm. 'We have kept you waiting already too long; you are looking quite pale. Hammond can take it,' he continued, ringing the bell. She sat down again, almost stunned with surprise.

'Whom is he going to marry?'

'I don't know. I didn't ask, and she didn't tell me.'

'That's so like a man. Why, half the character of the affair lies in the question of who it is that he is going to marry.'

'I daresay I ought to have asked. But somehow I'm not a good

one on such occasions. I was as sorry as could be for her, and yet
I couldn't tell what to say.'

'What did you say?'

'I gave her the best advice in my power.'

'Advice! you ought to have comforted her. Poor little Molly!'

'I think that, if advice is good, it's the best comfort.'

'That depends on what you mean by advice. Hush! here she is.'

To their surprise, Molly came in, trying hard to look as usual.
She had bathed her eyes, and arranged her hair, and was making
a great struggle to keep from crying, and to bring her voice into
order. She was unwilling to distress Mrs Hamley by the sight of
pain and suffering. She did not know that she was following
Roger's injunction to think more of others than of herself – but so
she was. Mrs Hamley was not sure if it was wise in her to begin
on the piece of news she had just heard from her son; but she was
too full of it herself to talk of anything else. 'So I hear your father
is going to be married, my dear? May I ask whom it is to?'

'Mrs Kirkpatrick. I think she was governess a long time ago at
the Countess of Cumnor's. She stays with them a great deal, and
they call her "Clare", and I believe they are very fond of her.'
Molly tried to speak of her future stepmother in the most favourable manner she knew how.

'I think I've heard of her. Then she's not very young? That's as
it should be. A widow, too. Has she any family?'

'One girl, I believe. But I know so little about her!'

Molly was very near crying again.

'Never mind, my dear. That will all come in good time. Roger,
you've hardly eaten anything; where are you going?'

'To fetch my dredging-net. It's full of things I don't want to
lose. Besides, I never eat much, as a general thing.' The truth was
partly told, not all. He thought he had better leave the other two
alone. His mother had such sweet power of sympathy that she
would draw the sting out of the girl's heart, when she had her
alone. As soon as he was gone, Molly lifted up her poor swelled
eyes, and, looking at Mrs Hamley, she said – 'He was so good to
me. I mean to try and remember all he said.'

'I'm glad to hear it, love; very glad. From what he told me, I
was afraid he had been giving you a little lecture. He has a good
heart, but he isn't so tender in his manner as Osborne. Roger is a
little rough sometimes.'

'Then I like roughness. It did me good. It made me feel how

badly – oh, Mrs Hamley, I did behave so badly to papa this morning!'

She rose up and threw herself into Mrs Hamley's arms, and sobbed upon her breast. Her sorrow was not now for the fact that her father was going to be married again, but for her own ill-behaviour.

If Roger was not tender in words, he was in deeds. Unreasonable, and possibly exaggerated, as Molly's grief had appeared to him, it was real suffering to her; and he took some pains to lighten it, in his own way, which was characteristic enough. That evening he adjusted his microscope, and put the treasures he had collected in his morning's ramble on a little table; and then he asked his mother to come and admire. Of course Molly came too, and this was what he had intended. He tried to interest her in his pursuit, cherished her first little morsel of curiosity, and nursed it into a very proper desire for further information. Then he brought out books on the subject, and translated the slightly pompous and technical language into homely every-day speech. Molly had come down to dinner, wondering how the long hours till bed-time would ever pass away: hours during which she must not speak on the one thing that would be occupying her mind to the exclusion of all others; for she was afraid that already she had wearied Mrs Hamley with it during their afternoon *tête-à-tête*. But prayers and bed-time came long before she expected; she had been refreshed by a new current of thought, and she was very thankful to Roger. And now there was tomorrow to come, and a confession of penitence to be made to her father.

But Mr Gibson did not want speech or words. He was not fond of expressions of feeling at any time, and perhaps, too, he felt that the less said the better on a subject about which it was evident that his daughter and he were not thoroughly and impulsively in harmony. He read her repentance in her eyes; he saw how much she had suffered; and he had a sharp pang at his heart in consequence. And he stopped her from speaking out her regret at her behaviour the day before, by a 'There, there, that will do. I know all you want to say. I know my little Molly – my silly little goosey – better than she knows herself. I've brought you an invitation. Lady Cumnor wants you to go and spend next Thursday at the Towers.'

'Do you wish me to go?' said she, her heart sinking.

'I wish you and Hyacinth to become better acquainted – to learn to love each other.'

'Hyacinth!' said Molly, entirely bewildered.

'Yes; Hyacinth! It's the silliest name I ever heard of; but it's hers, and I must call her by it. I can't bear Clare, which is what my lady and all the family at the Towers call her; and "Mrs Kirkpatrick" is formal and nonsensical too, as she'll change her name so soon.'

'When, papa?' asked Molly, feeling as if she were living in a strange, unknown world.

'Not till after Michaelmas.' And then, continuing on his own thoughts, he added, 'And the worst is, she's gone and perpetuated her own affected name by having her daughter called after her. Cynthia! One thinks of the moon, and the man in the moon with his bundle of faggots.* I'm thankful you're plain Molly, child.'

'How old is she – Cynthia, I mean?'

'Ay, get accustomed to the name. I should think Cynthia Kirkpatrick was about as old as you are. She's at school in France, picking up airs and graces. She's to come home for the wedding, so you'll be able to get acquainted with her then; though, I think, she's to go back again for another half-year or so.'

CHAPTER 11

Making Friendship

Mr Gibson believed that Cynthia Kirkpatrick was to return to England to be present at her mother's wedding; but Mrs Kirkpatrick had no such intention. She was not what is commonly called a woman of determination; but somehow what she disliked she avoided, and what she liked she tried to do, or to have. So although in the conversation, which she had already led to, as to the when and the how she was to be married, she had listened quietly to Mr Gibson's proposal that Molly and Cynthia should be the two bridesmaids, still she had felt how disagreeable it would be to her to have her young daughter flashing out her beauty by the side of the faded bride, her mother; and, as the further arrangements for the wedding became more definite, she saw further reasons in her own mind for Cynthia's remaining quietly at her school at Boulogne.

Mrs Kirkpatrick had gone to bed that first night of her engagement to Mr Gibson, fully anticipating a speedy marriage. She looked to it as a release from the thraldom of keeping school – keeping an unprofitable school, with barely pupils enough to pay for house-rent and taxes, food, washing, and the requisite masters. She saw no reason for ever going back to Ashcombe, except to wind up her affairs, and to pack up her clothes. She hoped that Mr Gibson's ardour would be such that he would press on the marriage, and urge her never to resume her school drudgery, but to relinquish it now and for ever. She even made up a very pretty, very passionate speech for him in her own mind; quite sufficiently strong to prevail upon her, and to overthrow the scruples which she felt she ought to have, at telling the parents of her pupils that she did not intend to resume school, and that they must find another place of education for their daughters, in the last week but one of the midsummer holidays.

It was rather like a douche of cold water on Mrs Kirkpatrick's plans, when the next morning at breakfast Lady Cumnor began to decide upon the arrangements and duties of the two middle-aged lovers.

'Of course you can't give up your school all at once, Clare. The wedding can't be before Christmas, but that will do very well. We shall all be down at the Towers; and it will be a nice amusement for the children to go over to Ashcombe, and see you married.'

'I think – I am afraid – I don't believe Mr Gibson will like waiting so long; men are so impatient under these circumstances.'

'Oh, nonsense! Lord Cumnor has recommended you to his tenants, and I'm sure he wouldn't like them to be put to any inconvenience. Mr Gibson will see that in a moment. He's a man of sense, or else he wouldn't be our family doctor. Now, what are you going to do about your little girl? Have you fixed yet?'

'No. Yesterday there seemed so little time, and when one is agitated it is so difficult to think of anything. Cynthia is nearly eighteen, old enough to go out as a governess, if he wishes it, but I don't think he will. He is so generous and kind.'

'Well! I must give you time to settle some of your affairs today. Don't waste it in sentiment; you're too old for that. Come to a clear understanding with each other; it will be for your happiness in the long run.'

So they did come to a clear understanding about one or two things. To Mrs Kirkpatrick's dismay, she found that Mr Gibson had no more idea than Lady Cumnor of her breaking faith with the parents of her pupils. Though he really was at a serious loss as to what was to become of Molly, till she could be under the protection of his new wife at her own home, and though his domestic worries teased him more and more every day, he was too honourable to think of persuading Mrs Kirkpatrick to give up school a week sooner than was right for his sake. He did not even perceive how easy the task of persuasion would be; with all her winning wiles, she could scarcely lead him to feel impatience for the wedding to take place at Michaelmas.

'I can hardly tell you what a comfort and relief it will be to me, Hyacinth, when you are once my wife – the mistress of my home – poor little Molly's mother and protector; but I wouldn't interfere with your previous engagements for the world. It wouldn't be right.'

'Thank you, my own love. How good you are! So many men would think only of their own wishes and interests! I'm sure the parents of my dear pupils will admire you – will be quite surprised at your consideration for their interests.'

'Don't tell them, then. I hate being admired. Why shouldn't you say it is your wish to keep on your school till they've had time to look out for another?'

'Because it isn't,' said she, daring all. 'I long to be making you happy; I want to make your home a place of rest and comfort to you; and I do so wish to cherish your sweet Molly, as I hope to do, when I come to be her mother. I can't take virtue to myself which doesn't belong to me. If I have to speak for myself, I shall say, "Good people, find a school for your daughters by Michaelmas – for after that time I must go and make the happiness of others." I can't bear to think of your long rides in November – coming home wet at night, with no one to take care of you. Oh! if you leave it to me, I shall advise the parents to take their daughters away from the care of one whose heart will be absent. Though I couldn't consent to any time before Michaelmas – that wouldn't be fair or right, and I'm sure you wouldn't urge me – you are too good.'

'Well, if you think that they will consider we have acted uprightly by them, let it be Michaelmas with all my heart. What does Lady Cumnor say?'

'Oh! I told her I was afraid you wouldn't like waiting, because of your difficulties with your servants, and because of Molly – it would be so desirable to enter on the new relationship with her as soon as possible.'

'To be sure, so it would. Poor child! I'm afraid the intelligence of my engagement has rather startled her.'

'Cynthia will feel it deeply, too,' said Mrs Kirkpatrick, unwilling to let her daughter be behind Mr Gibson's in sensibility and affection.

'We will have her over to the wedding! She and Molly shall be bridesmaids,' said Mr Gibson, in the unguarded warmth of his heart.

This plan did not quite suit Mrs Kirkpatrick: but she thought it best not to oppose it, until she had a presentable excuse to give, and perhaps also some reason would naturally arise out of future circumstances; so at this time she only smiled, and softly pressed the hand she held in hers.

It is a question whether Mrs Kirkpatrick or Molly wished the most for the day to be over which they were to spend together at the Towers. Mrs Kirkpatrick was rather weary of girls as a class. All the trials of her life were connected with girls in some way. She was very young when she first became a governess, and had been worsted in her struggles with her pupils, in the first place she ever went to. Her elegance of appearance and manner, and her accomplishments, more than her character and acquirements, had rendered it easier for her than for most to obtain good 'situations'; and she had been absolutely petted in some; but still she was constantly encountering naughty or stubborn, or over-conscientious, or severe-judging, or curious and observant girls. And again, before Cynthia was born, she had longed for a boy, thinking it possible that if some three or four intervening relations died, he might come to be a baronet; and instead of a son, lo and behold it was a daughter! Nevertheless, with all her dislike to girls in the abstract as 'the plagues of her life' (and her aversion was not diminished by the fact of her having kept a school for 'young ladies' at Ashcombe), she really meant to be as kind as she could be to her new step-daughter, whom she remembered principally as a black-haired, sleepy child, in whose eyes she had read admiration of herself. Mrs Kirkpatrick accepted Mr Gibson principally because she was tired of the struggle of earning her own livelihood; but she liked him personally – nay, she even loved him in her torpid way, and she intended to be good to his daughter, though she felt as if it would have been easier for her to have been good to his son.

Molly was bracing herself up in her way too. 'I will be like Harriet. I will think of others. I won't think of myself,' she kept repeating all the way to the Towers. But there was no selfishness in wishing that the day was come to an end, and that she did very heartily. Mrs Hamley sent her thither in the carriage, which was to wait and bring her back at night. Mrs Hamley wanted Molly to make a favourable impression, and she sent for her to come and show herself before she set out.

'Don't put on your silk gown – your white muslin will look the nicest, my dear.'

'Not my silk! it is quite new! I had it to come here.'

'Still, I think your white muslin suits you the best.' 'Anything but that horrid plaid silk' was the thought in Mrs Hamley's mind; and, thanks to her, Molly set off for the Towers, looking a little quaint, it is true, but thoroughly lady-like, if she was old-fashioned. Her father was to meet her there; but he had been detained, and she had to face Mrs Kirkpatrick by herself, the recollection of her last day of misery at the Towers fresh in her mind, as if it had been yesterday. Mrs Kirkpatrick was as caressing as could be. She held Molly's hand in hers, as they sate together in the library, after the first salutations were over. She kept stroking it from time to time, and purring out inarticulate sounds of loving satisfaction, as she gazed in the blushing face.

'What eyes! so like your dear father's! How we shall love each other – shan't we, darling? For his sake!'

'I'll try,' said Molly bravely; and then she could not finish her sentence.

'And you've just got the same beautiful black curling hair!' said Mrs Kirkpatrick, softly lifting one of Molly's curls from off her white temple.

'Papa's hair is growing grey,' said Molly.

'Is it? I never see it. I never shall see it. He will always be to me the handsomest of men.'

Mr Gibson was really a very handsome man, and Molly was pleased with the compliment; but she could not help saying –

'Still, he will grow old, and his hair will grow grey. I think he will be just as handsome, but it won't be as a young man.'

'Ah! that's just it, love. He'll always be handsome; some people always are. And he is so fond of you, dear.' Molly's colour flashed into her face. She did not want an assurance of her own father's love from this strange woman. She could not help being angry; all she could do was to keep silent. 'You don't know how he speaks of you; "his little treasure", as he calls you. I'm almost jealous sometimes.'

Molly took her hand away, and her heart began to harden; these speeches were so discordant to her. But she set her teeth together, and 'tried to be good'.

'We must make him so happy. I'm afraid he has had a great deal to annoy him at home; but we will do away with all that now. You must tell me,' seeing the cloud in Molly's eyes, 'what he likes and dislikes, for of course you will know.'

Molly's face cleared a little; of course she did know. She had not watched and loved him so long without believing that she understood him better than any one else: though, how he had come to like Mrs Kirkpatrick enough to wish to marry her, was an unsolved problem that she unconsciously put aside as inexplicable. Mrs Kirkpatrick went on – 'All men have their fancies and antipathies, even the wisest. I have known some gentlemen annoyed beyond measure by the merest trifles; leaving a door open, or spilling tea in their saucers, or a shawl crookedly put on. Why,' continued she, lowering her voice, 'I know of a house to which Lord Hollingford will never be asked again, because he didn't wipe his shoes on both the mats in the hall! Now you must tell me what your dear father dislikes most in these fanciful ways, and I shall take care to avoid it. You must be my little friend and helper in pleasing him. It will be such a pleasure to me to attend to his slightest fancies. About my dress, too – what colours does he like best? I want to do everything in my power with a view to his approval.'

Molly was gratified by all this, and began to think that really, after all, perhaps her father had done well for himself; and that, if she could help towards his new happiness, she ought to do it. So she tried very conscientiously to think over Mr Gibson's wishes and ways; to ponder over what annoyed him the most in his household.

'I think,' said she, 'papa isn't particular about many things; but, I think, our not having the dinner quite punctual – quite ready for him when he comes in – fidgets him more than anything. You see, he has often had a long ride, and there is another long ride to

come, and he has only half-an-hour – sometimes only a quarter –
to eat his dinner in.'

'Thank you, my own love! Punctuality! Yes; it's a great thing in
a household. It's what I've had to enforce with my young ladies at
Ashcombe. No wonder poor dear Mr Gibson has been displeased
at his dinner not being ready, and he so hard-worked!'

'Papa doesn't care what he has, if it's only ready. He would
take bread-and-cheese,* if cook would only send it in instead of
dinner.'

'Bread-and-cheese! Does Mr Gibson eat cheese?'

'Yes; he's very fond of it,' said Molly innocently. 'I've known
him eat toasted cheese when he has been too tired to fancy
anything else.'

'Oh! but, my dear, we must change all that. I shouldn't like to
think of your father eating cheese; it's such a strong-smelling,
coarse kind of thing. We must get him a cook who can toss him
up an omelette, or something elegant. Cheese is only fit for the
kitchen.'

'Papa is very fond of it,' persevered Molly.

'Oh! but we will cure him of that. I couldn't bear the smell of
cheese; and I'm sure he would be sorry to annoy me.'

Molly was silent; it did not do, she found, to be too minute in
telling about her father's likes or dislikes. She had better leave
them for Mrs Kirkpatrick to find out for herself. It was an
awkward pause; each was trying to find something agreeable to
say. Molly spoke at length. 'Please! I should so like to know
something about Cynthia – your daughter.'

'Yes, call her Cynthia. It's a pretty name, isn't it? Cynthia
Kirkpatrick. Not so pretty, though, as my old name, Hyacinth
Clare. People used to say it suited me so well. I must show you an
acrostic* that a gentleman – he was a lieutenant in the 53rd –
made upon it. Oh! we shall have a great deal to say to each other,
I foresee!'

'But about Cynthia?'

'Oh, yes! about dear Cynthia. What do you want to know, my
dear?'

'Papa said she was to live with us! When will she come?'

'Oh, was it not sweet of your kind father? I thought of nothing
else but Cynthia's going out as a governess when she had completed her education; she has been brought up for it, and has had
great advantages. But good, dear Mr Gibson wouldn't hear of it.

He said yesterday that she must come and live with us when she left school.'

'When will she leave school?'

'She went for two years. I don't think I must let her leave before next summer. She teaches English as well as learning French. Next summer she shall come home, and then shan't we be a happy little quartette!'

'I hope so,' said Molly. 'But she is to come to the wedding, isn't she?' she went on timidly, not knowing how far Mrs Kirkpatrick would like the allusion to her marriage.

'Your father has begged for her to come; but we must think about it a little more, before quite fixing it. The journey is a great expense!'

'Is she like you? I do so want to see her.'

'She is very handsome, people say. In the bright-coloured style – perhaps something like what I was. But I like the dark-haired, foreign kind of beauty best – just now,' touching Molly's hair, and looking at her with an expression of sentimental remembrance.

'Does Cynthia – is she very clever and accomplished?' asked Molly, a little afraid lest the answer should place Miss Kirkpatrick at too great a distance from her.

'She ought to be; I've paid ever so much money to have her taught by the best masters. But you will see her before long, and I'm afraid we must go now to Lady Cumnor. It has been very charming having you all to myself; but I know Lady Cumnor will be expecting us now, and she was very curious to see you – my future daughter, as she calls you.'

Molly followed Mrs Kirkpatrick into the morning-room, where Lady Cumnor was sitting – a little annoyed, because, having completed her toilette earlier than usual, Clare had not been aware by instinct of the fact, and so had not brought Molly Gibson for inspection a quarter of an hour before. Every small occurrence is an event in the day of a convalescent invalid, and a little while ago Molly would have met with patronising appreciation, where now she had to encounter criticism. Of Lady Cumnor's character as an individual she knew nothing; she only knew she was going to see and be seen by a live countess – nay, more, by 'the countess' of Hollingford.

Mrs Kirkpatrick led her into Lady Cumnor's presence by the

hand, and, in presenting her, said – 'My dear little daughter, Lady Cumnor!'

'Now, Clare, don't let me have any nonsense. She is not your daughter yet, and may never be – I believe that one-third of the engagements I have heard of have never come to marriages. Miss Gibson, I am very glad to see you, for your father's sake; when I know you better, I hope it will be for your own.'

Molly very heartily hoped that she might never be known any better by the stern-looking lady who sate so upright in the easy-chair prepared for lounging, which therefore gave all the more effect to her stiff attitude. Lady Cumnor luckily took Molly's silence for acquiescent humility, and went on speaking after a further little pause of inspection.

'Yes, yes, I like her looks, Clare. You may make something of her. It will be a great advantage to you, my dear, to have a lady who has trained up several young people of quality always about you just at the time when you are growing up. I'll tell you what, Clare!' – a sudden thought striking her – 'you and she must become better acquainted – you know nothing of each other at present; you are not to be married till Christmas, and what could be better than that she should go back with you to Ashcombe! She would be with you constantly, and have the advantage of the companionship of your young people, which would be a good thing for an only child! It's a capital plan; I'm very glad I thought of it!'

Now it would be difficult to say which of Lady Cumnor's two hearers was the more dismayed at the idea which had taken possession of her. Mrs Kirkpatrick had no fancy for being encumbered with a stepdaughter before her time. If Molly came to be an inmate of her house, farewell to many little background econom-ies, and a still more serious farewell to many little indulgences, that were innocent enough in themselves, but which Mrs Kirkpa-trick's former life had caused her to look upon as sins to be concealed: the dirty, dog's-eared delightful novel from the Ash-combe circulating library, the leaves of which she turned over with a pair of scissors; the lounging-chair which she had for use at her own home, straight and upright as she sate now in Lady Cumnor's presence; the dainty morsel, savoury and small, to which she treated herself for her own solitary supper – all these and many other similarly pleasant things would have to be foregone, if Molly came to be her pupil, parlour-boarder,* or visitor, as Lady Cumnor was planning. One – two things Clare was instinctively resolved upon: to be married at Michaelmas, and not to have Molly at Ashcombe. But she smiled as sweetly as if the plan proposed was the most charming project in the world, while all the time her poor brains were beating about in every bush for the reasons or excuses of which she should make use at some future time. Molly, however, saved her all this trouble. It was a question which of the three was the most surprised by the words which burst out of her lips. She did not mean to speak, but her heart was very full; and, almost before she was aware of her thought, she heard herself saying –

'I don't think it would be nice at all. I mean, my lady, that I should dislike it very much; it would be taking me away from papa just these very few last months. I will like you,' she went on, her eyes full of tears; and, turning to Mrs Kirkpatrick, she put her hand into her future step-mother's with the prettiest and most trustful action. 'I will try hard to love you, and to do all I can to make you happy; but you must not take me away from papa just this very last bit of time that I shall have him.'

Mrs Kirkpatrick fondled the hand thus placed in hers, and was grateful to the girl for her outspoken opposition to Lady Cumnor's plan. Clare was, however, exceedingly unwilling to back up Molly by any words of her own until Lady Cumnor had spoken and given the cue. But there was something in Molly's little speech, or in her straightforward manner, that amused instead of irritating Lady Cumnor in her present mood. Perhaps she was tired of the silkiness with which she had been shut up for so many days.

She put up her glasses, and looked at them both before speaking. Then she said – 'Upon my word, young lady! Why, Clare, you've got your work before you! Not but what there is a good deal of truth in what she says. It must be very disagreeable to a girl of her age to have a step-mother coming in between her father and herself, whatever may be the advantages to her in the long run.'

Molly almost felt as if she could make a friend of the stiff old countess, for her clearness of sight as to the plan proposed being a trial; but she was afraid, in her new-born desire of thinking for others, of Mrs Kirkpatrick being hurt. She need not have feared, as far as outward signs went; for the smile was still on that lady's pretty rosy lips, and the soft fondling of Molly's hand never stopped. Lady Cumnor was more interested in Molly, the more she looked at her; and her gaze was pretty steady through her gold-rimmed eye-glasses. She began a sort of catechism: a string of very straightforward questions, such as any lady under the rank of countess might have scrupled to ask, but which were not unkindly meant.

'You are sixteen, are you not?'

'No; I am seventeen. My birthday was three weeks ago.'

'Very much the same thing, I should think. Have you ever been to school?'

'No, never! Miss Eyre has taught me everything I know.'

'Umph! Miss Eyre was your governess, I suppose? I should not have thought your father could have afforded to keep a governess. But of course he must know his own affairs best.'

'Certainly, my lady,' replied Molly, a little touchy as to any reflections on her father's wisdom.

'You say "certainly"! as if it was a matter of course that every one should know their own affairs best. You are very young, Miss Gibson – very. You'll know better before you come to my age. And I suppose you've been taught music, and the use of globes, and French, and all the usual accomplishments, since you have had a governess? I never heard of such nonsense!' she went on, lashing herself up. 'An only daughter! If there had been half-a-dozen, there might have been some sense in it.'

Molly did not speak, but it was by a strong effort that she kept silence. Mrs Kirkpatrick fondled her hand more perseveringly than ever, hoping thus to express a sufficient amount of sympathy to prevent her from saying anything injudicious. But the caress had become wearisome to Molly, and only irritated her nerves. She took her hand out of Mrs Kirkpatrick's, with a slight manifestation of impatience.

It was, perhaps, fortunate for the general peace that just at this moment Mr Gibson was announced. It is odd enough to see how the entrance of a person of the opposite sex into an assemblage of either men or women calms down the little discordances and any disturbance of mood. It was the case now; at Mr Gibson's entrance my lady took off her glasses, and smoothed her brow; Mrs Kirkpatrick managed to get up a very becoming blush; and, as for Molly, her face glowed with delight, and the white teeth and pretty dimples came out like sunlight on a landscape.

Of course, after the first greeting, my lady had to have a private interview with her doctor; and Molly and her future stepmother wandered about in the gardens, with their arms round each other's waists, or hand in hand, like two babes in the wood;* Mrs Kirkpatrick active in such endearments, Molly passive, and feeling within herself very shy and strange; for she had that particular kind of shy modesty which makes any one uncomfortable at receiving caresses from a person towards whom the heart does not go forth with an impulsive welcome.

Then came the early dinner; Lady Cumnor having hers in the quiet of her own room, to which she was still a prisoner. Once or twice during the meal, the idea crossed Molly's mind that her father disliked his position as a middle-aged lover being made so evident to the men in waiting as it was by Mrs Kirkpatrick's affectionate speeches and innuendos. He tried to banish every tint of pink sentimentalism* from the conversation, and to confine it to matter of fact; and, when Mrs Kirkpatrick would persevere in referring to such particulars as had a bearing on their future relationship, he insisted upon viewing these things in the most matter-of-fact way; and this continued even after the men had left the room. An old rhyme Molly had heard Betty use would keep running in her head and making her uneasy –

> Two is company,
> Three is trumpery.*

But where could she go to in that strange house? What ought she to do? She was roused from this fit of wonder and abstraction by her father's saying – 'What do you think of this plan of Lady Cumnor's? She says she was advising you to have Molly as a visitor at Ashcombe until we are married.'

Mrs Kirkpatrick's countenance fell. If only Molly would be so good as to testify again, as she had done before Lady Cumnor! But, if the proposal was made by her father, it would come to his daughter from a different quarter than it had done from a strange lady, be she ever so great. Molly did not say anything; she only looked pale, and wistful, and anxious. Mrs Kirkpatrick had to speak for herself.

'It would be a charming plan, only – Well! we know why we would rather not have it; don't we, love? And we won't tell papa, for fear of making him vain. No! I think I must leave her with you, dear Mr Gibson, to have you all to herself for these last few weeks. It would be cruel to take her away.'

'But you know, my dear, I told you of the reason why it does not do to have Molly at home just at present,' said Mr Gibson eagerly. For, the more he knew of his future wife, the more he felt it necessary to remember that, with all her foibles, she would be able to stand between Molly and any such adventures as that which had occurred lately with Mr Coxe; so that one of the good reasons for the step he had taken was always present to him, while it had slipped off the smooth surface of Mrs Kirkpatrick's mirror-like mind without leaving any impression. She now recalled it, on seeing Mr Gibson's anxious face.

But what were Molly's feelings at these last words of her father's? She had been sent from home for some reason, kept a secret from her, but told to this strange woman. Was there to be perfect confidence between these two, and she to be for ever shut out? Was she, and what concerned her – though how she did not know – to be discussed between them for the future, and she to be kept in the dark? A bitter pang of jealousy made her heart-sick. She might as well go to Ashcombe, or anywhere else, now. Thinking more of others' happiness than of her own was very fine; but did it not mean giving up her very individuality, quenching all the warm love, the true desires, that made her herself? Yet in this deadness lay her only comfort; or so it seemed. Wandering in such mazes, she hardly knew how the conversation went on; a third was indeed 'trumpery', where there was entire confidence between the two who were company, from which the other was shut out. She was positively unhappy, and her father did not appear to see it; he seemed absorbed in his new plans and his new wife that was to be. But he did notice it, and was truly sorry for his little girl; only he thought that there was a greater chance for the future harmony of the household, if he did not lead Molly to define her present feelings by putting them into words. It was his general plan to repress emotion by not showing the sympathy he felt. Yet, when he had to leave, he took Molly's hand in his, and held it there, in such a different manner to that in which Mrs Kirkpatrick had held it; and his voice softened to his child as he bade her good-bye, and added the words (most unusual to him), 'God bless you, child!'

Molly had held up all the day bravely; she had not shown anger, or repugnance, or annoyance, or regret; but, when once more by herself in the Hamley carriage, she burst into a passion of tears, and cried her fill till she reached the village of Hamley. Then she tried in vain to smooth her face into smiles, and do away with the other signs of her grief. She only hoped she could run upstairs to her own room without notice, and bathe her eyes in cold water before she was seen. But at the Hall-door she was caught by the Squire and Roger, coming in from an after-dinner stroll in the garden, and hospitably anxious to help her to alight. Roger saw the state of things in an instant, and, saying –

'My mother has been looking for you to come back for this last hour,' he led the way to the drawing-room. But Mrs Hamley was not there; the Squire had stopped to speak to the coachman about one of the horses; they two were alone. Roger said –

'I'm afraid you've had a very trying day. I have thought of you several times, for I know how awkward these new relations are.'

'Thank you,' said she, with her lips trembling, and on the point of crying again. 'I did try to remember what you said, and to think more of others, but it is so difficult sometimes; you know it is, don't you?'

'Yes,' said he gravely. He was gratified by her simple confession of having borne his words of advice in mind, and tried to act up to them. He was but a very young man, and he was honestly flattered; perhaps this led him on to offer more advice, and this time it was evidently mingled with sympathy. He did not want to draw out her confidence, which he felt might very easily be done with such a simple girl; but he wished to help her by giving her a few of the principles on which he had learnt to rely. 'It is difficult,' he went on, 'but by-and-by you will be so much happier for it.'

'No, I shan't!' said Molly, shaking her head. 'It will be very dull when I shall have killed myself, as it were, and live only in trying to do, and to be, as other people like. I don't see any end to it. I might as well never have lived. And as for the happiness you speak of, I shall never be happy again.'

There was an unconscious depth in what she said, that Roger did not know how to answer at the moment; it was easier to address himself to the assertion of the girl of seventeen, that she should never be happy again.

'Nonsense: perhaps in ten years' time you will be looking back on this trial as a very light one – who knows?'

'I daresay it seems foolish; perhaps all our earthly trials will appear foolish to us after a while; perhaps they seem so now to angels. But we are ourselves, you know, and this is *now*, not some time to come, a long, long way off. And we are not angels, to be comforted by seeing the ends for which everything is sent.'

She had never spoken so long a sentence to him before; and, when she had said it, though she did not take her eyes away from his, as they stood steadily looking at each other, she blushed a little; she could not have told why. Nor did he tell himself why a sudden pleasure came over him, as he gazed at her simple, expressive face – and for a moment lost the sense of what she was saying, in the sensation of pity for her sad earnestness. In an instant more he was himself again. Only it is pleasant to the wisest, most reasonable youth of one or two and twenty to find himself looked up to as a Mentor* by a girl of seventeen.

'I know, I understand. Yes: it is *now* we have to do with. Don't let us go into metaphysics.' Molly opened her eyes wide at this. Had she been talking metaphysics without knowing it? 'One looks forward to a mass of trials, which will only have to be encountered one by one, little by little. Oh, here is my mother! she will tell you better than I can.'

And the *tête-à-tête* was merged into a trio. Mrs Hamley lay down; she had not been well all day – she had missed Molly, she said – and now she wanted to hear of all the adventures that had occurred to the girl at the Towers. Molly sate on a stool close to the head of the sofa, and Roger, though at first he took up a book and tried to read that he might be no restraint, soon found his reading all a pretence: it was so interesting to listen to Molly's little narrative, and, besides, if he could give her any help in her time of need, was it not his duty to make himself acquainted with all the circumstances of her case?

And so they went on during all the remaining time of Molly's stay at Hamley. Mrs Hamley sympathised, and liked to hear details; as the French say, her sympathy was given *en détail*, the Squire's *en gros*.* He was very sorry for her evident grief, and almost felt guilty, as if he had had a share in bringing it about, by the mention he had made of the possibility of Mr Gibson's marrying again, when first Molly came on her visit to them. He said to his wife more than once –

''Pon my word, now, I wish I'd never spoken those unlucky words that first day at dinner. Do you remember how she took them up? It was like a prophecy of what was to come, now, wasn't it? And she has looked pale from that day, and I don't think she has ever fairly enjoyed her food since. I must take more care what I say for the future. Not but what Gibson is doing the very best thing, both for himself and her, that he can do. I told him so only yesterday. But I'm very sorry for the little girl, though. I wish I'd never spoken about it, that I do! but it was like a prophecy, wasn't it?'

Roger tried hard to find out a reasonable and right method of comfort; for he, too, in his way, was sorry for the girl, who bravely struggled to be cheerful, in spite of her own private grief, for his mother's sake. He felt as if high principle and noble precept ought to perform an immediate work. But they do not, for there is always the unknown quantity of individual experience and feeling, which offer a tacit resistance, the amount incalculable by another, to all good counsel and high decree. But the bond between the Mentor and his Telemachus strengthened every day. He endeavoured to lead her out of morbid thought into interest in other than personal things; and, naturally enough, his own objects of interest came readiest to hand. She felt that he did her good, she did not know why or how; but, after a talk with him, she always fancied that she had got the clue to goodness and peace, whatever befell.

CHAPTER 12

Preparing for the Wedding

Meanwhile the love affairs of the middle-aged couple were prospering well, after a fashion; after the fashion that they liked best, although it might probably have appeared dull and prosaic to younger people. Lord Cumnor had come down in great glee at the news he had heard from his wife at the Towers. He, too, seemed to think he had taken an active part in bringing about the match by only speaking about it. His first words on the subject to Lady Cumnor were –

'I told you so. Now didn't I say what a good, suitable affair this affair between Gibson and Clare would be! I don't know when I've been so much pleased. You may despise the trade of match-maker, my lady, but I am very proud of it. After this, I shall go on looking out for suitable cases among the middle-aged people of my acquaintance. I shan't meddle with young folks, they are so apt to be fanciful; but I've been so successful in this, that I do think it's good encouragement to go on.'

'Go on – with what?' asked Lady Cumnor drily. 'Oh, planning!'

'You can't deny that I planned this match.'

'I don't think you are likely to do either much good or harm by planning,' she replied, with cool good-sense.

'It puts it into people's heads, my dear.'

'Yes, if you speak about your plans to them, of course it does. But in this case you never spoke to either Mr Gibson or Clare, did you?'

All at once the recollection of how Clare had come upon the passage in Lord Cumnor's letter flashed on his lady; but she did not say anything about it, but left her husband to flounder about as best he might.

'No! I never spoke to them; of course not.'

'Then you must be strongly mesmeric,* and your will acted upon theirs, if you are to take credit for any part in the affair,' continued his pitiless wife.

'I really can't say. It's no use looking back to what I said or did. I'm very well satisfied with it, and that's enough, and I mean to show them how much I'm pleased. I shall give Clare something towards her rigging-out, and they shall have a breakfast at Ashcombe Manor-house. I'll write to Preston about it. When did you say they were to be married?'

'I think they'd better wait till Christmas, and I have told them so. It would amuse the children, going over to Ashcombe for the wedding; and if it's bad weather during the holidays I'm always afraid of their finding it dull at the Towers. It's very different if it's a good frost, and they can go out skating and sledging in the park. But these last two years it has been so wet for them, poor dears!'

'And will the other poor dears be content to wait to make a holiday for your grandchildren? "To make a Roman holiday". Pope, or somebody else, has a line of poetry like that. "To make a Roman holiday",'* – he repeated, pleased with his unusual aptitude at quotation.

'It's Byron, and it's nothing to do with the subject in hand. I'm surprised at your lordship's quoting Byron – he was a very immoral poet.'

'I saw him take his oaths in the House of Lords,' said Lord Cumnor apologetically.

'Well! the less said about him the better,' said Lady Cumnor. 'I have told Clare that she had better not think of being married before Christmas; and it won't do for her to give up her school in a hurry either.'

But Clare did not intend to wait till Christmas; and for this once she carried her point against the will of the countess, and without many words, or any open opposition. She had a harder task in setting aside Mr Gibson's desire to have Cynthia over for the wedding, even if she went back to her school at Boulogne directly after the ceremony. At first she had said that it would be delightful, a charming plan; only she feared that she must give up her own wishes to have her child near her at such a time, on account of the expense of the double journey.

But Mr Gibson, economical as he was in his habitual expenditure, had a really generous heart. He had already shown it, in entirely relinquishing his future wife's life-interest in the very small property the late Mr Kirkpatrick had left, in favour of Cynthia; while he arranged that she should come to his home as a daughter, as soon as she left the school she was at. The life-interest was about thirty pounds a year. Now he gave Mrs Kirkpatrick three five-pounds notes, saying that he hoped they would do away with the objections to Cynthia's coming over to the wedding; and at the time Mrs Kirkpatrick felt as if they would, and caught the reflection of his strong wish, and fancied it was her own. If the letter could have been written and the money sent off that day while the reflected glow of affection lasted, Cynthia would have been bridesmaid to her mother. But a hundred little interruptions came in the way of letter-writing, and the value affixed to the money increased; money had been so much needed, so hardly earned in Mrs Kirkpatrick's life; while the perhaps necessary separation of mother and child had lessened the amount of affection the former had to bestow. So she persuaded herself, afresh, that it would be unwise to disturb Cynthia at her studies; to interrupt the fulfilment of her duties, just after the *semestre* had begun afresh; and she wrote a letter to Madame Lefèvre so well imbued with this persuasion, that an answer which was almost an echo of her words was returned, the sense of which being conveyed to Mr Gibson, who was no great French scholar, settled the vexed question, to his moderate but unfeigned regret. But the fifteen pounds were not returned. Indeed, not merely that sum, but a great part of the hundred which Lord Cumnor had given her for her trousseau, was required to pay off debts at Ashcombe; for the school had been anything but flourishing since Mrs Kirkpatrick had had it. It was very much to her credit that she preferred clearing herself from debt to purchasing wedding finery. But it was one of the few points to be respected in Mrs Kirkpatrick that she had always been careful in payment to the shops where she dealt; it was a little sense of duty cropping out. Whatever other faults might arise from her superficial and flimsy character, she was always uneasy till she was out of debt. Yet she had no scruple in appropriating her future husband's money to her own use, when it was decided that it was not to be employed as he intended. What new articles she bought for herself, were all such as would make a show, and an impression upon the ladies of Hollingford. She argued with herself that linen, and all underclothing, would never be seen; while she knew that every gown she had would give rise to much discussion, and would be counted in the little town.

So her stock of underclothing was very small, and scarcely any of it new; but it was made of dainty material, and was finely mended up by her deft fingers, many a night long after her pupils were in bed; inwardly resolving all the time she sewed, that hereafter some one else should do her plain-work. Indeed, many a little circumstance of former subjection to the will of others rose up before her during these quiet hours, as an endurance or a suffering never to occur again. So apt are people to look forward to a different kind of life from that to which they have been accustomed, as being free from care and trial! She recollected how, one time during this very summer at the Towers, after she was engaged to Mr Gibson, when she had taken above an hour to arrange her hair in some new mode carefully studied from Mrs Bradley's fashion-book – after all, when she came down looking her very best, as she thought, and ready for her lover, Lady Cumnor had sent her back again to her room, just if she had been a little child, to do her hair over again, and not make such a figure of fun of herself! Another time she had been sent to change her gown for one in her opinion far less becoming, but which suited Lady Cumnor's taste better. These were little things; but they were late samples of what in different shapes she had had to endure for many years; and her liking for Mr Gibson grew in proportion to her sense of the evils from which he was going to serve as a means of escape. After all, that interval of hope and plain-sewing, intermixed though it was with tuition, was not disagreeable. Her wedding-dress was secure. Her former pupils at the Towers were

going to present her with that; they were to dress her from head
to foot on the auspicious day. Lord Cumnor, as has been said,
had given her a hundred pounds for her trousseau, and had sent
Mr Preston a *carte-blanche* order for the wedding breakfast in the
old hall in Ashcombe Manor-house. Lady Cumnor – a little put
out by the marriage not being deferred till her grandchildren's
Christmas holidays – had nevertheless given Mrs Kirkpatrick an
excellent English-made watch and chain; more clumsy but more
serviceable than the little foreign elegance that had hung at her
side so long, and misled her so often.

Her preparations were thus in a very considerable state of
forwardness, while Mr Gibson had done nothing as yet towards
any new arrangement or decoration of his house for his intended
bride. He knew he ought to do something. But what? Where to
begin, when so much was out of order, and he had so little time
for superintendence? At length he came to the wise decision of
asking one of the Miss Brownings, for old friendship's sake, to
take the trouble of preparing what was immediately requisite; and
he resolved to leave all the more ornamental decorations that he
proposed to the taste of his future wife. But before making his
request, he had to tell of his engagement, which had hitherto been
kept a secret from the townspeople, who had set down his
frequent visits at the Towers to the score of the countess's health.
He felt how he should have laughed in his sleeve at any middle-
aged widower who came to him with a confession of the kind he
had now to make to Miss Brownings, and disliked the idea of the
necessary call; but it had to be done; so one evening he went in
'promiscuous',* as they called it, and told them his story. At the
end of the first chapter – that is to say, at the end of the story of
Mr Coxe's calf-love – Miss Browning held up her hands in
surprise.

'To think of Molly, as I have held in long-clothes, coming to
have a lover! Well, to be sure! Sister Phoebe' – she was just
coming into the room – 'here's a piece of news! Molly Gibson has
got a lover! One may almost say she's had an offer! Mr Gibson,
may not one? – and she's but sixteen!'

'Seventeen, sister,' said Miss Phoebe, who piqued herself on
knowing all about dear Mr Gibson's domestic affairs. 'Seventeen,
the 22nd of last June.'

'Well, have it your own way! Seventeen, if you like to call her
so!' said Miss Browning impatiently. 'The fact is still the same –

she's got a lover; and it seems to me she was in long-clothes only yesterday.'

'I'm sure I hope her course of true love will run smooth,'* said Miss Phoebe.

Now Mr Gibson came in; for his story was not half told, and he did not want them to run away too far with the idea of Molly's love-affair.

'Molly knows nothing about it. I haven't even named it to any one but you two, and to one other friend. I trounced Coxe well, and did my best to keep his attachment – as he calls it – in bounds. But I was sadly puzzled what to do about Molly. Miss Eyre was away, and I couldn't leave them in the house together without any older woman.'

'Oh, Mr Gibson! why did you not send her to us?' broke in Miss Browning. 'We would have done anything in our power for you; for your sake, as well as her poor dear mother's.'

'Thank you. I know you would, but it wouldn't have done to have had her in Hollingford, just at the time of Coxe's effervescence. He's better now. His appetite has come back with double force, after the fasting he thought it right to exhibit. He had three helpings of black-currant dumpling yesterday.'

'I am sure you are most liberal, Mr Gibson. Three helpings! And, I daresay, butcher's meat in proportion!'

'Oh! I only named it because, with such very young men, it's generally see-saw between appetite and love, and I thought the third helping a very good sign. But still, you know, what has happened once, may happen again.'

'I don't know. Phoebe had an offer of marriage once'—said Miss Browning.

'Hush! sister. It might hurt his feelings to have it spoken about.'

'Nonsense, child! It's five-and-twenty years ago; and his eldest daughter is married herself.'

'I own he has not been constant,' pleaded Miss Phoebe, in her tender, piping voice. 'All men are not – like you, Mr Gibson – faithful to the memory of their first love.'

Mr Gibson winced. Jeannie was his first love; but her name had never been breathed in Hollingford. His wife – good, pretty, sensible, and beloved as she had been – was not his second; no, nor his third love. And now he was come to make a confidence about his second marriage.

'Well, well,' said he; 'at any rate, I thought I must do something

to protect Molly from such affairs while she was so young, and
before I had given my sanction. Miss Eyre's little nephew fell ill of
scarlet fever' —

'Ah! by-the-by, how careless of me not to inquire! How is the
poor little fellow?'

'Worse – better. It doesn't signify to what I've got to say now;
the fact was, Miss Eyre couldn't come back to my house for some
time, and I cannot leave Molly altogether at Hamley.'

'Ah! I see now why there was that sudden visit to Hamley.
Upon my word, it's quite a romance.'

'I do like hearing of a love-affair,' murmured Miss Phoebe.

'Then if you'll let me get on with my story, you shall hear of
mine,' said Mr Gibson, quite beyond his patience with their
constant interruptions.

'Yours!' said Miss Phoebe faintly.

'Bless us and save us!' said Miss Browning, with less sentiment
in her tone; 'what next?'

'My marriage, I hope,' said Mr Gibson, choosing to take her
expression of intense surprise literally. 'And that's what I came to
speak to you about.'

A little hope darted up in Miss Phoebe's breast. She had often
said to her sister, in the confidence of curling-time* (ladies wore
curls in those days), 'that the only man who could ever bring her
to think of matrimony was Mr Gibson; but that, if he ever
proposed, she should feel bound to accept him, for poor dear
Mary's sake;' never explaining what exact style of satisfaction she
imagined she should give to her dead friend by marrying her late
husband. Phoebe played nervously with the strings of her black
silk apron. Like the Caliph in the Eastern story,* a whole lifetime
of possibilities passed through her mind in an instant, of which
possibilities the question of questions was, Could she leave her
sister? Attend, Phoebe, to the present moment, and listen to what
is being said before you distress yourself with a perplexity which
will never arise!

'Of course it has been an anxious thing for me to decide whom
I should ask to be the mistress of my family, the mother of my
girl; but I think I've decided rightly at last. The lady I have
chosen' —

'Tell us at once who she is, there's a good man,' said straightforward Miss Browning.

'Mrs Kirkpatrick,' said the bridegroom elect.

'What! the governess at the Towers, that the countess makes so much of?'

'Yes; she is much valued by them – and deservedly so. She keeps a school now at Ashcombe, and is accustomed to housekeeping. She has brought up the young ladies at the Towers, and has a daughter of her own, therefore it is probable she will have a kind, motherly feeling towards Molly.'

'She's a very elegant-looking woman,' said Miss Phoebe, feeling it incumbent upon her to say something laudatory, by way of concealing the thoughts that had just been passing through her mind. 'I've seen her in the carriage, riding backwards,* with the countess: a very pretty woman, I should say.'

'Nonsense, sister!' said Miss Browning. 'What has her elegance or prettiness to do with the affair? Did you ever know a widower marry again for such trifles as those? It's always from a sense of duty of one kind or another – isn't it, Mr Gibson? They want a housekeeper; or they want a mother for their children; or they think their last wife would have liked it.'

Perhaps the thought had passed through the elder sister's mind that Phoebe might have been chosen; for there was a sharp acrimony in her tone, not unfamiliar to Mr Gibson, but with which he did not choose to cope at this present moment.

'You must have it your own way, Miss Browning. Settle my motives for me. I don't pretend to be quite clear about them myself. But I am clear in wishing heartily to keep my old friends, and for them to love my future wife for my sake. I don't know any two women in the world, except Molly and Mrs Kirkpatrick, I regard as much as I do you. Besides, I want to ask you if you will let Molly come and stay with you till after my marriage?'

'You might have asked us before you asked Madam Hamley,' said Miss Browning, only half mollified. 'We are your old friends; and we were her mother's friends, too; though we are not county-folk.'

'That's unjust,' said Mr Gibson. 'And you know it is.'

'I don't know. You are always with Lord Hollingford, when you can get at him, much more than you ever are with Mr Goodenough, or Mr Smith. And you are always going over to Hamley.'

Miss Browning was not one to give in all at once.

'I seek Lord Hollingford as I should seek such a man, whatever his rank or position might be: usher to a school, carpenter, shoemaker, if it were possible for him to have had a similar character of mind developed by similar advantages. Mr Goodenough is a very clever attorney, with strong local interests and not a thought beyond.'

'Well, well; don't go on arguing; it always gives me a headache, as Phoebe knows. I didn't mean what I said; that's enough, isn't it? I'll retract anything sooner than be reasoned with. Where were we, before you began your arguments?'

'About dear little Molly coming to pay us a visit,' said Miss Phoebe.

'I should have asked you at first, only Coxe was so rampant with his love. I didn't know what he might do, or how troublesome he might be both to Molly and you. But he has cooled down now. Absence has had a very tranquillising effect, and I think Molly may be in the same town with him, without any consequences beyond a few sighs every time she's brought to his mind by meeting her. And I've got another favour to ask of you; so you see it would never do for me to argue with you, Miss Browning, when I ought to be a humble suppliant. Something must be done to the house to make it all ready for the future Mrs Gibson. It wants painting and papering shamefully, and I should think some new furniture, but I'm sure I don't know what. Would you be so very kind as to look over the place, and see how far a hundred pounds will go? The dining-room walls must be painted; we'll keep the drawing-room paper for her choice, and I've a little spare money for that room, for her to lay out; but all the rest of the house I'll leave to you, if you'll only be kind enough to help an old friend.'

This was a commission which exactly gratified Miss Browning's love of power. The disposal of money involved patronage of tradespeople, such as she had exercised in her father's lifetime, but had had very little chance of showing since his death. Her usual good-humour was quite restored by this proof of confidence in her taste and economy, while Miss Phoebe's imagination dwelt rather on the pleasure of a visit from Molly.

CHAPTER 13

Molly Gibson's New Friends

Time was speeding on; it was now the middle of August – if anything was to be done to the house, it must be done at once. Indeed, in several ways Mr Gibson's arrangements with Miss Browning had not been made too soon. The Squire had heard that Osborne might probably return home for a few days before going abroad; and, though the growing intimacy between Roger and Molly did not alarm him in the least, yet he was possessed by a very hearty panic lest the heir might take a fancy to the surgeon's daughter; and he was in such a fidget for her to leave the house before Osborne came home, that his wife lived in constant terror lest he should make it too obvious to their visitor.

Every young girl of seventeen or so, who is at all thoughtful, is very apt to make a Pope out of the first person who presents to her a new or larger system of duty than that by which she has been unconsciously guided hitherto. Such a Pope was Roger to Molly; she looked to his opinion, to his authority on almost every subject; yet he had only said one or two things in a terse manner which gave them the force of precepts – stable guides to her conduct – and had shown the natural superiority in wisdom and knowledge which is sure to exist between a highly educated young man of no common intelligence, and an ignorant girl of seventeen, who yet is well capable of appreciation. Still, although they were drawn together in this very pleasant relationship, each was imagining some one very different for the future owner of their whole heart – their highest and completest love. Roger looked to find a grand woman, his equal, and his empress; beautiful in person, serene in wisdom, ready for counsel, as was Egeria.* Molly's little wavering maiden-fancy dwelt on the unseen Osborne, who was now a troubadour, and now a knight, such as he wrote about in one of his own poems; some one like Osborne, perhaps, rather than Osborne himself, for she shrank from giving a personal form and name to the hero that was to be. The Squire was not unwise in wishing her well out of the house before Osborne came home, if he was considering her peace of mind. Yet, when she went away from the Hall he missed her constantly; it had been so pleasant to have her there fulfilling all the pretty offices of a daughter; cheering the meals, so often *tête-à-tête* betwixt him and Roger, with her innocent wise questions, her lively interest in their talk, her merry replies to his banter.

And Roger missed her too. Sometimes her remarks had sunk into his mind, and excited him to the deep thought in which he delighted; at other times he had felt himself of real help to her in her hours of need, and in making her take an interest in books which treated of higher things than the continual fiction and poetry which she had hitherto read. He felt something like an affectionate tutor suddenly deprived of his most promising pupil; he wondered how she would go on without him; whether she would be puzzled and disheartened by the books he had lent her to read; how she and her stepmother would get along together? She occupied his thoughts a good deal, those first few days after she left the Hall. Mrs Hamley regretted her more, and longer, than did the other two. She had given her the place of a daughter in her heart; and now she missed the sweet feminine companionship, the playful caresses, the never-ceasing attentions, the very need of sympathy in her sorrows, that Molly had shown so openly from time to time; all these things had extremely endeared her to the tender-hearted Mrs Hamley.

Molly, too, felt the change of atmosphere keenly; and she blamed herself for so feeling even more keenly still. But she could not help having a sense of refinement, which had made her appreciate the whole manner of being at the Hall. By her dear old friends the Miss Brownings she was petted and caressed so much that she became ashamed of noticing the coarser and louder tones in which they spoke, the provincialism of their pronunciation, the absence of interest in things, and their greediness of details about persons. They asked her questions, which she was puzzled enough to answer, about her future stepmother; her loyalty to her father forbidding her to reply fully and distinctly. She was always glad when they began to make inquiries as to every possible affair at the Hall. She had been so happy there; she had liked them all, down to the very dogs, so thoroughly, that it was easy work replying: she did not mind telling them everything, even to the style of Mrs Hamley's invalid dress, and what wine the Squire drank at dinner. Indeed, talking about these things helped her to recall the happiest time in her life. But one evening, as they were all sitting together after tea in the little upstairs drawing-room, looking into the High Street – Molly discoursing away on the various pleasures of Hamley Hall, and just then telling of all Roger's wisdom in natural science, and some of the curiosities he had shown her, she was suddenly pulled up by this little speech –

'You seem to have seen a great deal of Mr Roger, Molly?' said Miss Browning, in a way intended to convey a great deal of meaning to her sister and none at all to Molly. But –

> The man recovered of the bite;
> The dog it was that died.*

Molly was perfectly aware of Miss Browning's emphatic tone, though at first she was perplexed as to its cause; while Miss Phoebe was just then too much absorbed in knitting the heel of her stocking to be fully alive to her sister's words and winks.

'Yes; he was very kind to me,' said Molly slowly, pondering over Miss Browning's manner, and unwilling to say more, until she had satisfied herself to what the question tended.

'I daresay you will soon be going to Hamley Hall again? He's not the eldest son, you know, Phoebe! Don't make my head ache with your eternal "eighteen, nineteen", but attend to the conversation! Molly is telling us how much she saw of Mr Roger, and how kind he was to her. I've always heard he was a very nice young man, my dear. Tell us some more about him! Now, Phoebe, attend! How was he kind to you, Molly?'

'Oh, he told me what books to read; and one day he made me notice how many bees I saw' —

'Bees, child! What do you mean? Either you or he must have been crazy!'

'No, not at all. There are more than two hundred kinds of bees in England, and he wanted me to notice the difference between them and flies. – Miss Browning, I can't help seeing what you fancy,' said Molly, as red as fire; 'but it is very wrong; it is all a mistake. I won't speak another word about Mr Roger or Hamley at all, if it puts such silly notions into your head.'

'Highty-tighty! Here's a young lady to be lecturing her elders! Silly notions, indeed! They are in your head, it seems. And, let me tell you, Molly, you are too young to let your mind be running on lovers.'

Molly had been once or twice called saucy and impertinent, and certainly a little sauciness came out now.

'I never said what the "silly notion" was, Miss Browning; did I now, Miss Phoebe? Don't you see, dear Miss Phoebe, it is all her own interpretation, and according to her own fancy, this foolish talk about lovers?'

Molly was flaming with indignation; but she had appealed to the wrong person for justice. Miss Phoebe tried to make peace, after the fashion of weak-minded people, who would cover over the unpleasant sight of a sore, instead of trying to heal it.

'I'm sure I don't know anything about it, my dear. It seems to me that what Clarinda was saying was very true – very true indeed; and I think, love, you misunderstood her; or, perhaps, she misunderstood you; or I may be misunderstanding it altogether; so we'd better not talk any more about it. What price did you say you were going to give for the drugget in Mr Gibson's dining-room, sister?'

So Miss Browning and Molly went on till evening, each chafed and angry with the other. They wished each other good-night, going through the usual forms in the coolest manner possible. Molly went up to her little bed-room, clean and neat as a bed-room could be, with draperies of small delicate patchwork – bed-curtains, window-curtains, and counterpane; a japanned toilette-table, full of little boxes, with a small looking-glass affixed to it, that distorted every face that was so unwise as to look in it. This room had been to the child one of the most dainty and luxurious places ever seen, in comparison with her own bare, white-dimity bed-room; and now she was sleeping in it as a guest, and all the quaint adornments she had once peeped at as a great favour, as they were carefully wrapped up in cap-paper,* were set out for her use. And yet how little she had deserved this hospitable care; how impertinent she had been; how cross she had felt ever since! She was crying tears of penitence and youthful misery, when there came a low tap at the door. Molly opened it; and there stood Miss Browning, in a wonderful erection of a night-cap, and scantily attired in a coloured calico jacket over her scrimpy and short white petticoat.

'I was afraid you were asleep, child,' said she, coming in and shutting the door. 'But I wanted to say to you we've got wrong today, somehow; and I think it was perhaps my doing. It's as well Phoebe shouldn't know, for she thinks me perfect; and, when there's only two of us, we get along better if one of us thinks the other can do no wrong. But I rather think I was a little cross. We'll not say any more about it, Molly; only we'll go to sleep friends – and friends we'll always be, child, won't we? Now give me a kiss, and don't cry and swell your eyes up – and put out your candle carefully.'

'I was wrong – it was my fault,' said Molly, kissing her.

'Fiddlestick-ends! Don't contradict me! I say it was my fault, and I won't hear another word about it.'

The next day Molly went with Miss Browning to see the changes going on in her father's house. To her they were but dismal improvements. The faint grey of the dining-room walls, which had harmonised well enough with the deep crimson of the moreen curtains, and which, when well-cleaned, looked thinly-coated rather than dirty, was now exchanged for a pink salmon-colour of a very glowing hue; and the new curtains were of that pale sea-green just coming into fashion. 'Very bright and pretty', Miss Browning called it; and, in the first renewing of their love, Molly could not bear to contradict her. She could only hope that the green and brown drugget would tone down the brightness and prettiness. There was scaffolding here, scaffolding there, and Betty scolding everywhere.

'Come up now, and see your papa's bed-room. He's sleeping upstairs in yours, that everything may be done up afresh in his.'

Molly could just remember, in faint clear lines of distinctness, the being taken into this very room to bid farewell to her dying mother. She could see the white linen, the white muslin, surrounding the pale, wan, wistful face, with the large, longing eyes, yearning for one more touch of the little soft, warm child, whom she was too feeble to clasp in her arms, already growing numb in death. Many a time when Molly had been in this room since that sad day, had she seen in vivid fancy that same wan, wistful face lying on the pillow, the outline of the form beneath the clothes; and the girl had not shrunk from such visions, but rather cherished them, as preserving to her the remembrance of her mother's outward semblance. Her eyes were full of tears, as she followed Miss Browning into this room to see it under its new aspect. Nearly everything was changed – the position of the bed and the colour of the furniture; there was a grand toilette-table now, with a glass upon it, instead of the primitive substitute of the top of a chest of drawers, with a mirror above upon the wall, sloping downwards; these latter things had served her mother during her short married life.

'You see, we must have all in order for a lady who has passed so much of her time in the countess's mansion,' said Miss Browning, who was now quite reconciled to the marriage, thanks to the pleasant employment of furnishing that had devolved upon her in consequence. 'Cromer, the upholsterer, wanted to persuade me to have a sofa and a writing-table. These men will say anything is the fashion, if they want to sell an article. I said, "No, no, Cromer; bed-rooms are for sleeping in, and sitting-rooms are for sitting in. Keep everything to its right purpose, and don't try to delude me into nonsense." Why, my mother would have given us a fine scolding if she had ever caught us in our bed-rooms in the daytime. We kept our outdoor things in a closet downstairs; and there was a very tidy place for washing our hands, which is as much as one wants in the daytime. Stuffing up a bed-room with sofas and tables! I never heard of such a thing! Besides, a hundred pounds won't last for ever. I shan't be able to do anything for your room, Molly!'

'I'm right down glad of it,' said Molly. 'Nearly everything in it was what mamma had when she lived with my great-uncle. I wouldn't have had it changed for the world; I am so fond of it.'

'Well, there's no danger of it, now the money is run out. By the way, Molly, who's to buy you a bridesmaid's dress?'

'I don't know,' said Molly; 'I suppose I am to be a bridesmaid; but no one has spoken to me about my dress.'

'Then I shall ask your papa.'

'Please, don't! He must have to spend a great deal of money just now. Besides, I would rather not be at the wedding, if they'll let me stay away.'

'Nonsense, child! Why, all the town would be talking of it. You must go, and you must be well dressed, for your father's sake.'

But Mr Gibson had thought of Molly's dress, although he had said nothing about it to her. He had commissioned his future wife to get her what was requisite; and presently a very smart dress-maker came over from the county-town to try on a dress, which was both so simple and so elegant as at once to charm Molly. When it came home, all ready to put on, Molly had a private dressing-up, for the Miss Brownings' benefit; and she was almost startled when she looked into the glass, and saw the improvement in her appearance. 'I wonder if I'm pretty,' thought she. 'I almost think I am – in this kind of dress, I mean, of course. Betty would say, "Fine feathers make fine birds".'

When she went downstairs in her bridal attire, and with shy

blushes presented herself for inspection, she was greeted with a burst of admiration.

'Well, upon my word! I shouldn't have known you.' ('Fine feathers', thought Molly, and checked her rising vanity.)

'You are really beautiful – isn't she, sister?' said Miss Phoebe. 'Why, my dear, if you were always dressed-up, you would be prettier than your dear mamma, whom we always reckoned so very personable.'

'You're not a bit like her. You favour* your father, and white always sets off a brown complexion.'

'But isn't she beautiful?' persevered Miss Phoebe.

'Well! and if she is, Providence made her, and not she herself. Besides, the dressmaker must go shares. What a fine India muslin it is! it'll have cost a pretty penny!'

Mr Gibson and Molly drove over to Ashcombe the night before the wedding, in the one yellow post-chaise* that Hollingford possessed. They were to be Mr Preston's, or, rather, my lord's guests at the Manor-house. The Manor-house came up to its name, and delighted Molly at first sight. It was built of stone, had many gables and mullioned windows, and was covered over with Virginian creeper and late-blowing roses. Molly did not know Mr Preston, who stood in the doorway to greet her father. She took standing with him as a young lady at once, and it was the first time she had met with the kind of behaviour – half-complimentary, half-flirting – which some men think it necessary to assume with every woman under five-and-twenty. Mr Preston was very handsome, and knew it. He was a fair man, with light-brown hair and whiskers; grey, roving, well-shaped eyes, with lashes darker than his hair; and a figure rendered easy and supple by the athletic exercises in which his excellence was famous, and which had procured him admission into much higher society than he was otherwise entitled to enter. He was a capital cricketer; was so good a shot that any house desirous of reputation for its bags on the 12th or the 1st,* was glad to have him for a guest. He taught young ladies to play billiards on a wet day, or went in for the game in serious earnest when required. He knew half the private theatrical plays off by heart, and was invaluable in arranging impromptu charades and tableaux. He had his own private reasons for wishing to get up a flirtation with Molly just at this time; he had amused himself so much with the widow when she first came to Ashcombe, that he fancied that the sight of him, standing by her less polished, less handsome, middle-aged husband, might be too much of a contrast to be agreeable. Besides, he had really a strong passion for some one else; some one who would be absent; and that passion it was necessary for him to conceal. So that, altogether, he had resolved, even had 'Gibson's little girl' (as he called her) been less attractive than she was, to devote himself to her for the next sixteen hours.

They were taken by their host into a wainscoted parlour, where a wood fire crackled and burnt, and the crimson curtains shut out the waning day and the outer chill. Here the table was laid for dinner; snowy table-linen, bright silver, clear sparkling glass, wine and an autumnal dessert on the sideboard. Yet Mr Preston kept apologising to Molly for the rudeness of his bachelor home, for the smallness of the room, the great dining-room being already appropriated by his housekeeper, in preparation for the morrow's breakfast. And then he rang for a servant to show Molly to her room. She was taken into a most comfortable chamber; a wood fire on the hearth, candles lighted on the toilette-table, dark woolen curtains surrounding a snow-white bed, great vases of china standing here and there.

'This is my Lady Harriet's room when her ladyship comes to the Manor-house with my lord the earl,' said the housemaid, striking out thousands of brilliant sparks by a well-directed blow at a smouldering log. 'Shall I help you to dress, miss? I always helps her ladyship.'

Molly, quite aware of the fact that she had but her white muslin gown for the wedding besides that she had on, dismissed the good woman, and was thankful to be left to herself.

'Dinner' was it called? Why, it was nearly eight o'clock; and preparations for bed seemed a more natural employment than dressing at this hour of night. All the dressing she could manage was the placing of a red damask rose or two in the band of her grey stuff gown, from a great nosegay of choice autumnal flowers, standing on the toilette-table. She did try the effect of another crimson rose in her black hair, just above her ear; it was very pretty, but too coquettish, and so she put it back again. The dark oak-panels and wainscoting of the whole house seemed to glow in warm light; there were so many fires in different rooms, in the hall, and even one on the landing of the staircase. Mr Preston must have heard her step, for he met her in the hall, and led her into a small drawing-room, with close folding-doors on one side, opening into the larger drawing-room, as he told her. This room into which she entered reminded her a little of Hamley – yellow satin upholstery of seventy or a hundred years ago, all delicately kept and scrupulously clean; great Indian cabinets, and china jars, emitting spicy odours; a large blazing fire, before which her father stood in his morning dress, grave and thoughtful, as he had been all day.

'This room is that which Lady Harriet uses when she comes here with her father for a day or two,' said Mr Preston. And Molly tried to save her father by being ready to talk herself.

'Does she often come here?'

'Not often. But I fancy she likes being here, when she does. Perhaps she finds it an agreeable change after the more formal life she leads at the Towers.'

'I should think it was a very pleasant house to stay at,' said Molly, remembering the look of warm comfort that pervaded it. But, a little to her dismay, Mr Preston seemed to take it as a compliment to himself.

'I was afraid a young lady like you might perceive all the incongruities of a bachelor's home. I'm very much obliged to you, Miss Gibson. In general, I live pretty much in the room in which we shall dine; and I've a sort of agent's office in which I keep books and papers, and receive callers on business.'

Then they went in to dinner. Molly thought everything that was served was delicious, and cooked to the point of perfection; but it did not seem to satisfy Mr Preston, who apologised to his guests several times for the bad cooking of this dish, or the omission of a particular sauce to that; always referring to bachelor's house-keeping, bachelor's this, and bachelor's that, till Molly grew quite impatient at the word. Her father's depression, which was still continuing and rendering him very silent, made her uneasy; yet she wished to conceal it from Mr Preston; and so she talked away, trying to obviate the sort of personal bearing which their host would give to everything. She did not know when to leave the gentlemen, but her father made a sign to her; and she was conducted back to the yellow drawing-room by Mr Preston, who made many apologies for leaving her there alone. She enjoyed herself extremely, however, feeling at liberty to prowl about, and examine all the curiosities the room contained. Among other things was a Louis-Quinze cabinet with lovely miniatures in enamel let into the fine woodwork. She carried a candle to it, and was looking intently at these faces, when her father and Mr Preston came in. Her father still looked careworn and anxious; he came up and patted her on the back, looked at what she was looking at, and then went off to silence and the fire. Mr Preston took the candle out of her hand, and threw himself into her interests with an air of ready gallantry.

'That is said to be Mademoiselle de St. Quentin, a great beauty at the French Court. This is Madame du Barri.* Do you see any likeness in Mademoiselle de St. Quentin to any one you know?' He had lowered his voice a little, as he asked this question.

'No!' said Molly, looking at it again. 'I never saw any one half so beautiful.'

'But don't you see a likeness – in the eyes particularly?' he asked again, with some impatience.

Molly tried hard to find out a resemblance, and was again unsuccessful.

'It constantly reminds me of – of Miss Kirkpatrick.'

'Does it?' said Molly eagerly. 'Oh! I am so glad – I've never seen her, so of course I couldn't find out the likeness. You know her, then, do you? Please tell me all about her.'

He hesitated a moment before speaking. He smiled a little before replying.

'She's very beautiful; that of course is understood, when I say that this miniature does not come up to her for beauty.'

'And besides – Go on, please.'

'What do you mean by "besides"?'

'Oh! I suppose she's very clever and accomplished?'

That was not in the least what Molly wanted to ask; but it was difficult to word the vague vastness of her unspoken inquiry.

'She is clever naturally; she has picked up accomplishments. But she has such a charm about her, one forgets what she herself is in the halo that surrounds her. You ask me all this, Miss Gibson, and I answer truthfully; or else I should not entertain one young lady with my enthusiastic praises of another.'

'I don't see why not,' said Molly. 'Besides, if you wouldn't do it in general, I think you ought to do it in my case; for you, perhaps, don't know, but she is coming to live with us when she leaves school, and we are very nearly the same age; so it will be almost like having a sister.'

'She is to live with you, is she?' said Mr Preston, to whom this intelligence was news. 'And when is she to leave school? I thought she would surely have been at this wedding; but I was told she was not to come. When is she to leave school?'

'I think it is to be at Easter. You know she's at Boulogne, and it's a long journey for her to come alone; or else papa wished for her to be at the marriage very much indeed.'

'And her mother prevented it? – I understand.'

'No, it wasn't her mother; it was the French school-mistress, who didn't think it desirable.'

'It comes to pretty much the same thing. And she's to return and live with you after Easter?'

'I believe so. Is she a grave or a merry person?'

'Never very grave, as far as I have seen of her. "Sparkling" would be the word for her, I think. Do you ever write to her? If you do, pray remember me to her, and tell her how we have been talking about her – you and I.'

'I never write to her,' said Molly, rather shortly.

Tea came in; and after that they all went to bed. Molly heard her father exclaim at the fire in his bed-room, and Mr Preston's reply –

'I pique myself on my keen relish for all creature-comforts, and also on my power of doing without them, if need be. My lord's woods are ample, and I indulge myself with a fire in my bed-room for nine months in the year; yet I could travel in Iceland without wincing from the cold.'

CHAPTER 14

Molly Finds Herself Patronised

The wedding went off much as such affairs do. Lord Cumnor and Lady Harriet drove over from the Towers, so the hour for the ceremony was as late as possible. Lord Cumnor came in order to officiate as the bride's father, and was in more open glee than either bride or bridegroom, or any one else. Lady Harriet came as a sort of amateur bridesmaid, to 'share Molly's duties', as she called it. They went from the Manor-house in two carriages to the church in the park, Mr Preston and Mr Gibson in one, and Molly, to her dismay, shut up with Lord Cumnor and Lady Harriet in the other. Lady Harriet's gown of white muslin had seen one or

two garden-parties, and was not in the freshest order; it had been
rather a freak of the young lady's at the last moment. She was
very merry, and very much inclined to talk to Molly, by way of
finding out what sort of a little personage Clare was to have for
her future daughter. She began –

'We mustn't crush this pretty muslin dress of yours. Put it over
papa's knee; he doesn't mind it in the least.'

'What, my dear, a white dress! – no, to be sure not. I rather like
it. Besides, going to a wedding, who minds anything? It would be
different if we were going to a funeral.'

Molly conscientiously strove to find out the meaning of this
speech; but, before she had done so, Lady Harriet spoke again,
going to the point, as she always piqued herself on doing –

'I daresay it's something of a trial to you, this second marriage
of your father's; but you'll find Clare the most amiable of women.
She always let me have my own way, and I've no doubt she'll let
you have yours.'

'I mean to try and like her,' said Molly, in a low voice, striving
hard to keep down the tears that would keep rising to her eyes
this morning. 'I've seen very little of her yet.'

'Why, it's the very best thing for you that could have happened,
my dear,' said Lord Cumnor. 'You're growing up into a young
lady – and a very pretty young lady, too, if you'll allow an old
man to say so – and who so proper as your father's wife to bring
you out,* and show you off, and take you to balls, and that kind
of thing? I always said this match that is going to come off today
was the most suitable thing I ever knew; and it's even a better
thing for you than for the people themselves.'

'Poor child!' said Lady Harriet, who had caught a sight of
Molly's troubled face, 'the thought of balls is too much for her
just now; but you'll like having Cynthia Kirkpatrick for a companion, sha'n't you, dear?'

'Very much,' said Molly, cheering up a little. 'Do you know
her?'

'Oh, I've seen her over and over again when she was a little girl,
and once or twice since. She's the prettiest creature that you ever
saw, and with eyes that mean mischief, if I'm not mistaken. But
Clare kept her spirit under pretty well, when she was staying with
us – afraid of her being troublesome, I fancy.'

Before Molly could shape her next question, they were at the
church; and she and Lady Harriet went into a pew near the door

to wait for the bride, in whose train they were to proceed to the altar. The earl drove on alone to fetch her from her own house, not a quarter of a mile distant. It was pleasant to her to be led to the hymeneal altar by a belted earl, and pleasant to have his daughter as a volunteer bridesmaid. Mrs Kirkpatrick, in this flush of small gratifications, and on the brink of matrimony with a man whom she liked, and who would be bound to support her without any exertion of her own, looked beamingly happy and handsome. A little cloud came over her face at the sight of Mr Preston – the sweet perpetuity of her smile was rather disturbed, as he followed in Mr Gibson's wake. But his face never changed; he bowed to her gravely, and then seemed absorbed in the service. Ten minutes, and all was over. The bride and bridegroom were driving together to the Manor-house, Mr Preston was walking thither by a short cut, and Molly was again in the carriage with my lord, rubbing his hands and chuckling, and Lady Harriet, trying to be kind and consolatory, when her silence would have been the best comfort.

Molly found out, to her dismay, that the plan was for her to return with Lord Cumnor and Lady Harriet, when they went back to the Towers in the evening. In the meantime, Lord Cumnor had business to do with Mr Preston; and, after the happy couple had driven off on their week's holiday tour, she was to be left alone with the formidable Lady Harriet. When they were by themselves after all the others had been thus disposed of, Lady Harriet sate still over the drawing-room fire, holding a screen between it and her face, but gazing intently at Molly for a minute or two. Molly was fully conscious of this prolonged look, and was trying to get up her courage to return the stare, when Lady Harriet suddenly said –

'I like you – you are a little wild creature, and I want to tame you. Come here, and sit on this stool by me. What is your name? or what do they call you? – as North-country people would express it.'

'Molly Gibson. My real name is Mary.'

'Molly is a nice, soft-sounding name. People in the last century weren't afraid of homely names; now we are all so smart and fine: no more "Lady Bettys"* now. I almost wonder they haven't re-christened all the worsted and knitting-cotton that bears her name. Fancy Lady Constantia's cotton, or Lady Anna-Maria's worsted!'

'I didn't know there was a Lady Betty's cotton,' said Molly.

'That proves you don't do fancy-work! You'll find Clare will set you to it, though. She used to set me at piece after piece: knights kneeling to ladies; impossible flowers. But I must do her the justice to add that, when I got tired of them, she finished them herself. I wonder how you'll get on together?'

'So do I!' sighed out Molly, under her breath.

'I used to think I managed her, till one day an uncomfortable suspicion arose that all the time she had been managing me. Still it's easy work to let oneself be managed; at any rate till one wakens up to the consciousness of the process, and then it may become amusing, if one takes it in that light.'

'I should hate to be managed,' said Molly indignantly. 'I'll try and do what she wishes for papa's sake, if she'll only tell me outright; but I should dislike to be trapped into anything.'

'Now I,' said Lady Harriet, 'am too lazy to avoid traps; and I rather like to remark the cleverness with which they're set. But then, of course, I know that, if I choose to exert myself, I can break through the withes of green flax with which they try to bind me. Now, perhaps, you won't be able.'

'I don't quite understand what you mean,' said Molly.

'Oh, well – never mind; I daresay it's as well for you that you shouldn't. The moral of all I have been saying is, "Be a good girl, and suffer yourself to be led, and you'll find your new stepmother the sweetest creature imaginable." You'll get on capitally with her, I make no doubt. How you'll get on with her daughter is another affair; but I daresay very well. Now we'll ring for tea; for I suppose that heavy breakfast is to stand for our lunch.'

Mr Preston came into the room just at this time, and Molly was a little surprised at Lady Harriet's cool manner of dismissing him, remembering as she did how Mr Preston had implied his intimacy with her ladyship, the evening before at dinner-time.

'I cannot bear that sort of person,' said Lady Harriet, almost before he was out of hearing; 'giving himself airs of gallantry towards one to whom his simple respect is all his duty. I can talk to one of my father's labourers with pleasure, while with a man like that underbred fop I am all over thorns and nettles. What is it the Irish call that style of creature? They've some capital word for it, I know. What is it?'

'I don't know – I never heard it,' said Molly, a little ashamed of her ignorance.

'Oh! that shows you've never read Miss Edgeworth's tales* – now, have you? If you had, you'd have recollected that there was such a word, even if you didn't remember what it was. If you've never read those stories, they would be just the thing to beguile your solitude – vastly improving and moral, and yet quite sufficiently interesting. I'll lend them to you while you're all alone.'

'I'm not alone. I'm not at home, but on a visit to the Miss Brownings.'

'Then I'll bring them to you. I know the Miss Brownings; they used to come regularly on the school-day to the Towers. Pecksy and Flapsy* I used to call them. I like the Miss Brownings; one gets enough of respect from them at any rate; and I've always wanted to see the kind of *ménage** of such people. I'll bring you a whole pile of Miss Edgeworth's stories, my dear.'

Molly sate quite silent for a minute or two; then she mustered up courage to speak out what was in her mind.

'Your ladyship' (the title was the first-fruits of the lesson, as Molly took it, on paying due respect) – 'your ladyship keeps speaking of the sort of – the class of – people to which I belong, as if it was a kind of strange animal you were talking about; yet you talk so openly to me that' —

'Well, go on – I like to hear you.'

Still silence.

'You think me in your heart a little impertinent – now, don't you?' said Lady Harriet almost kindly.

Molly held her peace for two or three moments; then she lifted her beautiful, honest eyes to Lady Harriet's face, and said –

'Yes! – a little. But I think you a great many other things.'

'We'll leave the "other things" for the present. Don't you see, little one, I talk after my kind, just as you talk after your kind. It's only on the surface with both of us. Why, I daresay some of your good Hollingford ladies talk of the poor people in a manner which they would consider just as impertinent in their turn, if they could hear it. But I ought to be more considerate when I remember how often my blood has boiled at the modes of speech and behaviour of one of my aunts, mamma's sister, Lady—No! I won't name names. Any one who earns his livelihood by any exercise of head or hands, from professional people and rich merchants down to labourers, she calls "persons". She would never in her most slip-slop talk accord them even the conventional title of "gentlemen"; and the way in which she takes possession of human beings, "my woman", "my people" – but, after all, it is only a way of speaking.

I ought not to have used it to you; but somehow I separate you from all these Hollingford people.'

'But why?' persevered Molly. 'I'm one of them.'

'Yes, you are. But – now don't reprove me again for impertinence – most of them are so unnatural in their exaggerated respect
and admiration when they come up to the Towers, and put on so
much pretence by way of fine manners, that they only make
themselves objects of ridicule. You at least are simple and truthful,
and that's why I separate you in my own mind from them, and
have talked unconsciously to you as I would—well! now here's
another piece of impertinence – as I would to my equal – in rank,
I mean; for I don't set myself up in solid things as any better than
my neighbours. Here's tea, however, come in time to stop me
from growing too humble.'

It was a very pleasant little tea in the fading September twilight.

Just as it was ended, in came Mr Preston again –

'Lady Harriet, will you allow me the pleasure of showing you
some alterations I have made on the flower-garden – in which I
have tried to consult your taste – before it grows dark?'

'Thank you, Mr Preston. I will ride over with papa some day,
and we will see if we approve of them.'

Mr Preston's brow flushed. But he affected not to perceive Lady
Harriet's haughtiness, and, turning to Molly, he said –

'Will not you come out, Miss Gibson, and see something of the
gardens? You haven't been out at all, I think, excepting to church.'

Molly did not like the idea of going out for a walk with only
Mr Preston; yet she pined for a little fresh air, would have been
glad to see the gardens, and look at the Manor-house from
different aspects; and, besides this, much as she recoiled from Mr
Preston, she felt sorry for him under the repulse he had just
received.

While she was hesitating, and slowly tending towards consent,
Lady Harriet spoke –

'I cannot spare Miss Gibson. If she would like to see the place,
I will bring her over some day myself.'

When he had left the room, Lady Harriet said –

'I daresay it's my own lazy selfishness has kept you indoors all
day against your will. But, at any rate, you are not to go out
walking with that man. I've an instinctive aversion to him; not
entirely instinctive either; it has some foundation in fact; and I
desire you don't allow him ever to get intimate with you. He's a

very clever land-agent, and does his duty by papa, and I don't choose to be taken up for libel; but remember what I say!'

Then the carriage came round, and, after numberless last words from the earl – who appeared to have put off every possible direction to the moment when he stood, like an awkward Mercury,* balancing himself on the step of the carriage – they drove back to the Towers.

'Would you rather come in and dine with us – we should send you home, of course – or go home straight?' asked Lady Harriet of Molly. She and her father had both been sleeping, till they drew up at the bottom of the flight of steps.

'Tell the truth, now and evermore! Truth is generally amusing, if it's nothing else!'

'I would rather go back to the Miss Brownings' at once, please,' said Molly, with a nightmare-like recollection of the last, the only, evening she had spent at the Towers.

Lord Cumnor was standing on the steps, waiting to hand his daughter out of the carriage. Lady Harriet stopped to kiss Molly on the forehead, and to say –

'I shall come some day soon, and bring you a load of Miss Edgeworth's tales, and make further acquaintance with Pecksy and Flapsy.'

'No, don't, please,' said Molly, taking hold of her, to detain her. 'You must not come – indeed you must not.'

'Why not?'

'Because I would rather not – because I think that I ought not to have any one coming to see me who laughs at the friends I am staying with, and calls them names.' Molly's heart beat very fast, but she meant every word that she said.

'My dear little woman!' said Lady Harriet, bending over her and speaking quite gravely. 'I'm very sorry to have called them names – very, very sorry to have hurt you. If I promise you to be respectful to them in word and in deed – and in very thought, if I can – you'll let me come then, won't you?'

Molly hesitated. 'I'd better go home at once; I shall only say wrong things – and there's Lord Cumnor waiting all this time.'

'Let him alone; he's very well amused hearing all the news of the day from Brown. Then I shall come – under promise?'

So Molly drove off in solitary grandeur; and the Miss Brownings' knocker was loosened on its venerable hinges by the never-ending peal of Lord Cumnor's footman.

They were full of welcome, full of curiosity. All through the long day they had been missing their bright young visitor, and three or four times in every hour they had been wondering and settling what everybody was doing at that exact minute. What had become of Molly, during all the afternoon, had been a great perplexity to them; and they were very much oppressed with a sense of the great honour she had received in being allowed to spend so many hours alone with Lady Harriet. They were, indeed, more excited by this one fact than by all the details of the wedding, most of which they had known of beforehand and talked over with much perseverance during the day. Molly began to feel as if there was some foundation for Lady Harriet's inclination to ridicule the worship paid by the good people of Hollingford to their liege lord, and to wonder with what tokens of reverence they would receive Lady Harriet, if she came to pay her promised visit. She had never thought of concealing the probability of this call until the evening; but now she felt as if it would be better not to speak of the chance, as she was not at all sure that the promise would be fulfilled.

Before Lady Harriet's call was paid, Molly received another visit.

Roger Hamley came riding over one day with a note from his mother, and a wasps'-nest as a present from himself. Molly heard his powerful voice come sounding up the little staircase, as he asked if Miss Gibson was at home, from the servant-maid at the door; and she was half-amused and half-annoyed as she thought how this call of his would give colour to the Miss Brownings' fancies. 'I would rather never be married at all,' thought she, 'than marry an ugly man – and dear good Mr Roger is really ugly; I don't think one could even call him plain.' Yet the Miss Brownings, who did not look upon young men as if their natural costume was a helmet and a suit of armour, thought Mr Roger Hamley a very personable young fellow, as he came into the room, his face flushed with exercise, his white teeth showing pleasantly in the courteous bow and smile he gave to all around. He knew the Miss Brownings slightly, and talked pleasantly to them, while Molly read Mrs Hamley's little missive of sympathy and good wishes relating to the wedding; then he turned to her, and, though the Miss Brownings listened with all their ears, they could not find out anything remarkable either in the words he said or the tone in which they were spoken.

'I've brought you the wasps'-nest I promised you, Miss Gibson. There has been no lack of such things this year; we've taken seventy-four on my father's land alone; and one of the labourers, a poor fellow who ekes out his wages by bee-keeping, has had a sad misfortune – the wasps have turned the bees out of his seven hives, taken possession, and eaten up the honey.'

'What greedy little vermin!' said Miss Browning.

Molly saw Roger's eyes twinkle at the misapplication of the word; but, though he had a strong sense of humour, it never appeared to diminish his respect for the people who amused him.

'I'm sure they deserve fire and brimstone more than the poor dear innocent bees,' said Miss Phoebe. 'And then it seems so ungrateful of mankind, who are going to feast on the honey!' She sighed over the thought, as if it was too much for her.

While Molly finished reading her note, he explained its contents to Miss Browning.

'My brother and I are going with my father to an agricultural meeting at Canonbury on Thursday, and my mother desired me to say to you how very much obliged she would be, if you would spare her Miss Gibson for the day. She was very anxious to ask for the pleasure of your company, too, but she really is so poorly that we persuaded her to be content with Miss Gibson, as she wouldn't scruple leaving a young lady to amuse herself, which she would be unwilling to do if you and your sister were there.'

'I'm sure she's very kind; very. Nothing would have given us more pleasure,' said Miss Browning, drawing herself up in grati-fied dignity. 'Oh, yes, we quite understand, Mr Roger; and we fully recognise Mrs Hamley's kind intention. We will take the will for the deed, as the common people express it. I believe that there was an intermarriage between the Brownings and the Hamleys, a generation or two ago.'

'I daresay there was,' said Roger. 'My mother is very delicate, and obliged to humour her health, which has made her keep aloof from society.'

'Then I may go?' said Molly, sparkling with the idea of seeing her dear Mrs Hamley again, yet afraid of appearing too desirous of leaving her kind old friends.

'To be sure, my dear. Write a pretty note, and tell Mrs Hamley how much obliged to her we are for thinking of us.'

'I'm afraid I can't wait for a note,' said Roger. 'I must take a message instead, for I have to meet my father at one o'clock, and it's close upon it now.'

When he was gone, Molly felt so light-hearted at the thoughts of Thursday that she could hardly attend to what the Miss Brownings were saying. One was talking about the pretty muslin gown which Molly had sent to the wash only that morning, and contriving how it could be had back again in time for her to wear; and the other, Miss Phoebe, totally inattentive to her sister's speaking for a wonder, was piping out a separate strain of her own, and singing Roger Hamley's praises.

'Such a fine-looking young man, and so courteous and affable! Like the young men of our youth now, is he not, sister? And yet they all say Mr Osborne is the handsomest. What do you think, child?'

'I've never seen Mr Osborne,' said Molly, blushing, and hating herself for doing so. Why was it? She had never seen him, as she said. It was only that her fancy had dwelt on him so much.

He was gone – all the gentlemen were gone before the carriage, which came to fetch Molly on Thursday, reached Hamley Hall. But Molly was almost glad, she was so much afraid of being disappointed. Besides, she had her dear Mrs Hamley the more to herself; the quiet sit in the morning-room, talking poetry and romance; the midday saunter into the garden, brilliant with autumnal flowers and glittering dew-drops on the gossamer webs that stretched from scarlet to blue, and thence to purple and yellow petals. As they were sitting at lunch, a strange man's voice and step were heard in the hall; the door was opened, and a young man came in, who could be no other than Osborne. He was beautiful and languid-looking, almost as frail in appearance as his mother, whom he strongly resembled. This seeming delicacy made him appear older than he was. He was dressed to perfection, and yet with easy carelessness. He came up to his mother, and stood by her, holding her hand, while his eyes sought Molly, not boldly or impertinently, but as if appraising her critically.

'Yes! I'm back again. Bullocks, I find, are not in my line. I only disappointed my father in not being able to appreciate their merits, and, I'm afraid, I didn't care to learn. And the smell was insufferable on such a hot day.'

'My dear boy, don't make apologies to me; keep them for your father. I'm only too glad to have you back. Miss Gibson, this tall fellow is my son Osborne, as I daresay you have guessed. Osborne – Miss Gibson. Now, what will you have?'

He looked round the table as he sate down. 'Nothing here,' said he. 'Isn't there some cold game-pie? I'll ring for that.'

Molly was trying to reconcile the ideal with the real. The ideal was agile, yet powerful, with Greek features and an eagle eye, capable of enduring long fasting, and indifferent as to what he ate. The real was almost effeminate in movement, though not in figure; he had the Greek features, but his blue eyes had a cold, weary expression in them. He was dainty in eating, and had anything but a Homeric appetite.* However, Molly's hero was not to eat more than Ivanhoe, when he was Friar Tuck's guest;* and, after all, with a little alteration, she began to think Mr Osborne Hamley might turn out a poetical, if not a chivalrous, hero. He was extremely attentive to his mother, which pleased Molly; and, in return, Mrs Hamley seemed charmed with him to such a degree that Molly once or twice fancied that mother and son would have been happier in her absence. Yet, again, it struck the shrewd, if simple, girl, that Osborne was mentally squinting at her in the conversation which was directed to his mother. There were little turns and *fioriture** of speech which, Molly could not help feeling, were graceful antics of language not common in the simple daily intercourse between mother and son. But it was flattering rather than otherwise to perceive that a very fine young man, who was a poet to boot, should think it worth while to talk on the tight-rope* for her benefit. And before the afternoon was ended, without there having been any direct conversation between Osborne and Molly, she had reinstated him on his throne in her imagination; indeed, she had almost felt herself disloyal to her dear Mrs Hamley when, in the first hour after her introduction, she had questioned his claims on his mother's idolatry. His beauty came out more and more, as he became animated in some discussion with her; and all his attitudes, if a little studied, were graceful in the extreme. Before Molly left, the Squire and Roger returned from Canonbury.

'Osborne here!' said the Squire, red and panting. 'Why the deuce couldn't you tell us you were coming home? I looked about for you everywhere, just as we were going into the ordinary.* I wanted to introduce you to Grantley, and Fox, and Lord Forrest – men from the other side of the county, whom you ought to know; and Roger there missed above half his dinner hunting about for you; and, all the time, you'd stole away, and were quietly sitting here with the women. I wish you'd let me know, the next time you make off. I've lost half my pleasure in looking at as fine a lot of cattle as I ever saw, with thinking you might be having one of your old attacks of faintness.'

'I should have had one, I think, if I'd stayed longer in that atmosphere. But I'm sorry if I've caused you anxiety.'

'Well! well!' said the Squire, somewhat mollified. 'And Roger, too, there – I've been sending him here and sending him there all the afternoon.'

'I didn't mind it, sir. I was only sorry you were so uneasy. I thought Osborne had gone home, for I knew it wasn't much in his way,' said Roger.

Molly intercepted a glance between the two brothers – a look of true confidence and love, which suddenly made her like them both under the aspect of relationship – new to her observation.

Roger came up to her, and sat down by her.

'Well, and how are you getting on with Huber?* don't you find him very interesting?'

'I'm afraid,' said Molly penitently, 'I haven't read much. The Miss Brownings like me to talk; and, besides, there is so much to do at home before papa comes back; and Miss Browning doesn't like me to go without her. I know it sounds nothing; but it does take up a great deal of time.'

'When is your father coming back?'

'Next Tuesday, I believe. He cannot stay long away.'

'I shall ride over and pay my respects to Mrs Gibson,' said he. 'I shall come as soon as I may. Your father has been a very kind friend to me, ever since I was a boy. And, when I come, I shall expect my pupil to have been very diligent,' he concluded, smiling his kind, pleasant smile at idle Molly.

Then the carriage came round, and she had the long solitary drive back to the Miss Brownings'. It was dark out of doors, when she got there; but Miss Phoebe was standing on the stairs, with a lighted candle in her hand, peering into the darkness, to see Molly come in.

'Oh, Molly! I thought you'd never come back! Such a piece of news! Sister has gone to bed; she's had a headache – with the excitement, I think; but she says it's new bread. Come upstairs softly, my dear, and I'll tell you what it is! Who do you think has

been here – drinking tea with us, too, in the most condescending
manner?'

'Lady Harriet?' said Molly, suddenly enlightened by the word
'condescending'.

'Yes. Why, how did you guess it? But, after all, her call, at any
rate in the first instance, was upon you. Oh dear, Molly! if you're
not in a hurry to go to bed, let me sit down quietly and tell you
all about it; for my heart jumps into my mouth still, when I think
of how I was caught. She – that is, her ladyship – left the carriage
at the "George",* and took to her feet to go shopping – just as
you or I may have done many a time in our lives. And sister was
taking her forty winks;* and I was sitting with my gown up above
my knees and my feet on the fender, pulling out my grandmother's
lace, which I'd been washing. The worst has yet to be told. I'd
taken off my cap, for I thought it was getting dusk and no one
would come; and there was I in my black silk skull-cap, when
Nancy put her head in, and whispered, "There's a lady downstairs
– a real grand one, by her talk"; and in there came my Lady
Harriet, so sweet and pretty in her ways, it was some time before
I forgot I had never a cap on. Sister never wakened; or never
roused up, so to say. She says she thought it was Nancy bringing
in the tea, when she heard some one moving; for her ladyship, as
soon as she saw the state of the case, came and knelt down on the
rug by me, and begged my pardon so prettily for having followed
Nancy upstairs without waiting for permission; and was so taken
by my old lace, and wanted to know how I washed it, and where
you were, and when you'd be back, and when the happy couple
would be back; till sister wakened – she's always a little bit put
out, you know, when she first wakens from her afternoon nap –
and, without turning her head to see who it was, she said, quite
sharp – "Buzz, buzz, buzz! When will you learn that whispering is
more fidgeting than talking out loud? I've not been able to sleep
at all, for the chatter you and Nancy have been keeping up all this
time." You know that was a little fancy of sister's, for she'd been
snoring away as naturally as could be. So I went to her, and leant
over her, and said in a low voice –

'"Sister, it's her ladyship and me that has been conversing."

'"Ladyship here, ladyship there! have you lost your wits,
Phoebe, that you talk such nonsense – and in your skull-cap, too!"

'By this time she was sitting up – and, looking round her, she
saw Lady Harriet, in her velvets and silks, sitting on our rug,

smiling, her bonnet off, and her pretty hair all bright with the blaze of the fire. My word! sister was up on her feet directly; and she dropped her curtsey, and made her excuses for sleeping, as fast as might be, while I went off to put on my best cap; for sister might well say I was out of my wits, to go on chatting to an earl's daughter in an old black silk skull-cap! Black silk, too! when, if I'd only known she was coming, I might have put on my new brown silk, lying idle in my top drawer. And, when I came back, sister was ordering tea for her ladyship – our tea, I mean. So I took my turn at talk, and sister slipped out to put on her Sunday silk.* But I don't think we were quite so much at our ease with her ladyship as when I sat pulling out my lace in my skull-cap. And she was quite struck with our tea, and asked where we got it, for she had never tasted any like it before; and I told her we gave only 3s. 4d. a pound for it, at Johnson's* – (sister says I ought to have told her the price of our company-tea, which is 5s. a pound, only that is not what we were drinking; for, as ill-luck would have it, we'd none of it in the house) – and she said she would send us some of hers, all the way from Russia or Prussia, or some out-of-the-way place, and we were to compare and see which we liked best; and if we liked hers best, she could get it for us at 3s. a pound. And she left her love for you; and, though she was going away, you were not to forget her. Sister thought such a message would set you up too much, and told me she would not be chargeable for the giving it you. "But," I said, "a message is a message, and it's on Molly's own shoulders if she's set up by it. Let us show her an example of humility, sister, though we have been sitting cheek-by-jowl in such company." So sister humphed, and said she'd a headache, and went to bed. And now you may tell me your news, my dear.'

So Molly told her small events; which, interesting as they might have been at other times to the gossip-loving and sympathetic Miss Phoebe, were rather pale in the stronger light reflected from the visit of an earl's daughter.

CHAPTER 15

The New Mamma

On Tuesday afternoon, Molly returned home – to the home which was already strange, and what Warwickshire people would call 'unked',* to her. New paint, new paper, new colours; grim servants dressed in their best, and objecting to every change – from their master's marriage to the new oil-cloth in the hall, 'which tripped 'em up, and threw 'em down, and was cold to the feet, and smelt just abominable.' All these complaints Molly had to listen to, and it was not a cheerful preparation for the reception which she already felt to be so formidable.

The sound of their carriage-wheels was heard at last, and Molly went to the front door to meet them. Her father got out first, and took her hand and held it, while he helped his bride to alight. Then he kissed her fondly, and passed her on to his wife; but her veil was so securely (and becomingly) fastened down, that it was some time before Mrs Gibson could get her lips clear to greet her new daughter. Then there was the luggage to be seen about; and both the travellers were occupied in this, while Molly stood by, trembling with excitement, unable to help, and only conscious of Betty's rather cross looks, as heavy box after heavy box jammed up the passage.

'Molly, my dear, show – your mamma to her room!'

Mr Gibson had hesitated, because the question of the name by which Molly was to call her new relation had never occurred to him before. The colour flashed into Molly's face. Was she to call her 'mamma'? – the name long appropriated in her mind to some one else – to her own dead mother. The rebellious heart rose against it, but she said nothing. She led the way upstairs, Mrs Gibson turning round, from time to time, with some fresh direction as to which bag or trunk she needed most. She hardly spoke to Molly, till they were both in the newly-furnished bed-room, where a small fire had been lighted by Molly's orders.

'Now, my love, we can embrace each other in peace. O dear, how tired I am!' – (after the embrace had been accomplished). 'My spirits are so easily affected with fatigue; but your dear papa has been kindness itself. Dear! what an old-fashioned bed! And what a – But it doesn't signify. By-and-by we'll renovate the house – won't we, my dear? And you'll be my little maid tonight, and help me to arrange a few things; for I'm just worn out with the day's journey.'

'I've ordered a sort of tea-dinner to be ready for you,' said Molly. 'Shall I go and tell them to send it in?'

'I'm not sure if I can go down again tonight. It would be very comfortable to have a little table brought in here, and sit in my dressing-gown by this cheerful fire. But, to be sure, there's your dear papa! I really don't think he would eat anything, if I were not there. One must not think about oneself, you know. Yes, I'll come down in a quarter of an hour.'

But Mr Gibson had found a note awaiting him, with an immediate summons to an old patient, dangerously ill; and, snatching a mouthful of food while his horse was being saddled, he had to resume at once his old habits of attention to his profession above everything.

As soon as Mrs Gibson found that he was not likely to miss her presence – he had eaten a very tolerable lunch of bread and cold meat in solitude, so her fears about his appetite in her absence were not well-founded – she desired to have her meal upstairs in her own room; and poor Molly, not daring to tell the servants of this whim, had to carry up, first a table, which, however small, was too heavy for her, and afterwards all the choice portions of the meal, which she had taken great pains to arrange on the table, as she had seen such things done at Hamley, intermixed with fruit and flowers that had that morning been sent in from various great houses, where Mr Gibson was respected and valued. How pretty Molly had thought her handiwork an hour or two before! How dreary it seemed as, at last released from Mrs Gibson's conversation, she sate down in solitude to cold tea and the drumsticks of the chicken! No one to look at her preparations, and admire her deft-handedness and taste! She had thought that her father would be gratified by it, and, after all, he had never seen it! She had meant her cares as an offering of good-will to her stepmother, who even now was ringing her bell to have the tray taken away, and Miss Gibson summoned to her bed-room.

Molly hastily finished her meal, and went upstairs again.

'I feel so lonely, darling, in this strange house; do come and be with me, and help me to unpack. I think your dear papa might have put off his visit to Mr Craven Smith for just this one evening.'

'Mr Craven Smith couldn't put off his dying,' said Molly bluntly.

'You droll girl!' said Mrs Gibson, with a faint laugh. 'But, if this Mr Smith is dying, as you say, what's the use of your father's going off to him in such a hurry? Does he expect any legacy, or anything of that kind?'

Molly bit her lips, to prevent herself from saying something disagreeable. She only answered –

'I don't quite know that he is dying. The man said so; and papa can sometimes do something to make the last struggle easier. At any rate, it's always a comfort to the family to have him.'

'What dreary knowledge of death you have learned, for a girl of your age! Really, if I had heard all these details of your father's profession, I doubt if I could have brought myself to have him!'

'He doesn't make the illness or the death; he does his best against them. I call it a very fine thing to think of what he does or tries to do. And you will think so, too, when you see how he is watched for, and how people welcome him!'

'Well, don't let us talk any more of such gloomy things, tonight! I think I shall go to bed at once, I am so tired, if you will only sit by me till I get sleepy, darling. If you will talk to me, the sound of your voice will soon send me off.'

Molly got a book, and read her stepmother to sleep, preferring that to the harder task of keeping up a continual murmur of speech.

Then she stole down and went into the dining-room, where the fire was gone out; purposely neglected by the servants, to mark their displeasure at their new mistress's having had her tea in her own room. Molly managed to light it, however, before her father came home, and collected and rearranged some comfortable food for him. Then she knelt down again on the hearthrug, gazing into the fire in a dreamy reverie, which had enough of sadness about it to cause the tear to drop unnoticed from her eyes. But she jumped up, and shook herself into brightness, at the sound of her father's step.

'How is Mr Craven Smith?' she asked.

'Dead. He just recognised me. He was one of my first patients on my coming to Hollingford.'

Mr Gibson sate down in the arm-chair made ready for him, and warmed his hands at the fire, seeming neither to need food nor talk, as he went over a train of recollections. Then he roused

himself from his sadness, and, looking round the room, he said
briskly enough –

'And where's the new mamma?'

'She was tired, and went to bed early. Oh, papa! must I call her
"mamma"?'

'I should like it,' replied he, with a slight contraction of the
brows.

Molly was silent. She put a cup of tea near him; he stirred it,
and sipped it, and then he recurred to the subject.

'Why shouldn't you call her "mamma"? I'm sure she means to
do the duty of a mother to you. We all may make mistakes, and
her ways may not be quite all at once our ways; but at any rate
let us start with a family bond between us.'

What would Roger say was right? – that was the question that
rose to Molly's mind. She had always spoken of her father's new
wife as Mrs Gibson, and had once burst out at the Miss Brownings' with a protestation that she never would call her 'mamma'.
She did not feel drawn to her new relation by their intercourse of
that evening. She kept silence, though she knew her father was
expecting an answer. At last he gave up his expectation, and
turned to another subject; told about their journey, questioned her
as to the Hamleys, the Brownings, Lady Harriet, and the afternoon they had passed together at the Manor-house. But there was
a certain hardness and constraint in his manner, and in hers a
heaviness and absence of mind. All at once she said –

'Papa, I will call her "mamma"!'

He took her hand, and grasped it tight; but for an instant or
two he did not speak. Then he said –

'You won't be sorry for it, Molly, when you come to lie as poor
Craven Smith did tonight.'

For some time the murmurs and grumblings of the two elder
servants were confined to Molly's ears; then they spread to her
father's, who, to Molly's dismay, made summary work with them.

'You don't like Mrs Gibson's ringing her bell so often, don't
you? You've been spoilt, I'm afraid; but, if you don't conform to
my wife's desires, you have the remedy in your own hands, you
know.'

What servant ever resisted the temptation to give warning after
such a speech as that? Betty told Molly she was going to leave, in
as indifferent a manner as she could possibly assume towards the
girl whom she had tended and been about for the last sixteen

years. Molly had hitherto considered her former nurse as a fixture in the house; she would almost as soon have thought of her father's proposing to sever the relationship between them; and here was Betty coolly talking over whether her next place should be in town or country. But a great deal of this was assumed hardness. In a week or two Betty was in a flood of tears at the prospect of leaving her nursling, and would fain have stayed and answered all the bells in the house once every quarter of an hour. Even Mr Gibson's masculine heart was touched by the sorrow of the old servant, which made itself obvious to him, every time he came across her, by her broken voice and her swollen eyes.

One day he said to Molly, 'I wish you'd ask your mamma if Betty might not stay, if she made a proper apology, and all that sort of thing.'

'I don't much think it will be of any use,' said Molly, in a mournful voice. 'I know she is writing, or has written, about some under-housemaid at the Towers.'

'Well! – all I want is peace and a decent quantity of cheerfulness when I come home. I see enough of tears at other people's houses. After all, Betty has been with us sixteen years – a sort of service of the antique world.* But the woman may be happier elsewhere. Do as you like about asking mamma; only, if she agrees, I shall be quite willing.'

So Molly tried her hand at making a request to that effect to Mrs Gibson. Her instinct told her she would be unsuccessful; but surely favour was never refused in so soft a tone.

'My dear girl, I should never have thought of sending an old servant away – one who has had the charge of you from your birth, or nearly so. I could not have had the heart to do it. She might have stayed for ever for me, if she had only attended to all my wishes; and I am not unreasonable, am I? But, you see, she complained; and, when your dear papa spoke to her, she gave warning; and it is quite against my principles ever to take an apology from a servant who has given warning.'

'She is so sorry,' pleaded Molly; 'she says she will do anything you wish, and attend to all your orders, if she may only stay.'

'But, sweet one, you seem to forget that I cannot go against my principles, however much I may be sorry for Betty. She should not have given way to ill-temper, as I said before; although I never liked her, and considered her a most inefficient servant, thoroughly spoilt by having had no mistress for so long, I should have borne with her – at least, I think I should – as long as I could. Now I have all but engaged Maria, who was under-housemaid at the Towers; so don't let me hear any more of Betty's sorrow, or anybody else's sorrow, for I'm sure, what with your dear papa's sad stories and other things, I'm getting quite low.'

Molly was silent for a moment or two.

'Have you quite engaged Maria?' asked she.

'No – I said "all but engaged". Sometimes one would think you did not hear things, dear Molly!' replied Mrs Gibson petulantly. 'Maria is living in a place where they don't give her as much wages as she deserves. Perhaps they can't afford it, poor things! I'm always sorry for poverty, and would never speak hardly of those who are not rich; but I have offered her two pounds more than she gets at present, so I think she'll leave. At any rate, if they increase her wages, I shall increase my offer in proportion; so I think I'm sure to get her. Such a genteel girl! – always brings in a letter on a salver!'

'Poor Betty!' said Molly softly.

'Poor old soul! I hope she'll profit by the lesson, I'm sure,' sighed out Mrs Gibson; 'but it's a pity we hadn't Maria before the county-families began to call.'

Mrs Gibson had been highly gratified by the circumstance of so many calls 'from county-families'. Her husband was much respected; and many ladies from various halls, courts, and houses, who had profited by his services towards themselves and their families, thought it right to pay his new wife the attention of a call, when they drove into Hollingford to shop. The state of expectation into which these calls threw Mrs Gibson rather diminished Mr Gibson's domestic comfort. It was awkward to be carrying hot, savoury-smelling dishes from the kitchen to the dining-room at the very time when high-born ladies, with noses of aristocratic refinement, might be calling. Still more awkward was the accident which happened in consequence of clumsy Betty's haste to open the front door to a lofty footman's ran-tan,* which caused her to set down the basket containing the dirty plates right in his mistress's way, as she stepped gingerly through the comparative darkness of the hall; and then the young men, leaving the dining-room quietly enough, but bursting with long-repressed giggle, or no longer restraining their tendency to practical joking, no matter who might be in the passage when they made their exit! The remedy proposed by Mrs Gibson for all these distressing grievances was a late dinner. The luncheon for the young men, as she observed to her husband, might be sent into the surgery. A few elegant cold trifles for herself and Molly would not scent the house, and she would always take care to have some little dainty ready for him. He acceded, but unwillingly; for it was an innovation on the habits of a lifetime, and he felt as if he should never be able to arrange his rounds aright, with this new-fangled notion of a six o'clock dinner.

'Don't get any dainties for me, my dear; bread-and-cheese is the chief of my diet, as it was that of the old woman's.'*

'I know nothing of your old woman,' replied his wife; 'but really I cannot allow cheese to come beyond the kitchen.'

'Then I'll eat it there,' said he. 'It's close to the stable-yard; and, if I come in in a hurry, I can get it in a moment.'

'Really, Mr Gibson, it is astonishing to compare your appearance and manners with your tastes. You look such a gentleman, as dear Lady Cumnor used to say.'

Then the cook left – also an old servant, though not so old a one as Betty. The cook did not like the trouble of late dinners; and, being a Methodist, she objected on religious grounds to trying any of Mrs Gibson's new receipts* for French dishes. It was not scriptural, she said. There was a deal of mention of food in the Bible; but it was of sheep ready-dressed, which meant mutton, and of wine, and of bread-and-milk, and figs and raisins, of fatted calves, a good well-browned fillet of veal, and such-like; but it had always gone against her conscience to cook swine-flesh and make raised pork-pies; and now, if she was to be set to cook heathen dishes, after the fashion of the Papists, she'd sooner give it all up together. So the cook followed in Betty's track, and Mr Gibson had to satisfy his healthy English appetite on badly-made omelettes, rissoles, vol-au-vents, croquettes, and timbales;* never being exactly sure what he was eating.

He had made up his mind before his marriage to yield in trifles, and be firm in greater things. But the differences of opinion about trifles arose every day, and were perhaps more annoying than if they had related to things of more consequence. Molly knew her father's looks as well as she knew her alphabet; his wife did not; and being an unperceptive person, except when her own interests were dependent upon another person's humour, never found out how he was worried by all the small daily concessions which he made to her will or her whims. He never allowed himself to put any regret into shape, even in his own mind; he repeatedly reminded himself of his wife's good qualities, and comforted himself by thinking they should work together better as time rolled on; but he was very angry at a bachelor great-uncle of Mr Coxe's, who, after taking no notice of his red-headed nephew for years, suddenly sent for him, after the old man had partially recovered from a serious attack of illness, and appointed him his heir, on condition that his great-nephew remained with him during the rest of his life. This had happened almost directly after Mr and Mrs Gibson's return from their wedding journey, and once or twice since that time Mr Gibson had found himself wondering why the deuce old Benson could not have made up his mind sooner, and so have rid his house of the unwelcome presence of the young lover. To do Mr Coxe justice, in the very last conversation he had as a pupil with Mr Gibson, he said, with hesitating awkwardness, that perhaps the new circumstances in which he would be placed might make some difference with regard to Mr Gibson's opinion on –

'Not at all,' said Mr Gibson quickly. 'You are both of you too young to know your own minds; and, if my daughter was silly enough to be in love, she should never have to calculate her happiness on the chances of an old man's death. I dare say he'll disinherit you after all. He may do, and then you'd be worse off than ever. No! go away, and forget all this nonsense; and, when you've done, come back and see us!'

So Mr Coxe went away, with an oath of unalterable faithfulness in his heart; and Mr Gibson had unwillingly to fulfil an old promise made to a gentleman farmer in the neighbourhood a year or two before, and to take the second son of Mr Browne in young Coxe's place. He was to be the last of the race of pupils, and he was rather more than a year younger than Molly. Mr Gibson trusted that there would be no repetition of the Coxe romance.

CHAPTER 16

The Bride at Home

Among the 'county-people' (as Mrs Gibson termed them) who called upon her as a bride, were the two young Mr Hamleys. The

Squire, their father, had done his congratulations, as far as he ever intended to do them, to Mr Gibson himself when he came to the Hall; but Mrs Hamley, unable to go and pay visits herself, anxious to show attention to her kind doctor's new wife, and with perhaps a little sympathetic curiosity as to how Molly and her stepmother got on together, made her sons ride over to Hollingford with her cards and apologies. They came into the newly-furnished drawing-room, looking bright and fresh from their ride: Osborne first, as usual, perfectly dressed for the occasion, and with the sort of fine manner which sate so well upon him; Roger, looking like a strong-built, cheerful, intelligent country-farmer, followed in his brother's train. Mrs Gibson was dressed for receiving callers, and made the effect she always intended to produce, of a very pretty woman, no longer in her first youth, but with such soft manners and such a caressing voice that people forgot to wonder what her real age might be. Molly was better dressed than formerly; her stepmother saw after that. She disliked anything old or shabby, or out of taste about her; it hurt her eye; and she had already fidgeted Molly into a new amount of care about the manner in which she put on her clothes, arranged her hair, and was gloved and shod. Mrs Gibson had tried to put her through a course of rosemary washes and creams in order to improve her tanned complexion; but about that Molly was either forgetful or rebellious, and Mrs Gibson could not well come up to the girl's bed-room every night and see that she daubed her face and neck over with the cosmetics so carefully provided for her. Still, her appearance was extremely improved, even to Osborne's critical eye. Roger sought rather to discover in her looks and expression whether she was happy or not; his mother had especially charged him to note all these signs.

Osborne and Mrs Gibson made themselves agreeable to each other, according to the approved fashion when a young man calls on a middle-aged bride. They talked of the 'Shakspeare and musical glasses' of the day,* each vieing with the other in their knowledge of London topics. Molly heard fragments of their conversation, in the pauses of silence between Roger and herself. Her hero was coming out in quite a new character; no longer literary or poetical, or romantic or critical, he was now full of the last new play, of the singers at the opera. He had the advantage over Mrs Gibson, who, in fact, only spoke of these things from hearsay, from listening to the talk at the Towers; while Osborne had run up* from Cambridge two or three times to hear this, or to see that, wonder of the season. But she had the advantage over him in greater boldness of invention to eke out her facts; and, besides, she had more skill in the choice and arrangement of her words, so as to make it appear as if the opinions that were in reality quotations were formed by herself from actual experience of personal observation; for instance, in speaking of the mannerisms of a famous Italian singer, she would ask –

'Did you observe her constant trick of heaving her shoulders and clasping her hands together, before she took a high note?' – which was so said as to imply that Mrs Gibson herself had noticed this trick. Molly, who had a pretty good idea by this time of how her stepmother had passed the last year of her life, listened with no small bewilderment to this conversation; but at length decided that she must have misunderstood what they were saying, as she could not gather up the missing links, because of the necessity of replying to Roger's questions and remarks. Osborne was not the same Osborne he was when with his mother at the Hall.

Roger saw Molly glancing at his brother.

'You think my brother looking ill?' said he, lowering his voice.

'No – not exactly.'

'He is not well. Both my father and I are anxious about him. That run on the Continent did him harm, instead of good; and his disappointment at his examination has told upon him, I'm afraid.'

'I was not thinking he looked ill; only changed somehow.'

'He says he must go back to Cambridge soon. Possibly it may do him good; and I shall be off next week. This is a farewell visit to you, as well as one of congratulation to Mrs Gibson.'

'Your mother will feel your both going away, won't she? But, of course, young men will always have to live away from home.'

'Yes,' he replied. 'Still, she feels it a good deal; and I'm not satisfied about her health either. You will go out and see her sometimes, will you? she is very fond of you.'

'If I may,' said Molly, unconsciously glancing at her stepmother. She had an uncomfortable instinct that, in spite of Mrs Gibson's own perpetual flow of words, she could, and did, hear everything that fell from Molly's lips.

'Do you want any more books?' said he. 'If you do, make a list out, and send it to my mother before I leave, next Tuesday. After I am gone, there will be no one to go into the library and pick them out.'

As soon as they had left, Mrs Gibson began her usual comments on the departed visitors.

'I do like that Osborne Hamley! What a nice fellow he is! Somehow, I always do like eldest sons. He will have the estate, won't he? I shall ask your dear papa to encourage him to come about the house. He will be a very good, very pleasant acquaintance for you and Cynthia. The other is but a loutish young fellow, to my mind; there is no aristocratic bearing about him. I suppose he takes after his mother, who is but a parvenue, I've heard them say at the Towers.'

Molly was spiteful enough to have great pleasure in saying –

'I think I've heard her father was a Russian merchant,* and imported tallow and hemp. Mr Osborne Hamley is extremely like her.'

'Indeed! But there's no calculating these things. Anyhow, he is the perfect gentleman in appearance and manner. The estate is entailed,* is it not?'

'I know nothing about it,' said Molly.

A short silence ensued. Then Mrs Gibson said –

'Do you know, I almost think I must get dear papa to give a little dinner-party, and ask Mr Osborne Hamley? I should like to have him feel at home in this house. It would be something cheerful for him after the dulness and solitude of Hamley Hall. For the old people don't visit much, I believe?'

'He's going back to Cambridge next week,' said Molly.

'Is he? Well, then, we'll put off our little dinner till Cynthia comes home. I should like to have some young society for her, poor darling, when she returns.'

'When is she coming?' said Molly, who had always a longing curiosity for this same Cynthia's return.

'Oh! I'm not sure; perhaps at the New Year – perhaps not till Easter. I must get this drawing-room all new-furnished first; and then I mean to fit up her room and yours just alike. They are just the same size, only on opposite sides of the passage.'

'Are you going to new-furnish that room?' said Molly, in astonishment at the never-ending changes.

'Yes; and yours, too, darling; so don't be jealous!'

'Oh, please, mamma, not mine,' said Molly, taking in the idea for the first time.

'Yes, dear! You shall have yours done as well. A little French bed, and a new paper, and a pretty carpet, and a dressed-up toilet-table and glass, will make it look quite a different place.'

'But I don't want it to look different. I like it as it is. Pray don't do anything to it!'

'What nonsense, child! I never heard anything more ridiculous! Most girls would be glad to get rid of furniture only fit for the lumber-room.'

'It was my own mamma's, before she was married,' said Molly, in a very low voice; bringing out this last plea unwillingly, but with a certainty that it would not be resisted.

Mrs Gibson paused for a moment, before she replied –

'It's very much to your credit that you should have such feelings, I'm sure. But don't you think sentiment may be carried too far? Why, we should have no new furniture at all, and should have to put up with worm-eaten horrors! Besides, my dear, Hollingford will seem very dull to Cynthia, after pretty, gay France, and I want to make the first impressions attractive. I've a notion I can settle her down near here; and I want her to come in a good temper; for, between ourselves, my dear, she is a little, leetle, wilful. You need not mention this to your papa.'

'But can't you do Cynthia's room, and not mine? Please let mine alone.'

'No, indeed! I couldn't agree to that. Only think what would be said of me by everybody; petting my own child and neglecting my husband's! I couldn't bear it.'

'No one need know.'

'In such a tittle-tattle place as Hollingford! Really, Molly, you are either very stupid or very obstinate, or else you don't care what hard things may be said about me: and all for a selfish fancy of your own! No! I owe myself the justice of acting in this matter as I please. Every one shall know I'm not a common stepmother. Every penny I spend on Cynthia I shall spend on you too; so it's no use talking any more about it.'

So Molly's little white dimity bed, her old-fashioned chest of drawers, and her other cherished relics of her mother's maiden-days, were consigned to the lumber-room; and after a while, when Cynthia and her great French boxes had come home, the old furniture that had filled up the space required for the fresh importation of trunks, disappeared likewise into the same room.

All this time the family at the Towers had been absent; Lady Cumnor had been ordered to Bath for the early part of the winter, and her family were with her there. On dull, rainy days, Mrs Gibson used to bethink her of missing 'the Cumnors', for so she had taken to calling them since her position had become more independent of theirs. It marked a distinction between her intimacy with the family, and the reverential manner in which the townspeople were accustomed to speak of 'the earl' and 'the countess'. Both Lady Cumnor and Lady Harriet wrote to their 'dear Clare' from time to time. The former had generally some commissions that she wished to have executed at the Towers, or in the town; and no one could do them so well as Clare, who was acquainted with all the tastes and ways of the countess. These commissions were the cause of various bills for flys and cars* from the George Inn. Mr Gibson pointed out this consequence to his wife; but she, in return, bade him remark that a present of game was pretty sure to follow upon the satisfactory execution of Lady Cumnor's wishes. Somehow, Mr Gibson did not quite like this consequence either; but he was silent about it, at any rate. Lady Harriet's letters were short and amusing. She had that sort of regard for her old governess which prompted her to write from time to time, and to feel glad when the half-voluntary task was accomplished. So there was no real outpouring of confidence, but so much news of the family and gossip of the place she was in, as she thought would make Clare feel that she was not forgotten by her former pupils, intermixed with moderate but sincere expressions of regard. How those letters were quoted and referred to by Mrs Gibson in her conversations with the Hollingford ladies! She had found out their effect at Ashcombe; and it was not less at Hollingford. But she was rather perplexed at kindly messages to Molly, and at inquiries as to how the Miss Brownings liked the tea she had sent; and Molly had first to explain, and then to narrate at full length, all the occurrences of the afternoon at Ashcombe Manor-house,* and Lady Harriet's subsequent call upon her at the Miss Brownings'.

'What nonsense!' said Mrs Gibson, with some annoyance. 'Lady Harriet only went to see you out of a desire for amusement. She would only make fun of the Miss Brownings, and those two will be quoting her and talking about her, just as if she was their intimate friend.'

'I don't think she did make fun of them. She really seemed as if she had been very kind.'

'And you suppose you know her ways better than I do, who

have known her these fifteen years? I tell you, she turns every one into ridicule who does not belong to her set. Why, she used always to speak of the Miss Brownings as "Pecksy and Flapsy".'

'She promised me she would not,' said Molly, driven to bay.

'Promised you! – Lady Harriet! What do you mean?'

'Only – she spoke of them as Pecksy and Flapsy – and, when she talked of coming to call on me at their house, I asked her not to come if she was going to – to make fun of them.'

'Upon my word! with all my long acquaintance with Lady Harriet, I should never have ventured on such impertinence.'

'I didn't mean it as impertinence,' said Molly sturdily. 'And I don't think Lady Harriet took it as such.'

'You can't know anything about it. She can put on any kind of manner.'

Just then, Squire Hamley came in. It was his first call; and Mrs Gibson gave him a graceful welcome, and was quite ready to accept his apology for his tardiness, and to assure him that she quite understood the pressure of business on every land-owner who farmed his own estate. But no such apology was made. He shook her hand heartily, as a mark of congratulation on her good fortune in having secured such a prize as his friend Gibson, but said nothing about his long neglect of duty. Molly, who by this time knew the few strong expressions of his countenance well, was sure that something was the matter, and that he was very much disturbed. He hardly attended to Mrs Gibson's fluent opening of conversation, for she had already determined to make a favourable impression on the father of the handsome young man who was heir to an estate, besides possessing great personal agreeableness; but he turned to Molly and, addressing her, said – almost in a low voice, as if he was making a confidence to her that he did not intend Mrs Gibson to hear –

'Molly, we are all wrong at home! Osborne has lost the fellowship at Trinity he went back to try for. Then he has gone and failed miserably in his degree, after all that he said, and that his mother said; and I, like a fool, went and boasted about my clever son. I can't understand it. I never expected anything extraordinary from Roger; but Osborne—! And then it has thrown madam into one of her bad fits of illness; and she seems to have a fancy for you, child! Your father came to see her this morning. Poor things, she's very poorly, I'm afraid; and she told him how she should like to have you about her, and he said I might fetch you. You'll come, won't you, my dear? She's not a poor woman, such as many people think it's the only charity to be kind to; but she's just as forlorn of woman's care as if she was poor – worse, I daresay.'

'I'll be ready in ten minutes,' said Molly, much touched by the Squire's words and manner, never thinking of asking her step-mother's consent, now that she had heard that her father had given his. As she rose to leave the room, Mrs Gibson, who had only half heard what the Squire had said, and was a little affronted at the exclusiveness of his confidence, said –

'My dear, where are you going?'

'Mrs Hamley wants me, and papa says I may go,' said Molly; and almost at the same time the Squire replied –

'My wife is ill, and as she's very fond of your daughter, she begged Mr Gibson to allow her to come to the Hall for a little while, and he kindly said she might, and I'm come to fetch her.'

'Stop a minute, darling,' said Mrs Gibson to Molly – a slight cloud over her countenance, in spite of her caressing word. 'I am sure dear papa quite forgot that you were to go out with me tonight, to visit people,' continued she, addressing herself to the Squire, 'with whom I am quite unacquainted – and it is very uncertain if Mr Gibson can return in time to accompany me – so, you see, I cannot allow Molly to go with you.'

'I shouldn't have thought it would have signified. Brides are always brides, I suppose: and it's their part to be timid; but I shouldn't have thought it – in this case. And my wife sets her heart on things, as sick people do. Well, Molly' (in a louder tone, for these foregoing sentences were spoken *sotto voce*), 'we must put it off till tomorrow; and it's our loss, not yours,' he continued, as he saw the reluctance with which she slowly returned to her place. 'You'll be as gay as can be tonight, I daresay' –

'No, I shall not,' broke in Molly. 'I never wanted to go, and now I shall want it less than ever.'

'Hush, my dear,' said Mrs Gibson; and, addressing the Squire, she added, 'The visiting here is not all one could wish for so young a girl – no young people, no dances, nothing of gaiety; but it is wrong in you, Molly, to speak against such kind friends of your father's as I understand these Cockerells are. Don't give so bad an impression of yourself to the kind Squire.'

'Let her alone! let her alone!' quoth he. 'I see what she means.

She'd rather come and be in my wife's sickroom than go out for this visit tonight. Is there no way of getting her off?'

'None whatever,' said Mrs Gibson. 'An engagement is an engagement with me; and I consider that she is not only engaged to Mrs Cockerell, but to me – bound to accompany me, in my husband's absence.'

The Squire was put out; and, when he was put out, he had a trick of placing his hands on his knees and whistling softly to himself. Molly knew this phase of his displeasure, and only hoped he would confine himself to this wordless expression of annoyance. It was pretty hard work for her to keep the tears out of her eyes; and she endeavoured to think of something else rather than dwell on regrets and annoyances. She heard Mrs Gibson talking on in a sweet monotone, and wished to attend to what she was saying; but the Squire's visible annoyance struck sharper on her mind. At length, after a pause of silence, he started up, and said –

'Well! it's no use. Poor madam; she won't like it. She'll be disappointed! But it's but for one evening – but for one evening! She may come tomorrow, mayn't she? Or will the dissipation of such an evening as she describes be too much for her?'

There was a touch of savage irony in his manner which frightened Mrs Gibson into good behaviour.

'She shall be ready at any time you name. I am so sorry; my foolish shyness is in fault, I believe; but still, you must acknowledge that an engagement is an engagement.'

'Did I ever say an engagement was an elephant, madam? However, there's no use saying any more about it, or I shall forget my manners. I'm an old tyrant, and she – lying there in bed, poor girl – has always given me my own way. So you'll excuse me, Mrs Gibson, won't you; and let Molly come along with me at ten tomorrow morning?'

'Certainly,' said Mrs Gibson, smiling. But, when his back was turned, she said to Molly –

'Now, my dear, I must never have you exposing me to the ill-manners of such a man again! I don't call him a squire; I call him a boor, or a yeoman at best. You must not go on accepting or rejecting invitations, as if you were an independent young lady, Molly. Pay me the respect of a reference to my wishes another time, if you please, my dear!'

'Papa had said I might go,' said Molly, choking a little.

'As I am now your mamma, your references must be to me, for

the future. But, as you are to go, you may as well look well-dressed. I will lend you my new shawl for this visit, if you like it, and my set of green ribbons. I am always indulgent, when proper respect is paid to me. And, in such a house as Hamley Hall, no one can tell who may be coming and going, even if there is sickness in the family.'

'Thank you. But I don't want the shawl and the ribbons, please: there will be nobody there except the family. There never is, I think; and now that she is so ill' – Molly was on the point of crying at the thought of her friend lying ill and lonely, and looking for her arrival. Moreover, she was sadly afraid lest the Squire had gone off with the idea that she did not want to come – that she preferred that stupid, stupid party at the Cockerells'. Mrs Gibson, too, was sorry; she had an uncomfortable consciousness of having given way to temper before a stranger, and a stranger, too, whose good opinion she had meant to cultivate; and she was also annoyed at Molly's tearful face.

'What can I do for you, to bring you back into good temper?' she said. 'First, you insist upon knowing Lady Harriet better than I do – I, who have known her for eighteen or nineteen years at least. Then you jump at invitations without ever consulting me, or thinking of how awkward it would be for me to go stumping into a drawing-room all by myself; following my new name, too, which always makes me feel uncomfortable, it is such a sad come-down after Kirkpatrick! And then, when I offer you some of the prettiest things I have got, you say it does not signify how you are dressed! What can I do to please you, Molly? I, who delight in nothing more than peace in a family, to see you sitting there with despair upon your face!'

Molly could stand it no longer; she went upstairs to her own room – her own smart new room, which hardly yet seemed a familiar place; and began to cry so heartily and for so long a time, that she stopped at length for very weariness. She thought of Mrs Hamley wearying for her; of the old Hall whose very quietness might become oppressive to an ailing person; of the trust the Squire had had in her, that she would come off directly with him. And all this oppressed her much more than the querulousness of her stepmother's words.

CHAPTER 17

Trouble at Hamley Hall

If Molly thought that peace dwelt perpetually at Hamley Hall, she was sorely mistaken. Something was out of tune in the whole establishment; and, for a very unusual thing, the common irritation seemed to have produced a common bond. All the servants were old in their places, and were told by some one of the family, or gathered, from the unheeded conversation carried on before them, everything that affected master or mistress or either of the young gentlemen. Any one of them could have told Molly that the grievance which lay at the root of everything was the amount of the bills run up by Osborne at Cambridge, and which, now that all chance of his obtaining a fellowship was over, came pouring down upon the Squire. But Molly, confident of being told by Mrs Hamley herself anything which she wished her to hear, encouraged no confidences from any one else.

She was struck with the change in 'madam's' look, as soon as she caught sight of her in the darkened room, lying on the sofa in her dressing-room, all dressed in white, which almost rivalled the white wanness of her face. The Squire ushered Molly in with –

'Here she is at last!' and Molly had scarcely imagined that he had so much variety in the tones of his voice – the beginning of the sentence was spoken in a loud, congratulatory manner, while the last words were scarcely audible. He had seen the death-like pallor on his wife's face; not a new sight, and one which had been presented to him gradually enough, but which was now always giving him a fresh shock. It was a lovely, tranquil winter's day; every branch and every twig on the trees and shrubs was glittering with drops of the sun-melted hoar-frost; a robin was perched on a holly-bush, piping cheerily; but the blinds were down, and out of Mrs Hamley's windows nothing of all this was to be seen. There was even a large screen placed between her and the woodfire, to keep off that cheerful blaze. Mrs Hamley stretched out one hand to Molly, and held hers firm; with the other she shaded her eyes.

'She is not so well this morning,' said the Squire, shaking his head. 'But never fear, my dear one; here's the doctor's daughter, nearly as good as the doctor himself. Have you had your medicine? Your beef-tea?' he continued, going about on heavy tiptoe and peeping into every empty cup and glass. Then he returned to the sofa; looked at her for a minute or two, and then softly kissed her, and told Molly he would leave her in charge.

As if Mrs Hamley were afraid of Molly's remarks or questions, she began in her turn a hasty system of interrogatories.

'Now, dear child, tell me all; it's no breach of confidence, for I shan't mention it again, and I shan't be here long. How does it all go on – the new mother, the good resolutions? let me help you if I can. I think with a girl I could have been of use – a mother does not know boys. But tell me anything you like and will; don't be afraid of details!'

Even with Molly's small experience of illness, she saw how much of restless fever there was in this speech; and instinct, or some such gift, prompted her to tell a long story of many things – the wedding-day, her visit to the Miss Brownings', the new furniture, Lady Harriet, etc., all in an easy flow of talk which was very soothing to Mrs Hamley, inasmuch as it gave her something to think about beyond her own immediate sorrows. But Molly did not speak of her own grievances, nor of the new domestic relationship. Mrs Hamley noticed this.

'And you and Mrs Gibson get on happily together?'

'Not always,' said Molly. 'You know we didn't know much of each other, before we were put to live together.'

'I didn't like what the Squire told me last night. He was very angry.'

That sore had not yet healed over; but Molly resolutely kept silence, beating her brains to think of some other subject of conversation.

'Ah! I see, Molly,' said Mrs Hamley; 'you won't tell me your sorrows, and yet, perhaps, I could have done you some good.'

'I don't like,' said Molly, in a low voice. 'I think papa wouldn't like it. And, besides, you have helped me so much – you and Mr Roger Hamley. I often think of the things he said; they come in so usefully, and are such a strength to me.'

'Ah, Roger! yes. He is to be trusted, Oh, Molly! I've a great deal to say to you myself, only not now. I must have my medicine and try to go to sleep. Good girl! You are stronger than I am, and can do without sympathy.'

Molly was taken to another room; the maid who conducted her to it told her that Mrs Hamley had not wished her to have her nights disturbed, as they might very probably have been, if she had been in her former sleeping-room. In the afternoon Mrs Hamley sent for her, and, with the want of reticence common to invalids, especially to those suffering from long and depressing maladies, she told Molly of the family distress and disappointment.

She made Molly sit down near her on a little stool, and, holding her hand, and looking into her eyes to catch her spoken sympathy from their expression quicker than she could from her words, she said –

'Osborne has so disappointed us! I cannot understand it yet. And the Squire was so terribly angry! I cannot think how all the money was spent – advances through money-lenders, besides bills. The Squire does not show me how angry he is now, because he's afraid of another attack; but I know how angry he is. You see, he has been spending ever so much money in reclaiming that land at Upton Common, and is very hard pressed himself. But it would have doubled the value of the estate; and so we never thought anything of economies which would benefit Osborne in the long run. And now the Squire says he must mortgage some of the land; and you can't think how it cuts him to the heart. He sold a great deal of timber to send the two boys to college. Osborne – oh! what a dear, innocent boy he was; he was the heir, you know; and he was so clever, every one said he was sure of honours and a fellowship, and I don't know what all; and he did get a scholarship; and then all went wrong. I don't know how. That is the worst. Perhaps the Squire wrote too angrily, and that stopped up confidence. But he might have told me. He would have done, I think, Molly, if he had been here, face to face with me. But the Squire, in his anger, told him not to show his face at home, till he had paid off the debts he had incurred out of his allowance. Out of two hundred and fifty a year to pay off more than nine hundred, one way or another! And not to come home till then! Perhaps Roger will have debts too! He had but two hundred; but, then, he was not the eldest son. The Squire has given orders that the men are to be turned off the draining-works; and I lie awake thinking of their poor families this wintry weather. But what shall we do? I've never been strong, and perhaps I've been extravagant in my habits; and there were family traditions as to expenditure, and the reclaiming of this land. Oh, Molly! Osborne was such a sweet little baby, and such a loving boy: so clever, too! You know I read you some of his poetry: now, could a person who wrote like that do anything very wrong? And yet I'm afraid he has.'

'Don't you know, at all, how the money has gone?' asked Molly.

'No! not at all. That's the sting. There are tailors' bills, and bills for book-binding and wine and pictures – those come to four or five hundred; and, though this expenditure is extraordinary – inexplicable to such simple old folk as we are – yet it may be only the luxury of the present day. But the money for which he will give no account – of which, indeed, we only heard through the Squire's London agents, who found out that certain disreputable attorneys were making inquiries as to the entail of the estate; – oh, Molly! worse than all – I don't know how to bring myself to tell you – as to the age and health of the Squire, his dear father' – (she began to sob almost hysterically; yet she would go on talking, in spite of Molly's efforts to stop her) – 'who held him in his arms, and blessed him, even before I had kissed him; and thought always so much of him as his heir and first-born darling! How he has loved him! How I have loved him! I sometimes have thought of late, that we've almost done that good Roger injustice.'

'No! I'm sure you've not: only look at the way he loves you. Why, you are his first thought: he may not speak about it, but any one may see it. And dear, dear Mrs Hamley,' said Molly, determined to say out all that was in her mind, now that she had once got the word, 'don't you think that it would be better not to misjudge Mr Osborne Hamley? We don't know what he has done with the money; he is so good (is he not?) that he may have wanted it to relieve some poor person – some tradesman, for instance, pressed by creditors – some' —

'You forget, dear,' said Mrs Hamley, smiling a little at the girl's impetuous romance, but sighing the next instant, 'that all the other bills come from tradesmen, who complain piteously of being kept out of their money.'

Molly was non-plussed for the moment; but then she said –

'I daresay they imposed upon him. I'm sure I've heard stories of young men being made regular victims of by the shopkeepers in great towns.'

'You're a great darling, child,' said Mrs Hamley, comforted by Molly's strong partisanship, unreasonable and ignorant though it was.

'And, besides,' continued Molly, 'some one must be acting

wrongly in Osborne's – Mr Osborne Hamley's, I mean – I can't help saying Osborne sometimes, but, indeed, I always think of him as Mr Osborne'—

'Never mind, Molly, what you call him; only go on talking! It seems to do me good to hear the hopeful side taken. The Squire has been so hurt and displeased; strange-looking men coming into the neighbourhood, too, questioning the tenants, and grumbling about the last fall of timber,* as if they were calculating on the Squire's death.'

'That's just what I was going to speak about. Doesn't it show that they are bad men? and would bad men scruple to impose upon him, and to tell lies in his name, and to ruin him?'

'Don't you see, you only make him out weak, instead of wicked?'

'Yes; perhaps I do. But I don't think he is weak. You know yourself, dear Mrs Hamley, how very clever he really is. Besides, I would rather he was weak than wicked. Weak people may find themselves all at once strong in heaven, when they see things quite clearly; but I don't think the wicked will turn themselves into virtuous people all at once.'

'I think I've been very weak, Molly,' said Mrs Hamley, stroking Molly's curls affectionately. 'I've made such an idol of my beautiful Osborne; and he turns out to have feet of clay, not strong enough to stand on the firm ground. And that's the best view of his conduct, too!'

What with his anger against his son, and his anxiety about his wife, the difficulty of raising the money immediately required, and his irritation at the scarce-concealed inquiries made by strangers as to the value of his property, the poor Squire was in a sad state. He was angry and impatient with every one who came near him, and then was depressed at his own violent temper and unjust words. The old servants, who perhaps cheated him in many small things, were beautifully patient under his upbraidings. They could understand bursts of passion, and knew the cause of his variable moods as well as he did himself. The butler, who was accustomed to argue with his master about every fresh direction as to his work, now nudged Molly at dinner-time, to make her eat some dish which she had just been declining, and explained his conduct afterwards as follows –

'You see, miss, me and cook had planned a dinner as would tempt master to eat; but, when you say, "No, thank you", when I hand you anything, master never so much as looks at it. But if you take a thing, and eats with a relish, why first he waits, and then he looks, and by-and-by he smells; and then he finds out as he's hungry, and falls to eating as natural as a kitten takes to mewing. That's the reason, miss, as I gave you a nudge and a wink, which no one knows better nor me was not manners.'

Osborne's name was never mentioned during these cheerless meals. The Squire asked Molly questions about Hollingford people, but did not seem much to attend to her answers. He used also to ask her every day how she thought that his wife was; but if Molly told the truth – that every day seemed to make her weaker and weaker – he was almost savage with the girl. He could not bear it; and he would not. Nay, once he was on the point of dismissing Mr Gibson, because he insisted on a consultation with Dr Nicholls, the great physician of the county.

'It's nonsense thinking her so ill as that – you know it's only the delicacy she's had for years; and, if you can't do her any good in such a simple case – no pain – only weakness and nervousness – it is a simple case, eh? – don't look in that puzzled way, man! – you'd better give her up altogether, and I'll take her to Bath or Brighton, or somewhere for change; for in my opinion it's only moping and nervousness.'

But the Squire's bluff, florid face was pinched with anxiety, and worn with the effort of being deaf to the footsteps of fate, as he said these words which belied his fears.

Mr Gibson replied very quietly –

'I shall go on coming to see her, and I know you'll not forbid my visits. But I shall bring Dr Nicholls with me the next time I come. I may be mistaken in my treatment; and I wish to God he may say I am mistaken in my apprehensions.'

'Don't tell me them! I cannot bear them!' cried the Squire. 'Of course we must all die; and she must too. But the cleverest doctor in England shan't go about coolly meting out the life of such as her. I daresay I shall die first. I hope I shall. But I'll knock any one down who speaks to me of death sitting within me. And, besides, I think all doctors are ignorant quacks, pretending to knowledge they haven't got. Ay, you may smile at me. I don't care. Unless you can tell me I shall die first, neither you nor Dr Nicholls shall come prophesying and croaking about this house.'

Mr Gibson went away, heavy at heart from the thought of Mrs Hamley's approaching death, but thinking little enough of the

Squire's speeches. He had almost forgotten them, in fact, when about nine o'clock that evening, a groom rode in from Hamley Hall in hot haste, with a note from the Squire.

'DEAR GIBSON, – For God's sake forgive me if I was rude today. She is much worse. Come and spend the night here. Write for Nicholls, and all the physicians you want. Write before you start off. They may give her ease. There were Whitworth doctors* much talked of in my youth for curing people given up by the regular doctors; can't you get one of them? I put myself in your hands. Sometimes I think it is the turning point, and she'll rally after this bout. I trust all to you. – Yours ever,

'R. HAMLEY.

'P.S. – Molly is a treasure. – God help me!'

Of course Mr Gibson went; for the first time since his marriage cutting short Mrs Gibson's querulous lamentations over her life, as involved in that of a doctor called out at all hours of day and night.

He brought Mrs Hamley through this attack; and for a day or two the Squire's alarm and gratitude made him docile in Mr Gibson's hands. Then he returned to the idea of its being a crisis through which his wife had passed; and that she was now on the way to recovery. But the day after the consultation with Dr Nicholls, Mr Gibson said to Molly –

'Molly! I've written to Osborne and Roger. Do you know Osborne's address?'

'No, papa. He's in disgrace. I don't know if the Squire knows; and she has been too ill to write.'

'Never mind. I'll enclose it to Roger; whatever those lads may be to others, there's as strong a brotherly love, as ever I saw, between the two. Roger will know. And, Molly, they are sure to come home, as soon as they hear my report of their mother's state. I wish you'd tell the Squire what I've done. It's not a pleasant piece of work; and I'll tell madam myself in my own way. I'd have told him if he'd been at home; but you say he was obliged to go to Ashcombe on business.'

'Quite obliged. He was so sorry to miss you. But, papa, he will be so angry! You don't know how mad he is against Osborne.'

Molly dreaded the Squire's anger when she gave him her father's message. She had seen quite enough of the domestic relations of the Hamley family to understand that, underneath his old-fashioned courtesy and the pleasant hospitality he showed to her as a guest, there was a strong will, and a vehement passionate temper, along with that degree of obstinacy in prejudices (or 'opinions', as he would have called them) so common to those who have, neither in youth nor in manhood, mixed largely with their kind. She had listened, day after day, to Mrs Hamley's plaintive murmurs as to the deep disgrace in which Osborne was being held by his father – the prohibition of his coming home; and she hardly knew how to begin to tell him that the letter summoning Osborne had already been sent off.

Their dinners were *tête-à-tête*. The Squire tried to make them pleasant to Molly, feeling deeply grateful to her for the soothing comfort she was to his wife. He made merry speeches, which sank away into silence, and at which they each forgot to smile. He ordered up rare wines, which she did not care for, but tasted out of complaisance. He noticed that one day she had eaten some brown *beurré* pears as if she liked them; and, as his trees had not produced many this year, he gave directions that this particular kind should be sought for through the neighbourhood. Molly felt that, in many ways, he was full of goodwill towards her; but it did not diminish her dread of touching on the one sore point in the family. However, it had to be done, and that without delay.

The great log was placed on the after-dinner fire, the hearth swept up, the ponderous candles snuffed, and then the door was shut and Molly and the Squire were left to their dessert. She sat at the side of the table in her old place. That at the head was vacant; yet, as no orders had been given to the contrary, the plate and glasses and napkin were always arranged as regularly and methodically as if Mrs Hamley would come in as usual. Indeed, sometimes, when the door by which she used to enter was opened by any chance, Molly caught herself looking round, as if she expected to see the tall, languid figure in the elegant draperies of rich silk and soft lace, which Mrs Hamley was wont to wear of an evening.

This evening, it struck her, as a new thought of pain, that into that room she would come no more. She had fixed to give her father's message at this very point of time; but something in her throat choked her, and she hardly knew how to govern her voice. The Squire got up and went to the broad fire-place, to strike into the middle of the great log, and split it up into blazing, sparkling pieces. His back was towards her. Molly began, 'When papa was here today, he bade me tell you he had written to Mr Roger

Hamley, to say that – that he thought he had better come home; and he enclosed a letter to Mr Osborne Hamley, to say the same thing.'

The Squire put down the poker; but he still kept his back to Molly.

'He sent for Osborne and Roger?' he asked at length.

Molly answered, 'Yes.'

Then there was a dead silence, which Molly thought would never end. The Squire had placed his two hands on the high chimney-piece, and stood leaning over the fire.

'Roger would have been down from Cambridge on the 18th,' said he. 'And he has sent for Osborne, too! Did he know?' he continued, turning round to Molly, with something of the fierceness she had anticipated in voice and look. In another moment, he had dropped his voice. 'It's right; quite right. I understand. It has come at length. Come! Come! Osborne has brought it on, though,' with a fresh access of anger in his tones. 'She might have' (some word Molly could not hear – she thought it sounded like 'lingered') 'but for that. I can't forgive him; I cannot.'

And then he suddenly left the room. While Molly sat there still, very sad in her sympathy with all, he put his head in again –

'Go to her, my dear; I cannot – not just yet. But I will soon. Just this bit; and after that I won't lose a moment. You're a good girl. God bless you!'

It is not to be supposed that Molly had remained all this time at the Hall without interruption. Once or twice her father had brought her a summons home. Molly thought she could perceive that he brought it unwillingly; in fact, it was Mrs Gibson that had sent for her, almost, as it were, to preserve a 'right of way' through her actions.

'You shall come back tomorrow, or the next day,' her father had said. 'But mamma seems to think people will put a bad construction on your being so much away from home so soon after our marriage.'

'Oh, papa, I'm afraid Mrs Hamley will miss me! I do so like being with her.'

'I don't think it is likely she will miss you as much as she would have done a month or two ago. She sleeps so much now, that she is scarcely conscious of the lapse of time. I'll see that you come back here again in a day or two.'

So, out of the silence and the soft melancholy of the Hall, Molly returned into the all-pervading element of chatter and gossip at Hollingford. Mrs Gibson received her kindly enough. She had a smart new winter-bonnet ready to give her as a present; but she did not care to hear any particulars about the friends whom Molly had just left; and her few remarks on the state of affairs at the Hall jarred terribly on the sensitive Molly.

'What a time she lingers! Your papa never expected she would last half so long after that attack. It must be very wearing work to them all; I declare you look quite another creature since you were there. One can only wish it mayn't last, for their sakes.'

'You don't know how the Squire values every minute,' said Molly.

'Why, you say she sleeps a great deal, and doesn't talk much when she's awake, and there's not the slightest hope for her. And yet, at such times, people are kept on tenter-hooks with watching and waiting. I know it by my dear Kirkpatrick. There really were days, when I thought it never would end. But we won't talk any more of such dismal things; you've had quite enough of them, I'm sure, and it always makes me melancholy to hear of illness and death; and yet your papa seems sometimes as if he could talk of nothing else. I'm going to take you out tonight, though, and that will give you something of a change; and I've been getting Miss Rose to trim up one of my old gowns for you; it's too tight for me. There's some talk of dancing – it's at Mrs Edwards'.'

'Oh, mamma, I cannot go!' cried Molly. 'I've been so much with her; and she may be suffering so, or even dying – and I to be dancing!'

'Nonsense! You're no relation, so you need not feel it so much. I wouldn't urge you, if she was likely to know about it and be hurt; but as it is, it's all fixed that you are to go; and don't let us have any nonsense about it. We might sit twirling our thumbs, and repeating hymns all our lives long, if we were to do nothing else when people were dying.'

'I cannot go,' repeated Molly. And, acting upon impulse, and almost to her own surprise, she appealed to her father, who came into the room at this very time. He contracted his dark eyebrows, and looked annoyed, as both wife and daughter poured their different sides of the argument into his ears. He sat down in desperation of patience. When his turn came to pronounce a decision, he said –

'I suppose I can have some lunch? I went away at six this

morning, and there's nothing in the dining-room. I have to go off again directly.'

Molly started to the door; Mrs Gibson made haste to ring the bell.

'Where are you going, Molly?' said she sharply.

'Only to see about papa's lunch.'

'There are servants to do it; and I don't like your going into the kitchen.'

'Come, Molly! sit down and be quiet,' said her father. 'One comes home wanting peace and quietness – and food too. If I am to be appealed to, which I beg I may not be another time, I settle that Molly stops at home this evening. I shall come back late and tired. See that I have something ready to eat, goosey, and then I'll dress myself up in my best, and go and fetch you home, my dear. I wish all these wedding festivities were well over. Ready, is it? Then I'll go into the dining-room and gorge myself. A doctor ought to be able to eat like a camel, or like Major Dugald Dalgetty.'*

It was well for Molly that callers came in just at this time, for Mrs Gibson was extremely annoyed. They told her some little local piece of news, however, which filled up her mind; and Molly found that, if she only expressed wonder enough at the engagement they had both heard of from the departed callers, the previous discussion as to her accompanying her stepmother or not might be entirely passed over. Not entirely though; for the next morning she had to listen to a very brilliantly touched-up account of the dance and the gaiety which she had missed; and also to be told that Mrs Gibson had changed her mind about giving her the gown, and thought now that she should reserve it for Cynthia, if only it was long enough; but Cynthia was so tall – quite overgrown, in fact. The chances seemed equally balanced as to whether Molly might not have the gown after all.

CHAPTER 18

Mr Osborne's Secret

Osborne and Roger came to the Hall; Molly found Roger established there, when she returned after this absence at home. She gathered that Osborne was coming; but very little was said about him in any way. The Squire scarcely ever left his wife's room; he sat by her, watching her, and now and then moaning to himself. She was so much under the influence of opiates that she did not often rouse up; but, when she did, she almost invariably asked for Molly. On these rare occasions, she would ask after Osborne – where he was, if he had been told, and if he was coming? In her weakened and confused state of intellect she seemed to have retained two strong impressions – one, of the sympathy with which Molly had received her confidence about Osborne; the other, of the anger which her husband entertained against him. Before the Squire she never mentioned Osborne's name, nor did she seem at her ease in speaking about him to Roger; while, when she was alone with Molly, she hardly spoke of any one else. She must have had some sort of wandering idea that Roger blamed his brother, while she remembered Molly's eager defence, which she had thought hopelessly improbable at the time. At any rate, she made Molly her confidant about her first-born. She sent her to ask Roger how soon he would come, for she seemed to know perfectly well that he was coming.

'Tell me all Roger says. He will tell you.'

But it was several days before Molly could ask Roger any question; and meanwhile Mrs Hamley's state had materially altered. At length Molly came upon Roger sitting in the library, his head buried in his hands. He did not hear her footstep till she was close beside him. Then he lifted up his face, red, and stained with tears, his hair all ruffled up and in disorder.

'I've been wanting to see you alone,' she began. 'Your mother does so want some news of your brother Osborne. She told me last week to ask you about him; but I did not like to speak of him before your father.'

'She hardly ever named him to me.'

'I don't know why; for to me she used to talk of him perpetually. I have seen so little of her this week, and I think she forgets a great deal now. Still, if you don't mind, I should like to be able to tell her something, if she asks me again.'

He put his head again between his hands, and did not answer her for some time.

'What does she want to know?' said he, at last. 'Does she know that Osborne is coming soon – any day?'

'Yes. But she wants to know where he is.'

'I can't tell you. I don't exactly know. I believe he's abroad, but I'm not sure.'

'But you've sent papa's letter to him?'

'I've sent it to a friend of his, who will know better than I do where he's to be found. You must know that he isn't free from creditors, Molly. You can't have been one of the family, like a child of the house almost, without knowing that much. For that and for other reasons I don't exactly know where he is.'

'I will tell her so. You are sure he will come?'

'Quite sure. But, Molly, I think my mother may live some time yet; don't you? Dr Nicholls said so yesterday when he was here with your father. He said she had rallied more than he had ever expected. You're not afraid of any change that makes you so anxious for Osborne's coming?'

'No. It's only for her that I asked. She did seem so to crave for news of him. I think she dreamed of him; and then when she wakened it was a relief to her to talk about him to me. She always seemed to associate me with him. We used to speak so much of him when we were together.'

'I don't know what we should any of us have done without you. You've been like a daughter to my mother.'

'I do so love her,' said Molly softly.

'Yes; I see. Have you ever noticed that she sometimes calls you "Fanny"? It was the name of a little sister of ours who died. I think she often takes you for her. It was partly that, and partly because, at such a time as this, one can't stand on formalities, that made me call you Molly. I hope you don't mind it?'

'No; I like it. But will you tell me something more about your brother? She really hungers for news of him.'

'She'd better ask me herself. Yet, no! I am so involved by promises of secrecy, Molly, that I couldn't satisfy her if she once began to question me. I believe he's in Belgium, and that he went there about a fortnight ago, partly to avoid his creditors. You know my father has refused to pay his debts?'

'Yes: at least, I knew something like it.'

'I don't believe my father could raise the money all at once without having recourse to steps which he would exceedingly recoil from. Yet, for the time, it places Osborne in a very awkward position.'

'I think, what vexes your father a good deal is some mystery as to how the money was spent.'

'If my mother ever says anything about that part of the affair,' said Roger hastily, 'assure her from me that there's nothing of vice or wrong-doing about it. I can't say more: I'm tied. But set her mind at ease on that point!'

'I'm not sure if she remembers all her painful anxiety about this,' said Molly. 'She used to speak a great deal to me about him before you came, when your father seemed so angry. And now, whenever she sees me, she wants to talk on the old subject; but she doesn't remember so clearly. If she were to see him, I don't believe she would recollect why she was uneasy about him, while he was absent.'

'He must be here soon. I expect him every day,' said Roger uneasily.

'Do you think your father will be very angry with him?' asked Molly, with as much timidity as if the Squire's displeasure might be directed against her.

'I don't know,' said Roger. 'My mother's illness may alter him; but he didn't easily forgive us formerly. I remember once – but that is nothing to the purpose. I can't help fancying that he has put himself under some strong restraint for my mother's sake, and that he won't express much. But it doesn't follow that he will forget it. My father is a man of few affections, but what he has are very strong; he feels anything that touches him on these points deeply and permanently. That unlucky valuing of the property! It has given my father the idea of post-obits' —

'What are they?' asked Molly.

'Raising money to be paid on my father's death; which, of course, involves calculations as to the duration of his life.'

'How shocking!' said she.

'I'm as sure as I am of my own life that Osborne never did anything of the kind. But my father expressed his suspicions in language that irritated Osborne; and he doesn't speak out, and won't justify himself even as much as he might; and, much as he loves me, I've but little influence over him, or else he would tell my father all. Well, we must leave it to time,' he added, sighing. 'My mother would have brought us all right, if she'd been what she once was.'

He turned away, leaving Molly very sad. She knew that every member of the family she cared for so much was in trouble, out of which she saw no exit; and her small power of helping them was diminishing day by day, as Mrs Hamley sank more and more under the influence of opiates and stupefying illness. Her father had spoken to her, only this very day, of the desirableness of her returning home for good. Mrs Gibson wanted her – for no particular reason, but for many small fragments of reasons. Mrs Hamley had ceased to want her much, only occasionally appearing to remember her existence. Her position – so her father thought, for the idea had not entered her head – in a family of which the only woman was an invalid confined to bed, was becoming awkward. But Molly had begged hard to remain two or three days longer – only that – only till Friday. If Mrs Hamley should want her (she argued, with tears in her eyes), and should hear that she had left the house, she would think her so unkind, so ungrateful!

'My dear child, she's getting past wanting any one! The keenness of earthly feelings is deadened.'

'Papa, that is worst of all. I cannot bear it. I won't believe it. She may not ask for me again, and may quite forget me; but I'm sure, to the very last, if the medicines don't stupefy her, she will look round for the Squire and her children. For poor Osborne most of all; because he's in sorrow.'

Mr Gibson shook his head, but said nothing in reply. In a minute or two he asked –

'I don't like to take you away while you even fancy you can be of use or comfort to one who has been so kind to you; but, if she hasn't wanted you before Friday, will you be convinced, will you come home willingly?'

'If I go then, I may see her once again, even if she hasn't asked for me?' inquired Molly.

'Yes, of course. You must make no noise, no loud step; but you may go in and see her. I must tell you, I'm almost certain she won't ask for you.'

'But she may, papa. I will go home on Friday, if she does not. I think she will.'

So Molly hung about the house, trying to do all she could out of the sick-room, for the comfort of those in it. They only came out for meals, or for necessary business, and found little time for talking to her; so her life was solitary enough, waiting for the call that never came. The evening of the day on which she had had the above conversation with Roger, Osborne arrived. He came straight into the drawing-room, where Molly was seated on the rug, reading by the fire-light, as she did not like to ring for candles merely for her own use. Osborne came in, with a kind of hurry, which almost made him appear as if he would trip himself up and fall down. Molly rose. He had not noticed her before; now he came forwards, and took hold of both her hands, leading her into the full flickering light, and straining his eyes to look into her face.

'How is she? You will tell me – you must know the truth! I've travelled day and night, since I got your father's letter.'

Before she could frame her answer, he had sate down in the nearest chair, covering his eyes with his hand.

'She's very ill,' said Molly. 'That you know; but I don't think she suffers much pain. She has wanted you sadly.'

He groaned aloud. 'My father forbade me to come.'

'I know!' said Molly, anxious to prevent his self-reproach. 'Your brother was away, too. I think no one knew how ill she was – she had been an invalid for so long.'

'You know—Yes! she told you a great deal – she was very fond of you. And God knows how I loved her. If I had not been forbidden to come home, I should have told her all. Does my father know of my coming now?'

'Yes,' said Molly; 'I told him papa had sent for you.'

Just at that moment the Squire came in. He had not heard of Osborne's arrival, and was seeking Molly to ask her to write a letter for him.

Osborne did not stand up, when his father entered. He was too much exhausted, too much oppressed by his feelings, and also too much estranged by his father's angry, suspicious letters. If he had come forward with any manifestation of feeling at this moment, everything might have been different. But he waited for his father to see him, before he uttered a word. All that the Squire said, when his eye fell upon him at last, was –

'You here, sir!'

And, breaking off in the directions he was giving to Molly, he abruptly left the room. All the time, his heart was yearning after his first-born; but mutual pride kept them asunder. Yet he went straight to the butler, and asked of him when Mr Osborne had arrived, and how he had come, and if he had had any refreshment – dinner or what – since his arrival?

'For I think I forget everything now!' said the poor Squire, putting his hand up to his head. 'For the life of me, I can't remember whether we've had dinner or not; these long nights, and all this sorrow and watching, quite bewilder me.'

'Perhaps, sir, you will take some dinner with Mr Osborne? Mrs Morgan is sending up his directly. You hardly sate down at dinner-time, sir; you thought my mistress wanted something.'

'Ay! I remember now. No! I won't have any more. Give Mr Osborne what wine he chooses. Perhaps *he* can eat and drink!' So the Squire went away upstairs, with bitterness as well as sorrow in his heart.

When lights were brought, Molly was struck with the change in Osborne. He looked haggard and worn; perhaps with travelling and anxiety. Not quite such a dainty gentleman either, as Molly had thought him, when she had last seen him calling on her stepmother, two months before. But she liked him better now. The tone of his remarks pleased her more. He was simpler, and less ashamed of showing his feelings. He asked after Roger in a warm, longing kind of way. Roger was out: he had ridden to Ashcombe to transact some business for the Squire. Osborne evidently wished for his return; and hung about restlessly in the drawing-room, after he had dined.

'You're sure I mayn't see her tonight?' he asked Molly, for the third or fourth time.

'No, indeed. I will go up again, if you like it. But Mrs Jones, the nurse Dr Nicholls sent, is a very decided person. I went up, while you were at dinner; and Mrs Hamley had just taken her drops, and was on no account to be disturbed by seeing any one, much less by any excitement.'

Osborne kept walking up and down the long drawing-room, half talking to himself, half to Molly.

'I wish Roger would come! He seems to be the only one to give me a welcome. Does my father always live upstairs in my mother's rooms, Miss Gibson?'

'He has done since her last attack. I believe he reproaches himself for not having been enough alarmed before.'

'You heard all the words he said to me; they were not much of a welcome, were they? And my dear mother, who always – whether I was to blame or not—I suppose Roger is sure to come home tonight?'

'Quite sure.'

'You are staying here, are you not? Do you often see my mother, or does this omnipotent nurse keep you out too?'

'Mrs Hamley hasn't asked for me for three days now, and I

don't go into her room unless she asks. I'm leaving on Friday, I believe.'

'My mother was very fond of you, I know.'

After a while he said, in a voice that had a great deal of sensitive pain in its tone –

'I suppose – do you know whether she is quite conscious – quite herself?'

'Not always conscious,' said Molly tenderly. 'She has to take so many opiates. But she never wanders, only forgets, and sleeps.'

'Oh, mother, mother!' said he, stopping suddenly, and hanging over the fire, his hands on the chimney-piece.

When Roger came home, Molly thought it time to retire. Poor girl! it was getting time for her to leave this scene of distress in which she could be of no use. She sobbed herself to sleep, this Tuesday night. Two days more, and it would be Friday; and she would have to wrench up the roots she had shot down into this ground. The weather was bright the next morning; and morning and sunny weather cheer up young hearts. Molly sate in the dining-room, making tea for the gentlemen as they came down. She could not help hoping that the Squire and Osborne might come to a better understanding before she left; for after all, in the dissension between father and son lay a bitterer sting than in the illness sent by God. But, though they met at the breakfast-table, they purposely avoided addressing each other. Perhaps the natural subject of conversation between the two, at such a time, would have been Osborne's long journey the night before; but he had never spoken of the place he had come from, whether north, south, east, or west, and the Squire did not choose to allude to anything that might bring out what his son wished to conceal. Again, there was an unexpressed idea in both their minds that Mrs Hamley's present illness was much aggravated, if not entirely brought on, by the discovery of Osborne's debts; so, many inquiries and answers on that head were tabooed. In fact, their attempts at easy conversation were limited to local subjects, and principally addressed to Molly or Roger. Such intercourse was not productive of pleasure, or even of friendly feeling, though there was a thin outward surface of politeness and peace. Long before the day was over, Molly wished that she had acceded to her father's proposal, and gone home with him. No one seemed to want her. Mrs Jones, the nurse, assured her, time after time, that Mrs Hamley had never named her name; and her small services in the sick-room were not required since there was a regular nurse. Osborne and Roger seemed all in all to each other; and Molly now felt how much the short conversations she had had with Roger had served to give her something to think about, all during the remainder of her solitary days. Osborne was extremely polite, and even expressed his gratitude to her for her attentions to his mother in a very pleasant manner; but he appeared to be unwilling to show her any of the deeper feelings of his heart, and almost ashamed of his exhibition of emotion the night before. He spoke to her as any agreeable young man speaks to any pleasant young lady; but Molly almost resented this. It was only the Squire who seemed to make her of any account. He gave her letters to write, small bills to reckon up; and she could have kissed his hands for thankfulness.

The last afternoon of her stay at the Hall came. Roger had gone out on the Squire's business. Molly went into the garden, thinking over the last summer, when Mrs Hamley's sofa used to be placed under the old cedar-tree on the lawn, and when the warm air seemed to be scented with roses and sweetbriar. Now, the trees were leafless; there was no sweet odour in the keen frosty air; and, looking up at the house, there were the white sheets of blinds, shutting out the pale winter sky from the invalid's room. The thicket was tangled with dead weeds and rime and hoar-frost; and the beautiful fine articulations of branches and boughs and delicate twigs were all intertwined in leafless distinctness against the sky. Then she thought of the day her father had brought her the news of his second marriage. Could she ever be so passionately unhappy again? Was it goodness, or was it numbness, that made her feel as though life was too short to be troubled much about anything? Death seemed the only reality. She had neither energy nor heart to walk far or briskly; and turned back towards the house. The afternoon sun was shining brightly on the windows; and, stirred up to unusual activity by some unknown cause, the housemaids had opened the shutters and windows of the generally unused library. The middle window was also a door; the white-painted wood went half-way up. Molly turned along the little flag-paved path that led past the library windows to the gate in the white railings at the front of the house, and went in at the opened door. She had had leave given to choose out any books she wished to read, and to take them home with her; and it was just the sort of half-dawdling employment suited to her taste this afternoon.

She mounted on the ladder to get to a particular shelf, high up in a dark corner of the room; and, finding there some volume that looked interesting, she sat down on the step to read part of it. There she sat, in her bonnet and cloak, when Osborne suddenly came in. He did not see her at first; indeed, he seemed in such a hurry that he probably might not have noticed her at all, if she had not spoken.

'Am I in your way? I only came here for a minute to look for some books.' She came down the steps as she spoke, still holding the book in her hand.

'Not at all. It is I who am disturbing you. I must just write a letter for the post, and then I shall be gone. Is not this open door too cold for you?'

'Oh, no. It is so fresh and pleasant.'

She began to read again, sitting on the lowest step of the ladder; he to write at the large old-fashioned writing-table close to the window. There was a minute or two of profound silence, in which the rapid scratching of Osborne's pen upon the paper was the only sound. Then came a click of the gate, and Roger stood at the open door. His face was towards Osborne, sitting in the light; his back to Molly, crouched up in her corner. He held out a letter, and said in hoarse breathlessness –

'Here's a letter from your wife, Osborne. I went past the post-office and thought'—

Osborne stood up, angry dismay upon his face –

'Roger! what have you done? Don't you see her?'

Roger looked round, and Molly stood up in her corner, red, trembling, miserable, as though she were a guilty person. Roger entered the room. All three seemed to be equally dismayed. Molly was the first to speak; she came forward and said·–

'I am so sorry! I didn't wish to hear it, but I couldn't help it. You will trust me, won't you?' and, turning to Roger, she said to him, with tears in her eyes – 'Please say you know I shall not tell.'

'We can't help it,' said Osborne gloomily. 'Only, Roger, who knew of what importance it was, ought to have looked round him before speaking.'

'So I should,' said Roger. 'I'm more vexed with myself than you can conceive. Not but what I'm as sure of you as of myself,' continued he, turning to Molly.

'Yes; but,' said Osborne, 'you see how many chances there are that even the best-meaning persons may let out what it is of such consequence to me to keep secret.'

'I know you think it so,' said Roger.

'Well, don't let us begin that old discussion again – at any rate, before a third person.'

Molly had had hard work, all this time, to keep from crying. Now that she was alluded to as the third person before whom conversation was to be restrained, she said –

'I'm going away. Perhaps I ought not to have been here. I'm very sorry – very. But I'll try and forget what I've heard.'

'You can't do that,' said Osborne, still ungraciously. 'But will you promise me never to speak about it to any one – not even to me, or to Roger? Will you try to act and speak as if you had never heard it? I'm sure, from what Roger has told me about you, that, if you give me this promise, I may rely upon it.'

'Yes; I will promise,' said Molly, putting out her hand as a kind of pledge. Osborne took it, but rather as if the action was superfluous. She added, 'I think I should have done so, even without a promise. But it is, perhaps, better to bind oneself. I will go away now. I wish I'd never come into this room!'

She put down her book on the table very softly, and turned to leave the room, choking down her tears until she was in the solitude of her own chamber. But Roger was at the door before her, holding it open for her, and reading – she felt that he was reading – her face. He held out his hand for hers, and his firm grasp expressed both sympathy and regret for what had occurred.

She could hardly keep back her sobs till she reached her bed-room. Her feelings had been overwrought for some time past, without finding the natural vent in action. The leaving Hamley Hall had seemed so sad before; and now she was troubled with having to bear away a secret which she ought never to have known, and the knowledge of which had brought out a very uncomfortable responsibility. Then there would arise a very natural wonder as to who Osborne's wife was. Molly had not stayed so long and so intimately in the Hamley family without being well aware of the manner in which the future lady of Hamley was planned for. The Squire, for instance, partly in order to show that Osborne, his heir, was above the reach of Molly Gibson, the doctor's daughter, in the early days before he knew Molly well, had often alluded to the grand, the high, and the wealthy marriage which Hamley of Hamley, as represented by his clever, brilliant, handsome son Osborne, might be expected to make. Mrs Hamley, too, unconsciously on her part, showed the projects that she was constantly devising for the reception of the unknown daughter-in-law that was to be.

'The drawing-room must be refurnished when Osborne marries' – or, 'Osborne's wife will like to have the west suite of rooms to herself; it will perhaps be a trial to her to live with the old couple; but we must arrange it so that she will feel it as little as possible.' – 'Of course, when Mrs Osborne comes, we must try and give her a new carriage; the old one does well enough for us.' – These and similar speeches had given Molly the impression of the future Mrs Osborne as of some beautiful, grand young lady, whose very presence would make the old Hall into a stately, formal mansion, instead of the pleasant, unceremonious home that it was at present. Osborne, too, who had spoken with such languid criticism to Mrs Gibson about various country belles, and even in his own home was apt to give himself airs – only at home his airs were poetically fastidious, while with Mrs Gibson they had been socially fastidious – what unspeakably elegant beauty had he chosen for his wife? Who had satisfied him, and yet, satisfying him, had to have her marriage kept in concealment from his parents? At length Molly tore herself up from her wonderings. It was of no use: she could not find out; she might not even try. The blank wall of her promise blocked up the way. Perhaps it was not even right to wonder, and endeavour to remember slight speeches, casual mentions of a name, so as to piece them together into something coherent. Molly dreaded seeing either of the brothers again; but they all met at dinner-time, as if nothing had happened. The Squire was taciturn, either from melancholy or from displeasure. He had never spoken to Osborne since his return, excepting about the commonest trifles, when intercourse could not be avoided; and his wife's state oppressed him like a heavy cloud coming over the light of his day. Osborne put on an indifferent manner to his father, which Molly felt sure was assumed; but it was not conciliatory for all that. Roger, quiet, steady, and natural, talked more than all the others; but he too was uneasy, and in distress on many accounts. Today he principally addressed himself to Molly; entering into rather long narrations of late discoveries in natural history, which kept up the current of talk without requiring much reply from any one. Molly had expected Osborne to look something different from usual – conscious, or ashamed, or resentful, or even 'married' – but he was exactly the Osborne of the morning – handsome, elegant, languid in manner and in look; cordial with his brother, polite towards her, secretly uneasy at the state of things between his father and himself. She would never have guessed the concealed romance which lay *perdu** under that every-day behaviour. She had always wished to come into direct contact with a love-story; here she had, and she only found it very uncomfortable; there was a sense of concealment and uncertainty about it all; and her honest, straightforward father, her quiet life at Hollingford, which, even with all its drawbacks, was above-board, and where everybody knew what everybody was doing, seemed secure and pleasant in comparison. Of course she felt great pain at quitting the Hall, and at the mute farewell she had taken of her sleeping and unconscious friend. But leaving Mrs Hamley now was a different thing to what it had been a fortnight ago. Then, she was wanted at any moment, and felt herself to be of comfort. Now, her very existence seemed forgotten by the poor lady whose body appeared to be living so long after her soul.

She was sent home in the carriage, loaded with true thanks from every one of the family. Osborne ransacked the greenhouses for flowers for her; Roger had chosen her out books of every kind. The Squire himself kept shaking her hand, without being able to speak his gratitude, till at last he took her in his arms, and kissed her as he would have done a daughter.

CHAPTER 19

Cynthia's Arrival

Molly's father was not at home when she returned; and there was no one to give her a welcome. Mrs Gibson was out paying calls, the servants told Molly. She went upstairs to her own room, meaning to unpack and arrange her borrowed books. Rather to her surprise, she saw the chamber corresponding to her own being dusted; water and towels too were being carried in.

'Is any one coming?' she asked of the housemaid.

'Miss Kirkpatrick is coming tomorrow. Missus's daughter from France.'

Was Cynthia coming at last? Oh, what a pleasure it would be to have a companion, a girl, a sister of her own age!

Molly's depressed spirits sprang up again with bright elasticity. She longed for Mrs Gibson's return, to ask her all about it: it must be very sudden, for Mr Gibson had said nothing of it at the Hall the day before. No quiet reading now; the books were hardly put away with Molly's usual neatness. She went down into the drawing-room, and could not settle to anything. At last Mrs Gibson came home, tired out with her walk and her heavy velvet cloak. Until that was taken off, and she had rested herself for a few minutes, she seemed quite unable to attend to Molly's questions.

'Oh, yes! Cynthia is coming home tomorrow, by the 'Umpire',* which passes through at ten o'clock. What an oppressive day it is for the time of the year! I really am almost ready to faint. Cynthia heard of some opportunity, I believe, and was only too glad to leave school a fortnight earlier than we planned. She never gave me the chance of writing to say I did, or did not, like her coming so much before the time; and I shall have to pay for her just the same as if she had stopped. And I meant to have asked her to bring me a French bonnet; and then you could have had one made after mine. But I'm very glad she's coming, poor dear.'

'Is anything the matter with her?' asked Molly.

'Oh, no! Why should there be?'

'You called her "poor dear", and it made me afraid lest she might be ill.'

'Oh, no! It's only a way I got into, when Mr Kirkpatrick died. A fatherless girl – you know one always does call them 'poor dears'. Oh, no! Cynthia never is ill. She's as strong as a horse. She never would have felt today as I have done. Could you get me a glass of wine and a biscuit, my dear? I'm really quite faint.'

Mr Gibson was much more excited about Cynthia's arrival than her own mother was. He anticipated her coming as a great pleasure to Molly, on whom, in spite of his recent marriage and his new wife, his interests principally centred. He even found time to run upstairs and see the bed-rooms of the two girls; for the furniture of which he had paid a pretty round sum.

'Well, I suppose young ladies like their bed-rooms decked out in this way! It's very pretty certainly, but' —

'I liked my own old room better, papa; but perhaps Cynthia is accustomed to such decking-up.'

'Perhaps; at any rate, she'll see we've tried to make it pretty. Yours is like hers. That's right. It might have hurt her, if hers had been smarter than yours. Now, goodnight in your fine flimsy bed.'

Molly was up betimes – almost before it was light – arranging her pretty Hamley flowers in Cynthia's room. She could hardly eat her breakfast that morning. She ran upstairs and put on her things, thinking that Mrs Gibson was quite sure to go down to the 'Angel Inn',* where the 'Umpire' stopped, to meet her daughter after a two years' absence. But, to her surprise, Mrs Gibson had arranged herself at her great worsted-work frame, just as usual; and she, in her turn, was astonished at Molly's bonnet and cloak.

'Where are you going so early, child? The fog hasn't cleared away yet.'

'I thought you would go and meet Cynthia; and I wanted to go with you.'

'She will be here in half-an-hour; and dear papa has told the gardener to take the wheelbarrow down for her luggage. I'm not sure if he is not gone himself.'

'Then are not you going?' asked Molly, with a good deal of disappointment.

'No, certainly not. She will be here almost directly. And, besides, I don't like to expose my feelings to every passer-by in High Street. You forget, I have not seen her for two years, and I hate scenes in the market-place.'

She settled herself to her work again; and Molly, after some consideration, gave up her own grief, and employed herself in looking out of the downstairs window which commanded the approach from the town.

'Here she is – here she is!' she cried out at last. Her father was walking by the side of a tall young lady; William the gardener was wheeling along a great cargo of baggage. Molly flew to the front-door, and had it wide open to admit the new-comer, some time before she arrived.

'Well! here she is. Molly, this is Cynthia. Cynthia, Molly. You're to be sisters, you know.'

Molly saw the beautiful, tall, swaying figure, against the light of the open door, but could not see any of the features that were, for the moment, in shadow. A sudden gush of shyness had come over her just at the instant, and quenched the embrace she would have given a moment before. But Cynthia took her in her arms, and kissed her on both cheeks.

'Here's mamma,' she said, looking beyond Molly on to the stairs, where Mrs Gibson stood, wrapped up in a shawl, and shivering in the cold. She ran past Molly and Mr Gibson, who rather averted their eyes from this first greeting between mother and child.

Mrs Gibson said –

'Why, how you are grown, darling! You look quite a woman.'

'And so I am,' said Cynthia. 'I was, before I went away; I've hardly grown since – except, it is always to be hoped, in wisdom.'

'Yes! That we will hope,' said Mrs Gibson, in rather a meaning way. Indeed, there were evidently hidden allusions in their seemingly commonplace speeches. When they all came into the full light and repose of the drawing-room, Molly was absorbed in the contemplation of Cynthia's beauty. Perhaps her features were not regular; but the changes in her expressive countenance gave one no time to think of that. Her smile was perfect; her pouting charming; the play of the face was in the mouth. Her eyes were beautifully shaped, but their expression hardly seemed to vary. In colouring she was not unlike her mother; only she had not so much of the red-haired tints in her complexion, and her long-shaped, serious grey eyes were fringed with dark lashes, instead of her mother's insipid flaxen ones. Molly fell in love with her, so to speak, on the instant. She sate there warming her feet and hands, as much at her ease as if she had been there all her life; not particularly attending to her mother – who, all the time, was studying either her or her dress – measuring Molly and Mr Gibson with grave observant looks, as if guessing how she should like them.

'There's a hot breakfast ready for you in the dining-room, when you are ready for it,' said Mr Gibson. 'I'm sure you must want it after your night-journey.' He looked round at his wife, at Cynthia's mother; but she did not seem inclined to leave the warm room again.

'Molly will take you to your room, darling,' said she; 'it is near hers, and she has got her things to take off. I'll come down and sit in the dining-room, while you are having your breakfast; but I really am afraid of the cold now.'

Cynthia rose and followed Molly upstairs.

'I'm so sorry there isn't a fire for you,' said Molly, 'but – I suppose it wasn't ordered; and, of course, I don't give any orders. Here is some hot water, though.'

'Stop a minute,' said Cynthia, getting hold of both Molly's hands, and looking steadily into her face, but in such a manner that she did not dislike the inspection.

'I think I shall like you. I am so glad! I was afraid I should not. We're all in a very awkward position together, aren't we? I like your father's looks, though.'

Molly could not help smiling at the way this was said. Cynthia replied to her smile.

'Ah, you may laugh. But I don't know that I am easy to get on with; mamma and I didn't suit when we were last together. But perhaps we are each of us wiser now. Now, please leave me for a quarter of an hour. I don't want anything more.'

Molly went into her own room, waiting to show Cynthia down to the dining-room. Not that, in the moderate-sized house, there was any difficulty in finding the way. A very little trouble in conjecturing would enable a stranger to discover any room. But Cynthia had so captivated Molly, that she wanted to devote herself to the new-comer's service. Ever since she had heard of the probability of her having a sister – (she called her a sister, but whether it was a Scotch sister, or a sister *à la mode de Brétagne,** would have puzzled most people) – Molly had allowed her fancy to dwell much on the idea of Cynthia's coming; and in the short time since they had met, Cynthia's unconscious power of fascination had been exercised upon her. Some people have this power. Of course, its effects are only manifested in the susceptible. A school-girl may be found in every school who attracts and influences all the others, not by her virtues, nor her beauty, nor her sweetness, nor her cleverness, but by something that can neither be described nor reasoned upon. It is the something alluded to in the old lines: –

> Love me not for comely grace,
> For my pleasing eye and face;
> No, nor for my constant heart –
> For these may change, and turn to ill,
> And thus true love may sever;
> But love me on, and know not why,
> So hast thou the same reason still
> To dote upon me ever.*

A woman will have this charm, not only over men but over her own sex; it cannot be defined, or rather it is so delicate a mixture of many gifts and qualities that it is impossible to decide on the proportions of each. Perhaps it is incompatible with very high principle; as its essence seems to consist in the most exquisite power of adaptation to varying people and still more various moods – 'being all things to all men'.* At any rate, Molly might soon have been aware that Cynthia was not remarkable for unflinching morality; but the glamour thrown over her would have prevented Molly from any attempt at penetrating into and judging her companion's character, even had such processes been the least in accordance with her own disposition.

Cynthia was very beautiful, and was so well aware of this fact that she had forgotten to care about it; no one with such loveliness ever appeared so little conscious of it. Molly would watch her perpetually as she went about the room, with the free stately step of some wild animal of the forest – moving almost, as it were, to the continual sound of music. Her dress, too, though now to our ideas it would be considered ugly and disfiguring, was suited to her complexion and figure, and the fashion of it subdued within fit bounds by her exquisite taste. It was inexpensive enough, and the changes in it were but few. Mrs Gibson professed herself shocked to find that Cynthia had but four gowns, when she might have stocked herself so well, and brought over so many useful French patterns, if she had but patiently waited for her mother's answer to the letter which she had sent, announcing her return by the opportunity Madame had found for her. Molly was hurt for Cynthia at all these speeches; she thought they implied that the pleasure which her mother felt in seeing her a fortnight sooner, after her two years' absence, was inferior to that which she would have received from a bundle of silver-paper patterns. But Cynthia took no apparent notice of the frequent recurrence of these small complaints. Indeed, she received much of what her mother said with a kind of complete indifference, that made Mrs Gibson hold her rather in awe; and she was much more communicative to Molly than to her own child. With regard to dress, however, Cynthia soon showed that she was her mother's own daughter, in the manner in which she could use her deft and nimble fingers. She was a capital workwoman; and, unlike Molly, who excelled in plain-sewing, but had no notion of dress-making or millinery, she could repeat the fashions she had only seen in passing along the streets of Boulogne, with one or two pretty rapid movements of her hands as she turned and twisted the ribbons and gauze her mother furnished her with. So she refurbished Mrs Gibson's wardrobe; doing it all in a sort of contemptuous manner, the source of which Molly could not quite make out.

Day after day, the course of these small frivolities was broken in upon by the news Mr Gibson brought of Mrs Hamley's nearer approach to death. Molly – very often sitting by Cynthia, and surrounded by ribbon, and wire, and net – heard the bulletins, like the toll of a funeral bell at a marriage feast. Her father sympathised with her. It was the loss of a dear friend to him too; but he was so accustomed to death, that it seemed to him but as it was, the natural end of all things human. To Molly, the death of some one she had known so well and loved so much was a sad and gloomy phenomenon. She loathed the small vanities with which she was surrounded, and would wander out into the frosty garden, and pace the walk, which was both sheltered and concealed by evergreens.

At length – and yet it was not so long, not a fortnight since Molly had left the Hall – the end came. Mrs Hamley had sunk out of life, as gradually as she had sunk out of consciousness and her place in this world. The quiet waves closed over her, and her place knew her no more.*

'They all sent their love to you, Molly,' said her father. 'Roger said he knew how you would feel it.'

Mr Gibson had come in very late, and was having a solitary dinner in the dining-room. Molly was sitting near him, to keep him company. Cynthia and her mother were upstairs. The latter was trying on a head-dress which Cynthia had made for her.

Molly remained downstairs, after her father had gone out afresh on his final round among his town-patients. The fire was growing very low, and the lights were waning. Cynthia came softly in, and, taking Molly's listless hand, that hung down by her side, sat at her feet on the rug, chafing her chilly fingers without speaking. The tender action thawed the tears that had been gathering heavily at Molly's heart, and they came dropping down her cheeks.

'You loved her dearly, did you not, Molly?'

'Yes,' sobbed Molly; and then there was a silence.

'Had you known her long?'

'No, not a year. But I had seen a great deal of her. I was almost like a daughter to her; she said so. Yet I never bid her good-bye or anything. Her mind became weak and confused.'

'She had only sons, I think?'

'No; only Mr Osborne and Mr Roger Hamley. She had a daughter once – Fanny. Sometimes, in her illness, she used to call me "Fanny".'

The two girls were silent for some time, both gazing into the fire. Cynthia spoke first –

'I wish I could love people as you do, Molly!'

'Don't you?' said the other, in surprise.

'No. A good number of people love me, I believe, or at least they think they do; but I never seem to care much for any one. I do believe I love you, little Molly, whom I have only known for ten days, better than any one.'

'Not than your mother?' said Molly, in grave astonishment.

'Yes, than my mother!' replied Cynthia, half-smiling. 'It's very shocking, I daresay; but it is so. Now, don't go and condemn me. I don't think love for one's mother quite comes by nature; and remember how much I have been separated from mine! I loved my father, if you will,' she continued, with the force of truth in her tone, and then she stopped; 'but he died when I was quite a little thing, and no one believes that I remember him. I heard mamma say to a caller, not a fortnight after his funeral, "Oh, no, Cynthia is too young; she has quite forgotten him" – and I bit my lips, to keep from crying out, "Papa! papa! have I?" But it's of no use. Well, then mamma had to go out as a governess; she couldn't help it, poor thing! but she didn't much care for parting with me. I was a trouble, I daresay. So I was sent to a school at four years old; first one school, and then another; and, in the holidays, mamma went to stay at grand houses, and I was generally left with the schoolmistresses. Once I went to the Towers; and mamma lectured me continually, and yet I was very naughty, I believe. And so I never went again; and I was very glad of it, for it was a horrid place.'

'That it was!' said Molly, who remembered her own day of tribulation there.

'And once I went to London, to stay with my uncle Kirkpatrick. He is a lawyer, and getting on now; but then he was poor enough, and had six or seven children. It was winter-time, and we were all shut up in a small house in Doughty Street.* But, after all, that wasn't so bad.'

'But then you lived with your mother when she began school at
Ashcombe. Mr Preston told me that, when I stayed that day at the
Manor-house.'

'What did he tell you?' asked Cynthia, almost fiercely.

'Nothing but that. Oh, yes! He praised your beauty, and wanted
me to tell you what he had said.'

'I should have hated you if you had,' said Cynthia.

'Of course I never thought of doing such a thing,' replied Molly.
'I didn't like him; and Lady Harriet spoke of him the next day, as
if he wasn't a person to be liked.'

Cynthia was quite silent. At length she said –

'I wish I was good!'

'So do I,' said Molly simply. She was thinking again of Mrs
Hamley –

> Only the actions of the just
> Smell sweet and blossom in the dust;*

and 'goodness', just then, seemed to her to be the only enduring
thing in the world.

'Nonsense, Molly! You are good. At least, if you're not good,
what am I? There's a rule-of-three sum* for you to do! But it's no
use talking; I am not good, and I never shall be now. Perhaps I
might be a heroine still, but I shall never be a good woman, I
know.'

'Do you think it easier to be a heroine?'

'Yes, as far as one knows of heroines from history. I'm capable
of a great jerk, an effort, and then a relaxation – but steady,
every-day goodness is beyond me. I must be a moral kangaroo!'

Molly could not follow Cynthia's ideas; she could not distract
herself from the thoughts of the sorrowing group at the Hall.

'How I should like to see them all! and yet one can do nothing
at such a time! Papa says the funeral is to be on Tuesday, and
that, after that, Roger Hamley is to go back to Cambridge. It will
seem as if nothing had happened! I wonder how the Squire and
Mr Osborne Hamley will get on together.'

'He's the eldest son, is he not? Why shouldn't he and his father
get on well together?'

'Oh! I don't know. That is to say, I do know, but I think I
ought not to tell.'

'Don't be so pedantically truthful, Molly. Besides, your manner
shows when you speak truth and when you speak falsehood,

without troubling yourself to use words. I knew exactly what your "I don't know" meant. I never consider myself bound to be truthful; so I beg we may be on equal terms.'

Cynthia might well say she did not consider herself bound to be truthful; she literally said what came uppermost, without caring very much whether it was accurate or not. But there was no ill-nature, and, in a general way, no attempt at procuring any advantage for herself in all her deviations; and there was often such a latent sense of fun in them that Molly could not help being amused with them in fact, though she condemned them in theory. Cynthia's playfulness of manner glossed such failings over with a kind of charm; and yet, at times, she was so soft and sympathetic that Molly could not resist her, even when she affirmed the most startling things. The little account she made of her own beauty pleased Mr Gibson extremely; and her pretty deference to him won his heart. She was restless too, till she had attacked Molly's dress, after she had remodelled her mother's.

'Now for you, sweet one,' said she, as she began upon one of Molly's gowns. 'I've been working as connoisseur until now; now I begin as amateur.'

She brought down her pretty artificial flowers, plucked out of her own best bonnet to put into Molly's, saying they would suit her complexion, and that a knot of ribbons would do well enough for her. All the time she worked, she sang; she had a sweet voice in singing, as well as in speaking, and used to run up and down her gay French *chansons** without any difficulty; so flexible in the art was she. Yet she did not seem to care for music. She rarely touched the piano, on which Molly practised with daily conscientiousness. Cynthia was always willing to answer questions about her previous life, though, after the first, she rarely alluded to it of herself; but she was a most sympathetic listener to all Molly's innocent confidences of joys and sorrows: sympathising even to the extent of wondering how she could endure Mr Gibson's second marriage, and why she did not take some active steps of rebellion.

In spite of all this agreeable and pungent variety of companionship at home, Molly yearned after the Hamleys. If there had been a woman in that family, she would probably have received many little notes, and heard numerous details which were now lost to her, or summed up in condensed accounts of her father's visits at the Hall, which, since his dear patient was dead, were only occasional.

'Yes! The Squire is a good deal changed; but he's better than he was. There's an unspoken estrangement between him and Osborne; one can see it in the silence and constraint of their manners; but outwardly they are friendly – civil at any rate. The Squire will always respect Osborne as his heir, and the future representative of the family. Osborne doesn't look well; he says he wants change. I think he's weary of the domestic dulness, or domestic dissension. But he feels his mother's death acutely. It's a wonder that he and his father are not drawn together by their common loss. Roger's away at Cambridge too – examination for the mathematical tripos. Altogether the aspect of both people and place is changed; it is but natural!'

Such is perhaps the summing-up of the news of the Hamleys, as contained in many bulletins. They always ended in some kind message to Molly.

Mrs Gibson generally said, as a comment upon her husband's account of Osborne's melancholy –

'My dear! why don't you ask him to dinner here? A little quiet dinner, you know. Cook is quite up to it; and we would all of us wear blacks and lilacs; he couldn't consider that as gaiety.'

Mr Gibson took no more notice of these suggestions than by shaking his head. He had grown accustomed to his wife by this time, and regarded silence on his own part as a great preservative against long inconsequential arguments. But every time that Mrs Gibson was struck by Cynthia's beauty, she thought it more and more advisable that Mr Osborne Hamley should be cheered up by a quiet little dinner-party. As yet no one but the ladies of Hollingford and Mr Ashton, the vicar – that hopeless and impracticable old bachelor – had seen Cynthia; and what was the good of having a lovely daughter, if there were none but old women to admire her?

Cynthia herself appeared extremely indifferent upon the subject, and took very little notice of her mother's constant talk about the gaieties that were possible, and the gaieties that were impossible, in Hollingford. She exerted herself just as much to charm the two Miss Brownings as she would have done to delight Osborne Hamley, or any other young heir. That is to say, she used no exertion, but simply followed her own nature, which was to attract every one of those she was thrown amongst. The exertion seemed rather to be to refrain from doing so, and to protest, as she often did, by slight words and expressive looks against her mother's words and humours – alike against her folly and her caresses. Molly was almost sorry for Mrs Gibson, who seemed so unable to gain influence over her child. One day Cynthia read Molly's thought.

'I'm not good, and I told you so. Somehow, I cannot forgive her for her neglect of me as a child, when I would have clung to her. Besides, I hardly ever heard from her when I was at school. And I know she put a stop to my coming over to her wedding. I saw the letter she wrote to Madame Lefèbre. A child should be brought up with its parents, if it is to think them infallible when it grows up.'

'But, though it may know that there must be faults,' replied Molly, 'it ought to cover them over and try to forget their existence.'

'It ought. But, don't you see, I have grown up outside the pale of duty and "oughts". Love me as I am, sweet one; for I shall never be better.'

CHAPTER 20

Mrs Gibson's Visitors

One day, to Molly's infinite surprise, Mr Preston was announced as a caller. Mrs Gibson and she were sitting together in the drawing-room; Cynthia was out – gone into the town a-shopping – when the door was opened, the name given, and in walked the young man. His entrance seemed to cause more confusion than Molly could well account for. He came in with the same air of easy assurance with which he had received her and her father at Ashcombe Manor-house. He looked remarkably handsome in his riding-dress, and with the open-air exercise he had just had. But Mrs Gibson's smooth brows contracted a little at the sight of him, and her reception of him was much cooler than that which she usually gave to visitors. Yet there was a degree of agitation in it, which surprised Molly a little. Mrs Gibson was at her everlasting worsted-work frame when he entered the room; but, somehow, in rising to receive him, she threw down her basket of crewels,* and, declining Molly's offer to help her, she would pick up all the reels herself, before she asked her visitor to sit down. He stood there, hat in hand, affecting an interest in the recovery of the worsted which Molly was sure he did not feel; for all the time his eyes were glancing round the room, and taking note of the details in the arrangement.

At length they were seated, and conversation began.

'It is the first time I have been in Hollingford since your marriage, Mrs Gibson, or I should certainly have called to pay my respects sooner.'

'I know you are very busy at Ashcombe. I did not expect you to call. Is Lord Cumnor at the Towers? I have not heard from her ladyship for more than a week!'

'No! he seems still detained at Bath. But I had a letter from him giving me certain messages for Mr Sheepshanks. Mr Gibson is not at home, I'm afraid?'

'No. He is a great deal out – almost constantly, I may say. I had no idea that I should see so little of him. A doctor's wife leads a very solitary life, Mr Preston!'

'You can hardly call it solitary, I should think, when you have such a companion as Miss Gibson always at hand,' said he, bowing to Molly.

'Oh, but I call it solitude for a wife when her husband is away. Poor Mr Kirkpatrick was never happy, unless I always went with him; – in all his walks, all his visits, he liked me to be with him. But, somehow, Mr Gibson feels as if I should be rather in his way.'

'I don't think you could ride pillion behind him on Black Bess, mamma,' said Molly. 'And unless you could do that, you could hardly go with him in his rounds up and down all the rough lanes.'

'Oh! but he might keep a brougham!* I've often said so. And then I could use it for visiting in the evenings. Really it was one reason why I didn't go to the Hollingford Charity Ball. I couldn't bring myself to use the dirty fly from the Angel. We really must stir papa up against next winter, Molly; it will never do for you and' —

She pulled herself up suddenly, and looked furtively at Mr Preston, to see if he had taken any notice of her abruptness. Of course he had; but he was not going to show it. He turned to Molly, and said –

'Have you ever been to a public ball yet, Miss Gibson?'

'No!' said Molly.

'It will be a great pleasure to you, when the time comes.'

'I'm not sure. I shall like it, if I have plenty of partners; but I'm afraid I shan't know many people.'

'And you suppose that young men haven't their own ways and means of being introduced to pretty girls?'

It was exactly one of the speeches Molly had disliked him for before, and delivered, too, in that kind of under-bred manner which showed that it was meant to convey a personal compliment. Molly took great credit to herself for the unconcerned manner with which she went on with her tatting, exactly as if she had never heard it.

'I only hope I may be one of your partners at the first ball you go to. Pray remember my early application for that honour, when you are overwhelmed with requests for dances.'

'I don't choose to engage myself beforehand,' said Molly, perceiving, from under her dropped eyelids, that he was leaning forward and looking at her as though he was determined to have an answer.

'Young ladies are always very cautious in fact, however modest they may be in profession,' he replied, addressing himself in a nonchalant manner to Mrs Gibson. 'In spite of Miss Gibson's apprehension of not having many partners, she declines the certainty of having one. I suppose Miss Kirkpatrick will have returned from France before then?'

He said these last words exactly in the same tone as he had used before; but Molly's instinct told her that he was making an effort to do so. She looked up. He was playing with his hat, almost as if he did not care to have any answer to his question. Yet he was listening acutely, and with a half-smile on his face.

Mrs Gibson reddened a little, and hesitated –

'Yes; certainly. My daughter will be with us next winter, I believe; and I daresay she will go out with us.'

'Why can't she say at once that Cynthia is here now?' asked Molly of herself, yet glad that Mr Preston's curiosity was baffled.

He still smiled; but this time he looked up at Mrs Gibson, as he asked – 'You have good news from her, I hope?'

'Yes; very. By the way, how are our old friends the Robinsons? How often I think of their kindness to me at Ashcombe! Dear good people, I wish I could see them again.'

'I will certainly tell them of your kind inquiries. They are very well, I believe.'

Just at this moment, Molly heard the familiar sound of the click and opening of the front door. She knew it must be Cynthia; and, conscious of some mysterious reason which made Mrs Gibson wish to conceal her daughter's whereabouts from Mr Preston, and maliciously desirous to baffle him, she rose to leave the room, and meet Cynthia on the stairs; but one of the lost crewels of worsted had entangled itself in her gown and feet, and, before she had freed herself from the encumbrance, Cynthia had opened the drawing-room door, and stood in it, looking at her mother, at Molly, at Mr Preston, but not advancing one step. Her colour, which had been brilliant the first moment of her entrance, faded away as she gazed; but her eyes – her beautiful eyes – usually so soft and grave, seemed to fill with fire, and her brows to contract, as she took the resolution to come forward and take her place among the three, who were all looking at her with different emotions. She moved calmly and slowly forwards; Mr Preston went a step or two to meet her, his hand held out, and the whole expression of his face that of eager delight.

But she took no notice of the outstretched hand, nor of the chair that he offered her. She sate down on a little sofa in one of the windows, and called Molly to her.

'Look at my purchases!' said she. 'This green ribbon was fourteen-pence a yard, this silk three shillings,' and so she went on, forcing herself to speak about these trifles, as if they were all the world to her, and she had no attention to throw away on her mother and her mother's visitor.

Mr Preston took his cue from her. He, too, talked of the news of the day, the local gossip – but Molly, who glanced up at him from time to time, was almost alarmed by the bad expression of suppressed anger, nearly amounting to vindictiveness, which entirely marred his handsome looks. She did not wish to look again, and tried rather to back up Cynthia's efforts at maintaining a separate conversation. Yet she could not help overhearing Mrs Gibson's strain after increased civility, as if to make up for Cynthia's rudeness, and, if possible, to deprecate his anger. She talked perpetually, as though her object were to detain him; whereas, previous to Cynthia's return, she had allowed frequent pauses in the conversation, as if to give him the opportunity to take his leave.

In the course of the conversation between them, the Hamleys came up. Mrs Gibson was never unwilling to dwell upon Molly's intimacy with this county-family; and, when the latter caught the sound of her own name, her stepmother was saying –

'Poor Mrs Hamley could hardly do without Molly; she quite looked upon her as a daughter, especially towards the last, when, I am afraid, she had a good deal of anxiety. Mr Osborne Hamley – I daresay you have heard – he did not do so well at college, and they had expected so much – parents will, you know; but what did it signify? for he has not to earn his living! I call it a very foolish kind of ambition, when a young man has not to go into a profession.'

'Well, at any rate, the Squire must be satisfied now. I saw this morning's "Times", with the Cambridge examination lists in it. Isn't the second son called after his father, Roger?'

'Yes,' said Molly, starting up, and coming nearer.

'He's senior wrangler, that's all.' said Mr Preston, almost as though he were vexed with himself for having anything to say that could give her pleasure. Molly went back to her seat by Cynthia.

'Poor Mrs Hamley,' said she very softly, as if to herself. Cynthia took her hand, in sympathy with Molly's sad and tender look, rather than because she understood all that was passing in her mind; nor did Molly quite understand it herself. A death that had come out of time; a wonder whether the dead knew what passed upon the earth they had left – the brilliant Osborne's failure, Roger's success; the vanity of human wishes* – all these thoughts, and what they suggested, were inextricably mingled up in her mind. She came to herself in a few minutes. Mr Preston was saying all the unpleasant things he could think of about the Hamleys, in a tone of false sympathy.

'The poor old Squire – not the wisest of men – has woefully mismanaged his estate. And Osborne Hamley is too fine a gentleman to understand the means by which to improve the value of the land – even if he had the capital. A man who had practical knowledge of agriculture, and some thousands of ready money, might bring the rental up to eight thousand or so. Of course, Osborne will try and marry some one with money; the family is old and well-established, and he mustn't object to commercial descent, though I daresay the Squire will for him; but then the young fellow himself is not the man for the work. No! the family's going down fast; and it's a pity when these old Saxon houses vanish off the land; but it is "kismet"* with the Hamleys. Even the senior wrangler – if it is that Roger Hamley – he will have spent all his brains in one effort. You never hear of a senior wrangler being worth anything afterwards. He'll be a Fellow of his college, of course – that will be a livelihood for him, at any rate.'

'I believe in senior wranglers,' said Cynthia, her clear high voice ringing through the room. 'And from all I've ever heard of Mr Roger Hamley, I believe he will keep up the distinction he has earned. And I don't believe that the house of Hamley is so near extinction in wealth and fame, and good name.'

'They are fortunate in having Miss Kirkpatrick's good word,' said Mr Preston, rising to take his leave.

'Dear Molly,' said Cynthia, in a whisper, 'I know nothing about your friends the Hamleys, except that they are your friends, and what you have told me about them. But I won't have that man speaking of them so – and your eyes filling with tears all the time. I'd sooner swear to their having all the talents and good fortune under the sun.'

The only person of whom Cynthia appeared to be wholesomely afraid was Mr Gibson. When he was present, she was more careful in speaking, and showed more deference to her mother. Her evident respect for him, and desire to win his good opinion, made her curb herself before him; and in this manner she earned his favour as a lively, sensible girl, with just so much knowledge of the world as made her a very desirable companion for Molly. Indeed, she made something of the same kind of impression on all men. They were first struck with her personal appearance; and then with her pretty deprecating manner, which appealed to them much as if she had said, 'You are wise, and I am foolish – have mercy on my folly.' It was a way she had; it meant nothing really; and she was hardly conscious of it herself; but it was very captivating all the same. Even old Williams, the gardener, felt it; he said to his confidante, Molly –

'Eh, miss, but that be a rare young lady! She do have such pretty coaxing ways. I be to teach her to bud roses, come the season – and I'll warrant ye she'll learn sharp enough, for all she says she be's so stupid.'

If Molly had not had the sweetest disposition in the world, she might have become jealous of all the allegiance laid at Cynthia's feet; but she never thought of comparing the amount of admiration and love which they each received. Yet, once, she did feel a little as if Cynthia were poaching on her manor. The invitation to the quiet dinner had been sent to Osborne Hamley, and declined by him. But he thought it right to call soon afterwards. It was the first time Molly had seen any of the family since she left the Hall, just before Mrs Hamley's death; and there was so much that she wanted to ask. She tried to wait patiently till Mrs Gibson had exhausted the first gush of her infinite nothings; and then Molly came in with her modest questions. How was the Squire? Had he returned to his old habits? Had his health suffered? – putting each inquiry with as light and delicate a touch as if she had been dressing a wound. She hesitated a little, a very little, before speaking of Roger; for just one moment the thought flitted across her mind, that Osborne might feel the contrast between his own and his brother's college career too painfully to like to have it referred to; but then she remembered the generous brotherly love that had always existed between the two, and had just entered upon the subject, when Cynthia, in obedience to her mother's summons, came into the room, and took up her work. No one could have been quieter – she hardly uttered a word; but Osborne seemed to fall under her power at once. He no longer gave his undivided attention to Molly. He cut short his answers to her questions; and, by-and-by, without Molly's rightly understanding how it was, he had turned towards Cynthia, and was addressing himself to her. Molly saw the look of content on Mrs Gibson's face; perhaps it was her own mortification at not having heard all she wished to know about Roger, which gave her a keener insight than usual; but certain it is that all, at once, she perceived that Mrs Gibson would not dislike a marriage between Osborne and Cynthia, and considered the present occasion as an auspicious beginning. Remembering the secret which she had been let into so unwillingly, Molly watched his behaviour, almost as if she had been retained in the interest of the absent wife; but, after all, thinking as much of the possibility of his attracting Cynthia as of the unknown and mysterious Mrs Osborne Hamley. His manner was expressive of great interest and of strong prepossession in favour of the beautiful girl to whom he was talking. He was in deep mourning, which showed off his slight figure and delicate refined face. But there was nothing of flirting, as far as Molly understood the meaning of the word, in either looks or words.

Cynthia, too, was extremely quiet; she was always much quieter with men than with women; it was part of the charm of her soft allurement that she was so passive. They were talking of France. Mrs Gibson herself had passed two or three years of her girlhood there; and Cynthia's late return from Boulogne made it a very natural subject of conversation. But Molly was thrown out of it; and, with her heart still unsatisfied as to the details of Roger's success, she had to stand up at last, and receive Osborne's good-bye, scarcely longer or more intimate than his farewell to Cynthia. As soon as he was gone, Mrs Gibson began in his praise.

'Well, really, I begin to have some faith in long descent. What a gentleman he is! How agreeable and polite! So different from that forward Mr Preston,' she continued, looking a little anxiously at Cynthia. Cynthia, quite aware that her reply was being watched for, said coolly –

'Mr Preston doesn't improve on acquaintance. There was a time, mamma, when I think both you and I thought him very agreeable.'

'I don't remember. You've a clearer memory than I have. But we were talking of this delightful Mr Osborne Hamley. Why, Molly, you were always talking of his brother – it was Roger this, and Roger that – I can't think how it was you so seldom mentioned this young man.'

'I didn't know I had mentioned Mr Roger Hamley so often,' said Molly, blushing a little. 'But I saw much more of him – he was more at home.'

'Well, well! It's all right, my dear. I daresay he suits you best. But really, when I saw Osborne Hamley close to my Cynthia, I couldn't help thinking – but perhaps I'd better not tell you what I was thinking of. Only they are, each of them, so much above the average in appearance; and, of course, that suggests things.'

'I perfectly understand what you are thinking of, mamma,' said Cynthia, with the greatest composure; 'and so does Molly, I have no doubt.'

'Well! there's no harm in it, I'm sure. Did you hear him say that, though he did not like to leave his father alone just at present, yet, when his brother Roger came back from Cambridge, he should feel more at liberty! It was quite as much as to say, "If you will ask me to dinner then, I shall be delighted to come." And chickens will be so much cheaper, and cook has such a nice way of boning them, and doing them up with force-meat.* Everything seems to be falling out so fortunately. And Molly, my dear, you know I won't forget you. By-and-by, when Roger Hamley has taken his turn at stopping at home with his father, we will ask him to one of our little quiet dinners.'

Molly was very slow at taking this in; but in about a minute the sense of it had reached her brain, and she went all over very red and hot; especially as she saw that Cynthia was watching the light come into her mind with great amusement.

'I'm afraid Molly isn't properly grateful, mamma. If I were you, I wouldn't exert myself to give a dinner-party on her account. Bestow all your kindness upon me.'

Molly was often puzzled by Cynthia's speeches to her mother; and this was one of these occasions. But she was more anxious to say something for herself; she was so much annoyed at the implication in Mrs Gibson's last words.

'Mr Roger Hamley has been very good to me; he was a great deal at home when I was there, and Mr Osborne Hamley was very little there; that was the reason I spoke so much more of one than the other. If I had – if he had,' – losing her coherence in the difficulty of finding words – 'I don't think I should – oh, Cynthia, instead of laughing at me, I think you might help me to explain myself!'

Instead, Cynthia gave a diversion to the conversation.

'Mamma's paragon gives me an idea of weakness. I can't quite make out whether it's in body or mind. Which is it, Molly?'

'He's not strong, I know; but he's very accomplished and clever. Every one says that – even papa, who doesn't generally praise young men. That made the puzzle the greater, when he did so badly at college.'

'Then it's his character that is weak. I'm sure there's weakness somewhere; but he's very agreeable. It must have been very pleasant, staying at the Hall.'

'Yes, but it's all over now.'

'Oh, nonsense!' said Mrs Gibson, wakening up from counting the stitches in her pattern. 'We shall have the young men coming to dinner pretty often, you'll see. Your father likes them, and I shall always make a point of welcoming his friends. They can't go on mourning for a mother for ever. I expect we shall see a great deal of them, and that the two families will become very intimate. After all, these good Hollingford people are terribly behindhand and, I should say, rather common-place.'

CHAPTER 21

The Half-Sisters

It appeared as if Mrs Gibson's predictions were likely to be verified; for Osborne Hamley found his way to her drawing-room pretty frequently. To be sure, sometimes prophets can help on the fulfilment of their own prophecies; and Mrs Gibson was not passive.

Molly was altogether puzzled by his manners and ways. He spoke of occasional absences from the Hall, without exactly saying where he had been. But that was not her idea of the conduct of a married man; who, she imagined, ought to have a house and servants, and pay rent and taxes, and live with his wife. Who this mysterious wife might be, faded into insignificance before the wonder of where she was. London, Cambridge, Dover, nay, even France, were mentioned by him as places to which he had been on these different little journeys. These facts came out quite casually, almost as if he was unaware of what he was betraying. Sometimes he dropped out such sentences as these: – 'Ah, that would be the day I was crossing! It was stormy indeed! Instead of our being only two hours, we were nearly five.' Or, 'I met Lord Hollingford at Dover last week, and he said,' etc. 'The cold now is nothing to what it was in London on Thursday – the thermometer was down at 15°.' Perhaps, in the rapid flow of conversation, these small revelations were noticed by no one but Molly; whose interest and curiosity were always hovering over the secret she had become possessed of, in spite of all her self-reproach for allowing her thoughts to dwell on what was still to be kept as a mystery.

It was also evident to her that Osborne was not too happy at home. He had lost the slight touch of cynicism which he had affected when he was expected to do wonders at college; and that was one good result of his failure. If he did not give himself the trouble of appreciating other people and their performances, at any rate his conversation was not so amply sprinkled with critical pepper. He was more absent, not so agreeable, Mrs Gibson thought, but did not say. He looked ill in health; but that might be the consequence of the real depression of spirits which Molly occasionally saw peeping out through all his pleasant surface-talk. Now and then, when he was talking directly to her, he referred to 'the happy days that are gone' or 'to the time when my mother was alive'; and then his voice sank, and a gloom came over his countenance, and Molly longed to express her own deep sympathy. He did not often mention his father; and Molly thought she could read in his manner, when he did, that something of the painful restraint she had noticed, when she was last at the Hall, still existed between them. Nearly every particular she knew of the family interior she had heard from Mrs Hamley, and she was uncertain how far her father was acquainted with them; so she did not like to question him too closely; nor was he a man to be so questioned as to the domestic affairs of his patients. Sometimes she wondered if it was a dream – that short half-hour in the library at Hamley Hall – when she had learnt a fact which seemed so all-important to Osborne, yet which made so little difference in his way of life – either in speech or action. During the twelve or fourteen hours that she had remained at the Hall afterwards, no further allusion had been made to his marriage, either by himself or by Roger. It was, indeed, very like a dream. Probably Molly would have been rendered much more uncomfortable in the possession of her secret, if Osborne had struck her as particularly attentive in his devotion to Cynthia. She evidently amused and attracted him, but not in any lively or passionate kind of way. He admired her beauty, and seemed to feel her charm; but he would leave her side, and come to sit near Molly, if anything reminded him of his mother, about which he could talk to her, and to her alone. Yet he came so often to the Gibsons', that Mrs Gibson might be excused for the fancy she had taken into her head, that it was for Cynthia's sake. He liked the lounge, the friendliness, the company of two intelligent girls of beauty and manners above the average; one of whom stood in a peculiar relation to him, as having been especially beloved by the mother whose memory he cherished so fondly. Knowing himself to be out of the category of bachelors, he was, perhaps, too indifferent as to other people's ignorance and its possible consequences.

Somehow, Molly did not like to be the first to introduce Roger's name into the conversation; so she lost many an opportunity of hearing intelligence about him. Osborne was often so languid or so absent that he only followed the lead of talk; and, as an awkward fellow, who had paid her no particular attention, and, as a second son, Roger was not pre-eminent in Mrs Gibson's thoughts; Cynthia had never seen him, and the freak did not take her often to speak about him. He had not come home since he had obtained his high place in the mathematical lists; that Molly knew; and she knew, too, that he was working hard for something – she supposed a fellowship – and that was all. Osborne's tone in speaking of him was always the same: every word, every inflection of the voice breathed out affection and respect – nay, even admiration! And this from the *nil admirari** brother, who seldom carried his exertions so far!

'Ah, Roger!' he said one day. Molly caught the name in an instant, though she had not heard what had gone before. 'He is a fellow in a thousand – in a thousand, indeed! I don't believe there is his match anywhere, for goodness and real solid power combined.'

'Molly,' said Cynthia, after Mr Osborne Hamley had gone, 'what sort of a man is this Roger Hamley? One can't tell how much to believe of his brother's praises; for it is the one subject on which Osborne Hamley becomes enthusiastic. I've noticed it once or twice before.'

While Molly hesitated on which point of the large round to begin her description, Mrs Gibson struck in –

'It just shows what a sweet disposition Osborne Hamley is of – that he should praise his brother as he does. I daresay he is a senior wrangler, and much good may it do him – I don't deny that; but, as for conversation, he's as heavy as heavy can be. A great awkward fellow, to boot, who looks as if he did not know two and two made four, for all he is such a mathematical genius. You would hardly believe he was Osborne Hamley's brother, to see him! I should not think he has a profile at all.'

'What do you think of him, Molly?' said the persevering Cynthia.

'I like him,' said Molly. 'He has been very kind to me. I know he isn't handsome like Osborne.'

It was rather difficult to say all this quietly; but Molly managed to do it, quite aware that Cynthia would not rest till she had extracted some kind of an opinion out of her.

'I suppose he will come home at Easter,' said Cynthia, 'and then I shall see him for myself.'

'It's a great pity that their being in mourning will prevent their going to the Easter charity-ball,' said Mrs Gibson plaintively. 'I shan't like to take you two girls, if you are not to have any partners. It will put me in such an awkward position. I wish we could join on to the Towers party. That would secure you partners; for they always bring a number of dancing men, who might dance with you after they had done their duty by the ladies of the house. But really everything is so changed since dear Lady Cumnor has been an invalid, that, perhaps, they won't go at all.'

This Easter ball was a great subject of conversation with Mrs Gibson. She sometimes spoke of it as her first appearance in society as a bride, though she had been visiting once or twice a week all winter long. Then she shifted her ground, and said she felt so much interest in it, because she would then have the responsibility of introducing both her own and Mr Gibson's daughter to public notice, though the fact was that pretty nearly every one who was going to this ball had seen the two young ladies – though not their ball-dresses – before. But, aping the manners of the aristocracy as far as she knew them, she intended to 'bring out' Molly and Cynthia on this occasion, which she regarded in something of the light of a presentation at Court. 'They are not out yet', was her favourite excuse, when either of them was invited to any house to which she did not wish them to go, or when they were invited without her. She even made a difficulty about their 'not being out', when Miss Browning – that old friend of the Gibson family – came in one morning to ask the two girls to come to a friendly tea and a round game afterwards; this mild piece of gaiety being designed as an attention to three of Mrs Goodenough's grandchildren – two young ladies and their school-boy brother – who were staying on a visit to their grandmamma.

'You are very kind, Miss Browning; but, you see, I hardly like to let them go – they are not out, you know, till after the Easter ball.'

'Till when we are invisible,' said Cynthia, always ready with her mockery to exaggerate any pretension of her mother's. 'We are so high in rank that our sovereign must give us her sanction, before we can play a round-game at your house.'

Cynthia enjoyed the idea of her own full-grown size and stately gait, as contrasted with that of a meek, half-fledged girl in the nursery; but Miss Browning was half-puzzled and half-affronted.

'I don't understand it at all. In my days, girls went wherever it pleased people to ask them, without this farce of bursting out in all their new fine clothes at some public place. I don't mean but what the gentry took their daughters to York, or to Matlock,* or Bath, to give them a taste of gay society when they were growing up; and the quality went up to London, and their young ladies were presented to Queen Charlotte,* and went to a birth-day ball, perhaps. But for us little Hollingford people – why, we knew every child amongst us from the day of its birth; and many a girl of twelve or fourteen have I seen go out to a card-party, and sit quiet at her work, and know how to behave as well as any lady there. There was no talk of "coming out" in those days for any one under the daughter of a Squire.'

'After Easter, Molly and I shall know how to behave at a card-party, but not before,' said Cynthia demurely.

'You're always fond of your quips and your cranks,* my dear,' said Miss Browning, 'and I wouldn't quite answer for your behaviour; you sometimes let your spirits carry you away. But I'm quite sure Molly will be a little lady as she always is, and always was, and I have known her from a babe.'

Mrs Gibson took up arms on behalf of her own daughter, or, rather, she took up arms against Molly's praises.

'I don't think you would have called Molly a lady the other day, Miss Browning, if you had found her where I did: sitting up in a cherry-tree, six feet from the ground at least, I do assure you.'

'Oh! but that wasn't pretty,' said Miss Browning, shaking her head at Molly. 'I thought you'd left off those tom-boy ways.'

'She wants the refinement which good society gives in several ways,' said Mrs Gibson, returning to the attack on poor Molly. 'She's very apt to come upstairs two steps at a time.'

'Only two, Molly?' said Cynthia. 'Why, today I found I could manage four of these broad, shallow steps.'

'My dear child, what are you saying?'

'Only confessing that I, like Molly, want the refinements which good society gives; therefore, please do let us go to the Miss Brownings' this evening. I will pledge myself for Molly that she shan't sit in a cherry-tree; and Molly shall see that I don't go upstairs in an unladylike way. I will go upstairs as meekly as if I were a come-out young lady, and had been to the Easter ball.'

So it was agreed that they should go. If Mr Osborne Hamley had been named as one of the probable visitors, there would have been none of this difficulty about the affair.

But, though he was not there, his brother Roger was. Molly

saw him in a minute, when she entered the little drawing-room; but Cynthia did not.

'And see, my dears,' said Miss Phoebe Browning, turning them round to the side where Roger stood, waiting for his turn of speaking to Molly; 'we've got a gentleman for you after all! Wasn't it fortunate? – just as sister said that you might find it dull – you, Cynthia, she meant, because you know you come from France – then, just as if he had been sent from heaven, Mr Roger came in to call; and I won't say we laid violent hands on him, because he was too good for that; but really we should have been near it, if he had not stayed of his own accord.'

The moment Roger had done his cordial greeting to Molly, he asked her to introduce him to Cynthia.

'I want to know her – your new sister,' he added, with the kind smile that Molly remembered so well, since the very first day she had seen it directed towards her, as she sate crying under the weeping-ash. Cynthia was standing a little behind Molly, when Roger asked for this introduction. She was generally dressed with careless grace. Molly, who was delicate neatness itself, used sometimes to wonder how Cynthia's tumbled gowns, tossed away so untidily, had the art of looking so well, and falling in such graceful folds. For instance, the pale lilac muslin gown she wore this evening had been worn many times before, and had looked unfit to wear again till Cynthia put it on. Then the limpness became softness, and the very creases took the lines of beauty. Molly, in a daintily clean pink muslin, did not look half so elegantly dressed as Cynthia. The grave eyes that the latter raised, when she had to be presented to Roger, had a sort of childlike innocence and wonder about them, which did not quite belong to Cynthia's character. She put on her armour of magic that evening – involuntarily, as she always did; but, on the other side, she could not help trying her power on strangers. Molly had always felt that she should have a right to a good long talk with Roger, when she next saw him, and that he would tell her, or she should gather from him, all the details she so longed to hear about the Squire – about the Hall – about Osborne – about himself. He was just as cordial and friendly as ever with her. If Cynthia had not been there, all would have gone on as she had anticipated; but of all the victims to Cynthia's charms he fell most prone and abject. Molly saw it all, as she was sitting next to Miss Phoebe at the tea-table, acting right-hand, and passing cake, cream, sugar, with such

busy assiduity that every one besides herself thought that her
mind, as well as her hands, was fully occupied. She tried to talk
to the two shy girls, as in virtue of her two years' seniority she
thought herself bound to do; and the consequence was, she went
upstairs with the twain clinging to her arms, and willing to swear
an eternal friendship. Nothing would satisfy them but that she
must sit between them at vingt-un;* and they were so desirous of
her advice in the important point of fixing the price of the counters
that she could not ever have joined in the animated conversation
going on between Roger and Cynthia. Or, rather, it would be
more correct to say that Roger was talking in a most animated
manner to Cynthia, whose sweet eyes were fixed upon his face
with a look of great interest in all he was saying, while it was only
now and then that she made her low replies. Molly caught a few
words occasionally in intervals of business.

'At my uncle's, we always give a silver threepence* for three
dozen. You know what a silver threepence is, don't you, dear
Miss Gibson?'

'The three classes are published in the Senate-House at nine
o'clock on the Friday morning, and you can't imagine'—

'I think it will be thought rather shabby to play at anything less
than sixpence. That gentleman' (this in a whisper) 'is at Cambridge, and you know they always play very high there, and
sometimes ruin themselves, don't they, dear Miss Gibson?'

'Oh, on this occasion, the Master of Arts who precedes the
candidates for honours, when they go into the Senate House, is
called the Father of the College to which he belongs. I think I
mentioned that before, didn't I?'

So Cynthia was hearing all about Cambridge, and the very
examination about which Molly had felt such keen interest,
without having ever been able to have her questions answered by
a competent person; and Roger, to whom she had always looked
as the final and most satisfactory answerer, was telling the whole
of what she wanted to know, and she could not listen. It took all
her patience to make up little packets of counters, and settle, as
the arbiter of the game, whether it would be better for the round
or the oblong counters to be reckoned as six. And, when all was
done, and every one sate in their places round the table, Roger
and Cynthia had to be called twice before they came. They stood
up, it is true, at the first sound of their names; but they did not
move – Roger went on talking, Cynthia listening, till the second

call; when they hurried to the table and tried to appear, all on a sudden, quite interested in the great questions of the game – namely, the price of three dozen counters, and whether, all things considered, it would be better to call the round counters or the oblong half-a-dozen each. Miss Browning, drumming the pack of cards on the table, and quite ready to begin dealing, decided the matter by saying, 'Rounds are sixes, and three dozen counters cost sixpence. Pay up, if you please, and let us begin at once!' Cynthia sate between Roger and William Orford, the young school-boy, who bitterly resented on this occasion his sisters' habit of calling him 'Willie', as he thought it was this boyish sobriquet which prevented Cynthia from attending as much to him as to Mr Roger Hamley; he also was charmed by the charmer, who found leisure to give him one or two of her sweet smiles. On his return home to his grandmamma's, he gave out one or two very decided and rather original opinions, quite opposed – as was natural – to his sisters'. One was –

'That, after all, a senior wrangler was no great shakes.* Any man might be one if he liked; but there were a lot of fellows that he knew who would be very sorry to go in for anything so slow.'

Molly thought the game never would end. She had no particular turn for gambling in her; and, whatever her card might be, she regularly put on two counters, indifferent as to whether she won or lost. Cynthia, on the contrary, staked high, and was at one time very rich, but ended by being in debt to Molly something like six shillings. She had forgotten her purse, she said, and was obliged to borrow from the more provident Molly; who was aware that the round-game of which Miss Browning had spoken to her was likely to require money. If it was not a very merry affair for all the individuals concerned, it was a very noisy one on the whole. Molly thought it was going to last till midnight; but punctually, as the clock struck nine, the little maid-servant staggered in under the weight of a tray, loaded with sandwiches, cakes, and jelly. This brought on a general move; and Roger, who appeared to have been on the watch for something of the kind, came and took a chair by Molly.

'I am so glad to see you again – it seems such a long time since Christmas,' said he, dropping his voice, and not referring exactly to the day when she had left the Hall.

'It is a long time,' she replied; 'we are close to Easter now. I have so wanted to tell you how glad I was to hear about your honours at Cambridge. I once thought of sending you a message through your brother; but then I thought it might be making too much fuss, because I know nothing of mathematics, or of the value of a senior wranglership; and you were sure to have so many congratulations from people who did know.'

'I missed yours, though, Molly,' said he kindly. 'But I felt sure you were glad for me.'

'Glad and proud too,' she said. 'I should so like to hear something more about it. I heard you telling Cynthia'—

'Yes. What a charming person she is! I should think you must be happier than we expected long ago.'

'But tell me something about the senior wranglership, please,' said Molly.

'It's a long story, and I ought to be helping the Miss Brownings to hand sandwiches – besides, you wouldn't find it very interesting, it's so full of technical details.'

'Cynthia looked very much interested,' said Molly.

'Well! then I refer you to her, for I must go now. I can't for shame go on sitting here, and letting those good ladies have all the trouble. But I shall come and call on Mrs Gibson soon. Are you walking home tonight?'

'Yes, I think so,' replied Molly, eagerly foreseeing what was to come.

'Then I shall walk home with you. I left my horse at the Angel, and that's half-way. I suppose old Betty will allow me to accompany you and your sister? You used to describe her as something of a dragon.'

'Betty has left us,' said Molly sadly. 'She's gone to live at a place at Ashcombe.'

He made a face of dismay, and then went off to his duties. The short conversation had been very pleasant, and his manner had had just the brotherly kindness of old times; but it was not quite the manner he had to Cynthia; and Molly half-thought she would have preferred the latter. He was now hovering about Cynthia, who had declined the offer of refreshments from Willie Orford. Roger was tempting her, and with playful entreaties urging her to take something from him. Every word they said could be heard by the whole room; yet every word was said, on Roger's part at least, as if he could not have spoken it in that peculiar manner to any one else. At length, and rather more because she was weary of being entreated, than because it was his wish, Cynthia took a macaroon, and Roger seemed as happy as though she had crowned him with flowers. The whole affair was as trifling and commonplace as could be in itself; hardly worth noticing; and yet Molly did notice it, and felt uneasy; she could not tell why. As it turned out, it was a rainy night, and Mrs Gibson sent a fly for the two girls instead of old Betty's substitute. Both Cynthia and Molly thought of the possibility of their taking the two Orford girls back to their grandmother's, and so saving them a wet walk; but Cynthia got the start in speaking about it; and the thanks and the implied praise for thoughtfulness were hers.

When they got home, Mr and Mrs Gibson were sitting in the drawing-room, quite ready to be amused by any details of the evening.

Cynthia began –

'Oh! it wasn't very entertaining. One didn't expect that,' and she yawned wearily.

'Who were there?' asked Mr Gibson. 'Quite a young party – wasn't it?'

'They'd only asked Lizzie and Fanny Orford, and their brother; but Mr Roger Hamley had ridden over and called on the Miss Brownings, and they kept him to tea. No one else.'

'Roger Hamley there!' said Mr Gibson. 'He's come home then. I must make time to ride over and see him.'

'You'd much better ask him here,' said Mrs Gibson. 'Suppose you invite him and his brother to dine here on Friday, my dear. It would be a very pretty attention, I think.'

'My dear! these young Cambridge men have a very good taste in wine, and don't spare it. My cellar won't stand many of their attacks.'

'I didn't think you were so inhospitable, Mr Gibson.'

'I'm not inhospitable, I'm sure. If you'll put "bitter-beer" in the corner of your notes of invitation, just as the smart people put "quadrilles" as a sign of the entertainment offered, we'll have Osborne and Roger to dinner any day you like. And what did you think of my favourite, Cynthia? You hadn't seen him before, I think?'

'Oh! he's nothing like so handsome as his brother; nor so polished; nor so easy to talk to. He entertained me for more than an hour with a long account of some examination or other; but there's something one likes about him.'

'Well – and Molly,' said Mrs Gibson, who piqued herself on

being an impartial stepmother, and who always tried hard to make Molly talk as much as Cynthia – 'what sort of an evening have you had?'

'Very pleasant, thank you.' Her heart a little belied her, as she said this. She had not cared for the round-game; and she would have cared for Roger's conversation. She had had what she was indifferent to, and not had what she would have liked.

'We've had our unexpected visitor, too,' said Mr Gibson. 'Just after dinner, who should come in but Mr Preston! I fancy he's having more of the management of the Hollingford property than formerly. Sheepshanks is getting an old man. And, if so, I suspect we shall see a good deal of Preston. He's "no blate",* as they used to say in Scotland, and made himself quite at home tonight. If I'd asked him to stay, or, indeed, if I'd done anything but yawn, he'd have been here now. But I defy any man to stay, when I've a fit of yawning.'

'Do you like Mr Preston, papa?' asked Molly.

'About as much as I do half the men I meet. He talks well, and has seen a good deal. I know very little of him, though; except that he's my lord's steward, which is a guarantee for a good deal.'

'Lady Harriet spoke pretty strongly against him, that day I was with her at the Manor-house.'

'Lady Harriet's always full of fancies; she likes persons today, and dislikes them tomorrow,' said Mrs Gibson, who was touched on her sore point, whenever Molly quoted Lady Harriet, or said anything to imply ever so transitory an intimacy with her.

'You must know a good deal about Mr Preston, my dear. I suppose you saw a good deal of him at Ashcombe?'

Mrs Gibson coloured, and looked at Cynthia before she replied. Cynthia's face was set into a determination not to speak, however much she might be referred to.

'Yes; we saw a good deal of him – at one time, I mean. He's changeable, I think. But he always sent us game, and sometimes fruit. There were some stories against him, but I never believed them.'

'What kind of stories?' said Mr Gibson quickly.

'Oh, vague stories, you know; scandal, I daresay. No one ever believed them. He could be so agreeable, if he chose; and my lord, who is so very particular, would never have kept him as agent, if they were true; not that I ever knew what they were, for I consider all scandal as abominable gossip.'

'I'm very glad I yawned in his face,' said Mr Gibson. 'I hope he'll take the hint.'

'If it was one of your giant-gapes, papa, I should call it more than a hint,' said Molly. 'And if you want a yawning chorus the next time he comes, I'll join in; won't you, Cynthia?'

'I don't know,' replied the latter shortly, as she lighted her bed-candle. The two girls had usually some nightly conversation in one or other of their bed-rooms; but tonight Cynthia said some-thing or other about being terribly tired, and hastily shut her door.

The very next day, Roger came to pay his promised call. Molly was out in the garden with Williams, planning the arrangement of some new flower-beds, and deep in her employment of placing pegs upon the lawn to mark out the different situations, when, standing up to mark the effect, her eye was caught by the figure of a gentleman, sitting with his back to the light, leaning forwards, and talking, or listening, eagerly. Molly knew the shape of the head perfectly, and hastily began to put off her brown-holland gardening apron, emptying the pockets as she spoke to Williams.

'You can finish it now, I think,' said she. 'You know about the bright-coloured flowers being against the privet-hedge, and where the new rose-bed is to be?'

'I can't justly say as I do,' said he. 'Mebbe, you'll just go o'er it all once again, Miss Molly! I'm not so young as I onest was, and my head is not so clear now-a-days, and I'd be loath to make mistakes, when you're so set upon your plans.'

Molly gave up her impulse in a moment. She saw that the old gardener was really perplexed, yet that he was as anxious as he could be to do his best. So she went over the ground again, pegging and explaining till the wrinkled brow was smooth again, and he kept saying, 'I see, miss. All right, Miss Molly; I'se getten it in my head as clear as patch-work now.'

So she could leave him, and go in. But, just as she was close to the garden door, Roger came out. It really was for once a case of virtue its own reward, for it was far pleasanter to her to have him in a *tête-à-tête*, however short, than in the restraint of Mrs Gibson's and Cynthia's presence.

'I only just found out where you were, Molly. Mrs Gibson said you had gone out, but she didn't know where; and it was the greatest chance that I turned round and saw you.'

'I saw you some time ago, but I couldn't leave Williams. I think he was unusually slow today; and he seemed as if he couldn't understand my plans for the new flower-beds.'

'Is that the paper you've got in your hand? Let me look at it, will you? Ah, I see! you've borrowed some of your ideas from our garden at home, haven't you? This bed of scarlet geraniums, with the border of young oaks, pegged down? That was a fancy of my dear mother's.'

They were both silent for a minute or two. Then Molly said –

'How is the Squire? I've never seen him since.'

'No; he told me how much he wanted to see you, but he couldn't make up his mind to come and call. I suppose it would never do now for you to come and stay at the Hall, would it? It would give my father so much pleasure – he looks upon you as a daughter; and I'm sure both Osborne and I shall always consider you are like a sister to us, after all my mother's love for you, and your tender care of her at the last. But I suppose it wouldn't do?'

'No! certainly not,' said Molly hastily.

'I fancy, if you could come, it would put us a little to rights. You know, as I think I once told you, Osborne has behaved differently to what I should have done, though not wrongly – only what I call an error of judgment. But my father, I'm sure, has taken up some notion of—never mind; only the end of it is that he holds Osborne still in tacit disgrace, and is miserable himself all the time. Osborne, too, is sore and unhappy, and estranged from my father. It is just what my mother would have put right very soon, and perhaps you could have done it – unconsciously, I mean – for this wretched mystery that Osborne preserves about his affairs is at the root of it all. But there's no use talking about it; I don't know why I began.' Then, with a wrench, changing the subject, while Molly still thought of what he had been telling her, he broke out – 'I can't tell you how much I like Miss Kirkpatrick, Molly. It must be a great pleasure to you, having such a companion!'

'Yes,' said Molly, half-smiling. 'I'm very fond of her, and I think I like her better every day I know her. But how quickly you have found out her virtues!'

'I didn't say "virtues", did I?' asked he, reddening, but putting the question in all good faith. 'Yet I don't think one could be deceived in that face. And Mrs Gibson appears to be a very friendly person – she has asked Osborne and me to dine here on Friday.'

'Bitter-beer' came into Molly's mind; but what she said was, 'And are you coming?'

'Certainly, I am, unless my father wants me; and I've given Mrs Gibson a conditional promise for Osborne, too. So I shall see you all very soon again. But I must go now. I have to keep an appointment, seven miles from here, in half-an-hour's time. Good luck to your flower-garden, Molly!'

CHAPTER 22

The Old Squire's Troubles

Affairs were going on worse at the Hall than Roger had liked to tell. Moreover, very much of the discomfort there arose from 'mere manner', as people express it, which is always indescribable and indefinable. Quiet and passive as Mrs Hamley had always been in appearance, she was the ruling spirit of the house, as long as she lived. The directions to the servants, down to the most minute particulars, came from her sitting-room, or from the sofa on which she lay. Her children always knew where to find her; and to find her, was to find love and sympathy. Her husband, who was often restless and angry from one cause or another, always came to her to be smoothed down and put right. He was conscious of her pleasant influence over him, and became at peace with himself when in her presence; just as a child is at ease, when with some one who is both firm and gentle. But the keystone of the family arch was gone, and the stones of which it was composed began to fall apart. It is always sad, when a sorrow of this kind seems to injure the character of the mourning survivors. Yet, perhaps, this injury may be only temporary or superficial; the judgments so constantly passed upon the way in which people bear the loss of those whom they have deeply loved appear to be even more cruel, and wrongly meted out, than human judgments generally are. To careless observers, for instance, it would seem as though the Squire was rendered more capricious and exacting, more passionate and authoritative, by his wife's death. The truth was, that it occurred at a time when many things came to harass him, and some to bitterly disappoint him; and *she* was no longer there to whom he used to carry his sore heart for the gentle balm of her sweet words, if the sore heart ached and smarted intensely; and often, when he saw how his violent conduct affected others, he could have cried out for their pity, instead of their anger and resentment: 'Have mercy upon me, for I am very miserable!'* How often have such dumb thoughts gone up, from the hearts of those who have taken hold of their sorrow by the wrong end, as prayers against sin! And, when the Squire saw that his servants were learning to dread him, and his first-born to avoid him, he did not blame them. He knew he was becoming a domestic tyrant; it seemed as if all circumstances conspired against him, and as if he was too weak to struggle with them; else, why did everything indoors and out-of-doors go so wrong just now, when all he could have done, had things been prosperous, was to have submitted, in very imperfect patience, to the loss of his wife! But, just when he needed ready money to pacify Osborne's creditors, the harvest had turned out remarkably plentiful, and the price of corn had sunk down to a level it had not touched for years. The Squire had insured his life at the time of his marriage for a pretty large sum. It was to be a provision for his wife, if she survived him, and for their younger children. Roger was the only representative of these interests now; but the Squire was unwilling to lose the insurance by ceasing to pay the annual sum. He would not, if he could, have sold any part of the estate which he inherited from his father; and, besides, it was strictly entailed. He had sometimes thought how wise a step it would have been, could he have sold a portion of it, and with the purchase-money have drained and reclaimed the remainder; and at length, learning from some neighbour that Government would make certain advances for drainage, etc., at a very low rate of interest, on condition that the work was done, and the money repaid, within a given time, his wife had induced him to take advantage of the proffered loan. But, now that she was no longer there to encourage him, and take an interest in the progress of the work, he grew indifferent to it himself, and cared no more to go out on his stout roan cob, and sit square on his seat, watching the labourers on the marshy land, all overgrown with rushes; speaking to them from time to time in their own strong, nervous* country dialect; but the interest to Government had to be paid all the same, whether the men worked well or ill. Then the roof of the Hall let in the melted snow-water this winter; and, on examination it turned out that a new roof was absolutely requisite. The men who had come about the advances made to

Osborne by the London money lender had spoken disparagingly of the timber on the estate – 'Very fine trees – sound, perhaps, too, fifty years ago, but gone to rot now; had wanted lopping and clearing. Was there no wood-ranger or forester? They were nothing like the value young Mr Hamley had represented them to be.' The remarks had come round to the Squire's ears. He loved the trees he had played under as a boy, as if they were living creatures; that was on the romantic side of his nature. Merely looking at them as representing so many pounds sterling, he had esteemed them highly, and had had, until now, no opinion of another by which to correct his own judgment. So these words of the valuers cut him sharp, although he affected to disbelieve them, and tried to persuade himself that he did so. But, after all, these cares and disappointments did not touch the root of his deep resentment against Osborne. There is nothing like wounded affection for giving poignancy to anger. And the Squire believed that Osborne and his advisers had been making calculations, based upon his own death. He hated the idea so much – it made him so miserable – that he would not face it, and define it, and meet it with full inquiry and investigation. He chose rather to cherish the morbid fancy that he was useless in this world – born under an unlucky star – that all things went badly under his management. But he did not become humble in consequence. He put his misfortunes down to the score of Fate – not to his own; and he imagined that Osborne saw his failures, and that his first-born grudged him his natural term of life. All these fancies would have been set to rights, could he have talked them over with his wife; or even, had he been accustomed to mingle much in the society of those whom he esteemed his equals; but, as has been stated, he was inferior in education to those who should have been his mates; and perhaps the jealousy and *mauvaise honte*,* that this inferiority had called out long ago, extended itself in some measure to the feelings he entertained towards his sons – less to Roger than to Osborne, though the former was turning out by far the more distinguished man. But Roger was practical; interested in all out-of-door things; and he enjoyed the details, homely enough, which his father sometimes gave him of the every-day occurrences which the latter had noticed in the woods and the fields. Osborne, on the contrary, was, what is commonly called 'fine'; delicate almost to effeminacy in dress and in manner; careful in small observances. All this his father had been rather proud of in the

days when he looked forward to a brilliant career at Cambridge
for his son; he had, at that time, regarded Osborne's fastidiousness
and elegance as another stepping-stone to the high and prosperous
marriage which was to restore the ancient fortunes of the Hamley
family. But now that Osborne had barely obtained his degree; that
all the boastings of his father had proved vain; that the fastidiousness had led to unexpected expenses (to attribute the most innocent cause to Osborne's debts) – the poor young man's ways and
manners became a subject of irritation to his father. Osborne was
still occupied with his books and his writings, when he was at
home; and this mode of passing the greater part of the day gave
him but few subjects in common with his father, when they did
meet at meal-times, or in the evenings. Perhaps, if Osborne had
been able to have more out-of-door amusements it would have
been better; but he was short-sighted, and cared little for the
carefully observant pursuits of his brother; he knew but few young
men of his own standing in the county; his hunting even, of which
he was passionately fond, had been curtailed this season, as his
father had disposed of one of the two hunters he had been hitherto
allowed. The whole stable-establishment had been reduced; perhaps because it was the economy which told most on the enjoyment of both the Squire and Osborne, and which, therefore, the
former took a savage pleasure in enforcing. The old carriage – a
heavy family-coach bought in the days of comparative prosperity
– was no longer needed after Madam's death, and fell to pieces in
the cobwebbed seclusion of the coach-house. The best of the two
carriage-horses was taken for a gig, which the Squire now set up;
saying many a time, to all who might care to listen to him, that it
was the first time for generations that the Hamleys of Hamley had
not been able to keep their own coach. The other carriage-horse
was turned out to grass, being too old for regular work. Conqueror used to come whinnying up to the park-palings, whenever
he saw the Squire, who had always a piece of bread, or some
sugar, or an apple for the old favourite, and would make many a
complaining speech to the dumb animal, telling him of the change
of times since both were in their prime. It had never been the
Squire's custom to encourage his boys to invite their friends to the
Hall. Perhaps this, too, was owing to his *mauvaise honte*, and also
to an exaggerated consciousness of the deficiencies of his establishment, as compared with what he imagined these lads were accus-

tomed to at home. He explained this once or twice to Osborne and Roger, when they were at Rugby.

'You see, all you public schoolboys have a kind of free-masonry of your own, and outsiders are looked on by you much as I look on rabbits and all that isn't game. Ay, you may laugh, but it is so; and your friends will throw their eyes askance at me, and never think on my pedigree, which would beat theirs all to shivers, I'll be bound. No; I'll have no one here at the Hall who will look down on a Hamley of Hamley, even if he only knows how to make a cross instead of write his name.'

Then, of course, they must not visit at houses to whose sons the Squire could not, or would not, return a like hospitality. On all these points Mrs Hamley had used her utmost influence without avail; his prejudices were immovable. As regarded his position as head of the oldest family in three counties, his pride was invincible; as regarded himself personally – ill at ease in the society of his equals, deficient in manners, and in education – his morbid sensitiveness was too sore and too self-conscious to be called humility.

Take one instance from among many similar scenes of the state of feeling between him and his eldest son, which, if it could not be called active discord, showed at least passive estrangement.

It took place on an evening in the March succeeding Mrs Hamley's death. Roger was at Cambridge. Osborne had also been from home, and he had not volunteered any information as to his absence. The Squire believed that Osborne had been either at Cambridge with his brother, or in London; he would have liked to hear where his son had been, what he had been doing, and whom he had seen, precisely as pieces of news, and as some diversion from the domestic worries and cares which were pressing him hard; but he was too proud to ask any questions, and Osborne had not given him any details of his journey. This silence had aggravated the Squire's internal dissatisfaction, and he came home to dinner weary and sore-hearted a day or two after Osborne's return. It was just six o'clock, and he went hastily into his own little business-room on the ground-floor, and, after washing his hands, came into the drawing-room, feeling as if he were very late; but the room was empty. He glanced at the clock over the mantelpiece, as he tried to warm his hands at the fire. The fire had been neglected, and had gone out during the day; it was now piled up with half-dried wood, which sputtered and smoked instead of doing its duty in blazing and warming the room, through which the keen wind was cutting its way in all directions. The clock had stopped; no one had remembered to wind it up; but by the Squire's watch it was already past dinner time. The old butler put his head into the room; but, seeing the Squire alone, he was about to draw it back, and wait for Mr Osborne, before announcing dinner. He had hoped to do this unperceived; but the Squire caught him in the act.

'Why isn't dinner ready?' he called out sharply. 'It's ten minutes past six. And, pray, why are you using this wood? It's impossible to get oneself warm by such a fire as this.'

'I believe, sir, that Thomas'—

'Don't talk to me of Thomas! Send dinner in directly!'

About five minutes elapsed, spent by the hungry Squire in all sorts of impatient ways – attacking Thomas, who came in to look after the fire; knocking the logs about, scattering out sparks, but considerably lessening the chances of warmth; touching up the candles, which appeared to him to give a light unusually insufficient for the large cold room. While he was doing this, Osborne entered the room in full evening-dress. He always moved slowly; and this, to begin with, irritated the Squire. Then an uncomfortable consciousness of a black coat, drab trousers, checked cotton-cravat, and splashed boots, forced itself upon him, as he saw Osborne's point-device* costume. He chose to consider it affectation and finery in Osborne, and was on the point of bursting out with some remark, when the butler, who had watched Osborne downstairs before making the announcement, came in to say dinner was ready.

'It surely isn't six o'clock?' said Osborne, pulling out his dainty little watch. He was scarcely more unaware than it of the storm that was brewing.

'Six o'clock! It's more than a quarter-past,' growled out his father.

'I fancy your watch must be wrong, sir. I set mine by the Horse Guards* only two days ago.'

Now, impugning that old steady, turnip-shaped watch of the Squire's was one of the insults which, as it could not reasonably be resented, was not to be forgiven. That watch had been given him by his father, when watches were watches, long ago. It had given the law to house-clocks, stable-clocks, kitchen-clocks – nay, even to Hamley Church-clock in its day; and was it now, in its respectable old age, to be looked down upon by a little whipper-snapper of a French watch which could go into a man's waistcoat pocket, instead of having to be extricated with due efforts, like a respectable watch of size and position, from a fob in the waist-band! No! not if the whipper-snapper were backed by all the Horse Guards that ever were, with the Life Guards to boot! Poor Osborne might have known better than to cast this slur on his father's flesh and blood; for so dear did he hold his watch!

'My watch is like myself,' said the Squire, 'girning',* as the Scotch say – 'plain, but steady-going. At any rate, it gives the law in my house. The King may go by the Horse Guards if he likes.'

'I beg your pardon, sir,' said Osborne, really anxious to keep the peace, 'I went by my watch, which is certainly right by London time; and I'd no idea you were waiting for me; otherwise I could have dressed much quicker.'

'I should think so,' said the Squire, looking sarcastically at his son's attire. 'When I was a young man, I should have been ashamed to have spent as much time at my looking-glass as if I'd been a girl. I could make myself as smart as any one when I was going to a dance, or to a party where I was likely to meet pretty girls; but I should have laughed myself to scorn if I'd stood fiddle-faddling at a glass, smirking at my own likeness, all for my own pleasure.'

Osborne reddened, and was on the point of letting fly some caustic remark on his father's dress at the present moment; but he contented himself with saying, in a low voice –

'My mother always expected us all to dress for dinner. I got into the habit of doing it to please her, and I keep it up now.' Indeed, he had a certain kind of feeling of loyalty to her memory, in keeping up all the little domestic habits and customs she had instituted or preferred. But the contrast which the Squire thought was implied by Osborne's remark, put him beside himself.

'And I, too, try to attend to her wishes. I do; and in more important things. I did, when she was alive; and I do so now.'

'I never said you did not,' said Osborne, astonished at his father's passionate words and manner.

'Yes, you did, sir. You meant it. I could see by your looks. I saw you look at my morning-coat. At any rate, I never neglected any wish of hers in her lifetime. If she'd wished me to go to school again and learn my A, B, C, I would. By—I would; and I wouldn't have gone playing and lounging away my time, for fear of vexing and disappointing her. Yet some folks older than schoolboys—'

The Squire choked here; but, though the words would not come, his passion did not diminish. 'I'll not have you casting up your mother's wishes to me, sir. You, who went near to break her heart at last!'

Osborne was strongly tempted to get up and leave the room. Perhaps it would have been better if he had; it might then have brought about an explanation, and a reconciliation, between father and son. But he thought he did well in sitting still and appearing to take no notice. This indifference to what he was saying appeared to annoy the Squire still more; and he kept on grumbling and talking to himself, till Osborne, unable to bear it any longer, said, very quietly, but very bitterly—

'I am only a cause of irritation to you, and home is no longer home to me, but a place in which I am to be controlled in trifles, and scolded about trifles as if I were a child. Put me in a way of making a living for myself – that much your oldest son has a right to ask of you – I will then leave this house, and you shall be no longer vexed by my dress, or my want of punctuality.'

'You make your request pretty much as another son did long ago: "Give me the portion that falleth to me."* But I don't think what he did with his money is much encouragement for me to—' Then the thought of how little he could give his son his 'portion', or any part of it, stopped the Squire.

Osborne took up the speech.

'I'm as ready as any man to earn my living; only the preparation for any profession will cost money, and money I haven't got.'

'No more have I,' said the Squire shortly.

'What is to be done then?' said Osborne, only half believing his father's words.

'Why, you must learn to stop at home, and not take expensive journeys; and you must reduce your tailor's bill. I don't ask you to help me in the management of the land – you're far too fine a gentleman for that; but if you can't earn money, at least you needn't spend it.'

'I've told you I'm willing enough to earn money,' cried Osborne, passionately at last. 'But how am I to do it? You really are very unreasonable, sir.'

'Am I?' said the Squire – cooling in manner, though not in temper, as Osborne grew warm. 'But I don't set up for being reasonable; men who have to pay away money that they haven't got for their extravagant sons aren't likely to be reasonable. There's two things you've gone and done which put me beside myself, when I think of them; you've turned out next door to a dunce at college, when your poor mother thought so much of you – and when you might have pleased and gratified her so, if you had chosen, – and, well! I won't say what the other thing is.'

'Tell me, sir,' said Osborne, almost breathless with the idea that his father had discovered his secret marriage; but the father was thinking of the money-lenders, who were calculating how soon Osborne would come into the estate.

'No!' said the Squire. 'I know what I know, and I'm not going to tell you how I know it. Only, I'll just say this – your friends no more know a piece of good timber when they see it than you or I know how you could earn five pounds, if it was to keep you from starving. Now, there's Roger – we none of us made an ado about him; but he'll have his Fellowship now, I'll warrant him, and be a bishop, or a chancellor, or something, before we've found out he's clever – we've been so much taken up thinking about you. I don't know what's come over me to speak of "we" – "we" in this way,' said he, suddenly dropping his voice – a change of voice as sad as sad could be. 'I ought to say "I"; it will be "I" for evermore in this world.'

He got up and left the room in quick haste, knocking over his chair, and not stopping to pick it up. Osborne, who was sitting and shading his eyes with his hand, as he had been doing for some time, looked up at the noise, and then rose as quickly and hurried after his father, only in time to hear the study-door locked on the inside, the moment he reached it.

Osborne returned into the dining-room, chagrined and sorrowful. But he was always sensitive to any omission of the usual observances, which might excite remark; and, even with his heavy heart, he was careful to pick up the fallen chair, and restore it to its place near the bottom of the table, and afterwards so to disturb the dishes as to make it appear that they had been touched, before ringing for Robinson. When the latter came in, followed by Thomas, Osborne thought it necessary to say to him that his father was not well, and had gone into the study; and that he himself wanted no dessert, but would have a cup of coffee in the drawing-room. The old butler sent Thomas out of the room, and came up confidentially to Osborne.

'I thought master wasn't justly himself, Mr Osborne, before dinner. And, therefore, I made excuses for him – I did. He spoke to Thomas about the fire, sir, which is a thing I could in nowise put up with, unless by reason of sickness, which I am always ready to make allowances for.'

'Why shouldn't my father speak to Thomas?' said Osborne. 'He spoke angrily, I daresay; for I'm sure he's not well.'

'No, Mr Osborne, it wasn't that. I myself am given to anger; and I'm blessed with as good health as any man in my years. Besides, anger's a good thing for Thomas. He needs a deal of it. But it should come from the right quarter – and that is me, myself, Mr Osborne. I know my place, and I know my rights and duties as well as any butler that lives. And it's my duty to scold Thomas, and not master's. Master ought to have said, "Robinson! you must speak to Thomas about letting out the fire," and I'd ha' given it him well – as I shall do now, for that matter. But, as I said before, I make excuses for master, as being in mental distress and bodily ill-health; so I've brought myself round not to give warning, as I should ha' done, for certain, under happier circumstances.'

'Really, Robinson, I think it's all great nonsense,' said Osborne, weary of the long story the butler had told him, and to which he had not half-attended. 'What in the world does it signify whether my father speaks to you or to Thomas? Bring me coffee in the drawing-room, and don't trouble your head any more about scolding Thomas.'

Robinson went away, offended at his grievance being called nonsense. He kept muttering to himself in the intervals of scolding Thomas, and saying – 'Things is a deal changed since poor missis went. I don't wonder master feels it, for I'm sure I do. She was a lady who had always a becoming respect for a butler's position, and could have understood how he might be hurt in his mind. She'd never ha' called his delicacies of feelings nonsense – not she; no more would Mr Roger. He's not a merry young gentleman, and over-fond of bringing dirty, slimy creatures into the house; but he's always a kind word for a man who is hurt in his mind. He'd cheer up the Squire, and keep him from getting so cross and wilful. I wish Mr Roger was here, I do.'

The poor Squire, shut up with his grief, and his ill-temper as well, in the dingy, dreary study where he daily spent more and more of his indoors life, turned over his cares and troubles, till he was as bewildered with the process as a squirrel must be in going round in a cage. He had out day-books and ledgers, and was calculating up back-rents; and every time the sum-totals came to different amounts. He could have cried like a child over his sums; he was worn out and weary, angry and disappointed. He closed his books at last, with a bang.

'I'm getting old,' he said, 'and my head's less clear than it used to be. I think sorrow for her has dazed me. I never was much to boast on; but she thought a deal of me – bless her! She'd never let me call myself stupid; but, for all that, I am stupid. Osborne ought to help me. He's had money enough spent on his learning; but, instead, he comes down dressed like a popinjay, and never troubles his head to think how I'm to pay his debts. I wish I'd told him to earn his living as a dancing-master,' said the Squire, with a sad smile at his own wit. 'He's dressed for all the world like one. And how he's spent the money no one knows! Perhaps Roger will turn up some day with a heap of creditors at his heels. No, he won't – not Roger; he may be slow, but he's steady, is old Roger. I wish he was here! He's not the eldest son, but he'd take an interest in the estate; and he'd do up these weary accounts for me. I wish Roger was here!'

CHAPTER 23

Osborne Hamley Reviews His Position

Osborne had his solitary cup of coffee in the drawing-room. He was very unhappy too, after his fashion. He stood on the hearth-rug pondering over his situation. He was not exactly aware how hardly his father was pressed for ready-money; the Squire had never spoken to him on the subject without being angry; and many of his loose contradictory statements – all of which, however contradictory they might appear, had their basis in truth – were set down by his son to the exaggeration of passion. But it was uncomfortable enough to a young man of Osborne's age to feel himself continually hampered for want of a five-pound note. The principal supplies for the liberal – almost luxurious-table at the Hall came off the estate; so that there was no appearance of poverty as far as the household went; and, as long as Osborne was content at home, he had everything he could wish for; but he had a wife elsewhere – he wanted to see her continually – and that necessitated journeys. She, poor thing! had to be supported – where was the money for the journeys and for Aimée's modest wants to come from? That was the puzzle in Osborne's mind just now. While he had been at college, his allowance – heir of the Hamleys – had been three hundred, while Roger had to be content with a hundred less. The payment of these annual sums had given the Squire a good deal of trouble; but he thought of it as a merely temporary inconvenience; perhaps unreasonably thought so. Osborne was to do great things; take high honours, get a fellow-ship, marry a long-descended heiress, live in some of the many uninhabited rooms at the Hall, and help the Squire in the manage-ment of the estate that would some time be his. Roger was to be a clergyman; steady, slow Roger, was just fitted for that; and, when he declined entering the Church, preferring a life of more activity and adventure, Roger was to be anything; he was useful and practical, and fit for all the employments from which Osborne was shut out by his fastidiousness, and his (pseudo-) genius; so it was well he was an eldest son, for he would never have done to struggle through the world; and, as for his settling down to a profession, it would be like cutting blocks with a razor! And now here was Osborne, living at home, but longing to be elsewhere; his allowance stopped in reality; indeed, the punctual payment of it during the last year or two had been owing to his mother's exertions; but nothing had been said about its present cessation by either father or son; money-matters were too sore a subject between them. Every now and then the Squire threw him a ten-pound note or so; but the sort of suppressed growl with which it was given, and the entire uncertainty as to when he might receive such gifts, rendered any calculation based upon their receipt exceeding vague and uncertain.

'What in the world can I do to secure an income?' thought Osborne, as he stood on the hearth-rug, his back to a blazing fire; his cup of coffee sent up in the rare old china that had belonged to the Hall for generations; his dress finished, as dress of Osborne's could hardly fail to be. One could hardly have thought that this elegant young man, standing there in the midst of comfort that verged on luxury, should have been turning over that one great problem in his mind; but so it was. 'What can I do to be sure of a present income? Things cannot go on as they are. I should need support for two or three years, even if I entered myself at the Temple or Lincoln's Inn.* It would be impossible to live on my pay in the army; besides, I should hate that profession. In fact, there are evils attending all professions – I couldn't bring myself to become a member of any I've ever heard of. Perhaps I'm more fitted to take "orders" than anything else; but to be compelled to write weekly sermons whether one had anything to say or not, and, probably, doomed only to associate with people below one in refinement and education! Yet poor Aimée must have money! I can't bear to compare our dinners here, overloaded with joints and game and sweets, as Dawson will persist in sending them up, with Aimée's two little mutton-chops. Yet what would my father say, if he knew I'd married a French-woman? In his present mood he'd disinherit me, if that is possible; and he'd speak about her in a way I couldn't stand. A Roman Catholic, too! Well, I don't repent it. I'd do it again. Only, if my mother had been in good health – if she could have heard my story, and known Aimée! As it is, I must keep it secret; but where to get money? Where to get money?'

Then he bethought him of his poems – would they sell, and bring him in money? In spite of Milton,* he thought they might; and he went to fetch his MSS. out of his room. He sate down near the fire, trying to study them with a critical eye, to represent public opinion as far as he could. He had changed his style since the Mrs Hemans days. He was essentially imitative in his poetic faculty; and of late he had followed the lead of a popular writer of sonnets.* He turned his poems over; they were almost equivalent to an autobiographical passage in his life. Arranging them in their order, they came as follows: –

'To Aimée, Walking with a Little Child.'

'To Aimée, Singing at her Work.'

'To Aimée, Turning away from me while I told my Love.'

'Aimée's Confession.'

'Aimée in Despair.'

'The Foreign Land in which my Aimée dwells.'

'The Wedding-Ring.'

'The Wife.'

When he came to this last sonnet, he put down his bundle of papers and began to think. 'The wife'. Yes, and a French wife; and a Roman Catholic wife – and a wife who might be said to have been in service! And his father's hatred of the French, both collectively and individually – collectively, as tumultuous brutal ruffians, who had murdered their king, and committed all kinds of bloody atrocities – individually, as represented by 'Boney', and the various caricatures of 'Johnny Crapaud'* that had been in full circulation about five-and-twenty years before this time, when the Squire had been young and capable of receiving impressions. As for the form of religion in which Mrs Osborne Hamley had been brought up, it is enough to say that Catholic emancipation* had begun to be talked about by some politicians, and that the sullen roar of the majority of Englishmen, at the bare idea of it, was surging in the distance with ominous threatenings; the very mention of such a measure before the Squire was, as Osborne well knew, like shaking a red flag before a bull.

And then he considered that if Aimée had had the unspeakable, the incomparable, blessing of being born of English parents in the very heart of England – Warwickshire, for instance – and had never heard of priests, or mass, or confession, or the Pope, or Guy Fawkes, but had been born, baptized, and bred in the Church of England, without having ever seen the outside of a dissenting meeting-house, or a papist chapel – even with all these advantages, her having been a (what was the equivalent for '*bonne*' in English? nursery-governess was a term hardly invented) nursery-maid, with wages paid down once a quarter, liable to be dismissed at a month's warning, and having her tea and sugar doled out to her, would be a shock to his father's old ancestral pride that he would hardly ever get over.

'If he saw her!' thought Osborne. 'If he could but see her!' But if the Squire were to see Aimée, he would also hear her speak her pretty broken English – precious to her husband, as it was in it that she had confessed brokenly with her English tongue, that she loved him soundly with her French heart – and Squire Hamley piqued himself on being a good hater of the French. 'She would make such a loving, sweet, docile little daughter to my father – she would go as near as any one could towards filling up the blank void in this house, if he could but have her; but he won't; he never would; and he shan't have the opportunity of scouting her. Yet if I called her "Lucy"* in these sonnets; and if they made a great effect – were praised in *Blackwood* and the *Quarterly** – and all the world was agog to find out the author; and I told him my secret – I could if I were successful – I think then he would ask who Lucy was, and I could tell him all then. If – how I hate "ifs"! "If me no ifs", My life has been based on "whens"; and first they have turned to "ifs", and then they have vanished away. It was "when Osborne gets honours", and then "if Osborne", and then a failure altogether. I said to Aimée, "when my mother sees you", and now it is "if my father saw her", with a very faint prospect of its ever coming to pass.' So he let the evening hours flow on and disappear in reveries like these; winding up with a sudden determination to try the fate of his poems with a publisher, with the direct expectation of getting money for them, and an ulterior fancy that, if successful, they might work wonders with his father.

When Roger came home Osborne did not let a day pass before telling his brother of his plans. He never did conceal anything long from Roger; the feminine part of his character made him always desirous of a confidant, and as sweet sympathy as he could extract. But Roger's opinion had no effect on Osborne's actions; and Roger knew this full well. So when Osborne began with – 'I want your advice on a plan I have got in my head,' Roger replied: 'Some one told me that the Duke of Wellington's maxim was never to give advice unless he could enforce its being carried into effect; now I can't do that; and you know, old boy, you don't follow out my advice when you've got it.'

'Not always, I know. Not when it doesn't agree with my own opinion. You're thinking about this concealment of my marriage; but you're not up in all the circumstances. You know how fully I meant to have done it, if there hadn't been that row about my debts; and then my mother's illness and death. And now you've no conception how my father is changed – how irritable he has become! Wait till you've been at home a week! Robinson, Morgan – it's the same with them all; but worst of all with me.'

'Poor fellow!' said Roger; 'I thought he looked terribly changed: shrunken, and his ruddiness of complexion altered.'

'Why, he hardly takes half the exercise he used to do; so it's no wonder. He has turned away all the men of the new works, which used to be such an interest to him; and, because the roan cob stumbled with him one day, and nearly threw him, he won't ride it; and yet he won't sell it and buy another, which would be the sensible plan; so there are two old horses eating their heads off, while he is constantly talking about money and expense. And that brings me to what I was going to say. I'm desperately hard up for money, and so I've been collecting my poems – weeding them

well, you know – going over them quite critically, in fact; and I
want to know if you think Deighton* would publish them. You've
a name in Cambridge, you know; and I daresay he would look at
them if you offered them to him.'

'I can but try,' said Roger; 'but I'm afraid you won't get much
by them.'

'I don't expect much. I'm a new man, and must make my name.
I should be content with a hundred. If I'd a hundred pounds I'd
set myself to do something. I might keep myself and Aimée by my
writings, while I studied for the bar; or, if the worst came to the
worst, a hundred pounds would take us to Australia.'*

'Australia! Why, Osborne, what could you do there? And leave
my father! I hope you'll never get your hundred pounds, if that's
the use you're to make of it! Why, you'd break the Squire's heart.'

'It might have done once,' said Osborne gloomily, 'but it
wouldn't now. He looks at me askance, and shies away from
conversation with me. Let me alone for noticing and feeling this
kind of thing! It's this very susceptibility to outward things that
gives me what faculty I have; and it seems to me as if my bread,
and my wife's too, were to depend upon it. You'll soon see for
yourself the terms which I am on with my father!'

Roger did soon see. His father had slipped into a habit of silence
at meal-times – a habit which Osborne, who was troubled and
anxious enough for his own part, had not striven to break. Father
and son sate together, and exchanged all the necessary speeches
connected with the occasion civilly enough; but it was a relief to
them when their intercourse was over, and they separated – the
father to brood over his sorrow and his disappointment, which
were real and deep enough, and the injury he had received from
his boy, which was exaggerated in his mind by his ignorance of
the actual steps Osborne had taken to raise money. If the money-
lenders had calculated the chances of his father's life or death in
making their bargain, Osborne himself had thought only of how
soon and how easily he could get the money requisite for clearing
him from all imperious claims at Cambridge, and for enabling
him to follow Aimée to her home in Alsace, and for the subsequent
marriage. As yet, Roger had never seen his brother's wife; indeed,
he had only been taken into Osborne's full confidence after all
was decided in which his advice could have been useful. And now,
in the enforced separation, Osborne's whole thought, both the
poetical and practical sides of his mind, ran upon the little wife

who was passing her lonely days in farmhouse lodgings, wondering when her bridegroom husband would come to her next. With such an engrossing subject, it was, perhaps, no wonder that he unconsciously neglected his father; but it was none the less sad at the time, and to be regretted in its consequences.

'I may come in and have a pipe with you, sir, mayn't I?' said Roger, that first evening, pushing gently against the study-door, which his father held only half open.

'You'll not like it,' said the Squire, still holding the door against him, but speaking in a relenting tone. 'The tobacco I use isn't what young men like. Better go and have a cigar with Osborne.'

'No. I want to sit with you, and I can stand pretty strong tobacco.'

Roger pushed in, the resistance slowly giving way before him.

'It will make your clothes smell. You'll have to borrow Osborne's scents to sweeten yourself,' said the Squire grimly, at the same time pushing a short smart amber-mouthed pipe to his son.

'No; I'll have a churchwarden. Why, father, do you think I'm a baby to put up with a doll's head like this?' looking at the carving upon it.

The Squire was pleased in his heart, though he did not choose to show it. He only said, 'Osborne brought it me when he came back from Germany. That's three years ago.' and then for some time they smoked in silence. But the voluntary companionship of his son was very soothing to the Squire, though not a word might he said.

The next speech he made showed the direction of his thoughts; indeed, his words were always a transparent medium through which the current might be seen.

'A deal of a man's life comes and goes in three years – I've found that out;' and he puffed away at his pipe again. While Roger was turning over in his mind what answer to make to this truism, the Squire again stopped his smoking and spoke.

'I remember when there was all that fuss about the Prince of Wales being made Regent,* I read somewhere – I daresay it was in a newspaper – that kings and their heirs-apparent were always on bad terms. Osborne was quite a little chap then: he used to go out riding with me on White Surrey; – you won't remember the pony we called White Surrey?'*

'I remember it; but I thought it a tall horse in those days.'

'Ah! that was because you were such a small lad, you know. I'd seven horses in the stable then – not counting the farm-horses. I don't recollect having a care then, except – *she* was always delicate, you know. But what a beautiful boy Osborne was! He was always dressed in black velvet – it was a foppery, but it wasn't my doing, and it was all right, I'm sure. He's a handsome fellow now, but the sunshine has gone out of his face.'

'He's a good deal troubled about this money, and the anxiety he has given you,' said Roger, rather taking his brother's feelings for granted.

'Not he,' said the Squire, taking the pipe out of his mouth, and hitting the bowl so sharply against the hob that it broke in pieces. 'There! But never mind! I say, not he, Roger! He's none troubled about the money. It's easy getting money from Jews, if you're the eldest son and the heir. They just ask, "How old is your father, and has he had a stroke, or a fit?" and it's settled out of hand; and then they come prowling about a place, and running down the timber and land—Don't let us speak of him; it's no good, Roger. He and I are out of tune, and it seems to me as if only God Almighty could put us to rights. It's thinking of how he grieved *her* at last that makes me so bitter with him. And yet there's a deal of good in him! and he's so quick and clever, if only he'd give his mind to things. Now, you were always slow, Roger – all your masters used to say so.'

Roger laughed a little –

'Yes; I'd many a nickname at school for my slowness,' said he.

'Never mind!' said the Squire consolingly. 'I'm sure I don't. If you were a clever fellow like Osborne yonder, you'd be all for caring for books and writing, and you'd perhaps find it as dull as he does to keep company with a bumpkin Squire Jones like me. Yet, I daresay, they think a deal of you at Cambridge,' said he, after a pause, 'since you've got this fine wranglership; I'd nearly forgotten that – the news came at such a miserable time.'

'Well, yes! They're always proud of the senior wrangler of the year up at Cambridge. Next year I must abdicate.'

The Squire sat and gazed into the embers, still holding his useless pipe-stem. At last he said, in a low voice, as if scarcely aware he had got a listener – 'I used to write to her when she was away in London, and tell her the home news. But no letter will reach her now! Nothing reaches her!'

Roger started up.

'Where's the tobacco-box, father? Let me fill you another pipe!' and when he had done so, he stooped over his father and stroked his cheek. The Squire shook his head.

'You've only just come home, lad. You don't know me, as I am now-a-days! Ask Robinson – I won't have you asking Osborne, he ought to keep it to himself – but any of the servants will tell you I'm not like the same man, for getting into passions with them. I used to be reckoned a good master; but that's past now! Osborne was once a little boy, and she was once alive – and I was once a good master – a good master – yes! It's all past now.'

He took up his pipe, and began to smoke afresh; and Roger, after a silence of some minutes, began a long story about some Cambridge man's misadventure on the hunting-field, telling it with such humour that the Squire was beguiled into hearty laughing. When they rose to go to bed, his father said to Roger –

'Well, we've had a pleasant evening – at least, I have. But perhaps you haven't; for I'm but poor company now, I know.'

'I don't know when I've passed a happier evening, father,' said Roger. And he spoke truly, though he did not trouble himself to find out the cause of his happiness.

CHAPTER 24

Mrs Gibson's Little Dinner

All this had taken place before Roger's first meeting with Molly and Cynthia at the Miss Brownings', and the little dinner on the Friday at Mr Gibson's, which followed in due sequence.

Mrs Gibson intended the Hamleys to find this dinner pleasant; and they did. Mr Gibson was fond of the two young men, both for their parents' sake and their own, for he had known them since boyhood; and to those whom he liked Mr Gibson could be remarkably agreeable. Mrs Gibson really gave them a welcome – and cordiality in a hostess is a very becoming mantle for any other deficiencies there may be. Cynthia and Molly looked their best, which was all the duty Mrs Gibson absolutely required of them, as she was willing enough to take her full share in the conversation. Osborne fell to her lot, of course, and for some time he and she prattled on with all the ease of manner and commonplace-

ness of meaning which go far to make the 'art of polite conversation'.* Roger, who ought to have made himself agreeable to one
or the other of the young ladies, was exceedingly interested in
what Mr Gibson was telling him of a paper on comparative
osteology,* in some foreign journal of science which Lord Hollingford was in the habit of forwarding to his friend the country
surgeon. Yet, every now and then while he listened, he caught his
attention wandering to the face of Cynthia, who was placed
between his brother and Mr Gibson. She was not particularly
occupied with attending to anything that was going on; her eyelids
were carelessly dropped, as she crumbled her bread on the table-
cloth, and her beautiful long eyelashes were seen on the clear tint
of her oval cheek. She was thinking of something else; Molly was
trying to understand with all her might. Suddenly Cynthia looked
up, and caught Roger's gaze of intent admiration too fully for her
to be unaware that he was staring at her. She coloured a little;
but, after the first moment of rosy confusion at his evident
admiration of her, she flew to the attack, diverting his confusion
at thus being caught, to the defence of himself from her
accusation.

'It is quite true!' she said to him. 'I was not attending: you see I
don't know even the A B C of science. But please don't look so
severely at me, even if I am a dunce!'

'I didn't know – I didn't mean to look severely, I am sure,'
replied he, not knowing well what to say.

'Cynthia is not a dunce either,' said Mrs Gibson, afraid lest her
daughter's opinion of herself might be taken seriously. 'But I have
always observed that some people have a talent for one thing and
some for another. Now Cynthia's talents are not for science and
the severer studies. Do you remember, love, what trouble I had to
teach you the use of the globes?'

'Yes; and I don't know longitude from latitude now; and I'm
always puzzled as to which is perpendicular and which is
horizontal.'

'Yet, I do assure you,' her mother continued, rather addressing
herself to Osborne, 'that her memory for poetry is prodigious. I
have heard her repeat the "Prisoner of Chillon"* from beginning
to end.'

'It would be rather a bore to have to hear her, I think,' said Mr
Gibson, smiling at Cynthia, who gave him back one of her bright
looks of mutual understanding.

'Ah, Mr Gibson, I have found out before now that you have no soul for poetry; and Molly there is your own child. She reads such deep books – all about facts and figures; she'll be quite a blue-stocking by-and-by.'

'Mamma,' said Molly, reddening, 'you think it was a deep book, because there were the shapes of the different cells of bees in it! but it was not at all deep. It was very interesting.'

'Never mind, Molly,' said Osborne. 'I stand up for blue-stockings.'

'And I object to the distinction implied in what you say,' said Roger. 'It was not deep, *ergo*, it was very interesting. Now, a book may be both deep and interesting.'

'Oh, if you are going to chop logic and use Latin words, I think it is time for us to leave the room,' said Mrs Gibson.

'Don't let us run away as if we were beaten, mamma,' said Cynthia. 'Though it may be logic, I, for one, can understand what Mr Roger Hamley said just now; and I read some of Molly's books; and, whether it was deep or not, I found it very interesting – more so than I should think the "Prisoner of Chillon" now-a-days. I've displaced the Prisoner to make room for Johnnie Gilpin* as my favourite poem.'

'How could you talk such nonsense, Cynthia!' said Mrs Gibson, as the girls followed her upstairs. 'You know you are not a dunce. It is all very well not to be a blue-stocking, because gentle-people don't like that kind of woman; but running yourself down, and contradicting all I said about your liking for Byron, and poets and poetry – to Osborne Hamley of all men too!'

Mrs Gibson spoke quite crossly for her.

'But, mamma,' Cynthia replied, 'I am either a dunce, or I am not. If I am, I did right to own it; if I am not, he's a dunce if he doesn't find out I was joking.'

'Well,' said Mrs Gibson, a little puzzled by this speech, and wanting some elucidatory addition.

'Only that, if he's a dunce, his opinion of me is worth nothing. So, any way, it doesn't signify.'

'You really bewilder me with your nonsense, child. Molly is worth twenty of you.'

'I quite agree with you, mamma,' said Cynthia, turning round to take Molly's hand.

'Yes; but she ought not to be,' said Mrs Gibson, still irritated. 'Think of the advantages you've had!'

'I'm afraid I'd rather be a dunce than a blue-stocking,' said Molly; for the term had a little annoyed her, and the annoyance was rankling still.

'Hush; here they are coming: I hear the dining-room door! I never meant you were a blue-stocking, dear; so don't look vexed! – Cynthia, my love, where did you get those lovely flowers – anemones, are they? They suit your complexion so exactly.'

'Come, Molly, don't look so grave and thoughtful,' exclaimed Cynthia. 'Don't you perceive mamma wants us to be smiling and amiable?'

Mr Gibson had had to go out to his evening-round; and the young men were all too glad to come up into the pretty drawing-room; the bright little wood-fire; the comfortable easy-chairs which, with so small a party, might be drawn round the hearth; the good-natured hostess; the pretty, agreeable girls. Roger sauntered up to the corner where Cynthia was standing, playing with a hand-screen.

'There is a charity ball in Hollingford soon, isn't there?' asked he.

'Yes; on Easter Tuesday,' she replied.

'Are you going? I suppose you are?'

'Yes; mamma is going to take Molly and me.'

'You will enjoy it very much – going together?'

For the first time during this little conversation she glanced up at him – real honest pleasure shining out of her eyes.

'Yes; going together will make the enjoyment of the thing. It would be dull without her.'

'You are great friends, then?' he asked.

'I never thought I should like any one so much – any girl, I mean.'

She put in the final reservation in all simplicity of heart; and in all simplicity did he understand it. He came ever so little nearer, and dropped his voice a little.

'I was so anxious to know. I am so glad. I have often wondered how you two were getting on.'

'Have you?' said she, looking up again. 'At Cambridge? You must be very fond of Molly!'

'Yes, I am. She was with us so long; and at such a time! I look upon her almost as a sister.'

'And she is very fond of all of you. I seem to know you all, from hearing her talk about you so much.'

'All of you!' said she, laying an emphasis on 'all' to show that it included the dead as well as the living. Roger was silent for a minute or two.

'I didn't know you, even by hearsay. So you mustn't wonder that I was a little afraid. But, as soon as I saw you, I knew how it must be; and it was such a relief!'

'Cynthia,' said Mrs Gibson, who thought that the younger son had had quite his share of low, confidential conversation, 'come here, and sing that little French ballad to Mr Osborne Hamley.'

'Which do you mean, mamma? "*Tu t'en repentiras, Colin?*"'

'Yes; such a pretty, playful little warning to young men,' said Mrs Gibson, smiling up at Osborne. 'The refrain is –

> *Tu t'en repentiras, Colin,**
>   *Tu t'en repentiras;*
> *Car, si tu prends une femme, Colin,*
>   *Tu t'en repentiras.*

The advice may apply very well, when there is a French wife in the case; but not, I am sure, to an Englishman who is thinking of an English wife.'

This choice of a song was exceedingly *mal-àpropos*,* had Mrs Gibson but known it. Osborne and Roger, knowing that the wife of the former was a Frenchwoman, and conscious of each other's knowledge, felt doubly awkward; while Molly was as much confused as though she herself were secretly married. However, Cynthia carolled the saucy ditty out, and her mother smiled at it, in total ignorance of any application it might have. Osborne had instinctively gone to stand behind Cynthia, as she sate at the piano, so as to be ready to turn over the leaves of her music, if she required it. He kept his hands in his pockets and his eyes fixed on her fingers; his countenance clouded with gravity at all the merry quips which she so playfully sang. Roger looked grave as well, but was much more at his ease than his brother; indeed, he was half-amused by the awkwardness of the situation. He caught Molly's troubled eyes and heightened colour, and he saw that she was feeling this *contretemps* more seriously than she needed to do. He moved to a seat by her, and half whispered, 'Too late a warning, is it not?'

Molly looked up at him as he leant towards her, and replied in the same tone – 'Oh, I am so sorry!'

'You need not be. He won't mind it long; and a man must take the consequences, when he puts himself in a false position.'

Molly could not tell what to reply to this; so she hung her head and kept silence. Yet she could see that Roger did not change his attitude or remove his hand from the back of his chair, and, impelled by curiosity to find out the cause of his stillness, she looked up at him at length, and saw his gaze fixed on the two who were near the piano. Osborne was saying something eagerly to Cynthia, whose grave eyes were upturned to him with soft intentness of expression, and her pretty mouth half-open, with a sort of impatience for him to cease speaking, that she might reply.

'They are talking about France,' said Roger, in answer to Molly's unspoken question. 'Osborne knows it well, and Miss Kirkpatrick has been at school there, you know. It sounds very interesting; shall we go nearer and hear what they are saying?'

It was all very well to ask this civilly; but Molly thought it would have been better to wait for her answer. Instead of waiting, however, Roger went to the piano, and, leaning on it, appeared to join in the light merry talk, while he feasted his eyes, as much as he dared, by looking at Cynthia. Molly suddenly felt as if she could scarcely keep from crying – a minute ago he had been so near to her, and talking so pleasantly and confidentially; and now he almost seemed as if he had forgotten her existence. She thought that all this was wrong; and she exaggerated its wrongness to herself; 'mean', and 'envious of Cynthia', and 'ill-natured', and 'selfish', were the terms she kept applying to herself; but it did no good, she was just as naughty at the last as at the first.

Mrs Gibson broke into the state of things which Molly thought was to endure for ever. Her work had been intricate up to this time, and had required a great deal of counting; so she had had no time to attend to her duties, one of which she always took to be to show herself to the world as an impartial stepmother. Cynthia had played and sung, and now she must give Molly her turn of exhibition. Cynthia's singing and playing was light and graceful, but anything but correct; but she herself was so charming, that it was only fanatics for music who cared for false chords and omitted notes. Molly, on the contrary, had an excellent ear, though she had never been well taught; and, both from inclination and conscientious perseverance of disposition, she would go over an incorrect passage for twenty times. But she was very shy of playing in company; and, when forced to do it, she went through her performance heavily, and hated her handiwork more than any one.

'Now, you must play a little, Molly,' said Mrs Gibson; 'play us that beautiful piece of Kalkbrenner's,* my dear.'

Molly looked up at her stepmother with beseeching eyes; but it only brought out another form of request, still more like a command.

'Go at once, my dear! You may not play it quite rightly; and I know you are very nervous; but you're quite amongst friends.'

So there was a disturbance made in the little group at the piano, and Molly sate down to her martyrdom.

'Please, go away!' said she to Osborne, who was standing behind her, ready to turn over. 'I can quite well do it for myself. And oh! if you would but talk!'

Osborne remained where he was in spite of her appeal, and gave her what little approval she got; for Mrs Gibson, exhausted by her previous labour of counting her stitches, fell asleep in her comfortable sofa-corner near the fire; and Roger, who began at first to talk a little in compliance with Molly's request, found his conversation with Cynthia so agreeable, that Molly lost her place several times, in trying to catch a sudden glimpse of Cynthia sitting at her work, and Roger by her, intent on catching her low replies to what he was saying.

'There, now I've done!' said Molly, standing up quickly, as soon as she had finished the eighteen dreary pages; 'and I think I will never sit down to play again!'

Osborne laughed at her vehemence. Cynthia began to take some part in what was being said, and thus made the conversation general. Mrs Gibson wakened up gracefully, as was her way of doing all things, and slid into the subjects they were talking about so easily, that she almost succeeded in making them believe she had never been asleep at all.

CHAPTER 25

Hollingford in a Bustle

All Hollingford felt as if there was a great deal to be done before Easter this year. There was Easter proper, which always required new clothing of some kind, for fear of certain consequences from little birds, who were supposed to resent the impiety of those that did not wear some new article of dress on Easter-day. And most ladies considered it wiser that the little birds should see the new article for themselves, and not have to take it upon trust, as they would have to do if it were merely a pocket-handkerchief, or a petticoat, or any article of underclothing. So piety demanded a new bonnet, or a new gown, and was barely satisfied with an Easter pair of gloves. Miss Rose was generally very busy just before Easter in Hollingford. Then this year there was the charity ball. Ashcombe, Hollingford, and Coreham were three neighbouring towns, of about the same number of population, lying at the three equidistant corners of a triangle. In imitation of greater cities with their festivals, these three towns had agreed to have an annual ball for the benefit of the county-hospital, to be held in turn at each place; and Hollingford was to be the place this year.

It was a fine time for hospitality, and every house of any pretension was as full as it could hold, and flys were engaged long months before.

If Mrs Gibson could have asked Osborne, or in default, Roger Hamley to go to the ball with them and to sleep at their house – or if, indeed, she could have picked up any stray scion of a 'county family' to whom such an offer would have been a convenience, she would have restored her own dressing-room to its former use as the spare-room, with pleasure. But she did not think it was worth her while to put herself out for any of the humdrum and ill-dressed women who had been her former acquaintances at Ashcombe. For Mr Preston it might have been worth while to give up her room, considering him in the light of a handsome and prosperous young man, and a good dancer besides. But there were more lights in which he was to be viewed. Mr Gibson, who really wanted to return the hospitality shown to him by Mr Preston at the time of his marriage, had yet an instinctive distaste to the man, which no wish of freeing himself from obligation, nor even the more worthy feeling of hospitality, could overcome. Mrs Gibson had some old grudges of her own against him, but she was not one to retain angry feelings, or be very active in her retaliation; she was afraid of Mr Preston, and admired him at the same time. It was awkward too – so she said – to go into a ball-room without any gentleman at all, and Mr Gibson was so uncertain! On the whole – partly for this last-given reason, and partly because conciliation was the best policy, Mrs Gibson was slightly in favour of inviting Mr Preston to be their guest. But, as soon as Cynthia heard the question discussed – or rather, as soon as she heard it discussed in Mr Gibson's absence – she said that if Mr Preston came to be their visitor on the occasion, she for one would not go to the ball at all. She did not speak with vehemence or in anger; but with such quiet resolution that Molly looked up in surprise. She saw that Cynthia was keeping her eyes fixed on her work, and that she had no intention of meeting any one's gaze, or giving any further explanation. Mrs Gibson, too, looked perplexed, and once or twice seemed on the point of asking some question; but she was not angry, as Molly had fully expected. She watched Cynthia furtively and in silence for a minute or two, and then said that, after all, she could not conveniently give up her dressing-room; and, altogether, they had better say no more about it. So no stranger was invited to stay at Mr Gibson's at the time of the ball; but Mrs Gibson openly spoke of her regret at the unavoidable inhospitality, and hoped that they might be able to build an addition to their house before the next triennial Hollingford gaiety.

Another cause of unusual bustle at Hollingford this Easter was the expected return of the family to the Towers, after their unusually long absence. Mr Sheepshanks might be seen trotting up and down on his stout old cob, speaking to attentive masons, plasterers, and glaziers about putting everything – on the outside at least – about the cottages belonging to 'my lord', in perfect repair. Lord Cumnor owned the greater part of the town; and those who lived under other landlords, or in houses of their own, were stirred up by the dread of contrast to do up their dwellings. So the ladders of white-washers and painters were sadly in the way of the ladies tripping daintily along to make their purchases, and holding their gowns up in a bunch behind, after a fashion quite gone out in these days. The house-keeper and steward from the Towers might also be seen coming in to give orders at the various shops; and stopping here and there at those kept by favourites, to avail themselves of the eagerly-tendered refreshments.

Lady Harriet came to call on her old governess, the day after the arrival of the family at the Towers. Molly and Cynthia were out walking when she came – doing some errands for Mrs Gibson, who had a secret idea that Lady Harriet would call at the particular time she did, and had a not uncommon wish to talk to her ladyship without the corrective presence of any member of her own family.

Mrs Gibson did not give Molly the message of remembrance that Lady Harriet had left for her; but she imparted various pieces of news relating to the Towers with great animation and interest. The Duchess of Menteith and her daughter, Lady Alice, were coming to the Towers; would be there the day of the ball; would come to the ball; and the Menteith diamonds were famous. That was piece of news the first. The second was that ever so many gentlemen were coming to the Towers – some English, some French. This piece of news would have come first in order of importance, had there been much probability of their being dancing men, and, as such, possible partners at the coming ball. But Lady Harriet had spoken of them as Lord Hollingford's friends, useless scientific men in all probability. Then, finally, Mrs Gibson was to go to the Towers next day to lunch; Lady Cumnor had written a little note by Lady Harriet to beg her to come; if Mrs Gibson could manage to find her way to the Towers, one of the carriages in use should bring her back to her own home in the course of the afternoon.

'The dear countess!' said Mrs Gibson, with soft affection. It was a soliloquy, uttered after a minute's pause, at the end of all this information.

And all the rest of that day her conversation had an aristocratic perfume hanging about it. One of the few books* she had brought with her into Mr Gibson's house was bound in pink, and in it she studied, 'Menteith, Duke of, Adolphus George', etc., etc., till she was fully up in all the duchess's connections, and probable interests. Mr Gibson made his mouth up into a droll whistle when he came home at night, and found himself in a Towers atmosphere. Molly saw the shade of annoyance through the drollery; she was beginning to see it oftener than she liked, not that she reasoned upon it, or that she consciously traced the annoyance to its source; but she could not help feeling uneasy in herself when she knew that her father was in the least put out.

Of course a fly was ordered for Mrs Gibson. In the early afternoon she came home. If she had been disappointed in her interview with the countess, she never told her woe,* nor revealed the fact that, when she first arrived at the Towers, she had to wait for an hour in Lady Cumnor's morning-room, uncheered by any companionship save that of her old friend, Mrs Bradley, till suddenly, Lady Harriet coming in, she exclaimed – 'Why, Clare! you dear woman! are you here all alone? Does mamma know?' And, after a little more affectionate conversation, she rushed to find her ladyship, who was perfectly aware of the fact, but too deep in giving the duchess the benefit of her wisdom and experience in trousseaux to be at all mindful of the length of time Mrs Gibson had been passing in patient solitude. At lunch, Mrs Gibson was secretly hurt by my lord's supposing it to be her dinner, and calling out his urgent hospitality from the very bottom of the table, giving as a reason for it, that she must remember it was her dinner. In vain she piped out in her soft, high voice, 'Oh, my lord! I never eat meat in the middle of the day; I can hardly eat anything at lunch.' Her voice was lost, and the duchess might go away with the idea that the Hollingford doctor's wife dined early; that is to say, if her Grace ever condescended to have any idea on the subject at all; which presupposes that she was cognisant of the fact of there being a doctor at Hollingford, and that he had a wife, and that his wife was the pretty, faded, elegant-looking woman, sending away her plate of untasted food – food which she longed to eat, for she was really desperately hungry after her drive and her solitude.

And then after lunch there did come a *tête-à-tête* with Lady Cumnor, which was conducted after this wise: –

'Well, Clare! I am really glad to see you. I once thought I should never get back to the Towers; but here I am! There was such a clever man at Bath – a Doctor Snape – he cured me at last – quite set me up. I really think, if ever I am ill again, I shall send for him: it is such a thing to find a really clever medical man. Oh, by the way, I always forget you've married Mr Gibson – of course he is very clever, and all that. (The carriage to the door in ten minutes, Brown, and desire Bradley to bring my things down!) What was I asking you? Oh! how do you get on with the stepdaughter? She seemed to me to be a young lady with a pretty stubborn will of her own. I put a letter for the post down somewhere, and I cannot think where; do help me look for it, there's a good woman. Just run to my room, and see if Brown can find it, for it is of great consequence.'

Off went Mrs Gibson, rather unwillingly; for there were several things she wanted to speak about, and she had not heard half of what she had expected to learn of the family gossip. But all chance was gone; for, when she came back from her fruitless errand, Lady Cumnor and the duchess were in full talk, the former with the missing letter in her hand, which she was using something like a *bâton* to enforce her words.

'Every iota from Paris! Every i-o-ta!'

Lady Cumnor was too much of a lady not to apologise for useless trouble; but they were nearly the last words she spoke to Mrs Gibson, for she had to go out and drive with the duchess; and the brougham to take 'Clare' (as she persisted in calling Mrs Gibson) back to Hollingford followed the carriage to the door.

Lady Harriet came away from her *entourage* of young men and young ladies, all prepared for some walking-expedition, to wish Mrs Gibson good-bye.

'We shall see you at the ball,' she said. 'You'll be there with your two girls, of course, and I must have a little talk with you there; with all these visitors in the house, it has been impossible to see anything of you today, you know.'

Such were the facts; but rose-colour was the medium through which they were seen by Mrs Gibson's household listeners on her return.

'There are many visitors staying at the Towers – oh, yes! a great many: the duchess and Lady Alice, and Mr and Mrs Grey, and Lord Albert Monson and his sister, and my old friend, Captain James of the Blues* – many more in fact. But, of course, I preferred going to Lady Cumnor's own room, where I could see her and Lady Harriet quietly, and where we were not disturbed by the bustle downstairs. Of course we were obliged to go down to lunch; and then I saw my old friends, and renewed pleasant acquaintances. But I really could hardly get any connected conversation with any one. Lord Cumnor seemed so delighted to see me there again: though there were six or seven between us, he was always interrupting with some civil or kind speech especially addressed to me. And, after lunch, Lady Cumnor asked me all sorts of questions about my new life, with as much interest as if I had been her daughter. To be sure, when the duchess came in we had to leave off, and talk about the trousseau she is preparing for Lady Alice. Lady Harriet made such a point of our meeting at the ball; she is such a good, affectionate creature, is Lady Harriet!'

This last was said in a tone of meditative appreciation.

The afternoon of the day on which the ball was to take place, a servant rode over from Hamley with two lovely nosegays, 'with the Mr Hamleys' compliments to Miss Gibson and Miss Kirkpatrick.' Cynthia was the first to receive them. She came dancing into the drawing-room, flourishing the flowers about in either hand, and danced up to Molly, who was trying to settle to her reading, by way of helping on the time till the evening came.

'Look, Molly, look! Here are bouquets for us? Long life to the givers!'

'Who are they from?' asked Molly, taking hold of one, and examining it with tender delight at its beauty.

'Who from? Why, the two paragons of Hamleys to be sure. Isn't it a pretty attention?'

'How kind of them!' said Molly.

'I'm sure it is Osborne who thought of it. He has been so much abroad, where it is such a common compliment to send bouquets to young ladies.'

'I don't see why you should think it is Osborne's thought!' said Molly, reddening a little. 'Mr Roger Hamley used to gather nosegays constantly for his mother, and sometimes for me.'

'Well, never mind whose thought it was, or who gathered them; we've got the flowers, and that's enough. Molly, I'm sure these red flowers will just match your coral necklace and bracelets,' said Cynthia, pulling out some camellias, then a rare kind of flower.

'Oh, please, don't!' exclaimed Molly. 'Don't you see how carefully the colours are arranged – they have taken such pains; please don't.'

'Nonsense!' said Cynthia, continuing to pull them out; 'see, here are quite enough! I'll make you a little coronet of them – sewn on black velvet, which will never be seen – just as they do in France.'

'Oh, I am so sorry! It is quite spoilt,' said Molly.

'Never mind! I'll take this spoilt bouquet; I can make it up again just as prettily as ever; and you shall have this, which has never been touched.' Cynthia went on arranging the crimson buds and flowers to her taste. Molly said nothing, but kept watching Cynthia's nimble fingers tying up the wreath.

'There!' said Cynthia at last; 'when that is sewn on black velvet, to keep the flowers from dying, you'll see how pretty it will look. And there are enough red flowers in this untouched nosegay to carry out the idea!'

'Thank you' (very slowly). 'But sha'n't you mind having only the wrecks of the other?'

'Not I; red flowers would not go with my pink dress.'

'But – I daresay they arranged each nosegay so carefully!'

'Perhaps they did. But I never would allow sentiment to interfere with my choice of colours; and pink does tie one down. Now you, in white muslin, just tipped with crimson, like a daisy, may wear anything.'

Cynthia took the utmost pains in dressing Molly, leaving the clever housemaid to her mother's exclusive service. Mrs Gibson was more anxious about her attire than was either of the girls; it had given her occasion for deep thought and not a few sighs. Her deliberation had ended in her wearing her pearl-grey satin wedding-gown, with a profusion of lace, and white and coloured lilacs. Cynthia was the one who took the affair most lightly. Molly looked upon the ceremony of dressing for the first ball as rather a serious ceremony; certainly as an anxious proceeding. Cynthia was almost as anxious as herself; only Molly wanted her appearance to be correct and unnoticed; and Cynthia was desirous of setting off Molly's rather peculiar charms – her cream-coloured skin, her profusion of curly black hair, her beautiful long-shaped eyes, with their shy, loving expression. Cynthia took up so much time in dressing Molly to her mind, that she herself had to perform her toilet in a hurry. Molly, ready-dressed, sate on a low chair in Cynthia's room, watching the pretty creature's rapid movements, as she stood in her petticoat before the glass, doing up her hair, with quick certainty of effect. At length, Molly heaved a long sigh, and said –

'I should like to be pretty!'

'Why, Molly,' said Cynthia, turning round with an exclamation on the tip of her tongue; but when she caught the innocent, wistful look on Molly's face, she instinctively checked what she was going to say, and, half-smiling to her own reflection in the glass, she said – 'The French girls would tell you, to believe that you were pretty would make you so.'

Molly paused, before replying –

'I suppose they would mean that, if you knew you were pretty, you would never think about your looks; you would be so certain of being liked, and that it is caring—'

'Listen! that's eight o'clock striking. Don't trouble yourself with trying to interpret a French girl's meaning; but help me on with my frock, there's a dear one.'

The two girls were dressed, and standing over the fire waiting for the carriage in Cynthia's room, when Maria (Betty's successor) came hurrying into the room. Maria had been officiating as maid to Mrs Gibson; but she had had intervals of leisure, in which she had rushed upstairs, and, under the pretence of offering her services, had seen the young ladies' dresses, and the sight of so many nice clothes had sent her into a state of excitement which made her think nothing of rushing upstairs for the twentieth time, with a nosegay still more beautiful than the two previous ones.

'Here, Miss Kirkpatrick! No, it's not for you, miss!' as Molly, being nearer to the door, offered to take it and pass it to Cynthia. 'It's for Miss Kirkpatrick; and there's a note for her besides!'

Cynthia said nothing, but took the note and the flowers. She held the note so that Molly could read it at the same time she did.

'I send you some flowers; and you must allow me to claim the first dance after nine o'clock, before which time I fear I cannot arrive.

C.P.'

'Who is it?' asked Molly.

Cynthia looked extremely irritated, indignant, perplexed – what was it turned her cheek so pale, and made her eyes so full of fire?

'It is Mr Preston,' said she, in answer to Molly. 'I shall not dance with him; and here go his flowers' —

Into the very middle of the embers, which she immediately stirred down upon the beautiful shining petals as if she wished to annihilate them as soon as possible. Her voice had never been raised; it was as sweet as usual; nor, though her movements were prompt enough, were they hasty or violent.

'Oh!' said Molly, 'those beautiful flowers! We might have put them in water.'

'No,' said Cynthia; 'it's best to destroy them. We don't want them; and I can't bear to be reminded of that man.'

'It was an impertinent, familiar note,' said Molly. 'What right had he to express himself in that way – no beginning, no end, and only initials! Did you know him well, when you were at Ashcombe, Cynthia?'

'Oh, don't let us think any more about him,' replied Cynthia. 'It is quite enough to spoil my pleasure at the ball to think that he will be there. But I hope I shall get engaged before he comes, so that I can't dance with him – and don't you, either!'

'There! they are calling for us,' exclaimed Molly, and with quick step, yet careful of their draperies, they made their way downstairs to the place where Mr and Mrs Gibson awaited them. Yes; Mr Gibson was going – even if he had to leave them afterwards to attend to any professional call. And Molly suddenly began to admire her father as a handsome man, when she saw him now, in full evening attire. Mrs Gibson, too – how pretty she was! In short, it was true that no better-looking a party than these four people entered the Hollingford ball-room that evening.

CHAPTER 26

A Charity Ball

At the present time there are few people at a public ball besides the dancers and their chaperons, or relations in some degree interested in them. But in the days when Molly and Cynthia were young – before railroads were, and before their consequences, the excursion-trains,* which take every one up to London now-a-days, there to see their fill of gay crowds and fine dresses – going to an annual charity-ball, even though all thought of dancing had passed by years ago, and without any of the responsibilities of a chaperon, was a very allowable and favourite piece of dissipation to all the kindly old maids who thronged the country towns of England. They aired their old lace and their best dresses; they saw the aristocratic magnates of the country side; they gossipped with their coevals, and speculated on the romances of the young around them in a curious, yet friendly, spirit. The Miss Brownings would have thought themselves sadly defrauded of the gayest event of the year, if anything had prevented their attending the charity-ball; and Miss Browning would have been indignant, Miss Phoebe aggrieved, had they not been asked to Ashcombe and Coreham, by friends at each place, who had, like them, gone through the dancing-stage of life some five-and-twenty years before, buy who liked still to haunt the scenes of their former enjoyment, and see a younger generation dance on, 'regardless of their doom.'* They had come in one of the two sedan-chairs that yet lingered in use at Hollingford; such a night as this brought a regular harvest of gains to the two old men who, in what was called the 'town's livery', trotted backwards and forwards with their many loads of ladies and finery. There were some post-chaises, and some 'flys';

but, after mature deliberation, Miss Browning had decided to keep to the more comfortable custom of the sedan-chair, 'which,' as she said to Miss Piper, one of her visitors, 'came into the parlour, and got full of the warm air, and nipped you up and carried you tight and cosy into another warm room, where you could walk out without having to show your legs by going up steps, or down steps.' Of course, only one could go at a time; but here again a little of Miss Browning's good management arranged everything so very nicely, as Miss Horn-blower (their other visitor) remarked. She went first, and remained in the warm cloak-room until her hostess followed; and then the two ladies went arm-in-arm into the ball-room, finding out convenient seats whence they could watch the arrivals and speak to their passing friends, until Miss Phoebe and Miss Piper entered, and came to take possession of the seats reserved for them by Miss Browning's care. These two younger ladies came in, also arm-in-arm, but with a certain timid flurry in look and movement very different from the composed dignity of their seniors (by two or three years). When all four were once more assembled together, they took breath, and began to converse.

'Upon my word, I really do think this is a better room than our Ashcombe Court-house!'

'And how prettily it is decorated!' piped out Miss Piper. 'How well the roses are made! But you all have such taste at Hollingford.'

'There's Mrs Dempster,' cried Miss Hornblower; 'she said she and her two daughters were asked to stay at Mr Sheepshanks'. Mr Preston was to be there, too; but I suppose they could not all come at once. Look! and there is young Roscoe, our new doctor. I declare it seems as if all Ashcombe were here. Mr Roscoe! Mr Roscoe! come here and let me introduce you to Miss Browning, the friend we are staying with. We think very highly of our young doctor, I can assure you, Miss Browning.'

Mr Roscoe bowed and simpered at hearing his own praises. But Miss Browning had no notion of having any doctor praised who had come to settle on the very verge of Mr Gibson's practice; so she said to Miss Hornblower –

'You must be glad, I am sure, to have somebody you can call in, if you are in a sudden hurry, or for things that are too trifling to trouble Mr Gibson about; and I should think Mr Roscoe would feel it a great advantage to profit, as he will naturally have the opportunity of doing, by witnessing Mr Gibson's skill!'

Probably, Mr Roscoe would have felt more aggrieved by this speech than he really was, if his attention had not been called off, just then, by the entrance of the very Mr Gibson who was being spoken of. Almost before Miss Browning had ended her severe and depreciatory remark, she had asked his friend Miss Hornblower –

'Who is that lovely girl in pink, just come in?'

'Why, that's Cynthia Kirkpatrick!' said Miss Hornblower, taking up a ponderous gold eyeglass to make sure of her fact. 'How she has grown! To be sure, it is two or three years since she left Ashcombe – she was very pretty then – people did say Mr Preston admired her very much; but she was so young!'

'Can you introduce me?' asked the impatient young surgeon. 'I should like to ask her to dance.'

When Miss Hornblower returned from her greeting to her former acquaintance, Mrs Gibson, and had accomplished the introduction which Mr Roscoe had requested, she began her little confidences to Miss Browning.

'Well, to be sure! How condescending we are! I remember the time when Mrs Kirkpatrick wore old black silks, and was thankful and civil as became her place as a schoolmistress, and as having to earn her bread. And now she is in a satin; and she speaks to me as if she just could recollect who I was, if she tried very hard! It isn't so long ago since Mrs Dempster came to consult me as to whether Mrs Kirkpatrick would be offended, if she sent her a new breadth for her lilac silk-gown, in place of one that had been spoilt by Mrs Dempster's servant spilling the coffee over it the night before; and she took it and was thankful, for all she's dressed in pearl-grey satin now! and she would have been glad enough to marry Mr Preston in those days.'

'I thought you said he admired her daughter,' put in Miss Browning to her irritated friend.

'Well! perhaps I did, and perhaps it was so; I'm sure I can't tell; he was a great deal at the house. Miss Dixon keeps a school in the same house now, and I'm sure she does it a great deal better.'

'The earl and the countess are very fond of Mrs Gibson,' said Miss Browning, 'I know, for Lady Harriet told us when she came to drink tea with us last autumn; and they desired Mr Preston to be very attentive to her, when she lived at Ashcombe.'

'For goodness' sake, don't go and repeat what I've been saying about Mr Preston and Mrs Kirkpatrick to her ladyship! One may be mistaken, and you know I only said "people talked about it"'.

Miss Hornblower was evidently alarmed lest her gossip should be repeated to the Lady Harriet, who appeared to be on such an intimate footing with her Hollingford friends. Nor did Miss Browning dissipate the illusion. Lady Harriet had drunk tea with them, and might do it again; and, at any rate, the little fright she had put her friend into was not a bad return for that praise of Mr Roscoe, which had offended Miss Browning's loyalty to Mr Gibson.

Meanwhile Miss Piper and Miss Phoebe, who had not the character of *esprits-forts** to maintain, talked of the dresses of the people present, beginning by complimenting each other.

'What a lovely turban* you have got on, Miss Piper, if I may be allowed to say so: so becoming to your complexion!'

'Do you think so?' said Miss Piper, with ill-concealed gratification; it was something to have a 'complexion' at forty-five. 'I got it at Brown's, at Somerton, for this very ball. I thought I must have something to set off my gown, which isn't quite so new as it once was; and I have no handsome jewellery like you' – looking with admiring eyes at a large miniature, set round with pearls, which served as a shield to Miss Phoebe's breast.

'It is handsome,' that lady replied. 'It is a likeness of my dear mother; Dorothy has got my father on. The miniatures were both taken at the same time; and just about then my uncle died and left us each a legacy of fifty pounds, which we agreed to spend on the setting of our miniatures. But, because they are so valuable, Dorothy always keeps them locked up with the best silver, and hides the box somewhere; she never will tell me where, because, she says, I've such weak nerves, and that if a burglar, with a loaded pistol at my head, were to ask me where we kept our plate and jewels, I should be sure to tell him; and, she says, for her part, she would never think of revealing it under any circumstances. (I'm sure I hope she won't be tried.) But that's the reason I don't wear it often; it's only the second time I've had it on; and I can't even get at it, and look at it, which I should like to do. I shouldn't have had it on tonight, but that Dorothy gave it out to me, saying it was but a proper compliment to pay to the Duchess of Menteith, who is to be here in her diamonds.'

'Dear-ah-me! Is she really! Do you know I never saw a duchess

before!' And Miss Piper drew herself up and craned her neck, as
if resolved to 'behave herself properly', as she had been taught to
do at a boarding-school thirty years before, in the presence of 'her
Grace'. By-and-by, she said to Phoebe, with a sudden jerk out of
position – 'Look, look! that's our Mr Cholmley, the magistrate'
(he was the great man of Coreham); 'and that's Mrs Cholmley in
red satin, and Mr George and Mr Harry from Oxford, I do
declare; and Miss Cholmley; and pretty Miss Sophy. I should like
to go and speak to them, but then it's so formidable crossing a
room without a gentleman. And there is Coxe the butcher and his
wife! Why, all Coreham seems to be here! And how Mrs Coxe
can afford such a gown I can't make out, for one; for I know
Coxe had some difficulty in paying for the last sheep he bought of
my brother.'

Just at this moment the band, consisting of two violins, a harp,
and an occasional clarionet, having finished their tuning, and
brought themselves as nearly into accord as was possible, struck
up a brisk country-dance, and partners quickly took their places.
Mrs Gibson was secretly a little annoyed at Cynthia's being one
of those to stand up in this early dance, the performers in which
were principally the punctual plebeians of Hollingford, who, when
a ball was fixed to begin at eight, had no notion of being later,
and so losing part of the amusement for which they had paid their
money. She imparted some of her feelings to Molly, sitting by her,
longing to dance, and beating time to the spirited music with one
of her pretty little feet.

'Your dear papa is always so very punctual! Tonight it seems
almost a pity, for we really are here before there is any one come
that we know.'

'Oh! I see so many people here that I know. There are Mr and
Mrs Smeaton, and that nice good-tempered daughter.'

'Oh! booksellers and butchers, if you will.'

'Papa has found a great many friends to talk to.'

'Patients, my dear – hardly friends. There are some nice-looking
people here,' catching her eye on the Cholmleys; 'but I daresay
they have driven over from the neighbourhood of Ashcombe or
Coreham, and have hardly calculated how soon they would get
here. I wonder when the Towers party will come. Ah! there's Mr
Ashton, and Mr Preston. Come, the room is beginning to fill.'

So it was, for this was to be a very good ball, people said; and
a large party from the Towers was coming, and a duchess in

diamonds among the number. Every great house in the district was expected to be full of guests on these occasions; but, at this early hour, the townspeople had the floor almost entirely to themselves; the county-magnates came dropping in later; and chiefest among them all was the lord-lieutenant from the Towers. But tonight they were unusually late; and, the aristocratic ozone being absent from the atmosphere, there was a flatness about the dancing of all those who considered themselves above the plebeian ranks of the trades-people. They, however, enjoyed themselves thoroughly, and sprang and bounded, till their eyes sparkled and their cheeks glowed with exercise and excitement. Some of the more prudent parents, mindful of the next day's duties, began to consider at what hour they ought to go home; but with all there was an expressed or unexpressed curiosity to see the duchess and her diamonds; for the Menteith diamonds were famous in higher circles than that now assembled; and their fame had trickled down to it through the medium of lady's-maids and housekeepers. Mr Gibson had had to leave the ball-room for a time, as he had anticipated, but he was to return to his wife as soon as his duties were accomplished; and, in his absence, Mrs Gibson kept herself a little aloof from the Miss Brownings and those of her acquaintance who would willingly have entered into conversation with her, with the view of attaching herself to the skirts of the Towers party, when they should make their appearance. If Cynthia would not be so very ready in engaging herself to every possible partner who asked her to dance, there were sure to be young men staying at the Towers who would be on the look-out for pretty girls; and who could tell to what a dance might lead? Molly, too, though not so good a dancer as Cynthia, and, from her timidity, less graceful and easy, was becoming engaged pretty deeply; and, it must be confessed, she was longing to dance every dance, no matter with whom. Even she might not be available for the more aristocratic partners Mrs Gibson anticipated. She was feeling very much annoyed with the whole proceedings of the evening, when she was aware of some one standing by her; and, turning a little to one side, she saw Mr Preston keeping guard, as it were, over the seats which Molly and Cynthia had just quitted. He was looking so black that, if their eyes had not met, Mrs Gibson would have preferred not speaking to him; as it was, she thought it unavoidable.

'The rooms are not well lighted tonight; are they, Mr Preston?'

'No,' said he; 'but who could light such dingy old paint as this, loaded with evergreens, too, which always darken a room?'

'And the company, too! I always think that freshness and brilliancy of dress go as far as anything to brighten up a room. Look what a set of people are here: the greater part of the women are dressed in dark silks, really only fit for the morning. The place will be quite different by-and-by, when the county-families are in a little more force.'

Mr Preston made no reply. He had put his glass in his eye, apparently for the purpose of watching the dancers. If its exact direction could have been ascertained, it would have been found that he was looking intently and angrily at a flying figure in pink muslin; many a one was gazing at Cynthia with intentness besides himself, but no one in anger. Mrs Gibson was not so fine an observer as to read all this; but here was a gentlemanly and handsome young man, to whom she could prattle, instead of either joining herself on to objectionable people, or sitting all forlorn until the Towers party came. So she went on with her small remarks.

'You are not dancing, Mr Preston!'

'No! The partner I had engaged has made some mistake. I am waiting to have an explanation with her.'

Mrs Gibson was silent. An uncomfortable tide of recollections appeared to come over her; she, like Mr Preston, watched Cynthia; the dance was ended, and she was walking round the room in easy unconcern as to what might await her. Presently, her partner, Mr Harry Cholmley, brought her back to her seat. She took the one vacant next to Mr Preston, leaving that by her mother for Molly's occupation. The latter returned a moment afterwards to her place. Cynthia seemed entirely unconscious of Mr Preston's neighbourhood. Mrs Gibson leaned forwards, and said to her daughter –

'Your last partner was a gentleman, my dear. You are improving in your selection. I really was ashamed of you before, figuring away* with that attorney's clerk. Molly, do you know whom you have been dancing with? I have found out he is the Coreham bookseller.'

'That accounts for his being so well-up in all the books I've been wanting to hear about,' said Molly eagerly, but with a spice of malice in her mind. 'He really was very pleasant, mamma,' she added; 'and he looks quite a gentleman, and dances beautifully.'

'Very well. But remember, if you go on in this way, you will have to shake hands over the counter tomorrow morning with some of your partners of tonight,' said Mrs Gibson coldly.

'But I really don't know how to refuse when people are introduced to me and ask me, and I am longing to dance. You know tonight it is a charity-ball, and papa said everybody danced with everybody,' said Molly, in a pleading tone of voice; for she could not quite thoroughly enjoy herself, if she was out of harmony with any one. What reply Mrs Gibson would have made to this speech cannot now be ascertained; for, before she could answer, Mr Preston stepped a little forwards, and said, in a tone which he meant to be icily indifferent, but which trembled with anger –

'If Miss Gibson finds any difficulty in refusing a partner, she has only to apply to Miss Kirkpatrick for instructions.'

Cynthia lifted up her beautiful eyes, and, fixing them on Mr Preston's face, said, very quietly, as if only stating a matter of fact –

'You forget, I think, Mr Preston; Miss Gibson implied that she wished to dance with the person who asked her – that makes all the difference. I can't instruct her how to act in that difficulty.'

And to the rest of this little conversation Cynthia appeared to lend no ear; and she was almost directly claimed by her next partner. Mr Preston took the seat now left empty, much to Molly's annoyance. At first she feared lest he might be going to ask her to dance; but, instead, he put out his hand for Cynthia's nosegay, which she had left on rising, entrusted to Molly. It had suffered considerably from the heat of the room, and was no longer full and fresh; not so much so as Molly's, which had not, in the first instance, been pulled to pieces in picking out the scarlet flowers which now adorned her hair, and which had since been cherished with more care. Enough, however, remained of Cynthia's to show very distinctly that it was not the one Mr Preston had sent; and it was, perhaps, to convince himself of this, that he rudely asked to examine it. But Molly, faithful to what she imagined would be Cynthia's wish, refused to allow him to touch it; she only held it a little nearer.

'Miss Kirkpatrick has not done me the honour of wearing the bouquet I sent her, I see. She received it, I suppose, and my note?'

'Yes,' said Molly, rather intimidated by the tone in which this was said. 'But we had already accepted these two nosegays.'

Mrs Gibson was just the person to come to the rescue with her honeyed words, on such an occasion as the present. She evidently was rather afraid of Mr Preston, and wished to keep at peace with him.

'Oh, yes, we were so sorry! Of course, I don't mean to say we could be sorry for any one's kindness; but two such lovely nosegays had been sent from Hamley Hall – you may see how beautiful from what Molly holds in her hand – and they had come before yours, Mr Preston.'

'I should have felt honoured if you had accepted of mine, since the young ladies were so well provided for. I was at some pains in selecting the flowers at Green's; I think I may say it was rather more *recherché** than that of Miss Kirkpatrick's, which Miss Gibson holds so tenderly and securely in her hand.'

'Oh, because Cynthia would take out the most effective flowers to put in my hair!' exclaimed Molly eagerly.

'Did she?' said Mr Preston, with a certain accent of pleasure in his voice, as though he were glad she set so little store by the nosegay; and he walked off to stand behind Cynthia in the quadrille that was being danced; and Molly saw him making her reply to him – against her will, Molly was sure. But, somehow, his face and manner implied power over her. She looked grave, deaf, indifferent, indignant, defiant; but, after a half-whispered speech to Cynthia, at the conclusion of the dance, she evidently threw him an impatient consent to what he was asking, for he walked off with a disagreeable smile of satisfaction on his handsome face.

All this time, the murmurs were spreading at the lateness of the party from the Towers, and person after person came up to Mrs Gibson, as if she were the accredited authority as to the earl and countess's plans. In one sense this was flattering; but then the acknowledgment of common ignorance and wonder reduced her to the level of the inquirers. Mrs Goodenough felt herself particularly aggrieved; she had had her spectacles on for the last hour and a half, in order to be ready for the sight the very first minute any one from the Towers appeared at the door.

'I had a headache,' she complained, 'and I should have sent my money, and never stirred out o' doors tonight; for I've seen a many of these here balls, and my lord and my lady too, when they were better worth looking at nor they are now; but every one was talking of the duchess, and the duchess and her diamonds, and I thought I shouldn't like to be behindhand, and never ha' seen neither the duchess nor her diamonds; so I'm here, and coal and candle-light wasting away at home, for I told Sally to sit up for me; and, above everything, I cannot abide waste. I took it from my mother, who was such a one against waste as you never see now-a-days. She was a manager if ever there was a one; and brought up nine children on less than any one else could do, I'll be bound. Why! she wouldn't let us be extravagant – not even in the matter of colds. Whenever any on us had got a pretty bad cold, she took the opportunity and cut our hair; for, she said, said she, it was of no use having two colds when one would do – and cutting of our hair was sure to give us a cold. But, for all that, I wish the duchess would come.'

'Ah! but fancy what it is to me!' sighed out Mrs Gibson; 'so long as I have been without seeing the dear family – and seeing so little of them the other day when I was at the Towers (for the duchess would have my opinion on Lady Alice's trousseau, and kept asking me so many questions, it took up all the time) – and Lady Harriet's last words were a happy anticipation of our meeting tonight. It's nearly twelve o'clock!'

Every one of any pretensions to gentility was painfully affected by the absence of the family from the Towers; the very fiddlers seemed unwilling to begin playing a dance that might be interrupted by the entrance of the great folks. Miss Phoebe Browning had apologised for them – Miss Browning had blamed them with calm dignity; it was only the butchers and bakers and candlestick-makers who rather enjoyed the absence of restraint, and were happy and hilarious.

At last, there was a rumbling, and a rushing, and a whispering, and the music stopped; so the dancers were obliged to do so too; and in came Lord Cumnor in his state dress, with a fat, middle-aged woman on his arm; she was dressed almost like a girl – in a sprigged muslin, with natural flowers in her hair, but not a vestige of a jewel or a diamond. Yet it must be the duchess; but what was a duchess without diamonds? – and in a dress which Farmer Hodson's daughter might have worn! Was it the duchess? Could it be the duchess? The little crowd of inquirers around Mrs Gibson thickened, to hear her confirm their disappointing surmise. After the duchess came Lady Cumnor, looking like Lady Macbeth in black velvet – a cloud upon her brow, made more conspicuous by the lines of age, rapidly gathering on her handsome face; and Lady Harriet, and other ladies, amongst whom there was one dressed so like the duchess as to suggest the idea of a sister rather than a daughter, as far as dress went. There was Lord Hollingford, plain in face, awkward in person, gentlemanly in manner; and half-a-dozen younger men, Lord Albert Monson, Captain James, and others of their age and standing, who came in looking nothing if not critical. This long-expected party swept up to the seats reserved for them at the head of the room, apparently regardless of the interruption they caused; for the dancers stood aside, and almost dispersed back to their seats, and, when 'Monymusk'* struck up again, not half the former set of people stood up to finish the dance.

Lady Harriet, who was rather different to Miss Piper, and no more minded crossing the room alone than if the lookers-on were so many cabbages, spied the Gibson party pretty quickly out, and came across to them.

'Here we are at last. How d'ye do, dear? Why, little one' (to Molly), 'how nice you're looking! Aren't we shamefully late?'

'Oh! it's only just past twelve,' said Mrs Gibson, 'and I daresay you dined very late.'

'It wasn't that; it was that ill-mannered woman, who went to her own room after we came out from dinner; and she and Lady Alice stayed there invisible, till we thought they were putting on some splendid attire – as they ought to have done – and at half-past ten, when mamma sent up to them to say the carriages were at the door, the duchess sent down for some beef-tea, and at last appeared à l'enfant* as you see her. Mamma is so angry with her, and some of the others are so annoyed at not coming earlier, and one or two are giving themselves airs about coming at all. Papa is the only one who is not affected by it.' Then, turning to Molly, Lady Harriet asked –

'Have you been dancing much, Miss Gibson?'

'Yes; not every dance, but nearly all.'

It was a simple question enough; but Lady Harriet's speaking at all to Molly had become to Mrs Gibson almost like shaking a red rag at a bull; it was the one thing sure to put her out of temper. But she would not have shown this to Lady Harriet for the world; only she contrived to baffle any endeavours at further conversation between the two, by placing herself betwixt Lady Harriet and Molly, when the former asked to sit down in the absent Cynthia's room.

'I won't go back to those people, I am so mad with them; and, besides, I hardly saw you the other day, and I must have some gossip with you.' So she sat down by Mrs Gibson, and, as Mrs Goodenough afterwards expressed it, 'looked like anybody else'. Mrs Goodenough said this to excuse herself for a little misadventure she fell into. She had taken a deliberate survey of the grandees at the upper end of the room, spectacles on nose, and had inquired in no very measured voice, who everybody was, from Mr Sheepshanks, my lord's agent, and her very good neighbour, who in vain tried to check her loud ardour for information by replying to her in whispers. But she was rather deaf as well as blind; so his low tones only brought upon him fresh inquiries. Now, satisfied as far as she could be, and on her way to departure, and the extinguishing of fire and candle-light, she stopped opposite to Mrs Gibson, and thus addressed her by way of renewal of their former subject of conversation –

'Such a shabby thing for a duchess I never saw; not a bit of a diamond near her! They're none of 'em worth looking at except the countess, and she's always a personable woman, and not so lusty as she was. But they're not worth waiting up for till this time o' night.'

There was a moment's pause. Then Lady Harriet put her hand out, and said –

'You don't remember me, but I know you from having seen you at the Towers. Lady Cumnor is a good deal thinner than she was, but we hope her health is better for it.'

'It's Lady Harriet,' said Mrs Gibson to Mrs Goodenough, in reproachful dismay.

'Deary me, your ladyship! I hope I've given no offence! But, you see – that is to say, your ladyship sees – that it's late hours for such folks as me, and I only stayed out of my bed to see the duchess, and I thought she'd come in diamonds and a coronet; and it puts one out, at my age, to be disappointed in the only chance I'm likely to have of so fine a sight.'

'I'm put out too', said Lady Harriet. 'I wanted to have come early, and here we are as late as this! I'm so cross and ill-tempered, I should be glad to hide myself in bed as soon as you will do.'

She said this so sweetly that Mrs Goodenough relaxed into a smile, and her crabbedness into a compliment.

'I don't believe as ever your ladyship can be cross and ill-tempered with that pretty face. I'm an old woman, so you must let me say so.' Lady Harriet stood up, and made a low curtsey. Then holding out her hand, she said –

'I won't keep you up any longer; but I'll promise one thing in return for your pretty speech; if ever I am a duchess, I'll come and show myself to you in all my robes and gewgaws. Good night, madam!'

'There! I knew how it would be!' said she, not resuming her seat. 'And on the eve of a county election too!'

'Oh! you must not take old Mrs Goodenough as a specimen, dear Lady Harriet. She is always a grumbler! I am sure no one else would complain of your all being as late as you liked,' said Mrs Gibson.

'What do you say, Molly?' said Lady Harriet, suddenly turning her eyes on Molly's face. 'Don't you think we've lost some of our popularity – which at this time means votes – by coming so late? Come, answer me! you used to be a famous little truth-teller.'

'I don't know about popularity or votes,' said Molly, rather unwillingly. 'But I think many people were sorry you did not come sooner; and isn't that rather a proof of popularity?' she added.

'That's a very neat and diplomatic answer,' said Lady Harriet, smiling, and tapping Molly's cheek with her fan.

'Molly knows nothing about it,' said Mrs Gibson, a little off her guard. 'It would be very impertinent if she or any one else questioned Lady Cumnor's perfect right to come when she chose.'

'Well, all I know is, I must go back to mamma now; but I shall make another raid into these regions by-and-by, and you must keep a place for me. Ah! there are—the Miss Brownings; you see I don't forget my lesson, Miss Gibson.'

'Molly, I cannot have you speaking so to Lady Harriet,' said Mrs Gibson, as soon as she was left alone with her stepdaughter. 'You would never have known her at all, if if had not been for me, and don't be always putting yourself into our conversation.'

'But I must speak if she asks me questions,' pleaded Molly.

'Well! if you must, you must, I acknowledge. I'm candid about that at any rate. But there's no need for you to set up to have an opinion at your age.'

'I don't know how to help it,' said Molly.

'She's such a whimsical person; look there, if she's not talking to Miss Phoebe; and Miss Phoebe is so weak she'll be easily led away into fancying she's hand and glove with Lady Harriet. If there is one thing I hate more than another, it is the trying to make out an intimacy with great people.'

Molly felt innocent enough; so she offered no justification of herself, and made no reply. Indeed, she was more occupied in watching Cynthia. She could not understand the change that seemed to have come over her. She was dancing, it was true, with the same lightness and grace as before; but the smooth, bounding motion, as of a feather blown onwards by the wind, was gone. She was conversing with her partner, but without the soft animation that usually shone out upon her countenance. And, when she was brought back to her seat, Molly noticed her changed colour, and her dreamily abstracted eyes.

'What is the matter, Cynthia?' asked she, in a very low voice.

'Nothing,' said Cynthia, suddenly looking up, and in an accent of what, in her, was sharpness. 'Why should there be?'

'I don't know; but you look different to what you did – tired or something.'

'There's nothing the matter; or, if there is, don't talk about it! It's all your fancy.'

This was a rather contradictory speech, to be interpreted by intuition rather than by logic. Molly understood that Cynthia wished for quietness and silence. But what was her surprise, after the speeches that had passed before, and the implication of Cynthia's whole manner to Mr Preston, to see him come up to her, and, without a word, offer his arm and lead her away to dance! It appeared to strike Mrs Gibson as something remarkable; for, forgetting her late passage-at-arms with Molly, she asked, wonderingly, as if almost distrusting the evidence of her senses –

'Is Cynthia going to dance with Mr Preston?'

Molly had scarcely time to answer, before she herself was led off by her partner. She could hardly attend to him or to the figures of the quadrille, for watching for Cynthia among the moving forms.

Once she caught a glimpse of her standing still – downcast – listening to Mr Preston's eager speech. Again, she was walking languidly among the dancers, almost as if she took no notice of those around her. When she and Molly joined each other again, the shade on Cynthia's face had deepened to gloom. But, at the same time, if a physiognomist had studied her expression, he would have read in it defiance and anger, and perhaps also a little perplexity. While this quadrille was going on, Lady Harriet had been speaking to her brother.

'Hollingford!' she said, laying her hand on his arm, and drawing him a little apart from the well-born crowd amid which he stood silent and abstracted, 'you don't know how these good people here have been hurt and disappointed with our being so late, and with the duchess's ridiculous simplicity of dress.'

'Why should they mind it?' asked he, taking advantage of her being out of breath with eagerness.

'Oh, don't be so wise and stupid; don't you see, we're a show and a spectacle – it's like having a pantomime with harlequin and columbine in plain clothes.'

'I don't understand how' – he began.

'Then take it upon trust. They really are a little disappointed, whether they are logical or not in being so, and we must try and make it up to them; for one thing, because I can't bear our vassals to look dissatisfied and disloyal, and then there's the election in June.'

'I really would as soon be out of the House as in it.'

'Nonsense; it would grieve papa beyond measure – but there's no time to talk about that now. You must go and dance with some of the townspeople, and I'll ask Sheepshanks to introduce me to a respectable young farmer. Can't you get Captain James to make himself useful? There he goes with Lady Alice! If I don't get him introduced to the ugliest tailor's daughter I can find for the next dance!' She put her arm in her brother's as she spoke, as if to lead him to some partner. He resisted, however – resisted piteously.

'Pray don't, Harriet. You know I can't dance. I hate it; I always did. I don't know how to get through a quadrille.'

'It's a country dance!' said she resolutely.

'It's all the same. And what shall I say to my partner? I haven't a notion; I shall have no subject in common. Speak of being disappointed – they'll be ten times more disappointed, when they find I can neither dance nor talk!'

'I'll be merciful; don't be so cowardly. In their eyes a lord may dance like a bear – as some lords not very far from me do – if he likes, and they'll take it for grace. And you shall begin with Molly Gibson, your friend the doctor's daughter. She's a good, simple, intelligent little girl, which you'll think a great deal more of, I suppose, than of the frivolous fact of her being very pretty. Clare!

will you allow me to introduce my brother to Miss Gibson? He hopes to engage her for this dance. Lord Hollingford, Miss Gibson!'

Poor Lord Hollingford! there was nothing for him but to follow his sister's very explicit lead; and Molly and he walked off to their places, each heartily wishing their dance together well over. Lady Harriet flew off to Mr Sheepshanks to secure her respectable young farmer, and Mrs Gibson remained alone, wishing that Lady Cumnor would send one of her attendant gentlemen for her. It would be so much more agreeable to be sitting even at the fag-end of nobility than here on a bench with everybody; hoping that everybody would see Molly dancing away with a lord, yet vexed that the chance had so befallen that Molly instead of Cynthia was the young lady singled out; wondering if simplicity of dress was now become the highest fashion, and pondering on the possibility of cleverly inducing Lady Harriet to introduce Lord Albert Monson to her own beautiful daughter, Cynthia.

Molly found Lord Hollingford, the wise and learned Lord Hollingford, strangely stupid in understanding the mystery of 'Cross hands and back again, down the middle and up again.' He was constantly getting hold of the wrong hands, and as constantly stopping when he had returned to his place, quite unaware that the duties of society and laws of the game required that he should go on capering till he had arrived at the bottom of the room. He perceived that he had performed his part very badly, and apologised to Molly, when once they had arrived at that haven of comparative peace; and he expressed his regret so simply and heartily that she felt at her ease with him at once, especially when he confided to her his reluctance at having to dance at all, and his only doing it under his sister's compulsion. To Molly he was an elderly widower, almost as old as her father; and by-and-by they got into very pleasant conversation. She learnt from him that Roger Hamley had just been publishing a paper in some scientific periodical, which had excited considerable attention, as it was intended to confute some theory of a great French physiologist, and Roger's article proved the writer to be possessed of a most unusual amount of knowledge on the subject. This piece of news was of great interest to Molly; and, in her questions, she herself evinced so much intelligence, and a mind so well prepared for the reception of information, that Lord Hollingford, at any rate, would have felt his quest of popularity a very easy affair indeed, if he might have gone on talking quietly to Molly during the rest of the evening. When he took her back to her place, he found Mr Gibson there, and fell into talk with him, until Lady Harriet once more came to stir him up to his duties. Before very long, however, he returned to Mr Gibson's side, and began telling him of this paper of Roger Hamley's, of which Mr Gibson had not yet heard. In the midst of their conversation, as they stood close by Mrs Gibson, Lord Hollingford saw Molly in the distance, and interrupted himself to say, 'What a charming little lady that daughter of yours is! Most girls of her age are so difficult to talk to; but she is intelligent and full of interest in all sorts of sensible things; well read, too – she was up in the *Règne Animal** – and very pretty!'

Mr Gibson bowed, much pleased at such a compliment from such a man, were he lord or not. It is very likely that, if Molly had been a stupid listener, Lord Hollingford would not have discovered her beauty; or the converse might be asserted – if she had not been young and pretty, he would not have exerted himself to talk on scientific subjects in a manner which she could understand. But, in whatever way Molly had won his approbation and admiration, there was no doubt that she had earned it somehow. And, when she next returned to her place, Mrs Gibson greeted her with soft words and a gracious smile; for it does not require much reasoning power to discover that, if it is a very fine thing to be mother-in-law to a very magnificent three-tailed bashaw,* it presupposes that the wife who makes the connection between the two parties is in harmony with her mother. So far had Mrs Gibson's thoughts wandered into futurity! She only wished that the happy chance had fallen to Cynthia's instead of to Molly's lot. But Molly was a docile, sweet creature, very pretty, and remarkably intelligent, as my lord had said. It was a pity that Cynthia preferred making millinery to reading; but perhaps that could be rectified. And there was Lord Cumnor coming to speak to her, and Lady Cumnor nodding to her, and indicating a place by her side.

It was not an unsatisfactory ball upon the whole to Mrs Gibson, although she paid the usual penalty for sitting up beyond her ordinary hour in perpetual glare and movement. The next morning she awoke irritable and fatigued; and a little of the same feeling oppressed both Cynthia and Molly. The former was lounging in the window-seat, holding a three-days'-old newspaper in her hand, which she was making a pretence of reading, when she was startled by her mother's saying –

'Cynthia! can't you take up a book and improve yourself? I am sure your conversation will never be worth listening to unless you read something better than newspapers. Why don't you keep up your French? There was some French book that Molly was reading – *Le Règne Animal*, I think.'

'No! I never read it!' said Molly, blushing. 'Mr Roger Hamley sometimes read pieces out of it, when I was first at the Hall, and told me what it was about.'

'Oh! well. Then I suppose I was mistaken. But it comes to all the same thing. Cynthia, you really must learn to settle yourself to some improving reading every morning.'

Rather to Molly's surprise, Cynthia did not reply a word; but dutifully went and brought down from among her Boulogne school-books *Le Siècle de Louis XIV*.* But, after a while, Molly saw that this 'improving reading' was just as much a mere excuse for Cynthia's thinking her own thoughts as the newspaper had been.

CHAPTER 27

Father and Sons

Things were not going on any better at Hamley Hall. Nothing had occurred to change the state of dissatisfied feeling into which the Squire and his eldest son had respectively fallen; and the long continuance merely of dissatisfaction is sure of itself to deepen the feeling. Roger did all in his power to bring the father and son together, but sometimes wondered if it would not have been better to leave them alone; for they were falling into the habit of each making him their confidant, and so defining emotions and opinions which would have had less distinctness if they had been unexpressed. There was little enough relief in the daily life at the Hall to help them all to shake off the gloom; and it even told on the health of both the Squire and Osborne. The Squire became thinner, his skin as well as his clothes began to hang loose about him, and the freshness of his colour turned to red streaks; till his cheeks looked like Eardiston pippins, instead of resembling 'a

Katherine pear on the side that's next the sun.'* Roger thought
that his father sate indoors and smoked in his study more than
was good for him; but it had become difficult to get him far afield;
he was too much afraid of coming across some sign of the
discontinued drainage works, or being irritated afresh by the sight
of his depreciated timber. Osborne was wrapt up in the idea of
arranging his poems for the press, and so working out his wish
for independence. What with daily writing to his wife – taking his
letters himself to a distant post-office, and receiving hers there –
touching up his sonnets, etc., with fastidious care – and occasionally giving himself the pleasure of a visit to the Gibsons, and
enjoying the society of the two pleasant girls there, he found little
time for being with his father. Indeed, Osborne was too self-
indulgent, or 'sensitive', as he termed it, to bear well with the
Squire's gloomy fits or too frequent querulousness. The consciousness of his secret, too, made Osborne uncomfortable in his father's
presence. It was very well for all parties that Roger was not
'sensitive'; for, if he had been, there were times when it would
have been hard to bear little spurts of the domestic tyranny by
which his father strove to assert his power over both his sons.
One of these occurred very soon after the night of the Hollingford
charity-ball.

Roger had induced his father to come out with him; and the
Squire had, on his son's suggestion, taken with him his long-
unused spud. The two had wandered far afield; perhaps the elder
man had found the unwonted length of exercise too much for
him; for, as he approached the house, on his return, he became
what nurses call in children 'fractious', and ready to turn on his
companion for every remark he made. Roger understood the case
by instinct, as it were, and bore it all with his usual sweetness of
temper. They entered the house by the front door; it lay straight
on their line of march. On the old cracked yellow-marble slab
there lay a card with Lord Hollingford's name on it, which
Robinson, evidently on the watch for their return, hastened out of
his pantry to deliver to Roger.

'His lordship was very sorry not to see you, Mr Roger, and his
lordship left a note for you. Mr Osborne took it, I think, when he
passed through. I asked his lordship, if he would like to see Mr
Osborne, who was indoors, as I thought. But his lordship said he
was pressed for time, and told me to make his excuses.'

'Didn't he ask for me?' growled the Squire.

'No, sir; I can't say as his lordship did. He would never have thought of Mr Osborne, sir, if I hadn't named him. It was Mr Roger he seemed so keen after.'

'Very odd,' said the Squire. Roger said nothing, although he naturally felt some curiosity. He went into the drawing-room, not quite aware that his father was following him. Osborne sate at a table near the fire, pen in hand, looking over one of his poems, and dotting the *i*'s, crossing the *t*'s, and now and then pausing over the alteration of a word.

'Oh, Roger!' he said, as his brother came in, 'here's been Lord Hollingford wanting to see you.'

'I know,' replied Roger.

'And he's left a note for you. Robinson tried to persuade him it was for my father, so he's added a "junior" (Roger Hamley, Esq., junior) in pencil.' The Squire was in the room by this time, and what he had overheard rubbed him up still more the wrong way. Roger took his unopened note and read it.

'What does he say?' asked the Squire.

Roger handed him the note. It contained an invitation to dinner, to meet M. Geoffroi de St. H.,* whose views on certain subjects Roger had been advocating in the article Lord Hollingford had spoken about to Molly, when he danced with her at the Hollingford ball. M. Geoffroi de St. H. was in England now, and was expected to pay a visit at the Towers in the course of the following week. He had expressed a wish to meet the author of the paper which had already attracted the attention of the French comparative anatomists; and Lord Hollingford added a few words about his own desire to make the acquaintance of a neighbour whose tastes were so similar to his own; and then followed a civil message from Lord and Lady Cumnor.

Lord Hollingford's hand was cramped and rather illegible. The Squire could not read it all at once, and was enough put out to decline any assistance in deciphering it. At last he made it out.

'So my lord-lieutenant is taking some notice of the Hamleys at last. The election is coming on, is it? But, I can tell him, we're not to be got so easily. I suppose this trap is set for you, Osborne. What's this you've been writing that the French mounseer* is so taken with?'

'It is not me, sir!' said Osborne. 'Both note and call are for Roger.'

'I don't understand it,' said the Squire. 'These Whig fellows have never done their duty by me; not that I want it of them! The Duke of Debenham used to pay the Hamleys a respect due to 'em – the oldest landowners in the county – but since he died, and this shabby Whig lord has succeeded him, I've never dined at the lord-lieutenant's – no, not once.'

'But I think, sir, I've heard you say Lord Cumnor used to invite you – only you did not choose to go,' said Roger.

'Yes. What d'ye mean by that? Do you suppose I was going to desert the principles of my family, and curry favour with the Whigs? No! leave that to them! They can ask the heir of the Hamleys fast enough when a county election is coming on.'

'I tell you, sir,' said Osborne, in the irritable tone he sometimes used when his father was particularly unreasonable, 'it is not me Lord Hollingford is inviting; it is Roger. Roger is making himself known for what he is, a first-rate fellow,' continued Osborne – a sting of self-reproach mingling with his generous pride in his brother – 'and he's getting himself a name; he's been writing about these new French theories and discoveries, and this foreign *savant* very naturally wants to make his acquaintance, and so Lord Hollingford asks him to dine. It's as clear as can be,' lowering his tone, and addressing himself to Roger; 'it has nothing to do with politics, if my father would but see it.'

Of course the Squire heard this little aside with the unlucky uncertainty of hearing which is a characteristic of the beginning of deafness; and its effect on him was perceptible in the increased acrimony of his next speech.

'You young men think you know everything. I tell you it's a palpable Whig trick. And what business has Roger – if it is Roger the man wants – to go currying favour with the French? In my day we were content to hate 'em and lick 'em. But it's just like your conceit, Osborne, setting yourself up to say it's your younger brother they're asking, and not you; I tell you it's you. They think the eldest son was sure to be called after his father, Roger – Roger Hamley, junior. It's as plain as a pike-staff. They know they can't catch me with chaff, but they've got up this French dodge. What business had you to go writing about the French, Roger? I should have thought you were too sensible to take any notice of their fancies and theories; but, if it is you they've asked, I'll not have you going and meeting these foreigners at a Whig house. They ought to have asked Osborne. He's the representative of the Hamleys, if I'm not; and they can't get me, let 'em try ever so.

Besides, Osborne has got a bit of the mounseer about him, which he caught with being so fond of going off to the Continent, instead of coming back to his good old English home.'

He went on repeating much of what he had said before, till he left the room. Osborne had kept on replying to his unreasonable grumblings, which had only added to his anger; and, as soon as the Squire was fairly gone, Osborne turned to Roger, and said –

'Of course you'll go, Roger? Ten to one he'll be in another mind tomorrow.'

'No,' said Roger, bluntly enough – for he was extremely disappointed; 'I won't run the chance of vexing him. I shall refuse.'

'Don't be such a fool!' exclaimed Osborne. 'Really, my father is too unreasonable. You heard how he kept contradicting himself; and such a man as you to be kept under like a child by' —

'Don't let us talk any more about it, Osborne,' said Roger, writing away fast. When the note was written and sent off, he came and put his hand caressingly on Osborne's shoulder, as he sate pretending to read, but in reality vexed with both his father and his brother, though on very different grounds.

'How go the poems, old fellow? I hope they're nearly ready to bring out.'

'No, they're not; and if it weren't for the money, I shouldn't care if they were never published. What's the use of fame, if one mayn't reap the fruits of it?'

'Come now, we'll have no more of that; let's talk about the money. I shall be going up for my Fellowship examination next week, and then we'll have a purse in common; for they'll never think of not giving me a Fellowship now I'm senior wrangler. I'm short enough myself at present, and I don't like to bother my father; but, when I'm Fellow, you shall take me down to Winchester, and introduce me to the little wife.'

'It will be a month next Monday since I left her,' said Osborne, laying down his papers and gazing into the fire, as if by so doing he could call up her image. 'In her letter this morning she bids me give you such a pretty message. It won't bear translating into English; you must read it for yourself,' continued he, pointing out a line or two in a letter he drew from his pocket.

Roger suspected that one or two of the words were wrongly spelt; but their purport was so gentle and loving, and had such a touch of simple, respectful gratitude in them, that he could not help being drawn afresh to the little unseen sister-in-law, whose acquaintance Osborne had made by helping her to look for some missing article of the children's, whom she was taking for their daily walk in Hyde Park. For Mrs Osborne Hamley had been nothing more than a French *bonne*, very pretty, very graceful, and very much tyrannised over by the rough little boys and girls she had in charge. She was a little orphan girl, who had charmed the heads of a travelling English family, as she brought madame some articles of *lingerie* to an hotel; and she had been hastily engaged by them as *bonne* to their children, partly as a pet and plaything herself, partly because it would be so good for the children to learn French from a native (of Alsace!).* By-and-by her mistress ceased to take any particular notice of Aimée in the bustle of London and London gaiety; but, though feeling more and more forlorn in a strange land every day, the French girl strove hard to do her duty. One touch of kindness, however, was enough to set the fountain gushing; and she and Osborne naturally fell into an ideal state of love, to be rudely disturbed by the indignation of the mother, when accident discovered to her the attachment existing between her children's *bonne* and a young man of an entirely different class. Aimée answered truly to all her mistress's questions; but no worldly wisdom, nor any lesson to be learnt from another's experience, could in the least disturb her entire faith in her lover. Perhaps Mrs Townshend did no more than her duty in immediately sending Aimée back to Metz, where she had first met with her, and where such relations as remained to the girl might be supposed to be residing. But, altogether, she knew so little of the kind of people or life to which she was consigning her deposed *protégée* that Osborne, after listening with impatient indignation to the lecture which Mrs Townshend gave him, when he insisted on seeing her in order to learn what had become of his love, that the young man set off straight for Metz in hot haste, and did not let the grass grow under his feet, until he had made Aimée his wife. All this had occurred the previous autumn, and Roger did not know of the step his brother had taken until it was irrevocable. Then came the mother's death, which, besides the simplicity of its own overwhelming sorrow, brought with it the loss of the kind, tender mediatrix, who could always soften and turn his father's heart. It is doubtful, however, if even she could have succeeded in this; for the Squire looked high, and over-high, for the wife of his heir; he detested all foreigners, and moreover held all Roman

Catholics in a dread and abomination something akin to our ancestors' hatred of witchcraft. All these prejudices were strengthened by his grief. Argument would always have glanced harmless away off his shield of utter unreason; but a loving impulse, in a happy moment, might have softened his heart to what he most detested in the former days. But the happy moments came not now, and the loving impulses were trodden down by the bitterness of his frequent remorse, not less than by his growing irritability; so Aimée lived on solitary in the little cottage near Winchester in which Osborne had installed her, when she first came to England as his wife, and in the dainty furnishing of which he had run himself so deeply into debt. For Osborne consulted his own fastidious taste in his purchases rather than her simple childlike wishes and wants, and looked upon the little Frenchwoman rather as the future mistress of Hamley Hall, than as the wife of a man who was wholly dependent on others at present. He had chosen a southern county as being far removed from those midland shires where the name of Hamley of Hamley was well and widely known; for he did not wish his wife to assume, if only for a time, a name which was not justly and legally her own. In all these arrangements he had willingly striven to do his full duty by her; and she repaid him with passionate devotion and admiring reverence. If his vanity had met with a check, or his worthy desires for college honours had been disappointed, he knew where to go for a comforter; one who poured out praise, till her words were choked in her throat by the rapidity of her thoughts, and who emptied the small vials of her indignation on every one who did not acknowledge and bow down to her husband's merits. If she ever wished to go to the *château* – that was his home – and to be introduced to his family, Aimée never hinted a word of it to him. Only, she did yearn, and she did plead, for a little more of her husband's company; and the good reasons which had convinced her of the necessity of his being so much away, when he was present to urge them, failed in their efficacy, when she tried to reproduce them to herself in his absence.

The afternoon of the day on which Lord Hollingford called, Roger was going upstairs, three steps at a time, when, at a turn of the landing, he encountered his father. It was the first time he had seen him since their conversation about the Towers invitation to dinner. The Squire stopped his son, by standing right in the middle of the passage.

'Thou'rt going to meet the mounseer, my lad?' said he, half as affirmation, half as question.

'No, sir; I sent off James almost immediately with a note declining the invitation. I don't care about it – that's to say, not to signify.'

'Why did you take me up so sharp, Roger?' said his father pettishly. 'You all take me up so hastily, now-a-days. I think it hard that a man mustn't be allowed a bit of crossness, when he's tired and heavy at heart – that I do.'

'But, father, I should never like to go to a house where they had slighted you.'

'Nay, nay, lad,' said the Squire, brightening up a little; 'I think I slighted them. They asked me to dinner, after my lord was made Lieutenant, time after time; but I never would go near 'em. I call that my slighting them.'

And no more was said at the time; but the next day the Squire again stopped Roger.

'I've been making Jem try on his livery-coat that he hasn't worn this three or four years – he's got too stout for it now.'

'Well, he needn't wear it, need he? And Dawson's lad will be glad enough of it – he's sadly in want of clothes.'

'Ay, ay; but who's to go with you when you call at the Towers? It's but polite to call after Lord What's-his-name has taken the trouble to come here; and I shouldn't like you to go without a groom.'

'My dear father! I shouldn't know what to do with a man riding at my back. I can find my way to the stableyard for myself, or there'll be some man about to take my horse. Don't trouble yourself about that.'

'Well, you're not Osborne, to be sure. Perhaps it won't strike 'em as strange for you. But you must look up, and hold your own, and remember you're one of the Hamleys, who've been on the same land for hundreds of years, while they're but trumpery Whig folk, who only came into the county in Queen Anne's time.'

CHAPTER 28

Rivalry

For some days after the ball Cynthia seemed languid, and was very silent. Molly, who had promised herself fully as much enjoyment in talking over the past gaiety with Cynthia as in the evening itself, was disappointed when she found that all conversation on the subject was rather evaded than encouraged. Mrs Gibson, it is true, was ready to go over the ground as many times as any one liked; but her words were always like ready-made clothes, and never fitted individual thoughts. Anybody might have used them, and, with a change of proper names, they might have served to describe any ball. She repeatedly used the same language in speaking about it, till Molly knew the sentences and their sequence, even to irritation.

'Ah! Mr Osborne, you should have been there! I said to myself, many a time, how you really should have been there – you and your brother, of course.'

'I thought of you very often during the evening!'

'Did you? Now, that I call very kind of you. Cynthia, darling! Do you hear what Mr Osborne Hamley was saying?' as Cynthia came into the room just then. 'He thought of us all on the evening of the ball.'

'He did better than merely remember us then,' said Cynthia, with her soft, slow smile. 'We owe him thanks for those beautiful flowers, mamma.'

'Oh!' said Osborne, 'you must not thank me exclusively. I believe it was my thought, but Roger took all the trouble of it.'

'I consider the thought as everything,' said Mrs Gibson. 'Thought is spiritual, while action is merely material.'

This fine sentence took the speaker herself by surprise; but, in such conversation as was then going on, it is not necessary to accurately define the meaning of everything that is said.

'I'm afraid the flowers were too late to be of much use, though,' continued Osborne. 'I met Preston the next morning, and of course we talked about the ball. I was sorry to find he had been beforehand with us.'

'He only sent one nosegay, and that was for Cynthia,' said

Molly, looking up from her work. 'And it did not come till after
we had received the flowers from Hamley.' Molly caught a sight
of Cynthia's face, before she bent down again to her sewing. It
was scarlet in colour, and there was a flash of anger in her eyes.
Both she and her mother hastened to speak as soon as Molly had
finished; but Cynthia's voice was choked with passion, and Mrs
Gibson had the word.

'Mr Preston's bouquet was just one of those formal affairs any
one can buy at a nursery-garden, which always strike me as
having no sentiment in them. I would far rather have two or three
lilies of the valley gathered for me by a person I like than the most
expensive bouquet that could be bought!'

'Mr Preston had no business to speak as if he had forestalled
you,' said Cynthia. 'It came just as we were ready to go, and I put
it into the fire directly.'

'Cynthia, my dear love!' said Mrs Gibson (who had never heard
of the fate of the flowers until now), 'what an idea of yourself you
will give to Mr Osborne Hamley; but, to be sure, I can quite
understand it. You inherit my feeling – my prejudice – sentimental
I grant, against bought flowers.'

Cynthia was silent for a moment; then she said, 'I used some of
your flowers, Mr Hamley, to dress Molly's hair. It was a great
temptation, for the colour so exactly matched her coral ornaments; but I believe she thought it treacherous to disturb the
arrangement, so I ought to take all the blame on myself.'

'The arrangement was my brother's, as I told you; but I am sure
he would have preferred seeing them in Miss Gibson's hair rather
than in the blazing fire. Mr Preston comes off far the worst.'
Osborne was rather amused at the whole affair, and would have
liked to probe Cynthia's motives a little farther. He did not hear
Molly saying in as soft a voice as if she were talking to herself, 'I
wore mine just as they were sent,' for Mrs Gibson came in with a
total change of subject.

'Speaking of lilies of the valley, is it true that they grow wild in
Hurstwood? It is not the season for them to be in flower yet; but,
when it is, I think we must take a walk there – with our luncheon
in a basket – a little pic-nic, in fact. You'll join us, won't you?'
turning to Osborne. 'I think it's a charming plan! You could ride
to Hollingford and put up your horse here, and we could have a
long day in the woods, and all come home to dinner – dinner with
a basket of lilies in the middle of the table!'

'I should like it very much,' said Osborne; 'but I may not be at home. Roger is more likely to be here, I believe, at that time – a month hence.' He was thinking of the visit to London to sell his poems, and the run down to Winchester which he anticipated afterwards – the end of May had been the period fixed for this pleasure for some time, not merely in his own mind, but in writing to his wife.

'Oh, but you must be with us! We must wait for Mr Osborne Hamley, must not we, Cynthia?'

'I'm afraid the lilies won't wait,' replied Cynthia.

'Well, then, we must put it off till dog-rose and honey-suckle time. You will be at home then, won't you? Or does the London season present too many attractions?'

'I don't exactly know when dog-roses are in flower!'

'Not know, and you a poet! Don't you remember the lines –

> It was the time of roses,
> We plucked them as we went?'*

'Yes; but that doesn't specify the time of year that is the time of roses; and I believe my movements are guided more by the lunar calendar than the floral. You had better take my brother for your companion; he is practical in his love of flowers. I am only theoretical.'

'Does that fine word "theoretical" imply that you are ignorant?' asked Cynthia.

'Of course we shall be happy to see your brother; but why can't we have you too? I confess to a little timidity in the presence of one so deep and learned as your brother is, from all accounts. Give me a little charming ignorance, if we must call it by that hard word.'

Osborne bowed. It was very pleasant to him to be petted and flattered, even though he knew all the time that it was only flattery. It was an agreeable contrast to the home that was so dismal to him, to come to this house, where the society of two agreeable girls, and the soothing syrup of their mother's speeches, awaited him whenever he liked to come. To say nothing of the difference that struck upon his senses, poetical though he might esteem himself, of a sitting-room full of flowers, and tokens of women's presence, where all the chairs were easy, and all the tables well-covered with pretty things, to the great drawing-room at home, where the draperies were threadbare, and the seats uncomfortable, and where no sign of feminine presence ever now lent a grace to the stiff arrangement of the furniture. Then the meals, light and well-cooked, suited his taste and delicate appetite so much better than the rich and heavy viands prepared by the servants at the Hall, Osborne was becoming a little afraid of falling into the habit of paying too frequent visits to the Gibsons' (and that, not because he feared the consequences of his inter-course with the two young ladies; for he never thought of them excepting as friends; – the fact of his marriage was constantly present to his mind, and Aimée too securely enthroned in his heart, for him to remember that he might be looked upon by others in the light of a possible husband); but the reflection forced itself upon him occasionally, whether he was not trespassing too often on hospitality which he had at present no means of returning?

But Mrs Gibson, in her ignorance of the true state of affairs, was secretly exultant in the attraction which made him come so often and lounge away the hours in her house and garden. She had no doubt that it was Cynthia who drew him thither; and, if the latter had been a little more amenable to reason, her mother would have made more frequent allusions than she did to the crisis which she thought was approaching. But she was restrained by the intuitive conviction that, if her daughter became conscious of what was impending, and was made aware of Mrs Gibson's cautious and quiet efforts to forward the catastrophe, the wilful girl would oppose herself to it with all her skill and power. As it was, Mrs Gibson trusted that Cynthia's affections would become engaged before she knew where she was, and that in that case she would not attempt to frustrate her mother's delicate scheming, even though she did perceive it. But Cynthia had come across too many varieties of flirtation, admiration, and even passionate love, to be for a moment at fault as to the quiet, friendly nature of Osborne's attentions. She received him always as a sister might a brother. It was different when Roger returned from his election as a Fellow of Trinity. The trembling diffidence, the hardly sup-pressed ardour of his manner, made Cynthia understand before long with what kind of love she had now to deal. She did not put it into so many words – no, not even in her secret heart – but she recognised the difference between Roger's relation to her and Osborne's long before Mrs Gibson found it out. Molly was, however, the first to discover the nature of Roger's attentions. The first time they saw him after the ball, it came out to her observant eyes. Cynthia had not been looking well since that evening; she went slowly about the house, pale and heavy-eyed; and, fond as she usually was of exercise and the free fresh air, there was hardly any persuading her now to go out for a walk. Molly watched this fading with tender anxiety; but to all her questions as to whether she had felt over-fatigued with her dancing, whether anything had occurred to annoy her, and all such inquiries, she replied in languid negatives. Once, Molly touched on Mr Preston's name, and found that this was a subject on which Cynthia was raw; now Cynthia's face lighted up with spirit, and her whole body showed her ill-repressed agitation, but she only said a few sharp words, expressive of anything but kindly feeling towards the gentleman, and then bade Molly never name his name to her again. Still, the latter could not imagine that he was more than intensely distasteful to her friend, as well as to herself; he could not be the cause of Cynthia's present indisposition. But this indisposition lasted so many days without change or modification, that even Mrs Gibson noticed it, and Molly became positively uneasy. Mrs Gibson considered Cynthia's quietness and languor as the natural consequence of 'dancing with everybody who asked her' at the ball. Partners whose names were in the 'Red Book'* would apparently, according to Mrs Gibson's judgment, not have produced half the amount of fatigue; and, if Cynthia had been quite well, very probably she would have hit the blot in her mother's speech with one of her touches of sarcasm. Then, again, when Cynthia did not rally, Mrs Gibson grew impatient, and accused her of being fanciful and lazy. At length, and partly at Molly's instance, there came an appeal to Mr Gibson, and a professional examination of the supposed invalid, which Cynthia hated more than anything, especially when the verdict was, that there was nothing very much the matter, only a general lowness of tone and depression of health and spirits, which would soon be remedied by tonics, and meanwhile she was not to be roused to exertion.

'If there is one thing I dislike,' said Cynthia to Mr Gibson, after he had pronounced tonics to be the cure for her present state, 'it is the way doctors have of giving table-spoonfuls of nauseous mixtures as a certain remedy for sorrows and cares.' She laughed up in his face as she spoke; she had always a pretty word and smile for him, even in the midst of her loss of spirits.

'Come! you acknowledge you have "sorrows" by that speech;

we'll make a bargain: if you'll tell me your sorrows and cares, I'll try and find some other remedy for them than giving you what you are pleased to term my nauseous mixtures.'

'No,' said Cynthia, colouring; 'I never said I had sorrows and cares; I spoke generally. What should I have a sorrow about? – you and Molly are only too kind to me;' her eyes filling with tears.

'Well, well, we'll not talk of such gloomy things, and you shall have some sweet emulsion to disguise the taste of the bitters I shall be obliged to fall back upon.'

'Please don't! If you but knew how I dislike emulsions and disguises! I do want bitters – and if I sometimes – if I'm obliged to – if I'm not truthful myself, I do like truth in others – at least, sometimes!' She ended her sentence with another smile; but it was rather faint and watery.

Now, the first person out of the house to notice Cynthia's change of look and manner was Roger Hamley – and yet he did not see her until, under the influence of the 'nauseous mixture', she was beginning to recover. But his eyes were scarcely off her during the first five minutes he was in the room. All the time he was trying to talk to Mrs Gibson in reply to her civil platitudes, he was studying Cynthia; and at the first convenient pause he came and stood before Molly, so as to interpose his person between her and the rest of the room; for some visitors had come in subsequently to his entrance.

'Molly, how ill your sister is looking! What is it? Has she had advice? You must forgive me, but so often those who live together in the same house don't observe the first approaches of illness.'

Now, Molly's love for Cynthia was fast and unwavering; but, if anything tried it, it was the habit Roger had fallen into of always calling Cynthia Molly's sister in speaking to the latter. From any one else it would have been a matter of indifference to her, and hardly to be noticed; it vexed both ear and heart when Roger used the expression; and there was a curtness of manner as well as of words in her reply.

'Oh! she was over-tired by the ball. Papa has seen her, and says she will be all right very soon.'

'I wonder if she wants change of air!' said Roger meditatively. 'I wish – I do wish we could have her at the Hall; you and your mother too, of course. But I don't see how it would be possible – or else how charming it would be!'

Molly felt as if a visit to the Hall under such circumstances would be so entirely different an affair to all her former ones, that she could hardly tell if she should like it or not.

Roger went on –

'You got our flowers in time, did you not? Ah! you don't know how often I thought of you that evening! And you enjoyed it too, didn't you? – you had plenty of agreeable partners, and all that makes a first ball delightful? I heard that your sister danced every dance.'

'It was very pleasant,' said Molly quietly. 'But, after all, I'm not sure if I want to go to another just yet; there seems to be so much trouble connected with a ball.'

'Ah! you are thinking of your sister, and her not being well?'

'No, I was not,' said Molly, rather bluntly. 'I was thinking of the dress, and the dressing, and the weariness the next day.'

He might think her unfeeling, if he liked; she felt as if she had only too much feeling just then, for it was bringing on her a strange contraction of heart. But he was too inherently good himself to put any harsh construction on her speech. Just before he went away, while he was ostensibly holding her hand and wishing her good-bye, he said to her in a voice too low to be generally heard –

'Is there anything I could do for your sister? We have plenty of books, as you know, if she cares for reading.' Then, receiving no affirmative look or word from Molly in reply to this suggestion, he went on – 'Or flowers? she likes flowers. Oh! and our forced strawberries are just ready – I will bring some over tomorrow.'

'I am sure she will like them,' said Molly.

For some reason or other, unknown to the Gibsons, a longer interval than usual occurred between Osborne's visits, while Roger came nearly every day, always with some fresh offering by which he openly sought to relieve Cynthia's indisposition, as far as it lay in his power. Her manner to him was so gentle and gracious that Mrs Gibson became alarmed lest, in spite of his 'uncouthness' (as she was pleased to term it), he might come to be preferred to Osborne, who was so strangely neglecting his own interests in Mrs Gibson's opinion. In her quiet way, she contrived to pass many slights upon Roger; but the darts rebounded from his generous nature, which could not have imagined her motives, and fastened themselves on Molly. She had often been called naughty and passionate when she was a child; and she thought now that she began to understand that she really had a violent temper.

What seemed neither to hurt Roger nor annoy Cynthia made Molly's blood boil; and, now she had once discovered Mrs Gibson's wish to make Roger's visits shorter and less frequent, she was always on the watch for indications of this desire. She read her stepmother's heart, when the latter made allusions to the Squire's weakness, now that Osborne was absent from the Hall, and that Roger was so often away among his friends during the day –

'Mr Gibson and I should be so delighted, if you could have stopped to dinner; but, of course, we cannot be so selfish as to ask you to stay when we remember how your father would be left alone. We were saying yesterday we wondered how he bore his solitude, poor old gentleman!'

Or, as soon as Roger came with his bunch of early roses, it was desirable for Cynthia to go and rest in her own room, while Molly had to accompany Mrs Gibson on some improvised errand or call. Still, Roger, whose object was to give pleasure to Cynthia, and who had, from his boyhood, been always certain of Mr Gibson's friendly regard, was slow to perceive that he was not wanted. If he did not see Cynthia, that was his loss; at any rate, he heard how she was, and left her some little thing which he believed she would like, and was willing to risk the chance of his own gratification by calling four or five times in the hope of seeing her once. At last there came a day when Mrs Gibson went beyond her usual negative snubbiness, and when, in some unwonted fit of crossness, for she was a very placid-tempered person in general, she was guilty of positive rudeness.

Cynthia was very much better. Tonics had ministered to a mind diseased,* though she hated to acknowledge it; her pretty bloom and much of her light-heartedness had come back, and there was no cause remaining for anxiety. Mrs Gibson was sitting at her embroidery in the drawing-room, and the two girls were at the window, Cynthia laughing at Molly's earnest endeavour to imitate the French accent in which the former had been reading a page of Voltaire.* For the duty, or the farce, of settling to 'improving reading' in the mornings was still kept up, although Lord Hollingford, the unconscious suggester of the idea, had gone back to town without making any of the efforts to see Molly again that Mrs Gibson had anticipated on the night of the ball. That Alnaschar vision* had fallen to the ground. It was as yet early morning; a delicious, fresh, lovely June day, the air redolent with the scents of flower-growth and bloom; and, half the time the girls had been ostensibly employed in the French reading, they had been leaning out of the open window, trying to reach a cluster of climbing roses. They had secured them at last, and the buds lay on Cynthia's lap, but many of the petals had fallen off; so, though the perfume lingered about the window-seat, the full beauty of the flowers had passed away. Mrs Gibson had once or twice reproved them for the merry noise they were making, which hindered her in the business of counting the stitches in her pattern; and she had set herself a certain quantity to do that morning before going out, and was of that nature which attaches infinite importance to fulfilling small resolutions, made about indifferent trifles without any reason whatever.

'Mr Roger Hamley,' was announced. 'So tiresome!' said Mrs Gibson, almost in his hearing, as she pushed away her embroidery-frame. She put out her cold, motionless hand to him, with a half-murmured word of welcome, still eyeing her lost embroidery. He took no apparent notice, and passed on to the window.

'How delicious!' said he. 'No need for any more Hamley roses, now yours are out!'

'I agree with you,' said Mrs Gibson, replying to him before either Cynthia or Molly could speak, though he addressed his words to them. 'You have been very kind in bringing us flowers so long; but, now our own are out, we need not trouble you any more.'

He looked at her, with a little surprise clouding his honest face; it was perhaps more at the tone than the words. Mrs Gibson, however, had been bold enough to strike the first blow, and she determined to go on, as opportunity offered. Molly would perhaps have been more pained, if she had not seen Cynthia's colour rise. She waited for her to speak, if need were; for she knew that Roger's defence, if defence were required, might be safely entrusted to Cynthia's ready wit.

He put out his hand for the shattered cluster of roses that lay in Cynthia's lap.

'At any rate,' said he, 'my trouble – if Mrs Gibson considers it has been a trouble to me – will be overpaid, if I may have this.'

'Old lamps for new,'* said Cynthia, smiling as she gave it to him. 'I wish one could always buy nosegays such as you have brought us, as cheaply.'

'You forget the waste of time that, I think, we must reckon as part of the payment,' said her mother. 'Really, Mr Hamley, we must learn to shut our doors on you if you come so often, and at such early hours! I settle myself to my own employment regularly after breakfast till lunchtime; and it is my wish to keep Cynthia and Molly to a course of improving reading and study – so desirable for young people of their age, if they are ever to become intelligent, companionable women; but with early visitors it is quite impossible to observe any regularity of habits.'

All this was said in that sweet, false tone which of late had gone through Molly like the scraping of a slate-pencil on a slate. Roger's face changed. His ruddy colour grew paler for a moment, and he looked grave and not pleased. In another moment, the wonted frankness of expression returned. Why should not he, he asked himself, believe her? It was early to call; it did interrupt regular occupation. So he spoke, and said –

'I believe I have been very thoughtless – I'll not come so early again; but I had some excuse today: my brother told me you had made a plan for going to see Hurstwood when the roses were out, and they are earlier than usual this year – I've been round to see. He spoke of a long day there, going before lunch'—

'The plan was made with Mr Osborne Hamley. I could not think of going without him!' said Mrs Gibson coldly.

'I had a letter from him this morning, in which he named your wish, and he says he fears he cannot be at home till they are out of flower. I daresay they are not much to see in reality; but the day is so lovely I thought that the plan of going to Hurstwood would be a charming excuse for being out of doors.'

'Thank you! How kind you are! and so good, too, in sacrificing your natural desire to be with your father as much as possible.'

'I'm glad to say my father is so much better than he was in the winter, that he spends much of his time out of doors in his fields. He has been accustomed to go about alone, and I – we think that as great a return to his former habits as he can be induced to make is the best for him.'

'And when do you return to Cambridge?'

There was some hesitation in Roger's manner as he replied –

'It is uncertain. You probably know that I am a Fellow of Trinity now. I hardly yet know what my future plans may be; I am thinking of going up to London soon.'

'Ah! London is the true place for a young man,' said Mrs Gibson, with decision, as if she had reflected a good deal on the question. 'If it were not that we really are so busy this morning, I should have been tempted to make an exception to our general rule; one more exception, for your early visits have made us make too many already. Perhaps, however, we may see you again before you go?'

'Certainly I shall come,' replied he, rising to take his leave, and still holding the demolished roses in his hand. Then, addressing himself more especially to Cynthia, he added, 'My stay in London will not exceed a fortnight or so – is there anything I can do for you – or you?' turning a little to Molly.

'No, thank you very much,' said Cynthia, very sweetly; and then, acting on a sudden impulse, she leant out of the window, and gathered him some half-opened roses. 'You deserve these; do throw that poor shabby bunch away!'

His eyes brightened, his cheeks glowed. He took the offered buds, but did not throw away the other bunch.

'At any rate, I may come after lunch is over, and the afternoons and evenings will be the most delicious time of day a month hence.' He said this to both Molly and Cynthia, but in his heart he addressed it to the latter.

Mrs Gibson affected not to hear what he was saying, but held out her limp hand once more to him.

'I suppose we shall see you when you return; and pray tell your brother how we are longing to have a visit from him again.'

When he had left the room, Molly's heart was quite full. She had watched his face, and read something of his feelings: his disappointment at their non-acquiescence in his plan of a day's pleasure in Hurstwood; the delayed conviction that his presence was not welcome to the wife of his old friend, which had come so slowly upon him – perhaps, after all, these things touched Molly more keenly than they did him. His bright look when Cynthia gave him the rose-buds indicated a gush of sudden delight, more vivid than the pain he had shown by his previous increase of gravity.

'I can't think why he will come at such untimely hours,' said Mrs Gibson, as soon as she heard him fairly out of the house. 'It's different from Osborne; we are so much more intimate with him; he came and made friends with us all the time this stupid brother of his was muddling his brains with mathematics at Cambridge. Fellow of Trinity, indeed! I wish he would learn to stay there, and not come intruding here, and assuming that, because I asked

Osborne to join in a pic-nic, it was all the same to me which brother came.'

'In short, mamma, one man may steal a horse, but another must not look over the hedge,'* said Cynthia, pouting a little.

'And the two brothers have always been treated so exactly alike by their friends, and there has been such a strong friendship between them, that it is no wonder Roger thinks he may be welcome where Osborne is allowed to come at all hours,' continued Molly, in high dudgeon. 'Roger's "muddled brains", indeed! Roger, "stupid"!'

'Oh, very well, my dears! When I was young, it wouldn't have been thought becoming for girls of your age to fly out, because a little restraint was exercised as to the hours at which they should receive the calls of young men. And they would have supposed that there might be good reasons why their parents disapproved of the visits of certain gentlemen, even while they were proud and pleased to see some members of the same family.'

'But that was what I said, mamma,' said Cynthia, looking at her mother with an expression of innocent bewilderment on her face. 'One man may'—

'Be quiet, child! All proverbs are vulgar, and, I do believe, that is the vulgarest of all. You are really catching Roger Hamley's coarseness, Cynthia!'

'Mamma,' said Cynthia, roused to anger, 'I don't mind your abusing me, but Mr Roger Hamley has been very kind to me while I've not been well: I can't bear to hear him disparaged. If he's coarse, I've no objection to be coarse as well; for it seems to me it must mean kindliness and pleasantness, and the bringing of pretty flowers and presents.'

Molly's tears were brimming over at these words; she could have kissed Cynthia for her warm partisanship; but, afraid of betraying emotion, and 'making a scene', as Mrs Gibson called showing any signs of warm feeling, she laid down her book hastily, and ran upstairs to her room, and locked the door, in order to breathe freely. There were traces of tears upon her face, when she returned into the drawing-room half-an-hour afterwards, walking straight and demurely up to her former place, where Cynthia still sate and gazed idly out of the window, pouting and displeased; Mrs Gibson, meanwhile, counting her stitches aloud with great distinctness and vigour.

CHAPTER 29

Bush-Fighting*

During all the months that had elapsed since Mrs Hamley's death, Molly had wondered many a time about the secret she had so unwittingly become possessed of that last day in the Hall library. It seemed so utterly strange and unheard-of a thing to her inexperienced mind, that a man should be married, and yet not live with his wife – that a son should have entered into the holy state of matrimony without his father's knowledge, and without being recognised as the husband of some one known or unknown by all those with whom he came in daily contact, that she felt occasionally as if that little ten minutes of revelation must have been a vision in a dream. Roger had only slightly referred to it once, and Osborne had kept entire silence on the subject ever since. Not even a look betrayed any allusion to it; it even seemed to have passed out of his thoughts. There had been the great, sad event of his mother's death to fill their minds on the next occasion of his meeting Molly; and since then long pauses of intercourse had taken place; so that she sometimes felt as if both the brothers must have forgotten how she had come to know their important secret. She even found herself often entirely forgetting it; but perhaps the consciousness of it was present to her unawares, and enabled her to comprehend the real nature of Osborne's feelings towards Cynthia. At any rate, she never for a moment had supposed that his gentle kind manner towards Cynthia was anything but the courtesy of a friend. Strange to say, in these latter days Molly had looked upon Osborne's relation to herself as pretty much the same as that in which at one time she had regarded Roger's; and she thought of the former as of some one as nearly a brother both to Cynthia and herself as any young man could well be whom they had not known in childhood, and who was in nowise related to them. She thought that he was very much improved in manner, and probably in character, by his mother's death. He was no longer sarcastic, or fastidious, or vain, or self-confident. She did not know how often all these styles of talk or of behaviour are put on to conceal shyness or consciousness, and to veil the real self from strangers.

Osborne's conversation and ways might very possibly have been just the same as before, had he been thrown amongst new people; but Molly only saw him in their own circle, in which he was on terms of decided intimacy. Still, there was no doubt that he was really improved, though perhaps not to the extent for which Molly gave him credit; and this exaggeration on her part arose very naturally from the fact, that he, perceiving Roger's warm admiration for Cynthia, withdrew a little out of his brother's way, and used to go and talk to Molly, in order not to intrude himself between Roger and Cynthia. Of the two, perhaps, Osborne preferred Molly; to her he needed not to talk, if the mood was not on him – they were on those happy terms where silence is permissible, and where efforts to act against the prevailing mood of the mind are not required. Sometimes, indeed, when Osborne was in the humour to be critical and fastidious as of yore, he used to vex Roger by insisting upon it that Molly was prettier than Cynthia.

'You mark my words, Roger! Five years hence, the beautiful Cynthia's red and white will have become just a little coarse, and her figure will have thickened, while Molly's will only have developed into more perfect grace. I don't believe the girl has done growing yet; I'm sure she's taller than when I first saw her last summer.'

'Miss Kirkpatrick's eyes must always be perfection. I cannot fancy any could come up to them: soft, grave, appealing, tender; and such a heavenly colour – I often try to find something in nature to compare them to; they are not like violets – that blue in the eyes is too like physical weakness of sight; they are not like the sky – that colour has something of cruelty in it.'

'Come, don't go on trying to match her eyes as if you were a draper, and they a bit of ribbon; say at once "her eyes are loadstars",* and have done with it! I set up Molly's grey eyes and curling black lashes, long odds above the other young woman's; but, of course, it's all a matter of taste.'

And now both Osborne and Roger had left the neighbourhood. In spite of all that Mrs Gibson had said about Roger's visits being ill-timed and intrusive, she began to feel as if they had been a very pleasant variety, now that they had ceased altogether. He brought in a whiff of a new atmosphere from that of Hollingford. He and his brother had been always ready to do numberless little things which only a man can do for a woman; small services which Mr

Gibson was always too busy to render. For the good doctor's business grew upon him. He thought that this increase was owing to his greater skill and experience, and he would probably have been mortified if he could have known how many of his patients were solely biassed in sending for him, by the fact that he was employed at the Towers. Something of this sort must have been contemplated in the low scale of payment adopted long ago by the Cumnor family. Of itself the money he received for going to the Towers would hardly have paid him for horse-flesh;* but then, as Lady Cumnor in her younger days worded it –

'It is such a thing for a man just setting up in practice for himself to be able to say he attends at this house!'

So the prestige was tacitly sold and paid for; but neither buyer nor seller defined the nature of the bargain.

On the whole, it was as well that Mr Gibson spent so much of his time from home. He sometimes thought so himself, when he heard his wife's plaintive fret or pretty babble over totally indifferent things, and perceived of how flimsy a nature were all her fine sentiments. Still, he did not allow himself to repine over the step he had taken; he wilfully shut his eyes and waxed up his ears to many small things that he knew would have irritated him, if he had attended to them; and, in his solitary rides, he forced himself to dwell on the positive advantages that had accrued to him and his through his marriage. He had obtained an unexceptionable chaperon, if not a tender mother, for his little girl; a skilful manager of his previously disorderly household; a woman who was graceful and pleasant to look at for the head of his table. Moreover, Cynthia reckoned for something on the favourable side of the balance. She was a capital companion for Molly; and the two were evidently very fond of each other. The feminine companionship of the mother and daughter was agreeable to him as well as to his child – when Mrs Gibson was moderately sensible and not over-sentimental, he mentally added; and then he checked himself, for he would not allow himself to become more aware of her faults and foibles by defining them. At any rate, she was harmless, and wonderfully just to Molly for a stepmother. She piqued herself upon this indeed, and would often call attention to the fact of her being unlike other women in this respect. Just then sudden tears came into Mr Gibson's eyes, as he remembered how quiet and undemonstrative his little Molly had become in her general behaviour to him; but how once or twice, when they had met upon the stairs, or were otherwise unwitnessed, she had caught him and kissed him – hand or cheek – in a sad passionateness of affection. But in a moment he began to whistle an old Scotch air he had heard in his childhood, and which had never recurred to his memory since; and five minutes afterwards he was too busily treating a case of white swelling* in the knee of a little boy, and thinking how to relieve the poor mother, who went out charring all day, and had to listen to the moans of her child all night, to have any thought for his own cares, which, if they really existed, were of so trifling a nature compared to the hard reality of this hopeless woe.

Osborne came home first. He returned, in fact, not long after Roger had gone away; but he was languid and unwell, and, though he did not complain, he felt unequal to any exertion. Thus a week or more elapsed before any of the Gibsons knew that he was at the Hall; and then it was only by chance that they became aware of it. Mr Gibson met him in one of the lanes near Hamley; the acute surgeon noticed the gait of the man as he came near, before he recognised who it was. When he overtook him he said –

'Why, Osborne, is it you? I thought it was an old man of fifty loitering before me! I didn't know you had come back.'

'Yes,' said Osborne, 'I've been at home nearly ten days. I daresay I ought to have called on your people, for I made a half-promise to Mrs Gibson to let her know as soon as I returned; but the fact is, I'm feeling very good-for-nothing – this air oppresses me; I could hardly breathe in the house, and yet I'm already tired with this short walk.'

'You'd better get home at once; and I'll call and see you, as I come back from Rowe's.'

'No, you mustn't on any account!' said Osborne hastily; 'my father is annoyed enough about my going from home, so often, he says, though I hadn't been from it for six weeks. He puts down all my languor to my having been away – he keeps the purse-strings, you know,' he added, with a faint smile, 'and I'm in the unlucky position of a penniless heir, and I've been brought up so – In fact, I must leave home from time to time; and, if my father gets confirmed in this notion of his that my health is worse for my absence, he'll stop the supplies altogether.'

'May I ask where you do spend your time when you are not at

Hamley Hall?' asked Mr Gibson, with some hesitation in his manner.

'No!' replied Osborne reluctantly. 'I will tell you this: – I stay with friends in the country. I lead a life which ought to be conducive to health, because it is thoroughly simple, rational, and happy. And now I've told you more about it than my father himself knows. He never asks me where I've been; and I shouldn't tell him if he did – at least, I think not.'

Mr Gibson rode on by Osborne's side, not speaking for a moment or two.

'Osborne, whatever scrapes you may have got into, I should advise your telling your father boldly out. I know him; and I know he'll be angry enough at first, but he'll come round, take my word for it; and, somehow or another, he'll find money to pay your debts and set you free, if it's that kind of difficulty; and if it's any other kind of entanglement, why, still he's your best friend. It's this estrangement from your father that's telling on your health, I'll be bound.'

'No,' said Osborne, 'I beg your pardon; but it's not that; I am really out of order. I daresay my unwillingness to encounter any displeasure from my father is the consequence of my indisposition; but I'll answer for it, it is not the cause of it. My instinct tells me there is something really the matter with me.'

'Come, don't be setting up your instinct against the profession!' said Mr Gibson cheerily.

He dismounted, and throwing the reins of his horse round his arm, he looked at Osborne's tongue and felt his pulse, asking him various questions. At the end he said –

'We'll soon bring you about; though I should like a little more quiet talk with you, without this tugging brute for a third. If you'll manage to ride over and lunch with us tomorrow, Dr Nicholls will be with us; he's coming over to see old Rowe; and you shall have the benefit of the advice of two doctors instead of one. Go home now; you've had enough exercise for the middle of a day as hot as this is. And don't mope in the house, listening to the maunderings of your stupid instinct.'

'What else have I to do?' said Osborne. 'My father and I are not companions; one can't read and write for ever, especially when there's no end to be gained by it. I don't mind telling you – but in confidence, recollect – that I've been trying to get some of my poems published; but there's no one like a publisher for taking the conceit out of one. Not a man among them would have them as a gift.'

'Oho! so that's it, is it, Master Osborne! I thought there was some mental cause for this depression of health. I wouldn't trouble my head about it, if I were you; though that's always very easily said, I know. Try your hand at prose, if you can't manage to please the publishers with poetry; but, at any rate, don't go on fretting over spilt milk. But I mustn't lose my time here. Come over to us tomorrow, as I said; and, what with the wisdom of two doctors, and the wit and folly of three women, I think we shall cheer you up a bit.'

So saying, Mr Gibson remounted, and rode away at the long slinging trot* so well known to the country people as the doctor's pace.

'I don't like his looks,' thought Mr Gibson to himself at night, as over his daybooks he reviewed the events of the day. 'And then his pulse! But how often we're all mistaken; and, ten to one, my own hidden enemy lies closer to me than his does to him – even taking the worse view of the case!'

Osborne made his appearance a considerable time before luncheon the next morning; and no one objected to the earliness of his call. He was feeling better. There were few signs of the invalid about him; and what few there were disappeared under the bright pleasant influence of such a welcome as he received from all. Molly and Cynthia had much to tell him of the small proceedings since he went away, or to relate the conclusions of half-accomplished projects. Cynthia was often on the point of some gay, careless inquiry as to where he had been, and what he had been doing; but Molly, who conjectured the truth, as often interfered to spare him the pain of equivocation – a pain that her tender conscience would have felt for him, much more than he would have felt it for himself.

Mrs Gibson's talk was desultory, complimentary, and sentimental, after her usual fashion; but still, on the whole, though Osborne smiled to himself at much that she said, it was soothing and agreeable. Presently, Dr Nicholls and Mr Gibson came in; the former had had some conference with the latter on the subject of Osborne's health; and, from time to time, the skilful old physician's sharp and observant eyes gave a comprehensive look at Osborne.

Then there was lunch, when every one was merry and hungry,

excepting the hostess, who was trying to train her midday appetite into the genteelest of all ways, and thought (falsely enough) that Dr Nicholls was a good person to practise the semblance of ill-health upon; and that he would give her the proper civil amount of commiseration for her ailments, which every guest ought to bestow upon a hostess who complains of her delicacy of health. The old doctor was too cunning a man to fall into this trap. He would keep recommending her to try the coarsest viands on the table; and, at last, he told her, if she could not fancy the cold beef, to try a little with pickled onions. There was a twinkle in his eye as he said this, that would have betrayed his humour to any observer; but Mr Gibson, Cynthia, and Molly were all attacking Osborne on the subject of some literary preference he had expressed, and Dr Nicholls had Mrs Gibson quite at his mercy. She was not sorry, when luncheon was over, to leave the room to the three gentlemen; and ever afterwards she spoke of Dr Nicholls as 'that bear'.

Presently, Osborne came upstairs, and, after his old fashion, began to take up new books, and to question the girls as to their music. Mr Gibson had to go out and pay some calls, so he left the three together; and after a while they adjourned into the garden, Osborne lounging on a chair, while Molly employed herself busily in tying up carnations, and Cynthia gathered flowers in her careless, graceful way.

'I hope you notice the difference in our occupations, Mr Hamley? Molly, you see, devotes herself to the useful and I to the ornamental. Please, under what head do you class what you are doing? I think you might help one of us, instead of looking on like the *Grand Seigneur*.'*

'I don't know what I can do,' said he rather plaintively. 'I should like to be useful, but I don't know how; and my day is past for purely ornamental work. You must let me be, I'm afraid. Besides, I'm really rather exhausted by being questioned and pulled about by those good doctors.'

'Why, you don't mean to say they have been attacking you since lunch!' exclaimed Molly.

'Yes; indeed, they have; and they might have gone on till now, if Mr Gibson had not come in opportunely.'

'I thought mamma had gone out some time ago!' said Cynthia, catching wafts of the conversation, as she flitted hither and thither among the flowers.

'She came into the dining-room not five minutes ago. Do you want her, for I see her crossing the hall at this very moment?' and Osborne half-rose.

'Oh, not at all!' said Cynthia. 'Only she seemed to be in such a hurry to go out, I fancied she had set off long ago. She had some errand to do for Lady Cumnor, and she thought she could manage to catch the housekeeper, who is always in the town on Thursday.'

'Are the family coming to the Towers this autumn?'

'I believe so. But I don't know, and I don't much care. They don't take kindly to me,' continued Cynthia, 'and so I suppose I'm not generous enough to take kindly to them.'

'I should have thought that such a very unusual blot in their discrimination would have interested you in them as extraordinary people,' said Osborne, with a little air of conscious gallantry.

'Isn't that a compliment?' said Cynthia, after a pause of mock meditation. 'If any one pays me a compliment, please let it be short and clear! I'm very stupid at finding out hidden meanings.'

'Then such speeches as "you are very pretty", or "you have charming manners", are what you prefer. Now, I pique myself on wrapping up my sugar-plums delicately.'

'Then would you please to write them down, and at my leisure I'll parse them.'

'No! It would be too much trouble. I'll meet you halfway, and study clearness next time.'

'What are you two talking about?' said Molly, resting on her light spade.

'It's only a discussion on the best way of administering compliments,' said Cynthia, taking up her flower-basket again, but not going out of the reach of the conversation.

'I don't like them at all in any way,' said Molly. 'But, perhaps, it's rather sour grapes with me,' she added.

'Nonsense!' said Osborne. 'Shall I tell you what I heard of you at the ball?'

'Or shall I provoke Mr Preston,' said Cynthia, 'to begin upon you? It's like turning a tap, such a stream of pretty speeches flows out at the moment.' Her lip curled with scorn.

'For you, perhaps,' said Molly; 'but not for me.'

'For any woman. It's his notion of making himself agreeable. If you dare me, Molly, I'll try the experiment, and you'll see with what success.'

'No, don't, pray!' said Molly, in a hurry. 'I do so dislike him!'

'Why?' said Osborne, roused to a little curiosity by her vehemence.

'Oh! I don't know. He never seems to know what one is feeling.'

'He wouldn't care, if he did know,' said Cynthia. 'And he might know he is not wanted.'

'If he chooses to stay, he cares little whether he is wanted or not.'

'Come, this is very interesting,' said Osborne. 'It is like the strophe and anti-strophe in a Greek chorus.* Pray, go on.'

'Don't you know him?' asked Molly.

'Yes, by sight, and I think we were once introduced. But, you know, we are much farther from Ashcombe, at Hamley, than you are here, at Hollingford.'

'Oh, but he's coming to take Mr Sheepshanks' place; and then he'll live here altogether,' said Molly.

'Molly! who told you that?' said Cynthia, in quite a different tone of voice from that in which she had been speaking hitherto.

'Papa – didn't you hear him? Oh, no! it was before you were down this morning. Papa met Mr Sheepshanks yesterday, and he told him it was all settled; you know we heard a rumour about it in the spring!'

Cynthia was very silent after this. Presently, she said that she had gathered all the flowers she wanted, and that the heat was so great she would go indoors. And then Osborne went away. But Molly had set herself a task to dig up such roots as had already flowered, and to put down some bedding-out plants in their stead. Tired and heated as she was, she finished it, and then went upstairs to rest, and change her dress. According to her wont, she sought for Cynthia; there was no reply to her soft knock at the bedroom-door opposite to her own; and, thinking that Cynthia might have fallen asleep, and be lying uncovered in the draught of the open window, she went in softly. Cynthia was lying upon the bed, as if she had thrown herself down on it without caring for the ease or comfort of her position. She was very still; and Molly took a shawl, and was going to place it over her, when she opened her eyes, and spoke –

'Is that you, dear? Don't go. I like to know that you are there.'

She shut her eyes again, and remained quite quiet for a few minutes longer. Then she started up into a sitting posture, pushed her hair away from her forehead and burning eyes, and gazed intently at Molly.

'Do you know what I've been thinking, dear?' said she. 'I think I've been long enough here, and that I had better go out as a governess.'

'Cynthia! what do you mean?' asked Molly, aghast. 'You've been asleep – you've been dreaming. You're over-tired,' continued she, sitting down on the bed, and taking Cynthia's passive hand, and stroking it softly – a mode of caressing that had come down to her from her mother – whether as an hereditary instinct, or as a lingering remembrance of the tender ways of the dead woman, Mr Gibson often wondered within himself, when he observed it.

'Oh, how good you are, Molly! I wonder, if I had been brought up like you, whether I should have been as good. But I've been tossed about so.'

'Then, don't go and be tossed about any more,' said Molly softly.

'Oh, dear! I had better go. But, you see, no one ever loved me like you, and, I think, your father – doesn't he, Molly? And it's hard to be driven out.'

'Cynthia, I am sure you're not well, or else you're not half awake.'

Cynthia sate with her arms encircling her knees, and looking at vacancy.

'Well!' said she, at last, heaving a great sigh, but then smiling as she caught Molly's anxious face. 'I suppose there's no escaping one's doom; and anywhere else I should be much more forlorn and unprotected.'

'What do you mean by your doom?'

'Ah, that's telling, little one,' said Cynthia, who seemed now to have recovered her usual manner. 'I don't mean to have one, though. I think that, though I am an arrant coward at heart, I can show fight.'

'With whom?' asked Molly, really anxious to probe the mystery – if, indeed, there was one – to the bottom, in the hope of some remedy being found for the distress Cynthia was in, when first Molly entered.

Again Cynthia was lost in thought; then, catching the echo of Molly's last words in her mind, she said –

' "With whom?" – oh! show fight with whom? – why, my doom, to be sure. Am not I a grand young lady to have a doom? Why, Molly, child, how pale and grave you look!' said she, kissing her all of a sudden. 'You ought not to care so much for me; I'm not good enough for you to worry yourself about me. I've given myself up a long time ago as a heartless baggage!'

'Nonsense! I wish you wouldn't talk so, Cynthia!'

'And I wish you wouldn't always take me "at the foot of the letter",* as an English girl at school used to translate it. Oh, how hot it is! Is it never going to get cool again? My child! what dirty hands you've got, and face too; and I've been kissing you – I daresay I'm dirty with it, too. Now, isn't that like one of mamma's speeches? But, for all that, you look more like a delving Adam than a spinning Eve.'* This had the effect that Cynthia intended; the daintily clean Molly became conscious of her soiled condition, which she had forgotten while she had been attending to Cynthia, and she hastily withdrew to her own room. When she had gone, Cynthia noiselessly locked the door; and, taking her purse out of her desk, she began to count over her money. She counted it once – she counted it twice, as if desirous of finding out some mistake which should prove it to be more than it was; but the end of it all was a sigh.

'What a fool! – what a fool I was!' said she, at length. 'But, even if I don't go out as a governess, I shall make it up in time.'

Some weeks after the time he had anticipated when he spoke of his departure to the Gibsons, Roger returned back to the Hall. One morning when he called, Osborne told them that his brother had been at home for two or three days.

'And why has he not come here, then?' said Mrs Gibson. 'It is not kind of him not to come and see us as soon as he can. Tell him I say so – pray do.'

Osborne had gained one or two ideas as to her treatment of Roger the last time he had called. Roger had not complained of it, or even mentioned it till, that very morning when Osborne was on the point of starting and had urged Roger to accompany him, the latter had told him something of what Mrs Gibson had said. He spoke rather as if he was more amused than annoyed; but Osborne could read that he was chagrined at those restrictions placed upon calls which were the greatest pleasure of his life. Neither of them let out the suspicion which had entered both their minds – the well-grounded suspicion arising from the fact that Osborne's visits, be they paid early or late, had never yet been met with a repulse.

Osborne now reproached himself with having done Mrs Gibson injustice. She was evidently a weak, but probably a disinterested, woman; and it was only a little bit of ill-temper on her part which had caused her to speak to Roger as she had done.

'I daresay it was rather impertinent of me to call at such an untimely hour,' said Roger.

'Not at all; I call at all hours, and nothing is ever said about it. It was just because she was put out that morning. I'll answer for it she's sorry now, and I'm sure you may go there at any time you like in future.'

Still, Roger did not choose to go again for two or three weeks, and the consequence was that, the next time he called, the ladies were out. Once again he had the same ill-luck; and then he received a little pretty three-cornered note* from Mrs Gibson: –

'My dear Sir, – How is it that you are become so formal all of a sudden, leaving cards, instead of awaiting our return? Fie for shame! If you had seen the faces of disappointment that I did when the horrid little bits of pasteboard were displayed to our view, you would not have borne malice against me so long; for it is really punishing others as well as my naughty self. If you will come tomorrow – as early as you like – and lunch with us, I'll own I was cross, and acknowledge myself a penitent. – Yours ever,

'Hyacinth C. F. Gibson.'

There was no resisting this, even if there had not been strong inclination to back up the pretty words. Roger went, and Mrs Gibson caressed and petted him in her sweetest, silkiest manner. Cynthia looked lovelier than ever to him for the slight restriction that had been laid for a time on their intercourse. She might be gay and sparkling with Osborne; with Roger she was soft and grave. Instinctively she knew her men. She saw that Osborne was only interested in her because of her position in a family with whom he was intimate; that his friendship was without the least touch of sentiment; and that his admiration was only the warm criticism of an artist for unusual beauty. But she felt how different Roger's relation to her was. To him she was *the* one, alone, peerless. If his love was prohibited, it would be long years before he could sink down into tepid friendship; and to him her personal loveliness was only one of the many charms that made him tremble into passion. Cynthia was not capable of returning such feelings; she had had too little true love in her life, and perhaps too much admiration to do so; but she appreciated this honest ardour; this loyal worship that was new to her experience. Such appreciation, and such respect for his true and affectionate nature, gave a serious tenderness to her manner to Roger, which allured him with a fresh and separate grace. Molly sate by, and wondered how it would all end, or, rather, how soon it would all end, for she thought that no girl could resist such reverent passion; and on Roger's side there could be no doubt – alas! there could be no doubt. An older spectator might have looked far ahead, and thought of the question of pounds, shillings, and pence. Where was the necessary income for a marriage to come from? Roger had his Fellowship now, it is true; but the income of that would be lost, if he married; he had no profession, a life-interest in the two or three thousand pounds that he inherited from his mother, belonging to his father. This older spectator might have been a little surprised at the *empressement** of Mrs Gibson's manner to a younger son, always supposing this said spectator to have read to the depths of her worldly heart. Never had she tried to be more agreeable to Osborne; and, though her attempt was a great failure when practised upon Roger, and he did not know what to say in reply to the delicate flatteries which he felt to be insincere, he saw that she intended him to consider himself henceforward free of the house; and he was too glad to avail himself of this privilege, to examine over-closely into what might be her motives for her change of manner. He shut his eyes, and chose to believe that she was now desirous of making up for her little burst of temper on his previous visit.

The result of Osborne's conference with the two doctors had been certain prescriptions which appeared to have done him much good, and which would in all probability have done him yet more, could he have been free from the recollection of the little patient wife in her solitude near Winchester. He went to her whenever he could; and, thanks to Roger, money was far more plentiful with him now than it had been. But he still shrank, and perhaps even more and more, from telling his father of his marriage. Some bodily instinct made him dread all agitation inexpressibly. If he had not had this money from Roger, he might have been compelled to tell his father all, and to ask for the necessary funds to provide for the wife and the coming child. But, with enough in hand, and a secret, though remorseful, conviction that, as long as Roger had a penny his brother was sure to have half of it, he was more reluctant than ever to irritate his father by a revelation of his secret. 'Not just yet, not just at present,' he kept saying both to Roger and to himself. 'By-and-by, if we have a boy, I will call it Roger' – and then visions of poetical and romantic reconciliations brought about between father and son, through the medium of a child, the offspring of a forbidden marriage, became still more vividly possible to him, and at any rate it was a staving-off of an unpleasant thing. He atoned to himself for taking so much of Roger's Fellowship money by reflecting that, if Roger married, he would lose this source of revenue; yet Osborne was throwing no impediment in the way of this event, rather forwarding it, by promoting every possible means of his brother's seeing the lady of his love. Osborne ended his reflections by convincing himself of his own generosity.

CHAPTER 30

Old Ways and New Ways

Mr Preston was now installed in his new house at Hollingford; Mr Sheepshanks having entered into dignified idleness at the house of his married daughter, who lived in the county town. His successor had plunged with energy into all manner of improvements; and, among others, he fell to draining a piece of outlying waste and unreclaimed land of Lord Cumnor's, which was close to Squire Hamley's property – that very piece for which he had had the Government grant, but which now lay neglected, and only half-drained, with stacks of mossy tiles, and lines of upturned furrows telling of abortive plans. It was not often that the Squire rode in this direction now-a-days; but the cottage of a man who had been the Squire's gamekeeper in those more prosperous days when the Hamleys could afford to 'preserve',* was close to the rush-grown ground. This old servant and tenant was ill, and had sent a message up to the Hall, asking to see the Squire: not to reveal any secret, or to say anything particular, but only from the feudal loyalty which made it seem to the dying man as if it would be a comfort to shake the hand, and look once more into the eyes, of the lord and master whom he had served, and whose ancestors his own forbears had served, for so many generations. And the Squire was as fully alive as old Silas to the claims of the tie that existed between them. Though he hated the thought, and still more, should hate the sight of the piece of land, on the side of which Silas's cottage stood, the Squire ordered his horse, and rode off within half-an-hour of receiving the message. As he drew near the spot, he thought he heard the sound of tools and the hum of many voices, just as he used to hear them once, a year or two before. He listened with surprise. Yes! Instead of the still solitude he had expected, there was the clink of iron, the heavy gradual thud of the fall of barrowsful of soil – the cry and shout of labourers. But not on his land – better worth expense and trouble, by far than the reedy clay common on which the men were, in fact, employed. He knew it was Lord Cumnor's property; and he knew Lord Cumnor and his family had gone up in the world ('the Whig rascals!'), both in wealth and in station, as the Hamleys had gone down. But all the same – in spite of long-known facts, and in spite of reason – the Squire's ready anger rose high at the sight of his neighbour doing what he had been unable to do, and the fellow a Whig, and his family only in the county since Queen Anne's time. He went so far as to wonder whether they might not – the labourers he meant – avail themselves of his tiles, lying so conveniently close to hand. All these thoughts, regrets, and wonders were in his mind, as he rode up to the cottage he was bound to, and gave his horse in charge to a little lad, who had hitherto found his morning's business and amusement in playing at 'houses' with a still younger sister, with some of the Squire's neglected tiles. But he was old Silas's grandson, and he might have battered the rude red earthenware to pieces – a whole stack – one by one, and the Squire would have said little or nothing. It was only that he would not spare one to a labourer of Lord Cumnor's. No! not one!

Old Silas lay in a sort of closet, opening out of the family living room. The small window that gave it light looked right on to the 'moor', as it was called; and by day the check curtain was drawn aside, so that he might watch the progress of the labour. Everything about the old man was clean, of course; and, with Death, the leveller, so close at hand, it was the labourer who made the first advances, and put out his horny hand to the Squire.

'I thought you'd come, Squire. Your father came for to see my father, as he lay a-dying.'

'Come, come, my man!' said the Squire, easily affected, as he always was. 'Don't talk of dying; we shall soon have you out,

never fear! They've sent you up some soup from the Hall, as I
bade 'em, haven't they?'

'Ay, ay, I've had all as I could want for to eat and to drink. The
young squire and Master Roger was here yesterday.'

'Yes, I know.'

'But I'm a deal nearer heaven today, I am. I should like you to
look after th' covers* in th' West Spinney, Squire; them gorse, you
know, where th' old fox had her hole – her as give 'em so many a
run. You'll mind it, Squire, though you was but a lad. I could
laugh to think on her tricks yet.' And, with a weak attempt at a
laugh, he got himself into a violent fit of coughing, which alarmed
the Squire, who thought he would never get his breath again. His
daughter-in-law came in at the sound, and told the Squire that he
had these coughing-bouts very frequently, and that she thought he
would go off in one of them before long. This opinion of hers was
spoken simply out before the old man, who now lay gasping and
exhausted upon his pillow. Poor people acknowledge the inevi-
tableness and the approach of death in a much more straightforward manner than is customary among the more educated. The
Squire was shocked at her hard-heartedness, as he considered it;
but the old man himself had received much tender kindness from
his daughter-in-law; and what she had just said was no more news
to him than the fact that the sun would rise tomorrow. He was
more anxious to go on with his story.

'Them navvies – I call 'em navvies because some on 'em is
strangers, though some on 'em is th' men as was turned off your
own works, Squire, when there came orders to stop 'em last fall –
they're a-pulling up gorse and brush to light their fire for warming
up their messes. It's a long way off to their homes, and they
mostly dine here; and there'll be nothing of a cover left, if you
don't see after 'em. I thought I should like to tell ye, afore I died.
Parson's been here; but I did na tell him. He's all for the earl's
folk, and he'd not ha' heeded. It's the earl as put him into his
church, I reckon; for he said, what a fine thing it were for to see
so much employment a-given to the poor, and he never said
nought o' th' sort when your works were agait,* Squire.'

This long speech had been interrupted by many a cough and
gasp for breath; and, having delivered himself of what was on his
mind, he turned his face to the wall, and appeared to be going to
sleep. Presently, he roused himself with a start –

'I know I flogged him well, I did. But he were after pheasants' eggs, and I didn't know he were an orphan. Lord forgive me!'

'He's thinking on David Morton, the cripple, as used to go about trapping venison,' whispered the woman.

'Why, he died long ago – twenty year, I should think,' replied the Squire.

'Ay, but when grandfather goes off i' this way to sleep after a bout of talking he seems to be dreaming on old times. He'll not waken up yet, sir; you'd best sit down if you'd like to stay,' she continued, as she went into the houseplace and dusted a chair with her apron. 'He was very particular in bidding me wake him if he were asleep, and you or Mr Roger was to call. Mr Roger said he'd be coming again this morning – but he'll likely sleep an hour or more, if he's let alone.'

'I wish I'd said good-bye, I should like to have done that.'

'He drops off so sudden,' said the woman. 'But, if you'd be better pleased to have said it, Squire, I'll waken him up a bit.'

'No, no!' the Squire called out, as the woman was going to be as good as her word. 'I'll come again, perhaps tomorrow. And tell him I was sorry; for I am indeed. And be sure and send to the Hall for anything you want! Mr Roger is coming, is he? He'll bring me word how he is, later on. I should like to have bidden him goodbye.'

So, giving sixpence to the child who had held his horse, the Squire mounted. He sate still a moment, looking at the busy work going on before him, and then at his own half-completed drainage. It was a bitter pill. He had objected to borrowing from Government, in the first instance ; and then his wife had persuaded him to the step; and, after it was once taken, he was as proud as could be of the only concession to the spirit of progress he had ever made in his life. He had read and studied the subject pretty thoroughly, if also very slowly, during the time his wife had been influencing him. He was tolerably well up in agriculture, if in nothing else; and at one time he had taken the lead among the neighbouring landowners, when he first began tile-drainage.* In those days people used to speak of Squire Hamley's hobby; and at market-ordinaries, or county-dinners, they rather dreaded setting him off on long repetitions of arguments from the different pamphlets upon the subject which he had read. And now the proprietors all around him were draining – draining; his interest to Government was running on all the same, though his works were stopped, and his tiles deteriorating in value. It was not a soothing consideration, and the Squire was almost ready to quarrel with his shadow. He wanted a vent for his ill-humour; and, suddenly remembering the devastations on his covers, of which he had heard about not a quarter of an hour before, he rode towards the men busy at work on Lord Cumnor's land. Just before he got up to them he encountered Mr Preston, also on horseback, come to overlook his labourers. The Squire did not know him personally; but from the agent's manner of speaking, and the deference that was evidently paid to him, Mr Hamley saw that he was a responsible person. So he addressed the agent – 'I beg your pardon, I suppose you are the manager of these works?'

Mr Preston replied – 'Certainly. I am that and many other things besides, at your service. I have succeeded Mr Sheepshanks in the management of my lord's property. Mr Hamley of Hamley, I believe?'

The Squire bowed stiffly. He did not like his name to be asked, or presumed upon, in that manner. An equal might conjecture who he was, or recognise him; but, till he announced himself, an inferior had no right to do more than address him respectfully as 'sir'. That was the Squire's code of etiquette.

'I am Mr Hamley of Hamley. I suppose you are as yet ignorant of the boundary of Lord Cumnor's land, and so I will inform you that my property begins at the pond yonder – just where you see the rise in the ground.'

'I am perfectly acquainted with that fact, Mr Hamley,' said Mr Preston, a little annoyed at having such ignorance attributed to him. 'But may I inquire why my attention is called to it just now?'

The Squire was beginning to boil over; but he tried to keep his temper in. The effort was very much to be respected, for it was a great one. There was something in the handsome and well-dressed agent's tone and manner inexpressibly irritating to the Squire, and it was not lessened by an involuntary comparison of the capital roadster* on which Mr Preston was mounted with his own ill-groomed and aged cob.

'I have been told that your men out yonder do not respect these boundaries, but are in the habit of plucking up gorse from my covers to light their fires.'

'It is possible they may!' said Mr Preston, lifting his eyebrows, his manner being more nonchalant than his words. 'I daresay they think no great harm of it. However, I'll inquire.'

'Do you doubt my word, sir?' said the Squire, fretting his mare till she began to dance about. 'I tell you I've heard it only within this last half-hour.'

'I don't mean to doubt your word, Mr Hamley; it's the last thing I should think of doing. But you must excuse my saying that the argument which you have twice brought up for the authenticity of your statement, "that you have heard it within the last half-hour", is not quite so forcible as to preclude the possibility of a mistake.'

'I wish you'd only say in plain language that you doubt my word,' said the Squire, clenching and slightly raising his horsewhip. 'I can't make out what you mean – you use so many words.'

'Pray don't lose your temper, sir. I said I should inquire. You have not seen the men pulling up the gorse yourself, or you would have named it. I, surely, may doubt the correctness of your information until I have made some inquiry; at any rate, that is the course I shall pursue, and, if it gives you offence, I shall be sorry, but I shall do it just the same. When I am convinced that harm has been done to your property, I shall take steps to prevent it for the future, and of course, in my lord's name, I shall pay you compensation – it may probably amount to half-a-crown.' He added these last words in a lower tone, as if to himself, with a slight contemptuous smile on his face.

'Quiet, mare, quiet,' said the Squire, totally unaware that he was the cause of her impatient movements, by the way he was perpetually tightening her reins; and also, perhaps, he unconsciously addressed the injunction to himself.

Neither of them saw Roger Hamley, who was approaching them with long, steady steps. He had seen his father from the door of old Silas's cottage, and, as the poor fellow was still asleep, he was coming to speak to his father, and was near enough now to hear the next words.

'I don't know who you are, but I've known land-agents who were gentlemen, and I've known some who were not. You belong to this last set, young man,' said the Squire, 'that you do! I should like to try my horsewhip on you for your insolence.'

'Pray, Mr Hamley,' replied Mr Preston coolly, 'curb your temper a little, and reflect. I really feel sorry to see a man of your age in such a passion;' – moving a little farther off, however, but really more with a desire to save the irritated man from carrying his threat into execution, out of a dislike to the slander and excitement it would cause, than from any personal dread. Just at this moment Roger Hamley came close up. He was panting a little, and his eyes were very stern and dark; but he spoke quietly enough.

'Mr Preston, I can hardly understand what you mean by your last words. But, remember, my father is a gentleman of age and position, and not accustomed to receive advice as to the management of his temper from young men like you.'

'I desired him to keep his men off my land,' said the Squire to his son – his wish to stand well in Roger's opinion restraining his temper a little; but, though his words might be a little calmer, there were all other signs of passion present – the discoloured complexion, the trembling hands, the fiery cloud in his eyes. 'He refused, and doubted my word.'

Mr Preston turned to Roger, as if appealing from Philip drunk to Philip sober,* and spoke in a tone of cool explanation, which, though not insolent in words, was excessively irritating in manner.

'Your father has misunderstood me – perhaps it is no wonder,' trying to convey, by a look of intelligence at the son, his opinion that the father was in no state to hear reason. 'I never refused to do what was just and right. I only required further evidence as to the past wrong-doing; your father took offence at this' – and then he shrugged his shoulders, and lifted his eyebrows in a manner he had formerly learnt in France.

'At any rate, sir, I can scarcely reconcile the manner and words to my father, which I heard you use when I first came up, with the deference you ought to have shown to a man of his age and position. As to the fact of the trespass'—

'They are pulling up all the gorse, Roger – there'll be no cover whatever for game soon,' put in the Squire.

Roger bowed to his father, but took up his speech at the point it was at before the interruption.

'I will inquire into it myself at a cooler moment; and if I find that such trespass or damage has been committed, of course I shall expect that you will see it put a stop to. Come, father! I am going to see old Silas – perhaps you don't know that he is very ill.' So he endeavoured to wile the Squire away to prevent further words. He was not entirely successful.

Mr Preston was enraged by Roger's calm and dignified manner, and threw after them this parting shaft, in the shape of a loud soliloquy –

'Position, indeed! What are we to think of the position of a man who begins works like these without counting the cost, and comes to a stand-still, and has to turn off his labourers just at the beginning of winter, leaving'—

They were too far off to hear the rest. The Squire was on the point of turning back before this; but Roger took hold of the reins of the old mare, and led her over some of the boggy ground, as if to guide her into sure footing, but, in reality, because he was determined to prevent the renewal of the quarrel. It was well that the cob knew him, and was, indeed, old enough to prefer quietness to dancing; for Mr Hamley plucked hard at the reins, and at last broke out with an oath – 'Damn it, Roger! I'm not a child; I won't be treated as such! Leave go, I say!'

Roger let go; they were now on firm ground, and he did not wish any watchers to think that he was exercising any constraint over his father; and this quiet obedience to his impatient commands did more to soothe the Squire than anything else could have effected just then.

'I know I turned them off – what could I do? I'd no more money for their weekly wages; it's a loss to me, as you know. He doesn't know, no one knows, but I think your mother would, how it cut me to turn 'em off just before winter set in. I lay awake many a night thinking of it, and I gave them what I had – I did, indeed. I hadn't got money to pay 'em, but I had three barren cows fattened, and gave every scrap of meat to the men, and I let 'em go into the woods and gather what was fallen, and I winked at* their breaking off old branches – and now to have it cast up against me by that cur – that servant! But I'll go on with the works, by—, I will, if only to spite him. I'll show him who I am. "My position, indeed". A Hamley of Hamley takes a higher position than his master. I'll go on with the works; see if I don't! I'm paying between one and two hundred a year interest on Government money. I'll raise some more, if I go to the Jews; Osborne has shown me the way, and Osborne shall pay for it – he shall. I'll not put up with insults. You shouldn't have stopped me, Roger! I wish to heaven I'd horsewhipped the fellow!'

He was lashing himself again into an impotent rage, painful to a son to witness; but just then the little grandchild of Old Silas, who had held the Squire's horse during his visit to the sick man, came running up, breathless –

'Please, sir, please, Squire, mammy has sent me; grandfather has wakened up sudden, and mammy says he's dying, and would you please come; she says he'd take it as a kind compliment, she's sure.'

So they went to the cottage, the Squire speaking never a word, but suddenly feeling as if lifted out of a whirlwind and set down in a still and awful place.

CHAPTER 31

A Passive Coquette

It is not to be supposed that such an encounter as Mr Preston had just had with Roger Hamley sweetened the regards in which the two young men henceforward held each other. They had barely spoken to one another before, and but seldom met; for the land-agent's employment had hitherto lain at Ashcombe, some sixteen or seventeen miles from Hamley. He was older than Roger by several years; but, during the time he had lived in the country, Osborne and Roger had been at school and at college. Mr Preston was prepared to dislike the Hamleys for many unreasonable reasons. Cynthia and Molly had both spoken of the brothers with familiar regard, implying considerable intimacy; their flowers had been preferred to his on the occasion of the ball; most people spoke well of them; and Mr Preston had an animal's instinctive jealousy and combativeness against all popular young men. Their 'position' – poor as the Hamleys might be – was far higher than his own in the county; and, moreover, he was agent for the great Whig lord, whose political interests were diametrically opposed to those of the old Tory squire. Not that Lord Cumnor troubled himself much about his political interests. His family had obtained property and title from the Whigs at the time of the Hanoverian succession;* and so, traditionally, he was a Whig, and had belonged in his youth to Whig clubs, where he had lost consider-able sums of money to Whig gamblers. All this was satisfactory and consistent enough. And, if Lord Hollingford had not been returned for the county on the Whig interest – as his father had been before him, until he had succeeded to the title – it is quite probable Lord Cumnor would have considered the British consti-tution in danger, and the patriotism of his ancestors ungratefully ignored. But, excepting at elections, he had no notion of making Whig and Tory a party-cry. He had lived too much in London, and was of too sociable a nature, to exclude any man who jumped with his humour* from the hospitality he was always ready to offer, be the agreeable acquaintance Whig, Tory, or Radical. But in the county of which he was lord-lieutenant the old party distinction was still a shibboleth by which men were tested as to their fitness for social intercourse, as well as on the hustings. If by any chance a Whig found himself at a Tory dinner-table – or *vice versâ* – the food was hard of digestion, and the wine and viands were criticised rather than enjoyed. A marriage between the young people of the separate parties was almost as unheard-of and prohibited an alliance as that of Romeo and Juliet. And, of course, Mr Preston was not a man in whose breast such prejudices would die away. They were an excitement to him for one thing, and called out all his talent for intrigue on behalf of the party to which he was allied. Moreover, he considered it as loyalty to his employer to 'scatter his enemies'* by any means in his power. He had always hated and despised the Tories in general; and, after that interview on the marshy common in front of Silas's cottage, he hated the Hamleys, and Roger especially, with a very choice and particular hatred. 'That prig' – as hereafter he always designated Roger – 'he shall pay for it yet,' he said to himself by way of consolation, after the father and son had left him. 'What a lout it is!' – watching the receding figures. 'The old chap has twice as much spunk' – as the Squire tugged at his bridle reins. 'The old mare could make her way better without being led, my fine fellow! But I see through your dodge. You're afraid of your old father turning back and getting into another rage. "Position" indeed! a beggarly squire – a man who did turn off his men just before winter, to rot or starve, for all he cared – it's just like a venal old Tory!' And, under the cover of sympathy with the dismissed labourers, Mr Preston indulged his own private pique very pleasantly.

Mr Preston had many causes for rejoicing; he might have forgotten this discomfiture, as he chose to feel it, in the remembrance of an increase of income, and in the popularity he enjoyed in his new abode. All Hollingford came forward to do the earl's new agent honour. Mr Sheepshanks had been a crabbed, crusty old bachelor, frequenting inn-parlours on market-days, not unwilling to give dinners to three or four chosen friends and familiars, with whom, in return, he dined from time to time, and with whom, also, he kept up an amicable rivalry in the matter of wines. But he 'did not appreciate female society', as Miss Browning elegantly worded his unwillingness to accept the invitations of the Hollingford ladies. He was even unrefined enough to speak of these invitations to his intimate friends aforesaid as 'those old women's worrying'; but, of course, they never heard of this. Little quarter-of-sheet notes, without any envelopes – that invention was unknown in those days – but sealed in the corners when folded-up, instead of gummed (as they are fastened at present) – occasion-ally passed between Mr Sheepshanks and the Miss Brownings, Mrs Goodenough, or others. From the first-mentioned ladies the form ran as follows: – 'Miss Browning and her sister, Miss Phoebe Browning, present their respectful compliments to Mr Sheep-shanks, and beg to inform him that a few friends have kindly consented to favour them with their company at tea on Thursday next. Miss Browning and Miss Phoebe will take it very kindly if Mr Sheepshanks will join their little circle.'

Now for Mrs Goodenough:

'Mrs Goodenough's respects to Mr Sheepshanks, and hopes he is in good health. She would be very glad if he would favour her with his company to tea on Monday. My daughter, in Comberm-ere, has sent me a couple of guinea-fowls, and Mrs Goodenough hopes Mr Sheepshanks will stay and take a bit of supper.'

No need for the dates of the days of the month. The good ladies would have thought that the world was coming to an end, if the invitation had been sent out a week before the party therein named. But not even guinea-fowls for supper could tempt Mr Sheepshanks. He remembered the made-wines* he had tasted in former days at Hollingford parties, and shuddered. Bread-and-cheese, with a glass of bitter beer, or a little brandy-and-water, partaken of in his old clothes (which had worn into shapes of loose comfort, and smelt strongly of tobacco), he liked better than roast guinea-fowl and birch-wine,* even without throwing into the balance the stiff, uneasy coat, and the tight neckcloth and tighter shoes. So the ex-agent had been seldom, if ever, seen at the Hollingford tea-parties. He might have had his form of refusal stereotyped, it was so invariably the same.

'Mr Sheepshanks' duty to Miss Browning and her sister' (to Mrs Goodenough, or to others, as the case might be). 'Business of importance prevents him from availing himself of their polite invitation; for which he begs to return his best thanks.'

But now that Mr Preston had succeeded, and come to live in Hollingford, things were changed.

He accepted every civility right and left, and won golden opinions* accordingly. Parties were made in his honour, 'just as if he had been a bride,' Miss Phoebe Browning said; and to all of them he went.

'What's the man after?' said Mr Sheepshanks to himself, when he heard of his successor's affability, and sociability, and amiability, and a variety of other agreeable 'ilities' from the friends whom the old steward still retained at Hollingford. 'Preston's not a man to put himself out for nothing. He's deep. He'll be after something solider than popularity.'

The sagacious old bachelor was right. Mr Preston was 'after' something more than mere popularity. He went wherever he had a chance of meeting Cynthia Kirkpatrick.

It might be that Molly's spirits were more depressed at this time than they were in general; or that Cynthia was exultant, unawares to herself, in the amount of attention and admiration she was receiving, from Roger by day, from Mr Preston in the evening – but the two girls seemed to have parted company in cheerfulness. Molly was always gentle, but very grave and silent. Cynthia, on the contrary, was merry, full of pretty mockeries, and hardly ever silent. When first she came to Hollingford, one of her great charms had been that she was such a gracious listener; now her excitement, whatever its cause, made her too restless to hold her tongue; yet what she said was too pretty, too witty, not to be a winning and sparkling interruption, eagerly welcomed by those who were under her sway. Mr Gibson was the only one who observed this change, and reasoned upon it. 'She's in a mental fever of some kind,' thought he to himself. 'She's very fascinating, but I don't quite understand her.'

If Molly had not been so entirely loyal to her friend, she might have thought this constant brilliancy a little tiresome, when brought into everyday life; it was not the sunshiny rest of a placid lake – it was rather the glitter of the pieces of a broken mirror, which confuses and bewilders. Cynthia would not talk quietly about anything now; subjects of thought or conversation seemed to have lost their relative value. There were exceptions to this mood of hers, when she sank into deep fits of silence, that would have been gloomy, had it not been for the never varying sweetness of her temper. If there was a little kindness to be done to either Mr Gibson or Molly, Cynthia was just as ready as ever to do it; nor did she refuse to do anything her mother wished, however fidgety might be the humour that prompted the wish. But, in this latter case, Cynthia's eyes were not quickened by her heart.

Molly was dejected, she knew not why. Cynthia had drifted a little apart; that was not it. Her stepmother had whimsical moods; and, if Cynthia displeased her, she would oppress Molly with small kindnesses and pseudo-affection. Or else everything was wrong, the world was out of joint,* and Molly had failed in her mission to set it right, and was to be blamed accordingly. But Molly was of too steady a disposition to be much moved by the changeableness of an unreasonable person. She might be annoyed, or irritated; but she was not depressed. That was not it. The real cause was certainly this. As long as Roger was drawn to Cynthia, and sought her of his own accord, it had been a sore pain and bewilderment to Molly's heart; but it was a straightforward attraction, and one which Molly acknowledged, in her humility and great power of loving, to be the most natural thing in the world. She would look at Cynthia's beauty and grace, and feel as if no one could resist it. And, when she witnessed all the small signs of honest devotion which Roger was at no pains to conceal, she thought, with a sigh, that surely no girl could help relinquishing her heart to such tender, strong keeping as Roger's character ensured. She would have been willing to cut off her right hand, if need were, to forward his attachment to Cynthia; and the self-sacrifice would have added a strange zest to a happy crisis. She was indignant at what she considered Mrs Gibson's obtuseness to so much goodness and worth; and, when she called Roger a 'country lout', or any other depreciative epithet, Molly would pinch herself, in order to keep silent. But, after all, those were peaceful days compared to the present, when she, seeing the wrong side of the tapestry, after the wont of those who dwell in the same house with a plotter, became aware that Mrs Gibson had totally changed her behaviour to Roger, for some cause unknown to Molly.

But he was always exactly the same; 'steady as old Time', as Mrs Gibson called him, with her usual originality; 'a rock of strength, under whose very shadow there is rest',* as Mrs Hamley had once spoken of him. So the cause of Mrs Gibson's altered manner lay not in him. Yet now he was sure of a welcome, let him come at any hour he would. He was playfully reproved for having taken Mrs Gibson's words too literally, and for never coming before lunch. But he said he considered her reasons for such words to be valid, and should respect them. And this was done out of his simplicity, and with no tinge of malice. Then, in their family conversations at home, Mrs Gibson was constantly making projects for throwing Roger and Cynthia together, with so evident a betrayal of her wish to bring about an engagement, that Molly chafed at the net spread so evidently, and at Roger's blindness in coming so willingly to be entrapped. She forgot his previous willingness, his former evidences of manly fondness for the beautiful Cynthia; she only saw plots of which he was the victim, and Cynthia the conscious if passive bait. She felt as if she could not have acted as Cynthia did; no, not even to gain Roger's love! Cynthia heard and saw as much of the domestic background as she did, and yet she submitted to the *rôle* assigned to her! To be sure, this *rôle* would have been played by her unconsciously; the things prescribed were what she would naturally have done; but, because they were prescribed – by implication only, it is true – Molly would have resisted; have gone out, for instance, when she was expected to stay at home; or have lingered in the garden, when a long country walk was planned. At last – for she could not help loving Cynthia, come what would – she determined to believe that Cynthia was entirely unaware of all; but it was with an effort that she brought herself to believe it.

It may be all very pleasant 'to sport with Amaryllis in the shade, or with the tangles of Neaera's hair';* but young men at the outset of their independent life have many other cares in this prosaic England to occupy their time and their thoughts. Roger was Fellow at Trinity, to be sure; and, from the outside, it certainly appeared as if his position, as long as he chose to keep unmarried, was a very easy one. His was not a nature, however, to sink down into inglorious ease,* even had his Fellowship income been at his disposal. He looked forward to an active life; in what direction, he had not yet determined. He knew what were his talents and his tastes; and did not wish the former to lie buried, nor the latter, which he regarded as gifts, fitting him for some peculiar work, to be disregarded or thwarted. He rather liked awaiting an object, secure in his own energy to force his way to it, when once he saw it clearly. He reserved enough of money for his own personal needs, which were small, and for the ready furtherance of any project he might see fit to undertake; the rest of his income was Osborne's, given and accepted in the spirit which made the bond between these two brothers so rarely perfect. It was only the thought of Cynthia that threw Roger off his balance. A strong man in everything else, about her he was as a child. He knew that he could not marry and retain his Fellowship; his intention was to hold himself loose from any employment or profession, until he had found one to his mind; so there was no immediate prospect – no prospect for many years, indeed – that he would be able to marry. Yet he went on seeking Cynthia's sweet company, listening to the music of her voice, basking in her sunshine, and feeding his passion in every possible way, just like an unreasoning child. He knew that it was folly – and yet he did it; and it was perhaps this that made him so sympathetic with Osborne. Roger racked his brains about Osborne's affairs much more frequently than Osborne troubled himself. Indeed, he had become so ailing and languid of late, that even the Squire made only very faint objections to his desire for frequent change of scene, though formerly he used to grumble so much at the necessary expenditure it involved.

'After all, it doesn't cost much,' the Squire said to Roger one day. 'Choose how he does it, he does it cheaply; he used to come and ask me for twenty, where now he does it for five. But he and I have lost each other's language, that's what we have! and my dictionary' (only he called it 'dixonary') 'has all got wrong because of those confounded debts – which he will never explain to me, or talk about – he always holds me off at arm's length when I begin upon it – he does, Roger – me, his old dad, as was his primest favourite of all, when he was a little bit of a chap!'

The Squire dwelt so much upon Osborne's reserved behaviour to himself that, brooding over this one subject perpetually, he became more morose and gloomy than ever in his manner to his son, resenting the want of the confidence and affection that he thus repelled. So much so that Roger, who desired to avoid being made the receptacle of his father's complaints against Osborne – and Roger's passive listening was the sedative his father always sought – had often to have recourse to the discussion of the drainage works as a counter-irritant. The Squire had felt Mr Preston's speech about the dismissal of his work-people very keenly; it fell in with the reproaches of his own conscience, though, as he would repeat to Roger over and over again – 'I couldn't help it – how could I? – I was drained dry of ready money – I wish the land was drained as dry as I am!' said he, with a touch of humour that came out before he was aware, and at which he smiled sadly enough. 'What was I to do, I ask you, Roger? I know I was in a rage – I've had a deal to make me so – and maybe I didn't think as much about consequences as I should have done, when I gave orders for 'em to be sent off; but I couldn't have done otherwise, if I'd ha' thought for a twelvemonth in cool blood. Consequences! I hate consequences; they've always been against me; they have! I'm so tied up, I can't cut down a stick more – and that's a "consequence" of having the property so deucedly well settled; I wish I'd never had any ancestors! Ay, laugh, lad! it does me good to see thee laugh a bit, after Osborne's long face, which always grows longer at sight o' me.'

'Look here, father!' said Roger suddenly, 'I'll manage somehow about the money for the works. You trust to me; give me two months to turn myself in, and you shall have some money, at any rate, to begin with.'

The Squire looked at him, and his face brightened as a child's does at the promise of a pleasure, made to him by some one on whom he can rely. He became a little graver, however, as he said – 'But how will you get it? It's hard enough work.'

'Never mind; I'll get it – a hundred or so at first – I don't yet know how – but remember, father, I'm a senior wrangler, and a "very promising young writer", as that review called me. Oh, you don't know what a fine fellow you've got for a son! You should have read that review to know all my wonderful merits.'

'I did, Roger. I heard Gibson speaking of it, and I made him get it for me. I should have understood it better, if they could have called the animals by their English names, and not put so much of their French jingo into it.'

'But it was an answer to an article by a French writer,' pleaded Roger.

'I'd ha' let him alone!' said the Squire earnestly. 'We had to beat 'em, and we did it at Waterloo; but I'd not demean myself by answering any of their lies, if I was you. But I got through the review, for all their Latin and French – I did; and if you doubt me, you just look at the end of the great ledger, turn it upside down, and you'll find I've copied out all the fine words they said of you: "careful observer", "strong nervous English", "rising philosopher". Oh! I can nearly say it all off by heart; for, many a time when I'm frabbed* by bad debts, or Osborne's bills, or moidered with accounts, I turn the ledger wrong way up, and smoke a pipe over it, while I read those pieces out of the review which speak about you, lad!'

CHAPTER 32

Coming Events

Roger had turned over many plans in his mind, by which he thought that he could obtain sufficient money for the purpose he desired to accomplish. His careful grandfather, who had been a merchant in the city, had so tied up the few thousands he had left to his daughter that, although, in case of her death before her husband's, the latter might enjoy the life-interest thereof, yet, in case of both their deaths, their second son did not succeed to the property till he was five-and-twenty; and, if he died before that age, the money that then would have been his went to one of his cousins on the maternal side. In short, the old merchant had taken as many precautions about his legacy as if it had been for tens, instead of units, of thousands. Of course, Roger might have slipped through all these meshes by insuring his life until the specified age; and, probably, if he had consulted any lawyer, this course would have been suggested to him. But he disliked taking any one into his confidence on the subject of his father's want of ready money. He had obtained a copy of his grandfather's will at Doctors' Commons,* and he imagined that all the contingencies involved in it would be patent to the light of nature and common sense. He was a little mistaken in this, but not the less resolved that money in some way he would have, in order to fulfil his promise to his father, and for the ulterior purpose of giving the Squire some daily interest to distract his thoughts from the regrets and cares that were almost weakening his mind. It was 'Roger Hamley, senior wrangler and Fellow of Trinity, to the highest bidder, no matter what honest employment'; and presently it came down to 'any bidder at all'.

Another perplexity and distress at this time weighed upon Roger. Osborne, heir to the estate, was going to have a child. The

Hamley property was entailed on 'heirs-male born in lawful wedlock'. Was the 'wedlock' lawful? Osborne never seemed to doubt that it was – never seemed, in fact, to think twice about it. And if he, the husband, did not, how much less did Aimée, the trustful wife! Yet who could tell how much misery any shadows of illegality might cast into the future! One evening, Roger, sitting by the languid, careless, dilettante Osborne, began to question him as to the details of the marriage. Osborne knew instinctively at what Roger was aiming. It was not that he did not desire perfect legality in justice to his wife; it was that he was so indisposed at the time that he hated to be bothered. It was something like the refrain of Gray's Scandinavian Prophetess:*
'Leave me, leave me to repose!'

'But do try and tell me how you managed it.'

'How tiresome you are, Roger!' put in Osborne.

'Well, I daresay I am. Go on!'

'I've told you Morrison married us. You remember old Morrison at Trinity?'

'Yes; as good and blunder-headed a fellow as ever lived.'

'Well, he's taken orders; and the examination for priest's orders fatigued him so much that he got his father to give him a hundred or two for a tour on the Continent. He meant to get to Rome, because he had heard that there were such pleasant winters there. So he turned up at Metz in August.'

'I don't see why.'

'No more did he. He never was great in geography, you know; and, somehow, he thought that Metz, pronounced French fashion, must be on the road to Rome. Some one had told him so in fun. However, it was very well for me that I met with him there; for I was determined to be married, and that without loss of time.'

'But Aimée is a Catholic?'

'That's true! but you see I am not. You don't suppose I would do her any wrong, Roger?' asked Osborne, sitting up in his lounging-chair, and speaking rather indignantly to Roger, his face suddenly flushing red.

'No! I'm sure you would not mean it; but, you see, there's a child coming, and this estate is entailed on "heirs-male". Now, I want to know if the marriage is legal or not? and it seems to me it's a ticklish question.'

'Oh!' said Osborne, falling back into repose, 'if that's all, I suppose you're next heir-male, and I can trust you as I can myself.

You know my marriage is *bonâ fide* in intention, and I believe it to be legal in fact. We went over to Strasbourg! Aimée picked up a friend – a good middle-aged Frenchwoman – who served half as bridesmaid, half as chaperon, and then we went before the mayor – *préfet* – what do you call them? I think Morrison rather enjoyed the spree. I signed all manner of papers in the *préfecture*; I did not read them over, for fear lest I could not sign them conscientiously. It was the safest plan. Aimée kept trembling so, I thought she would faint; and then we went off to the nearest English chaplaincy, Carlsruhe, and the chaplain was away, so Morrison easily got the loan of the chapel, and we were married the next day.'

'But surely some registration or certificate was necessary?'

'Morrison said he would undertake all those forms; and he ought to know his own business. I know I tipped him pretty well for the job.'

'You must be married again,' said Roger, after a pause, 'and that before the child is born. Have you got a certificate of the marriage?'

'I daresay Morrison has got it somewhere. But I believe I'm legally married according to the laws both of England and France; I really do, old fellow. I've got the *préfet's* papers somewhere.'

'Never mind! you shall be married again in England. Aimée goes to the Roman Catholic chapel at Prestham, doesn't she?'

'Yes. She is so good I wouldn't disturb her in her religion for the world.'

'Then you shall be married both there and at the church of the parish in which she lives, as well,' said Roger decidedly.

'It's a great deal of trouble, unnecessary trouble, and unnecessary expense, I should say,' said Osborne. 'Why can't you leave well alone? Neither Aimée nor I are of the stuff to turn scoundrels and deny the legality of our marriage; and, if the child is a boy and my father dies, and I die, why I'm sure you'll do him justice, as sure as I am of myself, old fellow!'

'But if I die into the bargain? Make a hecatomb of the present Hamleys all at once, while you are about it! Who succeeds as heir-male?'

Osborne thought for a moment. 'One of the Irish Hamleys, I suppose. I fancy they are needy chaps. Perhaps you are right. But what need to have such gloomy forebodings?'

'The law makes one have foresight in such affairs,' said Roger. 'So I'll go down to Aimée next week when I'm in town, and I'll make all necessary arrangements before you come. I think you'll be happier, if it is all done.'

'I shall be happier if I've a chance of seeing the little woman; that I grant you. But what is taking you up to town? I wish I'd money to run about like you, instead of being shut up for ever in this dull old house.'

Osborne was apt occasionally to contrast his position with Roger's in a tone of complaint, forgetting that both were the results of character, and also that out of his income Roger gave up so large a portion for the maintenance of his brother's wife. But, if this ungenerous thought of Osborne's had been set clearly before his conscience, he would have smote his breast and cried 'Mea culpa!'* with the best of them; it was only that he was too indolent to keep an unassisted conscience.

'I shouldn't have thought of going up,' said Roger, reddening as if he had been accused of spending another's money instead of his own, 'if I hadn't had to go up on business. Lord Hollingford has written for me; he knows my great wish for employment, and has heard of something which he considers suitable; there's his letter if you care to read it. But it does not tell anything definitely.'

Osborne read the letter and returned it to Roger. After a moment or two of silence he said – 'Why do you want money? Are we taking too much from you? It's a great shame of me; but what can I do? Only suggest a career for me, and I'll follow it tomorrow.' He spoke as if Roger had been reproaching him.

'My dear fellow, don't get those notions into your head! I must do something for myself some time, and I've been on the look-out. Besides, I want my father to go on with his drainage; it would do good both to his health and his spirits. If I can advance any part of the money requisite, he and you shall pay me interest until you can return the capital.'

'Roger, you're the providence of the family,' exclaimed Osborne, suddenly struck by admiration of his brother's conduct, and forgetting to contrast it with his own.

So Roger went up to London, and Osborne followed him; and for two or three weeks the Gibsons saw nothing of the brothers. But, as wave succeeds to wave, so interest succeeds to interest. 'The family', as they were called, came down for their autumn-sojourn at the Towers, and again the house was full of visitors, and the Towers servants, and carriages, and liveries were seen in the two streets of Hollingford, just as they might have been seen for scores of autumns past.

So runs the round of life from day to day. Mrs Gibson found the chances of intercourse with the Towers rather more personally exciting than Roger's visits, or the rarer calls of Osborne Hamley. Cynthia had an old antipathy to the great family, who had made so much of her mother and so little of her; and whom she considered as in some measure the cause why she had seen so little of her mother, in the days when the little girl had craved for love and found none. Moreover, Cynthia missed her slave; although she did not care for Roger one thousandth part of what he did for her, yet she had found it not unpleasant to have a man whom she thoroughly respected, and whom men in general respected, the subject of her eye, the glad ministrant to each scarce-spoken wish, a person in whose sight all her words were pearls or diamonds, all her actions heavenly graciousness, and in whose thoughts she reigned supreme. She had no modest unconsciousness about her; and yet she was not vain. She knew of all this worship, and, when from circumstances she no longer received it, she missed it. The Earl and the Countess, Lord Hollingford and Lady Harriet, lords and ladies in general, liveries, dresses, bags of game, and rumours of riding parties, were as nothing to her, compared with Roger's absence. And yet she did not love him. No, she did not love him. Molly knew that Cynthia did not love him. Molly grew angry with her many and many a time, as the conviction of this fact was forced upon her. Molly did not know her own feelings; Roger had no overwhelming interest in what they might be; while his very life-breath seemed to depend on what Cynthia felt and thought. Therefore, Molly had keen insight into her 'sister's' heart, and she knew that Cynthia did not love Roger. Molly could have cried with passionate regret at the thought of the unvalued treasure lying at Cynthia's feet; and it would have been a merely unselfish regret. It was the old fervid tenderness: 'Do not wish for the moon, O my darling, for I cannot give it thee.' Cynthia's love was the moon Roger yearned for; and Molly saw that it was far away and out of reach, else would she have strained her heart-cords to give it to Roger.

'I am his sister,' she would say to herself. 'That old bond is not done away with, though he is too much absorbed by Cynthia to speak about it just now. His mother called me 'Fanny'; it was almost like an adoption. I must wait and watch, and see if I can do anything for my brother.'

One day Lady Harriet came to call on the Gibsons, or rather on Mrs Gibson; for the latter retained her old jealousy if any one else in Hollingford was supposed to be on intimate terms at the great house, or in the least acquainted with their plans. Mr Gibson might possibly know as much, but then he was professionally bound to secrecy. Out of the house she considered Mr Preston as her rival, and he was aware that she did so, and delighted in teasing her by affecting a knowledge of family-plans and details of affairs of which she was ignorant. Indoors, she was jealous of the fancy Lady Harriet had evidently taken for her stepdaughter, and she contrived to place quiet obstacles in the way of a too frequent intercourse between them. These obstacles were not unlike the shield of the knight in the old story; only, instead of the two sides presented to the two travellers approaching it from opposite quarters, one of which was silver, and one of which was gold, Lady Harriet saw the smooth and shining yellow radiance, while poor Molly only perceived a dull and heavy lead. To Lady Harriet it was 'Molly is gone out; she will be sorry to miss you, but she was obliged to go and see some old friends of her mother's whom she ought not to neglect; and I said to her, constancy is everything. It is Sterne, I think, who says, "Thine own and thy mother's friends forsake not".* But, dear Lady Harriet, you'll stop till she comes home, won't you? I know how fond you are of her; in fact' (with a little surface-playfulness) 'I sometimes say you come more to see her than your poor old Clare.'

To Molly it had previously been –

'Lady Harriet is coming here this morning. I can't have any one else coming in. Tell Maria to say I'm not at home. Lady Harriet has always so much to tell me; dear Lady Harriet! I've known all her secrets since she was twelve years old. You two girls must keep out of the way. Of course she'll ask for you, out of common civility; but you would only interrupt us if you came in, as you did the other day;' – now addressing Molly – 'I hardly like to say so, but I thought it was very forward.'

'Maria told me she had asked for me,' put in Molly simply.

'Very forward indeed!' continued Mrs Gibson, taking no further notice of the interruption, except to strengthen the words to which Molly's little speech had been intended as a correction.

'I think, this time, I must secure her ladyship from the chances

of such an intrusion, by taking care that you are out of the house,
Molly. You had better go to the Holly Farm, and speak about
those damsons I ordered, and which have never been sent.'

'I'll go,' said Cynthia. 'It's far too long a walk for Molly; she's
had a bad cold, and isn't as strong as she was a fortnight ago. I
delight in long walks. If you want Molly out of the way, mamma,
send her to the Miss Brownings; they are always glad to see her.'

'I never said I wanted Molly out of the way, Cynthia,' replied
Mrs Gibson. 'You always put things in such an exaggerated – I
might almost say, so coarse a manner. I am sure, Molly, my love,
you could never have so misunderstood me; it is only on Lady
Harriet's account.'

'I don't think I can walk as far as the Holly Farm; papa would
take the message; Cynthia need not go.'

'Well! I'm the last person in the world to tax any one's strength;
I'd sooner never see damson-preserve again. Suppose you do go
and see Miss Browning; you can pay her a nice long call, you
know she likes that; and ask after Miss Phoebe's cold from me,
you know. They were friends of your mother's, my dear, and I
would not have you break off old friendships for the world.
"Constancy above everything" is my motto, as you know, and the
memory of the dead ought always to be cherished.'

'Now, mamma, where am I to go?' asked Cynthia. 'Though
Lady Harriet doesn't care for me as much as she does for Molly –
indeed, quite the contrary, I should say – yet she might ask after
me, and I had better be safely out of the way.'

'True!' said Mrs Gibson meditatively, yet unconscious of any
satire in Cynthia's speech.

'She is much less likely to ask after you, my dear: I almost think
you might remain in the house, or you might go to the Holly
Farm; I really do want the damsons; or you might stay here in the
dining-room, you know, so as to be ready to arrange lunch
prettily, if she does take a fancy to stay for it. She is very fanciful,
is dear Lady Harriet! I would not like her to think we made any
difference in our meals because she stayed. "Simple elegance", as
I tell her, "always is what we aim at." But still you could put out
the best service, and arrange some flowers, and ask cook what
there is for dinner that she could send us for lunch, and make it
all look pretty, and impromptu, and natural. I think you had
better stay at home, Cynthia; and then you could fetch Molly

from the Miss Brownings' in the afternoon, you know, and you two could take a walk together.'

'After Lady Harriet was fairly gone! I understand, mamma. Off with you, Molly! Make haste, or Lady Harriet may come and ask for you as well as mamma! I'll take care and forget where you are going to, so that no one shall learn from me where you are, and I'll answer for mamma's loss of memory.'

'Child! what nonsense you talk; you quite confuse me with being so silly,' said Mrs Gibson, fluttered and annoyed as she usually was with the Lilliputian darts* Cynthia flung at her. She had recourse to her accustomed feckless piece of retaliation – bestowing some favour on Molly; and this did not hurt Cynthia one whit.

'Molly, darling, there's a very cold wind, though it looks so fine. You had better put on my Indian shawl; and it will look so pretty, too, on your grey gown – scarlet and grey; it's not everybody I would lend it to, but you're so careful.'

'Thank you,' said Molly: and she left Mrs Gibson in careless uncertainty as to whether her offer would be accepted or not.

Lady Harriet was sorry to miss Molly, as she was fond of the girl; but, as she perfectly agreed with Mrs Gibson's truism about 'constancy' and 'old friends', she saw no occasion for saying any more about the affair, but sat down in a little low chair with her feet on the fender. This said fender was made of bright, bright steel, and was strictly tabooed to all household and plebeian feet; indeed the position, if they assumed it, was considered low-bred and vulgar.

'That's right, dear Lady Harriet! you can't think what a pleasure it is to me to welcome you at my own fireside, into my humble home.'

'Humble! now, Clare, that's a little bit of nonsense, begging your pardon. I don't call this pretty little drawing-room a bit of a "humble home". It's as full of comforts, and of pretty things too, as any room of its size can be.'

'Ah! how small you must feel it! even I had to reconcile myself to it at first.'

'Well! perhaps your school-room was larger, but remember how bare it was, how empty of anything but deal tables, and forms, and mats. Oh, indeed, Clare, I quite agree with mamma, who always says you have done very well for yourself; and Mr Gibson too! What an agreeable, well-informed man!'

'Yes, he is,' said his wife slowly, as if she did not like to relinquish her *rôle* of a victim to circumstances quite immediately. 'He is very agreeable, very; only we see so little of him; and of course he comes home tired and hungry, and not inclined to talk to his own family, and apt to go to sleep.'

'Come, come!' said Lady Harriet, 'I'm going to have my turn now. We've had the complaint of a doctor's wife; now hear the moans of a peer's daughter! Our house is *so* overrun with visitors! and literally today I have come to you for a little solitude.'

'Solitude!' exclaimed Mrs Gibson. 'Would you rather be alone?' slightly aggrieved.

'No, you dear silly woman; my solitude requires a listener, to whom I may say, "how sweet is solitude!"* But I am tired of the responsibility of entertaining. Papa is so open-hearted, he asks every friend he meets with to come and pay us a visit. Mamma is really a great invalid; but she does not choose to give up her reputation for good health, having always considered illness a want of self-control. So she gets wearied and worried by a crowd of people who are all of them open-mouthed for amusement of some kind; just like a brood of fledglings in a nest; so I have to be parent-bird, and pop morsels into their yellow leathery bills, to find them swallowed down before I can think of where to find the next. Oh, it's "entertaining" in the largest, literalest, most dreariest, sense of the word! So I have told a few lies this morning, and come off here for quietness and the comfort of complaining!'

Lady Harriet threw herself back in her chair, and yawned; Mrs Gibson took one of her ladyship's hands in a soft sympathising manner, and murmured –

'Poor Lady Harriet!' and then she purred affectionately.

After a pause Lady Harriet started up and said – 'I used to take you as my arbiter of morals when I was a little girl. Tell me, do you think it wrong to tell lies?'

'Oh, my dear! how can you ask such questions? – of course it is very wrong – very wicked indeed, I think I may say. But I know you were only joking, when you said you had told lies.'

'No, indeed, I wasn't. I told as plump fat lies as you would wish to hear. I said I "was obliged to go into Hollingford on business"; when the truth was, there was no obligation in the matter, only an insupportable desire of being free from my visitors for an hour or two, and my only business was to come here, and yawn, and complain, and lounge at my leisure. I really think I'm unhappy at having told a story, as children express it.'

'But, my dear Lady Harriet,' said Mrs Gibson, a little puzzled as to the exact meaning of the words that were trembling on her tongue, 'I am sure you thought that you meant what you said, when you said it.'

'No, I didn't,' put in Lady Harriet.

'And besides, if you didn't, it was the fault of the tiresome people who drove you into such straits – yes, it was certainly their fault, not yours – and then you know the conventions of society – ah, what trammels they are!'

Lady Harriet was silent for a minute or two; then she said – 'Tell me, Clare; you've told lies sometimes, haven't you?'

'Lady Harriet! I think you might have known me better; but I know you don't mean it, dear.'

'Yes, I do. You must have told white lies, at any rate. How did you feel after them?'

'I should have been miserable, if I ever had. I should have died of self-reproach. "The truth, the whole truth, and nothing but the truth", has always seemed to me such a fine passage. But then I have so much that is unbending in my nature, and in our sphere of life there are so few temptations; if we are humble we are also simple, and unshackled by etiquette.'

'Then you blame me very much? If somebody else will blame me, I shan't be so unhappy at what I said this morning.'

'I am sure I never blamed you; not in my innermost heart, dear Lady Harriet. Blame you, indeed! That would be presumption in me.'

'I think I shall set up a confessor! and it shan't be you, Clare, for you have always been only too indulgent to me.'

After a pause she said – 'Can you give me some lunch, Clare? I don't mean to go home till three. My "business" will take me till then, as the people at the Towers are duly informed.'

'Certainly. I shall be delighted! but you know we are very simple in our habits.'

'Oh, I only want a little bread-and-butter, and perhaps a slice of cold meat – you must not give yourself any trouble, Clare – perhaps you dine now? let me sit down just like one of your family.'

'Yes, you shall; I won't make any alteration; – it will be so pleasant to have you sharing our family-meal, dear Lady Harriet.

But we dine late; we only lunch now. How low the fire is getting; I really am forgetting everything in the pleasure of this *tête-à-tête*!'

So she rang twice; with great distinctness, and with a long pause between the rings. Maria brought in coals.

But the signal was as well understood by Cynthia as the 'Hall of Apollo' was by the servants of Lucullus.* The brace of partridges that were to have been for the late dinner were instantly put down to the fire; and the prettiest china brought out, and the table decked with flowers and fruit, arranged with all Cynthia's usual dexterity and taste. So that, when the meal was announced, and Lady Harriet entered the room, she could not but think her hostess's apologies had been quite unnecessary, and be more and more convinced that Clare had done very well for herself. Cynthia now joined the party, pretty and elegant as she always was; but, somehow, she did not take Lady Harriet's fancy; she only noticed her on account of her being her mother's daughter. Her presence made the conversation more general, and Lady Harriet gave out several pieces of news, none of them of any great importance to her, but as what had been talked about by the circle of visitors assembled at the Towers.

'Lord Hollingford ought to have been with us,' she said, amongst other things; 'but he is obliged, or fancies himself obliged, which is all the same thing, to stay in town about this Crichton legacy!'

'A legacy? To Lord Hollingford? I am so glad!'

'Don't be in a hurry to be glad! It's nothing for him but trouble. Didn't you hear of that rich eccentric Mr Crichton, who died some time ago, and – fired by the example of the Duke of Bridgewater,* I suppose – left a sum of money in the hands of trustees, of whom my brother is one, to send out a man with a thousand fine qualifications, to make a scientific voyage, with a view to bringing back specimens of the fauna of distant lands, and so forming the nucleus of a museum which is to be called the Crichton Museum, and so perpetuate the founder's name. Such various forms does man's vanity take! Sometimes it simulates philanthropy; sometimes a love of science!'

'It seems to me a very laudable and useful object, I am sure,' said Mrs Gibson, safely.

'I daresay it is, taking it from the public-good view. But it's rather tiresome to us privately, for it keeps Hollingford in town – or between it and Cambridge – and each place as dull and empty as can be, just when we want him down at the Towers. The thing ought to have been decided long ago, and there's some danger of the legacy lapsing. The two other trustees have run away to the Continent, feeling, as they say, the utmost confidence in him, but in reality shirking their responsibilities. However, I believe he likes it, so I ought not to grumble. He thinks he is going to be very successful in the choice of his man – and he belongs to this county, too – young Hamley of Hamley, if he can only get his college to let him go, for he is a Fellow of Trinity, senior wrangler or something; and they're not so foolish as to send their crack man to be eaten up by lions and tigers!'

'It must be Roger Hamley!' exclaimed Cynthia, her eyes brightening, and her cheeks flushing.

'He's not the eldest son; he can scarcely be called Hamley of Hamley!' said Mrs Gibson.

'Hollingford's man is a Fellow of Trinity, as I said before.'

'Then it is Mr Roger Hamley,' said Cynthia; 'and he's up in London about some business! What news for Molly when she comes home!'

'Why, what has Molly to do with it?' asked Lady Harriet. 'Is' — and she looked into Mrs Gibson's face for an answer. Mrs Gibson in reply gave an intelligent and very expressive glance at Cynthia, who however did not perceive it.

'Oh, no! not at all;' and Mrs Gibson nodded a little at her daughter, as much as to say, 'If any one, that.'

Lady Harriet began to look at the pretty Miss Kirkpatrick with fresh interest; her brother had spoken in such a manner of this young Mr Hamley that every one connected with the phoenix was worthy of observation. Then, as if the mention of Molly's name had brought her afresh into her mind, Lady Harriet said – 'And where is Molly all this time? I should like to see my little mentor. I hear she is very much grown since those days.'

'Oh! when she once gets gossiping with the Miss Brownings, she never knows when to come home,' said Mrs Gibson.

'The Miss Brownings? Oh! I'm so glad you named them! I'm very fond of them. Pecksy and Flapsy; I may call them so in Molly's absence. I'll go and see them before I go home, and then perhaps I shall see my dear little Molly too. Do you know, Clare, I've quite taken a fancy to that girl!'

So Mrs Gibson, after all her precautions, had to submit to Lady Harriet's leaving her half-an-hour earlier than she otherwise would have done in order to 'make herself common' (as Mrs Gibson expressed it) by calling on the Miss Brownings.

But Molly had left, before Lady Harriet arrived.

Molly went the long walk to the Holly Farm, to order the damsons, out of a kind of penitence. She had felt conscious of anger at being sent out of the house by such a palpable manoeuvre as that which her stepmother had employed. Of course she did not meet Cynthia; so she went alone along the pretty lanes, with grassy sides and high-hedge banks not at all in the style of modern agriculture. At first, she made herself uncomfortable with questioning herself as to how far it was right to leave unnoticed the small domestic failings – the webs, the distortions of truth, which had prevailed in their household ever since her father's second marriage. She knew that very often she longed to protest, but did not do it, from the desire of sparing her father any discord; and she saw by his face that he, too, was occasionally aware of certain things that gave him pain, as showing that his wife's standard of conduct was not as high as he would have liked. It was a wonder to Molly, whether this silence was right or wrong. With a girl's want of toleration, and want of experience to teach her the force of circumstances, and of temptation, she had often been on the point of telling her stepmother some forcible home-truths. But, possibly, her father's example of silence, and often some piece of kindness on Mrs Gibson's part (for after her way, and when in a good temper, she was very kind to Molly), made her hold her tongue.

That night at dinner, Mrs Gibson repeated the conversation between herself and Lady Harriet, giving it a very strong individual colouring, as was her wont, and telling nearly the whole of what had passed, although implying that there was a great deal said which was so purely confidential, that she was bound in honour not to repeat it. Her three auditors listened to her without interrupting her much – indeed, without bestowing extreme attention on what she was saying, until she came to the fact of Lord Hollingford's absence in London, and the reason for it.

'Roger Hamley going off on a scientific expedition!' exclaimed Mr Gibson, suddenly awakened into vivacity.

'Yes. At least, it is not settled finally; but as Lord Hollingford is the only trustee who takes any interest – and being Lord Cumnor's son – it is next to certain.'

'I think, I must have a voice in the matter,' said Mr Gibson;

and he relapsed into silence, keeping his ears open, however, henceforward.

'How long will he be away?' asked Cynthia. 'We shall miss him sadly.'

Molly's lips formed an acquiescing 'yes' to this remark, but no sound was heard. There was a buzzing in her ears as if the others were going on with the conversation; but the words they uttered seemed indistinct and blurred; they were merely conjectures, and did not interfere with the one great piece of news. To the rest of the party she appeared to be eating her dinner as usual, and, if she were silent, there was one listener the more to Mrs Gibson's stream of prattle, and Mr Gibson's and Cynthia's remarks.

CHAPTER 33

Brightening Prospects

It was a day or two afterwards that Mr Gibson made time to ride round by Hamley, desirous to learn more exact particulars of this scheme for Roger than he could obtain from any extraneous source, and rather puzzled to know whether he should interfere in the project or not. The state of the case was this. Osborne's symptoms were, in Mr Gibson's opinion, signs of his having a fatal disease. Dr Nicholls had differed from him on this head, and Mr Gibson knew that the old physician had had long experience, and was considered very skilful in the profession. Still, he believed that he himself was right, and, if so, the complaint was one which might continue for years in the same state as at present, or might end the young man's life in an hour – a minute. Supposing that Mr Gibson was right, would it be well for Roger to be away where no sudden calls for his presence could reach him – away for two years? Yet, if the affair was concluded, the interference of a medical man might accelerate the very evil to be feared; and, after all, Dr Nicholls might be right, and the symptoms might proceed from some other cause. Might? Yes. Probably did? No. Mr Gibson could not bring himself to say 'yes' to this latter form of sentence. So he rode on, meditating; his reins slack, his head a little bent. It was one of those still and lovely autumn days, when the red and yellow leaves are hanging-pegs to dewy, brilliant gossamer-webs; when the hedges are full of trailing brambles, loaded with ripe blackberries; when the air is full of the farewell whistles and pipes of birds, clear and short – not the long full-throated warbles of spring; when the whirr of the partridge's wing is heard in the stubble-fields, as the sharp hoof-blows fall on the paved lanes; when here and there a leaf floats and flutters down to the ground, although there is not a single breath of wind. The country surgeon felt the beauty of the seasons, perhaps more than most men. He saw more of it by day, by night, in storm and sunshine, or in the still, soft cloudy weather. He never spoke about what he felt on the subject; indeed, he did not put his feelings into words, even to himself. But, if his mood ever approached to the sentimental, it was on such days as this. He rode into the stable-yard, gave his horse to a man, and went into the house by a side entrance. In the passage he met the Squire.

'That's capital, Gibson! What good wind blew you here? You'll have some lunch? it's on the table, I only just this minute left the room.' And he kept shaking Mr Gibson's hand all the time till he had placed him, nothing loth, at the well-covered dining-table.

'What's this I hear about Roger?' said Mr Gibson, plunging at once into the subject.

'Aha! so you've heard, have you? It's famous, isn't it? He's a boy to be proud of, is old Roger! Steady Roger; we used to think him slow, but it seems to me that slow and sure wins the race. But tell me; what have you heard; how much is known? Nay, you must have a glassful! It's old ale, such as we don't brew now-a-days; it's as old as Osborne. We brewed it that autumn, and we called it "the young Squire's ale". I thought to have tapped it on his marriage; but I don't know when that will come to pass, so we've tapped it now in Roger's honour.'

The old Squire had evidently been enjoying 'the young Squire's ale' to the verge of prudence. It was indeed, as he said, 'as strong as brandy'; and Mr Gibson had to sip it very carefully, as he ate his cold roast-beef.

'Well! and what have you heard? There's a deal to hear, and all good news; though I shall miss the lad, I know that.'

'I did not know that it was settled; I only heard that it was in progress.'

'Well, it was only in progress, as you call it, till last Tuesday. He never let me know anything about it, though; he says he thought I might be fidgety with thinking of the *pros* and *cons*. So

I never knew a word on't till I had a letter from my Lord Hollingford – where is it?' pulling out a great black leathern receptacle for all manner of papers. And, putting on his spectacles, he read aloud their headings.

'"Measurement of timber", – "new railways", "drench for cows, from Farmer Hayes", "Dobson's accounts", – 'um 'um – here it is. Now, read that letter!' handing it to Mr Gibson.

It was a manly, feeling, sensible letter, explaining to the old father in very simple language the services which were demanded by the terms of the will to which the writer and two or three others were trustees; the liberal allowance for expenses; the still more liberal reward for performance, which had tempted several men of considerable renown to offer themselves as candidates for the appointment. Lord Hollingford then went on to say that, having seen a good deal of Roger lately, since the publication of his article in reply to the French osteologist, he had had reason to think that in him the trustees would find united the various qualities required, in a greater measure than in any of the applicants who had at that time presented themselves. Roger had deep interest in the subject; much acquired knowledge, and at the same time, great natural powers of comparison and classification of facts; he had shown himself to be an observer of a fine and accurate kind; he was of the right age, in the very prime of health and strength, and unshackled by any family ties. Here Mr Gibson paused for consideration. He hardly cared to ascertain by what steps the result had been arrived at – he already knew what that result was; but his mind was again arrested, as his eye caught on the remuneration offered, which was indeed most liberal; and then he read with attention the high praise bestowed on the son in this letter to the father. The Squire had been watching Mr Gibson – waiting till he came to this part – and he rubbed his hands together, as he said –

'Ay! you've come to it at last. It's the best part of the whole, isn't it. God bless the boy! and from a Whig, mind you, which makes it the more handsome. And there's more to come still. I say, Gibson, I think my luck is turning at last,' passing him on yet another letter to read. 'That only came this morning; but I've acted on it already, I sent for the foreman of the drainage works at once, I did; and tomorrow, please God, they'll be at work again.'

Mr Gibson read the second letter, from Roger. To a certain

degree it was a modest repetition of what Lord Hollingford had said, with an explanation of how he had come to take so decided a step in life without consulting his father. He did not wish him to be in suspense for one reason. Another was that he felt, as no one else could feel for him, that, by accepting this offer, he entered upon the kind of life for which he knew himself to be most fitted. And then he merged the whole into business. He said that he knew well the suffering his father had gone through, when he had to give up his drainage works for want of money; that he, Roger, had been enabled at once to raise money upon the remuneration he was to receive on the accomplishment of two years' work; and that he had also insured his life, in order to provide for the repayment of the money he had raised, in case he did not live to return to England. He said that the sum he had borrowed on this security would at once be forwarded to his father.

Mr Gibson laid down the letter, without speaking a word for some time; then he said – 'He'll have to pay a pretty sum for insuring his life beyond seas.'

'He's got his Fellowship money,' said the Squire, a little depressed at Mr Gibson's remark.

'Yes; that's true. And he's a strong young fellow, as I know.'

'I wish I could tell his mother,' said the Squire in an undertone.

'It seems all settled now,' said Mr Gibson, more in reply to his own thoughts than to the Squire's remark.

'Yes!' said the Squire; 'and they're not going to let the grass grow under his feet. He's to be off, as soon as he can get his scientific traps* ready. I almost wish he wasn't to go. You don't seem quite to like it, doctor?'

'Yes, I do,' said Mr Gibson, in a more cheerful tone than before. 'It can't be helped now, without doing a mischief,' thought he to himself. 'Why, Squire, I think it a great honour to have such a son. I envy you, that's what I do! Here's a lad of three or four and twenty distinguishing himself in more ways than one, and as simple and affectionate at home as any fellow need to be – not a bit set-up!'

'Ay, ay; he's twice as much a son to me as Osborne, who has been all his life set up* on nothing at all, as one may say.'

'Come, Squire, I mustn't hear anything against Osborne; we may praise one, without hitting at the other. Osborne hasn't had the strong health which has enabled Roger to work as he has done. I met a man who knew his tutor at Trinity the other day, and of course we began cracking* about Roger – it's not every day that one can reckon a senior wrangler among one's friends, and I'm nearly as proud of the lad as you are. This Mr Mason told me, the tutor said that only half of Roger's success was owing to his mental powers; the other half was owing to his perfect health, which enabled him to work harder and more continuously than most men without suffering. He said that in all his experience he had never known any one with an equal capacity for mental labour; and that he could come again with a fresh appetite to his studies after shorter intervals of rest than most. Now I, being a doctor, trace a good deal of his superiority to the material cause of a thoroughly good constitution, which Osborne hasn't got.'

'Osborne might have, if he got out o' doors more,' said the Squire moodily; 'but, except when he can loaf into Hollingford, he doesn't care to go out at all. I hope,' he continued, with a glance of sudden suspicion at Mr Gibson, 'he's not after one of your girls? I don't mean any offence, you know; but he'll have the estate, and it won't be free, and he must marry money. I don't think I could allow it in Roger; but Osborne's the eldest son, you know.'

Mr Gibson reddened; he was offended for a moment. Then the partial truth of what the Squire said was presented to his mind, and he remembered their old friendship; so he spoke quietly, if shortly.

'I don't believe there's anything of the kind going on. I'm not much at home, you know; but I've never heard or seen anything that should make me suppose that there is. When I do, I'll let you know.'

'Now, Gibson, don't go and be offended! I'm glad for the boys to have a pleasant house to go to, and I thank you and Mrs Gibson for making it pleasant. Only keep off love; it can come to no good. That's all. I don't believe Osborne will ever earn a farthing to keep a wife during my life; and, if I were to die tomorrow, she would have to bring some money to clear the estate. And, if I do speak as I shouldn't have done formerly – a little sharp or so – why, it's because I've been worried by many a care no one knows anything of.'

'I'm not going to take offence,' said Mr Gibson; 'but let us understand each other clearly. If you don't want your sons to come as much to my house as they do, tell them so yourself. I like the lads, and am glad to see them; but, if they do come, you must take the consequences, whatever they are, and not blame me, or them either, for what may happen from the frequent intercourse between two young men and two young women; and, what is more, though, as I said, I see nothing whatever of the kind you fear at present, and have promised to tell you of the first symptoms I do see, yet farther than that I won't go. If there's an attachment at any future time, I won't interfere.'

'I shouldn't so much mind if Roger fell in love with your Molly. He can fight for himself, you see, and she's an uncommon nice girl. My poor wife was so fond of her,' answered the Squire. 'It's Osborne and the estate I'm thinking of!'

'Well, then, tell him not to come near us! I shall be sorry, but you will be safe.'

'I'll think about it; but he's difficult to manage. I've always to get my blood well up, before I can speak my mind to him.'

Mr Gibson was leaving the room; but at these words he turned and laid his hand on the Squire's arm.

'Take my advice, Squire! As I said, there's no harm done as yet, as far as I know. Prevention is better than cure. Speak out, but speak gently to Osborne, and do it at once! I shall understand how it is, if he doesn't show his face for some months in my house. If you speak gently to him, he'll take the advice as from a friend. If he can assure you there's no danger, of course he'll come just as usual, when he likes.'

It was all very fine giving the Squire this good advice; but, as Osborne had already formed the very kind of marriage his father most deprecated, it did not act quite as well as Mr Gibson had hoped. The Squire began the conversation with unusual self-control; but he grew irritated, when Osborne denied his father's right to interfere in any marriage he might contemplate; denied it with a certain degree of doggedness and weariness of the subject that drove the Squire into one of his passions; and although, on after reflection, he remembered that he had his son's promise and solemn word not to think of either Cynthia or Molly for his wife, yet the father and son had passed through one of those altercations which help to estrange men for life. Each had said bitter things to the other; and, if the brotherly affection had not been so true between Osborne and Roger, they too might have become alienated, in consequence of the Squire's exaggerated and injudicious comparison of their characters and deeds. But, as Roger in his boyhood had loved Osborne too well to be jealous of the praise and love which the eldest son, the beautiful brilliant lad, had received, to the disparagement of his own plain awkwardness and slowness: so now Osborne strove against any feeling of envy or jealousy with all his might; but his efforts were conscious, Roger's had been the simple consequence of affection, and the end to poor Osborne was that he became moody and depressed in mind and body. Both father and son, however, concealed their feelings in Roger's presence. When he came home just before sailing, busy and happy, the Squire caught his infectious energy, and Osborne looked up and was cheerful.

There was no time to be lost. He was bound to a hot climate, and must take all advantage possible of the winter months. He was to go first to Paris, to have interviews with some of the scientific men there. Some of his outfit, instruments, etc., were to follow him to Havre, from which port he was to embark, after transacting his business in Paris. The Squire learnt all his arrangements and plans, and even tried in after-dinner conversations to penetrate into the questions involved in the researches his son was about to make. But Roger's visit home could not be prolonged beyond two days.

The last day he rode into Hollingford earlier than he needed to have done to catch the London coach, in order to bid the Gibsons good-bye. He had been too actively busy for some time to have leisure to bestow much thought on Cynthia; but there was no need for fresh meditation on that subject. Her image as a prize to be worked for, to be served for seven years, and seven years more,* was safe and sacred in his heart. It was very bad, this going away, and wishing her good-bye for two long years; and he wondered much during his ride, how far he should be justified in telling her mother, perhaps in telling her own sweet self, what his feelings were, without expecting, nay, indeed deprecating, any answer on her part. Then she would know at any rate how dearly she was beloved by one who was absent; how in all difficulties or dangers the thought of her would be a polar star, high up in the heavens, and so on, and so on; for, with all a lover's quickness of imagination and triteness of fancy, he called her a star, a flower, a nymph, a witch, an angel, or a mermaid, a nightingale, a siren, as one or another of her attributes rose up before him.

CHAPTER 34

A Lover's Mistake

It was afternoon. Molly had gone out for a walk. Mrs Gibson had been paying some calls. Lazy Cynthia had declined accompanying either. A daily walk was not a necessity to her as it was to Molly. On a lovely day, or with an agreeable object, or when the fancy took her, she could go as far as any one; but these were exceptional cases; in general, she was not disposed to disturb herself from her indoor occupations. Indeed, not one of the ladies would have left the house, had they been aware that Roger was in the neighbourhood; for they were aware that he was to come down but once before his departure, and that his stay at home then would be but for a short time, and they were all anxious to wish him good-bye before his long absence. But they had understood that he was not coming to the Hall until the following week, and therefore they had left themselves at full liberty this afternoon to follow their own devices.

Molly chose a walk that had been a favourite with her ever since she was a child. Something or other had happened just before she left home that made her begin wondering how far it was right, for the sake of domestic peace, to pass over without comment the little deviations from right that people perceive in those whom they live with. Or whether, as they are placed in families for distinct purposes, not by chance merely, there are not duties involved in this aspect of their lot in life – whether by continually passing over failings their own standard is not lowered – the practical application of these thoughts being a dismal sort of perplexity on Molly's part, as to whether her father was quite aware of her stepmother's perpetual lapses from truth, and whether his blindness was wilful or not. Then she felt bitterly enough that, though she was as sure as could be that there was no real estrangement between her and her father, yet there were perpetual obstacles thrown in the way of their intercourse; and she thought, with a sigh, that, if he would but come in with authority, he might cut his way clear to the old intimacy with his daughter, and that they might have all the former walks and talks, and quips and cranks,* and glimpses of real confidence once again: things that her stepmother did not value, yet which she, like the dog in the manger, prevented Molly's enjoying. But, after all, Molly was a girl, not so far removed from childhood; and in the middle of her grave regrets and perplexities, her eye was caught by the sight of some fine ripe blackberries flourishing away, high up on the hedgebank among scarlet hips and green and russet leaves. She did not care much for blackberries herself; but she had heard Cynthia say that she liked them, and besides there was the charm of scrambling and gathering them; so she forgot all about her troubles, and went climbing up the banks, and clutching at her almost inaccessible prizes, and slipping down again triumphant, to carry them back to the large leaf which was to serve her as a basket. One or two of them she tasted, but they were as vapid to her palate as ever. The skirt of her pretty print gown was torn out of the gathers, and even with the fruit she had eaten 'her pretty lips with blackberries were all besmeared and dyed';* when, having gathered as many and more than she could possibly carry, she set off home, hoping to escape into her room and mend her gown, before it had offended Mrs Gibson's neat eye. The front-door was easily opened from the outside, and Molly was out of the clear light of the open air and in the shadow of the hall, when she saw a face peep out of the dining-room before she quite recognised whose it was; and then Mrs Gibson came softly out, sufficiently at least to beckon her into the room. When Molly had entered, Mrs Gibson closed the door. Poor Molly expected a reprimand for her torn gown and untidy appearance, but was soon relieved by the expression of Mrs Gibson's face – mysterious and radiant.

'I've been watching for you, dear. Don't go upstairs into the drawing-room, love! It might be a little interruption just now. Roger Hamley is there with Cynthia; and I've reason to think – in fact I did open the door unawares, but I shut it again softly, and I don't think they heard me. Isn't it charming? Young love, you know, ah, how sweet it is!'

'Do you mean that Roger has proposed to Cynthia?' asked Molly.

'Not exactly that. But I don't know; of course I know nothing. Only I did hear him say, that he had meant to leave England without speaking of his love, but that the temptation of seeing her alone had been too great for him. It was symptomatic, was it not, my dear? And all I wanted was, to let him come to a crisis without interruption. So I've been watching for you, to prevent your going in and disturbing them.'

'But I may go to my own room, mayn't I?' pleaded Molly.

'Of course,' said Mrs Gibson, a little testily. 'Only I had expected sympathy from you at such an interesting moment.'

But Molly did not hear these last words. She had escaped upstairs, and shut the door. Instinctively she had carried her leaf-full of blackberries – what would blackberries be to Cynthia now? She felt as if she could not understand it all; but as for that matter, what could she understand? Nothing. For a few minutes, her brain seemed in too great a whirl to comprehend anything but that she was being carried on in earth's diurnal course,* with rocks, and stones, and trees, with as little volition on her part as if she were dead. Then the room grew stifling, and instinctively she went to the open casement window, and leant out, gasping for breath. Gradually, the consciousness of the soft peaceful landscape stole into her mind, and stilled the buzzing confusion. There, bathed in the almost level rays of the autumn sunlight, lay the landscape she had known and loved from childhood; as quiet, as full of low, humming life as it had been at this hour for many generations. The autumn flowers blazed out in the garden below; the lazy cows were in the meadow adjoining, chewing their cud in the green aftermath; the evening fires had just been made up in the cottages beyond, in preparation for the husband's home-coming, and were sending up soft curls of blue smoke into the still air; the children, let loose from school, were shouting merrily in the distance, and she—Just then she heard nearer sounds; an opened door, steps on the lower flight of stairs. He could not have gone without even seeing her. He never, never would have done so cruel a thing – never would have forgotten poor little Molly, however happy he might be! No! there were steps and voices, and the drawing-room door was opened and shut once more. She laid down her head on her arms that rested upon the window-still, and cried – she had been so distrustful as to have let the idea enter her mind that he could go without wishing her good-bye – her, whom his mother had so loved, and called by the name of his little dead sister. And, as she thought of the tender love Mrs Hamley had borne her, she cried the more, for the vanishing of such love for her off the face of the earth. Suddenly, the drawing-room door opened, and some one was heard coming upstairs; it was Cynthia's step. Molly hastily wiped her eyes, and stood up and tried to look unconcerned; it was all she had time to do, before Cynthia, after a little pause at the closed door, had knocked and, on answer being given, had said, without opening the door – 'Molly! Mr Roger Hamley is here, and wants to wish you good-bye before he goes.' Then she went downstairs again, as if anxious, just at that moment, to avoid even so short a *tête-a-tête* with Molly. With a gulp and a fit of resolution, as when a child makes up its mind to swallow a nauseous dose of medicine, Molly went instantly down to the drawing-room.

Roger was talking earnestly to Mrs Gibson in the bow of the window when Molly entered; Cynthia was standing near, listening, but taking no part in the conversation. Her eyes were downcast, and she did not look up as Molly drew shyly near.

Roger was saying – 'I could never forgive myself, if I had accepted a pledge from her. She shall be free till my return; but the hope, the words, her sweet goodness, have made me happy beyond description. Oh, Molly!' suddenly becoming aware of her presence, and turning to her, and taking her hand in both of his – 'I think you have long guessed my secret, have you not? I once thought of speaking to you before I left, and confiding it all to you. But the temptation has been too great – I have told Cynthia how fondly I love her, as far as words can tell; and she says'— then he looked at Cynthia with passionate delight, and seemed to forget in that gaze that he had left his sentence to Molly half-finished.

Cynthia did not seem inclined to repeat her saying, whatever it was, but her mother spoke for her.

'My dear, sweet girl values your love as it ought to be valued, I am sure. And I believe,' looking at Cynthia and Roger with intelligent archness, 'I could tell tales as to the cause of her indisposition in the spring.'

'Mother,' said Cynthia suddenly, 'you know it was no such thing. Pray don't invent stories about me! I have engaged myself to Mr Roger Hamley, and that is enough.'

'Enough! more than enough!' said Roger. 'I will not accept your pledge. I am bound, but you are free. I like to feel bound; it makes me happy and at peace, but, with all the chances involved in the next two years, you must not shackle yourself by promises.'

Cynthia did not speak at once; she was evidently revolving something in her own mind. Mrs Gibson took up the word.

'You are very generous, I am sure. Perhaps it will be better not to mention it.'

'I would much rather have it kept a secret,' said Cynthia, interrupting.

'Certainly, my dear love. That was just what I was going to say. I once knew a young lady who heard of the death of a young man in America, whom she had known pretty well; and she immediately said she had been engaged to him, and even went so far as to put on weeds;* and it was a false report, for he came back well and merry, and declared to everybody he had never so much as thought about her. So it was very awkward for her. These things had much better be kept secret, until the proper time has come for divulging them.'

Even then and there Cynthia could not resist the temptation of saying – 'Mamma, I will promise you I won't put on weeds, whatever reports come of Mr Roger Hamley.'

'Roger, please!' he put in, in a tender whisper.

'And you will all be witnesses that he has professed to think of me, if he is tempted afterwards to deny the fact. But, at the same time, I wish it to be kept a secret until his return – and I am sure you will all be so kind as to attend to my wish. Please, *Roger*! Please, Molly! Mamma, I must especially beg it of you!'

Roger would have granted anything, when she asked him by that name, and in that tone. He took her hand in silent pledge of his reply. Molly felt as if she could never bring herself to name the affair as a common piece of news. So it was only Mrs Gibson that answered aloud –

'My dear child! why "especially" of poor me? You know I'm the most trustworthy person alive!'

The little pendule* on the chimney-piece struck the half-hour.

'I must go!' said Roger, in dismay. 'I had no idea it was so late. I shall write from Paris. The coach will be at the George by this time, and will only stay five minutes. Dearest Cynthia—' he took her hand; and then, as if the temptation was irresistible, he drew her to him and kissed her. 'Only remember you are free!' said he, as he released her and passed on to Mrs Gibson.

'If I had considered myself free,' said Cynthia, blushing a little, but ready with a repartee to the last – 'if I thought myself free, do you think I would have allowed that?'

Then Molly's turn came, and the old brotherly tenderness came back into his look, his voice, his bearing.

'Molly! you won't forget me, I know; I shall never forget you, nor your goodness to – her.' His voice began to quiver, and it was best to be gone. Mrs Gibson was pouring out unheard and unheeded words of farewell; Cynthia was re-arranging some flowers in a vase on the table, the defects in which had caught her artistic eye, without the consciousness penetrating to her mind. Molly stood, numb to the heart; neither glad nor sorry, nor anything but stunned. She felt the slackened touch of the warm grasping hand; she looked up – for till now her eyes had been downcast, as if there were heavy weights to their lids – and the place was empty where he had been; his quick step was heard on the stair, the front door was opened and shut; and then, as quick as lightning, Molly ran up to the front attic – the lumber-room, whose window commanded the street down which he must pass. The window-clasp was unused and stiff. Molly tugged at it – unless it was open, and her head put out, that last chance would be gone.

'I must see him again; I must! I must!' she wailed out, as she was pulling. There he was, running hard to catch the London coach; his luggage had been left at the George before he came up to wish the Gibsons good-bye. In all his hurry, Molly saw him turn round and shade his eyes from the level rays of the westering sun, and rake the house with his glances – in hopes, she knew, of catching one more glimpse of Cynthia. But apparently he saw no one, not even Molly at the attic casement; for she had drawn back when he turned, and kept herself in shadow; for she had no right to put herself forward as the one to watch and yearn for farewell signs. None came – another moment – he was out of sight for years!

She shut the window softly, and shivered all over. She left the attic and went to her own room; but she did not begin to take off her out-of-door things till she heard Cynthia's foot on the stairs. Then she hastily went to the toilet-table, and began to untie her bonnet-strings; but they were in a knot, and took time to undo. Cynthia's step stopped at Molly's door; she opened it a little and said – 'May I come in, Molly?'

'Certainly,' said Molly, longing to be able to say 'No' all the time. Molly did not turn to meet her; so Cynthia came up behind her and, putting her two hands round Molly's waist, peeped over her shoulder, putting out her lips to be kissed. Molly could not resist the action – the mute entreaty for a caress. But, in the moment before, she had caught reflections of the two faces in the glass: her own, red-eyed, pale, with lips dyed with blackberry-juice, her curls tangled, her bonnet pulled awry, her gown torn – and contrasted it with Cynthia's brightness and bloom, and the trim elegance of her dress. 'Oh! it is no wonder!' thought poor Molly, as she turned, and put her arms round Cynthia, and laid her head for an instant on her shoulder – the weary, aching head that sought a loving pillow in that supreme moment. The next, she had raised herself, and taken Cynthia's two hands, and was holding her off a little, the better to read her face.

'Cynthia! you do love him dearly, don't you?'

Cynthia winced a little aside from the penetrating steadiness of those eyes.

'You speak with all the solemnity of an adjuration, Molly!' said she, laughing a little at first, to cover her nervousness, and then looking up at Molly. 'Don't you think I've given a proof of it? But you know I've often told you I've not the gift of loving; I said pretty much the same thing to him. I can respect, and I fancy I can admire, and I can like; but I never feel carried off my feet by love for any one, not even for you, little Molly, and I'm sure I love you more than'—

'No, don't!' said Molly, putting her hand before Cynthia's mouth, in almost a passion of impatience. 'Don't, don't – I won't hear you – I ought not to have asked you – it makes you tell lies!'

'Why, Molly!' said Cynthia, in her turn seeking to read Molly's face, 'what's the matter with you? One might think you cared for him yourself.'

'I?' said Molly, all the blood rushing to her heart suddenly; then it returned, and she had courage to speak, and she spoke the truth as she believed it, though not the real actual truth.

'I do care for him: I think you have won the love of a prince amongst men. Why, I am proud to remember that he has been to me as a brother, and I love him as a sister, and I love you doubly because he has honoured you with his love.'

'Come, that's not complimentary!' said Cynthia, laughing, but not ill-pleased to hear her lover's praises, and even willing to depreciate him a little, in order to hear more.

'He's well enough, I daresay, and a great deal too learned and clever for a stupid girl like me; but even you must acknowledge he's very plain and awkward; and I like pretty things and pretty people.'

'Cynthia, I won't talk to you about him. You know you don't mean what you are saying, and only say it out of contradiction, because I praise him. He shan't be run down by you, even in joke.'

'Well, then, we won't talk of him at all. I was so surprised when he began to speak – so' —and Cynthia looked very lovely, blushing and dimpling-up as she remembered his words and looks. Suddenly she recalled herself to the present time, and her eye caught on the leaf full of blackberries – the broad, green leaf, so fresh and crisp when Molly had gathered it an hour or so ago, but now soft and flabby, and dying. Molly saw it, too, and felt a strange kind of sympathetic pity for the poor inanimate leaf.

'Oh! what blackberries! you've gathered them for me, I know!' said Cynthia, sitting down and beginning to feed herself daintily, touching them lightly with the ends of her taper fingers, and dropping each ripe berry into her open mouth. When she had eaten about half, she stopped suddenly short.

'How I should like to have gone as far as Paris with him!' she exclaimed. 'I suppose it wouldn't have been proper; but how pleasant it would have been! I remember at Boulogne' (another blackberry), 'how I used to envy the English who were going to Paris; it seemed to me then as if nobody stopped at Boulogne but dull, stupid, school-girls.'

'When will he be there?' asked Molly.

'On Wednesday, he said. I'm to write to him there; at any rate, he's going to write to me.'

Molly went about the adjustment of her dress in a quiet, business-like manner, not speaking much; Cynthia, although sitting still, seemed very restless. Oh! how much Molly wished that she would go!

'Perhaps, after all,' said Cynthia, after a pause of apparent meditation,'we shall never be married.'

'Why do you say that?' said Molly, almost bitterly. 'You have nothing to make you think so. I wonder how you can bear to think you won't, even for a moment.'

'Oh!' said Cynthia; 'you mustn't go and take me *au grand sérieux*.* I daresay I don't mean what I say, but, you see, everything seems a dream at present. Still, I think the chances are equal – the chances for and against our marriage, I mean. Two years! it's a long time! he may change his mind, or I may; or some one else may turn up, and I may get engaged to him: what should you think of that, Molly? I'm putting such a gloomy thing as death quite on one side, you see; yet in two years how much may happen!'

'Don't talk so, Cynthia, please don't,' said Molly piteously. 'One would think you didn't care for him, and he cares so much for you!'

'Why, did I say I didn't care for him? I was only calculating chances. I'm sure I hope nothing will happen to prevent the marriage. Only, you know, it may; and I thought I was taking a step in wisdom, in looking forward to all the evils that might befall. I'm sure, all the wise people I've ever known thought it a virtue to have gloomy prognostics of the future. But you're not in a mood for wisdom or virtue, I see; so I'll go and get ready for dinner, and leave you to your vanities of dress.'

She took Molly's face in both her hands, before Molly was aware of her intention, and kissed it playfully. Then she left Molly to herself.

CHAPTER 35

The Mother's Manoeuvre

Mr Gibson was not at home at dinner – detained by some patient, most probably. This was not an unusual occurence; but it *was* rather an unusual occurrence for Mrs Gibson to go down into the dining-room, and sit with him as he ate his deferred meal, when he came in an hour or two later. In general, she preferred her easy-chair, or her corner of the sofa, upstairs in the drawing-room; though it was very rarely that she would allow Molly to avail herself of her stepmother's neglected privilege. Molly would fain have gone down and kept her father company every night he had these solitary meals; but for peace and quietness she gave up her own wishes in the matter.

Mrs Gibson took a seat by the fire in the dining-room, and patiently waited for the auspicious moment when Mr Gibson, having satisfied his healthy appetite, turned from the table, and took his place by her side. She got up, and with unaccustomed attention moved the wine and glasses, so that he could help himself without moving from his chair.

'There, now! are you comfortable? for I have a great piece of news to tell you!' said she, when all was arranged.

'I thought there was something on hand,' said he, smiling. 'Now for it!'

'Roger Hamley has been here this afternoon to bid us goodbye.'

'Good-bye! Is he gone? I didn't know he was going so soon!' exclaimed Mr Gibson.

'Yes; never mind, that's not it.'

'But tell me; has he left this neighbourhood? I wanted to have seen him.'

'Yes, yes. He felt love and regret, and all that sort of thing for you. Now let me get on with my story: he found Cynthia alone, proposed to her, and was accepted.'

'Cynthia? Roger proposed to her, and she accepted him?' repeated Mr Gibson slowly.

'Yes, to be sure. Why not? you speak as if it was something so very surprising.'

'Did I? But I am surprised. He's a very fine young fellow, and I wish Cynthia joy; but do you like it? It will have to be a very long engagement.'

'Perhaps,' said she, in a knowing manner.

'At any rate, he will be away for two years,' said Mr Gibson.

'A great deal may happen in two years,' she replied.

'Yes! he will have to run many risks, and go into many dangers, and will come back no nearer to the power of maintaining a wife than when he went out.'

'I don't know that,' she replied, still in the arch manner of one possessing superior knowledge. 'A little bird did tell me that Osborne's life is not so very secure; and then – what will Roger be? Heir to the estate.'

'Who told you that about Osborne?' said he, facing round upon her, and frightening her by his sudden sternness of voice and manner. It seemed as if absolute fire came out of his long dark, sombre eyes. '*Who* told you, I say?'

She made a faint rally back into her former playfulness.

'Why? can you deny it? Is it not the truth?'

'I ask you again, Hyacinth: who told you that Osborne Hamley's life is in more danger than mine – or yours?'

'Oh, don't speak in that frightening way! My life is not in danger, I'm sure; nor yours either, love, I hope.'

He gave an impatient movement, and knocked a wine-glass off the table. For the moment she felt grateful for the diversion, and busied herself in picking up the fragments; 'bits of glass were so dangerous,' she said. But she was startled by a voice of command, such as she had never yet heard from her husband.

'Never mind the glass! I ask you again, Hyacinth: who told you anything about Osborne Hamley's state of health?'

'I am sure I wish no harm to him, and I daresay he is in very good health, as you say,' whispered she at last.

'Who told'—began he again, sterner than ever.

'Well, if you will know, and will make such a fuss about it,' said she, driven to extremity, 'it was you yourself – you or Dr Nicholls, I am sure I forget which.'

'I never spoke to you on the subject, and I don't believe Nicholls did. You'd better tell me at once what you're alluding to, for I'm resolved I'll have it out before we leave this room.'

'I wish I'd never married again!' she said, now fairly crying, and looking round the room, as if in vain search for a mouse-hole in which to hide herself. Then, as if the sight of the door into the store-room gave her courage, she turned and faced him.

'You should not talk your medical secrets so loud then, if you don't want people to hear them. I had to go into the store-room that day Dr Nicholls was here; cook wanted a jar of preserve, and stopped me just as I was going out – I am sure it was for no pleasure of mine, for I was sadly afraid of stickying my gloves – it was all that you might have a comfortable dinner.'

She looked as if she was going to cry again; but he gravely motioned her to go on, merely saying –

'Well! you overheard our conversation, I suppose?'

'Not much,' she answered eagerly, almost relieved by being thus helped out in her forced confession. 'Only a sentence or two.'

'What were they?' he asked.

'Why, you had just been saying something, and Dr Nicholls said, "If he has got aneurism of the aorta,* his days are numbered."'

'Well. Anything more?'

'Yes; you said, "I hope to God I may be mistaken; but there is a pretty clear indication of symptoms, in my opinion."'

'How do you know we were speaking of Osborne Hamley?' he asked; perhaps in hopes of throwing her off the scent. But as soon as she perceived that he was descending to her level of subterfuge, she took courage, and said, in quite a different tone to the cowed one which she had been using –

'Oh! I know. I heard his name mentioned by you both, before I began to listen.'

'Then you own you did listen?'

'Yes,' said she, hesitating a little now.

'And pray how do you come to remember so exactly the name of the disease spoken of?'

'Because I went—now don't be angry, I really can't see any harm in what I did'—

'There, don't deprecate anger! You went'—

'Into the surgery, and looked it out. Why might not I?'

Mr Gibson did not answer – did not look at her. His face was very pale, and both forehead and lips were contracted. At length he roused himself, sighed, and said –

'Well! I suppose as one brews one must bake.'

'I don't understand what you mean,' pouted she.

'Perhaps not,' he replied. 'I suppose that it was what you heard on that occasion that made you change your behaviour to Roger Hamley? I've noticed how much more civil you've been to him of late.'

'If you mean that I have ever got to like him as much as Osborne, you are very much mistaken; no, not even though he has offered to Cynthia, and is to be my son-in-law.'

'Let me know the whole affair. You overheard – I will own that it was Osborne about whom we were speaking, though I shall have something to say about that presently – and then, if I understand you rightly, you changed your behaviour to Roger, and made him more welcome to this house than you had ever done before, regarding him as proximate heir to the Hamley estates?'

'I don't know what you mean by "proximate".'

'Go into the surgery, and look in the dictionary, then,' said he, losing his temper for the first time during the conversation.

'I knew,' said she through sobs and tears, 'that Roger had taken a fancy to Cynthia; any one might see that; and as long as Roger was only a younger son, with no profession, and nothing but his Fellowship, I thought it right to discourage him, as any one would who had a grain of common sense in them; for a clumsier, more common, awkward, stupid fellow I never saw – to be called "county", I mean.'

'Take care; you'll have to eat your words presently, when you come to fancy he'll have Hamley some day.'

'No, I shan't,' said she, not perceiving his exact drift. 'You are vexed now because it is not Molly he's in love with; and I call it very unjust and unfair to my poor fatherless girl. I am sure I have always tried to further Molly's interests as if she was my own daughter.'

Mr Gibson was too indifferent to this accusation to take any notice of it. He returned to what was of far more importance to him.

'The point I want to be clear about is this. Did you or did you not alter your behaviour to Roger, in consequence of what you overheard of my professional conversation with Dr Nicholls? Have you not favoured his suit to Cynthia since then, on the understanding gathered from that conversation that he stood a good chance of inheriting Hamley?'

'I suppose I have,' said she sulkily. 'And if I did, I can't see any harm in it, that I should be questioned as if I were in a witness-box. He was in love with Cynthia long before that conversation, and she liked him so much. It was not for me to cross the path of true love. I don't see how you would have a mother show her love for her child, if she may not turn accidental circumstances to her advantage. Perhaps Cynthia might have died if she had been crossed in love; her poor father was consumptive.'

'Don't you know that all professional conversations are confidential? That it would be the most dishonourable thing possible for me to betray secrets which I learn in the exercise of my profession?'

'Yes, of course, you.'

'Well! and are not you and I one in all these respects? You cannot do a dishonourable act without my being inculpated in the disgrace. If it would be a deep disgrace for me to betray a professional secret, what would it be for me to trade on that knowledge?'

He was trying hard to be patient; but the offence was of that class which galled him insupportably.

'I don't know what you mean by trading. Trading in a daughter's affections is the last thing I should do; and I should have thought you would be rather glad than otherwise to get Cynthia well-married, and off your hands.'

Mr Gibson got up, and walked about the room, his hands in

his pockets. Once or twice he began to speak; but he stopped impatiently short without going on.

'I don't know what to say to you,' he said at length. 'You either can't or won't see what I mean. I'm glad enough to have Cynthia here. I have given her a true welcome, and I sincerely hope she will find this house as much a home as my own daughter does. But for the future I must look outside my doors, and double-lock the approaches, if I am so foolish as to—However, that's past and gone; and it remains with me to prevent its recurrence, as far as I can, for the future. Now let us hear the present state of affairs.'

'I don't think I ought to tell you anything about it. It is a secret, just as much as your mysteries are.'

'Very well; you have told me enough for me to act upon, which I most certainly shall do. It was only the other day I promised the Squire to let him know if I suspected anything – any love-affair, or entanglement, much less an engagement, between either of his sons and our girls.'

'But this is not an engagement; he would not let it be so; if you would only listen to me, I could tell you all. Only, I do hope you won't go and tell the Squire and everybody. Cynthia did so beg that it might not be known. It is only my unfortunate frankness that has led me into this scrape. I never could keep a secret from those whom I love.'

'I must tell the Squire. I shall not mention it to any one else. And do you quite think it was consistent with your general frankness to have overheard what you did, and never to have mentioned it to me? I could have told you then that Dr Nicholls' opinion was decidely opposed to mine, and that he believed that the disturbance about which I consulted him on Osborne's behalf was merely temporary. Dr Nicholls would tell you that Osborne is as likely as any man to live and marry and beget children.'

If there was any skill used by Mr Gibson so to word this speech as to conceal his own opinion, Mrs Gibson was not sharp enough to find it out. She was dismayed, and Mr Gibson enjoyed her dismay; it restored him to something like his usual frame of mind.

'Let us review this misfortune, for I see you consider it as such,' said he.

'No, not quite a misfortune,' said she. 'But certainly, if I had known Dr Nicholls' opinion'—she hesitated.

'You see the advantage of always consulting me,' he continued gravely. 'Here is Cynthia engaged'—

'Not engaged, I told you before. He would not allow it to be considered an engagement on her part.'

'Well, entangled in a love-affair with a lad of three-and-twenty, with nothing beyond his Fellowship and a chance of inheriting an encumbered estate; no profession even, abroad for two years, and I must go and tell his father all about it tomorrow.'

'Oh dear, pray say that, if he dislikes it, he has only to express his opinion.'

'I don't think you can act without Cynthia in the affair. And, if I am not mistaken, Cynthia will have a pretty stout will of her own on the subject.'

'Oh, I don't think she cares for him very much; she is not one to be always falling in love, and she does not take things very deeply to heart. But, of course, one would not do anything abruptly; two years' absence gives one plenty of time to turn oneself in.'

'But a little time ago we were threatened with consumption and an early death, if Cynthia's affections were thwarted.'

'Oh, you dear creature, how you remember all my silly words! It might be; you know poor dear Mr Kirkpatrick was consumptive, and Cynthia may have inherited it, and a great sorrow might bring out the latent seeds. At times I am so fearful. But I daresay it is not probable, for I don't think she takes things very deeply to heart.'

'Then I'm quite at liberty to give up the affair, acting as Cynthia's proxy, if the Squire disapproves of it?'

Poor Mrs Gibson was in a strait at this question.

'No!' she said at last. 'We cannot give it up. I am sure Cynthia would not; especially if she thought others were acting for her. And he really is very much in love. I wish he were in Osborne's place!'

'Shall I tell you what I should do?' said Mr Gibson, in real earnest. 'However it may have been brought about, here are two young people in love with each other. One is as fine a young fellow as ever breathed; the other a very pretty, lively, agreeable girl. The father of the young man must be told, and it is most likely he will bluster and oppose; for there is no doubt it is an imprudent affair, as far as money goes. But let them be steady and patient, and a better lot need await no young woman. I only wish it were Molly's good fortune to meet with such another!'

'I will try for her; I will indeed,' said Mrs Gibson, relieved by his change of tone.

'No, don't! That's one thing I forbid. I'll have no "trying" for Molly.'

'Well, don't be angry, dear! Do you know I was quite afraid you were going to lose your temper at one time.'

'It would have been of no use!' said he gloomily, getting up as if to close the sitting. His wife was only too glad to make her escape. The conjugal interview had not been satisfactory to either. Mr Gibson had been compelled to face and acknowledge the fact, that the wife he had chosen had a very different standard of conduct from that which he had upheld all his life, and had hoped to have seen inculcated in his daughter. He was more irritated than he chose to show; for there was so much of self-reproach in his irritation that he kept it to himself, brooded over it, and allowed a feeling of suspicious dissatisfaction with his wife to grow up in his mind, which extended itself by-and-by to the innocent Cynthia, and caused his manner to both mother and daughter to assume a certain curt severity, which took the latter at any rate with extreme surprise. But, on the present occasion, he followed his wife up to the drawing-room, and gravely congratulated the astonished Cynthia.

'Has mamma told you?' said she, shooting an indignant glance at her mother. 'It is hardly an engagement; and we all pledged ourselves to keep it a secret, mamma among the rest!'

'But my dearest Cynthia, you could not expect – you could not have wished me to keep a secret from my husband?' pleaded Mrs Gibson.

'No, perhaps not. At any rate, sir,' said Cynthia, turning towards him with graceful frankness, 'I am glad you should know it. You have always been a most kind friend to me, and I daresay I should have told you myself, but I did not want it named; if you please, it must still be a secret. In fact, it is hardly an engagement – he' (she blushed and sparkled a little at the pronoun, which implied that there was but one 'he' present in her thoughts at the moment) 'would not allow me to bind myself by any promise until his return!'

Mr Gibson looked gravely at her, irresponsive to her winning looks, which at the moment reminded him too forcibly of her mother's ways. Then he took her hand, and said, seriously enough – 'I hope you are worthy of him, Cynthia; for you have indeed drawn a prize. I have never known a truer or warmer heart than Roger's; and I have known him boy and man.'

Molly felt as if she could have thanked her father aloud for this testimony to the value of him who was gone away. But Cynthia pouted a little, before she smiled up in his face.

'You are not complimentary, are you, Mr Gibson?' said she. 'He thinks me worthy, I suppose; and, if you have so high an opinion of him, you ought to respect his judgement of me.' If she hoped to provoke a compliment she was disappointed; for Mr Gibson let go her hand in an absent manner, and sate down in an easy-chair by the fire, gazing at the wood embers, as if hoping to read the future in them. Molly saw Cynthia's eyes filled with tears, and followed her to the other end of the room, where she had gone to seek some working materials.

'Dear Cynthia,' was all she said; but she pressed her hand, while trying to assist in the search.

'Oh, Molly, I am so fond of your father; what makes him speak so to me tonight?'

'I don't know,' said Molly; 'perhaps he's tired.'

They were recalled from further conversation by Mr Gibson. He had roused himself from his reverie, and was addressing Cynthia.

'I hope you will not consider it a breach of confidence, Cynthia; but I must tell the Squire of – of what has taken place today between you and his son. I have bound myself by a promise to him. He was afraid – it's as well to tell you the truth – he was afraid' (an emphasis on this last word) 'of something of this kind between his sons and one of you two girls. It was only the other day I assured him there was nothing of the kind on foot; and I told him then I would inform him at once, if I saw any symptoms.'

Cynthia looked extremely annoyed.

'It was the one thing I stipulated for – secrecy.'

'But why?' said Mr Gibson. 'I can understand your not wishing to have it made public under the present circumstances. But the nearest friends on both sides! Surely you can have no objection to that?'

'Yes, I have,' said Cynthia; 'I would not have had any one know, if I could have helped it.'

'I'm almost certain Roger will tell his father.'

'No, he won't,' said Cynthia; 'I made him promise, and I think he is one to respect a promise' – with a glance at her mother, who, feeling herself in disgrace with both husband and child, was keeping a judicious silence.

'Well, at any rate, the story would come with so much better a grace from him that I shall give him the chance; I won't go over to the Hall till the end of the week; he may have written and told his father before then.'

Cynthia held her tongue for a little while. Then she said, with tearful pettishness –

'A man's promise is to override a woman's wish, then, is it?'

'I don't see any reason why it should not.'

'Will you trust in my reasons when I tell you it will cause me a great deal of distress if it gets known?' She said this in so pleading a voice that, if Mr Gibson had not been thoroughly displeased and annoyed by his previous conversation with her mother, he must have yielded to her. As it was, he said coldly – 'Telling Roger's father is not making it public. I don't like this exaggerated desire for such secrecy, Cynthia. It seems to me as if something more than is apparent was concealed behind it.'

'Come, Molly,' said Cynthia suddenly; 'let us sing that duet I've been teaching you; it's better than talking as we are doing.'

It was a little lively French duet. Molly sang it carelessly, with heaviness at her heart; but Cynthia sang it with spirit and apparent merriment; only she broke down in hysterics at last, and flew upstairs to her own room. Molly, heeding nothing else – neither her father nor Mrs Gibson's words – followed her, and found the door of her bedroom locked; and for all reply to her entreaties to be allowed to come in, she heard Cynthia sobbing and crying.

It was more than a week after the incidents just recorded, before Mr Gibson found himself at liberty to call on the Squire; and he heartily hoped that, long before then, Roger's letter might have arrived from Paris, telling his father the whole story. But he saw at the first glance that the Squire had heard nothing unusual to disturb his equanimity. He was looking better than he had done for months past; the light of hope was in his eyes, his face seemed of a healthy ruddy colour, gained partly by his resumption of outdoor employment in the superintendence of the works, and partly because the happiness he had lately had through Roger's means caused his blood to flow with regular vigour. He had felt Roger's going away, it is true; but, whenever the sorrow of parting with him pressed too heavily upon him, he filled his pipe, and smoked it out over a long, slow, deliberate re-perusal of Lord

Hollingford's letter, every word of which he knew by heart; but expressions in which he made a pretence to himself of doubting, that he might have an excuse for looking at his son's praises once again. The first greetings over, Mr Gibson plunged into his subject.

'Any news from Roger yet?'

'Oh, yes; here's his letter,' said the Squire, producing his black leather case, in which Roger's missive had been placed, along with the other very heterogeneous contents.

Mr Gibson read it, hardly seeing the words, after he had by one rapid glance assured himself that there was no mention of Cynthia in it.

'Hum! I see he doesn't name one very important event that has befallen him since he left you,' said Mr Gibson, seizing on the first words that came. 'I believe I'm committing a breach of confidence on one side; but I'm going to keep the promise I made the last time I was here. I find there is something – something of the kind you apprehended – you understand – between him and my step-daughter, Cynthia Kirkpatrick. He called at our house to wish us good-bye, while waiting for the London coach, found her alone, and spoke to her. They don't call it an engagement; but of course it is one.'

'Give me back the letter,' said the Squire, in a constrained kind of voice. Then he read it again, as if he had not previously mastered its contents, and as if there might be some sentence or sentences he had overlooked.

'No!' he said at last, with a sigh. 'He tells me nothing about it. Lads may play at confidences with their fathers, but they keep a deal back.' The Squire appeared more disappointed at not having heard of this straight from Roger than displeased at the fact itself, Mr Gibson thought. But he let him take his time.

'He's not the eldest son,' continued the Squire, talking as it were to himself. 'But it's not the match I should have planned for him. How came you, sir,' said he, firing round on Mr Gibson suddenly – 'to say when you were last here, that there was nothing between my sons and either of your girls? Why, this must have been going on all the time!'

'I'm afraid it was. But I was as ignorant about it as the babe unborn. I only heard of it on the evening of the day of Roger's departure.'

'And that's a week ago, sir. What's kept you quiet ever since?'

'I thought that Roger would tell you himself.'

'That shows you've no sons. More than half their life is unknown to their fathers. Why, Osborne there, we live together – that's to say, we have our meals together, and we sleep under the same roof – and yet – Well! well! life is as God has made it. You say it's not an engagement yet? But I wonder what I'm doing! Hoping for my lad's disappointment in the folly he's set his heart on – and just when he's been helping me! Is it a folly, or is it not? I ask you, Gibson, for you must know this girl. She hasn't much money, I suppose?'

'About thirty pounds a year, at my pleasure, during her mother's life.'

'Whew! It's well he's not Osborne. They'll have to wait. What family is she of? None of 'em in trade, I reckon, from her being so poor?'

'I believe her father was grandson of a certain Sir Gerald Kirkpatrick. Her mother tells me it is an old baronetcy. I know nothing of such things.'

'That's something. I do know something of such things, as you are pleased to call them. I like honourable blood.'

Mr Gibson could not help saying, 'But I'm afraid that only one-eighth of Cynthia's blood is honourable; I know nothing further of her relations excepting the fact that her father was a curate.'

'Professional. That's a step above trade at any rate. How old is she?'

'Eighteen or nineteen.'

'Pretty?'

'Yes, I think so; most people do; but it's all a matter of taste. Come, Squire, judge for yourself. Ride over and take lunch with us any day you like. I may not be in; but her mother will be there, and you can make acquaintance with your son's future wife.'

This was going too fast, however; presuming too much on the quietness with which the Squire had been questioning him. Mr Hamley drew back within his shell, and spoke in a surly manner as he replied –

'Roger's "future wife"! he'll be wiser by the time he comes home. Two years among the black folks will have put more sense in him.'

'Possible, but not probable, I should say,' replied Mr Gibson. 'Black folk are not remarkable for their powers of reasoning, I believe; so that they haven't much chance of altering his opinion by argument, even if they understood each other's language; and certainly, if he shares my taste, their peculiarity of complexion will only make him appreciate white skins the more.'

'But you said it was no engagement,' growled the Squire. 'If he thinks better of it, you won't keep him to it, will you?'

'If he wishes to break it off, I shall certainly advise Cynthia to be equally willing, that's all I can say. And I see no reason for discussing the affair further at present. I've told you how matters stand because I promised you I would, if I saw anything of this kind going on. But, in the present condition of things, we can neither make nor mar; we can only wait.' And he took up his hat to go. But the Squire was discontented.

'Don't go, Gibson! Don't take offence at what I've said, though I'm sure I don't know why you should. What's the girl like in herself?'

'I don't know what you mean,' said Mr Gibson. But he did; only he was vexed, and did not choose to understand.

'Is she – well, is she like your Molly? – sweet-tempered and sensible – with her gloves always mended, and neat about the feet, and ready to do anything one asks her, just as if doing it was the very thing she liked best in the world?'

Mr Gibson's face relaxed now, and he could understand all the Squire's broken sentences and unexplained meanings.

'She's much prettier than Molly to begin with, and has very winning ways. She's always well-dressed and smart-looking, and I know she hasn't much to spend on her clothes, and always does what she's asked to do, and is ready enough with her pretty, lively answers. I don't think I ever saw her out of temper; but then I'm not sure if she takes things keenly to heart, and a certain obtuseness of feeling goes a great way towards a character for good temper, I've noticed. Altogether I think Cynthia is one in a hundred.'

The Squire meditated a little. 'Your Molly is one in a thousand, to my mind. But then, you see, she comes of no family at all – and I don't suppose she'll have a chance of much money.' This he said as if he were thinking aloud, and without reference to Mr Gibson; but it nettled the latter, and he replied somewhat impatiently –

'Well, but, as there's no question of Molly in this business, I don't see the use of bringing her name in, and considering either her family or her fortune.'

'No, to be sure not,' said the Squire, rousing up. 'My wits had gone far afield, and I'll own I was only thinking what a pity it was she wouldn't do for Osborne. But, of course, it's out of the question – out of the question.'

'Yes,' said Mr Gibson, 'and if you will excuse me, Squire, I really must go now, and then you'll be at liberty to send your wits afield uninterrupted.' This time he was at the door, before the Squire called him back. He stood impatiently hitting his top-boots with his riding-whip, waiting for the interminable last words.

'I say, Gibson, we're old friends, and you're a fool if you take anything I say as an offence. Madam your wife and I didn't hit it off, the only time I ever saw her. I won't say she was silly; but I think one of us was silly, and it wasn't me. However, we'll pass that over. Suppose you bring her and this girl Cynthia (which is as outlandish a Christian name as I'd wish to hear), and little Molly, out here to lunch some day – I'm more at my ease in my own house – and I'm more sure to be civil, too. We need say nothing about Roger – neither the lass nor me – and you keep your wife's tongue quiet, if you can. It will only be like a compliment to you on your marriage, you know – and no one must take it for anything more. Mind, no allusion or mention of Roger, and this piece of folly! I shall see the girl then, and I can judge her for myself; for, as you say, that will be the best plan. Osborne will be here too; and he's always in his element talking to women. I sometimes think he's half a woman himself, he spends so much money and is so unreasonable.'

The Squire was pleased with his own speech and his own thought, and smiled a little as he finished speaking. Mr Gibson was both pleased and amused; and he smiled too, anxious as he was to be gone. The next Thursday was soon fixed upon as the day on which Mr Gibson was to bring his womenkind out to the Hall. He thought that, on the whole, the interview had gone off a good deal better than he expected, and felt rather proud of the invitation of which he was the bearer. Therefore Mrs Gibson's manner of receiving it was an annoyance to him. She, meanwhile, had been considering herself as an injured woman, ever since the evening of the day of Roger's departure; what business had any one had to speak as if the chances of Osborne's life being prolonged were infinitely small, if in fact the matter was uncertain? She liked Osborne extremely, much better than Roger, and would gladly have schemed to secure him for Cynthia, if she had not shrunk from the notion of her daughter's becoming a widow. For, if Mrs Gibson had ever felt anything acutely, it was the death of Mr Kirkpatrick; and, amiably callous as she was in most things, she recoiled from exposing her daughter wilfully to the same kind of suffering which she herself had experienced. But, if she had only known Dr Nicholls' opinion, she would never have favoured Roger's suit, never. And then Mr Gibson himself: why was he so cold and reserved in his treatment of her since that night of explanation? She had done nothing wrong; yet she was treated as though she were in disgrace. And everything about the house was flat just now. She even missed the little excitement of Roger's visits, and the watching of his attentions to Cynthia. Cynthia, too, was silent enough; and, as for Molly, she was absolutely dull and out of spirits – a state of mind so annoying to Mrs Gibson at present, that she vented some of her discontent upon the poor girl, from whom she feared neither complaint nor repartee.

CHAPTER 36

Domestic Diplomacy

The evening of the day on which Mr Gibson had been to see the Squire, the three women were alone in the drawing-room, for Mr Gibson had had a long round and was not as yet come in. They had had to wait dinner for him; and for some time after his return there was nothing done or said but what related to the necessary business of eating. Mr Gibson was, perhaps, as well satisfied with his day's work as any of the four; for this visit to the Squire had been weighing on his mind, ever since he heard of the state of things between Roger and Cynthia. He did not like the having to go and tell of a love-affair so soon after he had declared his belief that no such thing existed; it was a confession of fallibility which is distasteful to most men. If the Squire had not been of so unsuspicious and simple a nature, he might have drawn his own conclusions from the apparent concealment of facts, and felt doubtful of Mr Gibson's perfect honesty in the business; but, being what he was, there was no danger of such unjust misapprehension. Still Mr Gibson knew the hot hasty temper he had to deal with, and had expected more violence of language than he really encountered; and the last arrangement by which Cynthia, her mother, and Molly – who, as Mr Gibson thought to himself, and smiled at the thought, was sure to be a peace-maker, and a sweetener of intercourse – were to go to the Hall and make acquaintance with the Squire, appeared like a great success to Mr Gibson, for achieving which he took not a little credit to himself. Altogether, he was more cheerful and bland than he had been for many days; and, when he came up into the drawing-room for a few minutes after dinner, before going out again to see his town-patients, he whistled a little under his breath, as he stood with his back to the fire, looking at Cynthia, and thinking that he had not done her justice when describing her to the Squire. Now this soft, almost tuneless whistling, was to Mr Gibson what purring is to a cat. He could no more have done it with an anxious case on his mind, or when he was annoyed by human folly, or when he was hungry, than he could have flown through the air. Molly knew all this by instinct, and was happy without being aware of it, as soon as she heard the low whistle which was no music after all. But Mrs Gibson did not like this trick of her husband's; it was not refined, she thought, not even 'artistic'; if she could have called it by this fine word, it would have compensated her for the want of refinement. Tonight it was particularly irritating to her nerves; but, since her conversation with Mr Gibson about Cynthia's engagement, she had not felt herself in a sufficiently good position to complain.

Mr Gibson began – 'Well, Cynthia; I've seen the Squire today, and made a clean breast of it.'

Cynthia looked up quickly, questioning with her eyes; Molly stopped her netting* to listen; no one spoke.

'You're all to go there on Thursday to lunch; he asked you all, and I promised for you.'

Still no reply; natural, perhaps, but very flat.

'You'll be glad of that, Cynthia, shan't you?' asked Mr Gibson. 'It may be a little formidable; but I hope it will be the beginning of a good understanding between you.'

'Thank you!' said she, with an effort. 'But – but won't it make it public? I do so wish not to have it known or talked about, not till he comes back, or close upon the marriage.'

'I don't see how it should make it public,' said Mr Gibson. 'My wife goes to lunch with my friend, and takes her daughters with her – there's nothing in that, is there?'

'I am not sure that I shall go,' put in Mrs Gibson. She did not know why she said it, for she fully intended to go all the time;

but, having said it, she was bound to stick to it for a while; and, with such a husband as hers, the hard necessity was sure to fall upon her of having to find a reason for her saying. Then it came quick and sharp.

'Why not?' said he, turning round upon her.

'Oh, because – because I think he ought to have called on Cynthia first; I've that sort of sensitiveness I can't bear to think of her being slighted because she is poor.'

'Nonsense!' said Mr Gibson. 'I do assure you, no slight whatever was intended. He does not wish to speak about the engagement to any one – not even to Osborne – that's your wish too, isn't it, Cynthia? Nor does he intend to mention it to any of you when you go there; but, naturally enough, he wants to make acquaintance with his future daughter-in-law. If he deviated so much from his usual course as to come calling here'—

'I am sure I don't want him to come calling here,' said Mrs Gibson, interrupting. 'He was not so very agreeable, the only time he did come. But I am that sort of a character that I cannot put up with any neglect of persons I love, just because they are not smiled upon by fortune.' She sighed a little ostentatiously as she ended her sentence.

'Well, then, you won't go?' said Mr Gibson, provoked, but not wishing to have a long discussion, especially as he felt his temper going.

'Do you wish it, Cynthia?' said Mrs Gibson, anxious for an excuse to yield.

But her daughter was quite aware of this motive for the question, and replied quietly – 'Not particularly, mamma. I am quite willing to refuse the invitation.'

'It's already accepted,' said Mr Gibson, almost ready to vow that he would never again meddle in any affair in which women were concerned, which would effectually shut him out from all love-affairs for the future. He had been touched by the Squire's relenting, pleased with what he had thought would give others pleasure – and this was the end of it!

'Oh, do go, Cynthia!' said Molly, pleading with her eyes as well as her words. 'Do; I am sure you will like the Squire; and it is such a pretty place, and he'll be so much disappointed.'

'I should not like to give up my dignity,' said Cynthia demurely. 'And you heard what mamma said!'

It was very malicious of her. She fully intended to go, and was equally sure that her mother was already planning her dress for the occasion in her own mind. Mr Gibson, however, who, surgeon though he was, had never learnt to anatomise a woman's heart, took it all literally, and was excessively angry both with Cynthia and her mother; so angry that he durst not trust himself to speak. He went quickly to the door, intending to leave the room; but his wife's voice arrested him; she said –

'My dear, do you wish me to go? if you do, I will put my own feelings on one side.'

'Of course I do!' he said, short and stern, and left the room.

'Then I'll go!' said she, in the voice of a victim those words were meant for him, but he hardly heard them. 'And we'll have a fly from the George, and get a livery-coat for Thomas, which I've long been wanting; only dear Mr Gibson did not like it, but on an occasion like this I'm sure he won't mind; and Thomas shall go on the box, and' —

'But, mamma, I've my feelings too,' said Cynthia.

'Nonsense, child! when all is so nicely arranged, too.'

So they went on the day appointed. Mr Gibson was aware of the change of plans, and that they were going after all; but he was so much annoyed by the manner in which his wife had received an invitation that appeared to him so much kinder than he had expected from his previous knowledge of the Squire and his wishes on the subject of his son's marriage, that Mrs Gibson heard neither interest not curiosity expressed by her husband as to the visit itself, or the reception they met with. Cynthia's indifference as to whether the invitation was accepted or not had displeased Mr Gibson. He was not up to her ways with her mother, and did not understand how much of this said indifference had been assumed in order to countervent* Mrs Gibson's affectation and false sentiment. But for all his annoyance on the subject, he was, in fact, very curious to know how the visit had gone off, and took the first opportunity of being alone with Molly to question her about the lunch of the day before at Hamley Hall.

'And so you went to Hamley yesterday after all?'

'Yes; I thought you would have come. The Squire seemed quite to expect you.'

'I thought of going there at first; but I changed my mind like other people. I don't see why women are to have a monopoly of changeableness. Well! how did it go off? Pleasantly, I suppose, for both your mother and Cynthia were in high spirits last night.'

'Yes. The dear old Squire was in his best dress and on his best behaviour, and was so prettily attentive to Cynthia; and she looked so lovely, walking about with him, and listening to all his talk about the garden and farm. Mamma was tired, and stopped indoors, so they got on very well, and saw a great deal of each other.'

'And my little girl trotted behind?'

'Oh, yes. You know I was almost at home; and besides – of course—' Molly went very red, and left the sentence unfinished.

'Do you think she's worthy of him?' asked her father, just as if she had completed her speech.

'Of Roger, papa? oh, who is? But she's very sweet, and very, very charming.'

'Very charming if you will, but somehow I don't quite understand her. Why does she want all this secrecy? Why wasn't she more eager to go and pay her duty to Roger's father? She took it as coolly as if I'd asked her to go to church?'

'I don't think she did take it coolly; I believe I don't quite understand her either, but I love her dearly all the same.'

'Umph; I like to understand people thoroughly, but I know it's not necessary to women. D'ye really think she's worthy of him?'

'Oh, papa' – said Molly, and then she stopped; she wanted to speak in favour of Cynthia, but somehow she could form no reply that pleased her to this repeated inquiry. He did not seem much to care whether he got an answer or not; for he went on with his own thoughts, and the result was that he asked Molly if Cynthia had heard from Roger.

'Yes; on Wednesday morning.'

'Did she show it to you? But of course not. Besides, I read the Squire's letter, which told all about him.'

Now Cynthia, rather to Molly's surprise, had told her that she might read the letter if she liked, and Molly had shrunk from availing herself of the permission, for Roger's sake. She thought that he would probably have poured out his heart to the one sole person, and that it was not fair to listen, as it were, to his confidences.

'Was Osborne at home?' asked Mr Gibson. 'The Squire said he did not think he would have come back; but the young fellow is so uncertain'—

'No, he was still from home.' Then Molly blushed all over crimson, for it suddenly struck her that Osborne was probably with his wife – that mysterious wife, of whose existence she was cognisant, but of whom she knew so little, and of whom her father knew nothing. Mr Gibson noticed the blush with anxiety. What did it mean? It was troublesome enough to find that one of the Squire's precious sons had fallen in love within the prohibited ranks; and what would not have to be said and done, if anything fresh were to come out between Osborne and Molly! He spoke out at once, to relieve himself of this new apprehension.

'Molly, I was taken by surprise by this affair between Cynthia and Roger Hamley – if there's anything more on the *tapis*,* let me know at once, honestly and openly! I know it's an awkward question for you to reply to; but I wouldn't ask it, unless I had good reasons.' He took her hand, as he spoke. She looked up at him with clear, truthful eyes, which filled with tears as she spoke. She did not know why the tears came; perhaps it was because she was not so strong as formerly.

'If you mean that you're afraid that Osborne thinks of me as Roger thinks of Cynthia, papa, you are quite mistaken. Osborne and I are friends and nothing more, and never can be anything more. That's all I can tell you.'

'It's quite enough, little one. It's a great relief. I don't want to have my Molly carried off by any young man just yet; I should miss her sadly.' He could not help saying this, in the fulness of his heart just then; but he was surprised at the effect these few tender words produced. Molly threw her arms round his neck, and began to sob bitterly, her head lying on his shoulder. 'There, there!' said he, patting her on the back, and leading her to the sofa, 'that will do. I get quite enough of tears in the day, shed for real causes, not to want them at home, where, I hope, they are shed for no cause at all. There's nothing really the matter, is there, my dear?' he continued, holding her a little away from him, that he might look in her face. She smiled at him through her tears; and he did not see the look of sadness which returned to her face, after he had left her.

'Nothing, dear, dear papa – nothing now. It is such a comfort to have you all to myself – it makes me happy.'

Mr Gibson knew all implied in these words, and felt that there was no effectual help for the state of things which had arisen from his own act. It was better for them both that they should not speak out more fully. So he kissed her, and said –

'That's right, dear! I can leave you in comfort now, and indeed

I've stayed too long already gossiping. Go out and have a walk – take Cynthia with you, if you like. I must be off. Good-bye, little one!'

His commonplace words acted like an astringent on Molly's relaxed feelings. He intended that they should do so; it was the truest kindness to her; but he walked away from her with a sharp pang at his heart, which he turned into numbness as soon as he could, by throwing himself violently into the affairs and cares of others.

CHAPTER 37

A Fluke, and What Came of It

The honour and glory of having a lover of her own was soon to fall to Molly's share; though, to be sure, it was a little deduction from the honour, that the man who came with the full intention of proposing to her ended by making Cynthia an offer. It was Mr Coxe, who came back to Hollingford to follow out the purpose he had announced to Mr Gibson nearly two years before, of inducing Molly to become his wife, as soon as he should have succeeded to his uncle's estate. He was now a rich, though still a red-haired, young man. He came to the George Inn, bringing his horses and his groom; not that he was going to ride much, but that he thought such outward signs of his riches might help on his suit; and he was so justly modest in his estimation of himself, that he believed that he needed all extraneous aid. He piqued himself on his constancy; although, indeed, considering that he had been so much restrained by his duty and affection to, and his expectations from, his crabbed old uncle, that he had not been able to go much into society, and very rarely indeed into the company of young ladies, such fidelity to Molly was not very meritorious, except in his own eyes. Mr Gibson too was touched by it, and made it a point of honour to give him a fair field, all the time sincerely hoping that Molly would not be such a goose as to lend a willing ear to a youth who could never remember the difference between apophysis and epiphysis.* He thought it as well not to tell his wife more of Mr Coxe's antecedents than that he had been a former pupil; who had relinquished ('all that he knew of', understood) the medical profession, because an old uncle had left him enough of money to be idle. Mrs Gibson, who felt that she had somehow lost her place in her husband's favour, took it into her head that she could reinstate herself if she was successful in finding a good match for his daughter Molly. She knew that he had forbidden her to try for this end, as distinctly as words could express a meaning; but her own words so seldom expressed her meaning, or, if they did, she held to her opinions so loosely, that she had no idea but that it was the same with other people. Accordingly, she gave Mr Coxe a very sweet and gracious welcome.

'It is such a pleasure to me to make acquaintance with the former pupils of my husband. He has spoken to me so often of you that I quite feel as if you were one of the family, as indeed I am sure that Mr Gibson considers you.'

Mr Coxe felt much flattered, and took the words as a happy omen for his love-affair. 'Is Miss Gibson in?' asked he, blushing violently. 'I knew her formerly – that is to say, I lived in the same house with her, for more than two years, and it would be a great pleasure to – to – '

'Certainly, I am sure she will be so glad to see you. I sent her and Cynthia – you don't know my daughter Cynthia, I think, Mr Coxe? she and Molly are such great friends – out for a brisk walk this frosty day; but I think they will soon come back.' She went on saying agreeable nothings to the young man, who received her attentions with a certain complacency, but was all the time much more engaged in listening to the well-remembered click at the front door – the shutting it to again with household care, and the sound of the familiar bounding footstep on the stair. At last they came. Cynthia entered first, bright and blooming, fresh colour in her cheeks and lips, fresh brilliance in her eyes. She looked startled at the sight of a stranger, and for an instant she stopped short at the door, as if taken by surprise. Then in came Molly softly behind her, smiling, happy, dimpled; but not such a glowing beauty as Cynthia.

'Oh, Mr Coxe, is it you?' said she, going up to him with an outstretched hand, and greeting him with simple friendliness.

'Yes; it seems such a long time since I saw you. You are so much grown – so much – well, I suppose I mustn't say what,' he replied, speaking hurriedly, and holding her hand all the time, rather to her discomfiture. Then Mrs Gibson introduced her daughter, and the two girls spoke of the enjoyment of their walk. Mr Coxe marred his cause in that very first interview, if indeed he ever could have had any chance, by his precipitancy in showing his feelings; and Mrs Gibson helped him to mar it by trying to assist him. Molly lost her open friendliness of manner, and began to shrink away from him in a way which he thought was a very ungrateful return for all his faithfulness to her these two years past; and, after all, she was not the wonderful beauty his fancy or his love had painted her. That Miss Kirkpatrick was far more beautiful and much easier of access. For Cynthia put on all her pretty airs – her look of intent interest in what any one was saying to her, let the subject be what it would, as if it was the thing she cared most about in the whole world; her unspoken deference – in short, all the unconscious ways she possessed by instinct of tickling the vanity of men. So, while Molly quietly repelled him, Cynthia drew him to her by her soft attractive ways, and his constancy fell before her charms. He was thankful that he had not gone too far with Molly, and grateful to Mr Gibson for having prohibited all declarations two years ago; for Cynthia, and Cynthia alone, could make him happy. After a fortnight's time, during which he had entirely veered round in his allegiance, he thought it desirable to speak to Mr Gibson. He did so with a certain sense of exultation in his own correct behaviour in the affair, but at the same time feeling rather ashamed of the confession of his own changeableness which was naturally involved. Now, it so happened that Mr Gibson had been unusually little at home during the fortnight that Mr Coxe had ostensibly lodged at the George, but in reality had spent the greater part of his time at Mr Gibson's; so that he had seen very little of his former pupil, and on the whole he had thought him improved, especially after Molly's manner had made her father pretty sure that Mr Coxe stood no chance in that quarter. But Mr Gibson was quite ignorant of the attraction which Cynthia had had for the young man. If he had perceived it, he would have nipped it in the bud pretty quickly; for he had no notion of any girl, even though only partially engaged to one man, receiving offers from others, if a little plain speaking could prevent it. Mr Coxe had asked for a private interview; they were sitting in the old surgery, now called the consulting-room, but still retaining so much of its former self as to be the last place in which Mr Coxe could feel himself at ease. He was red up to the very roots of his red hair, and kept turning his glossy new hat round and round in his fingers, unable to find out the proper way of beginning his sentence; so at length he plunged in, grammar or no grammar.

'Mr Gibson, I dare say you'll be surprised, I'm sure I am, at – at what I want to say; but I think it's the part of an honourable man, as you said yourself, sir, a year or two ago, to – to speak to the father first, and as you, sir, stand in the place of a father to Miss Kirkpatrick, I should like to express my feelings, my hopes, or perhaps I should say wishes, in short' —

'Miss Kirkpatrick?' said Mr Gibson, a good deal surprised.

'Yes, sir!' continued Mr Coxe, rushing on now he had got so far. 'I know it may appear inconstant and changeable, but I do assure you, I came here with a heart as faithful to your daughter as ever beat in a man's bosom. I most fully intended to offer myself, and all that I had, to her acceptance before I left; but really, sir, if you had seen her manner to me every time I endeavoured to press my suit a little – it was more than coy, it was absolutely repellent, there could be no mistaking it – while Miss Kirkpatrick' — he looked modestly down, and smoothed the nap of his hat, smiling a little while he did so.

'While Miss Kirkpatrick' — repeated Mr Gibson, in such a stern voice, that Mr Coxe, landed esquire as he was now, felt as much discomfited as he used to do when he was an apprentice, and Mr Gibson had spoken to him in a similar manner.

'I was only going to say, sir, that, so far as one can judge from manner, and willingness to listen, and apparent pleasure in my visits – altogether, I think I may venture to hope that Miss Kirkpatrick is not quite indifferent to me – and I would wait – you have no objection, have you, sir, to my speaking to her, I mean?' said Mr Coxe, a little anxious at the expression on Mr Gibson's face. 'I do assure you, I haven't a chance with Miss Gibson,' he continued, not knowing what to say, and fancying that his inconstancy was rankling in Mr Gibson's mind.

'No! I don't suppose you have. Don't go and fancy it is that which is annoying me. You're mistaken about Miss Kirkpatrick, however. I don't believe she could ever have meant to give you encouragement!'

Mr Coxe's face grew perceptibly paler. His feelings, if evanescent, were evidently strong.

'I think, sir, if you could have seen her – I don't consider myself vain, and manner is so difficult to describe. At any rate, you can have no objection to my taking my chance, and speaking to her.'

'Of course, if you won't be convinced otherwise, I can have no objection. But, if you'll take my advice, you will spare yourself the pain of a refusal. I may, perhaps, be trenching on confidence, but I think I ought to tell you that her affections are otherwise engaged.'

'It cannot be!' said Mr Coxe. 'Mr Gibson, there must be some mistake. I have gone as far as I durst in expressing my feelings, and her manner has been most gracious. I don't think she could have misunderstood my meaning. Perhaps she has changed her mind. It is possible that, after consideration, she has learnt to prefer another, is it not?'

'By "another", you mean yourself, I suppose. I can believe in such inconstancy' (he could not help, in his own mind, giving a slight sneer at the instance before him), 'but I should be very sorry to think that Miss Kirkpatrick could be guilty of it.'

'But she may – it is a chance. Will you allow me to see her?'

'Certainly, my poor fellow' – for, intermingled with a little contempt, was a good deal of respect for the simplicity, the unworldliness, the strength of feeling, even though the feeling was evanescent – 'I will send her to you directly.'

'Thank you, sir! God bless you for a kind friend!'

Mr Gibson went upstairs to the drawing-room, where he was pretty sure he should find Cynthia. There she was, as bright and careless as usual, making up a bonnet for her mother, and chattering to Molly as she worked.

'Cynthia, you will oblige me by going down into my consulting-room at once. Mr Coxe wants to speak to you.'

'Mr Coxe?' said Cynthia. 'What can he want with me?'

Evidently, she answered her own question as soon as it was asked, for she coloured, and avoided meeting Mr Gibson's severe, uncompromising look. As soon as she had left the room, Mr Gibson sat down, and took up a new *Edinburgh** lying on the table, as an excuse for silence. Was there anything in the article that made him say, after a minute or two, to Molly, who sat silent and wondering – 'Molly, you must never trifle with the love of an honest man. You don't know what pain you may give.'

Presently Cynthia came back into the drawing-room, looking very much confused. Most likely she would not have returned, if she had known that Mr Gibson was still there; but it was such an unheard-of thing for him to be sitting in that room in the middle of the day, reading or making pretence to read, that she had never thought of his remaining. He looked up at her the moment she came in; so there was nothing for it but putting a bold face on it, and going back to her work.

'Is Mr Coxe still downstairs?' asked Mr Gibson.

'No. He is gone. He asked me to give you both his kind regards. I believe he is leaving this afternoon.' Cynthia tried to make her manner as commonplace as possible; but she did not look up, and her voice trembled a little.

Mr Gibson went on looking at his book for a few minutes; but Cynthia felt that more was coming, and only wished it would come quickly, for the severe silence was very hard to bear. It came at last.

'I trust this will never occur again, Cynthia!' said he, in grave displeasure. 'I should not feel satisfied with the conduct of any girl, however free, who could receive marked attentions from a young man with complacency, and so lead him on to make an offer which she never meant to accept. But what must I think of a young woman in your position, engaged – yet "accepting most graciously", for that was the way Coxe expressed it – the overtures of another man? Do you consider what unnecessary pain you have given him by your thoughtless behaviour? I call it thoughtless – but it's the mildest epithet I can apply to it. I beg that such a thing may not occur again, or I shall be obliged to characterise it more severely.'

Molly could not imagine what 'more severely' could be, for her father's manner appeared to her almost cruel in its sternness. Cynthia coloured up extremely, then went pale, and at length raised her beautiful appealing eyes full of tears to Mr Gibson. He was touched by that look; but he resolved immediately not to be mollified by any of her physical charms of expression, but to keep to his sober judgment of her conduct.

'Please, Mr Gibson, hear my side of the story before you speak so harshly to me. I did not mean to – to flirt. I merely meant to make myself agreeable – I can't help doing that – and that goose of a Mr Coxe seems to have fancied I meant to give him encouragement.'

'Do you mean that you were not aware that he was falling in love with you?' Mr Gibson was melting into a readiness to be convinced by that sweet voice and pleading face.

'Well, I suppose I must speak truly.' Cynthia blushed and smiled – ever so little – but it was a smile, and it hardened Mr Gibson's heart again. 'I did think once or twice that he was becoming a little more complimentary than the occasion required; but I hate throwing cold water on people, and I never thought he could take it into his silly head to fancy himself seriously in love, and to make such a fuss at the last, after only a fortnight's acquaintance.'

'You seem to have been pretty well aware of his silliness (I should rather call it simplicity). Don't you think you should have remembered that it might lead him to exaggerate what you were doing and saying into encouragement?'

'Perhaps. I daresay I'm all wrong, and he's all right,' said Cynthia, piqued and pouting. 'We used to say in France, that "*les absens ont toujours tort*",* but really it seems as if here' – she stopped. She was unwilling to be impertinent to a man whom she respected and liked. She took up another point of her defence, and rather made matters worse. 'Besides, Roger would not allow me to consider myself as finally engaged to him; I would willingly have done it, but he would not let me.'

'Nonsense! Don't let us go on talking about it, Cynthia! I've said all I mean to say. I believe that you were only thoughtless, as I told you before. But don't let it happen again.' He left the room at once, to put a stop to the conversation, the continuance of which would serve no useful purpose, and perhaps end by irritating him.

'Not guilty, but we recommend the prisoner not to do it again. It's pretty much that, isn't it, Molly?' said Cynthia, letting her tears down fall, even while she smiled. 'I do believe your father might make a good woman of me yet, if he would only take the pains, and wasn't quite so severe. And to think of that stupid little fellow making all this mischief! He pretended to take it to heart, as if he had loved me for years instead of only for days. I daresay only for hours, if the truth were told!'

'I was afraid he was becoming very fond of you,' said Molly; 'at least it struck me once or twice; but I knew he could not stay long, and I thought it would only make you uncomfortable, if I said anything about it. But now I wish I had!'

'It wouldn't have made a bit of difference,' replied Cynthia. 'I knew he liked me, and I like to be liked; it's born in me to try to make every one I come near fond of me; but then they shouldn't carry it too far, for it becomes very troublesome if they do. I shall

hate red-haired people for the rest of my life. To think of such a
man as that being the cause of your father's displeasure with me!'

Molly had a question at her tongue's end that she longed to
put; she knew it was indiscreet, but at last out it came almost
against her will –

'Shall you tell Roger about it?'

Cynthia replied, 'I've not thought about it – no! I don't think I
shall – there's no need. Perhaps, if we are ever married'–

'Ever married!' said Molly, under her breath. But Cynthia took
no notice of the exclamation until she had finished the sentence
which it interrupted.

'–and I can see his face and know his mood, I may tell it him
then; but not in writing, and when he is absent; it might annoy
him.'

'I am afraid it would make him uncomfortable,' said Molly
simply. 'And yet it must be so pleasant to be able to tell him
everything – all your difficulties and troubles.'

'Yes; only I don't worry him with these things; it's better to
write him merry letters, and cheer him up among the black folk.
You repeated "Ever married", a little while ago; do you know,
Molly, I don't think I ever shall be married to him? I don't know
why, but I have a strong presentiment; so it's just as well not to
tell him all my secrets, for it would be awkward for him to know
them, if it never came off!'

Molly dropped her work, and sat silent, looking into the future;
at length she said, 'I think it would break his heart, Cynthia!'

'Nonsense! Why, I'm sure that Mr Coxe came here with the
intention of falling in love with you – you needn't blush so
violently. I'm sure you saw it as plainly as I did; only you made
yourself disagreeable, and I took pity on him, and consoled his
wounded vanity.'

'Can you – do you dare to compare Roger Hamley to Mr
Coxe?' asked Molly indignantly.

'No, no, I don't!' said Cynthia in a moment. 'They are as
different as men can be. Don't be so dreadfully serious over
everything, Molly! You look as oppressed with sad reproach, as if
I had been passing on to you the scolding your father gave me.'

'Because I don't think you value Roger as you ought, Cynthia!'
said Molly stoutly, for it required a good deal of courage to force
herself to say this, although she could not tell why she shrank so
from speaking.

'Yes, I do! It's not in my nature to go into ecstasies, and I don't suppose I shall ever be what people call "in love". But I am glad he loves me, and I like to make him happy, and I think him the best and most agreeable man I know, always excepting your father when he isn't angry with me. What can I say more, Molly? would you like me to say I think him handsome?'

'I know most people think him plain, but'—

'Well, I'm of the opinion of most people then, and small blame to them! But I like his face – oh, ten thousand times better than Mr Preston's handsomeness!' For the first time during the conversation Cynthia seemed thoroughly in earnest. Why Mr Preston was introduced neither she nor Molly knew; it came up and out by a sudden impulse; but a fierce look came into the eyes, and the soft lips contracted themselves as Cynthia named his name. Molly had noticed this look before, always at the mention of this one person.

'Cynthia, what makes you dislike Mr Preston so much?'

'Don't you? Why do you ask me? and yet, Molly,' said she, suddenly relaxing into depression, not merely in tone and look, but in the droop of her limbs – 'Molly, what should you think of me if I married him after all?'

'Married him! Has he ever asked you?' But Cynthia, instead of replying to this question, went on, uttering her own thoughts.

'More unlikely things have happened. Have you never heard of strong wills mesmerising weaker ones into submission? One of the girls at Madame Lefèbre's went out as a governess to a Russian family, who lived near Moscow. I sometimes think I'll write to her to find me a situation in Russia, just to get out of the daily chance of seeing that man!'

'But sometimes you seem quite intimate with him, and talk to him'—

'How can I help it?' said Cynthia impatiently. Then, recovering herself, she added – 'We knew him so well at Ashcombe, and he's not a man to be easily thrown off, I can tell you. I must be civil to him; it's not from liking, and he knows it's not, for I've told him so. However, we won't talk about him. I don't know how we came to do it, I'm sure; the mere fact of his existence, and of his being within half a mile of us, is bad enough. Oh! I wish Roger was at home, and rich, and could marry me at once, and carry me away from that man! If I'd thought of it, I really believe I would have taken poor red-haired Mr Coxe.'

'I don't understand it at all,' said Molly. 'I dislike Mr Preston; but I should never think of taking such violent steps as you speak of, to get away from the neighbourhood in which he lives.'

'No, because you are a reasonable little darling,' said Cynthia, resuming her usual manner, and coming up to Molly, and kissing her. 'At least you'll acknowledge I'm a good hater!'

'Yes. But still I don't understand it.'

'Oh, never mind! There are old complications with our affairs at Ashcombe. Money matters are at the root of it all. Horrid poverty – do let us talk of something else! Or, better still, let me go and finish my letter to Roger, or I shall be too late for the African mail!'

'Isn't it gone? Oh, I ought to have reminded you! It will be too late. Did you not see the notice at the post-office that letters ought to be in London on the morning of the 10th instead of the evening? Oh, I am so sorry!'

'So am I, but it can't be helped. It is to be hoped it will be the greater treat when he does get it. I've a far greater weight on my heart, because your father seems so displeased with me. I was fond of him, and now he is making me quite a coward. You see, Molly,' continued she, a little piteously, 'I've never lived with people with such a high standard of conduct before; and I don't quite know how to behave.'

'You must learn,' said Molly, tenderly. 'You'll find Roger quite as strict in his notions of right and wrong.'

'Ah, but he's in love with me!' said Cynthia, with a pretty consciousness of her power. Molly turned away her head, and was silent; it was of no use combating the truth, and she tried rather not to feel it – not to feel, poor girl, that she too had a great weight on her heart, into the cause of which she shrank from examining. That whole winter long, she had felt as if her sun was all shrouded over with grey mist, and could no longer shine brightly for her. She wakened up in the morning with a dull sense of something being wrong; the world was out of joint,* and, if she were born to set it right, she did not know how to do it. Blind herself as she would, she could not help perceiving that her father was not satisfied with the wife he had chosen. For a long time Molly had been surprised at his apparent contentment; sometimes she had been unselfish enough to be glad that he was satisfied; but still more frequently nature would have its way, and she was almost irritated at what she considered his blindness. Something, however, had changed him now; something that had arisen at the time of Cynthia's engagement. He had become nervously sensitive to his wife's failings, and his whole manner had grown dry and sarcastic, not merely to her, but sometimes to Cynthia – and even, but this very rarely, to Molly herself. He was not a man to go into passions, or ebullitions of feeling; they would have relieved him, even while degrading him in his own eyes; but he became hard and occasionally bitter in his speeches and ways. Molly now learnt to long after the vanished blindness in which her father had passed the first year of his marriage; yet there were no outrageous infractions of domestic peace. Some people might say that Mr Gibson 'accepted the inevitable'; he told himself in more homely phrase 'that it was no use crying over spilt milk'; and he, from principle, avoided all actual dissensions with his wife, preferring to cut short a discussion by a sarcasm, or by leaving the room. Moreover, Mrs Gibson had a very tolerable temper of her own, and her cat-like nature purred and delighted in smooth ways and pleasant quietness. She had no great facility for understanding sarcasm; it is true it disturbed her; but, as she was not quick at deciphering any depth of meaning, and felt it unpleasant to think about it, she forgot it as soon as possible. Yet she saw she was often in some kind of disfavour with her husband, and it made her uneasy. She resembled Cynthia in this: she liked to be liked; and she wanted to regain the esteem which she did not perceive she had lost for ever. Molly sometimes took her stepmother's part in secret; she felt as if she herself could never have borne her father's hard speeches so patiently; they would have cut her to the heart, and she must either have demanded an explanation, and probed the sore to the bottom, or sat down despairing and miserable. Instead of which Mrs Gibson, after her husband had left the room, on these occasions would say in a manner more bewildered than hurt –

'I think dear papa seems a little put out today; we must see that he has a dinner that he likes when he comes home. I have often perceived that everything depends on making a man comfortable in his own house.'

And thus she went on, groping about to find the means of reinstating herself in his good graces – really trying according to her lights, till Molly was often compelled to pity her in spite of herself, and although she saw that her stepmother was the cause of her father's increased astringency of disposition. For, indeed, he had got into that kind of exaggerated susceptibility with regard to his wife's faults, which may be best typified by the state of bodily irritation that is produced by the constant recurrence of any particular noise: those who are brought within hearing of it are apt to be always on the watch for the repetition, if they are once made to notice it, and are in an irritable state of nerves.

So that poor Molly had not passed a cheerful winter, independently of any private sorrows that she might have in her own heart. She did not look well, either: she was gradually falling into low health, rather than bad health. Her heart beat more feebly and slower; the vivifying stimulant of hope – even unacknowledged hope – was gone out of her life. It seemed as if there was not, and never could be in this world, any help for the dumb discordancy between her father and his wife. Day after day, month after month, year after year, would Molly have to sympathise with her father, and pity her stepmother, feeling acutely for both, and certainly more than Mrs Gibson felt for herself. Molly could not imagine how she had at one time wished for her father's eyes to be opened, and how she could ever have fancied that, if they were, he would be able to change things in Mrs Gibson's character. It was all hopeless, and the only attempt at a remedy was to think about it as little as possible. Then Cynthia's ways and manner about Roger gave Molly a great deal of uneasiness. She did not believe that Cynthia cared enough for him; at any rate, not with the sort of love that she herself would have bestowed, if she had been so happy – no, that was not it – if she had been in Cynthia's place. She felt as if she should have gone to him, both hands held out, full and brimming over with tenderness, and been grateful for every word of precious confidence bestowed on her. Yet Cynthia received his letters with a kind of carelessness, and read them with a strange indifference, while Molly sat at her feet, so to speak, looking up with eyes as wistful as a dog's waiting for crumbs and such chance beneficences.

She tried to be patient on these occasions, but at last she must ask – 'Where is he, Cynthia? What does he say?' By this time Cynthia had put down the letter on the table by her, smiling a little from time to time, as she remembered the loving compliments it contained.

'Where? Oh, I didn't look exactly – somewhere in Abyssinia – Huon.* I can't read the word, and it doesn't much signify, for it would give me no idea.'

'Is he well?' asked greedy Molly.

'Yes, now. He has had a slight touch of fever, he says; but it's all over now, and he hopes he is getting acclimatised.'

'Of fever! – and who took care of him? he would want nursing – and so far from home! Oh, Cynthia!'

'Oh, I don't fancy he had any nursing, poor fellow! One doesn't expect nursing, and hospitals, and doctors in Abyssinia; but he had plenty of quinine with him, and I suppose that is the best specific. At any rate he says he is quite well now!'

Molly sat silent for a minute or two.

'What is the date of the letter, Cynthia?'

'I didn't look. December the – December the 10th.'

'That's nearly two months ago,' said Molly.

'Yes; but I determined I wouldn't worry myself with useless anxiety, when he went away. If anything did – go wrong, you know,' said Cynthia, using a euphemism for death as most people do (it is an ugly word to speak plain out in the midst of life), 'it would be all over before I even heard of his illness, and I could be of no use to him – could I, Molly?'

'No. I daresay it is all very true; only I should think the Squire could not take it so easily.'

'I always write him a little note, when I hear from Roger; but I don't think I'll name this touch of fever – shall I, Molly?'

'I don't know,' said Molly. 'People say one ought; but I almost wish I hadn't heard it. Please, does he say anything else that I may hear?'

'Oh, lovers' letters are so silly, and I think this is sillier than usual,' said Cynthia, looking over her letter again. 'Here's a piece you may read, from that line to that,' indicating two places. 'I haven't read it myself, for it looked dullish – all about Aristotle and Pliny* – and I want to get this bonnet-cap made-up, before we go out to pay our calls.'

Molly took the letter, the thought crossing her mind that he had touched it, had had his hands upon it, in those far distant desert lands, where he might be lost to sight and to any human knowledge of his fate; even now her pretty brown fingers almost caressed the flimsy paper with their delicacy of touch, as she read. She saw references made to books which, with a little trouble, would be accessible to her here in Hollingford. Perhaps the details and the references would make the letter dull and dry to some people, but not to her, thanks to his former teaching and the interest he had excited in her for his pursuits. But, as he said in apology, what had he to write about in that savage land, but his love, and his researches, and travels? There was no society, no gaiety, no new books to write about, no gossip in Abyssinian wilds.

Molly was not in strong health, and perhaps this made her a little fanciful; but certain it is that her thoughts by day and her dreams by night were haunted by the idea of Roger, lying ill and unattended in those savage lands. From a heart as true as that of the real mother in King Solomon's judgment,* who pleaded, 'O my lord! give her the living child, and in no wise slay it,' came Molly's constant prayer, 'Let him live, let him live, even though I may never set eyes upon him again! Have pity upon his father! Grant that he may come home safe, and live happily with her whom he loves so tenderly – so tenderly, O God.' And then she would burst into tears, and drop asleep at last, sobbing.

CHAPTER 38

Mr Kirkpatrick, Q.C.

Cynthia was always the same with Molly: kind, sweet-tempered, ready to help, professing a great deal of love for her, and probably feeling as much as she did for any one in the world. But Molly had reached to this superficial depth of affection and intimacy in the first few weeks of Cynthia's residence in her father's house; and, if she had been of a nature prone to analyse the character of one whom she loved dearly, she might have perceived that, with all Cynthia's apparent frankness, there were certain limits beyond which her confidence did not go; where her reserve began, and her real self was shrouded in mystery. For instance, her relations with Mr Preston were often very puzzling to Molly. She was sure that there had been a much greater intimacy between them formerly at Ashcombe, and that the remembrance of this was often very galling and irritating to Cynthia, who was evidently desirous of forgetting it as he was anxious to make her remember it. But why this intimacy had ceased, why Cynthia disliked him so extremely now, and many other unexplained circumstances connected with these two facts, were Cynthia's secrets; and she effectually baffled all Molly's innocent attempts, during the first glow of her friendship for Cynthia, to learn the girlish antecedents of her companion's life. Every now and then Molly came to a dead wall, beyond which she could not pass – at least with the delicate instruments which were all she chose to use. Perhaps Cynthia might have told all there was to tell to a more forcible curiosity, which knew how to improve every slip of the tongue and every fit of temper to its own gratification. But Molly's was the interest of affection, not the coarser desire of knowing everything for a little excitement; and, as soon as she saw that Cynthia did not wish to tell her anything about that period of her life, Molly left off referring to it. But, if Cynthia had preserved a sweet tranquillity of manner and an unvarying kindness for Molly during the winter in question, at present she was the only person to whom the beauty's ways were unchanged. Mr Gibson's influence had been good for her as long as she saw that he liked her; she had tried to keep as high a place in his good opinion as she could, and had curbed many a little sarcasm against her mother, and many a twisting of the absolute truth, when he was by. Now there was a constant uneasiness about her, which made her more cowardly than before; and even her partisan, Molly, could not help being aware of the distinct equivocations she occasionally used when anything in Mr Gibson's words or behaviour pressed her too hard. Her repartees to her mother were less frequent than they had been, but there was often the unusual phenomenon of pettishness in her behaviour to her. These changes in humour and disposition, here described all at once, were in themselves a series of delicate alterations of relative conduct spread over many months – many winter months of long evenings and bad weather, which bring out discords of character, as a dash of cold water brings out the fading colours of an old fresco.

During much of this time Mr Preston had been at Ashcombe; for Lord Cumnor had not been able to find an agent whom he liked, to replace Mr Preston; and, while the inferior situation remained vacant, Mr Preston had undertaken to do the duties of both. Mrs Goodenough had had a serious illness; and the little society at Hollingford did not care to meet, while one of their habitual set was scarcely out of danger. So there had been very little visiting; and though Miss Browning said that the absence of the temptations of society was very agreeable to cultivated minds, after the dissipations of the previous autumn, when there were parties every week to welcome Mr Preston, yet Miss Phoebe let out in confidence that she and her sister had fallen into the habit of going to bed at nine o'clock, for they found cribbage night after night, from five o'clock till ten, rather too much of a good thing. To tell the truth, that winter, if peaceful, was monotonous in Hollingford; and the whole circle of gentility there was delighted to be stirred up in March by the intelligence that Mr Kirkpatrick, the newly-made Q.C., was coming on a visit for a couple of days to his sister-in-law, Mrs Gibson. Mrs Goodenough's room was the very centre of gossip; gossip had been her daily bread through her life, gossip was meat and wine to her now.

'Dear-ah-me!' said the old lady, rousing herself so as to sit upright in her easy-chair, and propping herself with her hands on the arms; 'who would ha' thought she'd such grand relations! Why, Mr Ashton told me once that a Queen's counsel was as like to be a judge as a kitten is like to be a cat. And to think of her being as good as sister to a judge! I saw one oncst; and I know I thought as I shouldn't wish for a better winter-cloak than his old robes would make me, if I could only find out where I could get 'em second-hand. And I know she'd her silk gowns turned and dyed and cleaned, and, for aught I know, turned again, while she lived at Ashcombe. Keeping a school, too, and so near akin to this Queen's counsel all the time! Well, to be sure, it wasn't much of a school – only ten young ladies at the best o' times; so perhaps he never heard of it.'

'I've been wondering what they'll give him to dinner,' said Miss Browning. 'It is an unlucky time for visitors; no game to be had, and lamb so late this year, and chicken hardly to be had for love or money.'

'He'll have to put up with calf's head, that he will,' said Mrs Goodenough solemnly. 'If I'd ha' got my usual health, I'd copy out a recipe of my grandmother's for a rolled calf's head,* and send it to Mrs Gibson – the doctor has been very kind to me all through this illness – I wish my daughter in Combermere would send me some autumn chickens – I'd pass 'em on to the doctor, that I would; but she's been a-killing of 'em all, and a-sending of them to me, and the last she sent she wrote me word was the last.'

'I wonder if they'll give a party for him!' suggested Miss Phoebe. 'I should like to see a Queen's counsel for once in my life. I have seen javelin-men,* but that's the greatest thing in the legal line I ever came across.'

'They'll ask Mr Ashton, of course,' said Miss Browning. 'The three black graces,* Law, Physic, and Divinity, as the song calls them. Whenever there's a second course, there's always the clergyman of the parish invited in any family of gentility.'

'I wonder if he's married!' said Mrs Goodenough. Miss Phoebe had been feeling the same wonder, but had not thought it maidenly to express it, even to her sister, who was the source of knowledge, having met Mrs Gibson in the street on her way to Mrs Goodenough's.

'Yes, he's married, and must have several children, for Mrs Gibson said that Cynthia Kirkpatrick had paid them a visit in London, to have lessons with her cousins. And she said that his wife was a most accomplished woman, and of good family, though she brought him no fortune.'

'It's a very creditable connection, I'm sure; it's only a wonder to me as how we've heard so little talk of it before,' said Mrs Goodenough. 'At the first look of the thing, I shouldn't ha' thought Mrs Gibson was one to hide away her fine relations under a bushel;* indeed, for that matter we're all of us fond o' turning the best breadth o' the gown to the front. I remember, speaking o' breadths, how I've undone my skirts, many a time and oft,* to put a stain or a grease spot next to poor Mr Goodenough. He'd a soft kind of heart, when first we was married; and he said, says he, "Patty, link thy right arm into my left one, then thou'lt be nearer to my heart;" and so we kept up the habit, when, poor man, he'd a deal more to think on than romancing on which side his heart lay; so, as I said, I always put my damaged breadths on the right hand, and, when we walked arm in arm, as we always did, no one was never the wiser.'

'I should not be surprised, if he invited Cynthia to pay him another visit in London,' said Miss Browning. 'If he did it when he was poor, he's twenty times more likely to do it now he's a Queen's counsel.'

'Ay, work it by the rule o' three,* and she stands a good chance. I only hope it won't turn her head; going up visiting in London at her age. Why, I was fifty before ever I went!'

'But she has been in France; she's quite a travelled young lady,' said Miss Phoebe.

Mrs Goodenough shook her head for a whole minute, before she gave vent to her opinion.

'It's a risk,' said she, 'a great risk. I don't like saying so to the doctor, but I shouldn't like having my daughter, if I was him, so cheek-by-jowl with a girl as was brought up in the country where Robespierre and Bonyparte* was born.'

'But Bonaparte was a Corsican,' said Miss Browning, who was much farther advanced both in knowledge and in liberality of opinions than Mrs Goodenough. 'And there's a great opportunity for cultivation of the mind afforded by intercourse with foreign countries. I always admire Cynthia's grace of manner, never too shy to speak, yet never putting herself forwards; she's quite a help to a party; and, if she has a few airs and graces, why they're natural at her age! Now, as for dear Molly, there's a kind of awkwardness about her – she broke one of our best china cups last time she was at a party at our house, and spilt the coffee on the new carpet; and then she got so confused that she hardly did anything but sit in a corner and hold her tongue all the rest of the evening.'

'She was so sorry for what she'd done, sister,' said Miss Phoebe, in a gentle tone of reproach; she was always faithful to Molly.

'Well, and did I say she wasn't? but was there any need for her to be stupid all the evening after?'

'But you were rather sharp – rather displeased' —

'And I think it my duty to be sharp, ay, and cross too, when I see young folks careless. And, when I see my duty clear, I do it; I'm not one to shrink from it, and they ought to be grateful to me. It's not every one that will take the trouble of reproving them, as Mrs Goodenough knows. I'm very fond of Molly Gibson, very, for her own sake and for her mother's too; I'm not sure if I don't think she's worth half-a-dozen Cynthias; but for all that she shouldn't break my best china teacup, and then sit doing nothing for her livelihood all the rest of the evening.'

By this time, Mrs Goodenough gave evident signs of being tired; Molly's misdemeanours and Miss Browning's broken teacup were not as exciting subjects of conversation as Mrs Gibson's newly-discovered good luck in having a successful London lawyer for a relation.

Mr Kirkpatrick had been, like many other men, struggling on in his profession, and encumbered with a large family of his own; he was ready to do a good turn for his connections, if it occasioned him no loss of time, and if (which was, perhaps, a primary condition) he remembered their existence. Cynthia's visit to Doughty Street, nine or ten years ago, had not made much impression upon him after he had once suggested its feasibility to his good-natured wife. He was even rather startled, every now and then, by the appearance of a pretty little girl amongst his own children, as they trooped in to dessert, and had to remind himself who she was. But, as it was his custom to leave the table almost immediately and to retreat into a small back-room called his study, to immerse himself in papers for the rest of the evening, the child had not made much impression upon him; and probably the next time he remembered her existence was, when Mrs Kirkpatrick wrote to him to beg him to receive Cynthia for a night on her way to school at Boulogne. The same request was repeated on her return; but it so happened that he had not seen her either time; and he only dimly remembered some remarks which his wife had made on one of these occasions, that it seemed to her rather hazardous to send so young a girl on so long a journey, without making more provision for her safety than Mrs Kirkpatrick had done. He knew that his wife would fill up all deficiencies in this respect, as if Cynthia had been her own daughter, and thought no more about her, until he received an invitation to attend Mrs Kirkpatrick's wedding with Mr Gibson, the highly-esteemed surgeon of Hollingford, etc., etc. – an attention which irritated instead of pleasing him. 'Does the woman think I have nothing to do but run about the country in search of brides and bridegrooms, when this great case of Houghton v. Houghton is coming on, and I haven't a moment to spare?' he asked of his wife.

'Perhaps she never heard of it,' suggested Mrs Kirkpatrick.

'Nonsense! the case has been in the paper for days.'

'But she mayn't know you are engaged in it.'

'She mayn't,' said he meditatively – such ignorance was possible.

But now the great case of Houghton v. Houghton was a thing of the past; the hard struggle was over, the comparative table-land of Q.C.-dom gained, and Mr Kirkpatrick had leisure for family feeling and recollection. One day in the Easter vacation he found himself near Hollingford; he had a Sunday to spare, and he wrote to offer himself as a visitor to the Gibsons from Friday till Monday; expressing strongly (what he really felt, in a less degree) his wish to make Mr Gibson's acquaintance. Mr Gibson, though often overwhelmed with professional business, was always hospitable; and, moreover, it was always a pleasure to him to get out of the somewhat confined mental atmosphere which he had breathed over and over again, and have a whiff of fresh air: a glimpse of what was passing in the great world beyond his daily limits of thought and action. So he was ready to give a cordial reception to his unknown relation. Mrs Gibson was in a flutter of sentimental delight, which she fancied was family affection, but which might not have been quite so effervescent, if Mr Kirkpatrick had remained in his former position of struggling lawyer, with seven children, living in Doughty Street.

When the two gentlemen met, they were attracted towards each other by a similarity of character, with just enough difference in their opinions to make the experience of each, on which such opinions were based, valuable to the other. To Mrs Gibson, although the bond between them counted for very little in their intercourse, Mr Kirkpatrick paid very polite attention; and he was, in fact, very glad that she had done so well for herself as to marry a sensible and agreeable man, who was able to keep her in comfort, and to behave to her daughter in so liberal a manner. Molly struck him as a delicate-looking girl, who might be very pretty if she had a greater look of health and animation; indeed, looking at her critically, there were beautiful points about her face – long soft grey eyes, black curling eyelashes, rarely-showing dimples, perfect teeth; but there was a languor over all, a slow depression of manner, which contrasted unfavourably with the brightly-coloured Cynthia, sparkling, quick, graceful, and witty. As Mr Kirkpatrick expressed it afterwards to his wife, he was quite in love with that girl; and Cynthia, as ready to captivate strangers as any little girl of three or four, rose to the occasion, forgot all her cares and despondencies, remembered no longer her regret at having lost something of Mr Gibson's good opinion, and listened eagerly and made soft replies, intermixed with naïve sallies and droll humour, till Mr Kirkpatrick was quite captivated. He left Hollingford, almost surprised to have performed a duty, and found it a pleasure. For Mrs Gibson and Molly he had a general friendly feeling; but he did not care if he never saw them again. But for Mr Gibson he had a warm respect, a strong personal liking, which he would be glad to have ripen into a friendship, if there was time for it in this bustling world. And he fully resolved to see more of Cynthia; his wife must know her; they must have her up to stay with them in London, and show her something of the world. But, on returning home, Mr Kirkpatrick found so much work awaiting him that he had to lock up embryo friendships and kindly plans in some safe closet of his mind, and give himself up, body and soul, to the immediate work of his profession. But, in May, he found time to take his wife to the Academy Exhibition;* and, some portrait there striking him as being like Cynthia, he told his wife more about her and his visit to Hollingford than he had ever had leisure to do before; and the result was that on the next day a letter was sent off to Mrs Gibson, inviting Cynthia to pay a visit to her cousins in London, and reminding her of many little circumstances that had occurred when she was with them as a child, so as to carry on the clue of friendship from that time to the present.

On its receipt, this letter was greeted in various ways by the four people who sate round the breakfast-table. Mrs Gibson read it to herself first. Then, without telling what its contents were, so that her auditors were quite in the dark as to what her remarks applied, she said –

'I think they might have remembered that I am a generation nearer to them than she is; but nobody thinks of family affection now-a-days; and I liked him so much, and bought a new cookery-book, all to make it pleasant and agreeable and what he was used to.' She said all this in a plaintive, aggrieved tone of voice; but, as no one knew to what she was referring, it was difficult to offer her consolation. Her husband was the first to speak.

'If you want us to sympathise with you, tell us what is the nature of your woe.'

'Why, I daresay it's what he means as a very kind attention, only I think I ought to have been asked before Cynthia,' said she, reading the letter over again.

'Who's *he*? and what's meant for a "kind attention"?'

'Mr Kirkpatrick, to be sure. This letter is from him; and he wants Cynthia to go and pay them a visit, and never says anything about you or me, my dear. And I'm sure we did our best to make it pleasant; and he should have asked us first, I think.'

'As I couldn't possibly have gone, it makes very little difference to me.'

'But I could have gone; and, at any rate, he should have paid us the compliment: it's only a proper mark of respect, you know. So ungrateful, too, when I gave up my dressing-room on purpose for him!'

'And I dressed for dinner every day he was here, if we are each to recapitulate all our sacrifices on his behalf. But, for all that, I didn't expect to be invited to his house. I shall be only too glad, if he will come again to mine.'

'I've a great mind not to let Cynthia go,' said Mrs Gibson, reflectively.

'I can't go, mamma,' said Cynthia, colouring. 'My gowns are all so shabby, and my old bonnet must do for the summer.'

'Well, but you can buy a new one; and I'm sure it is high time you should get yourself another silk gown. You must have been saving up a great deal, for I don't know when you've had any new clothes.'

Cynthia began to say something, but stopped short. She went on buttering her toast, but she held it in her hand without eating it; without looking up either, as, after a minute or two of silence, she spoke again –

'I cannot go. I should like it very much; but I really cannot go. Please, mamma, write at once, and refuse it.'

'Nonsense, child! When a man in Mr Kirkpatrick's position comes forward to offer a favour, it does not do to decline it without giving a sufficient reason. So kind of him as it is, too!'

'Suppose you offer to go instead of me?' proposed Cynthia.

'No, no! that won't do,' said Mr Gibson decidedly. 'You can't transfer invitations in that way. But, really, this excuse about your clothes does appear to be very trivial, Cynthia, if you have no other reason to give.'

'It is a real, true reason to me,' said Cynthia, looking up at him as she spoke. 'You must let me judge for myself. It would not do to go there in a state of shabbiness; for even in Doughty Street, I remember, my aunt was very particular about dress; and now that Margaret and Helen are grown up, and they visit so much – pray don't say anything more about it, for I know it would not do.'

'What have you done with all your money, I wonder?' said Mrs Gibson. 'You've twenty pounds a year, thanks to Mr Gibson and me; and I'm sure you haven't spent more than ten.'

'I hadn't many things when I came back from France,' said Cynthia, in a low voice, and evidently troubled by all this questioning. 'Pray let it be decided at once; I can't go, and there's an end of it.' She got up, and left the room rather suddenly.

'I don't understand it at all,' said Mrs Gibson. 'Do you, Molly?'

'No. I know she doesn't like spending money on her dress, and is very careful.' Molly said this much, and then was afraid she had made mischief.

'But then she must have got the money somewhere. It always has struck me that, if you have not extravagant habits, and do not live up to your income, you must have a certain sum to lay by at the end of the year. Have I not often said so, Mr Gibson?'

'Probably.'

'Well, then, apply the same reasoning to Cynthia's case; and then, I ask, what has become of the money?'

'I cannot tell,' said Molly, seeing that she was appealed to. 'She may have given it away to some one who wants it.'

Mr Gibson put down his newspaper.

'It's very clear that she has neither got the dress nor the money necessary for this London visit, and that she doesn't want any more inquiries to be made on the subject. She likes mysteries, in fact, and I detest them. Still, I think it's a desirable thing for her to keep up the acquaintance, or friendship, or whatever it is to be called, with her father's family; and I shall gladly give her ten pounds; and if that's not enough, why, either you must help her out, or she must do without some superfluous article of dress or another.'

'I'm sure there never was such a kind, dear, generous man as you are, Mr Gibson,' said his wife. 'To think of your being a stepfather! and so good to my poor fatherless girl! But, Molly my dear, I think you'll acknowledge that you, too, are very fortunate in your stepmother. Are not you, love? And what happy *tête-à-têtes* we shall have together when Cynthia goes to London! I'm not sure if I don't get on better with you even than with her, though she is my own child; for, as dear papa says so truly, there is a love of mystery about her; and, if I hate anything, it is the slightest concealment or reserve. Ten pounds! Why, it will quite set her up, buy her a couple of gowns and a new bonnet, and I don't know what all! Dear Mr Gibson, how generous you are!'

Something very like 'Pshaw!' was growled out from behind the newspaper.

'May I go and tell her?' said Molly, rising up.

'Yes, do, love! Tell her it would be so ungrateful to refuse; and tell her that your father wishes her to go; and tell her, too, that it would be quite wrong not to avail herself of an opening which may by-and-by be extended to the rest of the family. I am sure, if they ask me – which certainly they ought to do – I won't say before they asked Cynthia, because I never think of myself, and am really the most forgiving person in the world, in forgiving slights; – but, when they do ask me, which they are sure to do, I shall never be content till, by putting in a little hint here and a little hint there, I've induced them to send you an invitation. A month or two in London would do you so much good, Molly.'

Molly had left the room, before this speech was ended, and Mr Gibson was occupied with his newspaper; but Mrs Gibson finished it to herself very much to her own satisfaction; for, after all, it was better to have some one of the family going on the visit, though she might not be the right person, than to refuse it altogether, and never to have the opportunity of saying anything about it. As Mr Gibson was so kind to Cynthia, she too would be kind to Molly, and dress her becomingly, and invite young men to the house; do all the things, in fact, which Molly and her father did not want to have done, and throw the old stumbling-blocks in the way of their unrestrained intercourse, which was the one thing they desired to have, free and open, and without the constant dread of her jealousy.

CHAPTER 39

Secret Thoughts Ooze Out

Molly found Cynthia in the drawing-room, standing in the bow-window, looking out on the garden. She started as Molly came up to her.

'Oh, Molly,' she said, putting her arms out towards her, 'I am always so glad to have you with me!'

It was outbursts of affection such as these that always called Molly back, if she had been ever so unconsciously wavering in her allegiance to Cynthia. She had been wishing downstairs that Cynthia would be less reserved, and not have so many secrets; but now it seemed almost like treason to have wanted her to be anything but what she was. Never had any one more than Cynthia the power spoken of by Goldsmith when he wrote –

> He threw off his friends like a huntsman his pack,
> For he knew when he liked he could whistle them back.*

'Do you know, I think you'll be glad to hear what I've got to tell you,' said Molly. 'I think you would really like to go to London; shouldn't you?'

'Yes, but it's of no use "liking",' said Cynthia. 'Don't you begin about it, Molly, for the thing is settled; and I can't tell you why, but I can't go.'

'It is only the money, dear. And papa has been so kind about it. He wants you to go; he thinks you ought to keep up relationships; and he is going to give you ten pounds.'

'How kind he is!' said Cynthia. 'But I ought not to take it. I wish I had known you years ago; I should have been different to what I am.'

'Never mind that! We like you as you are; we don't want you different. You'll really hurt papa, if you don't take it. Why do you hesitate? Do you think Roger won't like it?'

'Roger! no, I wasn't thinking about him! Why should he care? I shall be there and back again before he even hears about it.'

'Then you will go?' said Molly.

Cynthia thought for a minute or two. 'Yes, I will,' said she, at length. 'I daresay it's not wise; but it will be pleasant, and I'll go. Where is Mr Gibson? I want to thank him. Oh, how kind he is! Molly, you're a lucky girl!'

'I?' said Molly, quite startled at being told this; for she had been feeling as if so many things were going wrong – almost as if they would never go right again.

'There he is!' said Cynthia. 'I hear him in the hall!' And down she flew, and, laying her hands on Mr Gibson's arm, she thanked him with such warm impulsiveness, and in so pretty and caressing a manner, that something of his old feeling of personal liking for her returned, and he forgot for a time the reasons for disapproval he had against her.

'There, there!' said he, 'that's enough, my dear! It's quite right you should keep up with your relations; there's nothing more to be said about it.'

'I do think your father is the most charming man I know,' said Cynthia, on her return to Molly; 'and it's that which always makes me so afraid of losing his good opinion, and fret so when I think he is displeased with me. And now let us think all about this London visit. It will be delightful, won't it? I can make ten pounds go ever so far; and in some ways it will be such a comfort to get out of Hollingford.'

'Will it?' said Molly, rather wistfully.

'Oh, yes! You know I don't mean that it will be a comfort to leave you; that will be anything but a comfort. But, after all, a country town is a country town, and London is London. You need not smile at my truisms; I've always had a sympathy with M. de la Palisse –

> M. de la Palisse est mort
>   En perdant sa vie;
> Un quart d'heure avant sa mort
>   Il était en vie' – *

sang she, in so gay a manner that she puzzled Molly, as she often did, by her change of mood from the gloomy decision with which she had refused to accept the invitation only half-an-hour ago. She suddenly took Molly round the waist, and began waltzing about the room with her, to the imminent danger of the various little tables, loaded with '*objets d'art*' (as Mrs Gibson delighted to call them) with which the drawing-room was crowded. She avoided them, however, with her usual skill; but they both stood still at last, surprised at Mrs Gibson's surprise, as she stood at the door, looking at the whirl going on before her.

'Upon my word, I only hope you are not going crazy, both of you! What's all this about, pray?'

'Only because I'm so glad I'm going to London, mamma,' said Cynthia demurely.

'I'm not sure if it's quite the thing for an engaged young lady to be so much beside herself at the prospect of gaiety. In my time, our great pleasure in our lovers' absence was in thinking about them.'

'I should have thought that would have given you pain, because you would have had to remember that they were away, which ought to have made you unhappy. Now, to tell you the truth, just at the moment I had forgotten all about Roger. I hope it wasn't very wrong. Osborne looks as if he did all my share as well as his own of the fretting after Roger. How ill he looked yesterday!'

'Yes,' said Molly; 'I didn't know if any one besides me had noticed it. I was quite shocked.'

'Ah,' said Mrs Gibson, 'I'm afraid that young man won't live long – very much afraid,' and she shook her head ominously.

'Oh, what will happen if he dies?' exclaimed Molly, suddenly sitting down, and thinking of that strange, mysterious wife who never made her appearance, whose very existence was never spoken about – and Roger away too!

'Well, it would be very sad, of course, and we should all feel it very much, I've no doubt; for I've always been very fond of Osborne; in fact, before Roger became, as it were, my own flesh and blood, I liked Osborne better; but we must not forget the living, dear Molly,' (for Molly's eyes were filling with tears at the dismal thoughts presented to her). 'Our dear good Roger would, I am sure, do all in his power to fill Osborne's place in any way; and his marriage need not be so long delayed.'

'Don't speak of that in the same breath as Osborne's life, mamma,' said Cynthia hastily.

'Why, my dear, it is a very natural thought. For poor Roger's sake, you know, one wishes it not to be so very, very long an engagement; and I was only answering Molly's question, after all. One can't help following out one's thoughts. People must die, you know – young, as well as old.'

'If I ever suspected Roger of following out his thoughts in a similar way,' said Cynthia, 'I'd never speak to him again.'

'As if he would!' said Molly, warm in her turn. 'You know he never would; and you shouldn't suppose it of him, Cynthia – no, not even for a moment!'

'I can't see the great harm of it all, for my part,' said Mrs Gibson plaintively. 'A young man strikes us all as looking very ill – and I'm sure I'm sorry for it; but illness very often leads to death. Surely you agree with me there, and what's the harm of saying so? Then Molly asks what will happen, if he dies; and I try to answer her question. I don't like talking or thinking of death any more than any one else; but I should think myself wanting in strength of mind, if I could not look forward to the consequences of death. I really think we're commanded to do so, somewhere in the Bible or the Prayer-book.'

'Do you look forward to the consequences of my death, mamma?' asked Cynthia.

'You really are the most unfeeling girl I ever met with,' said Mrs Gibson, really hurt. 'I wish I could give you a little of my own sensitiveness, for I have too much for my happiness. Don't let us speak of Osborne's looks again; ten to one it was only some temporary over-fatigue, or some anxiety about Roger, or perhaps a little fit of indigestion. I was very foolish to attribute it to anything more serious, and dear papa might be displeased, if he knew I had done so. Medical men don't like other people to be making conjectures about health; they consider it as trenching on their own particular province, and very proper, I'm sure. Now let us consider about your dress, Cynthia; I could not understand how you had spent your money, and made so little show with it.'

'Mamma! it may sound very cross, but I must tell Molly, and you, and everybody, once for all, that, as I don't want and didn't ask for more than my allowance, I'm not going to answer any questions about what I do with it.' She did not say this with any want of respect; but she said it with a quiet determination which subdued her mother for the time; though often afterwards, when Mrs Gibson and Molly were alone, the former would start the wonder as to what Cynthia could possibly have done with her money, and hunt each poor conjecture through woods and valleys of doubt, till she was wearied out; and the exciting sport was given up for the day. At present, however, she confined herself to the practical matter in hand; and the genius for millinery and dress, inherent in both mother and daughter, soon settled a great many knotty points of contrivance and taste, and then they all three set to work to 'gar auld claes look amaist as weel's the new.'*

Cynthia's relations with the Squire had been very stationary, ever since the visit she had paid to the Hall the previous autumn. He had received them all at that time with hospitable politeness, and he had been more charmed with Cynthia than he liked to acknowledge to himself, when he thought the visit all over afterwards.

'She's a pretty lass, sure enough,' thought he, 'and has pretty ways about her too, and likes to learn from older people, which is a good sign; but, somehow, I don't like madam her mother; but still she is her mother, and the girl's her daughter; yet she spoke to her once or twice as I shouldn't ha' liked our little Fanny to have spoken, if it had pleased God for her to ha' lived. No, it's not the right way, and it may be a bit old-fashioned, but I like the right way. And then again she took possession o' me, as I may say, and little Molly had to run after us in the garden walks that are too narrow for three, just like a little four-legged doggie; and the other was so full of listening to me, she never turned round for to speak a word to Molly. I don't mean to say they're not fond of each other; and that's in Roger's sweetheart's favour, and it's very ungrateful in me to go and find fault with a lass who was

so civil to me, and had such a pretty way with her of hanging on
every word that fell from my lips. Well! a deal may come and go
in two years! and the lad says nothing to me about it. I'll be as
deep as him, and take no more notice of the affair till he comes
home and tells me himself.'

So, although the Squire was always delighted to receive the little
notes which Cynthia sent him every time she heard from Roger,
and although this attention on her part was melting the heart he
tried to harden, he controlled himself into writing her the briefest
acknowledgments. His words were strong in meaning, but formal
in expression; she herself did not think much about them, being
satisfied to do the kind actions that called them forth. But her
mother criticised them and pondered them. She thought she had
hit on the truth, when she decided in her own mind that it was a
very old-fashioned style, and that he and his house and his
furniture all wanted some of the brightening up and polishing
which they were sure to receive, when – she never quite liked to
finish the sentence definitely, although she kept repeating to herself
that 'there was no harm in it'.

To return to the Squire. Occupied as he now was, he recovered
his former health, and something of his former cheerfulness. If
Osborne had met him half-way, it is probable that the old bond
between father and son might have been renewed; but Osborne
either was really an invalid, or had sunk into invalid habits, and
made no effort to rally. If his father urged him to go out – nay,
once or twice he gulped down his pride, and asked Osborne to
accompany him – Osborne would go to the window and find out
some flaw or speck in the wind or weather, and make that an
excuse for stopping indoors over his books. He would saunter out
on the sunny side of the house, in a manner that the Squire
considered as both indolent and unmanly. Yet, if there was a
prospect of his leaving home, which he did pretty often about this
time, he was seized with a hectic energy: the clouds in the sky, the
easterly wind, the dampness of the air, were nothing to him then;
and, as the Squire did not know the real secret cause of this
anxiety to be gone, he took it into his head that it arose from
Osborne's dislike to Hamley and to the monotony of his father's
society.

'It was a mistake,' thought the Squire. 'I see it now. I was never
great at making friends myself; I always thought those Oxford
and Cambridge men turned up their noses at me for a country-

booby, and I'd get the start and have none o'them. But when the boys went to Rugby and Cambridge, I should ha' let them have their own friends about 'em, even though they might ha' looked down on me; it was the worst they could ha' done to me; and now, what few friends I had have fallen off from me, by death or somehow, and it is but dreary work for a young man, I grant it. But he might try not to show it so plain to me as he does. I'm getting case-hardened; but it does cut me to the quick sometimes – it does. And he so fond of his dad as he was once! If I can but get the land drained, I'll make him an allowance, and let him go to London, or where he likes. Maybe he'll do better this time, or maybe he'll go to the dogs altogether; but perhaps it will make him think a bit kindly of the old father at home – I should like him to do that, I should!'

It is possible that Osborne might have been induced to tell his father of his marriage during their long solitary intercourse, if the Squire, in an unlucky moment, had not given him his confidence about Roger's engagement with Cynthia. It was on one wet Sunday afternoon, when the father and son were sitting together in the large empty drawing-room: Osborne had not been to church in the morning; the Squire had, and he was now trying hard to read one of Blair's sermons.* They had dined early; they always did on Sundays; and either that, or the sermon, or the hopeless wetness of the day, made the afternoon seem interminably long to him. He had certain unwritten rules for the regulation of his conduct on Sundays. Cold meat, sermon-reading, no smoking till after evening-prayers, as little thought as possible as to the state of the land and the condition of the crops, and as much respectable sitting-indoors in his best clothes as was consistent with going to church twice a day, and saying the responses louder than the clerk. Today, it had rained so unceasingly that he had remitted the afternoon church; but oh, even with the luxury of a nap, how long it seemed before he saw the Hall servants trudging homewards, along the field-path, a covey of umbrellas! He had been standing at the window for the last half-hour, his hands in his pockets, and his mouth often contracting itself into the traditional sin of a whistle, but as often checked into sudden gravity – ending, nine times out of ten, in a yawn. He looked askance at Osborne, who was sitting near the fire absorbed in a book. The poor Squire was something like the little boy in the child's story, who asks all sorts of birds and beasts to come and play with him; and, in every

case, receives the sober answer, that they are too busy to have
leisure for trivial amusements. The father wanted the son to put
down his book, and talk to him: it was so wet, so dull, and a little
conversation would so wile away the time! But Osborne, with his
back to the window where his father was standing, saw nothing
of all this, and went on reading. He had assented to his father's
remark that it was a very wet afternoon, but had not carried on
the subject into all the varieties of truisms of which it was
susceptible. Something more rousing must be started, and this the
Squire felt. The recollection of the affair between Roger and
Cynthia came into his head, and, without giving it a moment's
consideration, he began –

'Osborne! Do you know anything about this – this attachment
of Roger's?'

Quite successful. Osborne laid down his book in a moment,
and turned round to his father.

'Roger! an attachment! No! I never heard of it – I can hardly
believe it – that is to say, I suppose it is to'—

And then he stopped; for he thought he had no right to betray
his own conjecture, that the object was Cynthia Kirkpatrick.

'Yes. He is, though. Can you guess who to? Nobody that I
particularly like – not a connection to my mine – yet she's a very
pretty girl; and I suppose I was to blame in the first instance.'

'Is it'—

'It's no use beating about the bush. I've gone so far, I may as
well tell you all. It's Miss Kirkpatrick, Gibson's step-daughter. But
it's not an engagement, mind you'—

'I'm very glad – I hope she likes Roger back again'—

' "Like"! It's only too good a connection for her not to like it: if
Roger is of the same mind when he comes home, I'll be bound
she'll be only too happy!'

'I wonder Roger never told me,' said Osborne, a little hurt, now
he began to consider himself.

'He never told me either,' said the Squire. 'It was Gibson, who
came here, and made a clean breast of it, like a man of honour.
I'd been saying to him, I couldn't have either of you two lads
taking up with his lasses. I'll own it was you I was afraid of – it's
bad enough with Roger, and maybe will come to nothing after all;
but, if it had been you, I'd ha' broken with Gibson and every
mother's son of 'em, sooner than have let it go on; and so I told
Gibson.'

'I beg your pardon for interrupting you; but, once for all, I claim the right of choosing my wife for myself, subject to no man's interference,' said Osborne, hotly.

'Then you'll keep your wife with no man's interference, that's all; for ne'er a penny will you get from me, my lad, unless you marry to please me a little, as well as yourself a great deal. That's all I ask of you. I'm not particular as to beauty, or as to cleverness, and piano-playing, and that sort of thing; if Roger marries this girl, we shall have enough of that in the family. I shouldn't much mind her being a bit older than you; but she must be well-born, and the more money she brings the better for the old place.'

'I say again, father, I choose my wife for myself, and I don't admit any man's right of dictation.'

'Well, well!' said the Squire, getting a little angry in his turn. 'If I'm not to be father in this matter, thou shan't be son. Go against me in what I've set my heart on, and you'll find there's the devil to pay, that's all. But don't let us get angry, it's Sunday afternoon for one thing, and it's a sin; and, besides that, I've not finished my story.'

For Osborne had taken up his book again, and under pretence of reading, was fuming to himself. He hardly put it away, even at his father's request.

'As I was saying, Gibson said, when first we spoke about it, that there was nothing on foot between any of you four, and that, if there was, he would let me know; so by-and-by he comes and tells me of this.'

'Of what? I don't understand how far it has gone?'

There was a tone in Osborne's voice the Squire did not quite like, and he began answering rather angrily.

'Of this, to be sure – of what I'm telling you – of Roger going and making love to this girl, that day he left, after he had gone away from here, and was waiting for the "Umpire" in Hollingford. One would think you quite stupid at times, Osborne.'

'I can only say that these details are quite new to me; you never mentioned them before, I assure you.'

'Well; never mind whether I did or not. I'm sure I said Roger was attached to Miss Kirkpatrick, and be hanged to her; and you might have understood all the rest as a matter of course.'

'Possibly,' said Osborne politely. 'May I ask if Miss Kirkpatrick, who appeared to me to be a very nice girl, responds to Roger's affection?'

'Fast enough, I'll be bound,' said the Squire sulkily. 'A Hamley of Hamley isn't to be had every day. Now, I'll tell you what, Osborne, you're the only marriageable one left in the market, and I want to hoist the old family up again. Don't go against me in this; it really will break my heart if you do.'

'Father, don't talk so!' said Osborne. 'I'll do anything I can to oblige you, except'—

'Except the only thing I've set my heart on your doing?'

'Well, well, let it alone for the present. There's no question of my marrying just at this moment. I'm out of health, and I'm not up to going into society, and meeting young ladies and all that sort of thing, even if I had an opening into fitting society.'

'You should have an opening fast enough. There'll be more money coming in, in a year or two, please God. And as for your health, why, what's to make you well, if you cower over the fire all day, and shudder away from a good honest tankard as if it were poison?'

'So it is to me,' said Osborne languidly, playing with his book as if he wanted to end the conversation and take it up again. The Squire saw the movements, and understood them.

'Well,' said he, 'I'll go and have a talk with Will about poor old Black Bess. It's Sunday work enough, asking after a dumb animal's aches and pains.'

But, after his father had left the room, Osborne did not take up his book again. He laid it down on the table by him, leant back in his chair, and covered his eyes with his hand. He was in a state of health which made him despondent about many things, though, least of all, about what was most in danger. The long concealment of his marriage from his father made the disclosure of it far, far more difficult than it would have been at first. Unsupported by Roger, how could he explain it all to one so passionate as the Squire? how tell of the temptation, the stolen marriage, the consequent happiness, and alas! the consequent suffering? – for Osborne had suffered, and did suffer, greatly in the untoward circumstances in which he had placed himself. He saw no way out of it all, excepting by the one strong stroke of which he felt himself incapable. So, with a heavy heart, he addressed himself to his book again. Everything seemed to come in his way, and he was not strong enough in character to overcome obstacles. The only overt step he took, in consequence of what he had heard from his father, was to ride over to Hollingford the first fine day after he had received the news, and go to see Cynthia and the Gibsons. He had not been there for a long time; bad weather and languor combined had prevented him. He found them full of preparations and discussions about Cynthia's visit to London, and Cynthia herself not at all in the sentimental mood proper to respond to his delicate intimations of how glad he was in his brother's joy. Indeed, it was so long after the time, that Cynthia scarcely perceived that to him the intelligence was recent, and that the first bloom of his emotions had not yet passed away. With her head a little on one side, she was contemplating the effect of a knot of ribbons, when he began, in a low whisper, and leaning forward towards her as he spoke – 'Cynthia – I may call you Cynthia now, mayn't I? – I'm so glad of this news; I've only just heard of it, but I'm so glad.'

'What news do you mean?' She had her suspicions; but she was annoyed to think that from one person her secret was passing to another and another, till, in fact, it was becoming no secret at all. Still, Cynthia could always conceal her annoyance when she chose. 'Why are you to begin calling me Cynthia now?' she went on, smiling. 'The terrible word has slipped out from between your lips before, do you know?'

This light way of taking his tender congratulation did not quite please Osborne, who was in a sentimental mood; and for a minute or so he remained silent. Then, having finished making her bow of ribbon, she turned to him, and continued in a quick low voice, anxious to take advantage of a conversation between her mother and Molly –

'I think I can guess why you made that pretty little speech just now. But do you know you ought not to have been told? And, moreover, things are not quite arrived at the solemnity of – of – well – an engagement. He would not have it so. Now, I shan't say any more; and you must not. Pray remember, you ought not to have known; it is my own secret, and I particularly wished it not to be spoken about; and I don't like its being so talked about. Oh, the leaking of water through one small hole!'

And then she plunged into the talk of the other two, making the conversation general. Osborne was rather discomfited at the non-success of his congratulations; he had pictured to himself the unbosoming of a love-sick girl, full of rapture, and glad of a sympathising confidant. He little knew Cynthia's nature. The more she suspected that she was called upon for a display of emotion, the less would she show; and her emotions were generally under the control of her will. He had made an effort to come and see her; and now he leant back in his chair, weary and a little dispirited.

'You poor dear young man,' said Mrs Gibson, coming up to him with her soft, soothing manner; 'how tired you look! Do take some of that eau-de-cologne and bathe your forehead. This spring weather overcomes me too. '*Primavera*', I think the Italians call it. But it is very trying for delicate constitutions, as much from its associations as from its variableness of temperature. It makes me sigh perpetually; but then I am so sensitive. Dear Lady Cumnor always used to say I was like a thermometer. You've heard how ill she has been?'

'No,' said Osborne, not very much caring either.

'Oh, yes, she is better now; but the anxiety about her has tried me so: detained here by what are, of course, my duties, but far away from all intelligence, and not knowing what the next post might bring.'

'Where was she, then?' asked Osborne, becoming a little more sympathetic.

'At Spa.* Such a distance off! Three days' post! Can't you conceive the trial? Living with her as I did for years; bound up in the family as I was!'

'But Lady Harriet said, in her last letter, that they hoped she would be stronger than she had been for years,' said Molly innocently.

'Yes – Lady Harriet – of course – every one who knows Lady Harriet knows that she is of too sanguine a temperament for her statements to be perfectly relied on. Altogether – strangers are often deluded by Lady Harriet – she has an off-hand manner which takes them in; but she does not mean half she says.'

'We will hope she does in this instance,' said Cynthia shortly. 'They're in London now, and Lady Cumnor hasn't suffered from the journey.'

'They say so,' said Mrs Gibson, shaking her head, and laying an emphasis on the word 'say'. 'I am perhaps over-anxious, but I wish – I wish I could see and judge for myself. It would be the only way of calming my anxiety. I almost think I shall go up with you, Cynthia, for a day or two, just to see her with my own eyes. I don't quite like your travelling alone either. We will think about it, and you shall write to Mr Kirkpatrick, and propose it, if we determine upon it. You can tell him of my anxiety; and it will be only sharing your bed for a couple of nights.'

CHAPTER 40

Molly Gibson Breathes Freely

That was the way in which Mrs Gibson first broached her intention of accompanying Cynthia up to London for a few days' visit. She had a trick of producing the first sketch of any new plan before an outsider to the family circle; so that the first emotions of others, if they disapproved of her projects, had to be repressed, until the idea had become familiar to them. To Molly it seemed too charming a proposal ever to come to pass. She had never allowed herself to recognise the restraint she was under in her stepmother's presence; but all at once she found it out, when her heart danced at the idea of three whole days – for that it would be at the least – of perfect freedom of intercourse with her father; of old times come back again; of meals without perpetual fidgetiness after details of ceremony and correctness of attendance.

'We'll have bread-and-cheese for dinner, and eat it on our knees; we'll make up for having had to eat sloppy puddings with a fork instead of a spoon all this time, by putting our knives in our mouths till we cut ourselves. Papa shall pour his tea into his saucer if he's in a hurry; and, if I'm thirsty, I'll take the slop-basin. And oh, if I could but get, buy, borrow, or steal any kind of an old horse; my grey skirt isn't new, but it will do; – that would be too delightful! After all, I think I can be happy again; for months and months it has seemed as if I had got too old ever to feel pleasure, much less happiness again.'

So thought Molly. Yet she blushed, as if with guilt, when Cynthia, reading her thoughts, said to her one day—

'Molly, you're very glad to get rid of us, are not you?'

'Not of you, Cynthia; at least, I don't think I am. Only, if you but knew how I love papa, and how I used to see a great deal more of him than I ever do now'—

'Ah! I often think what interlopers we must seem, and are in fact'—

'I don't feel you as such. You, at any rate, have been a new delight to me – a sister; and I never knew how charming such a relationship could be.'

'But mamma?' said Cynthia, half-suspiciously, half-sorrowfully.

'She is papa's wife,' said Molly quietly. 'I don't mean to say I'm not often very sorry to feel I'm no longer first with him; but it was' – the violent colour flushed into her face, till even her eyes burnt, and she suddenly found herself on the point of crying; the weeping ash-tree, the misery, the slow dropping comfort, and the comforter came all so vividly before her – 'it was Roger!' – she went on looking up at Cynthia, as she overcame her slight hesitation at mentioning his name – 'Roger, who told me how I ought to take papa's marriage, when I was first startled and grieved at the news. Oh, Cynthia, what a great thing it is to be loved by him!'

Cynthia blushed, and looked fluttered and pleased.

'Yes, I suppose it is. At the same time, Molly, I'm afraid he'll expect me to be always as good as he fancies me now, and I shall have to walk on tiptoe all the rest of my life.'

'But you are good, Cynthia,' put in Molly.

'No, I'm not. You're just as much mistaken as he is; and some day I shall go down in your opinions with a run, just like the hall-clock the other day, when the spring broke.'

'I think he'll love you just as much,' said Molly.

'Could you? Would you be my friend, if – if it turned out even that I had done very wrong things? Would you remember, how very difficult it has sometimes been to me to act rightly?' (she took hold of Molly's hand as she spoke). 'We won't speak of mamma, for your sake as much as mine or hers; but you must see she isn't one to help a girl with much good advice, or good—Oh, Molly, you don't know how I was neglected, just at a time when I wanted friends most. Mamma does not know it; it is not in her to know what I might have been, if I had only fallen into wise, good hands. But I know it; and, what's more,' continued she, suddenly ashamed of her unusual exhibition of feeling, 'I try not to care, which I daresay is really the worst of all; but I could worry myself to death, if I once took to serious thinking.'

'I wish I could help you, or even understand you,' said Molly, after a moment or two of sad perplexity.

'You can help me,' said Cynthia, changing her manner abruptly. 'I can trim bonnets, and make head-dresses; but somehow my hands can't fold up gowns and collars, like your deft fingers.

Please will you help me to pack? That's a real, tangible piece of kindness, and not sentimental consolation for sentimental distresses, which are, perhaps, imaginary after all.'

In general, it is the people that are left behind stationary, who give way to low spirits at any parting; the travellers, however bitterly they may feel the separation, find something in the change of scene to soften regret in the very first hour of separation. But, as Molly walked home with her father from seeing Mrs Gibson and Cynthia off to London by the 'Umpire' coach, she almost danced along the street.

'Now, papa!' said she, 'I'm going to have you all to myself for a whole week. You must be very obedient.'

'Don't be tyrannical, then! You're walking me out of breath, and we're cutting Mrs Goodenough, in our hurry.'

So they crossed over the street, to speak to Mrs Goodenough.

'We've just been seeing my wife and her daughter off to London. Mrs Gibson has gone up for a week!'

'Deary, deary, to London, and only for a week! Why, I can remember its being a three days' journey! It'll be very lonesome for you, Miss Molly, without your young companion!'

'Yes!' said Molly, suddenly feeling as if she ought to have taken this view of the case. 'I shall miss Cynthia very much.'

'And you, Mr Gibson; why, it'll be like being a widower once again! You must come and drink tea with me some evening. We must try and cheer you up a bit amongst us. Shall it be Tuesday?'

In spite of the sharp pinch which Molly gave his arm, Mr Gibson accepted the invitation, much to the gratification of the old lady.

'Papa, how could you go and waste one of our evenings! We have but six in all, and now but five; and I had so reckoned on our doing all sorts of things together.'

'What sort of things?'

'Oh, I don't know: everything that is unrefined and ungenteel,' added she, slily looking up into her father's face.

His eyes twinkled, but the rest of his face was perfectly grave. 'I'm not going to be corrupted. With toil and labour I've reached a very fair height of refinement. I won't be pulled down again.'

'Yes, you will papa. We'll have bread-and-cheese for lunch this very day. And you shall wear your slippers in the drawing-room every evening you'll stay quietly at home; and oh, papa, don't you think I could ride Nora Creina?* I've been looking out the old grey skirt, and I think I could make myself tidy.'

'Where is the side-saddle to come from?'

'To be sure, the old one won't fit that great Irish mare. But I'm not particular, papa. I think I could manage somehow.'

'Thank you. But I'm not quite going to return into barbarism. It may be a depraved taste, but I should like to see my daughter properly mounted.'

'Think of riding together down the lanes – why, the dog-roses must be all out in flower, and the honeysuckles, and the hay – how I should like to see Merriman's farm again! Papa, do let me have one ride with you! Please do! I'm sure we can manage it somehow.'

And 'somehow' it was managed. 'Somehow' all Molly's wishes came to pass; there was only one little drawback to this week of holiday and happy intercourse with her father. Everybody would ask them out to tea. They were quite like bride and bridegroom; for the fact was, that the late dinners which Mrs Gibson had introduced into her own house were a great inconvenience in the calculations of the small tea-drinkings at Hollingford. How ask people to tea at six, who dined at that hour? How, when they refused cake and sandwiches at half-past eight, how induce other people who were really hungry to commit a vulgarity before those calm and scornful eyes? So there had been a great lull of invitations for the Gibsons to Hollingford tea-parties. Mrs Gibson, whose object was to squeeze herself into 'county society', had taken this being left out of the smaller festivities with great equanimity; but Molly missed the kind homeliness of the parties to which she had gone from time to time as long as she could remember; and though, as each three-cornered note was brought in, she grumbled a little over the loss of another charming evening with her father, she really was glad to go again in the old way among old friends. Miss Browning and Miss Phoebe were especially compassionate towards her in her loneliness. If they had had their will, she would have dined there every day; and she had to call upon them very frequently, in order to prevent their being hurt at her declining the dinners. Mrs Gibson wrote twice during her week's absence to her husband. That piece of news was quite satisfactory to the Miss Brownings, who had of late held themselves a great deal aloof from a house where they chose to suppose that their presence was not wanted. In their winter evenings they had often talked over Mr Gibson's household, and, having little besides conjecture to go upon, they found the subject interminable, as they could vary the possibilities every day. One of their wonders was, how Mr and Mrs Gibson really got on together; another was, whether Mrs Gibson was extravagant or not. Now two letters during the week of her absence showed what was in those days considered a very proper amount of conjugal affection. Yet not too much – at elevenpence-halfpenny postage.* A third letter would have been extravagant. Sister looked to sister with an approving nod, as Molly named the second letter, which arrived in Hollingford the very day before Mrs Gibson was to return. They had settled between themselves that two letters would show the right amount of good feeling and proper understanding in the Gibson family: more would have been excessive; only one would have been a mere matter of duty. There had been rather a question between Miss Browning and Miss Phoebe as to which person the second letter (supposing it came) was to be addressed to. It would be very conjugal to write twice to Mr Gibson; and yet it would be very pretty, if Molly came in for her share.

'You've had another letter, you say, my dear?' asked Miss Browning. 'I daresay Mrs Gibson has written to you this time?'

'It is a large sheet, and Cynthia has written on one half to me, and all the rest is to papa.'

'A very nice arrangement, I'm sure. And what does Cynthia say? Is she enjoying herself?'

'Oh, yes, I think so. They've had a dinner-party; and one night, when mamma was at Lady Cumnor's, Cynthia went to the play with her cousins.'

'Upon my word! and all in one week? I do call that dissipation. Why, Thursday would be taken up with the journey, and Friday with resting, and Sunday is Sunday all the world over; and they must have written on Tuesday. Well! I hope Cynthia won't find Hollingford dull, that's all, when she comes back.'

'I don't think it's likely,' said Miss Phoebe, with a little simper and a knowing look, which sate oddly on her kindly innocent face. 'You see a great deal of Mr Preston, don't you, Molly?'

'Mr Preston!' said Molly, flushing up with surprise. 'No! not much. He's been at Ashcombe all the winter, you know! He has but just come back to settle here. What should make you think so?'

'Oh! a little bird told us,' said Miss Browning. Molly knew that little bird from her childhood, and had always hated it, and longed to wring its neck. Why could not people speak out and say that they did not mean to give up the name of their informant? But it was a very favourite form of fiction with the Miss Brownings, and to Miss Phoebe it was the very acme of wit.

'The little bird was flying about one day in Heath Lane, and it saw Mr Preston and a young lady – we won't say who – walking together in a very friendly manner; that is to say, he was on horseback, but the path is raised above the road, just where there is the little wooden bridge over the brook' —

'Perhaps Molly is in the secret, and we ought not to ask her about it,' said Miss Phoebe, seeing Molly's extreme discomfiture and annoyance.

'It can be no great secret,' said Miss Browning, dropping the little-bird formula, and assuming an air of dignified reproval at Miss Phoebe's interruption, 'for Miss Hornblower says Mr Preston owns to being engaged' —

'At any rate it isn't to Cynthia, that I know positively,' said Molly, with some vehemence. 'And pray put a stop to any such reports; you don't know what mischief they may do. I do so hate that kind of chatter!' It was not very respectful of Molly to speak in this way, certainly; but she thought only of Roger, and the distress any such reports might cause, should he ever hear of them (in the centre of Africa!) made her colour up scarlet with vexation.

'Heighty-teighty! Miss Molly! don't you remember that I am old enough to be your mother, and that it is not pretty behaviour to speak so to us – to me! "Chatter" to be sure. Really, Molly' —

'I beg your pardon,' said Molly, only half-penitent.

'I daresay you did not mean to speak so to sister,' said Miss Phoebe, trying to make peace.

Molly did not answer all at once. She wanted to explain how much mischief might be done by such reports.

'But don't you see,' she went on, still flushed by vexation, 'how bad it is to talk of such things in such a way? Supposing one of them cared for some one else, and that might happen, you know; Mr Preston, for instance, may be engaged to some one else.'

'Molly! I pity the woman! Indeed I do. I have a very poor opinion of Mr Preston,' said Miss Browning, in a warning tone of voice; for a new idea had come into her head.

'Well, but the woman, or young lady, would not like to hear such reports about Mr Preston.'

'Perhaps not. But for all that, take my word for it, he's a great flirt, and young ladies had better not have much to do with him.'

'I daresay it was all accident, their meeting in Heath Lane,' said Miss Phoebe.

'I know nothing about it,' said Molly, 'and I dare say I have been impertinent; only please don't talk about it any more. I have my reasons for asking you.' She got up, for by the striking of the church-clock she had just found out that it was later than she had thought, and she knew that her father would be at home by this time. She bent down and kissed Miss Browning's grave and passive face.

'How you are growing, Molly!' said Miss Phoebe, anxious to cover over her sister's displeasure. 'As tall and as straight as a poplar tree!'* as the old song says.

'Grow in grace, Molly, as well as in good looks!' said Miss Browning, watching her out of the room. As soon as she was fairly gone, Miss Browning got up and shut the door quite securely, and then sitting down near her sister, she said, in a low voice, 'Phoebe, it was Molly herself that was with Mr Preston in Heath Lane, that day when Mrs Goodenough saw them together!'

'Gracious goodness me!' exclaimed Miss Phoebe, receiving it at once as gospel. 'How do you know?'

'By putting two and two together. Didn't you notice how red Molly went, and then pale, and how she said she knew for a fact that Mr Preston and Cynthia Kirkpatrick were not engaged?'

'Perhaps not engaged; but Mrs Goodenough saw them loitering together, all by their own two selves' —

'Mrs Goodenough only crossed Heath Lane at the Shire Oak, as she was riding in her phaeton,'* said Miss Browning sententiously. 'We all know what a coward she is in a carriage, so that most likely she had only half her wits about her, and her eyes are none of the best when she is standing steady on the ground. Molly and Cynthia have got their new plaid shawls just alike, and they trim their bonnets alike, and Molly is grown as tall as Cynthia since Christmas. I was always afraid she'd be short and stumpy; but she's now as tall and slender as any one need be. I'll answer for it, Mrs Goodenough saw Molly, and took her for Cynthia.'

When Miss Browning 'answered for it', Miss Phoebe gave up doubting. She sate some time in silence revolving her thoughts. Then she said —

'It wouldn't be such a very bad match after all, sister.' She spoke very meekly, awaiting her sister's sanction to her opinion.

'Phoebe, it would be a bad match for Mary Pearson's daughter. If I had known what I know now, we'd never have had him to tea last September.'

'Why, what do you know?' asked Miss Phoebe.

'Miss Hornblower told me many things; some that I don't think you ought to hear, Phoebe. He was engaged to a very pretty Miss Gregson, at Henwick, where he comes from; and her father made inquiries, and heard so much that was bad about him that he made his daughter break off the match, and she's dead since!'

'How shocking!' said Miss Phoebe, duly impressed.

'Besides, he plays at billiards, and he bets at races, and some people do say he keeps race-horses.'

'But isn't it strange that the earl keeps him on as his agent?'

'No! perhaps not. He's very clever about land, and very sharp in all law affairs; and my lord isn't bound to take notice – if indeed he knows – of the manner in which Mr Preston talks, when he has taken too much wine.'

'Taken too much wine! Oh, sister, is he a drunkard? and we have had him to tea!'

'I didn't say he was a drunkard, Phoebe,' said Miss Browning pettishly. 'A man may take too much wine occasionally, without being a drunkard. Don't let me hear you using such coarse words, Phoebe!'

Miss Phoebe was silent for a time after this rebuke.

Presently she said, 'I do hope it wasn't Molly Gibson!'

'You may hope as much as you like; but I'm pretty sure it was. However, we'd better say nothing about it to Mrs Goodenough; she has got Cynthia into her head, and there let her rest. Time enough to set reports afloat about Molly when we know there's some truth in them. Mr Preston might do for Cynthia, who's been brought up in France, though she has such pretty manners; but it may have made her not particular. He must not, and he shall not, have Molly, if I go into church and forbid the banns myself; but I'm afraid – I'm afraid, there's something between her and him. We must keep on the look-out, Phoebe. I'll be her guardian angel, in spite of herself.'

CHAPTER 41

Gathering Clouds

Mrs Gibson came back full of rose-coloured accounts of London. Lady Cumnor had been gracious and affectionate, 'so touched by my going up to see her so soon after her return to England'; Lady Harriet charming and devoted to her old governess; Lord Cumnor 'just like his dear usual hearty self'; and, as for the Kirkpatricks, no Lord Chancellor's house was ever grander than theirs, and the silk-gown of the Q.C. had floated over housemaids and footmen. Cynthia, too, was so much admired; and, as for her dress, Mrs Kirkpatrick had showered down ball-dresses and wreaths, and pretty bonnets and mantles, like a fairy-godmother. Mr Gibson's poor present of ten pounds shrank into very small dimensions, compared with all this munificence.

'And they're so fond of her, I don't know when we shall have her back!' was Mrs Gibson's winding-up sentence. 'And now, Molly, what have you and papa been doing? Very gay, you sounded in your letter. I had not time to read it in London; so I put it in my pocket, and read it in the coach coming home. But, my dear child, you do look so old-fashioned with your gown made all tight, and your hair all tumbling about in curls. Curls are quite gone out. We must do your hair differently,' she continued, trying to smooth Molly's black waves into straightness.

'I sent Cynthia an African letter,' said Molly timidly. 'Did you hear anything of what was in it?'

'Oh, yes, poor child! It made her very uneasy, I think; she said she did not feel inclined to go to Mr Rawson's ball, which was on that night, and for which Mrs Kirkpatrick had given her the ball-dress. But there was really nothing for her to fidget herself about. Roger only said he had had another touch of fever, but was better when he wrote. He says every European has to be acclimatised by fever, in that part of Abyssinia where he is.'

'And did she go?' asked Molly.

'Yes, to be sure. It is not an engagement; and, if it were, it is not acknowledged. Fancy her going and saying, "A young man that I know has been ill for a few days in Africa, two months ago, therefore I don't want to go to the ball tonight!" It would have seemed like affectation of sentiment; and, if there's one thing I hate, it is that.'

'She would hardly enjoy herself,' said Molly.

'Oh, yes, but she did! Her dress was white gauze, trimmed with lilacs, and she really did look – a mother may be allowed a little natural partiality – most lovely. And she danced every dance, although she was quite a stranger. I am sure she enjoyed herself, from her manner of talking about it the next morning.'

'I wonder if the Squire knows!'

'Knows what? Oh, yes, to be sure – you mean about Roger. I daresay he doesn't; and there's no need to tell him, for I've no doubt it is all right now.' And she went out of the room, to finish her unpacking.

Molly let her work fall, and sighed. 'It will be a year the day after tomorrow, since he came here to propose our going to Hurst Wood, and mamma was so vexed at his calling before lunch. I wonder if Cynthia remembers it as well as I do. And now perhaps—Oh, Roger, Roger! I wish – I pray that you were safe home again! How could we all bear it, if—'

She covered her face with her hands, and tried to stop thinking. Suddenly she got up, as if stung by a venomous fancy.

'I don't believe she loves him as she ought, or she could not – could not have gone and danced. What shall I do if she does not? What shall I do? I can bear anything but that!'

But she found the long suspense as to his health hard enough to endure. They were not likely to hear from him for a month at least, and before that time had elapsed Cynthia would be at home again. Molly learnt to long for her return, before a fortnight of her absence was over. She had had no idea that perpetual *tête-à-têtes* with Mrs Gibson could, by any possibility, be so tiresome as she found them. Perhaps Molly's state of delicate health, consequent upon her rapid growth during the last few months, made her irritable; but, really, often she had to get up and leave the room, to calm herself down after listening to a long series of words, more frequently plaintive or discontented in tone than cheerful, and which at the end conveyed no distinct impression of either the speaker's thought or feeling. Whenever anything had gone wrong; whenever Mr Gibson had coolly persevered in anything to which she had objected; whenever the cook had made a mistake about the dinner, or the housemaid broken any little frangible* article; whenever Molly's hair was not done to her liking, or her dress did not become her, or the smell of dinner pervaded the house, or the wrong callers came, or the right callers did not come – in fact, whenever anything went wrong – poor Mr Kirkpatrick was regretted and mourned over, nay, almost blamed, as if, had he only given himself the trouble of living, he could have helped it.

'When I look back to those happy days, it seems to me as if I had never valued them as I ought. To be sure – youth, love – what did we care for poverty! I remember dear Mr Kirkpatrick walking five miles into Stratford to buy me a muffin, because I had such a fancy for one after Cynthia was born. I don't mean to complain of dear papa – but I don't think – but perhaps I ought not to say it to you. If Mr Kirkpatrick had but taken care of that cough of his; but he was so obstinate! Men always are, I think. And it really was selfish of him. Only, I daresay, he did not consider the forlorn state in which I should be left. It came harder upon me than upon most people, because I always was of such an affectionate, sensitive nature. I remember a little poem of Mr Kirkpatrick's, in which he compared my heart to a harpstring, vibrating to the slightest breeze.'

'I thought harpstrings required a pretty strong finger to make them sound,' said Molly.

'My dear child, you've no more poetry in you than your father. And as for your hair! it's worse than ever. Can't you drench it in water, to take those untidy twists and twirls out of it?'

'It only makes it curl more and more, when it gets dry,' said Molly, sudden tears coming into her eyes as a recollection came before her like a picture seen long ago and forgotten for years – a young mother watching and dressing her little girl; placing the half-naked darling on her knee, and twining the wet rings of dark hair fondly round her fingers, and then, in an ecstasy of fondness, kissing the little curly head.

The receipt of Cynthia's letters made very agreeable events. She did not write often, but her letters were tolerably long when they did come, and very sprightly in tone. There was constant mention made of many new names, which conveyed no idea to Molly, though Mrs Gibson would try and enlighten her by running commentaries like the following –

'Mrs Green! ah, that's Mr Jones's pretty cousin, who lives in Russell Square with the fat husband. They keep their carriage; but I'm not sure if it is not Mr Green who is Mrs Jones's cousin. We can ask Cynthia, when she comes home. Mr Henderson! to be sure – a young man with black whiskers, a pupil of Mr Kirkpatrick's formerly – or was he a pupil of Mr Murray's? I know they said he had read law with somebody. Ah, yes! they are the people who called the day after Mr Rawson's ball, and who admired Cynthia so much, without knowing I was her mother. She was very handsomely dressed indeed, in black satin; and the son had a glass eye, but he was a young man of good property. Coleman! yes, that was the name.'

No more news of Roger, until some time after Cynthia had returned from her London visit. She came back, looking fresher and prettier than ever, beautifully dressed, thanks to her own good taste and her cousins' generosity, full of amusing details of the gay life she had been enjoying, yet not at all out of spirits at having left it behind her. She brought home all sorts of pretty and dainty devices for Molly: a neck-ribbon made up in the newest fashion, a pattern for a tippet, a delicate pair of tight gloves, embroidered as Molly had never seen gloves embroidered before, and many another little sign of remembrance during her absence. Yet somehow or other, Molly felt that Cynthia was changed in her relation to her. Molly was aware that she had never had Cynthia's full confidence, for with all her apparent frankness and *naïveté* of manner, Cynthia was extremely reserved and reticent. She knew this much of herself, and had often laughed about it to Molly, and the latter had by this time found out the truth of her friend's assertion. But Molly did not trouble herself much about it. She too knew that there were many thoughts and feelings that flitted through her mind which she should never think of telling to any one, except perhaps – if they were ever very much thrown together – to her father. She knew that Cynthia withheld from her more than thoughts and feelings – that she withheld facts. But then, as Molly reflected, these facts might involve details of struggle and suffering – might relate to her mother's neglect – and altogether be of so painful a character, that it would be well if Cynthia could forget her childhood altogether, instead of fixing it in her mind by the relation of her grievances and troubles. So it was not now by any want of confidence that Molly felt distanced, as it were. It was because Cynthia rather avoided than sought her companionship; because her eyes shunned the straight, serious, loving look of Molly's; because there were certain subjects on which she evidently disliked speaking – not particularly interesting things, as far as Molly could perceive; but it almost seemed as if they lay on the road to points to be avoided. Molly felt a sort of sighing pleasure in noticing Cynthia's changed manner of talking about Roger. She spoke of him tenderly now – 'poor Roger', as she called him; and Molly thought that she must be referring to the illness which he had mentioned in his last letter. One morning in the first week after Cynthia's return home, just as he was going out, Mr Gibson ran up into the drawing-room, booted and spurred, and hastily laid an open pamphlet down before her; pointing out a particular passage with his finger, but not speaking a word before he rapidly quitted the room. His eyes were sparkling, and had an amused as well as pleased expression. All this Molly noticed, as well as Cynthia's flush of colour, as she read what was thus pointed out to her. Then she pushed it a little on one side, not closing the book, however, and went on with her work.

'What is it? may I see it?' asked Molly, stretching out her hand for the pamphlet, which lay within her reach. But she did not take it, until Cynthia had said –

'Certainly; I don't suppose there are any great secrets in a scientific journal, full of reports of meetings.' And she gave the book a little push towards Molly.

'Oh, Cynthia!' said Molly, catching her breath as she read, 'are you not proud?' For it was an account of an annual gathering of the Geographical Society,* and Lord Hollingford had read a letter he had received from Roger Hamley, dated from Arracuoba, a district in Africa, hitherto unvisited by any intelligent European traveller, and about which Mr Hamley sent many curious particulars. The reading of this letter had been received with the greatest interest, and several subsequent speakers had paid the writer very high compliments.

But Molly might have known Cynthia better than to expect an answer responsive to the feelings that prompted her question. Let Cynthia be ever so proud, ever so glad, or so grateful, or even indignant, remorseful, grievous or sorry, the very fact that she was expected by another to entertain any of these emotions, would have been enough to prevent her expressing them.

'I'm afraid I'm not as much struck by the wonder of the thing as you are, Molly. Besides, it is not news to me; at least, not entirely. I heard of the meeting before I left London; it was a good deal talked about in my uncle's set; to be sure, I didn't hear all the fine things they say of him there – but then, you know, that's a mere fashion of speaking, which means nothing; somebody is bound to pay compliments, when a lord takes the trouble to read one of his letters aloud.'

'Nonsense!' said Molly. 'You know you don't believe what you are saying, Cynthia.'

Cynthia gave that pretty little jerk of her shoulders, which was her equivalent for a French shrug, but did not lift up her head from her sewing. Molly began to read the report over again.

'Why, Cynthia!' she said, 'you might have been there; ladies were there. It says "many ladies were present". Oh, couldn't you have managed to go? If your uncle's set cared about these things, wouldn't some of them have taken you?'

'Perhaps, if I had asked them. But I think they would have been rather astonished at my sudden turn for science.'

'You might have told your uncle how matters really stood; he wouldn't have talked about it, if you had wished him not, I am sure, and he could have helped you.'

'Once for all, Molly,' said Cynthia, now laying down her work, and speaking with quick authority, 'do learn to understand that it is, and always has been my wish, not to have the relation which Roger and I bear to each other, mentioned or talked about. When the right time comes, I will make it known to my uncle, and to everybody whom it may concern; but I am not going to make mischief, and get myself into trouble – even for the sake of hearing compliments paid to him – by letting it out before the time. If I'm pushed to it, I'd sooner break it off altogether at once, and have done with it. I can't be worse off than I am now.' Her angry tone had changed into a kind of desponding complaint, before she had ended her sentence. Molly looked at her with dismay.

'I can't understand you, Cynthia,' she said at length.

'No, I daresay you can't,' said Cynthia, looking at her with tears in her eyes, and very tenderly, as if in atonement for her late vehemence. 'I am afraid – I hope – you never will.'

In a moment, Molly's arms were round her. 'Oh, Cynthia,' she murmured, 'have I been plaguing you? Have I vexed you? Don't say you're afraid of my knowing you! Of course you've your faults, everybody has; but I think I love you the better for them.'

'I don't know that I am so very bad,' said Cynthia, smiling a little through the tears that Molly's words and caresses had forced to overflow from her eyes. 'But I've got into scrapes. I'm in a scrape now. I do sometimes believe I shall always be in scrapes; and, if they ever come to light, I shall seem to be worse than I really am, and I know your father will throw me off, and I – no, I won't be afraid that you will, Molly.'

'I'm sure I shan't. Are they – do you think – how would Roger take it?' asked Molly, very timidly.

'I don't know. I hope he will never hear of it. I don't see why he should, for in a little while I shall be quite clear again. It all came about without my ever thinking I was doing wrong. I've a great mind to tell you all about it, Molly.'

Molly did not like to urge it, though she longed to know, and to see if she could not offer help; but, while Cynthia was hesitating, and perhaps, to say the truth, rather regretting that she had even made this slight advance towards bestowing her confidence, Mrs Gibson came in, full of some manner of altering a gown of hers, so as to make it into the fashion of the day, as she had seen it during her visit to London. Cynthia seemed to forget her tears and her troubles, and to throw her soul into millinery.

Cynthia's correspondence went on pretty briskly with her London cousins, according to the usual rate of correspondence in those days. Indeed, Mrs Gibson was occasionally inclined to complain of the frequency of Helen Kirkpatrick's letters; for, before the penny post came in, the recipient had to pay the postage of letters; and elevenpence-halfpenny three times a week came, according to Mrs Gibson's mode of reckoning when annoyed, to a sum 'between three and four shillings'. But these complaints were only for the family; they saw the wrong side of the tapestry. Hollingford in general, the Miss Brownings in particular, heard of 'dear Helen's enthusiastic friendship for Cynthia', and of 'the real pleasure it was to receive such constant news – relays of news, indeed – from London. It was almost as good as living there!'

'A great deal better, I should think,' said Miss Browning, with some severity. For she had got many of her notions of the metropolis from the British Essayists,* where town is so often represented as the centre of dissipation, corrupting country-wives and squires' daughters, and unfitting them for all their duties by the constant whirl of its not always innocent pleasures. London was a sort of moral pitch, which few could touch and not be defiled. Miss Browning had been on the watch for the signs of deterioration in Cynthia's character, ever since her return home.

But, except in a greater number of pretty and becoming articles of dress, there was no great change for the worse to be perceived. Cynthia had been 'in the world', had 'beheld the glare and glitter and dazzling display of London', yet had come back to Hollingford, as ready as ever to place a chair for Miss Browning, or to gather flowers for a nosegay for Miss Phoebe, or to mend her own clothes. But all this was set down to the merits of Cynthia, not to the credit of London-town.

'As far as I can judge of London,' said Miss Browning, sententiously continuing her tirade against the place, 'it's no better than a pick-pocket and a robber dressed up in the spoils of honest folk. I should like to know where my Lord Hollingford was bred, and Mr Roger Hamley. Your good husband lent me that report of the meeting, Mrs Gibson, where so much was said about them both; and he was as proud of their praises as if he had been akin to them; and Phoebe read it aloud to me, for the print was too small for my eyes; she was a good deal perplexed with all the new names of places, but I said she'd better skip them, for we had never heard of them before, and probably should never hear of them again; but she read out the fine things they said of my lord, and Mr Roger – and I put it to you, where were they born and bred? Why, within eight miles of Hollingford; it might have been Molly there or me; it's all a chance; and then they go and talk about the pleasures of intellectual society in London, and the distinguished people up there that it is such an advantage to know, and all the time I know it's only shops and the play that's the real attraction. But that's neither here nor there. We all put our best foot foremost, and, if we have a reason to give that looks sensible, we speak it out like men, and never say anything about the silliness we are hugging to our heart. But I ask you again, where does this fine society come from, and these wise men, and these distinguished travellers? Why, out of country parishes like this! London picks 'em all up, and decks herself with them, and then calls out to the folks she's robbed, and says, "Come and see how fine I am". "Fine", indeed! I've no patience with London: Cynthia is much better out of it; and I'm not sure, if I were you, Mrs Gibson, if I wouldn't stop those London letters: they'll only be unsettling her.'

'But perhaps she may live in London some of these days, Miss Browning,' simpered Mrs Gibson.

'Time enough then to be thinking of London. I wish her an

honest country husband, with enough to live upon, and a little to lay by, and a good character to boot. Mind that, Molly,' said she, firing round upon the startled Molly; 'I wish Cynthia a husband with a good character; but she's got a mother to look after her; you've none, and when your mother was alive she was a dear friend of mine: so I'm not going to let you throw yourself away upon any one whose life isn't clear and aboveboard, you may depend upon it!'

This last speech fell like a bomb into the quiet little drawing-room, it was delivered with such vehemence. Miss Browning, in her secret heart, meant it as a warning against the intimacy she believed that Molly had formed with Mr Preston; but, as it happened that Molly had never dreamed of any such intimacy, the girl could not imagine why such severity of speech should be addressed to her. Mrs Gibson, who always took up the points of every word or action where they touched her own self (and called it sensitiveness), broke the silence that followed Miss Browning's speech by saying, plaintively –

'I'm sure, Miss Browning, you are very much mistaken, if you think that any mother could take more care of Molly than I do. I don't – I can't think there is any need for any one to interfere to protect her; and I have not an idea why you have been talking in this way, just as if we were all wrong and you were all right. It hurts my feelings, indeed it does; for Molly can tell you there is not a thing or a favour that Cynthia has, that she has not. And, as for not taking care of her, why, if she were to go up to London tomorrow, I should make a point of going with her to see after her; and I never did it for Cynthia, when she was at school in France; and her bed-room is furnished just like Cynthia's, and I let her wear my red shawl whenever she likes – she might have it oftener, if she would. I can't think what you mean, Miss Browning.'

'I did not mean to offend you, but I meant just to give Molly a hint. She understands what I mean.'

'I'm sure I don't,' said Molly boldly. 'I haven't a notion what you meant, if you were alluding to anything more than you said straight out – that you do not wish me to marry any one who hasn't a good character, and that, as you were a friend of mamma's, you would prevent my marrying a man with a bad character, by every means in your power. I'm not thinking of marrying; I don't want to marry anybody at all; but, if I did, and he were not a good man, I should thank you for coming and warning me of it.'

'I shall not stand on warning you, Molly. I shall forbid the banns in church, if need be,' said Miss Browning, half convinced of the clear transparent truth of what Molly had said – blushing all over, it is true, but with her steady eyes fixed on Miss Browning's face while she spoke.

'Do!' said Molly.

'Well, well, I won't say any more. Perhaps I was mistaken. We won't say any more about it. But remember what I have said, Molly; there's no harm in that, at any rate. I'm sorry I hurt your feelings, Mrs Gibson. As stepmothers go, I think you try and do your duty. Good morning. Good-bye to you both, and God bless you!'

If Miss Browning thought that her final blessing would secure peace in the room she was leaving, she was very much mistaken; Mrs Gibson burst out with –

'Try and do my duty, indeed! I should be much obliged to you, Molly, if you would take care not to behave in such a manner as to bring down upon me such impertinence as I have just been receiving from Miss Browning.'

'But I don't know what made her talk as she did, mamma,' said Molly.

'I'm sure I don't know, and I don't care either. But I know that I never was spoken to as if I was trying to do my duty before – "trying", indeed! everybody always knew that I did it, without talking about it before my face in that rude manner. I've that deep feeling about duty, that I think it ought only to be talked about in church, and in such sacred places as that; not to have a common caller startling one with it, even though she was an early friend of your mother's. And as if I didn't look after you quite as much as I look after Cynthia! Why, it was only yesterday I went up into Cynthia's room and found her reading a letter that she put away in a hurry as soon as I came in, and I didn't even ask her who it was from; and I'm sure I should have made you tell me.'

Very likely. Mrs Gibson shrank from any conflicts with Cynthia, pretty sure that she would be worsted in the end; while Molly generally submitted, sooner than have any struggle for her own will.

Just then Cynthia came in.

'What's the matter?' said she quickly, seeing that something was wrong.

'Why, Molly has been doing something which has set that impertinent Miss Browning off into lecturing me on trying to do my duty! If your poor father had but lived, Cynthia, I should never have been spoken to as I have been. "A stepmother trying to do her duty, indeed!" That was Miss Browning's expression.'

Any allusion to her father took from Cynthia all desire of irony. She came forward, and again asked Molly what was the matter.

Molly, herself ruffled, made answer –

'Miss Browning seemed to think I was likely to marry some one whose character was objectionable'—

'You, Molly?' said Cynthia.

'Yes – she once before spoke to me, – I suspect she has got some notion about Mr Preston in her head'—

Cynthia sate down quite suddenly. Molly went on – 'And she spoke, as if mamma did not look enough after me, – I think she was rather provoking'—

'Not rather, but very – very impertinent,' said Mrs Gibson, a little soothed by Molly's recognition of her grievance.

'What could have put it into her head?' said Cynthia, very quietly, taking her sewing as she spoke.

'I don't know,' said her mother, replying to the question after her own fashion. 'I'm sure I don't always approve of Mr Preston; but, even if it was him she was thinking about, he's far more agreeable than she is; and I had much rather have him coming to call than an old maid like her any day.'

'I don't know that it was Mr Preston she was thinking about,' said Molly. 'It was only a guess. When you were both in London, she spoke about him – I thought she had heard something about you and him, Cynthia.' Unseen by her mother, Cynthia looked up at Molly, her eyes full of prohibition, her cheeks full of angry colour. Molly stopped short suddenly. After that look she was surprised at the quietness with which Cynthia said, almost immediately –

'Well, after all, it is only your fancy that she was alluding to Mr Preston, so perhaps we had better not say any more about him; and, as for her advice to mamma to look after you better, Miss Molly, I'll stand bail for your good behaviour; for both mamma and I know you're the last person to do any foolish things in that way. And now, don't let us talk any more about it. I was coming to tell you that Hannah Brand's little boy has been badly burnt, and his sister is downstairs asking for old linen.'

Mrs Gibson was always kind to poor people, and she immediately got up and went to her stores, to search for the article wanted.

Cynthia turned quietly round to Molly.

'Molly, pray don't ever allude to anything between me and Mr Preston, – not to mamma, nor to any one! Never do! I've a reason for it, – don't say anything more about it, ever!'

Mrs Gibson came back at this moment, and Molly had to stop short again on the brink of Cynthia's confidence; uncertain indeed this time, whether she would have been told anything more, and only sure that she had annoyed Cynthia a good deal.

But the time was approaching, when she would know all.

CHAPTER 42

The Storm Bursts

The autumn drifted away through all its seasons. The golden corn-harvest; the walks through the stubble-fields, and rambles into hazel-copses in search of nuts; the stripping of the apple-orchards of their ruddy fruit, amid the joyous cries and shouts of watching children, and the gorgeous tulip-like colouring of the later time, had now come on with the shortening days. There was comparative silence in the land, excepting for the distant shots and the whirr of the partridges as they rose up from the field.

Ever since Miss Browning's unlucky conversation, things had been ajar in the Gibsons' house. Cynthia seemed to keep every one out at (mental) arms'-length, and particularly avoided any private talks with Molly. Mrs Gibson, still cherishing a grudge against Miss Browning for her implied accusation of not looking enough after Molly, chose to exercise a most wearying supervision over the poor girl. It was, 'Where have you been, child?' 'Who did you see?' 'Who was that letter from?' 'Why were you so long out, when you had only to go to so-and-so?' just as if Molly had really been detected in carrying on some underhand intercourse. She answered every question asked of her with the simple truthfulness of perfect innocence; but the inquiries (although she read their motive, and knew that they arose from no especial suspicion of her conduct, but were only made, that Mrs Gibson might be able to say that she looked well after her stepdaughter,) chafed her inexpressibly. Very often she did not go out at all, sooner than have to give a plan of her intended proceedings, when perhaps she had no plan whatever – only thought of wandering out at her own sweet will,* and of taking pleasure in the bright solemn fading of the year. It was a very heavy time for Molly – zest and life had fled, and left so many of the old delights mere shells of seeming. She thought it was that her youth had fled – at nineteen! Cynthia was no longer the same, somehow: and perhaps Cynthia's change would injure her in the distant Roger's opinion. Her stepmother seemed almost kind, in comparison with Cynthia's withdrawal of her heart; Mrs Gibson worried her, to be sure, with all these forms of watching over her; but in every other way, she, at any rate, was the same. Yet Cynthia herself seemed anxious and careworn, though she would not speak of her anxieties to Molly. And then the poor girl, in her goodness, would blame herself for feeling Cynthia's change of manner; for, as Molly said to herself, 'If it is hard work for me to help always fretting after Roger, and wondering where he is, and how he is, what must it be for her?'

One day Mr Gibson came in, bright and swift.

'Molly,' said he, 'where's Cynthia?'

'Gone out to do some errands'—

'Well, it's a pity – but never mind! Put on your bonnet and cloak as fast as you can! I've had to borrow old Simpson's dog-cart – there would have been room both for you and Cynthia; but, as it is, you must walk back alone. I'll drive you as far on the Barford road as I can, and then you must jump down. I can't take you on to Broadhurst's; I may be kept there for hours.'

Mrs Gibson was out of the room; out of the house, it might be, for all Molly cared, now she had her father's leave and command. Her bonnet and cloak were on in two minutes, and she was sitting by her father's side, the back-seat shut up, and the light-weight going swiftly and merrily bumping over the stone-paved lanes.

'Oh, this is charming!' said Molly, after a toss-up on her seat from a tremendous bump.

'For youth, but not for crabbed age,'* said Mr Gibson. 'My bones are getting rheumatic, and would rather go smoothly over macadamized streets.'*

'That's treason to this lovely view and this fine pure air, papa! Only I don't believe you!'

'Thank you. As you are so complimentary, I think I shall put you down at the foot of this hill; we've passed the second mile-stone from Hollingford.'

'Oh, let me just go up to the top! I know we can see the blue range of the Malverns from it, and Dorrimer Hall among the woods; the horse will want a minute's rest, and then I will get down without a word.'

She went up to the top of the hill; and there they sate still a minute or two, enjoying the view, without much speaking. The woods were golden; the old house of purple-red brick, with its twisted chimneys, rose up from among them facing on to green lawns, and a placid lake; beyond again were the Malvern Hills.

'Now jump down, lassie, and make the best of your way home before it gets dark! You'll find the cut over Croston Heath shorter than the road we've come by.'

To reach Croston Heath, Molly had to go down a narrow lane overshadowed by trees, with picturesque old cottages dotted here and there on the steep sandy banks; and then there came a small wood, and then there was a brook to be crossed on a plank-bridge, and up the steeper fields on the opposite side were cut steps in the turfy path; these ended, she was on Croston Heath, a wide-stretching common skirted by labourers' dwellings, past which a near road to Hollingford lay.

The loneliest part of the road was the first – the lane, the wood, the little bridge, and the clambering through the upland fields. But Molly cared little for loneliness. She went along the lane under the overarching elm-branches, from which, here and there, a yellow leaf came floating down upon her very dress; past the last cottage where a little child had tumbled down the sloping bank, and was publishing the accident with frightened cries. Molly stooped to pick it up, and, holding it in her arms in a manner which caused intense surprise to take the place of alarm in its little breast, she carried it up the rough flag-steps towards the cottage which she supposed to be its home. The mother came running in from the garden behind the house, still holding the late damsons she had been gathering in her apron; but, on seeing her, the little creature held out its arms to go to her, and she dropped her damsons all about as she took it, and began to soothe it as it cried afresh, interspersing her lulling with thanks to Molly. She called her by her name; and, on Molly asking the woman how she came to know it, she replied that before her marriage she had been a servant of Mrs Goodenough, and so was 'bound to know Dr Gibson's daughter by sight.' After the exchange of two or three more words, Molly ran down the lane, and pursued her way, stopping here and there to gather a nosegay of such leaves as struck her for their brilliant colouring. She entered the wood. As she turned a corner in the lonely path, she heard a passionate voice of distress; and in an instant she recognised Cynthia's tones. She stood still and looked around. There were some thick holly bushes shining out dark-green in the midst of the amber and scarlet foliage. If any one was there, it must be behind these. So Molly left the path, and went straight, plunging through the brown tangled growth of ferns and underwood, and turned the holly-bushes. There stood Mr Preston and Cynthia; he holding her hands tight, each looking as if just silenced in some vehement talk by the rustle of Molly's footsteps.

For an instant no one spoke. Then Cynthia said –

'Oh, Molly, Molly, come and judge between us!'

Mr Preston let go Cynthia's hands slowly, with a look that was more of a sneer than a smile; and yet he, too, had been strongly agitated, whatever was the subject in dispute. Molly came forward and took Cynthia's arm, her eyes steadily fixed on Mr Preston's face. It was fine to see the fearlessness of her perfect innocence. He could not bear her look, and said to Cynthia –

'The subject of our conversation does not well admit of a third person's presence. As Miss Gibson seems to wish for your company now, I must beg you to fix some other time and place where we can finish our discussion.'

'I will go, if Cynthia wishes me,' said Molly.

'No, no; stay – I want you to stay – I want you to hear it all – I wish I had told you sooner.'

'You mean that you regret that she has not been made aware of our engagement – that you promised long ago to be my wife. Pray remember that it was you who made me promise secrecy, not I you!'

'I don't believe him, Cynthia. Don't, don't cry, if you can help it; I don't believe him.'

'Cynthia,' said he, suddenly changing his tone to fervid tenderness, 'pray, pray do not go on so; you can't think how it distresses me!' He stepped forward, to try and take her hand and soothe her; but she shrank away from him, and sobbed the more irrepressibly. She felt Molly's presence so much to be a protection that now she dared to let herself go, and weaken herself by giving way to her emotion.

'Go away!' said Molly. 'Don't you see you make her worse?' But he did not stir; he was looking at Cynthia so intently that he did not seem even to hear Molly. 'Go!' said she, vehemently, 'if it really distresses you to see her cry. Don't you see it's you who are the cause of it?'

'I will go, if Cynthia tells me,' said he at length.

'Oh, Molly, I don't know what to do,' said Cynthia, taking down her hands from her tear-stained face, and appealing to Molly, and sobbing worse than ever; in fact, she became hysterical, and, though she tried to speak coherently, no intelligible words would come.

'Run to that cottage in the trees, and fetch her a cup of water,' said Molly. He hesitated a little.

'Why don't you go?' said Molly impatiently.

'I have not done speaking to her; you will not leave before I come back?'

'No. Don't you see she can't move in this state?'

He went quickly, if reluctantly.

Cynthia was some time before she could check her sobs enough to speak. At length she said –

'Molly, I do hate him!'

'But what did he mean by saying you were engaged to him? Don't cry, dear, but tell me; if I can help you, I will; but I can't imagine what it all really is.'

'It's too long a story to tell now, and I'm not strong enough. Look! he's coming back. As soon as I can, let us get home!'

'With all my heart,' said Molly.

He brought the water, and Cynthia drank, and was restored to calmness.

'Now,' said Molly, 'we had better go home, as fast as you can manage it; it's getting dark quickly.'

If she hoped to carry Cynthia off so easily, she was mistaken. Mr Preston was resolute on this point. He said –

'I think, since Miss Gibson has made herself acquainted with this much, we had better let her know the whole truth – that you are engaged to marry me as soon as you are twenty; otherwise your being here with me, and by appointment too, may appear strange – even equivocal – to her.'

'As I know that Cynthia is engaged to another man, you can hardly expect me to believe what you say, Mr Preston.'

'Oh, Molly,' said Cynthia, trembling all over, but trying to be calm, 'I am not engaged – neither to the person you mean, nor to Mr Preston.'

Mr Preston forced a smile. 'I think I have some letters that would convince Miss Gibson of the truth of what I have said; and which will convince Mr Osborne Hamley, if necessary – I conclude it is to him she is alluding.'

'I am quite puzzled by you both,' said Molly. 'The only thing I do know is, that we ought not to be standing here at this time of evening, and that Cynthia and I must go home directly. If you want to talk to Miss Kirkpatrick, Mr Preston, why don't you come to my father's house, and ask to see her openly, and like a gentleman?'

'I am perfectly willing,' said he; 'I shall only be too glad to explain to Mr Gibson on what terms I stand in relation to her. If I have not done it sooner, it is because I have yielded to her wishes.'

'Pray, pray don't, Molly – you don't know all – you don't know anything about it; you mean well and kindly, I know, but you are only making mischief. I am quite well enough to walk, do let us go; I will tell you all about it, when we are at home.' She took Molly's arm and tried to hasten her away; but Mr Preston followed, talking as he walked by their side.

'I do not know what you will say at home; but can you deny that you are my promised wife? can you deny that it has only been at your earnest request that I have kept the engagement secret so long?' He was unwise – Cynthia stopped, and turned at bay.

'Since you will have it out – since I must speak, I own that what you say is literally true; that, when I was a neglected girl of sixteen, you – whom I believed to be a friend – lent me money at my need, and made me give you a promise of marriage.'

' "Made you"!' said he, laying an emphasis on the first word.

Cynthia turned scarlet. ' "Made" is not the right word, I confess. I liked you then – you were almost my only friend – and, if it had been a question of immediate marriage, I dare say I should never have objected. But I know you better now; and you have persecuted me so of late, that I tell you once for all (as I have told you before, till I am sick of the very words), that nothing shall ever make me marry you. Nothing! I see there's no chance of escaping exposure and, I dare say, losing my character and, I know, losing all the few friends I have.'

'Never me,' said Molly, touched by the wailing tone of despair that Cynthia was falling into.

'It is hard,' said Mr Preston. 'You may believe all the bad things you like about me, Cynthia, but I don't think you can doubt my real, passionate, disinterested love for you.'

'I do doubt it,' said Cynthia, breaking out with fresh energy. 'Ah! when I think of the self-denying affection I have seen – I have known – affection that thought of others before itself—'

Mr Preston broke in at the pause she made. She was afraid of revealing too much to him.

'You do not call it love which has been willing to wait for years – to be silent while silence was desired – to suffer jealousy and to bear neglect, relying on the solemn promise of a girl of sixteen – for "solemn" say "flimsy", when that girl grows older! Cynthia, I have loved you, and I do love you, and I can't give you up. If you will but keep your word, and marry me, I'll swear I'll make you love me in return.'

'Oh, I wish – I wish I'd never borrowed that unlucky money; it was the beginning of it all. Oh, Molly, I have saved and scrimped to repay it, and he won't take it now; I thought, if I could but repay it, it would set me free.'

'You seem to imply you sold yourself for twenty pounds,' he said. They were nearly on the common now, close to the protection of the cottages, in very hearing of their inmates; if neither of the other two thought of this, Molly did, and resolved in her mind to call in at one of them, and ask for the labourer's protection home; at any rate, his presence must put a stop to this miserable altercation.

'I did not "sell" myself; I liked you then. But oh, how I do hate you now!' cried Cynthia, unable to contain her words.

He bowed and turned back, vanishing rapidly down the field staircase. At any rate, that was a relief. Yet the two girls hastened on, as if he was still pursuing them. Once, when Molly said something to Cynthia, the latter replied –

'Molly, if you pity me – if you love me – don't say anything more just now! We shall have to look as if nothing had happened when we get home. Come to my room, when we go upstairs to bed, and I'll tell you all. I know you'll blame me terribly; but I will tell you all.'

So Molly did not say another word till they reached home; and then, comparatively at ease, inasmuch as no one perceived how late was their return to the house, each of the girls went up into their separate rooms, to rest and calm themselves before dressing for the necessary family-gathering at dinner. Molly felt as if she were so miserably shaken that she could not have gone down at all, if her own interests only had been at stake. She sate by her dressing-table, holding her head in her hands, her candles unlighted, and the room in soft darkness, trying to still her beating heart, and to recall all she had heard, and what would be its bearing on the lives of those whom she loved. Roger! Oh, Roger! – far away in the mysterious darkness of distance – loving as he did, (ah, that was love! that was the love to which Cynthia had referred, as worthy of the name!) and the object of his love claimed by another – false to one she must be! How could it be? What would he think and feel if ever he came to know it? It was of no use trying to imagine his pain – that could do no good. What lay before Molly was, to try and extricate Cynthia, if she could help her by thought, or advice, or action; not to weaken herself by letting her fancy run into pictures of possible, probable, suffering.

When she went into the drawing-room before dinner, she found Cynthia and her mother by themselves. There were candles in the room, but they were not lighted; for the wood-fire blazed merrily and fitfully, and they were waiting for Mr Gibson's return, which might be expected at any minute. Cynthia sate in the shade; so it was only by her sensitive ear that Molly could judge of her state of composure. Mrs Gibson was telling some of her day's adventures – whom she had found at home in the calls she had been making; who had been out; and the small pieces of news she had heard. To Molly's quick sympathy Cynthia's voice sounded languid and weary; but she made all the proper replies, and expressed the proper interest at the right places; and Molly came to the rescue, chiming in, with an effort, it is true, but Mrs Gibson was not one to notice slight shades or differences in manner. When Mr Gibson returned, the relative positions of the parties were altered. It was Cynthia now who raised herself into liveliness, partly from a consciousness that he would have noticed any depression, and partly because Cynthia was one of those natural coquettes, who, from their cradle to their grave, instinctively bring out all their prettiest airs and graces, in order to stand well with any man, young or old, who may happen to be present. She listened to his remarks and stories with all the sweet intentness of happier days, till Molly, silent and wondering, could hardly believe that the Cynthia before her was the same girl as she who was sobbing and crying as if her heart would break, but two hours before. It is true, she looked pale and heavy-eyed; but that was the only sign she gave of her past trouble, which yet must be a present care, thought Molly. After dinner, Mr Gibson went out to his town-patients; Mrs Gibson subsided into her arm-chair, holding a sheet of the *Times* before her, behind which she took a quiet and lady-like doze. Cynthia had a book in one hand, with the other she shaded her eyes from the light. Molly alone could neither read, nor sleep, nor work. She sate in the seat in the bow window; the blind was not drawn down, for there was no danger of their being overlooked. She gazed into the soft outer darkness, and found herself striving to discern the outlines of objects – the cottage at the end of the garden – the great beech-tree with the seat round it – the wire-arches, up which the summer-roses had clambered; each came out faint and dim against the dusky velvet of the atmosphere. Presently tea came, and there was the usual nightly bustle. The table was cleared, Mrs Gibson roused herself, and made the same remark about dear papa that she had done at the same hour for weeks past. Cynthia too did not look different from usual. And yet, what a hidden mystery did her calmness hide! thought Molly. At length came bed-time, and the customary little speeches. Both Molly and Cynthia went to their own rooms without exchanging a word. When Molly was in hers, she had forgotten whether she was to go to Cynthia, or Cynthia to come to her. She took off her gown and put on her dressing-gown, and stood and waited, and even sat down for a minute or two: but Cynthia did not come, so Molly went and knocked at the opposite door, which, to her surprise, she found shut. When she entered the room, Cynthia sate by her dressing-table, just as she had come up from the drawing-room. She had been leaning her head on her arms, and seemed almost to have forgotten the tryst she had made with Molly, for she looked up as if startled, and her face did seem full of worry and distress; in her solitude she made no more exertion, but gave way to thoughts of care.

CHAPTER 43

Cynthia's Confession

'You said I might come,' said Molly, 'and that you would tell me all.'

'You know all, I think,' said Cynthia heavily. 'Perhaps you don't know what excuses I have, but at any rate you know what a scrape I am in.'

'I've been thinking a great deal,' said Molly, timidly and doubtfully. 'And I can't help fancying if you told papa' —

Before she could go on, Cynthia had stood up.

'No!' said she. 'That I won't. Unless I'm to leave here at once. And you know I have not another place to go to — without warning, I mean. I daresay my uncle would take me in; he's a relation, and would be bound to stand by me, in whatever disgrace I might be; or perhaps I might get a governess's situation — a pretty governess I should be!'

'Pray, please, Cynthia, don't go off into such wild talking. I don't believe you've done so very wrong. You say you have not, and I believe you. That horrid man has managed to get you involved in some way; but I am sure papa could set it to rights, if you would only make a friend of him, and tell him all' —

'No, Molly,' said Cynthia, 'I can't, and there's an end of it. You may if you like; only, let me leave the house first; give me that much time.'

'You know I would never tell anything you wished me not to tell, Cynthia,' said Molly, deeply hurt.

'Would you not, darling?' said Cynthia, taking her hand. 'Will you promise me that? quite a sacred promise? — for it would be such a comfort to me to tell you all, now you know so much.'

'Yes! I'll promise not to tell. You should not have doubted me,' said Molly, still a little sorrowfully.

'Very well. I trust to you. I know I may.'

'But do think of telling papa, and getting him to help you,' persevered Molly.

'Never,' said Cynthia resolutely, but more quietly than before. 'Do you think I forget what he said at the time of that wretched Mr Coxe; how severe he was, and how long I was in disgrace, if indeed I'm out of it now? I am one of those people, as mamma says sometimes – I cannot live with persons who don't think well of me. It may be a weakness, or a sin, – I'm sure I don't know, and I don't care; but I really cannot be happy in the same house with any one who knows my faults, and thinks they are greater than my merits. Now, you know your father would do that. I have often told you that he (and you too, Molly,) have a higher standard than I had ever known. Oh, I couldn't bear it; if he were to know, he would be so angry with me – he would never get over it, and I have so liked him! I do so like him!'

'Well, never mind, dear; he shall not know,' said Molly, for Cynthia was again becoming hysterical – 'at least, we'll say no more about it now.'

'And you'll never say any more – never – promise me!' said Cynthia, taking her hand eagerly.

'Never, till you give me leave! Now do let me see if I cannot help you. Lie down on the bed, and I'll sit by you, and let us talk it over.'

But Cynthia sat down again in the chair by the dressing-table.

'When did it all begin?' said Molly, after a long pause of silence.

'Long ago – four or five years. I was such a child to be left all to myself. It was the holidays, and mamma was away visiting, and the Donaldsons asked me to go with them to the Worcester Festival.* You can't fancy how pleasant it all sounded, especially to me. I had been shut up in that great dreary house at Ashcombe, where mamma had her school; it belonged to Lord Cumnor, and Mr Preston as his agent had to see it all painted and papered; but, besides that, he was very intimate with us; I believe mamma thought – no, I'm not sure about that, and I have enough blame to lay at her door, to prevent my telling you anything that may be only fancy—'

Then she paused and sate still for a minute or two, recalling the past. Molly was struck by the aged and careworn expression which had taken temporary hold of the brilliant and beautiful face; she could see from that how much Cynthia must have suffered from this hidden trouble of hers.

'Well! at any rate we were intimate with him, and he came a great deal about the house, and knew as much as any one of mamma's affairs, and all the ins and outs of her life. I'm telling you this, in order that you may understand how natural it was for me to answer his questions, when he came one day and found me, not crying, for you know I'm not much given to that – in spite of today's exposure of myself – but fretting and fuming because, though mamma had written word I might go with the Donaldsons, she had never said how I was to get any money for the journey, much less for anything of dress, and I had outgrown all my last year's frocks, and, as for gloves and boots – in short, I really had hardly clothes decent enough for church' —

'Why didn't you write to her and tell her all this?' said Molly, half afraid of appearing to cast blame by her very natural question.

'I wish I had her letter to show you; you must have seen some of mamma's letters, though; don't you know how she always seems to leave out just the important point of every fact? In this case she descanted largely on the enjoyment she was having, and the kindness she was receiving, and her wish that I could have been with her, and her gladness that I too was going to have some pleasure; but the only thing that would have been of real use to me she left out, and that was where she was going to next. She mentioned that she was leaving the house she was stopping at the day after she wrote, and that she should be at home by a certain date; but I got the letter on a Saturday, and the festival began the next Tuesday' —

'Poor Cynthia!' said Molly. 'Still, if you had written, your letter might have been forwarded. I don't mean to be hard, only I do so dislike the thought of your ever having made a friend of that man.'

'Ah!' said Cynthia, sighing. 'How easy it is to judge rightly, after one sees what evil comes from judging wrongly! I was only a young girl, hardly more than a child, and he was a friend to us then – excepting mamma, the only friend I knew; the Donaldsons were only kind and good-natured acquaintances.'

'I am sorry,' said Molly humbly, 'I have been so happy with papa. I hardly can understand how different it must have been with you.'

'Different! I should think so! The worry about money made me sick of my life. We might not say we were poor, it would have injured the school; but I would have stinted and starved if mamma and I had got on as happily together as we might have done – as you and Mr Gibson do. It was not the poverty; it was that she never seemed to care to have me with her. As soon as the holidays came round, she was off to some great house or another; and I daresay I was at a very awkward age for her to have me lounging about in the drawing-room, when callers came. Girls at the age I was then are so terribly keen at scenting out motives, and putting in their disagreeable questions as to the little twistings and twirlings and vanishings of conversation; they've no distinct notion of what are the truths and falsehoods of polite life. At any rate, I was very much in mamma's way, and I felt it. Mr Preston seemed to feel it too for me; and I was very grateful to him for kind words and sympathetic looks – crumbs of kindness which would have dropped under your table unnoticed. So this day, when he came to see how the workmen were getting on, he found me in the deserted schoolroom, looking at my faded summer-bonnet and some old ribbons I had been sponging, and half-worn-out gloves – a sort of rag-fair spread out on the deal table. I was in a regular passion with only looking at that shabbiness. He said he was so glad to hear I was going to this festival with the Donaldsons; old Sally, our servant, had told him the news, I believe. But I was so perplexed about money, and my vanity was so put out about my shabby dress, that I was in a pet,* and said I shouldn't go. He sate down on the table, and little by little he made me tell him all my troubles. I do sometimes think he was very nice in those days. Somehow, I never felt as if it was wrong or foolish or anything to accept his offer of money at the time. He had twenty pounds in his pocket, he said, and really didn't know what to do with it – shouldn't want it for months; I could repay it, or rather mamma could, when it suited her, She must have known I should want money, and most likely thought I should apply to him. Twenty pounds wouldn't be too much, I must take it all, and so on. I knew – at least I thought I knew – that I should never spend twenty pounds; but I thought I could give him back what I didn't want, and so – well, that was the beginning! It doesn't sound so very wrong, does it, Molly?'

'No,' said Molly hesitatingly. She did not wish to make herself into a hard judge, and yet she did so dislike Mr Preston. Cynthia went on –

'Well, what with boots and gloves, and a bonnet and a mantle, and a white muslin gown, which was made for me before I left on Tuesday, and a silk gown that followed to the Donaldsons', and my journeys, and all, there was very little left of the twenty pounds, especially when I found I must get a ball-dress in Worcester, for we were all to go to the Ball. Mrs Donaldson gave me my ticket, but she rather looked grave at my idea of going to the Ball in my white muslin, which I had already worn two evenings at their house. Oh dear! how pleasant it must be to be rich! You know,' continued Cynthia, smiling a very little, 'I can't help being aware that I'm pretty, and that people admire me very much. I found it out first at the Donaldsons'. I began to think I did look pretty in my fine new clothes, and I saw that other people thought so too. I was certainly the belle of the house, and it was very pleasant to feel my power. The last day or two of that gay week Mr Preston joined our party. The last time he had seen me was when I was dressed in shabby clothes too small for me, half-crying in my solitude, neglected and penniless. At the Donaldsons' I was a little queen; and, as I said, fine feathers make fine birds, and all the people were making much of me; and at that Ball, which was the first night he came, I had more partners than I knew what to do with. I suppose he really did fall in love with me then. I don't think he had done so before. And then I began to feel how awkward it was to be in his debt. I couldn't give myself airs to him as I did to others. Oh! it was so awkward and uncomfortable! But I liked him, and felt him as a friend all the time. The last day, I was walking in the garden along with the others, and I thought I could tell him how much I had enjoyed myself, and how happy I had been, all thanks to his twenty pounds (I was beginning to feel like Cinderella when the clock was striking twelve), and could tell him it should be repaid to him as soon as possible; though I turned sick at the thought of telling mamma, and knew enough of our affairs to understand how very difficult it would be to muster up the money. The end of our talk came very soon; for, almost to my terror, he began to talk violent love to me, and to beg me to promise to marry him. I was so frightened, that I ran away to the others. But that night I got a letter from him, apologising for startling me, renewing his offer, his entreaties for a promise of marriage, to be fulfilled at any date I would please to name – in fact, a most urgent love-letter, and in it a reference to my unlucky debt, which was to be a debt no longer, only an advance of the money to be hereafter mine if only — You can fancy it all, Molly, better than I can remember it to tell it you.'

'And what did you say?' asked Molly, breathless.

'I did not answer it at all, until another letter came, entreating for a reply. By that time mamma had returned home, and the old daily pressure and plaint of poverty had come on. Mary

Donaldson wrote to me often, singing the praises of Mr Preston as enthusiastically as if she had been bribed to do it. I had seen him a very popular man in their set, and I liked him well enough, and felt grateful to him. So I wrote and gave him my promise to marry him when I was twenty, but it was to be a secret till then. And I tried to forget I had ever borrowed money of him; but somehow, as soon as I felt pledged to him, I began to hate him. I couldn't endure his eagerness of greeting, if ever he found me alone; and mamma began to suspect, I think. I cannot tell you all the ins and outs; in fact, I didn't understand them at the time, and I don't remember clearly how it all happened now. But I know that Lady Cuxhaven sent mamma some money, to be applied to my education, as she called it; and mamma seemed very much put out and in very low spirits, and she and I didn't get on at all together. So, of course, I never ventured to name the hateful twenty pounds to her, but went on trying to think that, if I was to marry Mr Preston, it need never be paid – very mean and wicked, I daresay; but oh, Molly, I've been punished for it, for now I abhor that man.'

'But why? When did you begin to dislike him? You seem to have taken it very passively all this time.'

'I don't know. It was growing upon me, before I went to that school at Boulogne. He made me feel as if I was in his power; and, by too often reminding me of my engagement to him, he made me critical of his words and ways. There was an insolence in his manner to mamma, too. Ah! you're thinking that I'm not too respectful a daughter – and perhaps not; but I couldn't bear his covert sneers at her faults, and I hated his way of showing what he called his "love" for me. Then, after I had been a *semestre** at Mdme. Lefèbre's, a new English girl came – a cousin of his, who knew but little of me. Now, Molly, you must forget as soon as I've told you what I'm going to say; and she used to talk so much and perpetually about her cousin Robert – he was the great man of the family, evidently – and how he was so handsome, and every lady of the land in love with him – a lady of title into the bargain'—

'Lady Harriet! I daresay,' said Molly indignantly.

'I don't know,' said Cynthia wearily. 'I didn't care at the time, and I don't care now; for she went on to say there was a very pretty widow too, who made desperate love to him. He had often laughed with them at all her little advances, which she thought he didn't see through. And, oh! and this was the man I had promised to marry, and gone into debt to, and written love-letters to! So now you understand it all, Molly.'

'No, I don't yet. What did you do, on hearing how he had spoken about your mother?'

'There was but one thing to do. I wrote and told him I hated him, and would never, never marry him, and would pay him back his money and the interest on it as soon as ever I could.'

'Well?'

'And Mdme. Lefèbre brought me back my letter, unopened, I will say; and told me that she didn't allow letters to gentleman to be sent by the pupils of her establishment unless she had previously seen their contents. I told her he was a family friend, the agent who managed mamma's affairs – I really could not stick at the truth; but she wouldn't let it go; and I had to see her burn it, and to give her my promise I wouldn't write again before she would consent not to tell mamma. So I had to calm down and wait till I came home.'

'But you didn't see him them; at least, not for some time?'

'No, but I could write; and I began to try and save up my money to pay him.'

'What did he say to your letter?'

'Oh, at first he pretended not to believe I could be in earnest; he thought it was only pique, or a temporary offence, to be apologised for and covered over with passionate protestations.'

'And afterwards?'

'He condescended* to threats; and, what is worse, then I turned coward. I couldn't bear to have it all known and talked about, and my silly letters shown – oh, such letters! I cannot bear to think of them, beginning, "My dearest Robert", to that man' —

'But, oh, Cynthia, how could you go and engage yourself to Roger?' asked Molly.

'Why not?' said Cynthia, sharply turning round upon her. 'I was free – I am free; it seemed a way of assuring myself that I was quite free; and I did like Roger – it was such a comfort to be brought into contact with people who could be relied upon; and I was not a stock or a stone that I could fail to be touched by his tender, unselfish love, so different to Mr Preston's. I know you don't think me good enough for him; and, of course, if all this comes out, he won't think me good enough either' (falling into a plaintive tone, very touching to hear); 'and sometimes I think I'll give him up, and go off to some fresh life amongst strangers; and once or twice I've thought I would marry Mr Preston out of pure revenge, and have him for ever in my power – only I think I should have the worst of it; for he is cruel in his very soul – tigerish, with his beautiful striped skin and relentless heart. I have so begged and begged him to let me go without exposure.'

'Never mind the exposure,' said Molly. 'It will recoil far more on him than harm you.'

Cynthia went a little paler. 'But I said things in those letters about mamma. I was quick-eyed enough to all her faults, and hardly understood the force of her temptations; and he says he will show those letters to your father, unless I consent to acknowl-edge our engagement.'

'He shall not!' said Molly, rising up in her indignation, and standing before Cynthia almost as resolutely fierce as if she were in the very presence of Mr Preston himself. 'I am not afraid of him. He dare not insult me, or if he does I don't care. I will ask him for those letters, and see if he will dare to refuse me.'

'You don't know him,' said Cynthia, shaking her head. 'He has made many an appointment with me, just as if he would take back the money – which has been sealed up ready for him this four months; or as if he would give me back my letters. Poor, poor Roger! How little he thinks of all this! When I want to write words of love to him, I pull myself up; for I have written words as affectionate to that other man. And, if Mr Preston ever guessed that Roger and I were engaged, he would manage to be revenged on both him and me, by giving us as much pain as he could with those unlucky letters – written when I was not sixteen, Molly – only seven of them! They are like a mine under my feet, which may blow up any day; and down will come father and mother and all.'* She ended bitterly enough, though her words were so light.

'How can I get them?' said Molly, thinking: 'for get them I will. With papa to back me, he dare not refuse.'

'Ah! But that's just the thing. He knows I'm afraid of your father's hearing of it all, more than of any one else.'

'And yet he thinks he loves you!'

'It is his way of loving. He says often enough, he doesn't care what he does so he gets me to be his wife; and that, after that, he is sure he can make me love him.' Cynthia began to cry, out of weariness of body and despair of mind. Molly's arms were round her in a minute, and she pressed the beautiful head to her bosom, and laid her own cheek upon it, and hushed her up with lulling words, just as if she were a little child.

'Oh, it is such a comfort to have told you all!' murmured Cynthia. And Molly made reply – 'I am sure we have right on our side; and that makes me certain he must and shall give up the letters.'

'And take the money?' added Cynthia, lifting her head, and looking eagerly into Molly's face. 'He must take the money. Oh, Molly, you can never manage it all without its coming out to your father! And I would far rather go out to Russia as a governess. I almost think I would rather – no, not that,' said she, shuddering away from what she was going to say. 'But he must not know – please, Molly, he must not know. I couldn't bear it. I don't know what I might not do. You'll promise me never to tell him – or mamma?'

'I never will. You do not think I would for anything short of saving—' She was going to have said, 'saving you and Roger from pain.' But Cynthia broke in –

'For nothing! No reason whatever must make you tell your father. If you fail, you fail, and I will love you for ever for trying; but I shall be no worse off than before. Better, indeed; for I shall have the comfort of your sympathy. But promise me not to tell Mr Gibson.'

'I have promised once,' said Molly, 'but I promise again; so now do go to bed, and try and rest. You are looking as white as a sheet; you'll be ill, if you don't get some rest; and it's past two o'clock, and you're shivering with cold.'

So they wished each other good-night. But when Molly got into her room, all her spirit left her; and she threw herself down on her bed, dressed as she was, for she had no heart left for anything. If Roger ever heard of it all by any chance, she felt how it would disturb his love for Cynthia. And yet was it right to conceal it from him? She must try and persuade Cynthia to tell it all straight out to him, as soon as he returned to England. A full confession on her part would wonderfully lessen any pain he might have on first hearing of it. She lost herself in thoughts of Roger – how he would feel, what he would say, how that meeting would come to pass, where he was at that very time, and so on, till she suddenly plucked herself up, and recollected what she herself had offered and promised to do. Now that the first *furor* was over, she saw the difficulties clearly; and the foremost of all was how she was to manage to have an interview with Mr Preston. How had Cynthia managed? and the letters that had passed between them, too? Unwillingly, Molly was compelled to perceive that there must have been a good deal of underhand work going on beneath Cynthia's apparent openness of behaviour; and still more unwillingly she began to be afraid that she herself might be led into the practice. But she would try and walk in a straight path; and, if she did wander out of it, it should only be to save pain to those whom she loved.

CHAPTER 44

Molly Gibson to the Rescue

It seemed strange enough, after the storms of the night, to meet in smooth tranquillity at breakfast. Cynthia was pale; but she talked as quietly as usual about all manner of different things, while Molly sate silent, watching and wondering, and becoming convinced that Cynthia must have gone through a long experience of concealing her real thoughts and secret troubles, before she could have been able to put on such a semblance of composure. Among the letters that came in that morning was one from the London Kirkpatricks; but not from Helen, Cynthia's own particular correspondent. Her sister wrote to apologise for Helen, who was not well, she said: had had the influenza, which had left her very weak and poorly.

'Let her come down here for a change of air,' said Mr Gibson. 'The country at this time of the year is better than London, except when the place is surrounded by trees. Now our house is well drained, high up, gravel-soil, and I'll undertake to doctor her for nothing.'

'It would be charming,' said Mrs Gibson, rapidly revolving in her mind the changes necessary in her household economy before receiving a young lady accustomed to such a household as Mr Kirkpatrick's – calculating the consequent inconveniences, and weighing them against the probable advantages, even while she spoke. 'Should not you like it, Cynthia? and Molly too? You then, dear, would become acquainted with one of the girls, and I have no doubt you would be asked back again, which would be so very nice!'

'And I shouldn't let her go,' said Mr Gibson, who had acquired an unfortunate facility of reading his wife's thoughts.

'Dear Helen!' went on Mrs Gibson, 'I should so like to nurse her! We would make your consulting-room into her own private sitting-room, my dear.' – (It is hardly necessary to say that the scales had been weighed down by the inconveniences of having a person behind the scenes for several weeks.) 'For with an invalid so much depends on tranquillity. In the drawing-room, for instance, she might constantly be disturbed by callers; and the dining-room is so – so what shall I call it? so dinnery, – the smell of meat never seems to leave it; it would have been different, if dear papa had allowed me to throw out that window'—

'Why can't she have the dressing-room for her bedroom, and the little room opening out of the drawing-room for her sitting-room?' asked Mr Gibson.

'The library?' – for by this name Mrs Gibson chose to dignify what had formerly been called the book-closet – 'why, it would hardly hold a sofa, besides the books and the writing-table; and there are draughts everywhere. No, my dear, we had better not ask her at all; her own home is comfortable, at any rate!'

'Well, well!' said Mr Gibson, seeing that he was to be worsted, and not caring enough about the matter to show fight. 'Perhaps you're right. It's a case of luxury *versus* fresh air. Some people suffer more from want of the one than from want of the other. You know I shall be glad to see her, if she likes to come and take us as we are; but I can't give up the consulting-room. It's a necessity and daily bread!'

'I'll write and tell them how kind Mr Gibson is,' said his wife, in high contentment, as her husband left the room. 'They'll be just as much obliged to him as if she had come.'

Whether it was from Helen's illness, or some other cause, after breakfast Cynthia became very flat and absent, and this lasted all day long. Molly understood now why her moods had been so changeable for many months, and was tender and forbearing with her accordingly. Towards evening, when the two girls were left alone, Cynthia came and stood over Molly, so that her face could not be seen.

'Molly,' said she, 'will you do it? Will you do what you said last night? I've been thinking of it all day, and sometimes I believe he would give you back the letters if you asked him; he might fancy – at any rate it's worth trying, if you don't very much dislike it.'

Now it so happened that, with every thought she had given to it, Molly disliked the idea of the proposed interview with Mr Preston more and more; but it was, after all, her own offer, and she neither could nor would draw back from it; it might do good, she did not see how it could possibly do harm. So she gave her consent, and tried to conceal her distaste, which grew upon her even more as Cynthia hastily arranged the details.

'You shall meet him in the avenue leading from the park lodge up to the Towers. He can come in one way from the Towers, where he has often business – he has pass-keys everywhere – you can go in, as we have often done, by the lodge – you need not go far.'

It did strike Molly that Cynthia must have had some experience in making all these arrangements; and she ventured to ask how he was to be informed of all this. Cynthia only reddened and replied, 'Oh! never mind! He will only be too glad to come; you heard him say he wished to discuss the affair more; it is the first time the appointment has come from my side. If I can but once be free – oh, Molly, I will love you, and be grateful to you all my life!'

Molly thought of Roger, and that thought prompted her next speech.

'It must be horrible – I think I'm very brave – but I don't think I could have – could have accepted even Roger, with a half-cancelled engagement hanging over me.' She blushed as she spoke.

'You forget how I detest Mr Preston!' said Cynthia. 'It was that, more than any excess of love for Roger, that made me thankful to be at least as securely pledged to some one else. He did not want to call it an engagement; but I did; because it gave me the feeling of assurance that I was free from Mr Preston. And so I am! all but these letters. Oh! if you can but make him take back his abominable money, and get me my letters! Then we would bury it all in oblivion, and he could marry somebody else, and I would marry Roger, and no one would be the wiser. After all, it was only what people call "youthful folly". And you may tell Mr Preston that, as soon as he makes my letters public, shows them to your father or anything, I'll go away from Hollingford, and never come back.'

Loaded with many such messages, which she felt that she would never deliver, not really knowing what she should say, hating the errand, not satisfied with Cynthia's manner of speaking about her relations to Roger, oppressed with shame and complicity in conduct which appeared to her deceitful, yet willing to bear all and brave all, if she could once set Cynthia in a straight path – in a clear space, and almost more pitiful to her friend's great distress and possible disgrace, than able to give her that love which involves perfect sympathy: Molly set out on her walk towards the appointed place. It was a cloudy, blustering day; and the noise of the blowing wind among the nearly leafless branches of the great trees filled her ears, as she passed through the park-gates and entered the avenue. She walked quickly, instinctively wishing to get her blood up, and have no time for thought. But there was a bend in the avenue, about a quarter of a mile from the lodge; after that bend it was a straight line up to the great house, now emptied of its inhabitants. Molly did not like going quite out of sight of the lodge, and she stood facing it, close by the trunk of one of the trees. Presently, she heard a step coming on the grass. It was Mr Preston. He saw a woman's figure half-behind the trunk of a tree, and made no doubt that it was Cynthia. But when he came near, almost close, the figure turned round, and, instead of the brilliantly-coloured face of Cynthia, he met the pale, resolved look of Molly. She did not speak to greet him; but, though he felt sure from the general aspect of pallor and timidity that she was afraid of him, her steady grey eyes met his with courageous innocence.

'Is Cynthia unable to come?' asked he, perceiving that she expected him.

'I did not know you thought that you should meet her,' said Molly, a little surprised. In her simplicity she believed that Cynthia had named that it was she, Molly Gibson, who would meet Mr Preston at a given time and place; but Cynthia had been too worldly-wise for that, and had decoyed him thither by a vaguely-worded note, which, while avoiding actual falsehood, led him to suppose that she herself would give him the meeting.

'She said she should be here,' said Mr Preston, extremely annoyed at being entrapped, as he now felt he had been, into an interview with Miss Gibson. Molly hesitated a little before she spoke. He was determined not to break the silence; as she had intruded herself into the affair, she should find her situation as awkward as possible.

'At any rate, she sent me here to meet you,' said Molly. 'She has told me exactly how matters stand between you and her.'

'Has she?' sneered he. 'She is not always the most open or reliable person in the world!'

Molly reddened. She perceived the impertinence of the tone; and her temper was none of the coolest. But she mastered herself and gained courage by so doing.

'You should not speak so of the person you profess to wish to have for your wife. But, putting all that aside, you have some letters of hers that she wishes to have back again.'

'I dare say.'

'And that you have no right to keep.'

'No legal, or no moral right? which do you mean?'

'I do not know; simply you have no right at all, as a gentleman, to keep a girl's letters when she asks for them back again, much less to hold them over her as a threat.'

'I see you do know all, Miss Gibson,' said he, changing his manner to one of more respect. 'At least she has told you her story from her point of view, her side; now you must hear mine. She promised me as solemnly as ever woman'—

'She was not a woman, she was only a girl, barely sixteen.'

'Old enough to know what she was doing; but I'll call her a girl if you like. She promised me solemnly to be my wife, making the one stipulation of secrecy, and a certain period of waiting; she wrote me letters repeating this promise, and confidential enough to prove that she considered herself bound to me by such an implied relation. I don't give in to humbug – I don't set myself up as a saint – and in most ways I can look after my own interests pretty keenly; you know enough of her position as a penniless girl, and at that time with no influential connections to take the place of wealth and help me on in the world. It was as sincere and unworldly a passion as ever man felt; she must say so herself. I might have married two or three girls with plenty of money; one of them was handsome enough, and not at all reluctant.'

Molly interrupted him: she was chafed at the conceit of his manner. 'I beg your pardon, but I don't want to hear accounts of young ladies whom you might have married; I come here simply on behalf of Cynthia, who does not like you, and who does not wish to marry you.'

'Well, then, I must make her "like" me, as you call it. She did 'like' me once, and made promises which she will find it requires the consent of two people to break. I don't despair of making her love me as much as ever she did – according to her letters, at least – when we are married.'

'She will never marry you,' said Molly firmly.

'Then, if she ever honours any one else with her preference, he shall be allowed the perusal of her letters to me.'

Molly almost could have laughed, she was so secure and certain that Roger would never read the letters offered to him under these circumstances; but then she thought that he would feel such pain at the whole affair, and at the contact with Mr Preston, especially if he had not heard of it from Cynthia first; and that, if she, Molly, could save him this pain, she would. Before she could settle what to say, Mr Preston spoke again.

'You said the other day that Cynthia was engaged. May I ask whom to?'

'No,' said Molly, 'you may not. You heard her say it was not an engagement. It is not exactly; and if it were a full engagement, do you think, after what you last said, I should tell you to whom? But you may be sure of this, he would never read a line of your letters. He is too——No! I won't speak of him before you. You could never understand him.'

'It seems to me that this mysterious "he" is a very fortunate person to have such a warm defender in Miss Gibson, to whom he is not at all engaged,' said Mr Preston, with so disagreeable a look on his face that Molly suddenly found herself on the point of bursting into tears. But she rallied herself, and worked on – for Cynthia first, and for Roger as well.

'No honourable man or woman will read your letters; and, if any people do read them, they will be so much ashamed of it that they won't dare to speak of them. What use can they be of to you?'

'They contain Cynthia's reiterated promises of marriage,' replied he.

'She says she would rather leave Hollingford for ever, and go out to earn her bread, than marry you.'

His face fell a little. He looked so bitterly mortified, that Molly was almost sorry for him.

'Does she say that to you in cold blood? Do you know you are telling me very hard truths, Miss Gibson? If they are truths, that is to say,' he continued, recovering himself a little. 'Young ladies are very fond of the words "hate" and "detest". I've known many who have applied them to men whom they were hoping all the time to marry.'

'I cannot tell about other people,' said Molly; 'I only know that Cynthia does' – here she hesitated for a moment; she felt for his pain, and so she hesitated; but then she brought it out – 'does as nearly hate you as anybody like her ever does hate.'

'Like her?' said he, repeating the words almost unconsciously, seizing on anything to try and hide his mortification.

'I mean I should hate worse,' said Molly in a low voice.

But he did not attend much to her answer. He was working the point of his stick into the turf, and his eyes were bent on it.

'So now would you mind sending her back the letters by me? I do assure you that you cannot make her marry you.'

'You are very simple, Miss Gibson,' said he, suddenly lifting up his head. 'I suppose you don't know that there is any other feeling that can be gratified, except love. Have you never heard of revenge? Cynthia has cajoled me with promises, and little as you or she may believe me – well, it's no use speaking of that. I don't mean to let her go unpunished. You may tell her that. I shall keep the letters, and make use of them as I see fit when the occasion arises.'

Molly was miserably angry with herself for her mis-management of the affair. She had hoped to succeed; she had only made matters worse. What new argument could she use? Meanwhile he went on, lashing himself up as he thought how the two girls must have talked him over, wounded vanity thus adding to the rage of disappointed love.

'Mr Osborne Hamley may hear of their contents, though he may be too honourable to read them. Nay, even your father may hear whispers; and if I remember them rightly, Miss Cynthia Kirkpatrick does not always speak in the most respectful terms of the lady who is now Mrs Gibson. There are'—

'Stop,' said Molly. 'I won't hear anything out of these letters, written, when she was almost without friends, to you, whom she looked upon as a friend! But I have thought of what I will do next. I give you fair warning. If I had not been foolish, I should have told my father; but Cynthia made me promise that I would not. So I will tell it all, from beginning to end, to Lady Harriet, and ask her to speak to her father. I feel sure that she will do it; and I don't think you will dare to refuse Lord Cumnor.'

He felt at once that he should not dare; that, clever land-agent

as he was, and high up in the earl's favour on that account, yet
the conduct of which he had been guilty in regard to the letters
and the threats which he had held out respecting them, were just
what no gentleman, no honourable man, no manly man, could
put up with in any one about him. He knew that much, and he
wondered how she, the girl standing before him, had been clever
enough to find it out. He forgot himself for an instant in admiration of her. There she stood, frightened, yet brave, not letting go
her hold on what she meant to do, even when things seemed most
against her; and, besides, there was something that struck him
most of all perhaps, and which shows the kind of man he was –
he perceived that Molly was as unconscious that he was a young
man, and she a young woman, as if she had been a pure angel
from heaven. Though he felt that he would have to yield, and give
up the letters, he was not going to do it at once; and, while he
was thinking what to say, so as still to evade making any
concession till he had had time to think over it, he, with his quick
senses all about him, heard the trotting of a horse crunching
quickly along over the gravel of the drive. A moment afterwards,
Molly's perception overtook his. He could see the startled look
overspread her face; and in an instant she would have run away;
but, before the first rush was made, Mr Preston laid his hand
firmly on her arm.

'Keep quiet. You must be seen. You, at any rate, have done
nothing to be ashamed of.'

As he spoke, Mr Sheepshanks came round the bend of the road
and was close upon them. Mr Preston saw, if Molly did not, the
sudden look of intelligence that dawned upon the shrewd ruddy
face of the old gentleman – saw, but did not much heed. He went
forwards and spoke to Mr Sheepshanks, who made a halt right
before them.

'Miss Gibson! your servant. Rather a blustering day for a young
lady to be out – and cold, I should say, for standing still too long;
eh, Preston?' poking his whip at the latter in a knowing manner.

'Yes,' said Mr Preston; 'and I'm afraid I've kept Miss Gibson
too long standing.'

Molly did not know what to say or do; so she only bowed a
silent farewell, and turned away to go home, feeling very heavy at
heart at the non-success of her undertaking. For she did not know
how she had conquered, in fact, although Mr Preston might not

as yet acknowledge it even to himself. Before she was out of hearing, she heard Mr Sheepshanks say –

'Sorry to have disturbed your *tête-à-tête*, Preston;' but, though she heard the words, their implied sense did not sink into her mind; she was only feeling how she had gone out glorious and confident, and was coming back to Cynthia defeated.

Cynthia was on the watch for her return, and, rushing downstairs, dragged Molly into the dining-room.

'Well, Molly? Oh! I see you haven't got them. After all, I never expected it.' She sate down, as if she could get over her disappointment better in that position, and Molly stood like a guilty person before her.

'I am so sorry; I did all I could; we were interrupted at last – Mr Sheepshanks rode up.'

'Provoking old man! Do you think you should have persuaded him to give up the letters, if you had had more time?'

'I don't know. I wish Mr Sheepshanks hadn't come up just then. I didn't like his finding me standing talking to Mr Preston.'

'Oh! I dare say he'd never think anything about it. What did he – Mr Preston – say?'

'He seemed to think you were fully engaged to him, and that these letters were the only proof he had. I think he loves you in his way.'

'His way, indeed!' said Cynthia scornfully.

'The more I think of it, the more I see it would be better for papa to speak to him. I did say I would tell it all to Lady Harriet, and get Lord Cumnor to make him give up the letters. But it would be very awkward.'

'Very!' said Cynthia gloomily. 'But he would see it was only a threat.'

'But I will do it in a moment, if you like. I meant what I said; only I feel that papa would manage it best of all, and more privately.'

'I'll tell you what, Molly – you're bound by promise, you know, and cannot tell Mr Gibson without breaking your solemn word – but it's just this: I'll leave Hollingford and never come back again, if ever your father hears of this affair; there!' Cynthia stood up now, and began to fold up Molly's shawl, in her nervous excitement.

'Oh, Cynthia – Roger!' was all that Molly said.

'Yes, I know! you need not remind me of him. But I'm not

going to live in the house with any one who may be always casting
up in his mind the things he has heard against me – things – faults,
perhaps – which sound so much worse than they really are. I was
so happy, when I first came here; you all liked me, and admired
me, and thought well of me, and now—Why, Molly, I can see the
difference in you already. You carry your thoughts in your face –
I have read them there these two days – you've been thinking,
"How Cynthia must have deceived me; keeping up a correspondence all this time – having half-engagements to two men!"
You've been more full of that, than of pity for me as a girl who
has always been obliged to manage for herself, without any friend
to help her and protect her.'

Molly was silent. There was a great deal of truth in what
Cynthia was saying: and yet a great deal of falsehood. For,
through all this long forty-eight hours, Molly had loved Cynthia
dearly, and had been more weighed down by the position the
latter was in than Cynthia herself. She also knew – but this was a
second thought following on the other – that she had suffered
much pain in trying to do her best in this interview with Mr
Preston. She had been tried beyond her strength: and the great
tears welled up into her eyes, and fell slowly down her cheeks.

'Oh! what a brute I am!' said Cynthia, kissing them away. 'I see
– I know it is the truth, and I deserve it – but I need not reproach
you.'

'You did not reproach me!' said Molly, trying to smile. 'I have
thought something of what you said – but I do love you dearly –
dearly, Cynthia – I should have done just the same as you did.'

'No, you would not. Your grain is different, somehow.'

CHAPTER 45

Confidences

All the rest of that day, Molly was depressed and not well. Having
anything to conceal was so unusual – almost so unprecedented a
circumstance with her that it preyed upon her in every way.

It was a nightmare that she could not shake off; she did so wish
to forget it all, and yet every little occurrence seemed to remind
her of it. The next morning's post brought several letters; one

from Roger for Cynthia; and Molly, letterless herself, looked at Cynthia as she read it, with wistful sadness. It appeared to Molly as though Cynthia should have no satisfaction in these letters, until she had told him what was her exact position with Mr Preston; yet Cynthia was colouring and dimpling up, as she always did at any pretty words of praise, or admiration, or love. But Molly's thoughts and Cynthia's reading were both interrupted by a little triumphant sound from Mrs Gibson, as she pushed a letter she had just received to her husband, with a –

'There! I must say I expected that!' Then, turning to Cynthia, she explained – 'It is a letter from uncle Kirkpatrick, love. So kind, wishing you to go and stay with them, and help them to cheer up Helen. Poor Helen! I am afraid she is very far from well. But we could not have had her here, without disturbing dear papa in his consulting-room; and though I could have relinquished my dressing-room – he – well! so I said in my letter how you were grieved – you above all of us, because you are such a friend of Helen's you know – and how you longed to be of use – as I am sure you do – and so now they want you to go up directly, for Helen has quite set her heart upon it.'

Cynthia's eyes sparkled. 'I shall like going,' said she – 'all but leaving you, Molly,' she added, in a lower tone, as if suddenly smitten with some compunction.

'Can you be ready to go by the Bang-up* tonight?' said Mr Gibson; 'for, curiously enough, after more than twenty years of quiet practice at Hollingford, I am summoned up today for the first time to a consultation in London tomorrow. I am afraid Lady Cumnor is worse, my dear.'

'You don't say so? Poor dear lady! What a shock it is to me! I'm so glad I've had some breakfast. I could not have eaten anything.'

'Nay, I only say she is worse. With her complaint, being worse may only be a preliminary to being better. Don't take my words for more than their literal meaning.'

'Thank you. How kind and reassuring dear papa always is! About your gowns, Cynthia?'

'Oh, they're all right, mamma, thank you. I shall be quite ready by four o'clock. Molly, will you come with me and help me to pack? I wanted to speak to you, dear,' said she, as soon as they had gone upstairs. 'It is such a relief to get away from a place haunted by that man; but I'm afraid you thought I was glad to leave you; and indeed I am not.' There was a little flavour of 'protesting too much'* about this; but Molly did not perceive it. She only said, 'Indeed I did not. I know from my own feelings how you must dislike meeting a man in public in a different manner from what you have done in private. I shall try not to see Mr Preston again for a long, long time, I'm sure. But, Cynthia, you haven't told me one word out of Roger's letter. Please, how is he? Has he quite got over his attack of fever?'

'Yes, quite. He writes in very good spirits. A great deal about birds and beasts, as usual, habits of natives, and things of that kind. You may read from there' (indicating a place in the letter) 'to there, if you can. And I'll tell you what, I'll trust you with it, Molly, while I pack; and that shows my sense of your honour – not but what you might read it all, only you'd find the love-making dull; but make a little account of where he is, and what he is doing, date, and that sort of thing, and send it to his father.'

Molly took the letter down without a word, and began to copy it at the writing-table; often reading over what she was allowed to read; often pausing, her cheek on her hand, her eyes on the letter, and letting her imagination rove to the writer, and all the scenes in which she had either seen him herself, or in which her fancy had painted him. She was startled from her meditations by Cynthia's sudden entrance into the drawing-room, looking the picture of glowing delight. 'No one here? What a blessing! Ah, Miss Molly, you're more eloquent than you believe yourself. Look here!' holding up a large full envelope, and then quickly replacing it in her pocket, as if she was afraid of being seen. 'What's the matter, sweet one?' coming up and caressing Molly. 'Is it worrying itself over that letter? Why, don't you see these are my very own horrible letters, that I am going to burn directly, that Mr Preston has had the grace to send me, thanks to you, little Molly – cuishla ma chree, pulse of my heart – the letters that have been hanging over my head like somebody's sword* for these two years?'

'Oh, I am so glad!' said Molly, rousing up a little. 'I never thought he would have sent them. He's better than I believed him. And now it is all over. I am so glad! You quite think he means to give up all claim over you by this, don't you, Cynthia?'

'He may claim, but I won't be claimed; and he has no proofs now. It is the most charming relief; and I owe it all to you, you precious little lady! Now there's only one thing more to be done;

and, if you would but do it for me—' (coaxing and caressing while she asked the question).

'Oh, Cynthia, don't ask me; I cannot do any more. You don't know how sick I go when I think of yesterday, and Mr Sheepshanks' look.'

'It is only a very little thing. I won't burden your conscience with telling you how I got my letters, but it is not through a person I can trust with money; and I must force him to take back his twenty-three pounds odd shillings. I have put it together at the rate of five per cent, and it's sealed up. Oh, Molly, I should go off with such a light heart, if you would only try to get it safely to him. It's the last thing; there would be no immediate hurry, you know. You might meet him by chance in a shop, in the street, even at a party – and, if you only had it with you in your pocket, there would be nothing so easy.'

Molly was silent. 'Papa would give it to him. There would be no harm in that. I would tell him he must ask no questions as to what it was.'

'Very well,' said Cynthia, 'have it your own way. I think my way is the best: for, if any of this affair comes out—But you've done a great deal for me already, and I won't blame you now for declining to do any more!'

'I do so dislike having these underhand dealings with him,' pleaded Molly.

'Underhand! just simply giving him a letter from me! If I left a note for Miss Browning, should you dislike giving it to her?'

'You know that's very different. I could do it openly.'

'And yet there might be writing in that; and there wouldn't be a line with the money. It would only be the winding-up – the honourable, honest winding-up-of an affair which has worried me for years. But do as you like!'

'Give it me!' said Molly. 'I will try.'

'There's a darling! You can but try; and, if you can't give it to him in private, without getting yourself into a scrape, why, keep it till I come back again. He shall have it then, whether he will or no!'

Molly looked forward to her two days alone with Mrs Gibson with very different anticipations from those with which she had welcomed the similar intercourse with her father. In the first place, there was no accompanying the travellers to the inn from which the coach started; leave-taking in the market-place was quite out of the bounds of Mrs Gibson's sense of propriety. Besides this, it was a gloomy, rainy evening, and candles had to be brought in at an unusually early hour. There would be no break for six hours – no music, no reading; but the two ladies would sit at their worsted work, pattering away at small-talk, with not even the usual break of dinner; for, to suit the requirements of those who were leaving, they had already dined early. But Mrs Gibson really meant to make Molly happy, and tried to be an agreeable companion; only Molly was not well, and was uneasy about many apprehended cares and troubles – and, at such hours of indisposition as she was then passing through, apprehensions take the shape of certainties, lying await in our paths. Molly would have given a good deal to have shaken off all these feelings, unusual enough to her; but the very house and furniture, and rain-blurred outer landscape, seemed steeped with unpleasant associations, most of them dating from the last few days.

'You and I must go on the next journey, I think, my dear,' said Mrs Gibson, almost chiming in with Molly's wish that she could get away from Hollingford into some new air and life, for a week or two. 'We have been stay-at-homes for a long time, and variety of scene is so desirable for the young! But I think the travellers will be wishing themselves at home by this nice bright fireside. "There's no place like home",* as the poet says. "Mid pleasures and palaces though I may roam", it begins, and it's both very pretty and very true. It's a great blessing to have such a dear little home as this, is not it, Molly?'

'Yes,' said Molly, rather drearily, having something of the 'toujours perdrix'* feeling at the moment. If she could but have gone away with her father, just for two days, how pleasant it would have been!

'To be sure, love, it would be very nice for you and me to go a little journey all by ourselves. You and I. No one else. If it were not such miserable weather, we would have gone off on a little impromptu tour. I've been longing for something of the kind for some weeks; but we live such a restricted kind of life here! I declare sometimes I get quite sick of the very sight of the chairs and tables that I know so well. And one misses the others, too! It seems so flat and deserted without them!'

'Yes! We are very forlorn tonight; but I think it's partly owing to the weather!'

'Nonsense, dear! I can't have you giving in to the silly fancy of being affected by weather. Poor dear Mr Kirkpatrick used to say, "a cheerful heart makes its own sunshine." He would say it to me, in his pretty way, whenever I was a little low – for I am a complete barometer – you may really judge of the state of the weather by my spirits, I have always been such a sensitive creature! It is well for Cynthia that she does not inherit it; I don't think her easily affected in any way, do you?'

Molly thought for a minute or two, and then replied – 'No, she certainly is not easily affected – not deeply affected, perhaps I should say.'

'Many girls, for instance, would have been touched by the admiration she excited – I may say the attentions she received – when she was at her uncle's last summer.'

'At Mr Kirkpatrick's?'

'Yes. There was Mr Henderson, that young lawyer; that's to say, he is studying law, but he has a good private fortune and is likely to have more; so he can only be what I call playing at law. Mr Henderson was over head and ears in love with her. It is not my fancy, although I grant mothers are partial: both Mr and Mrs Kirkpatrick noticed it; and, in one of Mrs Kirkpatrick's letters, she said that poor Mr Henderson was going into Switzerland for the long vacation, doubtless to try and forget Cynthia; but she really believed he would find it only "dragging at each remove a lengthening chain."*I thought it such a refined quotation, and altogether worded so prettily. You must know aunt Kirkpatrick some day, Molly, my love; she is what I call a woman of a truly elegant mind.'

'I can't help thinking it was a pity that Cynthia did not tell them of her engagement.'

'It is not an engagement, my dear! How often must I tell you that?'

'But what am I to call it?'

'I don't see why you need to call it anything. Indeed, I don't understand what you mean by "it". You should always try to express yourself intelligibly. It really is one of the first principles of the English language. In fact, philosophers might ask what is language given us for at all, if it is not that we may make our meaning understood?'

'But there is something between Cynthia and Roger; they are more to each other than I am to Osborne, for instance. What am I to call it?'

'You should not couple your name with that of any unmarried young man; it is so difficult to teach you delicacy, child. Perhaps one may say there is a peculiar relation between dear Cynthia and Roger, but it is very difficult to characterise it; I have no doubt that is the reason she shrinks from speaking about it. For, between ourselves, Molly, I really sometimes think it will come to nothing. He is so long away, and, privately speaking, Cynthia is not very, very constant. I once knew her very much taken before – that little affair is quite gone by; and she was very civil to Mr Henderson, in her way; I fancy she inherits it, for when I was a girl I was beset by lovers, and could never find in my heart to shake them off. You have not heard dear papa say anything of the old Squire, or dear Osborne, have you? It seems so long since we have heard or seen anything of Osborne. But he must be quite well, I think, or we should have heard of it.'

'I believe he is quite well. Some one said the other day that they had met him riding – it was Mrs Goodenough, now I remember – and that he was looking stronger than he had done for years.'

'Indeed! I am truly glad to hear it. I always was fond of Osborne; and, do you know, I never really took to Roger? I respected him and all that, of course; but to compare him with Mr Henderson! Mr Henderson is so handsome and well-bred, and gets all his gloves from Houbigant!'*

It was true that they had not seen anything of Osborne Hamley for a long time; but, as it often happens, just after they had been speaking about him he appeared. It was on the day following Mr Gibson's departure that Mrs Gibson received one of the notes, not so common now as formerly, from the family in town, asking her to go over to the Towers, and find a book, or a manuscript, or something or other that Lady Cumnor wanted with all an invalid's impatience. It was just the kind of employment she required for an amusement on a gloomy day, and it put her into a good humour immediately. There was a certain confidential importance about it, and it was a variety, and it gave her the pleasant drive in a fly up the noble avenue, and the sense of being the temporary mistress of all the grand rooms once so familiar to her. She asked Molly to accompany her, out of an access of kindness, but was not at all sorry when Molly excused herself and preferred stopping at home. At eleven o'clock Mrs Gibson was off, all in her Sunday best (to use the servants' expression, which she herself would so have contemned), well-dressed in order to impose on the servants at the Towers, for there was no one else to see or to be seen by.

'I shall not be at home until the afternoon, my dear! But I hope you will not find it dull. I don't think you will; for you are something like me, my love – "never less alone than when alone", as one of the great authors has justly expressed it.'

Molly enjoyed the house to herself fully as much as Mrs Gibson would enjoy having the Towers to herself. She ventured on having her lunch brought up on a tray into the drawing-room, so that she might eat her sandwiches while she went on with her book. In the middle, Mr Osborne Hamley was announced. He came in, looking wretchedly ill in spite of purblind Mrs Goodenough's report of his healthy appearance.

'This call is not on you, Molly,' said he, after the first greetings were over. 'I was in hopes I might have found your father at home; I thought lunch-time was the best hour.' He had sate down, as if thoroughly glad of the rest, and fallen into a languid stooping position, as if it had become so natural to him that no sense of what were considered good manners sufficed to restrain him now.

'I hope you did not want to see him professionally?' said Molly, wondering if she was wise in alluding to his health, yet urged to it by her real anxiety.

'Yes, I did. I suppose I may help myself to a biscuit and a glass of wine? No, don't ring for more. I could not eat it if it was here. But I just want a mouthful; this is quite enough, thank you. When will your father be back?'

'He was summoned up to London. Lady Cumnor is worse. I fancy there is some operation going on; but I don't know. He will be back tomorrow night.'

'Very well. Then I must wait. Perhaps I shall be better by that time. I think it's half fancy; but I should like your father to tell me so. He will laugh at me, I dare say; but I don't think I shall mind that. He always is severe on fanciful patients, isn't he, Molly?'

Molly thought that, if he saw Osborne's looks just then, he would hardly think him fanciful, or be inclined to be severe. But she only said – 'Papa enjoys a joke at everything, you know. It is a relief after all the sorrow he sees.'

'Very true. There is a great deal of sorrow in the world. I don't think it's a very happy place after all. So Cynthia is gone to London?' he added, after a pause. 'I think I should like to have seen her again. Poor old Roger! He loves her very dearly, Molly,' he said. Molly hardly knew how to answer him in all this; she was so struck by the change in both voice and manner.

'Mamma has gone to the Towers,' she began at length. 'Lady Cumnor wanted several things that mamma only can find. She will be sorry to miss you. We were speaking of you only yesterday, and she said how long it was since we had seen you.'

'I think I've grown careless; I've often felt so weary and ill that it was all I could do to keep up a brave face before my father.'

'Why did you not come and see papa?' said Molly; 'or write to him?'

'I cannot tell. I drifted on, sometimes better, and sometimes worse, till today I mustered up pluck, and came to hear what your father has got to tell me; and for no use it seems.'

'I am very sorry. But it is only for two days. He shall go and see you, as soon as ever he returns.'

'He must not alarm my father; remember, Molly,' said Osborne, lifting himself by the arms of his chair into an upright position, and speaking eagerly for the moment. 'I wish to God Roger was at home!' said he, falling back into the old posture.

'I can't help understanding you,' said Molly. 'You think yourself ill; but isn't it that you are tired just now?' She was not sure if she ought to have understood what was passing in his mind; but, as she did, she could not help speaking a true reply.

'Well, sometimes I do think I'm very ill; and then, again, I think it's only the moping life sets me fancying and exaggerating.' He was silent for some time. Then, as if he had taken a sudden resolution, he spoke again. 'You see, there are others depending upon me – upon my health. You haven't forgotten what you heard that day in the library at home? No, I know you haven't. I have seen the thought of it in your eyes often since then. I didn't know you at that time. I think I do now.'

'Don't go on talking so fast,' said Molly. 'Rest. No one will interrupt us; I will go on with my sewing; when you want to say anything more, I shall be listening.' For she was alarmed at the strange pallor that had come over his face.

'Thank you.' After a time he roused himself, and began to speak very quietly, as if on an indifferent matter of fact.

'The name of my wife is Aimée. Aimée Hamley, of course. She lives at Bishopfield, a village near Winchester. Write it down, but keep it to yourself. She is a French-woman, a Roman Catholic, and was a servant. She is a thoroughly good woman. I must not say how dear she is to me. I dare not. I meant once to have told Cynthia; but she didn't seem quite to consider me as a brother. Perhaps she was shy of a new relation; but you'll give my love to her, all the same. It is a relief to think that some one else has my secret; and you are like one of us, Molly. I can trust you almost as I can trust Roger. I feel better already, now I feel that some one else knows the whereabouts of my wife and child.'

'Child!' said Molly, surprised. But before he could reply, Maria had announced, 'Miss Phoebe Browning.'

'Fold up that paper,' said he quickly, putting something into her hands. 'It is only for yourself.'

CHAPTER 46

Hollingford Gossips

'My dear Molly, why didn't you come and dine with us? I said to sister I would come and scold you well. Oh, Mr Osborne Hamley, is that you?' and a look of mistaken intelligence at the *tête-à-tête* she had disturbed came so perceptibly over Miss Phoebe's face, that Molly caught Osborne's sympathetic eye, and both smiled at the notion.

'I'm sure I – well! one must sometimes – I see our dinner would have been'—Then she recovered herself into a connected sentence. 'We only just heard of Mrs Gibson's having a fly from the George, because sister sent our Betty to pay for a couple of rabbits Tom Ostler had snared, (I hope we shan't be taken up for poachers, Mr Osborne – snaring doesn't require a licence,*I believe?) and she heard he was gone off with the fly to the Towers with your dear mamma; for Coxe, who drives the fly in general, has sprained his ankle. We had just finished dinner; but, when Betty said Tom Ostler would not be back till night, I said, "Why, there's that poor dear girl left all alone by herself, and her mother such a friend of ours" – when she was alive, I mean. But I'm sure I'm glad I'm mistaken.'

Osborne said – 'I came to speak to Mr Gibson, not knowing he had gone to London, and Miss Gibson kindly gave me some of her lunch. I must go now.'

'Oh dear! I am so sorry,' fluttered out Miss Phoebe, 'I disturbed you; but it was with the best intentions. I always was *mal-àpropos**from a child.' But Osborne was gone, before she had finished her apologies. As he left, his eyes met Molly's with a strange look of yearning farewell that struck her at the time, and that she remembered strongly afterwards. 'Such a nice suitable thing, and I came in the midst, and spoilt it all. I am sure you're very kind, my dear, considering' —

'Considering what, my dear Miss Phoebe? If you are conjecturing a love-affair between Mr Osborne Hamley and me, you never were more mistaken in your life. I think I told you so once before. Please do believe me.'

'Oh, yes! I remember. And somehow sister got it into her head it was Mr Preston. I recollect.'

'One guess is just as wrong as the other,' said Molly, smiling, and trying to look perfectly indifferent, but going extremely red at the mention of Mr Preston's name. It was very difficult for her to keep up any conversation, for her heart was full of Osborne – his changed appearance, his melancholy words of foreboding, and his confidences about his wife – French, Catholic, servant. Molly could not help trying to piece these strange facts together by imaginations of her own, and found it very hard work to attend to kind Miss Phoebe's unceasing patter. She came up to the point, however, when the voice ceased, and could recall, in a mechanical manner, the echo of the last words which, both from Miss Phoebe's look, and from the dying accent that lingered in Molly's ear, she perceived to be a question. Miss Phoebe was asking her if she would go out with her. She was going to Grinstead's, the bookseller of Hollingford; who, in addition to his regular business, was the agent for the Hollingford Book Society,*received their subscriptions, kept their accounts, ordered their books from London, and, on payment of a small salary, allowed the Society to keep their volumes on shelves in his shop. It was the centre of news, and the club, as it were, of the little town. Everybody who pretended to gentility in the place belonged to it. It was a test of gentility, indeed, rather than of education or a love of literature. No shopkeeper would have thought of offering himself as a member, however great his general intelligence and love of reading; while it boasted on its list of subscribers most of the county-families in the neighbourhood, some of whom subscribed to it as a sort of duty belonging to their station, without often using their privilege of reading the books; while there were residents in the

little town, such as Mrs Goodenough, who privately thought
reading a great waste of time, that might be much better employed
in sewing, and knitting, and pastry-making, but who nevertheless
belonged to it as a mark of station, just as these good, motherly
women would have thought it a terrible come-down in the world,
if they had not had a pretty young servant-maid to fetch them
home from the tea-parties at night. At any rate, Grinstead's was a
very convenient place for a lounge. In that view of the Book
Society every one agreed.

Molly went upstairs to get ready to accompany Miss Phoebe;
and, on opening one of her drawers, she saw Cynthia's envelope,
containing the money she owed to Mr Preston, carefully sealed-up
like a letter. This was what Molly had so unwillingly promised to
deliver – the last final stroke to the affair. Molly took it up, hating
it. For a time she had forgotten it; and now it was here, facing
her, and she must try and get rid of it. She put it into her pocket
for the chances of the walk and the day, and fortune for once
seemed to befriend her; for, on their entering Grinstead's shop, in
which two or three people were now, as always, congregated,
making play of examining the books, or business of writing down
the titles of new works in the order-book, there was Mr Preston.
He bowed as they came in. He could not help that; but, at the
sight of Molly, he looked as ill-tempered and out of humour as a
man well could do. She was connected in his mind with defeat
and mortification; and, besides, the sight of her called up what he
desired now, above all things, to forget; namely, the deep conviction, received through Molly's simple earnestness, of Cynthia's
dislike to him. If Miss Phoebe had seen the scowl upon his
handsome face, she might have undeceived her sister in her
suppositions about him and Molly. But Miss Phoebe, who did not
consider it quite maidenly to go and stand close to Mr Preston,
and survey the shelves of books in such close proximity to a
gentleman, found herself an errand at the other end of the shop,
and occupied herself in buying writing-paper. Molly fingered her
valuable letter, as it lay in her pocket; did she dare to cross over
to Mr Preston, and give it to him, or not? While she was still
undecided, shrinking always just at the moment when she thought
she had got her courage up for action, Miss Phoebe, having
finished her purchase, turned round, and after looking a little
pathetically at Mr Preston's back, said to Molly in a whisper – 'I
think we'll go to Johnson's now, and come back for the books in

a little while.' So across the street to Johnson's they went; but, no sooner had they entered the draper's shop, than Molly's conscience smote her for her cowardice, and loss of a good opportunity. 'I'll be back directly,' said she, as soon as Miss Phoebe was engaged with her purchases; and Molly ran across to Grinstead's, without looking either to the right or the left; she had been watching the door, and she knew that no Mr Preston had issued forth. She ran in; he was at the counter now, talking to Grinstead himself; Molly put the letter into his hand, to his surprise, and almost against his will, and turned round to go back to Miss Phoebe. At the door of the shop stood Mrs Goodenough, arrested in the act of entering, staring, with her round eyes, made still rounder and more owl-like by spectacles, to see Molly Gibson giving Mr Preston a letter, which he, conscious of being watched, and favouring underhand practices habitually, put quickly into his pocket, unopened. Perhaps, if he had had time for reflection, he would not have scrupled to put Molly to open shame, by rejecting what she so eagerly forced upon him.

There was another long evening to be got through with Mrs Gibson; but on this occasion there was the pleasant occupation of dinner, which took up at least an hour; for it was one of Mrs Gibson's fancies – one which Molly chafed against – to have every ceremonial gone through in the same stately manner for two as for twenty. So, although Molly knew full well, and her stepmother knew full well, and Maria knew full well, that neither Mrs Gibson nor Molly touched dessert, it was set on the table with as much form as if Cynthia had been at home, who delighted in almonds and raisins, or Mr Gibson had been there, who never could resist dates, though he always protested against 'persons in their station of life having a formal dessert set out before them every day.'

And Mrs Gibson herself apologised, as it were, to Molly today, in the same words she had often used to Mr Gibson – 'It's no extravagance, for we need not eat it – I never do. But it looks well, and makes Maria understand what is required in the daily life of every family of position.'

All through the evening, Molly's thoughts wandered far and wide, though she managed to keep up a show of attention to what Mrs Gibson was saying. She was thinking of Osborne, and his abrupt, half-finished confidence, and his ill-looks; she was wondering when Roger would come home, and longing for his return, as much (she said to herself) for Osborne's sake as for her own. And then she checked herself. What had she to do with Roger? Why should she long for his return? It was Cynthia who was doing this; only, somehow, he was such a true friend to Molly, that she could not help thinking of him as a staff and a stay in the troublous times which appeared to lie not far ahead – this evening. Then Mr Preston and her little adventure with him came uppermost. How angry he looked! How could Cynthia have liked him even enough to get into this abominable scrape, which was, however, all over now! And so she ran on in her fancies and imaginations, little dreaming that that very night much talk was going on, not half-a-mile from where she sate sewing, which could prove that the 'scrape' (as she called it, in her girlish phraseology) was not all over.

Scandal sleeps in the summer, comparatively speaking. Its nature is the reverse of that of the dormouse. Warm ambient air, loiterings abroad, gardenings, flowers to talk about, and preserves to make, soothed the wicked imp to slumber in the parish of Hollingford in summer-time. But when evenings grew short, and people gathered round the fires, and put their feet in a circle – not on the fenders, that was not allowed – then was the time for confidential conversation! Or, in the pauses allowed for the tea-trays to circulate among the card-tables – when those who were peaceably inclined tried to stop the warm discussions about 'the odd trick', and the rather wearisome feminine way of 'shouldering the crutch, and showing how fields were won'* – small crumbs and scraps of daily news came up to the surface, such as 'Martindale has raised the price of his best joints a halfpenny in the pound;' or, 'It's a shame of Sir Harry to order in another book on farriery into the Book Society; Phoebe and I tried to read it, but really there is no general interest in it;' or, 'I wonder what Mr Ashton will do, now Nancy is going to be married! Why, she's been with him these seventeen years! It's a very foolish thing for a woman of her age to be thinking of matrimony; and so I told her, when I met her in the market-place this morning!'

So said Miss Browning on the night in question; her hand of cards lying by her on the puce baize-covered table, while she munched the rich pound-cake*of a certain Mrs Dawes, lately come to inhabit Hollingford.

'Matrimony's not so bad as you think for, Miss Browning,' said Mrs Goodenough, standing up for the holy estate into which she had twice entered. 'If I'd ha' seen Nancy, I should ha' given her my mind very different. It's a great thing to be able to settle what you'll have for dinner, without never a one interfering with you.'

'If that's all!' said Miss Browning, drawing herself up, 'I can do that; and, perhaps, better than a woman who has a husband to please.'

'No one can say as I didn't please my husbands – both on 'em, though Jeremy was tickler*in his tastes than poor Harry Beaver. But, as I used to say to 'em, "Leave the victual to me; it's better for you than knowing what's to come beforehand. The stomach likes to be taken by surprise." And neither of 'em ever repented 'em of their confidence. You may take my word for it, beans and bacon will taste better (to Mr Ashton's Nancy in her own house) than all the sweetbreads and spring-chickens she's been a-doing for him this seventeen years. But, if I chose, I could tell you of something as would interest you all a deal more than Nancy's marriage to a widower with nine children – only, as the young folks themselves is meeting in private, clandestine-like, it's perhaps not for me to tell their secrets.'

'I'm sure I don't want to hear of clandestine meetings between young men and young women,' said Miss Browning, throwing up her head. 'It's disgrace enough to the people themselves, I consider, if they enter on a love-affair without the proper sanction of parents. I know public opinion has changed on the subject; but, when poor Gratia was married to Mr Byerley, he wrote to my father without ever having so much as paid her a compliment, or said more than the most trivial and commonplace things to her; and my father and mother sent for her into my father's study, and she said she was never so much frightened in her life – and they said it was a very good offer, and Mr Byerley was a very worthy man, and they hoped she would behave properly to him when he came to supper that night. And, after that, he was allowed to come twice a week till they were married. My mother and I sate at our work in the bow-window of the Rectory drawing-room, and Gratia and Mr Byerley at the other end; and my mother always called my attention to some flower or plant in the garden when it struck nine, for that was his time for going. Without offence to the present company, I am rather inclined to look upon matrimony as a weakness to which some very worthy people are prone; but, if they must be married, let them make the best of it, and go through the affair with dignity and propriety: or, if there are misdoings and clandestine meetings, and such things, at any rate, never let me hear about them! I think it's you to play, Mrs Dawes. You'll excuse my frankness on the subject of matrimony! Mrs Goodenough there can tell you I'm a very out-spoken person.'

'It's not the out-speaking, it's what you say that goes against me, Miss Browning,' said Mrs Goodenough, affronted, yet ready to play her card as soon as needed. And as for Mrs Dawes, she was too anxious to get into the genteelest of all (Hollingford) society to object to whatever Miss Browning (who, in right of being a deceased rector's daughter, rather represented the selectest circle of the little town) advocated, whether celibacy, marriage, bigamy, or polygamy.

So the remainder of the evening passed over without any further reference to the secret Mrs Goodenough was burning to disclose, unless a remark made *àpropos de rien**by Miss Browning, during the silence of a deal, could be supposed to have connection with the previous conversation. She said, suddenly and abruptly –

'I don't know what I have done that any man should make me his slave.' If she was referring to any prospect of matrimonial danger she saw opening before her fancy, she might have been comforted. But it was a remark of which no one took any notice, all being far too much engaged in the rubber. Only when Miss Browning took her early leave (for Miss Phoebe had a cold, and was an invalid at home), Mrs Goodenough burst out with –

'Well! now I may speak out my mind, and say as how, if there was a slave between us two, when Goodenough was alive, it wasn't me; and I don't think as it was pretty in Miss Browning to give herself such airs on her virginity when there was four widows in the room, – who've had six honest men among 'em for husbands. No offence, Miss Airy!' addressing an unfortunate little spinster, who found herself the sole representative of celibacy, now that Miss Browning was gone. 'I could tell her of a girl as she's very fond on, who's on the high road to matrimony; and in as cunning a way as ever I heard on: going out at dusk to meet her sweetheart, just as if she was my Betty, or your Jenny. And her name is Molly*too – which, as I have often thought, shows a low taste in them as first called her so; – she might as well be a scullery-maid at oncest. Not that she's picked up anybody common; she's looked about her for a handsome fellow, and a smart young man enough!'

Every one around the table looked curious and intent on the disclosures being made, except the hostess, Mrs Dawes, who smiled intelligence with her eyes, and knowingly pursed up her mouth until Mrs Goodenough had finished her tale. Then she said demurely –

'I suppose you mean Mr Preston and Miss Gibson?'

'Why, who told you?' said Mrs Goodenough, turning round upon her in surprise. 'You can't say as I did. There's many a Molly in Hollingford, beside her – though none, perhaps, in such a genteel station of life. I never named her, I'm sure.'

'No. But I know. I could tell my tale too,' continued Mrs Dawes.

'No! could you, really?' said Mrs Goodenough, very curious and a little jealous.

'Yes. My uncle Sheepshanks came upon them in the Park Avenue – he startled 'em a good deal, he said; and, when he taxed Mr Preston with being with his sweetheart, he didn't deny it.'

'Well! Now so much has come out, I'll tell you what I know. Only, ladies, I wouldn't wish to do the girl an unkind turn, – so you must keep what I've got to tell you a secret.' Of course they promised; that was easy.

'My Hannah, as married Tom Oakes, and lives in Pearson's Lane, was a-gathering of damsons only a week ago, and Molly Gibson was a-walking fast down the lane – quite in a hurry like to meet some one – and Hannah's little Anna-Maria fell down, and Molly (who's a kind-hearted lass enough) picked her up; so, if Hannah had had her doubts before, she had none then.'

'But there was no one with her, was there?' asked one of the ladies anxiously, as Mrs Goodenough stopped to finish her piece of cake, just at this crisis.

'No; I said she looked as if she was going to meet some one – and by-and-by comes Mr Preston running out of the wood just beyond Hannah's, and, says he, "A cup of water, please, good woman, for a lady has fainted, or is 'sterical or something." Now, though he didn't know Hannah, Hannah knew him. "More folks know Tom Fool, than Tom Fool knows,"* asking Mr Preston's pardon; for he's no fool whatever he be. And I could tell you more – and what I've see'd with my own eyes. I see'd her give him a letter in Grinstead's shop, only yesterday; and he looked as black as thunder at her, for he see'd me if she didn't.'

'It's a very suitable kind of thing,' said Miss Airy; 'why do they make such a mystery of it?'

'Some folks like it,' said Mrs Dawes; 'it adds zest to it all, to do their courting underhand.'

'Ay, it's like salt to their victual,' put in Mrs Goodenough. 'But I didn't think Molly Gibson was one of that sort, I didn't.'

'The Gibsons hold themselves very high?' cried Mrs Dawes, more as an inquiry than as an assertion. 'Mrs Gibson has called upon me.'

'Ay, you're like to be a patient of the doctor's,' put in Mrs Goodenough.

'She seemed to me very affable, though she is so intimate with the Countess and the family at the Towers; and is quite the lady herself; dines late, I've heard, and everything in style.'

'Style! very different style to what Bob Gibson, her husband, was used to when first he came here – glad of a mutton-chop in his surgery, for I doubt if he'd a fire anywhere else; we called him "Bob Gibson" then, but none on us dare "Bob" him now; I'd as soon think o' calling him "sweep"!'

'I think it looks very bad for Miss Gibson!' said one lady, rather anxious to bring back the conversation to the more interesting present time. But, as soon as Mrs Goodenough heard this natural comment on the disclosures she had made, she fired round on the speaker –

'Not at all "bad", and I'll trouble you not to use such a word as that about Molly Gibson, as I've known her all her life. It's odd, if you will. I was odd myself as a girl; I never could abide a plate of gathered gooseberries, but I must needs go and skulk behind a bush and gather 'em for myself. It's some folk's taste, though it mayn't be Miss Browning's, who'd have all the courting done under the nose of the family. All as ever I said was, that I was surprised at it in Molly Gibson; and that I'd ha' thought it was liker that pretty piece of a Cynthia, as they call her; indeed, at one time I was ready to swear as it was her Mr Preston was after. And now, ladies, I'll wish you a very good night. I cannot abide waste; and I'll venture for it Hetty's letting the candle in the lantern run all to grease, instead of putting it out, as I've told her to do, if ever she's got to wait for me.'

So, with formal dipping curtseys, the ladies separated, but not without thanking Mrs Dawes for the pleasant evening they had had; a piece of old-fashioned courtesy always gone through in those days.

CHAPTER 47

Scandal and Its Victims

When Mr Gibson returned to Hollingford, he found an accumulation of business waiting for him, and he was much inclined to complain of the consequences of the two days' comparative holiday, which had resulted in over-work for the week to come. He had hardly time to speak to his family, he had so immediately to rush off to pressing cases of illness. But Molly managed to arrest him in the hall, standing there with his greatcoat held out ready for him to put on, but whispering as she did so –

'Papa! Mr Osborne Hamley was here to see you yesterday. He looks very ill, and he's evidently frightened about himself.'

Mr Gibson faced about, and looked at her for a moment; but all he said was –

'I'll go and see him; don't tell your mother where I am gone; you've not mentioned this to her, I hope?'

'No,' said Molly, for she had only told Mrs Gibson of Osborne's call, not of the occasion for it.

'Don't say anything about it; there's no need. Now I think of it, I can't possibly go today – but I will go.'

Something in her father's manner disheartened Molly, who had persuaded herself that Osborne's evident illness was partly 'nervous', by which she meant imaginary. She had dwelt upon his looks of enjoyment at Miss Phoebe's perplexity, and thought that no one really believing himself to be in danger could have given the merry glances which he had done; but, after seeing the seriousness of her father's face, she recurred to the shock she had experienced on first seeing Osborne's changed appearance. All this time Mrs Gibson was busy reading a letter from Cynthia which Mr Gibson had brought from London; for every opportunity of private conveyance was seized upon, when postage was so high; and Cynthia had forgotten so many things in her hurried packing, that she now sent a list of the clothes which she required. Molly almost wondered that it had not come to her; but she did not understand the sort of reserve that was springing up in Cynthia's mind towards her. Cynthia herself struggled with the feeling, and tried to fight against it by calling herself 'ungrateful'; but the truth

was, she believed that she no longer held her former high place in
Molly's estimation, and she could not help turning away from one
who knew things to her discredit. She was fully aware of Molly's
prompt decision and willing action, where action was especially
disagreeable, on her behalf; she knew that Molly would never
bring up the past errors and difficulties; but still, the consciousness
that the good, straightforward girl had learnt that Cynthia had
been guilty of so much underhand work cooled her regard, and
restrained her willingness of intercourse. Reproach herself with
ingratitude as she would, she could not help feeling glad to be
away from Molly; it was awkward to speak to her as if nothing
had happened; it was awkward to write to her about forgotten
ribbons and laces, when their last conversation had been on such
different subjects, and had called out such vehement expressions
of feeling. So Mrs Gibson held the list in her hand, and read out
the small fragments of news that were intermixed with notices of
Cynthia's requirements.

'Helen cannot be so very ill,' said Molly at length, 'or Cynthia
would not want her pink muslin and daisy wreath.'

'I don't see that that follows, I'm sure,' replied Mrs Gibson
rather sharply. 'Helen would never be so selfish as to tie Cynthia
to her side, however ill she was. Indeed, I should not have felt that
it was my duty to let Cynthia go to London at all, if I had thought
she was to be perpetually exposed to the depressing atmosphere
of a sick-room. Besides, it must be so good for Helen to have
Cynthia coming in with bright pleasant accounts of the parties she
has been to – even if Cynthia disliked gaiety, I should desire her
to sacrifice herself and go out as much as she could, for Helen's
sake. My idea of nursing is that one should not be always thinking
of one's own feelings and wishes, but doing those things which
will most serve to beguile the weary hours of an invalid. But then
so few people have had to consider the subject so deeply as I have
done!'

Mrs Gibson here thought fit to sigh, before going on with
Cynthia's letter. As far as Molly could make any sense out of this
rather incoherent epistle, very incoherently read aloud to her,
Cynthia was really pleased, and glad to be of use and comfort to
Helen, but at the same time very ready to be easily persuaded into
the perpetual small gaieties which abounded in her uncle's house
in London, even at this dead season of the year. Mrs Gibson came
upon Mr Henderson's name once, and then went on with a

running 'um-um-um' to herself, which sounded very mysterious, but which might as well have been omitted, as all that Cynthia really said about him was, 'Mr Henderson's mother has advised my aunt to consult a certain Dr Donaldson, who is said to be very clever in such cases as Helen's; but my uncle is not sufficiently sure of the professional etiquette, etc.' Then there came a very affectionate, carefully worded message to Molly – implying a good deal more than was said of loving gratitude for the trouble she had taken on Cynthia's behalf. And that was all; and Molly went away a little depressed; she knew not why.

The operation on Lady Cumnor had been successfully performed, and in a few days they hoped to bring her down to the Towers to recruit her strength in the fresh country air. The case was one which interested Mr Gibson extremely, and in which his opinion had been proved to be right, in opposition to that of one or two great names in London. The consequence was that he was frequently consulted and referred to during the progress of her recovery; and, as he had much to do in the immediate circle of his Hollingford practice, as well as to write thoughtful letters to his medical brethren in London, he found it difficult to spare the three or four hours necessary to go over to Hamley to see Osborne. He wrote to him, however, begging him to reply immediately and detail his symptoms; and from the answer he received he did not imagine that the case was immediately pressing. Osborne, too, deprecated his coming over to Hamley for the express purpose of seeing him. So the visit was deferred to that 'more convenient season' which is so often too late.

All these days the buzzing gossip about Molly's meetings with Mr Preston, her clandestine correspondence, the secret interviews in lonely places, had been gathering strength, and assuming the positive form of scandal. The simple, innocent girl, who walked through the quiet streets without a thought of being the object of mysterious implications, became for a time the unconscious black sheep of the town. Servants heard part of what was said in their mistresses' drawing-rooms, and exaggerated the sayings amongst themselves with the coarse strengthening of expression common with uneducated people. Mr Preston himself became aware that her name was being coupled with his, though hardly of the extent to which the love of excitement and gossip had carried people's speeches; he chuckled over the mistake, but took no pains to correct it. 'It serves her right,' said he to himself, 'for meddling with other folk's business,' and he felt himself avenged for the discomfiture which her menace of appealing to Lady Harriet had caused him, and the mortification he had experienced in learning from her plain-speaking lips, how he had been talked over by Cynthia and herself, with personal dislike on the one side, and evident contempt on the other. Besides, if any denial of Mr Preston's stirred up an examination as to the real truth, more might come out of his baffled endeavours to compel Cynthia to keep to her engagement to him than he cared to have known. He was angry with himself for still loving Cynthia; loving her in his own fashion, be it understood. He told himself that many a woman of more position and wealth would be glad enough to have him; some of them pretty women too. And he asked himself why he was such a confounded fool to go on hankering after a penniless girl, who was as fickle as the wind? The answer was silly enough, logically; but forcible in fact. Cynthia was Cynthia, and not Venus herself could have been her substitute. In this one thing Mr Preston was more really true than many a worthy man, who, seeking to be married, turns with careless facility from the unattainable to the attainable, and keeps his feelings and fancy tolerably loose, till he finds a woman who consents to be his wife. But no one would ever be to Mr Preston what Cynthia had been, and was; and yet he could have stabbed her in certain of his moods. So Molly, who had come between him and the object of his desire, was not likely to find favour in his sight, or to obtain friendly action from him.

There came a time – not very distant from the evening at Mrs Dawes' – when Molly felt that people looked askance at her. Mrs Goodenough openly pulled her grand-daughter away, when the young girl stopped to speak to Molly in the street, and an engagement which the two had made for a long walk together was cut very short by a very trumpery excuse. Mrs Goodenough explained her conduct in the following manner to some of her friends: –

'You see, I don't think the worse of a girl for meeting her sweetheart here and there and everywhere, till she gets talked about; but then, when she does – and Molly Gibson's name is in everybody's mouth – I think it's only fair to Bessy, who has trusted me with Annabella, not to let her daughter be seen with a lass who has managed her matters so badly as to set folk talking about her. My maxim is this, – and it's a very good working one, you may depend on't – women should mind what they're about, and never be talked of; and, if a woman's talked of, the less her friends have to do with her till the talk has died away, the better. So Annabella is not to have anything to do with Molly Gibson this visit at any rate.'

For a good while, the Miss Brownings were kept in ignorance of the evil tongues that whispered hard words about Molly. Miss Browning was known to 'have a temper', and by instinct every one who came in contact with her shrank from irritating that temper by uttering the slightest syllable against the smallest of those creatures over whom she spread the aegis of her love. She would and did reproach them herself; she used to boast that she never spared them; but no one else might touch them with the slightest slur of a passing word. But Miss Phoebe inspired no such terror; the great reason why she did not hear of the gossip against Molly as early as any one, was that, although she was not the rose, she lived near the rose.* Besides, she was of so tender a nature that even thick-skinned Mrs Goodenough was unwilling to say what would give her pain; and it was the new-comer, Mrs Dawes, who in all ignorance alluded to the town's talk, as to something of which Miss Phoebe must be aware. Then Miss Phoebe poured down her questions, although she protested, even with tears, her total disbelief in all the answers she received. It was a small act of heroism on her part to keep all that she then learnt a secret from her sister Dorothy, as she did for four or five days; till Miss Browning attacked her one evening with the following speech –

'Phoebe! either you've some reason for puffing yourself out with sighs, or you've not. If you have a reason, it's your duty to tell it me directly; and if you haven't a reason, you must break yourself of a bad habit that is growing upon you.'

'Oh, sister! do you think it is really my duty to tell you? it would be such a comfort; but then I thought I ought not; it will distress you so.'

'Nonsense. I am so well prepared for misfortune by the frequent contemplation of its possibility, that I believe I can receive any ill news with apparent equanimity and real resignation. Besides, when you said yesterday at breakfast-time that you meant to give up the day to making your drawers tidy, I was aware that some misfortune was impending, though of course I could not judge of its magnitude. Is the Highchester Bank broken?'*

'Oh no, sister!' said Miss Phoebe, moving to a seat close to her sister's on the sofa. 'Have you really been thinking that? I wish I had told you what I heard at the very first, if you've been fancying that!'

'Take warning, Phoebe, and learn to have no concealments from me. I did think we must be ruined, from your ways of going on: eating no meat at dinner, and sighing continually. And now what is it?'

'I hardly know how to tell you, Dorothy. I really don't.'

Miss Phoebe began to cry; Miss Browning took hold of her arm, and gave her a little sharp shake.

'Cry as much as you like, when you've told me; but don't cry now, child, when you're keeping me on the tenter-hooks.'

'Molly Gibson has lost her character, sister. That's it.'

'Molly Gibson has done no such thing,' said Miss Browning indignantly. 'How dare you repeat such stories about poor Mary's child? Never let me hear you say such things again.'

'I can't help it: Mrs Dawes told me; and she says it's all over the town. I told her I did not believe a word of it. And I kept it from you; and I think I should have been really ill, if I'd kept it to myself any longer. Oh, sister! what are you going to do?'

For Miss Browning had risen without speaking a word, and was leaving the room in a stately and determined fashion.

'I'm going to put on my bonnet and things, and then I shall call upon Mrs Dawes, and confront her with her lies.'

'Oh, don't call them "lies", sister; it's such a strong, ugly word. Please call them tarradiddles,*for I don't believe she meant any harm. Besides – besides – if they should turn out to be truth? Really, sister, that's the weight on my mind; so many things sounded as if they might be true.'

'What things?' said Miss Browning, still standing with judicial erectness of position in the middle of the floor.

'Why – one story was that Molly had given him a letter.'

'Who's him? How am I to understand a story told in that silly way?' Miss Browning sat down on the nearest chair, and made up her mind to be patient if she could.

'Him is Mr Preston. And that must be true; because I missed her from my side, when I wanted to ask if she thought blue would look green by candlelight, as the young man said it would; and she had run across the street, and Mrs Goodenough was just going into the shop, just as she said she was.'

Miss Browning's distress was overcoming her anger; so she only said. 'Phoebe, I think you'll drive me mad. Do tell me what you heard from Mrs Dawes, in a sensible and coherent manner, for once in your life.'

'I'm sure I'm trying with all my might to tell you everything just as it happened.'

'What did you hear from Mrs Dawes?'

'Why, that Molly and Mr Preston were keeping company just as if she was a maid-servant and he was a gardener: meeting at all sorts of improper times and places, and fainting away in his arms, and out at night together, and writing to each other, and slipping their letters into each other's hands; and that was what I was talking about, sister, for I next door to saw that done once. I saw her with my own eyes run across the street to Grinstead's, where he was, for we had just left him there; with a letter in her hand, too, which was not there when she came back, all fluttered and blushing. But I never thought anything of it at the time; but now all the town is talking about it, and crying shame, and saying they ought to be married.' Miss Phoebe sank into sobbing again; but was suddenly roused by a good box on her ear. Miss Browning was standing over her almost trembling with passion.

'Phoebe, if ever I hear you say such things again, I'll turn you out of the house that minute.'

'I only said what Mrs Dawes said, and you asked me what it was,' replied Miss Phoebe, humbly and meekly. 'Dorothy, you should not have done that.'

'Never mind whether I should or I shouldn't. That's not the matter in hand. What I've got to decide is, how to put a stop to all these lies.'

'But, Dorothy, they are not all "lies" – if you will call them so; I'm afraid some things are true; though I stuck to their being false when Mrs Dawes told me of them.'

'If I go to Mrs Dawes, and she repeats them to me, I shall slap her face or box her ears, I'm afraid, for I couldn't stand tales being told of poor Mary's daughter, as if they were just a stirring piece of news, like James Horrock's pig with two heads,' said Miss Browning, meditating aloud. 'That would do harm instead of good. Phoebe, I'm really sorry I boxed your ears; only I should do it again, if you said the same things.' Phoebe sate down by her sister, and took hold of one of her withered hands, and began caressing it, which was her way of accepting her sister's expression of regret. 'If I speak to Molly, the child will deny it, if she's half as good-for-nothing as they say; and, if she's not, she'll only worry herself to death. No, that won't do. Mrs Goodenough – but she's a donkey; and, if I convinced her, she could never convince any one else. No; Mrs Dawes, who told you, shall tell me, and I'll tie my hands together inside my muff, and bind myself over to keep the peace. And, when I've heard what is to be heard, I'll put the matter into Mr Gibson's hands. That's what I'll do. So it's no use your saying anything against it, Phoebe, for I shan't attend to you.'

Miss Browning went to Mrs Dawes's and began, civilly enough, to make inquiries concerning the reports current in Hollingford about Molly and Mr Preston; and Mrs Dawes fell into the snare, and told all the real and fictitious circumstances of the story in circulation, quite unaware of the storm that was gathering and ready to fall upon her as soon as she stopped speaking. But she had not the long habit of reverence for Miss Browning, which would have kept so many Hollingford ladies from justifying themselves if she found fault. Mrs Dawes stood up for herself and her own veracity, bringing out fresh scandal, which she said she did not believe, but that many did; and adducing so much evidence as to the truth of what she had said and did believe, that Miss Browning was almost quelled, and sate silent and miserable at the end of Mrs Dawes's justification of herself.

'Well!' she said at length, rising up from her chair as she spoke, 'I'm very sorry I've lived till this day; it's a blow to me, just as if I had heard of such goings-on in my own flesh and blood. I suppose I ought to apologise to you, Mrs Dawes, for what I said; but I've no heart to do it today. I ought not to have spoken as I did; but that's nothing to this affair, you see.'

'I hope you do me the justice to perceive that I only repeated what I had heard on good authority, Miss Browning,' said Mrs Dawes in reply.

'My dear, don't repeat evil on any authority, unless you can do some good by speaking about it,' said Miss Browning, laying her hand on Mrs Dawes's shoulder. 'I'm not a good woman, but I know what is good, and that advice is. And now I think I can tell you that I beg your pardon for flying out upon you so; but God knows what pain you were putting me to. You'll forgive me, won't you, my dear?' Mrs Dawes felt the hand trembling on her shoulder, and saw the real distress of Miss Browning's mind; so it was not difficult for her to grant the requested forgiveness. Then Miss Browning went home, and said but a few words to Phoebe, who indeed saw well enough that her sister had heard the reports confirmed, and needed no further explanation of the cause of scarcely-tasted dinner, and short replies, and saddened looks. Presently, Miss Browning sate down and wrote a short note. Then she rang the bell, and told the little maiden who answered it to take it to Mr Gibson and, if he was out, to see that it was given to him as soon as ever he came home. And then she went and put on her Sunday-cap; and Miss Phoebe knew that her sister had written to ask Mr Gibson to come and be told of the rumours affecting his daughter. Miss Browning was sadly disturbed at the information she had received, and the task that lay before her; she was miserably uncomfortable to herself and irritable to Miss Phoebe, and the netting-cotton she was using kept continually snapping and breaking from the jerks of her nervous hands. When the knock at the door was heard – the well-known doctor's knock – Miss Browning took off her spectacles, and dropped them on the carpet, breaking them as she did so; and then she bade Miss Phoebe leave the room, as if her presence had cast the evil-eye, and caused the misfortune. She wanted to look natural, and was distressed at forgetting whether she usually received him sitting or standing.

'Well!' said he, coming in cheerfully, and rubbing his cold hands as he went straight to the fire, 'and what is the matter with us? It's Phoebe, I suppose? I hope none of those old spasms? But, after all, a dose or two will set that to rights.'

'Oh! Mr Gibson, I wish it was Phoebe, or me either!' said Miss Browning, trembling more and more.

He sate down by her patiently, when he saw her agitation, and took her hand in a kind, friendly manner.

'Don't hurry yourself – take your time. I daresay it's not so bad as you fancy; but we'll see about it. There's a great deal of help in the world, much as we abuse it.'

'Mr Gibson,' said she, 'it's your Molly I'm so grieved about. It's out now, and God help us both, and the poor child too; for I'm sure she's been led astray, and not gone wrong by her own free will!'

'Molly!' said he, fighting against her words. 'What's my little Molly been doing or saying?'

'Oh! Mr Gibson, I don't know how to tell you. I never would

have named it, if I had not been convinced, sorely, sorely against my will.'

'At any rate, you can let me hear what you've heard,' said he, putting his elbow on the table, and screening his eyes with his hand. 'Not that I'm a bit afraid of anything you can hear about my girl,' continued he. 'Only, in this little nest of gossip, it's as well to know what people are talking about.'

'They say – oh, how shall I tell you?'

'Go on, can't you?' said he, removing his hand from his blazing eyes. 'I'm not going to believe it, so don't be afraid!'

'But I fear you must believe it. I would not, if I could help it. She's been carrying on a clandestine correspondence with Mr Preston'—

'Mr Preston!' exclaimed he.

'And meeting him at all sorts of unseemly places and hours, out of doors – in the dark – fainting away in his – his arms, if I must speak out. All the town is talking of it.' Mr Gibson's hand was over his eyes again, and he made no sign; so Miss Browning went on, adding touch to touch. 'Mr Sheepshanks saw them together. They have exchanged notes in Grinstead's shop; she ran after him there.'

'Be quiet, can't you?' said Mr Gibson, taking his hand away, and showing his grim, set face. 'I've heard enough. Don't go on. I said I shouldn't believe it, and I don't. I suppose I must thank you for telling me; but I can't yet.'

'I don't want your thanks,' said Miss Browning, almost crying. 'I thought you ought to know; for, though you're married again, I can't forget you were dear Mary's husband once upon a time; and Molly's her child.'

'I'd rather not speak any more about it, just at present,' said he, not at all replying to Miss Browning's last speech. 'I may not control myself as I ought. I only wish I could meet Preston and horsewhip him within an inch of his life. I wish I'd the doctoring of these slanderous gossips – I'd make their tongues lie still for a while! My little girl! What harm has she done them all, that they should go and foul her fair name?'

'Indeed, Mr Gibson, I'm afraid it's all true. I would not have sent for you if I hadn't examined into it. Do ascertain the truth before you do anything violent, such as horse-whipping or poisoning.'

With all the *inconséquence** of a man in a passion, Mr Gibson laughed out, 'What have I said about horse-whipping or poisoning? Do you think I'd have Molly's name dragged about the streets in connection with any act of violence on my part? Let the report die away as it arose! Time will prove its falsehood.'

'But I don't think it will, and that's the pity of it,' said Miss Browning. 'You must do something; but I don't know what.'

'I shall go home and ask Molly herself what's the meaning of it all; that's all I shall do. It's too ridiculous – knowing Molly as I do, it's perfectly ridiculous.' He got up and walked about the room with hasty steps, laughing short unnatural laughs from time to time. 'Really, what will they say next? "Satan finds some mischief still for idle tongues to do." '*

'Don't talk of Satan, please, in this house. No one knows what may happen, if he's lightly spoken about,' pleaded Miss Browning.

He went on, without noticing her, talking to himself – 'I've a great mind to leave the place; – and what food for scandal that piece of folly would give rise to!' Then he was silent for a time; his hands in his pockets, his eyes on the ground, as he continued his quarter-deck march.* Suddenly he stopped close to Miss Browning's chair: 'I'm thoroughly ungrateful to you, for as true a mark of friendship as you've ever shown me. True or false, it was right I should know the wretched scandal that is being circulated; and it couldn't have been pleasant for you to tell it me. Thank you from the bottom of my heart!'

'Indeed, Mr Gibson, if it was false, I would never have named it, but let it die away.'

'It's not true, though!' said he doggedly, letting drop the hand he had taken in his effusion of gratitude.

She shook her head. 'I shall always love Molly for her mother's sake,' she said. And it was a great concession from the correct Miss Browning. But her father did not understand it as such.

'You ought to love her for her own. She has done nothing to disgrace herself. I shall go straight home, and probe into the truth.'

'As if the poor girl who has been led away into deceit already would scruple much at going on in falsehood!' was Miss Browning's remark on this last speech of Mr Gibson's; but she had discretion enough not to make it, until he was well out of hearing.

CHAPTER 48

An Innocent Culprit

With his head bent down – as if he were facing some keen-blowing wind – and yet there was not a breath of air stirring – Mr Gibson went swiftly to his own home. He rang at the door-bell; an unusual proceeding on his part. Maria opened the door. 'Go and tell Miss Molly she's wanted in the dining-room. Don't say who it is that wants her.' There was something in Mr Gibson's manner that made Maria obey him to the letter, in spite of Molly's surprised question –

'Wants me? Who is it, Maria?'

Mr Gibson went into the dining-room, and shut the door, for an instant's solitude. He went up to the chimney-piece, took hold of it, and laid his head on his hands, and tried to still the beating of his heart.

The door opened. He knew that Molly stood there, before he heard her tone of astonishment.

'Papa!'

'Hush!' said he, turning round sharply. 'Shut the door. Come here.'

She came to him wondering what was amiss. Her thoughts went to the Hamleys immediately. 'Is it Osborne?' she asked, breathless. If Mr Gibson had not been too much agitated to judge calmly, he might have deduced comfort from these three words.

But, instead of allowing himself to seek for comfort from collateral evidence, he said – 'Molly, what is this I hear? That you have been keeping up a clandestine intercourse with Mr Preston – meeting him in out-of-the-way places; exchanging letters with him in a stealthy way?'

Though he had professed to disbelieve all this, and did disbelieve it at the bottom of his soul, his voice was hard and stern, his face was white and grim, and his eyes fixed Molly's with the terrible keenness of their search. Molly trembled all over, but she did not attempt to evade his penetration. If she was silent for a moment, it was because she was rapidly reviewing her relation with regard to Cynthia in the matter. It was but a moment's pause of silence, but it seemed long minutes to one who was craving for a burst of indignant denial. He had taken hold of her two arms just above her wrists, as she had advanced towards him; he was unconscious of this action; but, as his impatience for her words grew upon him, he grasped her more and more tightly in his vice-like hands, till she made a little involuntary sound of pain. And then he let go; and she looked at her soft bruised flesh, with tears gathering fast to her eyes, to think that he, her father, should have hurt her so. At the instant, it appeared to her stranger that he should inflict bodily pain upon his child, than that he should have heard the truth – even in an exaggerated form. With a childish gesture, she held out her arm to him; but, if she expected pity, she received none.

'Pooh!' said he, as he just glanced at the mark, 'that is nothing – nothing. Answer my question. Have you – have you met that man in private?'

'Yes, papa, I have; but I don't think it was wrong.'

He sate down now. 'Wrong!' he echoed bitterly. 'Not wrong? Well! I must bear it somehow. Your mother is dead. That's one comfort. It is true, then, is it? Why, I didn't believe it – not I! I laughed in my sleeve at their credulity; and I was the dupe all the time!'

'Papa, I cannot tell you all. It is not my secret, or you should know it directly. Indeed, you will be sorry some time – I have never deceived you yet, have I?' trying to take one of his hands; but he kept them tightly in his pockets, his eyes fixed on the pattern of the carpet before him. 'Papa!' said she, pleading again, 'have I ever deceived you?'

'How can I tell? I hear of this from the town's talk. I don't know what next may come out!'

'The town's talk!' said Molly in dismay. 'What business is it of theirs?'

'Every one makes it their business to cast dirt on a girl's name, who has disregarded the commonest rules of modesty and propriety.'

'Papa, you are very hard. Modesty disregarded! I will tell you exactly what I have done. I met Mr Preston once – that evening when you put me down to walk over Croston Heath – and there was another person with him. I met him a second time – and that time by appointment – nobody but our two selves – in the Towers Park. That is all, papa. You must trust me. I cannot explain more. You must trust me indeed.'

He could not help relenting at her words; there was such truth in the tone in which they were spoken. But he neither spoke nor stirred for a minute or two. Then he raised his eyes to hers, for the first time since she had acknowledged the external truth of what he charged her with. Her face was very white, but it bore the impress of the final sincerity of death, when the true expression prevails without the poor disguises of time.

'The letters?' he said – but almost as if he were ashamed to question that countenance any further.

'I gave him one letter – of which I did not write a word – which, in fact, I believe to have been merely an envelope, without any writing whatever inside. The giving that letter – the two interviews I have named – make all the private intercourse I have had with Mr Preston. Oh! papa, what have they been saying that has grieved – shocked you so much?'

'Never mind. As the world goes, what you say you have done, Molly, is ground enough. You must tell me all. I must be sure to refute these rumours point by point.'

'How are they to be refuted, when you say that the truth which I have acknowledged is ground enough for what people are saying?'

'You say you were not acting for yourself, but for another. If you tell me who the other was – if you tell me everything out fully, I will do my utmost to screen her – for of course I guess it was Cynthia – while I am exonerating you.'

'No, papa!' said Molly, after some little consideration; 'I have told you all I can tell; all that concerns myself; and I have promised not to say one word more.'

'Then your character will be impugned. It must be, unless the fullest explanation of these secret meetings is given. I've a great mind to force the whole truth out of Preston himself.'

'Papa! once again I beg you to trust me. If you ask Mr Preston, you will be very likely to hear the whole truth; but that is just what I have been trying so hard to conceal, for it will only make several people very unhappy, if it is known, and the whole affair is over and done with now.'

'Not your share in it. Miss Browning sent for me this evening, to tell me how people were talking about you. She implied that it was a complete loss of your good name. You don't know, Molly, how slight a thing may blacken a girl's reputation for life. I'd hard work to stand all she said, even though I didn't believe a word of it at the time. And now you've told me that much of it is true.'

'But I think you are a brave man, papa. And you believe me, don't you? We shall outlive these rumours, never fear.'

'You don't know the power of ill-natured tongues, child,' said he.

'Oh, now you've called me "child" again, I don't care for anything. Dear, dear papa, I'm sure it is best and wisest to take no notice of these speeches. After all, they may not mean them ill-naturedly. I am sure Miss Browning would not. By-and-by they'll quite forget how much they made out of so little – and even if they don't, you would not have me break my solemn word, would you?'

'Perhaps not. But I cannot easily forgive the person who, by practising on your generosity, led you into this scrape. You are very young, and look upon these things as merely temporary evils. I have more experience.'

'Still, I don't see what I can do now, papa. Perhaps I've been foolish; but, what I did, I did of my own self. It was not suggested to me. And I'm sure it was not wrong in morals, whatever it might be in judgment. As I said, it's all over now; what I did ended the affair, I am thankful to say; and it was with that object I did it. If people choose to talk about me, I must submit; and so must you, dear papa.'

'Does your mother – does Mrs Gibson – know anything about it?' asked he, with sudden anxiety.

'No; not a bit; not a word. Pray don't name it to her. That might lead to more mischief than anything else. I have really told you everything I am at liberty to tell.'

It was a great relief to Mr Gibson to find that this sudden fear that his wife might have been privy to it all was ill-founded. He had been seized by a sudden dread that she, whom he had chosen to marry in order to have a protectress and guide for his daughter, had been cognisant of this ill-advised adventure with Mr Preston – nay, more, that she might even have instigated it to save her own child; for that Cynthia was, somehow or other, at the bottom of it all he had no doubt whatever. But now, at any rate, Mrs Gibson had not been playing a treacherous part; that was all the comfort he could extract out of Molly's mysterious admission, that much mischief might result from Mrs Gibson's knowing anything about these meetings with Mr Preston.

'Then, what is to be done?' said he. 'The reports are abroad, –
am I to do nothing to contradict them? Am I to go about smiling
and content with all this talk about you passing from one idle
gossip to another?'

'I'm afraid so. I'm very sorry, for I never meant you to have
known anything about it, and I can see now how it must distress
you. But surely, when nothing more happens, and nothing comes
of what has happened, the wonder and the gossip must die away.
I know you believe every word I have said, and you must trust
me, papa. Please, for my sake, be patient with all this gossip and
cackle!'

'It will try me hard, Molly,' said he.

'For my sake, papa!'

'I don't see what else I can do,' replied he moodily, 'unless I get
hold of Preston.'

'That would be the worst of all. That would make a talk. And,
after all, perhaps he was not so much to blame. Yes! he was. But
he behaved well to me, as far as that goes,' said she, suddenly
recollecting his speech, when Mr Sheepshanks came up in the
Towers Park – 'Don't stir, you have done nothing to be ashamed
of.'

'That's true. A quarrel between men which drags a woman's
name into notice is to be avoided at any cost. But, sooner or later,
I must have it out with Preston. He shall find it not so pleasant to
have placed my daughter in equivocal circumstances.'

'He didn't place me. He didn't know I was coming; didn't
expect to meet me either time; and would far rather not have
taken the letter I gave him, if he could have helped himself.'

'It's all a mystery. I hate to have you mixed-up in mysteries.'

'I hate to be mixed-up. But what can I do? I know of another
mystery which I'm pledged not to speak about. I cannot help
myself.'

'Well, all I can say is, never be the heroine of a mystery that
you can avoid, if you can't help being an accessory. Then, I
suppose I must yield to your wishes and let this scandal wear itself
out without any notice from me?'

'What else can you do, under the circumstances?'

'Ay; what else, indeed? How shall you bear it?'

For an instant the quick hot tears sprang into her eyes: to have
everybody – all her world – thinking evil of her, did seem hard to

the girl who had never thought or said an unkind thing of them. But she smiled as she made answer –

'It's like tooth-drawing; it will be over some time. It would be much worse, if I really had been doing wrong.'

'Cynthia shall beware'—he began; but Molly put her hand before his mouth.

'Papa, Cynthia must not be accused, or suspected; you will drive her out of your house if you do; she is so proud, and so unprotected, except by you. And Roger – for Roger's sake, you will never do or say anything to send Cynthia away, when he has trusted us all to take care of her, and love her in his absence. Oh! I think, if she were really wicked, and I did not love her at all, I should feel bound to watch over her, he loves her so dearly. And she is really good at heart, and I do love her dearly. You must not vex or hurt Cynthia, papa – remember she is dependent upon you!'

'I think the world would get on tolerably well, if there were no women in it. They plague the life out of one. You've made me forget, amongst you – poor old Job Houghton, that I ought to have gone to see an hour ago.'

Molly put up her mouth to be kissed. 'You're not angry with me now, papa, are you?'

'Get out of my way' (kissing her all the same), 'If I'm not angry with you, I ought to be; for you've caused a great deal of worry, which won't be over yet awhile, I can tell you.'

For all Molly's bravery at the time of this conversation, it was she that suffered more than her father. He kept out of the way of hearing gossip; but she was perpetually thrown into the small society of the place. Mrs Gibson herself had caught cold, and moreover was not tempted by the quiet old-fashioned visiting which was going on just about this time, provoked by the visit of two of Mrs Dawes's pretty unrefined nieces, who laughed, and chattered, and ate, and would fain have flirted with Mr Ashton, the vicar, could he have been brought by any possibility to understand his share in the business. Mr Preston did not accept the invitations to Hollingford tea-drinkings with the same eager gratitude as he had done a year before: or else the shadow which hung over Molly would not have extended to him, her co-partner in the clandestine meetings which gave such umbrage to the feminine virtue in the town. Molly herself was invited, because it would not do to pass any apparent slight on either Mr or Mrs

Gibson; but there was a tacit and underhand protest against her being received on the old terms. Every one was civil to her, but no one was cordial; there was a very perceptible film of difference in their behaviour to her from what it was formerly; nothing that had outlines and could be defined. But Molly, for all her clear conscience and her brave heart, felt acutely that she was only tolerated, not welcomed. She caught the buzzing whispers of the two Miss Oakeses, who, when they first met the heroine of the prevailing scandal, looked at her askance, and criticised her pretensions to good looks, with hardly an attempt at undertones. Molly tried to be thankful that her father was not in the mood for visiting. She was even glad that her stepmother was too much of an invalid to come out, when she felt thus slighted, and, as it were, degraded from her place. Miss Browning herself, that true old friend, spoke to her with chilling dignity, and much reserve; for she had never heard a word from Mr Gibson, since the evening when she had put herself to so much pain to tell him of the disagreeable rumours affecting his daughter.

Only Miss Phoebe would seek out Molly with even more than her former tenderness; and this tried Molly's calmness more than all the slights put together. The soft hand, pressing hers under the table – the continual appeals to her, so as to bring her back into the conversation – touched Molly almost to shedding tears. Sometimes, the poor girl wondered to herself whether this change in the behaviour of her acquaintances was not a mere fancy of hers; whether, if she had never had that conversation with her father, in which she had borne herself so bravely at the time, she should have discovered the difference in their treatment of her. She never told her father how she felt these perpetual small slights: she had chosen to bear the burden of her own free will; nay, more, she had insisted on being allowed to do so; and it was not for her to grieve him now, by showing that she shrank from the consequences of her own act. So she never even made an excuse for not going into the small gaieties, or mingling with the society of Hollingford. Only, she suddenly let go the stretch of restraint she was living in, when one evening her father told her that he was really anxious about Mrs Gibson's cough, and should like Molly to give up a party at Mrs Goodenough's, to which they were all three invited, but to which Molly alone was going. Molly's heart leaped up at the thought of stopping at home, even though the next moment she had to blame herself for rejoicing at a reprieve that was purchased by another's suffering. However, the remedies prescribed by her husband did Mrs Gibson good; and she was particularly grateful and caressing to Molly.

'Really, dear!' said she, stroking Molly's head, 'I think your hair is getting softer, and losing that disagreeable crisp, curly feeling.'

Then Molly knew that her stepmother was in high good-humour; the smoothness or curliness of her hair was a sure test of the favour in which Mrs Gibson held her at the moment.

'I am so sorry to be the cause of detaining you from this little party; but dear papa is so over-anxious about me. I have always been a kind of pet with gentlemen, and poor Mr Kirkpatrick never knew how to make enough of me. But I think Mr Gibson is even more foolishly fond; his last words were, "Take care of yourself, Hyacinth;" and then he came back again, to say, "If you don't attend to my directions, I won't answer for the consequences." I shook my fore-finger at him, and said, "Don't be so anxious, you silly man."'

'I hope we have done everything he told us to do,' said Molly.

'Oh yes! I feel so much better. Do you know, late as it is, I think you might go to Mrs Goodenough's yet! Maria could take you, and I should like to see you dressed; when one has been wearing dull warm gowns for a week or two, one gets quite a craving for bright colours and evening dress. So go and get ready, dear, and then perhaps you'll bring me back some news; for really, shut up as I have been with only papa and you for the last fortnight, I've got quite moped* and dismal, and I can't bear to keep young people from the gaieties suitable to their age.'

'Oh, pray, mamma! I had so much rather not go!'

'Very well! very well! Only I think it is rather selfish of you, when you see I am so willing to make the sacrifice for your sake.'

'But you say it is a sacrifice to you, and I don't want to go.'

'Very well; did I not say you might stop at home? only pray don't chop logic; nothing is so fatiguing to a sick person.'

Then they were silent for some time. Mrs Gibson broke the silence by saying, in a languid voice –

'Can't you think of anything amusing to say, Molly?'

Molly pumped up from the depths of her mind a few little trivialities which she had nearly forgotten; but she felt that they were anything but amusing, and so Mrs Gibson seemed to feel them; for presently she said –

'I wish Cynthia was at home!' And Molly felt it as a reproach to her own dulness.

'Shall I write to her and ask her to come back?'

'Well, I'm not sure; I wish I knew a great many things. You've not heard anything of poor dear Osborne Hamley lately, have you?'

Remembering her father's charge not to speak of Osborne's health, Molly made no reply, nor was any needed, for Mrs Gibson went on thinking aloud –

'You see, if Mr Henderson has been as attentive as he was in the spring – and the chances about Roger – I shall be really grieved if anything happens to that young man, uncouth as he is; but it must be owned that Africa is not merely an unhealthy, it is a savage – and even in some parts a cannibal – country. I often think of all I've read of it in geography books, as I lie awake at night; and if Mr Henderson is really becoming attached—The future is hidden from us by infinite wisdom, Molly, or else I should like to know it; one would calculate one's behaviour at the present time so much better, if one only knew what events were to come. But I think, on the whole, we had better not alarm Cynthia. If we had only known in time, we might have planned for her to have come down with Lord Cumnor and my lady.'

'Are they coming? Is Lady Cumnor well enough to travel?'

'Yes, to be sure; or else I should not have considered whether or no Cynthia could have come down with them. It would have sounded very well – more than respectable, and would have given her a position among that lawyer set in London.'

'Then Lady Cumnor is better?'

'Of course. I should have thought papa would have mentioned it to you; but, to be sure, he is always so scrupulously careful not to speak about his patients. Quite right too – quite right and delicate! Why, he hardly ever tells me how they are going on. Yes! the Earl and the Countess, and Lady Harriet and Lord and Lady Cuxhaven, and Lady Agnes; and I've ordered a new winter bonnet and a black satin cloak.'

CHAPTER 49

Molly Gibson Finds a Champion

Lady Cumnor had so far recovered from the violence of her attack, and from the consequent operation, as to be able to be removed to the Towers for change of air; and accordingly she was brought thither by her whole family, with all the pomp and state becoming an invalid peeress. There was every probability that 'the family' would make a longer residence at the Towers than they had done for several years, during which time they had been wanderers hither and thither in search of health. Somehow, after all, it was very pleasant and restful to come to the old ancestral home, and every member of the family enjoyed it in his or her own way; Lord Cumnor most especially. His talent for gossip and his love of small details had scarcely fair play in the hurry of a London life, and were much nipped in the bud during his Continental sojournings, as he neither spoke French fluently, nor understood it easily when spoken. Besides, he was a great proprietor, and liked to know how his land was going on; how his tenants were faring in the world. He liked to hear of their births, marriages, and deaths, and had something of a royal memory for faces. In short, if ever a peer was an old woman, Lord Cumnor was that peer; but he was a very good-natured old woman, and rode about on his stout old cob, with his pockets full of halfpence for the children,* and little packets of snuff for the old people. Like an old woman, too, he enjoyed an afternoon cup of tea in his wife's sitting-room, and over his gossip's beverage he would repeat all that he had learnt in the day. Lady Cumnor was exactly in that state of convalescence when such talk as her lord's was extremely agreeable to her; but she had condemned the habit of listening to gossip so severely all her life, that she thought it due to consistency to listen first, and enter a supercilious protest afterwards. It had, however, come to be a family habit for all of them to gather together in Lady Cumnor's room on their return from their daily walks, or drives, or rides, and, over the fire, sipping their tea at her early meal, to recount the morsels of local intelligence they had heard during the morning. When they had said all that they had to say (and not before), they had always to

listen to a short homily from her ladyship on the well-worn texts
– the poorness of conversation about persons – the probable
falsehood of all they had heard, and the degradation of character
implied by its repetition. On one of these November evenings they
were all assembled in Lady Cumnor's room. She was lying – all
draped in white, and covered up with an Indian shawl – on a sofa
near the fire. Lady Harriet sate on the rug, close before the wood-
fire, picking up fallen embers with a pair of dwarf tongs, and
piling them on the red and odorous heap in the centre of the
hearth. Lady Cuxhaven, a notable* from girlhood, was using the
blind man's holiday* to net fruit-nets* for the walls at Cuxhaven
Park. Lady Cumnor's woman was trying to see to pour out tea by
the light of one small wax-candle in the background (for Lady
Cumnor could not bear much light to her weakened eyes); and
the great leafless branches of the trees outside the house kept
sweeping against the windows, moved by the wind that was
gathering.

It was always Lady Cumnor's habit to snub those she loved
best. Her husband was perpetually snubbed by her, yet she missed
him now that he was later than usual, and professed not to want
her tea; but they all knew that it was only because he was not
there to hand it to her, and be found fault with for his invariable
stupidity in forgetting that she liked to put sugar in, before she
took any cream. At length he burst in –

'I beg your pardon, my lady – I'm later than I should have been,
I know. Why! haven't you had your tea yet?' he exclaimed,
bustling about to get the cup for his wife.

'You know I never take cream before I've sweetened it,' said
she, with even more emphasis on the 'never' than usual.

'Oh, dear! What a simpleton I am! I think I might have
remembered it by this time! You see I met old Sheepshanks, and
that's the reason of it.'

'Of your handing me the cream before the sugar?' asked his
wife. It was one of her grim jokes.

'No, no! ha, ha! You're better this evening, I think, my dear.
But, as I was saying, Sheepshanks is such an eternal talker, there's
no getting away from him, and I had no idea it was so late!'

'Well, I think the least you can do is to tell us something of Mr
Sheepshanks's conversation, now you have torn yourself away
from him.'

'Conversation! did I call it conversation? I don't think I said much. I listened. He really has always a great deal to say. More than Preston, for instance. And, by the way, he was telling me something about Preston; – old Sheepshanks thinks he'll be married before long – he says there's a great deal of gossip going on about him and Gibson's daughter. They've been caught meeting in the park, and corresponding, and all that kind of thing that is likely to end in a marriage.'

'I shall be very sorry,' said Lady Harriet. 'I always liked that girl; and I can't bear papa's model land-agent.'

'I daresay it's not true,' said Lady Cumnor, in a very audible aside to Lady Harriet. 'Papa picks up stories one day, to contradict them the next.'

'Ah, but this did sound like truth. Sheepshanks said all the old ladies in the town had got hold of it, and were making a great scandal out of it.'

'I don't think it does sound quite a nice story. I wonder what Clare could be doing to allow such goings-on,' said Lady Cuxhaven.

'I think it's much more likely that Clare's own daughter – that pretty, pawky* Miss Kirkpatrick – is the real heroine of this story,' said Lady Harriet. 'She always looks like a heroine of genteel comedy; and those young ladies were capable of a good deal of innocent intriguing, if I remember rightly. Now, little Molly Gibson has a certain *gaucherie** about her which would disqualify her at once from any clandestine proceedings. Besides, "clandestine"! why, the child is truth itself. Papa, are you sure Mr Sheepshanks said it was Miss Gibson that was exciting Hollingford scandal? Wasn't it Miss Kirkpatrick? The notion of her and Mr Preston making a match of it doesn't sound so incongruous; but, if it's my little friend Molly, I'll go to church and forbid the banns.'

'Really, Harriet, I can't think what always makes you take such an interest in all these petty Hollingford affairs.'

'Mamma, it's only tit for tat. They take the most lively interest in all our sayings and doings. If I were going to be married, they would want to know every possible particular – when we first met, what we first said to each other, what I wore, and whether he offered by letter or in person. I'm sure those good Miss Brownings were wonderfully well-informed as to Mary's methods of managing her nursery, and educating her girls; so it's only a proper return of the compliment to want to know on our side how they are going on. I'm quite of papa's faction. I like to hear all the local gossip.'

'Especially when it is flavoured with a spice of scandal and impropriety, as in this case,' said Lady Cumnor, with the momentary bitterness of a convalescent invalid. Lady Harriet coloured with annoyance. But then she rallied her courage, and said with more gravity than before –

'I am really interested in this story about Molly Gibson, I own. I both like and respect her: and I do not like to hear her name coupled with that of Mr Preston. I can't help fancying papa has made some mistake.'

'No, my dear. I'm sure I'm repeating what I heard. I'm sorry I said anything about it, if it annoys you or my lady there. Sheepshanks did say Miss Gibson, though, and he went on to say it was a pity the girl had got herself so talked about; for it was the way they had carried on that gave rise to all the chatter. Preston himself was a very fair match for her, and nobody could have objected to it. But I'll try and find a more agreeable piece of news. Old Marjory at the lodge is dead; and they don't know where to find some one to teach clear-starching at your school; and Robert Hall made forty pounds last year by his apples.' So they drifted away from Molly and her affairs; only Lady Harriet kept turning what she had heard over in her own mind with interest and wonder.

'I warned her against him, the day of her father's wedding. And what a straightforward, out-spoken child it was then! I don't believe it; it's only one of old Sheepshanks's stories, half invention and half deafness.'

The next day Lady Harriet rode over to Hollingford, and, for the settling of her curiosity, she called on the Miss Brownings, and introduced the subject. She would not have spoken about the rumour she had heard to any who was not a warm friend of Molly's. If Mr Sheepshanks had chosen to allude to it when she had been riding with her father, she could very soon have silenced him by one of the haughty looks she knew full well how to assume. But she felt as if she must know the truth, and accordingly she began thus abruptly to Miss Browning –

'What is all this I hear about my little friend Molly Gibson and Mr Preston?'

'Oh, Lady Harriet! have you heard of it? We are so sorry!'

'Sorry for what?'

'I think, begging your ladyship's pardon, we had better not say any more till we know how much you know,' said Miss Browning.

'Nay,' replied Lady Harriet, laughing a little, 'I shan't tell what I know till I am sure you know more. Then we'll make an exchange if you like.'

'I'm afraid it's no laughing matter for poor Molly,' said Miss Browning, shaking her head. 'People do say such things!'

'But I don't believe them; indeed I don't,' burst in Miss Phoebe, half-crying.

'No more will I, then,' said Lady Harriet, taking the good lady's hand.

'It's all very fine, Phoebe, saying you don't believe them; but I should like to know who it was that convinced me – sadly against my will, I am sure.'

'I only told you the facts as Mrs Goodenough told them me, sister; but I'm sure, if you had seen poor patient Molly as I have done, sitting up in a corner of a room, looking at the "Beauties of England and Wales"* till she must have been sick of them, and no one speaking to her; and she as gentle and sweet as ever at the end of the evening, though maybe a bit pale – facts or no facts, I won't believe anything against her!'

So there sate Miss Phoebe, in tearful defiance of facts.

'And, as I said before, I'm quite of your opinion,' said Lady Harriet.

'But how does your ladyship explain away her meetings with Mr Preston in all sorts of unlikely and open-air places?' asked Miss Browning – who, to do her justice, would have been only too glad to join Molly's partisans, if she could have preserved her character for logical deduction at the same time. 'I went so far as to send for her father and tell him all about it. I thought at least he would have horsewhipped Mr Preston; but he seems to have taken no notice of it.'

'Then we may be quite sure he knows some way of explaining matters that we don't,' said Lady Harriet decisively. 'After all, there may be a hundred and fifty perfectly natural and justifiable explanations.'

'Mr Gibson knew of none, when I thought it my duty to speak to him,' said Miss Browning.

'Why, suppose that Mr Preston is engaged to Miss Kirkpatrick, and Molly is confidante and messenger?'

'I don't see that your ladyship's supposition much alters the blame. Why, if he is honourably engaged to Cynthia Kirkpatrick, does he not visit her openly at her home in Mr Gibson's house? Why does Molly lend herself to clandestine proceedings?'

'One can't account for everything,' said Lady Harriet, a little impatiently, for reason was going hard against her. 'But I choose to have faith in Molly Gibson. I'm sure she's not done anything very wrong. I've a great mind to go and call on her – Mrs Gibson is confined to her room with this horrid influenza – and take her with me on a round of calls through the little gossiping town – on Mrs Goodenough, or Badenough, who seems to have been propagating all these stories. But I've not time today. I've to meet papa at three, and it's three now. Only remember, Miss Phoebe, it's you and I against the world, in defence of a distressed damsel.'

'Don Quixote and Sancho Panza!'* said she to herself as she ran lightly down the Miss Brownings' old-fashioned staircase.

'Now, I don't think that's pretty of you, Phoebe,' said Miss Browning in some displeasure, as soon as she was alone with her sister. 'First, you convince me against my will, and make me very unhappy; and I have to do unpleasant things, all because you've made me believe that certain statements are true; and, then, you turn round and cry, and say you don't believe a word of it all, making me out a regular ogre and backbiter. No! it's of no use. I shan't listen to you.' So she left Miss Phoebe in tears, and locked herself up in her own room.

Lady Harriet, meanwhile, was riding homewards by her father's side, apparently listening to all he chose to say, but in reality turning over the probabilities and possibilities that might account for these strange interviews between Molly and Mr Preston. It was a case of *parlez de l'âne, et l'on en voit les oreilles.** At a turn in the road, they saw Mr Preston a little way before them, coming towards them on his good horse, point device, in his riding attire.

The earl, in his threadbare coat, and on his old brown cob, called out cheerfully –

'Aha! here's Preston. Good-day to you! I was just wanting to ask you about that slip of pasture-land on the Home Farm. John Brickkill wants to plough it up and crop it. It's not two acres at the best.'

While they were talking over this bit of land, Lady Harriet came to her resolution. As soon as her father had finished, she said – 'Mr Preston, perhaps you will allow me to ask you one or two questions, to relieve my mind, for I am in some little perplexity at present.'

'Certainly; I shall only be too happy to give you any information in my power.' But the moment after he had made this polite speech, he recollected Molly's speech – that she would refer her case to Lady Harriet. But the letters had been returned, and the affair was now wound up. She had come off conqueror, he the vanquished. Surely she would never have been so ungenerous as to appeal after that!

'There are reports about Miss Gibson and you current among the gossips of Hollingford. Are we to congratulate you on your engagement to that young lady?'

'Ah! by the way, Preston, we ought to have done it before,' interrupted Lord Cumnor, in hasty goodwill. But his daughter said quietly, 'Mr Preston has not yet told us, if the reports are well founded, papa.'

She looked at him with the air of a person expecting an answer, and expecting a truthful answer.

'I am not so fortunate,' replied he, trying to make his horse appear fidgety, without incurring observation.

'Then I may contradict that report?' asked Lady Harriet quickly. 'Or is there any reason for believing that in time it may come true? I ask, because such reports, if unfounded, do harm to young ladies.'

'Keep other sweethearts off,' put in Lord Cumnor, looking a good deal pleased at his own discernment. Lady Harriet went on –

'And I take a great interest in Miss Gibson.'

Mr Preston saw from her manner that he was 'in for it', as he expressed it to himself. The question was, how much or how little did she know?

'I have no expectation or hope of ever having a nearer interest in Miss Gibson than I have at present. I shall be glad if this straightforward answer relieves your ladyship from your perplexity.'

He could not help the touch of insolence that accompanied these last words. It was not in the words themselves, nor in the tone in which they were spoken, nor in the look which accompanied them; it was in all; it implied a doubt of Lady Harriet's right to question him as she did; and there was something of defiance in it as well. But this touch of insolence put Lady

Harriet's mettle up; and she was not one to check herself, in any course, for the opinion of an inferior.

'Then, sir! are you aware of the injury you may do to a young lady's reputation, if you meet her, and detain her in long conversations, when she is walking by herself, unaccompanied by any one? You give rise – you have given rise to reports.'

'My dear Harriet, are not you going too far? You don't know – Mr Preston may have intentions – acknowledged intentions.'

'No, my lord. I have no intentions with regard to Miss Gibson. She may be a very worthy young lady – I have no doubt she is. Lady Harriet seems determined to push me into such a position that I cannot but acknowledge myself to be – it is not enviable – not pleasant to own – but I am, in fact, a jilted man; jilted by Miss Kirkpatrick, after a tolerably long engagement. My interviews with Miss Gibson were not of the most agreeable kind – as you may conclude, when I tell you she was, I believe, the instigator – certainly, she was the agent – in this last step of Miss Kirkpatrick's. Is your ladyship's curiosity' (with an emphasis on this last word) 'satisfied with this rather mortifying confession of mine?'

'Harriet, my dear, you've gone too far – we had no right to pry into Mr Preston's private affairs.'

'No more I had,' said Lady Harriet, with a smile of winning frankness – the first smile she had accorded to Mr Preston for many a long day; ever since the time, years ago, when, presuming on his handsomeness, he had assumed a tone of gallant familiarity with Lady Harriet, and paid her personal compliments as he would have done to an equal.

'But he will excuse me, I hope,' continued she, still in that gracious manner which made him feel that he now held a much higher place in her esteem than he had had at the beginning of their interview, 'when he learns that the busy tongues of the Hollingford ladies have been speaking of my friend, Miss Gibson, in the most unwarrantable manner; drawing unjustifiable inferences from the facts of that intercourse with Mr Preston, the nature of which he has just conferred such a real obligation on me by explaining.'

'I think I need hardly request Lady Harriet to consider this explanation of mine as confidential,' said Mr Preston.

'Of course, of course!' said the earl: 'every one will understand that.' And he rode home, and told his wife and Lady Cuxhaven the whole conversation between Lady Harriet and Mr Preston; in

the strictest confidence, of course. Lady Harriet had to stand a
good many strictures on manners and proper dignity for a few
days after this. However, she consoled herself by calling on the
Gibsons; and, finding that Mrs Gibson (who was still an invalid)
was asleep at the time, she experienced no difficulty in carrying
off the unconscious Molly for a walk, which Lady Harriet so
contrived that they twice passed along the whole length of the
principal street of the town, loitered at Grinstead's for half-an-
hour, and wound up by Lady Harriet's calling on the Miss
Brownings, who, to her regret, were not at home.

'Perhaps it's as well,' said she, after a minute's consideration.
'I'll leave my card, and put your name down underneath it, Molly.'

Molly was a little puzzled by the manner in which she had been
taken possession of, like an inanimate chattel, for all the afternoon, and exclaimed – 'Please, Lady Harriet – I never leave cards;
I have not got any; and on the Miss Brownings, of all people!
why, I am in and out whenever I like.'

'Never mind, little one. Today you shall do everything properly,
and according to full etiquette.'

'And now tell Mrs Gibson to come out to the Towers for a long
day; we will send the carriage for her, whenever she will let us
know that she is strong enough to come. Indeed, she had better
come for a few days: at this time of the year it doesn't do for an
invalid to be out in the evenings, even in a carriage.' So spoke
Lady Harriet, standing on the white doorsteps at the Miss Brownings', and holding Molly's hand while she wished her good-bye.
'You'll tell her, dear, that I came partly to see her – but that,
finding her asleep, I ran off with you, and don't forget about her
coming to stay with us for change of air – mamma will like it, I'm
sure – and the carriage, and all that. And now good-bye, we've
done a good day's work! And better than you're aware of,'
continued she, still addressing Molly, though the latter was quite
out of hearing. 'Hollingford is not the place I take it to be, if it
doesn't veer round in Miss Gibson's favour after my today's
trotting of that child about.'

CHAPTER 50

Cynthia at Bay

Mrs Gibson was slow in recovering her strength after the influenza; and, before she was well enough to accept Lady Harriet's invitation to the Towers, Cynthia came home from London. If Molly had thought her manner of departure was scarcely as affectionate and considerate as it might have been – if such a thought had crossed Molly's fancy for an instant, she was repentant for it, as soon as ever Cynthia returned; and the girls met together face to face, with all the old familiar affection, going upstairs to the drawing-room, with their arms round each other's waists, and sitting there together hand in hand. Cynthia's whole manner was more quiet than it had been, when the weight of her unpleasant secret rested on her mind, and made her alternately despondent or flighty.

'After all,' said Cynthia, 'there's a look of home about these rooms which is very pleasant. But I wish I could see you looking stronger, mamma! that's the only unpleasant thing. Molly, why didn't you send for me?'

'I wanted to do'—began Molly.

'But I wouldn't let her,' said Mrs Gibson. 'You were much better in London than here, for you could have done me no good; and your letters were very agreeable to read; and now Helen is better, and I'm nearly well, and you've come home just at the right time, for everybody is full of the charity ball.'

'But we are not going this year, mamma,' said Cynthia decidedly. 'It's on the 25th, isn't it? and I'm sure you'll never be well enough to take us.'

'You really seem determined to make me out worse than I am, child,' said Mrs Gibson, rather querulously, she being one of those who, when their malady is only trifling, exaggerate it, but when it is really of some consequence, are unwilling to sacrifice any pleasures by acknowledging it. It was well for her in this instance that her husband had wisdom and authority enough to forbid her going to this ball, on which she had set her heart; but the consequence of his prohibition was an increase of domestic plaintiveness and low spirits, which seemed to tell on Cynthia – the bright, gay Cynthia herself – and it was often hard work for Molly to keep up the spirits of two other people as well as her own. Ill-health might account for Mrs Gibson's despondency; but why was Cynthia so silent, not to say so sighing? Molly was puzzled to account for it; and all the more perplexed, because from time to time Cynthia kept calling upon her for praise for some unknown and mysterious virtue that she had practised; and Molly was young enough to believe that, after any exercise of virtue, the spirits rose, cheered up by an approving conscience. Such was not the case with Cynthia, however. She sometimes said such things as these, when she had been particularly inert and desponding: –

'Ah, Molly, you must let my goodness lie fallow for a while! It has borne such a wonderful crop this year. I have been so pretty-behaved – if you knew all!' Or, 'Really, Molly, my virtue must come down from the clouds! It was strained to the utmost in London; and I find it is like a kite – after soaring aloft for some time, it suddenly comes down, and gets tangled in all sorts of briars and brambles; which things are an allegory – unless you can bring yourself to believe in my extraordinary goodness, while I was away, giving me a sort of right to fall foul of all mamma's briars and brambles now.'

But Molly had had some experience of Cynthia's whim of perpetually hinting at a mystery which she did not mean to reveal, in the Mr Preston days, and, although she was occasionally piqued into curiosity, Cynthia's allusions at something more in the background fell in general on rather deaf ears. One day the mystery burst its shell, and came out in the shape of an offer made to Cynthia by Mr Henderson – and refused. Under all the circumstances, Molly could not appreciate the heroic goodness so often alluded to. The revelation of the secret at last took place in this way. Mrs Gibson breakfasted in bed: she had done so ever since she had had the influenza; and, consequently, her own private letters always went up on her breakfast-tray. One morning she came into the drawing-room earlier than usual, with an open letter in her hand.

'I've had a letter from Aunt Kirkpatrick, Cynthia. She sends me my dividends* – your uncle is so busy. But what does she mean by this, Cynthia?' (holding out the letter to her, with a certain paragraph indicated by her finger). Cynthia put her netting on one side, and looked at the writing. Suddenly her face turned scarlet, and then became of a deadly white. She looked at Molly, as if to gain courage from the strong serene countenance.

'It means – mamma, I may as well tell you at once – Mr Henderson offered to me while I was in London, and I refused him.'

'Refused him – and you never told me, but let me hear it by chance! Really, Cynthia, I think you're very unkind. And pray, what made you refuse Mr Henderson? Such a fine young man, and such a gentleman! Your uncle told me he had a very good private fortune besides.'

'Mamma, do you forget that I have promised to marry Roger Hamley?' said Cynthia quietly.

'No! of course I don't – how can I, with Molly always dinning the word "engagement" into my ears? But really, when one considers all the uncertainties – and after all it was not a distinct promise – he seemed almost as if he might have looked forward to something of this sort.'

'Of what sort, mamma?' said Cynthia sharply.

'Why, of a more eligible offer. He must have known you might change your mind, and meet with some one you liked better: so little as you had seen of the world.' Cynthia made an impatient movement, as if to stop her mother.

'I never said I liked him better – how can you talk so, mamma? I'm going to marry Roger, and there's an end of it. I will not be spoken to about it again.' She got up and left the room.

'Going to marry Roger! That's all very fine. But who is to guarantee his coming back alive? And if he does, what have they to marry upon, I should like to know? I don't wish her to have accepted Mr Henderson, though I am sure she liked him; and true love ought to have its course, and not be thwarted; but she need not have quite finally refused him until – well, until we had seen how matters turn out. Such an invalid as I am too! It has given me quite a palpitation at the heart. I do call it quite unfeeling of Cynthia.'

'Certainly' – began Molly; but then she remembered that her stepmother was far from strong, and unable to bear a protest in favour of the right course without irritation. So she changed her speech into a suggestion of remedies for palpitation; and curbed her impatience to speak out her indignation at the contemplated falsehood to Roger. But, when they were alone, and Cynthia began upon the subject, Molly was less merciful. Cynthia said –

'Well, Molly, and now you know all! I've been longing to tell you – and yet somehow I could not.'

'I suppose it was a repetition of Mr Coxe?' said Molly gravely. 'You were agreeable – and he took it for something more.'

'I don't know,' sighed Cynthia. 'I mean, I don't know if I was agreeable or not. He was very kind – very pleasant – but I didn't expect it all to end as it did. However, it's of no use thinking of it.'

'No!' said Molly simply; for in her mind the pleasantest and kindest person in the world, put in comparison with Roger, was as nothing; he stood by himself. Cynthia's next words, – and they did not come very soon – were on quite a different subject, and spoken in rather a pettish tone. Nor did she allude again in jesting sadness to her late efforts at virtue.

In a little while, Mrs Gibson was able to accept the often-repeated invitation from the Towers to go and stay there for a day or two. Lady Harriet told her that it would be a kindness to Lady Cumnor to come and bear her company in the life of seclusion the latter was still compelled to lead; and Mrs Gibson was flattered and gratified with a dim unconscious sense of being really wanted, not merely deluding herself into a pleasing fiction. Lady Cumnor was in that state of convalescence common to many invalids. The spring of life had begun again to flow, and with the flow returned the old desires and projects and plans, which had all become mere matters of indifference during the worst part of her illness. But as yet her bodily strength was not sufficient to be an agent to her energetic mind, and the difficulty of driving the ill-matched pair of body and will – the one weak and languid, the other strong and stern – made her ladyship often very irritable. Mrs Gibson herself was not quite strong enough for a '*souffre-douleur*';* and the visit to the Towers was not, on the whole, quite so happy a one as she had anticipated. Lady Cuxhaven and Lady Harriet, each aware of their mother's state of health and temper, but only alluding to it as slightly as was absolutely necessary in their conversations with each other, took care not to leave 'Clare' too long with Lady Cumnor; but several times, when one or the other went to relieve guard, they found Clare in tears, and Lady Cumnor holding forth on some point on which she had been meditating during the silent hours of her illness, and on which she seemed to consider herself born to set the world to rights. Mrs Gibson was always apt to consider these remarks as addressed with a personal direction at some error of her own, and defended the fault in question with a feeling of property in it, whatever it might happen to be. The second and the last day of her stay at the Towers, Lady Harriet came in, and found her mother haranguing in an excited tone of voice, and Clare looking submissive and miserable and oppressed.

'What's the matter, dear mamma? Are not you tiring yourself with talking?'

'No, not at all! I was only speaking of the folly of people dressing above their station. I began by telling Clare of the fashions of my grandmother's days, when every class had a sort of costume of its own – and servants did not ape tradespeople, nor tradespeople professional men, and so on – and what must the foolish woman do but begin to justify her own dress; as if I had been accusing her, or even thinking about her at all! Such nonsense! Really, Clare, your husband has spoilt you sadly, if you can't listen to any one without thinking they are alluding to you. People may flatter themselves just as much by thinking that their faults are always present to other people's minds, as if they believe that the world is always contemplating their individual charms and virtues.'

'I was told, Lady Cumnor, that this silk was reduced in price. I bought it at Waterloo House* after the season was over,' said Mrs Gibson, touching the very handsome gown she wore, in deprecation of Lady Cumnor's angry voice, and blundering on to the very source of irritation.

'Again, Clare! How often must I tell you I had no thought of you or your gowns, or whether they cost much or little; your husband has to pay for them, and it is his concern if you spend more on your dress than you ought to do.'

'It was only five guineas for the whole dress,' pleaded Mrs Gibson.

'And very pretty it is,' said Lady Harriet, stooping to examine it, and so hoping to soothe the poor aggrieved woman. But Lady Cumnor went on.

'No! you ought to have known me better by this time. When I think a thing, I say it out. I don't beat about the bush. I use straightforward language. I will tell you where I think you have been in fault, Clare, if you like to know.' Like it or not, the plain speaking was coming now. 'You have spoilt that girl of yours till she does not know her own mind. She has behaved abominably to Mr Preston; and it is all in consequence of the faults in her education. You have much to answer for.'

'Mamma, mamma!' said Lady Harriet, 'Mr Preston did not wish it spoken about.' And at the same moment Mrs Gibson exclaimed, 'Cynthia – Mr Preston!' in such a tone of surprise, that, it Lady Cumnor had been in the habit of observing the revelations made by other people's tones and voices, she would have found out that Mrs Gibson was ignorant of the affair to which she was alluding.

'As for Mr Preston's wishes, I do not suppose I am bound to regard them when I feel it my duty to reprove error,' said Lady Cumnor loftily to Lady Harriet. 'And, Clare, do you mean to say that you are not aware that your daughter has been engaged to Mr Preston for some time – years, I believe – and has at last chosen to break it off – and has used the Gibson girl – I forget her name – as a cat's-paw, and made both her and herself the town's talk – the butt for all the gossip of Hollingford? I remember, when I was young, there was a girl called Jilting Jessie. You'll have to watch over your young lady, or she will get some such name. I speak to you like a friend, Clare, when I tell you it's my opinion that girl of yours will get herself into some more mischief yet, before she's safely married. Not that I care one straw for Mr Preston's feelings. I don't even know if he's got feelings or not; but I know what is becoming in a young woman, and jilting is not. And now you may both go away and send Dawson to me, for I'm tired, and want to have a little sleep.'

'Indeed, Lady Cumnor – will you believe me? – I do not think Cynthia was ever engaged to Mr Preston. There was an old flirtation. I was afraid' —

'Ring the bell for Dawson,' said Lady Cumnor wearily: her eyes closed, Lady Harriet had too much experience of her mother's moods not to lead Mrs Gibson away almost by main force, she protesting all the while that she did not think there was any truth in the statement, though it was dear Lady Cumnor that said it.

Once in her own room, Lady Harriet said, 'Now, Clare, I'll tell you all about it; and I think you'll have to believe it, for it was Mr Preston himself who told me. I heard of a great commotion in Hollingford about Mr Preston; and I met him riding out, and asked him what it was all about; he didn't want to speak about it, evidently. No man does, I suppose, when he's been jilted; and he made both papa and me promise not to tell; but papa did – and that's what mamma has for a foundation; you see, a really good one.'

'But Cynthia is engaged to another man – she really is. And another – a very good match indeed – has just been offering to her in London. Mr Preston is always at the root of mischief.'

'Nay! I do think in this case it must be that pretty Miss Cynthia of yours who has drawn on one man to be engaged to her – not to say two – and another to make her an offer. I can't endure Mr Preston; but I think it's rather hard to accuse him of having called up the rivals, who are, I suppose, the occasion of his being jilted.'

'I don't know; I always feel as if he owed me a grudge, and men have so many ways of being spiteful. You must acknowledge that, if he had not met you, I should not have had dear Lady Cumnor so angry with me.'

'She only wanted to warn you about Cynthia. Mamma has always been very particular about her own daughters. She has been very severe on the least approach to flirting, and Mary will be like her!'

'But Cynthia will flirt, and I can't help it. She is not noisy, or giggling; she is always a lady – that everybody must own. But she has a way of attracting men she must have inherited from me, I think.' And here she smiled faintly, and would not have rejected a confirmatory compliment; but none came. 'However, I will speak to her; I will get to the bottom of the whole affair. Pray tell Lady Cumnor that it has so fluttered me the way she spoke, about my dress and all. And it only cost five guineas after all, reduced from eight!'

'Well, never mind now. You are looking very much flushed; quite feverish! I left you too long in mamma's hot room. But, do you know, she is so much pleased to have you here!' And so Lady Cumnor really was, in spite of the continual lectures which she gave 'Clare', and which poor Mrs Gibson turned under as helplessly as the typical worm.* Still it was something to have a countess to scold her; and that pleasure would endure, when the worry was past. And then Lady Harriet petted her more than usual, to make up for what she had to go through in the convalescent's room; and Lady Cuxhaven talked sense to her, with dashes of science and deep thought intermixed, which was very flattering, although generally unintelligible; and Lord Cumnor, good-natured, good-tempered, kind, and liberal, was full of gratitude to her for her kindness in coming to see Lady Cumnor, and his gratitude took the tangible shape of a haunch of venison, to say nothing of lesser game. When she looked back upon her visit, as she drove home in the solitary grandeur of the Towers carriage, there had been but one great enduring rub* – Lady Cumnor's crossness – and she chose to consider Cynthia as the cause of that, instead of seeing the truth, which had been so often set before her by the members of her ladyship's family, that it took its origin in her state of health. Mrs Gibson did not exactly mean to visit this one discomfort upon Cynthia, nor did she quite mean to upbraid her daughter for conduct as yet unexplained, and which might have some justification; but, finding her quietly sitting in the drawing-room, she sate down despondingly in her own little easy-chair, and in reply to Cynthia's quick pleasant greeting of –

'Well, mamma, how are you? We didn't expect you so early! Let me take off your bonnet and shawl!' she replied dolefully –

'It has not been such a happy visit that I should wish to prolong it.' Her eyes were fixed on the carpet, and her face was as irresponsive to the welcome offered as she could make it.

'What has been the matter?' asked Cynthia, in all good faith.

'You! Cynthia – you! I little thought, when you were born, how I should have to bear to hear you spoken about.'

Cynthia threw back her head, and angry light came into her eyes.

'What business have they with me? How came they to talk about me in any way?'

'Everybody is talking about you; it is no wonder they are. Lord Cumnor is sure to hear about everything always. You should take more care about what you do, Cynthia, if you don't like being talked about.'

'It rather depends upon what people say,' said Cynthia, affecting a lightness which she did not feel; for she had a prevision of what was coming.

'Well! I don't like it, at any rate. It is not pleasant for me to hear first of my daughter's misdoings from Lady Cumnor, and then to be lectured about her, and her flirting, and her jilting, as if I had anything to do with it. I can assure you it has quite spoilt my visit. No! don't touch my shawl. When I go to my room I can take it myself.'

Cynthia was brought to bay, and sate down; remaining with her mother, who kept sighing ostentatiously from time to time.

'Would you mind telling me what they said? If there are

accusations abroad against me, it is as well I should know what they are. Here's Molly' (as the girl entered the room, fresh from a morning's walk). 'Molly, mamma has come back from the Towers, and my lord and lady have been doing me the honour to talk over my crimes and mis-demeanors, and I am asking mamma what they have said. I don't set up for more virtue than other people; but I can't make out what an earl and a countess have to do with poor little me.'

'It was not for your sake!' said Mrs Gibson. 'It was for mine. They felt for me, for it is not pleasant to have one's child's name in everybody's mouth.'

'As I said before, that depends upon how it is in everybody's mouth. If I were going to marry Lord Hollingford, I make no doubt every one would be talking about me, and neither you nor I should mind it in the least.'

'But this is no marriage with Lord Hollingford, so it is nonsense to talk as if it was. They say you've gone and engaged yourself to Mr Preston, and now refuse to marry him; and they call that jilting.'

'Do you wish me to marry him, mamma?' asked Cynthia, her face in a flame, her eyes cast down. Molly stood by, very hot, not fully understanding it; and only kept where she was by the hope of coming in as sweetener or peacemaker, or helper of some kind.

'No,' said Mrs Gibson, evidently discomfited by the question. 'Of course I don't; you've gone and entangled yourself with Roger Hamley, a very worthy young man; but nobody knows where he is, and if he's dead or alive; and he has not a penny, if he is alive.'

'I beg your pardon. I know that he has some fortune from his mother; it may not be much, but he is not penniless; and he is sure to earn fame and great reputation, and with it money will come,' said Cynthia.

'You've entangled yourself with him, and you've done something of the sort with Mr Preston, and got yourself into such an imbroglio' (Mrs Gibson could not have said 'mess' for the world, although the word was present to her mind), 'that when a really eligible person comes forward – handsome, agreeable, and quite the gentleman, and a good private fortune into the bargain – you have to refuse him. You'll end an old maid, Cynthia, and it will break my heart.'

'I dare say I shall,' said Cynthia quietly. 'I sometimes think I'm the kind of person of which old maids are made!' She spoke seriously, and a little sadly.

Mrs Gibson began again. 'I don't want to know your secrets, as long as they are secrets; but, when all the town is talking about you, I think I ought to be told.'

'But, mamma, I didn't know I was such a subject of conversation; and even now I can't make out how it has come about.'

'No more can I. I only know that they say you've been engaged to Mr Preston, and ought to have married him, and that I can't help it, if you did not choose, any more than I could have helped your refusing Mr Henderson; and yet I am constantly blamed for your misconduct. I think it's very hard.' Mrs Gibson began to cry. Just then her husband came in.

'You here, my dear! Welcome back,' said he, coming up to her courteously, and kissing her cheek. 'Why, what's the matter? Tears?' and he heartily wished himself away again.

'Yes!' said she, raising herself up, and clutching after sympathy of any kind, at any price. 'I'm come home again, and I'm telling Cynthia how Lady Cumnor has been so cross to me, and all through her. Did you know she had gone and engaged herself to Mr Preston, and then broken it off! Everybody is talking about it, and they know it up at the Towers.'

For one moment his eyes met Molly's, and he comprehended it all. He made his lips into a whistle, but no sound came. Cynthia had quite lost her defiant manner, since her mother had spoken to Mr Gibson. Molly sate down by her.

'Cynthia,' said he, very seriously.

'Yes!' she answered softly.

'Is this true? I had heard something of it before – not much; but there is scandal enough about to make it desirable that you should have some protector – some friend who knows the whole truth.'

No answer. At last she said, 'Molly knows it all.'

Mrs Gibson, too, had been awed into silence by her husband's grave manner, and she did not like to give vent to the jealous thought in her mind, that Molly had known the secret of which she was ignorant. Mr Gibson replied to Cynthia with some sternness.

'Yes! I know that Molly knows it all, and that she has had to bear slander and ill words for your sake, Cynthia. But she refused to tell me more.'

'She told you that much, did she?' said Cynthia, aggrieved.

'I could not help it,' said Molly.

'She didn't name your name,' said Mr Gibson. 'At the time, I believe, she thought she had concealed it – but there was no mistaking who it was.'

'Why did she speak about it at all?' said Cynthia, with some bitterness. Her tone – her question stirred up Mr Gibson's passion.

'It was necessary for her to justify herself to me – I heard my daughter's reputation attacked for the private meetings she had given to Mr Preston – I came to her for an explanation. There's no need to be ungenerous, Cynthia, because you've been a flirt and a jilt, even to the degree of dragging Molly's name down into the same mire.'

Cynthia lifted her bowed-down head, and looked at him.

'You say that of me, Mr Gibson? Not knowing what the circumstances are, you say that?'

He had spoken too strongly; he knew it. But he could not bring himself to own it just at that moment. The thought of his sweet innocent Molly, who had borne so much patiently, prevented any retraction of his words at the time.

'Yes!' he said, 'I do say it. You cannot tell what evil constructions are put upon actions ever so slightly beyond the bounds of maidenly propriety. I do say that Molly has had a great deal to bear, in consequence of this clandestine engagement of yours, Cynthia – there may be extenuating circumstances, I acknowledge – but you will need to remember them all to excuse your conduct to Roger Hamley, when he comes home. I asked you to tell me the full truth, in order that, until he comes, and has a legal right to protect you, I may do so.' No answer. 'It certainly requires explanation,' continued he. 'Here are you engaged to two men at once, to all appearances!' Still no answer. 'To be sure, the gossips of the town haven't yet picked out the fact of Roger Hamley's being your accepted lover; but scandal has been resting on Molly, and ought to have rested on you, Cynthia – for a concealed engagement to Mr Preston – necessitating meetings in all sorts of places unknown to your friends.'

'Papa,' said Molly, 'if you knew all, you wouldn't speak so to Cynthia. I wish she would tell you herself all that she has told me.'

'I am ready to hear whatever she has to say,' said he. But Cynthia said –

'No! you have prejudged me; you have spoken to me as you

had no right to speak. I refuse to give you my confidence or accept your help. People are very cruel to me' – her voice trembled for a moment – 'I did not think you would have been. But I can bear it.'

And then, in spite of Molly, who would have detained her by force, she tore herself away, and hastily left the room.

'Oh, papa!' said Molly, crying, and clinging to him, 'do let me tell you all!' And then she suddenly recollected the awkwardness of telling some of the details of the story before Mrs Gibson, and stopped short.

'I think, Mr Gibson, you have been very, very unkind to my poor fatherless child,' said Mrs Gibson, emerging from behind her pocket-handkerchief. 'I only wish her poor father had been alive, and all this would never have happened.'

'Very probably. Still I cannot see of what either she or you have to complain. As much as we could, I and mine have sheltered her; I have loved her; I do love her, almost as if she were my own child – as well as Molly, I do not pretend to do.'

'That's it, Mr Gibson! you do not treat her like your own child.' But in the midst of this wrangle Molly stole out, and went in search of Cynthia. She thought she bore an olive-branch of healing in the sound of her father's just spoken words: 'I do love her almost as if she were my own child.' But Cynthia was locked into her room, and refused to open the door.

'Open to me, please,' pleaded Molly. 'I have something to say to you – I want to see you – do open!'

'No!' said Cynthia. 'Not now. I am busy. Leave me alone. I don't want to hear what you have got to say. I don't want to see you. By-and-by we shall meet, and then'—Molly stood quite quietly, wondering what new words of more persuasion she could use. In a minute or two Cynthia called out, 'Are you there still, Molly?' and when Molly answered 'Yes', and hoped for a relenting, the same hard, metallic voice, telling of resolution and repression, spoke out, 'Go away. I cannot bear the feeling of your being there – waiting and listening. Go downstairs – out of the house – anywhere away. It is the most you can do for me now.'

CHAPTER 51

'Troubles Never Come Alone'

Molly had her out-of-door things on, and she crept away, as she was bidden. She lifted her heavy weight of heart and body along till she came to a field, not so very far off, – where she had sought the comfort of loneliness ever since she was a child; and there, under the hedge-bank, she sate down, burying her face in her hands, and quivering all over as she thought of Cynthia's misery, which she might not try to touch or assuage. She never knew how long she sate there; but it was long past lunch-time, when once again she stole up to her room. The door opposite was open wide – Cynthia had quitted the chamber. Molly arranged her dress and went down into the drawing-room. Cynthia and her mother sate there in the stern repose of an armed neutrality. Cynthia's face looked made of stone, for colour and rigidity; but she was netting away, as if nothing unusual had occurred. Not so Mrs Gibson; her face bore evident marks of tears, and she looked up and greeted Molly's entrance with a faint smiling notice. Cynthia went on, as though she had never heard the opening of the door, or felt the approaching sweep of Molly's dress. Molly took up a book – not to read, but to have the semblance of some employment which should not necessitate conversation.

There was no measuring the duration of the silence that ensued. Molly grew to fancy it was some old enchantment that weighed upon their tongues and kept them still. At length Cynthia spoke, but she had to begin again before her words came clear.

'I wish you both to know, that henceforward all is at an end between me and Roger Hamley.'

Molly's book went down upon her knees; with open eyes and lips, she strove to draw in Cynthia's meaning. Mrs Gibson spoke querulously, as if injured.

'I could have understood this if it had happened three months ago – when you were in London; but now it's just nonsense, Cynthia, and you know you don't mean it!'

Cynthia did not reply; nor did the resolute look on her face change when Molly spoke at last.

'Cynthia – think of him! It will break his heart!'

'No!' said Cynthia, 'it will not. But, even if it did, I cannot help it.'

'All this talk will soon pass away!' said Molly; 'and, when he knows the truth from your own self'—

'From my own self he shall never hear it. I do not love him well enough to go through the shame of having to excuse myself – to plead that he will reinstate me in his good opinion. Confession may be – well! I can never believe it pleasant – but it may be an ease of mind if one makes it to some people – to some person – and it may not be a mortification to sue for forgiveness. I cannot tell. All I know is – and I know it clearly, and will act upon it inflexibly – that—' And here she stopped short.

'I think you might finish your sentence,' said her mother, after a silence of five seconds.

'I cannot bear to exculpate myself to Roger Hamley. I will not submit to his thinking less well of me than he has done – however foolish his judgment may have been. I would rather never see him again, for these two reasons. And the truth is, I do not love him. I like him, I respect him; but I will not marry him. I have written to tell him so. That was merely as a relief to myself, for when or where the letter will reach him—And I have written to old Mr Hamley. The relief is the one good thing come out of it all. It is such a relief to feel free again. It wearied me so to think of straining up to his goodness. "Extenuate my conduct!"' she concluded, quoting Mr Gibson's words. Yet, when Mr Gibson came home, after a silent dinner, she asked to speak with him, alone, in his consulting-room; and there laid bare the exculpation of herself which she had given to Molly many weeks before. When she had ended, she said –

'And now, Mr Gibson – I still treat you like a friend – help me to find some home far away, where all the evil talking and gossip mamma tells me of cannot find me and follow me. It may be wrong to care for people's good opinion – but it is me, and I cannot alter myself. You, Molly – all the people in the town – I haven't the patience to live through the nine days' wonder. I want to go away and be a governess.'

'But, my dear Cynthia – how soon Roger will be back – a tower of strength!'

'Has not mamma told you I have broken it all off with Roger? I wrote this morning. I wrote to his father. That letter will reach tomorrow. I wrote to Roger. If he ever receives that letter, I hope to be far away by that time; in Russia, may be.'

'Nonsense. An engagement like yours cannot be broken off, except by mutual consent. You've only given others a great deal of pain without freeing yourself. Nor will you wish it in a month's time. When you come to think calmly, you'll be glad to think of the stay and support of such a husband as Roger. You have been in fault, and have acted foolishly at first – perhaps wrongly afterwards; but you don't want your husband to think you faultless?'

'Yes, I do,' said Cynthia. 'At any rate, my lover must think me so. And it is just because I do not love him even as so light a thing as I could love, that I feel that I couldn't bear to have to tell him I'm sorry, and stand before him, like a chidden child, to be admonished and forgiven.'

'But here you are, just in such a position before me, Cynthia!'

'Yes! but I love you better than Roger; I've often told Molly so. And I would have told you, if I hadn't expected and hoped to leave you all before long. I should see if the recollection of it all came up before your mind; I should see it in your eyes, I should know it by instinct. I have a fine instinct for reading the thoughts of others, when they refer to me. I almost hate the idea of Roger judging me by his own standard, which wasn't made for me, and graciously forgiving me at last.'

'Then I do believe it's right for you to break it off,' said Mr Gibson, almost as if he were thinking to himself. 'That poor, poor lad! But it'll be best for him too. And he'll get over it. He has a good, strong heart. Poor old Roger!'

For a moment Cynthia's wilful fancy stretched after the object passing out of her grasp – Roger's love became for the instant a treasure; but, again, she knew that in its entirety of high undoubting esteem, as well as of passionate regard, it would no longer be hers; and, for the flaw which she herself had made, she case it away, and would none of it. Yet often in after years, when it was too late, she wondered and strove to penetrate the inscrutable mystery of 'what would have been.'

'Still, take till tomorrow before you act upon your decision,' said Mr Gibson slowly. 'What faults you have fallen into have been mere girlish faults at first – leading you into much deceit, I grant.'

'Don't give yourself the trouble to define the shades of blackness,' said Cynthia bitterly. 'I'm not so obtuse but what I know them all, better than any one can tell me. And, as for my decision, I acted upon it at once. It may be long before Roger gets my letter – but I hope he is sure to get it at last – and, as I said, I have let his father know; it won't hurt him! Oh, sir! I think, if I had been differently brought up, I shouldn't have had the sore angry heart I have now. No, don't! I don't want reasoning comfort. I can't stand it. I should always have wanted admiration and worship, and men's good opinion. Those unkind gossips! To visit Molly with their hard words! Oh, dear! I think life is very dreary.'

She put her head down on her hands; tired out, mentally as well as bodily. So Mr Gibson thought. He felt was if much speech from him would only add to her excitement, and make her worse. He left the room, and called Molly, from where she was sitting, dolefully. 'Go to Cynthia!' he whispered, and Molly went. She took Cynthia into her arms with gentle power, and laid her head against her own breast, as if the one had been a mother, and the other a child.

'Oh, my darling!' she murmured. 'I do so love you, dear, dear Cynthia!' and she stroked her hair, and kissed her eyelids; Cynthia passive all the while, till suddenly she started up, stung with a new idea, and looking Molly straight in the face, she said –

'Molly, Roger will marry you! See if it isn't so! You two good'—

But Molly pushed her away, with a sudden violence of repulsion. 'Don't!' she said. She was crimson with shame and indignation. 'Your husband this morning! Mine tonight! What do you take him for?'

'A man!' smiled Cynthia. 'And therefore, if you won't let me call him changeable, I'll coin a word and call him consolable!' But Molly gave her back no answering smile. At this moment, the servant Maria entered the consulting-room, where the two girls were. She had a scared look.

'Isn't master here?' asked she, as if she distrusted her eyes.

'No!' said Cynthia. 'I heard him go out. I heard him shut the front door, not five minutes ago.'

'Oh, dear!' said Maria. 'And there's a man come on horseback from Hamley Hall, and he says as Mr Osborne is dead, and that master must go off to the Squire straight away.'

'Osborne Hamley dead!' said Cynthia, in awed surprise. Molly was out at the front door, seeking the messenger through the dusk, round into the stable-yard, where the groom sate motionless on his dark horse, flecked with foam, made visible by the lantern placed on the steps near, where it had been left by the servants, who were dismayed at this news of the handsome young man, who had frequented their master's house, so full of sportive elegance and winsomeness. Molly went up to the man, whose thoughts were lost in recollection of the scene he had left at the place he had come from.

She laid her hand on the hot damp skin of the horse's shoulder; the man started.

'Is the doctor coming, Miss?' For he saw who it was by the dim light.

'He is dead, is he not?' asked Molly in a low voice.

'I'm afeard he is – leastways, there is no doubt according to what they said. But I've ridden hard! there may be a chance. Is the doctor coming, Miss?'

'He is gone out. They are seeking him, I believe. I will go myself. Oh! the poor old Squire!' She went into the kitchen – went over the house with swift rapidity, to gain news of her father's whereabouts. The servants knew no more than she did. Neither she nor they had heard what Cynthia, ever quick of perception, had done. The shutting of the front door had fallen on deaf ears, as far as others were concerned. Upstairs sped Molly to the drawing-room, where Mrs Gibson stood at the door, listening to the unusual stir in the house.

'What is it, Molly? Why, how white you look, child!'

'Where's papa?'

'Gone out. What's the matter?'

'Where?'

'How should I know? I was asleep; Jenny came upstairs on her way to the bedroom; she's a girl who never keeps to her work, and Maria takes advantage of her.'

'Jenny, Jenny!' cried Molly, frantic at the delay.

'Don't shout, dear – ring the bell. What can be the matter?'

'Oh, Jenny!' said Molly, half-way up the stairs to meet her, 'who wanted papa?'

Cynthia came to join the group; she too had been looking for traces or tidings of Mr Gibson.

'What is the matter?' said Mrs Gibson. 'Can nobody speak and answer a question?'

'Osborne Hamley is dead!' said Cynthia gravely.

'Dead! Osborne! Poor fellow! I knew it would be so, though – I was sure of it. But Mr Gibson can do nothing, if he's dead. Poor young man! I wonder where Roger is now? He ought to come home.'

Jenny had been blamed for coming into the drawing-room instead of Maria, whose place it was, and so had lost the few wits she had. To Molly's hurried questions her replies had been entirely unsatisfactory. A man had come to the back door – she could not see who it was – she had not asked his name; he wanted to speak to master – master seemed in a hurry, and only stopped to get his hat.

'He will not be long away,' thought Molly, 'or he would have left word where he was going. But oh! the poor father all alone!' And then a thought came into her head, which she acted upon straight. 'Go to James, tell him to put the side-saddle I had in November on Nora Creina! Don't cry, Jenny! There's no time for that. No one is angry with you. Run!'

So, down into the cluster of collected women Molly came, equipped in her jacket and skirt; quick determination in her eyes; controlled quivering about the corners of her mouth.

'Why, what in the world' – said Mrs Gibson – 'Molly, what are you thinking about?' But Cynthia had understood it at a glance, and was arranging Molly's hastily assumed dress, as she passed along.

'I am going. I must go. I cannot bear to think of him alone. When papa comes back, he is sure to go to Hamley, and if I am not wanted, I can come back with him.' She heard Mrs Gibson's voice following her in remonstrance, but she did not stay for words. She had to wait in the stable-yard, and she wondered how the messenger could bear to eat and drink the food and beer, brought out to him by the servants. Her coming out had evidently interrupted the eager talk – the questions and answers passing sharp to and fro; but she caught the words, 'all amongst the tangled grass', and 'the Squire would let none on us touch him; he took him up, as if he was a baby; he had to rest many a time, and once he sate him down on the ground; but still he kept him in his arms; but we thought we should ne'er have gotten him up again – him and the body.'

'The body!'

Molly had never felt that Osborne was really dead, till she heard these words. They rode quick under the shadows of the hedgerow trees; but, when they slackened speed, to go up a brow, or to give their horses breath, Molly heard these two little words again in her ears, and said them over again to herself, in hopes of forcing the sharp truth into her unwilling sense. But, when they came in sight of the square stillness of the house, shining in the moonlight – the moon had risen by this time – Molly caught at her breath, and for an instant she thought she never could go in, and face the presence in that dwelling. One yellow light burnt steadily, spotting the silver shining with its earthly coarseness. The man pointed it out; it was almost the first word he had spoken since they had left Hollingford.

'It's the old nursery. They carried him there. The Squire broke down at the stair-foot, and they took him to the readiest place. I'll be bound for it, the Squire is there hisself, and old Robin too. They fetched him, as a knowledgable man among dumb beasts, till th' regular doctor came.'

Molly dropped down from her seat, before the man could dismount to help her. She gathered up her skirts, and did not stay again to think of what was before her. She ran along the once familiar turns, and swiftly up the stairs, and through the doors, till she came to the last; then she stopped and listened. It was a deathly silence. She opened the door – the Squire was sitting alone at the side of the bed, holding the dead man's hand, and looking straight before him at vacancy. He did not stir or move, even so much as an eyelid, at Molly's entrance. The truth had entered his soul before this,* and he knew that no doctor, be he ever so cunning, could, with all his striving, put the breath into that body again. Molly came up to him with the softest steps, the most hushed breath that ever she could. She did not speak, for she did not know what to say. She felt that he had no more hope from earthly skill; so what was the use of speaking of her father and the delay in his coming? After a moment's pause, standing by the old man's side, she slipped down to the floor, and sat at his feet. Possibly, her presence might have some balm in it; but uttering of words was as a vain thing. He must have been aware of her being there, but he took no apparent notice. There they sate, silent and still, he in his chair, she on the floor; the dead man, beneath the sheet, for a third. She fancied that she must have disturbed the father in his contemplation of the quiet face, now more than half, but not fully, covered up out of sight. Time had never seemed so without measure, silence had never seemed so noiseless as it did to Molly, sitting there. In the acuteness of her senses she heard a step mounting a distant staircase, coming slowly, coming nearer. She knew it not to be her father's, and that was all she cared about. Nearer and nearer – close to the outside of the door – a pause, and a soft hesitating tap. The great, gaunt figure sitting by her side quivered at the sound. Molly rose and went to the door: it was Robinson, the old butler, holding in his hand a covered basin of soup.

'God bless you, Miss,' said he; 'make him touch a drop o' this; he's gone since breakfast without food, and it's past one in the morning now.'

He softly removed the cover, and Molly took the basin back with her to her place at the Squire's side. She did not speak; for she did not well know what to say, or how to present this homely want of nature before one so rapt in grief. But she put a spoonful to his lips, and touched them with the savoury food, as if he had been a sick child, and she the nurse; and, instinctively, he took down the first spoonful of the soup. But in a minute he said, with a sort of cry, and almost overturning the basin Molly held, by his passionate gesture as he pointed to the bed –

'He will never eat again – never.'

Then he threw himself across the corpse, and wept in such a terrible manner that Molly trembled, lest he also should die – should break his heart there and then. He took no more notice of her words, of her tears, of her presence, than he did of that of the moon, looking through the unclosed window, with passionless stare. Her father stood by them both, before either of them was aware.

'Go downstairs, Molly,' said he gravely; but he stroked her head tenderly as she rose. 'Go into the dining-room.' Now she felt the reaction from all her self-control. She trembled with fear, as she went along the moonlit passages. It seemed to her as if she should meet Osborne, and hear it all explained: how he came to die – what he now felt and thought and wished her to do. She did get down to the dining-room – the last few steps with a rush of terror – senseless terror of what might be behind her; and there she found supper laid out, and candles lit, and Robinson bustling about, decanting some wine. She wanted to cry; to get into some quiet place, and weep away her over-excitement; but she could hardly do so there. She only felt very much tired, and to care for nothing in this world any more. But vividness of life came back, when she found Robinson holding a glass to her lips as she sat in the great leather easy-chair, to which she had gone instinctively as to a place of rest.

'Drink, Miss. It's good old Madeira. Your papa said as how you was to eat a bit. Says he, "My daughter may have to stay here, Mr Robinson, and she's young for the work. Persuade her to eat something, or she'll break down utterly." Those was his very words.'

Molly did not say anything. She had not energy enough for resistance. She drank and she ate, at the old servant's bidding; and then she asked him to leave her alone, and went back to her easy-chair and let herself cry, and so ease her heart.

CHAPTER 52

Squire Hamley's Sorrow

It seemed very long before Mr Gibson came down. He went and stood with his back to the empty fireplace, and did not speak for a minute or two.

'He's gone to bed,' said he at length. 'Robinson and I have got him there. But, just as I was leaving him, he called me back and asked me to let you stop. I'm sure I don't know – but one doesn't like to refuse at such a time.'

'I wish to stay,' said Molly.

'Do you? There's a good girl. But how will you manage?'

'Oh, never mind that! I can manage. Papa' – she paused – 'what did Osborne die of?' She asked the question in a low, awe-stricken voice.

'Something wrong about the heart. You wouldn't understand if I told you. I apprehended it for some time; but it's better not to talk of such things at home. When I saw him on Thursday week, he seemed better than I've seen him for a long time. I told Dr Nicholls so. But one never can calculate in these complaints.'

'You saw him on Thursday week? Why, you never mentioned it!' said Molly.

'No. I don't talk of my patients at home. Besides, I didn't want him to consider me as his doctor, but as a friend. Any alarm about his own health would only have hastened the catastrophe.'

'Then, didn't he know that he was ill – ill of a dangerous complaint, I mean: one that might end as it has done?'

'No; certainly not. He would only have been watching his symptoms – accelerating matters, in fact.'

'Oh, papa!' said Molly, shocked.

'I've no time to go into the question,' Mr Gibson continued. 'And, until you know what has to be said on both sides and in every instance, you are not qualified to judge. We must keep our attention on the duties in hand now. You sleep here for the remainder of the night, which is more than half-gone already?'

'Yes.'

'Promise me to go to bed just as usual. You may not think it, but most likely you'll go to sleep at once. People do at your age.'

'Papa, I think I ought to tell you something. I know a great secret of Osborne's, which I promised solemnly not to tell; but, the last time I saw him, I think he must have been afraid of something like this.' A fit of sobbing came upon her, which her father was afraid would end in hysterics. But suddenly she mastered herself, and looked up into his anxious face, and smiled to reassure him.

'I could not help it, papa!'

'No. I know. Go on with what you were saying. You ought to be in bed; but, if you've a secret on your mind, you won't sleep.'

'Osborne was married,' said she, fixing her eyes on her father. 'That is the secret.'

'Married! Nonsense! What makes you think so?'

'He told me. That's to say, I was in the library – was reading there, some time ago; and Roger came and spoke to Osborne about his wife. Roger did not see me, but Osborne did. They made me promise secrecy. I don't think I did wrong.'

'Don't worry yourself about right or wrong just now; tell me more about it, at once.'

'I knew no more till six months ago – last November, when you went up to Lady Cumnor. Then he called, and gave me his wife's address, but still under promise of secrecy; and, except those two times, and once when Roger just alluded to it, I have never heard any one mention the subject. I think he would have told me more that last time, only Miss Phoebe came in.'

'Where is this wife of his?'

'Down in the south; near Winchester, I think. He said she was

a Frenchwoman and a Roman Catholic; and I think he said she
was a servant,' added Molly.

'Phew!' Her father made a long whistle of dismay.

'And,' continued Molly, 'he spoke of a child. Now you know as
much as I do, papa, except the address. I have it written down
safe at home.'

Forgetting, apparently, what time of night it was, Mr Gibson
sate down, stretched out his legs before him, put his hands in his
pockets, and began to think. Molly sate still without speaking, too
tired to do more than wait.

'Well!' said he at last, jumping up, 'nothing can be done tonight;
by tomorrow morning, perhaps, I may find out. Poor little pale
face!' – taking it between both his hands and kissing it; 'poor,
sweet, little pale face!' Then he rang the bell, and told Robinson
to send some maid-servant to take Miss Gibson to her room.

'He won't be up early,' said he, in parting. 'The shock has
lowered him too much to be energetic. Send breakfast up to him
in his own room. I'll be here again before ten.'

Late as it was before he left, he kept his word.

'Now, Molly,' he said, 'you and I must tell him the truth
between us. I don't know how he will take it; it may comfort him,
but I've very little hope: either way, he ought to know it at once.'

'Robinson says he has gone into the room again, and he is
afraid he has locked the door on the inside.'

'Never mind. I shall ring the bell, and send up Robinson to say
that I am here, and wish to speak to him.'

The message returned was, 'The Squire's kind love, and he
could not see Mr Gibson just then.' Robinson added, 'It was a
long time before he'd answer at all, sir.'

'Go up again, and tell him I can wait his convenience. Now,
that's a lie,' Mr Gibson said, turning round to Molly, as soon as
Robinson had left the room. 'I ought to be far enough away at
twelve; but, if I'm not much mistaken, the innate habits of a
gentleman will make him uneasy at the idea of keeping me waiting
his pleasure, and will do more to bring him out of that room into
this than any entreaties or reasoning.' Mr Gibson was growing
impatient, though, before they heard the Squire's footstep on the
stairs; he was evidently coming slowly and unwillingly. He came
in almost like one blind, groping along, and taking hold of chair
or table for support or guidance, till he reached Mr Gibson. He

did not speak when he held the doctor by the hand; he only hung down his head, and kept on a feeble shaking of welcome.

'I'm brought very low, sir. I suppose it's God's doing; but it comes hard upon me. He was my firstborn child.' He said this almost as if speaking to a stranger, and informing him of facts of which he was ignorant.

'Here's Molly,' said Mr Gibson, choking a little himself, and pushing her forwards.

'I beg your pardon; I did not see you at first. My mind is a good deal occupied just now.' He state heavily down, and then seemed almost to forget they were there. Molly wondered what was to come next. Suddenly her father spoke –

'Where's Roger?' said he. 'Is he not likely to be soon at the Cape?'* He got up and looked at the directions of one or two unopened letters brought by that morning's post; among them was one in Cynthia's handwriting. Both Molly and he saw it at the same time. How long it was since yesterday! But the Squire took no notice of their proceedings or their looks.

'You will be glad to have Roger at home as soon as may be, I think, sir. Some months must elapse first; but I'm sure he will return as speedily as possible.'

The Squire said something in a very low voice. Both father and daughter strained their ears to hear what it was. They both believed it to be, 'Roger isn't Osborne!' And Mr Gibson spoke on that belief. He spoke more quietly than Molly had ever heard him do before.

'No! we know that. I wish that anything that Roger could do, or that I could do, or that any one could do, would comfort you; but it is past human comfort.'

'I do try to say, God's will be done, sir,' said the Squire, looking up at Mr Gibson for the first time, and speaking with more life in his voice; 'but it's harder to be resigned than happy people think.' They were all silent for a while. The Squire himself was the first to speak again – 'He was my first child, sir; my eldest son. And of late years we weren't' – his voice broke down, but he controlled himself – 'we weren't quite as good friends as could be wished; and I'm not sure – not sure that he knew how I loved him.' And now he cried aloud, with an exceeding bitter cry.*

'Better so!' whispered Mr Gibson to Molly. 'When he's a little calmer, don't be afraid; tell him all you know, exactly as it happened.'

Molly began. Her voice sounded high and unnatural to herself, as if some one else was speaking; but she made her words clear. The Squire did not attempt to listen, at first, at any rate.

'One day when I was here, at the time of Mrs Hamley's last illness' (the Squire here checked his convulsive breathing), 'I was in the library, and Osborne came in. He said he had only come in for a book, and that I was not to mind him; so I went on reading. Presently, Roger came along the flagged garden-path just outside the window (which was open). He did not see me in the corner where I was sitting, and said to Osborne, "Here's a letter from your wife!"'

Now the Squire was all attention; for the first time his tear-swollen eyes met the eyes of another, and he looked at Molly with searching anxiety, as he repeated, 'His wife! Osborne married!' Molly went on –

'Osborne was angry with Roger for speaking out before me, and they made me promise never to mention it to any one, or to allude to it to either of them again. I never named it to papa till last night.'

'Go on,' said Mr Gibson. 'Tell the Squire about Osborne's call – what you told me!' Still the Squire hung on her lips, listening with open mouth and eyes.

'Some months ago Osborne called. He was not well, and wanted to see papa. Papa was away, and I was alone. I don't exactly remember how it came about, but he spoke to me of his wife for the first and only time since the affair in the library.' She looked at her father, as if questioning him as to the desirableness of telling the few further particulars that she knew. The Squire's mouth was dry and stiff, but he tried to say, 'Tell me all – everything.' And Molly understood the half-formed words.

'He said his wife was a good woman, and that he loved her dearly; but she was a French Roman Catholic, and a' – another glance at her father – 'she had been a servant once. That was all; except that I have her address at home. He wrote it down and gave it me.'

'Well! well!' moaned the Squire. 'It's all over now. All over. All past and gone. We'll not blame him – no; but I wish he'd ha' told me; he and I to live together with such a secret in one of us! It's no wonder to me now – nothing can be a wonder again, for one never can tell what's in a man's heart. Married so long! and we sitting together at meals – and living together! Why, I told him everything! Too much, may be; for I showed him all my passions and ill-tempers. Married so long! Oh, Osborne, Osborne, you should have told me!'

'Yes, he should!' said Mr Gibson. 'But I dare say he knew how much you would dislike such a choice as he had made. But he should have told you!'

'You know nothing about it, sir,' said the Squire sharply. 'You don't know the terms we were on. Not hearty or confidential. I was cross to him many a time; angry with him for being dull, poor lad – and he with all this weight on his mind. I won't have people interfering and judging between me and my sons. And Roger too! He could know it all, and keep it from me!'

'Osborne evidently had bound him down to secrecy, just as he bound me,' said Molly; 'Roger could not help himself.'

'Osborne was such a fellow for persuading people, and winning them over,' said the Squire dreamily. 'I remember – but what's the use of remembering? It's all over, and Osborne's dead without opening his heart to me. I could have been tender to him, I could. But he'll never know it now!'

'But we can guess what wish he had strongest in his mind at the last, from what we do know of his life,' said Mr Gibson.

'What, sir?' said the Squire, with sharp suspicion of what was coming.

'His wife must have been his last thought, must she not?'

'How do I know she was his wife? Do you think he'd go and marry a French baggage of a servant? It may be all a tale trumped up.'

'Stop, Squire! I don't care to defend my daughter's truth or accuracy. But, with the dead man's body lying upstairs – his soul with God – think twice before you say more hasty words, impugning his character; if she was not his wife, what was she?'

'I beg your pardon. I hardly know what I'm saying. Did I accuse Osborne? Oh, my lad, my lad – thou might have trusted thy old dad! He used to call me his "old dad", when he was a little chap not bigger than this,' indicating a certain height with his hand. 'I never meant to say he was not – not what one would wish to think him now – his soul with God, as you say very justly – for I'm sure it is there' –

'Well, but, Squire,' said Mr Gibson, trying to check the other's rambling, 'to return to his wife' —

'And the child,' whispered Molly to her father. Low as the whisper was, it struck on the Squire's ear.

'What?' said he, turning round to her suddenly, ' – child? You never named that? Is there a child? Husband and father, and I never knew! God bless Osborne's child! I say, God bless it!' He stood up reverently, and the other two instinctively rose. He closed his hands, as if in momentary prayer. Then, exhausted, he sate down again, and put out his hand to Molly.

'You're a good girl. Thank you. – Tell me what I ought to do, and I'll do it.' This to Mr Gibson.

'I'm almost as much puzzled as you are, Squire,' replied he. 'I fully believe the whole story; but I think there must be some written confirmation of it, which perhaps ought to be found at once, before we act. Most probably this is to be discovered among Osborne's papers. Will you look over them at once? Molly shall return with me, and find the address that Osborne gave her, while you are busy'—

'She'll come back again?' said the Squire eagerly. 'You – she – won't leave me to myself?'

'No! She shall come back this evening. I'll manage to send her somehow. But she has no clothes but the habit she came in, and I want my horse that she rode away upon.'

'Take, the carriage,' said the Squire. 'Take anything! I'll give orders. You'll come back again, too?'

'No, I'm afraid not today. I'll come tomorrow, early. Molly shall return this evening, whenever it suits you to send for her.'

'This afternoon; the carriage shall be at your house at three. I dare not look at Osborne's – at the papers without one of you with me; and yet I shall never rest till I know more.'

'I'll send the desk* in by Robinson, before I leave. And – can you give me some lunch, before I go?'

Little by little, he led the Squire to eat a morsel or so of food; and so, strengthening him physically, and encouraging him mentally, Mr Gibson hoped that he could begin his researches during Molly's absence.

There was something touching in the Squire's wistful looks after Molly, as she moved about. A stranger might have imagined her to be his daughter instead of Mr Gibson's. The meek, broken-down, considerate ways of the bereaved father never showed themselves more strongly than when he called them back to his chair, out of which he seemed too languid to rise, and said, as if by an after-thought: 'Give my love to Miss Kirkpatrick; tell her I look upon her as quite one of the family. I shall be glad to see her after – after the funeral. I don't think I can before.'

'He knows nothing of Cynthia's resolution to give up Roger,' said Mr Gibson, as they rode away. 'I had a long talk with her last night; but she was as resolute as ever. From what your mamma tells me, there is a third lover in London, whom she's already refused. I'm thankful that you've no lover at all, Molly, unless that abortive attempt of Mr Coxe's at an offer, long ago, can be called a lover.'

'I never heard of it, papa!' said Molly.

'Oh, no; I forgot. What a fool I was! Why, don't you remember the hurry I was in to get you off to Hamley Hall, the very first time you ever went? It was all because I got hold of a desperate love-letter from Coxe, addressed to you.'

But Molly was to tired to be amused, or even interested. She could not get over the sight of the straight body covered with a sheet, which yet let the outlines be seen – all that remained of Osborne. Her father had trusted too much to the motion of the ride and the change of scene from the darkened house. He saw his mistake.

'Some one must write to Mrs Osborne Hamley,' said he. 'I believe her to have a legal right to the name, but, whether or no, she must be told that the father of her child is dead. Shall you do it, or I?'

'Oh, you, please, papa!'

'I will, if you wish. But she may have heard of you as a friend of her dead husband's; while of me – a mere country doctor – it's very probable she has never heard the name.'

'If I ought I will do it.' Mr Gibson did not like this ready acquiescence given in so few words, too.

'There's Hollingford church-spire,' said she presently, as they drew near the town, and caught a glimpse of the church through the trees. 'I think I never wish to go out of sight of it again.'

'Nonsense!' said he. 'Why, you've all your travelling to do yet; and, if these new-fangled railways spread, as they say they will, we shall all be spinning about the world; "sitting on tea-kettles", as Phoebe Browning calls it. Miss Browning wrote such a capital letter of advice to Miss Hornblower. I heard of it at the Millers'. Miss Hornblower was going to travel by railroad for the first time; and Dorothy was very anxious, and sent her directions for her conduct; one piece of advice was not to sit on the boiler.'

Molly laughed a little, as she was expected to do. 'Here we are at home, at last.'

Mrs Gibson gave Molly a warm welcome. For one thing, Cynthia was in disgrace; for another, Molly came from the centre of news; for a third, Mrs Gibson was really fond of the girl, in her way, and sorry to see her pale, heavy looks.

'To think of it all being so sudden at last! Not but what I always expected it! And so provoking! Just when Cynthia had given up Roger! If she had only waited a day! What does the Squire say to it all?'

'He is beaten down with grief,' replied Molly.

'Indeed! I should not have fancied he had liked the engagement so much.'

'What engagement?'

'Why, Roger to Cynthia, to be sure. I asked you how the Squire took her letter, announcing the breaking of it off?'

'Oh – I made a mistake. He hasn't opened his letters today. I saw Cynthia's among them.'

'Now that I call positive disrespect.'

'I don't know. He did not mean it for such. Where is Cynthia?'

'Gone out into the meadow-garden. She'll be in directly. I wanted her to do some errands for me, but she flatly refused to go into the town. I am afraid she mismanages her affairs badly. But she won't allow me to interfere. I hate to look at such things in a mercenary spirit, but it is provoking to see her throw over two such good matches. First Mr Henderson and now Roger Hamley. When does the Squire expect Roger? Does he think he will come back sooner for poor dear Osborne's death?'

'I don't know. He hardly seems to think of anything but Osborne. He appears to me to have almost forgotten every one else. But perhaps the news of Osborne's being married, and of the child, may rouse him up.'

Molly had no doubt that Osborne was really and truly married, nor had she any idea that her father had never breathed the facts of which she had told him on the previous night to his wife or Cynthia. But Mr Gibson had been slightly dubious of the full legality of the marriage, and had not felt inclined to speak of it to his wife, until that had been ascertained one way or another. So

Mrs Gibson exclaimed, 'What *do* you mean, child? Married! Osborne married! Who says so?'

'Oh, dear! I suppose I ought not to have named it. I'm very stupid today. Yes! Osborne has been married a long time; but the Squire did not know of it till this morning. I think it has done him good. But I don't know.'

'Who is the lady? Why, I call it a shame to go about as a single man, and be married all the time! If there is one thing that revolts me, it is duplicity. Who is the lady? Do tell me all you know about it, there's a dear.'

'She is French, and a Roman Catholic,' said Molly.

'French! They are such beguiling women; and he was so much abroad! You said there was a child – is it a boy or a girl?'

'I did not hear. I did not ask.'

Molly did not think it necessary to do more than answer questions; indeed, she was vexed enough to have told anything of what her father evidently considered it desirable to keep a secret. Just then, Cynthia came wandering into the room with a careless, hopeless look in her face, which Molly noticed at once. She had not heard of Molly's arrival, and had no idea that she was returned, until she saw her sitting there.

'Molly, darling! Is that you? You're as welcome as the flowers in May, though you've not been gone twenty-four hours. But the house isn't the same, when you are away!'

'And she brings us such news too!' said Mrs Gibson. 'I'm really almost glad you wrote to the Squire yesterday; for, if you had waited till today – I thought you were in too great a hurry at the time – he might have thought you had some interested reason for giving up your engagement. Osborne Hamley was married all this time unknown to everybody, and has got a child too.'

'Osborne married!' exclaimed Cynthia. 'If ever a man looked a bachelor he did. Poor Osborne! with his fair delicate elegance – he looked so young and boyish!'

'Yes! it was a great piece of deceit, and I can't easily forgive him for it. Only think! If he had paid either of you any particular attention, and you had fallen in love with him! Why, he might have broken your heart, or Molly's either. I can't forgive him, even though he is dead, poor fellow!'

'Well, as he never did pay either of us any particular attention, and as we neither of us did fall in love with him, I think I only feel sorry that he had all the trouble and worry of concealment.'

Cynthia spoke with a pretty keen recollection of how much trouble and worry her concealment had cost her.

'And now of course it is a son, and will be the heir, and Roger will just be as poorly off as ever. I hope you'll take care and let the Squire know Cynthia was quite ignorant of these new facts that have come out, when she wrote those letters, Molly? I should not like a suspicion of worldliness to rest upon any one with whom I had any concern.'

'He hasn't read Cynthia's letter yet. Oh, do let me bring it home unopened!' said Molly. 'Send another letter to Roger – now – at once; it will reach him at the same time; he will get both when he arrives at the Cape, and make him understand which is the last – the real one. Think! he will hear of Osborne's death at the same time – two such sad things! Do, Cynthia!'

'No, my dear,' said Mrs Gibson. 'I could not allow that, even if Cynthia felt inclined for it. Asking to be re-engaged to him! At any rate, she must wait now until he proposes again, and we see how things turn out.'

But Molly kept her pleading eyes fixed on Cynthia.

'No!' said Cynthia firmly, but not without consideration. 'It cannot be. I've felt more content this last night than I've done for weeks past. I'm glad to be free. I dreaded Roger's goodness, and learning, and all that. It was not in my way, and I don't believe I should have ever married him, even without knowing of all these ill-natured stories that are circulating about me, and which he would hear of, and expect me to explain, and be sorry for, and penitent and humble. I know he could not have made me happy, and I don't believe he would have been happy with me. It must stay as it is. I would rather be a governess than married to him. I should get weary of him every day of my life.'

'Weary of Roger!' said Molly to herself. 'It is best as it is, I see,' she answered aloud. 'Only I'm very sorry for him, very. He did love you so. You will never get any one to love you like him!'

'Very well. I must take my chance. And too much love is rather oppressive to me, I believe. I like a great deal, widely spread about; not all confined to one individual lover.'

'I don't believe you,' said Molly. 'But don't let us talk any more about it. It is best as it is. I thought – I almost felt sure – you would be sorry this morning. But we will leave it alone now.' She sate silently looking out of the window, her heart sorely stirred, she scarcely knew how or why. But she could not have spoken.

Most likely she would have begun to cry, if she had spoken. Cynthia stole softly up to her after a while.

'You are vexed with me, Molly,' she began in a low voice. But Molly turned sharply round –

'I! I have no business at all in the affair. It is for you to judge. Do what you think right. I believe you have done right. Only I don't want to discuss it, and paw it over with talk. I'm very much tired, dear' – gently now she spoke – 'and I hardly know what I say. If I speak crossly, don't mind it.' Cynthia did not reply at once. Then she said –

'Do you think I might go with you, and help you? I might have done yesterday; and you say he hasn't opened my letter, so he has not heard as yet. And I was always fond of poor Osborne, in my way, you know.'

'I cannot tell; I have no right to say,' replied Molly, scarcely understanding Cynthia's motives, which, after all, were only impulses in this case. 'Papa would be able to judge; I think, perhaps, you had better not. But don't go by my opinion; I can only tell what I should wish to do in your place.'

'It was as much for your sake as any one's, Molly,' said Cynthia.

'Oh, then, don't! I am tired today with sitting up; but tomorrow I shall be all right; and I should not like it, if, for my sake, you came into the house at so solemn a time.'

'Very well!' said Cynthia, half-glad that her impulsive offer was declined; for, as she said, thinking to herself, 'It would have been awkward, after all.' So Molly went back in the carriage alone, wondering how she should find the Squire; wondering what discoveries he had made among Osborne's papers, and at what conviction he would have arrived.

CHAPTER 53

Unlooked-for Arrivals

Robinson opened the door for Molly almost before the carriage had fairly drawn up at the Hall, and told her that the Squire had been very anxious for her return, and had more than once sent him to an upstairs window, from which a glimpse of the hill-road between Hollingford and Hamley could be caught, to know if the

carriage was not yet in sight. Molly went into the drawing-room.
The Squire was standing in the middle of the floor, awaiting her –
in fact, longing to go out and meet her, but restrained by a feeling
of solemn etiquette, which prevented his moving about as usual in
that house of mourning. He held a paper in his hands, which were
trembling with excitement and emotion; and four or five open
letters were strewed on a table near him.

'It's all true,' he began; 'she's his wife, and he's her husband –
was her husband – that's the word for it – was! Poor lad! poor
lad! it's cost him a deal. Pray God, it wasn't my fault. Read this,
my dear. It's a certificate. It's all regular – Osborne Hamley to
Marie-Aimée Scherer, – parish-church and all, and witnessed. Oh,
dear!' He sate down in the nearest chair and groaned. Molly took
a seat by him, and read the legal paper, the perusal of which was
not needed to convince her of the fact of the marriage. She held it
in her hand after she had finished reading it, waiting for the
Squire's next coherent words; for he kept talking to himself in
broken sentences. 'Ay, ay! that comes o' temper and crabbedness.
She was the only one as could – and I've been worse since she was
gone. Worse! worse! and see what it has come to! He was afraid
of me – ay – afraid. That's the truth of it – afraid. And it made
him keep all to himself, and care killed him. They may call it
heart-disease – Oh my lad, my lad, I know better now; but it's too
late – that's the sting of it – too late, too late!' He covered his
face, and moved himself backward and forward till Molly could
bear it no longer.

'There are some letters,' said she; 'may I read any of them?' At
another time she would not have asked; but she was driven to it
now by her impatience of the speechless grief of the old man.

'Ay, read 'em, read 'em,' said he. 'Maybe you can. I can only
pick out a word here and there. I put 'em there for you to look at;
and tell me what is in 'em.'

Molly's knowledge of written French of the present day was
not so great as her knowledge of the French of the *Mémoires de
Sully*,* and neither the spelling nor the writing of the letters was
of the best; but she managed to translate into good enough
colloquial English some innocent sentences of love, and submission to Osborne's will – as if his judgment was infallible – and
of faith in his purposes; little sentences in 'little language' that
went home to the Squire's heart. Perhaps, if Molly had read
French more easily, she might not have translated them into such

touching, homely, broken words. Here and there, there were expressions in English; these the hungry-hearted Squire had read, while waiting for Molly's return. Every time she stopped, he said 'Go on'. He kept his face shaded, and only repeated these two words at every pause. She got up to find some more of Aimée's letters. In examining the papers, she came upon one in particular. 'Have you seen this, sir? This certificate of baptism' (reading aloud) 'of Roger Stephen Osborne Hamley, born June 21, 183 – , child of Osborne Hamley and Marie-Aimée his wife'—

'Give it me,' said the Squire, his voice breaking now, and stretching forth his eager hand. ' "Roger", that's me, "Stephen", that's my poor old father; he died when he was not so old as I am; but I've always thought on him as very old. He was main and fond of Osborne, when he was quite a little one. It's good of the lad to have thought on my father Stephen. Ay! that was his name. And Osborne – Osborne Hamley! One Osborne Hamley lies dead on his bed – and t'other – t'other I've never seen, and never heard on till today. He must be called Osborne, Molly. There is a Roger – there's two for that matter; but one is a good-for-nothing old man; and there's never an Osborne any more, unless this little thing is called Osborne; we'll have him here, and get a nurse for him; and make his mother comfortable for life in her own country. I'll keep this, Molly. You're a good lass for finding it. Osborne Hamley! And if God will give me grace, he shall never hear a cross word from me – never! He shan't be afeard of me. Oh, *my* Osborne, *my* Osborne' (he burst out), 'do you know how bitter and sore is my heart for every hard word as I ever spoke to you? Do you know how I loved you – my boy – my boy?'

From the general tone of the letters, Molly doubted if the mother would consent, so easily as the Squire seemed to expect, to be parted from her child. They were not very wise, perhaps (though of this Molly never thought), but a heart full of love spoke tender words in every line. Still, it was not for Molly to talk of this doubt of hers just then; but rather to dwell on the probable graces and charms of the little Roger Stephen Osborne Hamley. She let the Squire exhaust himself in wondering as to the particulars of every event, helping him out in conjectures; and both of them, from their imperfect knowledge of possibilities, made the most curious, fantastic, and improbable guesses at the truth. And so that day passed over, and the night came.

There were not many people who had any claim to be invited

to the funeral, and of these Mr Gibson and the Squire's hereditary man of business had taken charge. But when Mr Gibson came, early on the following morning, Molly referred the question to him, which had suggested itself to her mind, though apparently not to the Squire's, what intimation of her loss should be sent to the widow, living solitarily near Winchester, watching and waiting, if not for his coming who lay dead in his distant home, at least for his letters. One from her had already come, in her foreign handwriting, to the post-office to which all her communications were usually sent; but of course they at the Hall knew nothing of this.

'She must be told,' said Mr Gibson, musing.

'Yes, she must,' replied his daughter. 'But how?'

'A day or two of waiting will do no harm,' said he, almost as if he were anxious to delay the solution of the problem. 'It will make her anxious, poor thing, and all sorts of gloomy possibilities will suggest themselves to her mind – amongst them the truth; it will be a kind of preparation.'

'For what? Something must be done at last,' said Molly.

'Yes; true. Suppose you write, and say he's very ill; write tomorrow. I daresay they've indulged themselves in daily postage, and then she'll have had three days' silence. Say how you come to know all you do about it; I think she ought to know he is very ill – in great danger, if you like; and you can follow it up next day with the full truth. I wouldn't worry the Squire about it. After the funeral we will have a talk about the child.'

'She will never part with it,' said Molly.

'Whew! Till I see the woman, I can't tell,' said her father; 'some women would. It will be well provided for, according to what you say. And she's a foreigner, and may very likely wish to go back to her own people and kindred. There's much to be said on both sides.'

'So you always say, papa! But, in this case, I think you'll find I'm right. I judge from her letters; but I think I'm right.'

'So you always say, daughter! Time will show. So the child is a boy? Mrs Gibson told me particularly to ask. It will go far to reconciling her to Cynthia's dismissal of Roger. But, indeed, it is quite as well for both of them, though of course he will be a long time before he thinks so. They were not suited to each other. Poor Roger! It was hard work writing to him yesterday; and who knows what may have become of him! Well, well! one has to get through the world somehow. I'm glad, however, this little lad has turned up to be the heir. I shouldn't have liked the property to go to the Irish Hamleys, who are the next heirs, as Osborne once told me. Now write that letter, Molly, to the poor little French-woman out yonder. It will prepare her for it; and we must think a bit how to spare her the shock, for Osborne's sake.'

The writing this letter was rather difficult work for Molly, and she tore up two or three copies before she could manage it to her satisfaction; and at last, in despair of ever doing it better, she sent it off without re-reading it. The next day was easier; the fact of Osborne's death was told briefly and tenderly. But, when this second letter was sent off, Molly's heart began to bleed for the poor creature, bereft of her husband, in a foreign land, and he at a distance from her, dead and buried without her ever having had the chance of printing his dear features on her memory by one last long lingering look.* With her thoughts full of the unknown Aimée, Molly talked much about her that day to the Squire. He would listen for ever to any conjecture, however wild, about the grandchild, but perpetually winced away from all discourse about 'the Frenchwoman', as he called her; not unkindly, but to his mind she was simply the Frenchwoman – chattering, dark-eyed, demonstrative, and possibly even rouged. He would treat her with respect as his son's widow, and would try even not to think upon the female inveiglement in which he believed. He would make her an allowance to the extent of his duty: but he hoped and trusted he might never be called upon to see her. His solicitor, Gibson, anybody and everybody, should be called upon to form a phalanx of defence against that danger.

And all this time a little young grey-eyed woman was making her way – not towards him, but towards the dead son, whom as yet she believed to be her living husband. She knew she was acting in defiance of his expressed wish; but he had never dismayed her with any expression of his own fears about his health; and she, bright with life, had never contemplated death coming to fetch away one so beloved. He was ill – very ill, the letter from the strange girl said that; but Aimée had nursed her parents, and knew what illness was. The French doctor had praised her skill and neat-handedness as a nurse; and, even if she had been the clumsiest of women, was he not her husband – her all? And was she not his wife, whose place was by his pillow? So, without even as much reasoning as has been here given, Aimée made her preparations, swallowing down the tears that would overflow her eyes, and drop into the little trunk she was packing so neatly. And by her side, on the ground, sate the child, now nearly two years old; and for him Aimée had always a smile and a cheerful word. Her servant loved her and trusted her; and the woman was of an age to have had experience of humankind. Aimée had told her that her husband was ill, and the servant had known enough of the household history to be aware that, as yet, Aimée was not his acknowledged wife. But she sympathised with the prompt decision of her mistress to go to him directly, wherever he was. Caution comes from education of one kind or another, and Aimée was not dismayed by warnings; only the woman pleaded hard for the child to be left. 'He was such company,' she said; 'and he would so tire his mother in her journeyings; and maybe his father would be too ill to see him.' To which Aimée replied, 'Good company for you, but better for me. A woman is never tired with carrying her own child' (which was not true; but there was sufficient truth in it to make it believed by both mistress and servant), 'and, if Monsieur could care for anything, he would rejoice to hear the babble of his little son.' So Aimée caught the evening coach to London at the nearest cross-road, Martha standing by as chaperon and friend to see her off, and handing her in the large lusty child, already crowing with delight at the sight of the horses. There was a '*lingerie*' shop, kept by a Frenchwoman, whose acquaintance Aimée had made in the days when she was a London nursemaid; and thither she betook herself, rather than to an hotel, to spend the few night hours that intervened before the Birmingham coach started at early morning. She slept or watched on a sofa in the parlour, for spare-bed there was none; but Madame Pauline came in betimes with a good cup of coffee for the mother, and of '*soupe blanche*'* for the boy; and they went off again into the wide world, only thinking of, only seeking the 'him', who was everything human to both. Aimée remembered the sound of the name of the village, where Osborne had often told her that he alighted from the coach to walk home; and, though she could never have spelt the strange, uncouth word, yet she spoke it with pretty slow distinctness to the guard, asking him in her broken English when they should arrive there? Not till four o'clock. Alas! and what might happen before then! Once with him, she would have no fear; she was sure that she could bring him round; but what might not happen, before he was in her tender care? She was a very capable person in many ways, though so childish and innocent in others. She made up her mind to the course she should take, when the coach set her down at Feversham. She asked for a man to carry her trunk, and show her the way to Hamley Hall.

'Hamley Hall!' said the innkeeper. 'Eh! there's a deal o' trouble there just now.'

'I know, I know,' said she, hastening off after the wheelbarrow in which her trunk was going, and breathlessly struggling to keep up with it, her heavy child asleep in her arms. Her pulses beat all over her body; she could hardly see out of her eyes. To her, a foreigner, the drawn blinds of the house, when she came in sight of it, had no significance; she hurried, stumbled on.

'Back-door or front, missus?' asked the boots* from the inn.

'The most nearest,' said she. And the front-door was 'the most nearest'. Molly was sitting with the Squire in the darkened drawing-room, reading out her translations of Aimée's letters to her husband. The Squire was never weary of hearing them; the very sound of Molly's voice soothed and comforted him, it was so sweet and low. And he pulled her up, much as a child does, if on a second reading of the same letter she substituted one word for another. The house was very still this afternoon – still, as it had been now for several days; every servant in it, however needlessly, moving about on tiptoe, speaking below the breath, and shutting doors as softly as might be. The nearest noise or stir of active life was that of the rooks in the trees, who were beginning their spring-chatter of business. Suddenly, through this quiet, there came a ring at the front-door bell that sounded, and went on sounding, through the house, pulled by an ignorant, vigorous hand. Molly stopped reading; she and the Squire looked at each other in surprised dismay. Perhaps a thought of Roger's sudden (and impossible) return was in the mind of each; but neither spoke. They heard Robinson hurrying to answer the unwonted summons. They listened; but they heard no one. There was little more to hear. When the old servant opened the door, a lady with a child in her arms stood there. She gasped out her ready-prepared English sentence.

'Can I see Mr Osborne Hamley? He is ill, I know; but I am his wife.'

Robinson had been aware that there was some mystery, long-suspected by the servants, and come to light at last to the master, – he had guessed that there was a young woman in the case; but, when she stood there before him, asking for her dead husband as if he were living, any presence of mind Robinson might have had forsook him; he could not tell her the truth – he could only leave the door open, and say to her, 'Wait awhile, I'll come back', and betake himself to the drawing-room where Molly was, he knew. He went up to her in a flutter and a hurry, and whispered something to her which turned her white with dismay.

'What is it? What is it?' said the Squire, trembling with excitement. 'Don't keep it from me! I can bear it. Roger' —

They both thought he was going to faint; he had risen up and came close to Molly; suspense would be worse than anything.

'Mrs Osborne Hamley is here,' said Molly. 'I wrote to tell her her husband was very ill, and she has come.'

'She does not know what has happened, seemingly,' said Robinson.

'I can't see her – I can't see her,' said the Squire, shrinking away into a corner. 'You will go, Molly, won't you? You'll go?'

Molly stood for a moment or two, irresolute. She, too, shrank from the interview. Robinson put in his word: 'She looks but a weakly thing, and has carried a big baby, choose how far,* I didn't stop to ask.'

At this instant the door softly opened, and right into the midst of them came the little figure in grey, looking ready to fall with the weight of her child.

'You are Molly,' said she, not seeing the Squire at once. 'The lady who wrote the letter; he spoke of you sometimes. You will let me go to him.'

Molly did not answer, except that at such moments the eyes speak solemnly and comprehensively. Aimée read their meaning. All she said was – 'He is not – oh, my husband – my husband!' Her arms relaxed, her figure swayed, the child screamed and held out his arms for help. That help was given him by his grandfather, just before Aimée fell senseless on the floor.

'*Maman, maman!*' cried the little fellow, now striving and fighting to get back to her, where she lay; he fought so lustily that the Squire had to put him down, and he crawled to the poor inanimate body, behind which sat Molly, holding the head; whilst Robinson rushed away for water, wine, and more womankind.

'Poor thing, poor thing!' said the Squire, bending over her, and crying afresh over her suffering. 'She is but young, Molly, and she must ha' loved him dearly.'

'To be sure!' said Molly quickly. She was untying the bonnet, and taking off the worn, but neatly-mended gloves; there was the soft luxuriant black hair, shading the pale, innocent face, – the little, notable-looking brown hands, with the wedding-ring for sole ornament. The child clustered his fingers round one of hers, and nestled up against her with his plaintive cry, getting more and more into a burst of wailing: '*Maman, maman*!' At the growing acuteness of his imploring, her hand moved, her lips quivered, consciousness came partially back. She did not open her eyes; but great, heavy tears stole out from beneath her eyelashes. Molly held her head against her own breast; and they tried to give her wine, which she shrank from; water, which she did not reject, that was all. At last she tried to speak. 'Take me away,' she said, 'into the dark! Leave me alone!'

So Molly and the women lifted her up and carried her away, and laid her on the bed, in the best bed-chamber in the house, and darkened the already-shaded light. She was like an unconscious corpse herself, in that she offered neither assistance nor resistance to all that they were doing. But, just before Molly was leaving the room, to take up her watch outside the door, she felt rather than heard that Aimée spoke to her.

'Food – bread-and-milk for baby!' But, when they brought her food herself, she only shrank away and turned her face to the wall without a word. In the hurry, the child had been left with Robinson and the Squire. For some unknown, but most fortunate reason, he took a dislike to Robinson's red face and hoarse voice, and showed a most decided preference for his grandfather. When Molly came down, she found the Squire feeding the child, with more of peace upon his face than there had been for all these days. The boy was every now and then leaving off taking his bread-and-milk, to show his dislike to Robinson by word and gesture: a proceeding which only amused the old servant, while it highly delighted the more favoured Squire.

'She is lying very still, but she will neither speak nor eat. I don't even think she is crying,' said Molly, volunteering this account; for the Squire was, for the moment, too much absorbed in his grandson to ask many questions.

Robinson put in his word: 'Dick Hayward, he's Boots at the Hamley Arms, says the coach she come by started at five this morning from London, and the passengers said she'd been crying a deal on the road, when she thought folks were not noticing; and she never came in to meals with the rest, but stopped feeding her child.'

'She'll be tired out; we must let her rest,' said the Squire. 'And I do believe this little chap is going to sleep in my arms. God bless him!' But Molly stole out, and sent off a lad to Hollingford with a note to her father. Her heart had warmed towards the poor stranger, and she felt uncertain as to what ought to be the course pursued in her case.

She went up from time to time to look at the girl, scarce older than herself, who lay there with her eyes open, but as motionless as death. She softly covered her over, and let her feel the sympathetic presence from time to time; and that was all she was allowed to do. The Squire was curiously absorbed in the child, but Molly's supreme tenderness was for the mother. Not but what she admired the sturdy, gallant, healthy little fellow, whose every limb and square-inch of clothing showed the tender and thrifty care that had been taken of him. By-and-by, the Squire said in a whisper –

'She's not like a Frenchwoman, is she, Molly?'

'I don't know. I don't know what Frenchwomen are like. People say Cynthia is French.'

'And she didn't look like a servant? We won't speak of Cynthia, since she's served my Roger so. Why, I began to think, as soon as I could think after *that*, how I would make Roger and her happy, and have them married at once; and then came that letter! I never wanted her for a daughter-in-law, not I. But he did, it seems; and he wasn't one for wanting many things for himself. But it's all over now; only we won't talk of her; and maybe, as you say, she was more French than English. This poor thing looks like a gentlewoman, I think. I hope she's got friends who'll take care of her, – she can't be above twenty. I thought she must be older than my poor lad!'

'She's a gentle, pretty creature,' said Molly. 'But – but I sometimes think it has killed her; she lies like one dead.' And Molly could not keep from crying softly at the thought.

'Nay, nay!' said the Squire. 'It's not so easy to break one's heart. Sometimes I've wished it were. But one has to go on living – "all the appointed days",* as is said in the Bible. But we'll do our best for her. We'll not think of letting her go away, till she's fit to travel.'

Molly wondered in her heart about this going away, on which the Squire seemed fully resolved. She was sure that he intended to keep the child; perhaps he had a legal right to do so – but would the mother ever part from it? Her father, however, would solve the difficulty – her father, whom she always looked to as so clear-seeing and experienced. She watched and waited for his coming. The February evening drew on; the child lay asleep in the Squire's arms, till his grandfather grew tired and laid him down on the sofa – the large square-cornered yellow sofa upon which Mrs Hamley used to sit, supported by pillows, in a half-reclining position. Since her time, it had been placed against the wall, and had served merely as a piece of furniture to fill up the room. But once again a human figure was lying upon it: a little human creature, like a cherub in some old Italian picture. The Squire remembered his wife, as he put the child down. He thought of her as he said to Molly –

'How pleased she would have been!' But Molly thought of the poor young widow upstairs. Aimée was her 'she' at the first moment. Presently – but it seemed a long, long time first – she heard the quick, prompt sounds which told of her father's arrival. In he came – to the room as yet only lighted by the fitful blaze of the fire.

CHAPTER 54

Molly Gibson's Worth Is Discovered

Mr Gibson came in rubbing his hands after his frosty ride. Molly judged from the look in his eye, that he had been fully informed of the present state of things at the Hall by some one. But he simply went up to and greeted the Squire, and waited to hear what was said to him. The Squire was fumbling at the taper on the writing-table; and, before he answered much, he lighted it and, signing to his friend to follow him, went softly to the sofa and showed him the sleeping child, taking the utmost care not to arouse it by flare or sound.

'Well! this is a fine young gentleman,' said Mr Gibson, returning to the fire rather sooner than the Squire expected. 'And you've got the mother here, I understand. Mrs Osborne Hamley, as we must call her, poor thing! It's a sad coming home to her; for I hear she knew nothing of his death.' He spoke without exactly addressing any one, so that either Molly or the Squire might answer as they liked. The Squire said –

'Yes! She's felt it a terrible shock. She's upstairs in the best bedroom. I should like you to see her, Gibson, if she'll let you. We must do our duty by her, for my poor lad's sake. I wish he could have seen his boy lying there; I do. I dare say it preyed on him to have to keep it all to himself. He might ha' known me, though. He might ha' known my bark was waur* than my bite. It's all over now, though; and God forgive me if I was too sharp! I'm punished now.'

Molly grew impatient on the mother's behalf.

'Papa, I feel as if she was very ill; perhaps worse than we think. Will you go and see her at once?'

Mr Gibson followed her upstairs, and the Squire came too, thinking that he would do his duty now, and even feeling some self-satisfaction at conquering his desire to stay with the child. They went into the room where she had been taken. She lay quite still, in the same position as at first. Her eyes were open and tearless, fixed on the wall. Mr Gibson spoke to her, but she did not answer; he lifted her hand to feel her pulse; she never noticed.

'Bring me some wine at once, and order some beef-tea,' he said to Molly.

But when he tried to put the wine into her mouth, as she lay there on her side, she made no effort to receive or swallow it, and it ran out upon the pillow. Mr Gibson left the room abruptly; Molly chafed the little inanimate hand; the Squire stood by in dumb dismay, touched in spite of himself by the death-in-life of one so young, and who must have been so much beloved.

Mr Gibson came back two steps at a time; he was carrying the half-awakened child in his arms. He did not scruple to rouse him into yet further wakefulness – did not grieve to hear him begin to wail and cry. His eyes were on the figure upon the bed, which at that sound quivered all through; and, when her child was laid at her back, and began caressingly to scramble yet closer, Aimée turned round, and took him in her arms, and lulled him and soothed him with the soft wont of mother's love.

Before she lost this faint consciousness, which was habit or instinct rather than thought, Mr Gibson spoke to her in French. The child's one word of '*maman*' had given him this clue. It was the language sure to be most intelligible to her dulled brain; and, as it happened – only Mr Gibson did not think of that – it was the language in which she had been commanded, and had learnt to obey.

Mr Gibson's tongue was a little stiff at first, but, by-and-by, he spoke it with more readiness. He extorted from her short answers at first, then longer ones, and from time to time he plied her with little drops of wine, until some further nourishment should be at hand. Molly was struck by her father's low tones of comfort and sympathy, although she could not follow what was said quickly enough to catch the meaning of what passed.

By-and-by, however, when her father had done all that he could, and they were once more downstairs, he told them more about her journey than they yet knew. The hurry, the sense of acting in defiance of a prohibition, the overmastering anxiety, the broken night, and fatigue of the journey, had ill prepared her for the shock at last, and Mr Gibson was seriously alarmed for the consequences. She had wandered strangely in her replies to him; he had perceived that she was wandering, and had made great efforts to recall her senses; but Mr Gibson foresaw that some bodily illness was coming on, and stopped late that night, arranging many things with Molly and the Squire. One – the only – comfort arising from her state was, the probability that she would be entirely unconscious by the morrow – the day of the funeral. Worn out by the contending emotions of the day, the Squire seemed now unable to look beyond the wrench and trial of the next twelve hours. He sate with his head in his hands, declining to go to bed, refusing to dwell on the thought of his grandchild – not three hours ago such a darling in his eyes. Mr Gibson gave some instructions to one of the maid-servants as to the watch she was to keep by Mrs Osborne Hamley, and insisted on Molly's going to bed. When she pleaded the apparent necessity of staying up, he said –

'Now, Molly, look how much less trouble the dear old Squire would give if he would obey orders. He is only adding to anxiety by indulging himself. One pardons everything to extreme grief, however. But you will have enough to do to occupy all your strength for days to come; and go to bed you must now. I only wish I saw my way as clearly through other things as I do to your nearest duty. I wish I'd never let Roger go wandering off; he'll wish it too, poor fellow! Did I tell you, Cynthia is going off in hot haste to her uncle Kirkpatrick's. I suspect a visit to him will stand in lieu of going out to Russia as a governess.'

'I am sure she was quite serious in wishing for that.'

'Yes, yes! at the time. I've no doubt she thought she was sincere in intending to go. But the great thing was to get out of the unpleasantness of the present time and place; and uncle Kirkpatrick's will do this as effectually, and more pleasantly, than a situation at Nishni-Novgorod in an ice-palace.'

He had given Molly's thoughts a turn, which was what he wanted to do. Molly could not help remembering Mr Henderson, and his offer, and all the consequent hints; and wondering and wishing – what did she wish? or had she been falling asleep? Before she had quite ascertained this point, she was asleep in reality.

After this, long days passed over in a monotonous round of care; for no one seemed to think of Molly's leaving the Hall during the woeful illness that befell Mrs Osborne Hamley. It was not that her father allowed her to take much active part in the nursing; the Squire gave him *carte-blanche*, and he engaged two efficient hospital-nurses to watch over the unconscious Aimée; but Molly was needed to receive the finer directions as to her treatment and diet. It was not that she was wanted for the care of the little boy; the Squire was too jealous of the child's exclusive love for that, and one of the housemaids was employed in the actual physical charge of him; but he needed some one to listen to his incontinence of language, both when his passionate regret for his dead son came uppermost, and also when he had discovered some extraordinary charm in that son's child; and, again, when he was oppressed with the uncertainty of Aimée's long-continued illness. Molly was not so good or so bewitching a listener to ordinary conversation as Cynthia; but, where her heart was interested, her sympathy was deep and unfailing. In this case, she only wished that the Squire could really feel that Aimée was not the encumbrance which he evidently considered her to be. Not that he would have acknowledged the fact, if it had been put before him in plain words. He fought against the dim consciousness of what was in his mind; he spoke repeatedly of patience, when no one but himself was impatient; he would often say that, when she grew better, she must not be allowed to leave the Hall, until she was perfectly strong, when no one was even contemplating the remotest chance of her leaving her child, excepting only himself. Molly once or twice asked her father, if she might not speak to the Squire and represent the hardship of sending her away, the improbability that she would consent to quit her boy, and so on; but Mr Gibson only replied –

'Wait quietly. Time enough, when nature and circumstance have had their chance, and have failed.'

It was well that Molly was such a favourite with the old servants; for she had frequently to restrain and to control. To be sure, she had her father's authority to back her; and they were aware that, where her own comfort, ease, or pleasure was concerned, she never interfered, but submitted to their will. If the Squire had known of the want of attendance to which she submitted with the most perfect meekness, as far as she herself was the only sufferer, he would have gone into a towering rage. But Molly hardly thought of it, so anxious was she to do all she could for others, and to remember the various charges which her father gave her in his daily visits. Perhaps he did not spare her enough; she was willing and uncomplaining; but, one day, after Mrs Osborne Hamley had 'taken the turn',* as the nurses called it, when she was lying weak as a new-born baby, but with her faculties all restored, and her fever gone – when spring buds were blooming out, and spring birds sang merrily – Molly answered to her father's sudden questioning, that she felt unaccountably weary; that her head ached heavily, and that she was aware of a sluggishness of thought which it required a painful effort to overcome.

'Don't go on,' said Mr Gibson, with a quick pang of anxiety, almost of remorse. 'Lie down here – with your back to the light. I'll come back and see you before I go.' And off he went, in search of the Squire. He had a good long walk, before he came upon Mr Hamley in a field of spring wheat, where the women were weeding, his little grandson holding to his finger in the intervals of short walks of inquiry into the dirtiest places, which was all his sturdy little limbs could manage.

'Well, Gibson, and how goes the patient? Better? I wish we could get her out of doors, such a fine day as it is! It would make her strong as soon as anything. I used to beg my poor lad to come out more. Maybe, I worried him; but the air is the finest thing for strengthening that I know of. Though, perhaps, she'll not thrive in English air as if she'd been born here; and she'll not be quite right, till she gets back to her native place, wherever that is.'

'I don't know. I begin to think we shall get her quite round here; and I don't know that she could be in a better place. But it's not about her. May I order the carriage for my Molly?' Mr Gibson's voice sounded as if he was choking a little, as he said these last words.

'To be sure,' said the Squire, setting the child down. He had been holding him in his arms the last few minutes; but now he wanted all his eyes to look into Mr Gibson's face. 'I say,' said he, catching hold of Mr Gibson's arm, 'what's the matter, man? Don't twitch up your face like that, but speak!'

'Nothing's the matter,' said Mr Gibson hastily. 'Only I want her at home under my own eye'; and he turned away to go to the house. But the Squire left his field and his weeders, and kept at Mr Gibson's side. He wanted to speak, but his heart was so full he did not know what to say. 'I say, Gibson,' he got out at last, 'your Molly is liker a child of mine than a stranger; and I reckon we've all on us been coming too hard upon her. You don't think there's much amiss, do you?'

'How can I tell?' said Mr Gibson, almost savagely. But any hastiness of temper was instinctively understood by the Squire; and he was not offended, though he did not speak again till they reached the house. Then he went to order the carriage, and stood by, sorrowful enough, while the horses were being put in. He felt as if he should not know what to do without Molly; he had never known her value, he thought, till now'. But he kept silence on this view of the case; which was a praiseworthy effort on the part of one who usually let bystanders see and hear as much of his passing feelings as if he had had a window in his breast.* He stood by, while Mr Gibson helped the faintly-smiling, tearful Molly into the carriage. Then the Squire mounted on the step and kissed her hand; but when he tried to thank her and bless her, he broke down; and, as soon as he was once more safely on the ground, Mr Gibson cried out to the coachman to drive on. And so Molly left Hamley Hall. From time to time her father rode up to the window, and made some little cheerful, and apparently careless, remark. When they came within two miles of Hollingford, he put spurs to his horse, and rode briskly past the carriage windows, kissing his hand to the occupant as he did so. He went on to prepare her home for Molly; when she arrived, Mrs Gibson was ready to greet her. Mr Gibson had given one or two of his bright, imperative orders, and Mrs Gibson was feeling rather lonely 'without either of her two dear girls at home', as she phrased it, to herself as well as to others.

'Why, my sweet Molly, this is an unexpected pleasure. Only this morning I said to papa, "When do you think we shall see our Molly back?" He did not say much – he never does, you know; but I am sure he thought directly of giving me this surprise, this pleasure. You're looking a little – what shall I call it? I remember such a pretty line of poetry, "Oh, call her fair not pale!"* so we'll call you fair.'

'You'd better not call her anything, but let her get to her own room and have a good rest as soon as possible. Haven't you got a trashy novel or two in the house? That's the literature to send her to sleep.'

He did not leave her, till he had seen her laid on a sofa in a darkened room, with some slight pretence of reading in her hand. Then he came away, leading his wife, who turned round at the door to kiss her hand to Molly, and make a little face of unwillingness to be dragged away.

'Now, Hyacinth,' said he, as he took his wife into the drawing-room, 'she will need much care. She has been overworked, and I've been a fool. That's all. We must keep her from all worry and care – but I won't answer for it that she'll not have an illness, for all that!'

'Poor thing! she does look worn out. She is something like me, her feelings are too much for her. But, now she is come home, she shall find us as cheerful as possible. I can answer for myself; and you really must brighten up your doleful face, my dear – nothing so bad for invalids as the appearance of depression in those around them! I have had such a pleasant letter from Cynthia today. Uncle Kirkpatrick really seems to make so much of her, he treats her just like a daughter; he has given her a ticket for the Concerts of Ancient Music;* and Mr Henderson has been to call on her, in spite of all that has gone before.'

For an instant Mr Gibson thought that it was easy enough for his wife to be cheerful, with the pleasant thoughts and evident anticipations she had in her mind, but a little more difficult for him to put off his doleful looks, while his own child lay in a state of suffering and illness which might be the precursor of a still worse malady. But he was always a man for immediate action, as soon as he had resolved on the course to be taken; and he knew that 'some must watch, while some must sleep; so runs the world away.'*

The illness which he apprehended came upon Molly; not vio-

lently or acutely, so that there was any immediate danger to be
dreaded; but making a long pull upon her strength, which seemed
to lessen day by day, until at last her father feared that she might
become a permanent invalid. There was nothing very decided or
alarming to tell Cynthia, and Mrs Gibson kept the dark side from
her in her letters. 'Molly was feeling the spring weather'; or 'Molly
had been a good deal overdone with her stay at the Hall, and was
resting'; such little sentences told nothing of Molly's real state.
But then, as Mrs Gibson said to herself, it would be a pity to
disturb Cynthia's pleasure by telling her much about Molly;
indeed, there was not much to tell, one day was so like another.
But it so happened that Lady Harriet – who came, whenever she
could, to sit awhile with Molly, at first against Mrs Gibson's will,
and afterwards with her full consent – for reasons of her own,
Lady Harriet wrote a letter to Cynthia, to which she was urged
by Mrs Gibson. It fell out in this manner: – One day, when Lady
Harriet was sitting in the drawing-room for a few minutes, after
she had been with Molly, she said –

'Really, Clare, I spend so much time in your house that I'm
going to establish a work-basket here. Mary has infected me with
her notability,* and I'm going to work mamma a footstool. It is
to be a surprise; and so, if I do it here, she will know nothing
about it. Only I cannot match the gold beads I want for the
pansies in this dear little town; and Hollingford, who could send
me down stars and planets if I asked him, I make no doubt, could
no more match beads than'—

'My dear Lady Harriet! you forget Cynthia! Think what a
pleasure it would be to her to do anything for you.'

'Would it? Then she shall have plenty of it; but mind, it is you
who have answered for her. She shall get me some wool too; how
good I am to confer so much pleasure on a fellow-creature! But,
seriously, do you think I might write and give her a few commissions? Neither Agnes nor Mary is in town'—

'I am sure she would be delighted,' said Mrs Gibson, who also
took into consideration the reflection of aristocratic honour that
would fall upon Cynthia, if she had a letter from Lady Harriet,
while at Mr Kirkpatrick's. So she gave the address, and Lady
Harriet wrote. All the first part of the letter was taken up with
apology and commissions; but then, never doubting but that
Cynthia was aware of Molly's state, she went on to say –

'I saw Molly this morning. Twice I have been forbidden admittance, as she was too ill to see any one out of her own family. I wish we could begin to perceive a change for the better; but she looks more fading every time, and I fear Mr Gibson considers it a very anxious case.'

The day but one after this letter was despatched, Cynthia walked into the drawing-room at home, with as much apparent composure as if she had left it not an hour before. Mrs Gibson was dozing, but believing herself to be reading; she had been with Molly the greater part of the morning, and now, after her lunch, and the invalid's pretence of early dinner, she considered herself entitled to some repose. She started up as Cynthia came in.

'Cynthia! Dear child, where have you come from? Why in the world have you come? My poor nerves! My heart is quite fluttering; but, to be sure, it's no wonder with all this anxiety I have to undergo. Why have you come back?'

'Because of the anxiety you speak of, mamma. I never knew – you never told me – how ill Molly was.'

'Nonsense! I beg your pardon, my dear, but it's really nonsense. Molly's illness is only nervous, Mr Gibson says. A nervous fever; but you must remember nerves are mere fancy, and she's getting better. Such a pity for you to have left your uncle's. Who told you about Molly?'

'Lady Harriet. She wrote about some wool' —

'I know – I know. But you might have known she always exaggerates things. Not but what I have been almost worn out with nursing. Perhaps, after all, it is a very good thing you have come, my dear; and now you shall come down into the dining-room and have some lunch, and tell me all the Hyde Park Street news – into my room – don't go into yours yet – Molly is so sensitive to noise!'

While Cynthia ate her lunch, Mrs Gibson went on questioning. 'And your aunt, how is her cold? And Helen, quite strong again? Margaretta as pretty as ever? The boys are at Harrow, I suppose? And my old favourite, Mr Henderson?' She could not manage to slip in this last inquiry naturally; in spite of herself, there was a change of tone, an accent of eagerness. Cynthia did not reply on the instant; she poured herself out some water with great deliberation, and then said –

'My aunt is quite well; Helen is as strong as she ever is, and Margaretta very pretty. The boys are at Harrow, and I conclude that Mr Henderson is enjoying his usual health, for he was to dine at my uncle's today.'

'Take care, Cynthia. Look how you are cutting that gooseberry tart,' said Mrs Gibson, with sharp annoyance; not provoked by Cynthia's present action, although it gave excuse for a little vent of temper. 'I can't think how you could come off in this sudden kind of way; I am sure it must have annoyed your uncle and aunt. I daresay they'll never ask you again.'

'On the contrary, I am to go back there as soon as ever I can be easy to leave Molly.'

' "Easy to leave Molly." Now that really is nonsense, and rather uncomplimentary to me, I must say: nursing her as I have been, daily, and almost nightly; for I have been wakened, times out of number, by Mr Gibson getting up, and going to see if she had had her medicine properly.'

'I'm afraid she has been very ill?' asked Cynthia.

'Yes, she has, in one way; but not in another. It was what I call more a tedious, than an interesting illness. There was no immediate danger, but she lay much in the same state from day to day.'

'I wish I had known!' sighed Cynthia. 'Do you think I might go and see her now?'

'I'll go and prepare her. You'll find her a good deal better than she has been. Ah; here's Mr Gibson!' He came into the dining-room, hearing voices. Cynthia thought that he looked much older.

'You here!' said he, coming forward to shake hands. 'Why, how did you come?'

'By the "Umpire". I never knew Molly had been so ill, or I would have come directly.' Her eyes were full of tears. Mr Gibson was touched: he shook her hand again, and murmured, 'You're a good girl, Cynthia.'

'She's heard one of dear Lady Harriet's exaggerated accounts,' said Mrs Gibson, 'and come straight off. I tell her it's very foolish, for Molly is a great deal better now.'

'Very foolish,' said Mr Gibson, echoing his wife's words, but smiling at Cynthia. 'But sometimes one likes foolish people for their folly, better than wise people for their wisdom.'

'I am afraid folly always annoys me,' said his wife. 'However, Cynthia is here, and what is done, is done.'

'Very true, my dear. And now I'll run up and see my little girl, and tell her the good news. You'd better follow me in a couple of minutes.' This to Cynthia.

Molly's delight at seeing her showed itself, first in a few happy tears, and then in soft caresses and inarticulate sounds of love. Once or twice she began, 'It is such a pleasure,' and there she stopped short. But the eloquence of these five words sank deep into Cynthia's heart. She had returned just at the right time, when Molly wanted the gentle fillip of the society of a fresh and yet a familiar person. Cynthia's tact made her talkative or silent, gay or grave, as the varying humour of Molly required. She listened, too, with the semblance, if not the reality, of unwearied interest, to Molly's continual recurrence to all the time of distress and sorrow at Hamley Hall, and to the scenes which had then so deeply impressed themselves upon her susceptible nature. Cynthia instinctively knew that the repetition of all these painful recollections would ease the oppressed memory, which refused to dwell on anything but what had occurred at a time of feverish disturbance of health. So she never interrupted Molly, as Mrs Gibson had so frequently done, with – 'You told me all that before, my dear. Let us talk of something else;' or, 'Really I cannot allow you to be always dwelling on painful thoughts. Try and be a little more cheerful. Youth is gay. You are young, and therefore you ought to be gay. That is put in a famous form of speech;* I forget exactly what it is called.'

So Molly's health and spirits improved rapidly after Cynthia's return; and, although she was likely to retain many of her invalid habits during the summer, she was able to take drives, and enjoy the fine weather; it was only her as yet tender spirits that required a little management. All the Hollingford people forgot that they had ever thought of her except as the darling of the town; and each in his or her way showed kind interest in her father's child. Miss Browning and Miss Phoebe considered it quite a privilege that they were allowed to see her a fortnight or three weeks before any one else; Mrs Goodenough, spectacles on nose, stirred dainty messes in a silver saucepan for Molly's benefit; the Towers sent books, and forced fruit, and new caricatures, and strange and delicate poultry; humble patients of 'the doctor', as Mr Gibson was usually termed, left the earliest cauliflowers they could grow in their cottage gardens, with 'their duty for Miss'.

The last of all, though strongest in regard, most piteously eager in interest, came Squire Hamley himself. When she was at the worst, he rode over every day to hear the smallest detail, facing even Mrs Gibson (his abomination), if her husband was not at home, to ask and hear, and ask and hear, till the tears were unconsciously stealing down his cheeks. Every resource of his heart, or his house, or his lands, was searched and tried, if it could bring a moment's pleasure to her; and, whatever it might be that came from him, at her very worst time, it brought out a dim smile upon her face.

CHAPTER 55

An Absent Lover Returns

And now it was late June; and to Molly's and her father's extreme urgency in pushing, and Mr and Mrs Kirkpatrick's affectionate persistency in pulling, Cynthia had yielded, and had gone back to finish her interrupted visit in London, but not before the bruit of her previous sudden return to nurse Molly had told strongly in her favour in the fluctuating opinion of the little town. Her affair with Mr Preston was thrust into the shade; while every one was speaking of her warm heart. Under the gleam of Molly's recovery everything assumed a rosy hue, as indeed became the time when actual roses were fully in bloom.

One morning, Mrs Gibson brought Molly a great basket of flowers, that had been sent from the Hall. Molly still breakfasted in bed, but she had just come down, and was now well enough to arrange the flowers for the drawing-room, and, as she did so with these blossoms, she made some comments on each.

'Ah! these white pinks! They were Mrs Hamley's favourite flower; and so like her! This little bit of sweet briar, it quite scents the room. It has pricked my fingers, but never mind! Oh, mamma, look at this rose! I forget its name, but it is very rare, and grows up in the sheltered corner of the wall, near the mulberry-tree. Roger bought the tree for his mother with his own money when he was quite a boy; he showed it me, and made me notice it.'

'I daresay it was Roger who got it now. You heard papa say he had seen him yesterday.'

'No! Roger! Roger come home!' said Molly, turning first red, then very white.

'Yes. Oh, I remember you had gone to bed before papa came

in, and he was called off early to tiresome Mrs Beale. Yes, Roger turned up at the Hall the day before yesterday.'

But Molly leaned back against her chair, too faint to do more at the flowers for some time. She had been startled by the suddenness of the news. 'Roger come home!'

It happened that Mr Gibson was unusually busy on this particular day, and he did not come home till late in the afternoon. But Molly kept her place in the drawing-room all the time, not even going to take her customary siesta, so anxious was she to hear everything about Roger's return, which as yet appeared to her almost incredible. But it was quite natural in reality; the long monotony of her illness had made her lose all count of time. When Roger left England, his idea was to coast round Africa on the eastern side until he reached the Cape, and thence to make what further journey or voyage might seem to him best in pursuit of his scientific objects. To Cape Town all his letters had been addressed of late; and there, two months before, he had received the intelligence of Osborne's death, as well as Cynthia's hasty letter of relinquishment. He did not consider that he was doing wrong in returning to England immediately, and reporting himself to the gentlemen who had sent him out, with a full explanation of the circumstances relating to Osborne's private marriage and sudden death. He offered, and they accepted his offer, to go out again for any time that they might think equivalent to the five months he was yet engaged to them for. They were most of them gentlemen of property, and saw the full importance of proving the marriage of an eldest son, and installing his child as the natural heir to a long-descended estate. This much information, but in a more condensed form, Mr Gibson gave to Molly, in a very few minutes. She sat up on her sofa, looking very pretty with the flush on her cheeks, and the brightness in her eyes.

'Well!' said she, when her father stopped speaking.

'Well! what?' asked he playfully.

'Oh! why, such a number of things! I've been waiting all day to ask you all about everything. How is he looking?'

'If a young man of twenty-four ever does take to growing taller, I should say that he was taller. As it is, I suppose it's only that he looks broader, stronger – more muscular.'

'Oh! is he changed?' asked Molly, a little disturbed by this account.

'No, not changed; and yet not the same. He's as brown as a

berry for one thing; caught a little of the negro tinge, and a beard as fine and sweeping as my bay-mare's tail.'

'A beard! but go on, papa! Does he talk as he used to do? I should know his voice amongst ten thousand.'

'I didn't catch any Hottentot* twang, if that's what you mean. Nor did he say, "Caesar and Pompey berry much alike,* 'specially Pompey," which is the only specimen of negro language I can remember just at this moment.'

'And which I never could see the wit of,' said Mrs Gibson, who had come into the room after the conversation had begun, and did not understand what it was aiming at. Molly fidgeted; she wanted to go on with her questions and keep her father to definite and matter-of-fact answers, and she knew that, when his wife chimed into a conversation, Mr Gibson was very apt to find out that he must go about some necessary piece of business.

'Tell me, how are they all getting on together?' It was an inquiry which she did not make in general before Mrs Gibson, for Molly and her father had tacitly agreed to keep silence on what they knew, or had observed, respecting the three who formed the present family at the Hall.

'Oh!' said Mr Gibson, 'Roger is evidently putting everything to rights in his firm, quiet way.'

' "Things to rights." Why, what's wrong?' asked Mrs Gibson quickly. 'The Squire and the French daughter-in-law don't get on well together, I suppose? I am always so glad Cynthia acted with the promptitude she did; it would have been very awkward for her to have been mixed up with all these complications. Poor Roger! to find himself supplanted by a child when he comes home!'

'You were not in the room, my dear, when I was telling Molly of the reasons for Roger's return; it was to put his brother's child at once into his rightful and legal place. So now, when he finds the work partly done to his hands, he is happy and gratified in proportion.'

'Then he is not much affected by Cynthia's breaking off her engagement?' (Mrs Gibson could afford to call it an 'engagement' now.) 'I never did give him credit for very deep feelings.'

'On the contrary, he feels it very acutely. He and I had a long talk about it, yesterday.'

Both Molly and Mrs Gibson would have liked to have heard something more about this conversation; but Mr Gibson did not choose to go on with the subject. The only point which he disclosed was, that Roger had insisted on his right to have a personal interview with Cynthia; and, on hearing that she was in London at present, had deferred any further explanation or expostulation by letter, preferring to await her return.

Molly went on with her questions on other subjects. 'And Mrs Osborne Hamley? How is she?'

'Wonderfully brightened-up by Roger's presence. I don't think I've ever seen her smile before; but she gives him the sweetest smiles from time to time. They are evidently good friends; and she loses her strange startled look when she speaks to him. I suspect she has been quite aware of the Squire's wish that she should return to France, and has been hard put to it to decide whether to leave her child or not. The idea that she would have to make some such decision came upon her, when she was completely shattered by grief and illness; and she hasn't had any one to consult as to her duty until Roger came, upon whom she has evidently firm reliance. He told me something of this himself.'

'You seem to have had quite a long conversation with him, papa!'

'Yes. I was going to see old Abraham, when the Squire called to me over the hedge, as I was jogging along. He told me the news; and there was no resisting his invitation to come back and lunch with them. Besides, one gets a great deal of meaning out of Roger's words; it didn't take so very long a time to hear this much.'

'I should think he would come and call upon us soon,' said Mrs Gibson to Molly, 'and then we shall see how much we can manage to hear.'

'Do you think he will, papa?' said Molly, more doubtfully. She remembered the last time he was in that very room, and the hopes with which he left it; and she fancied that she could see traces of this thought in her father's countenance at his wife's speech.

'I can't tell, my dear. Until he's quite convinced of Cynthia's intentions, it can't be very pleasant for him to come on mere visits of ceremony to the house in which he has known her; but he's one who will always do what he thinks right, whether pleasant or not.'

Mrs Gibson could hardly wait till her husband had finished his sentence, before she testified against a part of it.

'Convinced of Cynthia's intentions! I should think she had made them pretty clear! What more does the man want?'

'He's not as yet convinced that the letter wasn't written in a fit of temporary feeling. I've told him that this was true; although I didn't feel it my place to explain to him the causes of that feeling. He believes that he can induce her to resume the former footing. I don't; and I've told him so; but, of course, he needs the full conviction that she alone can give him.'

'Poor Cynthia! My poor child!' said Mrs Gibson, plaintively. 'What she has exposed herself to by letting herself be over-persuaded by that man!'

Mr Gibson's eyes flashed fire. But he kept his lips tight closed; and only said, 'That man, indeed!' quite below his breath.

Molly, too, had been damped by an expression or two in her father's speech. 'Mere visits of ceremony!' Was it so, indeed? A 'mere visit of ceremony!' Whatever it was, the call was paid before many days were over. That he felt all the awkwardness of his position towards Mrs Gibson – that he was in reality suffering pain all the time – was but too evident to Molly; but, of course, Mrs Gibson saw nothing of this in her gratification at the proper respect paid to her by one whose name was in the newspapers that chronicled his return, and about whom already Lord Cumnor and the Towers family had been making inquiry.

Molly was sitting in her pretty white invalid's dress, half-reading, half-dreaming; for the June air was so clear and ambient, the garden so full of bloom, the trees so full of leaf, that reading by the open window was only a pretence at such a time; besides which, Mrs Gibson continually interrupted her with remarks about the pattern of her worsted-work. It was after lunch – orthodox calling time – when Maria ushered in Mr Roger Hamley. Molly started up; and then stood shyly and quietly in her place, while a bronzed, bearded, grave man came into the room, in whom she at first had to seek for the merry boyish face she knew by heart only two years ago. But months in the climates in which Roger had been travelling age as much as years in more temperate regions. And constant thought and anxiety, while in daily peril of life, deepen the lines of character upon the face. Moreover, the circumstances that had of late affected him personally were not of a nature to make him either buoyant or cheerful. But his voice was the same; that was the first point of the old friend Molly caught, when he addressed her in a tone far softer than he used in speaking conventional politenesses to her stepmother.

'I was so sorry to hear how ill you had been! You are looking but delicate!' letting his eyes rest upon her face with affectionate examination. Molly felt herself colour all over with the consciousness of his regard. To do something to put an end to it, she looked up, and showed him her beautiful soft grey eyes, which he never remembered to have noticed before. She smiled at him, as she blushed still deeper, and said –

'Oh! I am quite strong now to what I was. It would be a shame to be ill when everything is in its full summer beauty.'

'I have heard how deeply we – I am indebted to you – my father can hardly praise you'—

'Please don't!' said Molly, the tears coming into her eyes in spite of herself. He seemed to understand her at once; he went on as if speaking to Mrs Gibson: 'Indeed, my little sister-in-law is never weary of talking about '*Monsieur le Docteur*', as she calls your husband!'

'I have not had the pleasure of making Mrs Osborne Hamley's acquaintance yet,' said Mrs Gibson, suddenly aware of a duty which might have been expected from her, 'and I must beg you to apologise to her for my remissness. But Molly has been such a care and anxiety to me – for, you know, I look upon her quite as my own child – that I really have not gone anywhere; excepting to the Towers, perhaps I should say, which is just like another home to me. And then I understood that Mrs Osborne Hamley was thinking of returning to France before long? Still it was very remiss.'

The little trap thus set for news of what might be going on in the Hamley family was quite successful. Roger answered her thus –

'I am sure Mrs Osborne Hamley will be very glad to see any friends of the family, as soon as she is a little stronger. I hope she will not go back to France at all. She is an orphan, and I trust we shall induce her to remain with my father. But at present nothing is arranged.' Then, as if glad to have got over his 'visit of ceremony', he got up and took leave. When he was at the door, he looked back, having, as he thought, a word more to say; but he quite forgot what it was, for he surprised Molly's intent gaze, and sudden confusion at discovery, and went away as soon as he could.

'Poor Osborne was right!' said he. 'She has grown into delicate fragrant beauty, just as he said she would; or is it the character which has formed her face? Now, the next time I enter these doors, it will be to learn my fate!'

Mr Gibson had told his wife of Roger's desire to have a personal interview with Cynthia, rather with a view to her repeating what he said to her daughter. He did not see any exact necessity for this, it is true; but he thought it might be advisable that she should know all the truth in which she was concerned, and he told his wife this. But she took the affair into her own management, and, although she apparently agreed with Mr Gibson, she never named the affair to Cynthia; all that she said to her was –

'Your old admirer, Roger Hamley, has come home in a great hurry, in consequence of poor dear Osborne's unexpected decease. He must have been rather surprised to find the widow and her little boy established at the Hall. He came to call here the other day, and made himself really rather agreeable, although his manners are not improved by the society he has kept on his travels. Still, I prophesy he will be considered as a fashionable 'lion', and perhaps the very uncouthness which jars against my sense of refinement may even become admired in a scientific traveller, who has been into more desert places, and eaten more extraordinary food, than any other Englishman of the day. I suppose he has given up all chance of inheriting the estate, for I hear he talks of returning to Africa and becoming a regular wanderer. Your name was not mentioned; but I believe he inquired about you from Mr Gibson.'

'There!' said she to herself, as she folded up and directed her letter. 'That can't disturb her or make her uncomfortable. And it's all the truth too, or very near it. Of course he'll want to see her when she comes back; but, by that time, I do hope Mr Henderson will have proposed again, and that that affair will all be settled.'

But Cynthia returned to Hollingford one Tuesday morning, and, in answer to her mother's anxious inquiries on the subject, would only say that Mr Henderson had not offered again. Why should he? She had refused him once, and he did not know the reason of her refusal, at least one of the reasons. She did not know if she should have taken him, if there had been no such person as Roger Hamley in the world. No! Uncle and aunt Kirkpatrick had never heard anything about Roger's offer – nor had her cousins. She had always declared her wish to keep it a secret, and she had not mentioned it to any one, whatever other people might have done. Underneath this light and careless vein there were other feelings; but Mrs Gibson was not one to probe beneath the surface. She had set her heart on Mr Henderson's marrying Cynthia, very early in their acquaintance; and to know, first, that the same wish had entered into his head, and that Roger's attachment to Cynthia, with its consequences, had been the obstacle; and secondly, that Cynthia herself, with all the opportunities of propinquity which she had lately had, had failed to provoke a repetition of the offer – was, as Mrs Gibson said, 'enough to provoke a saint'. All the rest of the day, she alluded to Cynthia as a disappointing and ungrateful daughter; Molly could not make out why, and resented it for Cynthia, until the latter said, bitterly, 'Never mind, Molly. Mamma is only vexed because Mr—because I have not come back an engaged young lady.'

'Yes; and I am sure you might have done – there's the ingratitude! I am not so unjust as to want you to do what you can't do!' said Mrs Gibson querulously.

'But where's the ingratitude, mamma? I'm very much tired, and perhaps that makes me stupid; but I cannot see the ingratitude.' Cynthia spoke very wearily, leaning her head back on the sofa-cushions, as if she did not care to have an answer.

'Why, don't you see we are doing all we can for you; dressing you well, and sending you to London; and, when you might relieve us of the expense of all this, you don't.'

'No! Cynthia, I will speak,' said Molly, all crimson with indignation, and pushing away Cynthia's restraining hand. 'I am sure papa does not feel, and does not mind, any expense he incurs about his daughters. And I know quite well that he does not wish us to marry, unless—' She faltered and stopped.

'Unless what?' said Mrs Gibson, half-mocking.

'Unless we love some one very dearly indeed,' said Molly, in a low, firm tone.

'Well, after this tirade – really rather indelicate, I must say – I have done. I will neither help nor hinder any love-affairs of you two young ladies. In my days, we were glad of the advice of our elders.' And she left the room, to put into fulfilment an idea which had just struck her: to write a confidential letter to Mrs Kirkpatrick, giving her her version of Cynthia's 'unfortunate entanglement', and 'delicate sense of honour', and hints of her entire indifference to all the masculine portion of the world, Mr Henderson being dexterously excluded from the category.

'Oh, dear!' said Molly, throwing herself back in a chair, with a sigh of relief, as Mrs Gibson left the room; 'how cross I do get since I've been ill! But I couldn't bear her to speak as if papa grudged you anything.'

'I'm sure he doesn't, Molly. You need not defend him on my account. But I'm sorry mamma still looks upon me as "an encumbrance", as the advertisements in the *Times* always call us unfortunate children. But I've been an encumbrance to her all my life. I'm getting very much into despair about everything, Molly. I shall try my luck in Russia. I've heard of a situation as English governess at Moscow, in a family owning whole provinces of land, and serfs by the hundred. I put off writing my letter till I came home; I shall be as much out of the way there as if I was married. Oh, dear! travelling all night isn't good for the spirits. How's Mr Preston?'

'Oh, he has taken Cumnor Grange, three miles away, and he never comes in to the Hollingford tea-parties now. I saw him once in the street, but it's a question which of us tried the harder to get out of the other's way.'

'You've not said anything about Roger, yet.'

'No; I didn't know if you would care to hear. He is very much older-looking; quite a strong grown-up man. And papa says he is much graver. Ask me any questions, if you want to know, but I have only seen him once.'

'I was in hopes he would have left the neighbourhood by this time. Mamma said he was going to travel again.'

'I can't tell,' said Molly. 'I suppose you know,' she continued, but hesitating a little before she spoke, 'that he wishes to see you?'

'No! I never heard. I wish he would have been satisfied with my letter. It was as decided as I could make it. If I say I won't see him, I wonder if his will or mine will be the stronger?'

'His,' said Molly. 'But you must see him; you owe it to him. He will never be satisfied without it.'

'Suppose he talks me round into resuming the engagement? I should only break it off again.'

'Surely, you can't be talked "round", if your mind is made up. But perhaps it is not really, Cynthia?' asked she, with a little wistful anxiety betraying itself in her face.

'It is quite made up. I am going to teach little Russian girls, and am never going to marry nobody.'

'You are not serious, Cynthia. And yet it is a very serious thing.'

But Cynthia went into one of her wild moods, and no more reason or sensible meaning was to be got out of her at the time.

CHAPTER 56

'Off with the Old Love, and on with the New'*

The next morning saw Mrs Gibson in a much more contented frame of mind. She had written and posted her letter, and the next thing was to keep Cynthia in what she called a reasonable state, or, in other words, to try and cajole her into docility. But it was so much labour lost. Cynthia had already received a letter from Mr Henderson before she came down to breakfast – a declaration of love, a proposal of marriage as clear as words could make it; together with an intimation that, unable to wait for the slow delays of the post, he was going to follow her down to Hollingford, and would arrive at the same time that she had done herself on the previous day. Cynthia said nothing about this letter to any one. She came late into the breakfast-room, after Mr and Mrs Gibson had finished the actual business of the meal; but her unpunctuality was quite accounted for by the fact that she had been travelling all the last night but one. Molly was not as yet strong enough to get up so early. Cynthia hardly spoke, and did not touch her food. Mr Gibson went about his daily business, and Cynthia and her mother were left alone.

'My dear,' said Mrs Gibson, 'you are not eating your breakfast as you should do. I am afraid our meals seem very plain and homely to you, after those in Hyde Park Street?'

'No,' said Cynthia; 'I'm not hungry, that's all.'

'If we were as rich as your uncle, I should feel it to be both a duty and a pleasure to keep an elegant table; but limited means are a sad clog to one's wishes. I don't suppose that, work as he will, Mr Gibson can earn more than he does at present; while the capabilities of the law are boundless. Lord Chancellor! Titles, as well as fortune!'

Cynthia was almost too much absorbed in her own reflections to reply, but she did say – 'Hundreds of briefless barristers. Take the other side, mamma.'

'Well; but I have noticed that many of these have private fortunes.'

'Perhaps. Mamma, I expect Mr Henderson will come and call this morning.'

'Oh, my precious child! But how do you know? My darling Cynthia, am I to congratulate you?'

'No! I suppose I must tell you. I have had a letter this morning from him, and he's coming down by the "Umpire" today.'

'But he has offered? He surely must mean to offer, at any rate?'

Cynthia played with her tea-spoon before she replied; then she looked up, like one startled from a dream, and caught the echo of her mother's question.

'Offered! yes, I suppose he has.'

'And you accept him? Say "yes", Cynthia, and make me happy!'

'I shan't say "yes" to make any one happy except myself, and the Russian scheme has great charms for me.' She said this, to plague her mother, and lessen Mrs Gibson's exuberance of joy, it must be confessed; for her mind was pretty well made up. But it did not affect Mrs Gibson, who affixed even less truth to it than there really was. The idea of a residence in a new, strange country, among new, strange people, was not without allurement to Cynthia.

'You always look nice, dear; but don't you think you had better put on that pretty lilac silk?'

'I shall not vary a thread or a shred from what I have got on now.'

'You dear, wilful creature! you know you always look lovely in whatever you put on.' So, kissing her daughter, Mrs Gibson left the room, intent on the lunch which should impress Mr Henderson at once with an idea of family refinement.

Cynthia went upstairs to Molly; she was inclined to tell her about Mr Henderson, but she found it impossible to introduce the subject naturally, so she left it to time to reveal the future as gradually as it might. Molly was tired with a bad night; and her father, in his flying visit to his darling before going out, had advised her to stay upstairs for the greater part of the morning, and to keep quiet in her own room till after her early dinner; so Time had not a fair chance of telling her what he had in store in his budget.* Mrs Gibson sent an apology to Molly for not paying her her usual morning visit, and told Cynthia to give Mr Henderson's probable coming as a reason for her occupation downstairs. But Cynthia did no such thing. She kissed Molly, and sate silently by her, holding her hand; till at length she jumped up, and said, 'You shall be left alone now, little one. I want you to be very well and very bright this afternoon; so rest now.' And Cynthia left her, and went to her own room, locked the door, and began to think.

Some one was thinking about her at the same time, and it was not Mr Henderson. Roger had heard from Mr Gibson that Cynthia had come home, and he was resolving to go to her at once, and make one strong, manly attempt to overcome the obstacles whatever they might be – and of their nature he was not fully aware – that she had conjured up against the continuance of their relation to each other. He left his father – he left them all – and went off into the woods, to be alone until the time came when he might mount his horse and ride over to put his fate to the touch.* He was as careful as ever not to interfere with the morning hours that were tabooed to him of old; but waiting was very hard work when he knew that she was so near, and the time so close at hand.

Yet he rode slowly, compelling himself to quietness and patience, when he was once really on the way to her.

'Mrs Gibson at home? Miss Kirkpatrick?' he asked of the servant, Maria, who opened the door. She was confused; but he did not notice it.

'I think so – I'm not sure! Will you walk up into the drawing-room, sir? Miss Gibson is there, I know.'

So he went upstairs, all his nerves on the strain for the coming interview with Cynthia. It was either a relief or a disappointment, he was not sure which, to find only Molly in the room: – Molly, half-lying on the couch in the bow-window which commanded the garden; draped in soft white drapery, very white herself, and a laced half-handkerchief tied over her head, to save her from any ill effects of the air that blew in through the open window. He was so ready to speak to Cynthia that he hardly knew what to say to any one else.

'I'm afraid you are not so well,' he said to Molly, who sat up to receive him, and who suddenly began to tremble with emotion.

'I'm a little tired, that's all,' said she; and then she was quite silent, hoping that he might go, and yet somehow wishing him to stay. But he took a chair and placed it near her, opposite to the window. He thought that surely Maria would tell Miss Kirkpatrick that she was wanted, and that at any moment he might hear her light quick footstep on the stairs. He felt he ought to talk, but he could not think of anything to say. The pink flush came out on Molly's cheeks; once or twice she was on the point of speaking, but again she thought better of it; and the pauses between their faint disjointed remarks became longer and longer. Suddenly, in one of these pauses, the merry murmur of distant happy voices in the garden came nearer and nearer; Molly looked more and more uneasy and flushed, and in spite of herself kept watching Roger's face. He could see over her into the garden. A sudden deep colour overspread him, as if his heart had sent its blood out coursing at full gallop. Cynthia and Mr Henderson had come in sight; he, eagerly talking to her as he bent forward to look into her face; she, her looks half averted in pretty shyness, was evidently coquetting about some flowers, which she either would not give, or would not take. Just then, for the lovers had emerged from the shrubbery into comparatively public life, Maria was seen approaching; apparently she had feminine tact enough to induce Cynthia to leave her present admirer, and to go a few steps to meet her and receive the whispered message that Mr Roger Hamley was there, and wished to speak to her. Roger could see her startled gesture; she turned back to say something to Mr Henderson before coming towards the house. Now Roger spoke to Molly – spoke hurriedly, spoke hoarsely.

'Molly, tell me! Is it too late for me to speak to Cynthia? I came on purpose. Who is that man?'

'Mr Henderson. He only came today – but now he is her accepted lover. Oh, Roger, forgive me the pain!'

'Tell her I have been, and am gone. Send out word to her. Don't let her be interrupted.'

And Roger ran downstairs at full speed, and Molly heard the passionate clang of the outer door. He had hardly left the house, before Cynthia entered the room, pale and resolute.

'Where is he?' she said, looking around, as if he might yet be hidden.

'Gone!' said Molly, very faint.

'Gone. Oh, what a relief! It seems to be my fate never to be off with the old lover before I am on with the new, and yet I did write as decidedly as I could. Why, Molly, what's the matter?' for now Molly had fainted away utterly. Cynthia flew to the bell, summoned Maria, water, salts, wine, anything; and as soon as Molly, gasping and miserable, became conscious again, she wrote a little pencil-note to Mr Henderson, bidding him return to the George, whence he had come in the morning, and saying that, if he obeyed her at once, he might be allowed to call again in the evening; otherwise, she would not see him till the next day. This she sent down by Maria, and the unlucky man never believed but that it was Miss Gibson's sudden indisposition in the first instance that had deprived him of his charmer's company. He comforted himself for the long solitary afternoon by writing to tell all his friends of his happiness, and amongst them uncle and aunt Kirkpatrick, who received his letter by the same post as that discreet epistle of Mrs Gibson's, which she had carefully arranged to reveal as much as she wished, and no more.

'Was he very terrible?' asked Cynthia, as she sate with Molly in the stillness of Mrs Gibson's dressing-room.

'Oh, Cynthia, it was such pain to see him, he suffered so!'

'I don't like people of deep feelings,' said Cynthia, pouting. 'They don't suit me. Why couldn't he let me go without this fuss? I'm not worth his caring for!'

'You've the happy gift of making people love you. Remember Mr Preston – he too wouldn't give up hope.'

'Now, I won't have you classing Roger Hamley and Mr Preston together in the same sentence. One was as much too bad for me as the other is too good. Now I hope that man in the garden is the *juste milieu** – I'm that myself; for I don't think I'm vicious, and I know I'm not virtuous.'

'Do you really like him enough to marry him?' asked Molly earnestly. 'Do think, Cynthia! It won't do to go on throwing your lovers off; you give pain that I'm sure you do not mean to do – that you cannot understand.'

'Perhaps I can't. I'm not offended. I never set up for what I am not, and I know I'm not constant. I've told Mr Henderson so' — She stopped, blushing and smiling at the recollection.

'You have! and what did he say?'

'That he liked me just as I was; so you see he's fairly warned. Only he's a little afraid, I suppose – for he wants me to be married very soon; almost directly, in fact. But I don't know if I shall give way – you hardly saw him, Molly – but he's coming again tonight, and mind, I'll never forgive you, if you don't think him very charming. I believe I cared for him when he offered all those months ago, but I tried to think I didn't; only sometimes I really was so unhappy, I thought I must put an iron band round my heart to keep it from breaking, like the Faithful John of the German story* – do you remember, Molly? – how, when his master came to his crown and his fortune and his lady-love, after innumerable trials and disgraces, and was driving away from the church where he'd been married in a coach-and-six, with Faithful John behind, the happy couple heard three great cracks in succession, and, on inquiring, they were the iron bands round his heart, that Faithful John had worn all during the time of his master's tribulation to keep it from breaking.'

In the evening Mr Henderson came. Molly had been very curious to see him; and, when she saw him, she was not sure whether she liked him or not. He was handsome, without being conceited; gentlemanly, without being foolishly fine. He talked easily, and never said a silly thing. He was perfectly well-appointed, yet never seemed to have given a thought to his dress. He was good-tempered and kind; not without some of the cheerful flippancy of repartee which belonged to his age and profession, and which his age and profession are apt to take for wit. But he wanted something in Molly's eyes – at any rate, in this first interview, and in her heart of hearts she thought him rather commonplace. But of course she said nothing of this to Cynthia, who was evidently as happy as she could be. Mrs Gibson, too, was in the seventh heaven of ecstasy, and spoke but little; but what she did say expressed the highest sentiments in the finest language. Mr Gibson was not with them for long; but, while he was there, he was evidently studying the unconscious Mr Henderson with his dark penetrating eyes. Mr Henderson behaved exactly as he ought to have done to everybody: respectful to Mr Gibson, deferential to Mrs Gibson, friendly to Molly, devoted to Cynthia.

The next time Mr Gibson found Molly alone, he began – 'Well! and how do you like the new relation that is to be?'

'It's difficult to say. I think he's very nice in all his bits, but – rather dull on the whole.'

'I think him perfection,' said Mr Gibson, to Molly's surprise; but in an instant afterwards she saw that he had been speaking ironically. He went on – 'I don't wonder she preferred him to Roger Hamley. Such scents! such gloves! And then his hair and cravat!'

'Now, papa, you're not fair. He's a great deal more than that. One could see that he had very good feeling; and he's very handsome, and very much attached to her.'

'So was Roger. However, I must confess I shall be only too glad to have her married. She's a girl who'll always have some love affair on hand, and will always be apt to slip through a man's fingers if he doesn't look sharp; as I was saying to Roger'—

'You have seen him, then, since he was here?'

'Met him in the street.'

'How was he?'

'I don't suppose he'd be going through the pleasantest thing in the world; but he'll get over it before long. He spoke with sense and resignation, and didn't say much about it; but one could see that he was feeling it pretty sharply. He's had three months to think it over, remember. The Squire, I should guess, is showing more indignation. He is boiling over, that any one should reject his son. The enormity of the sin never seems to have been apparent to him till now, when he sees how Roger is affected by it. Indeed, with the exception of myself, I don't know one reasonable father; eh, Molly?'

Whatever else Mr Henderson might be, he was an impatient lover; he wanted to marry Cynthia directly – next week – the week after; at any rate before the long vacation, so that they could go abroad at once. Trousseaux, and preliminary ceremonies, he gave to the winds. Mr Gibson, generous as usual, called Cynthia aside a morning or two after her engagement, and put a hundred-pound note into her hands.

'There, that's to pay your expenses to Russia and back. I hope you'll find your pupils obedient.'

To his surprise and rather to his discomfiture, Cynthia threw her arms round his neck and kissed him.

'You are the kindest person I know,' said she; 'and I don't know how to thank you in words.'

'If you tumble my shirt-collars again in that way, I'll charge you for the washing. Just now, too, when I'm trying so hard to be trim and elegant, like your Mr Henderson.'

'But you do like him, don't you?' said Cynthia pleadingly. 'He does so like you.'

'Of course. We're all angels just now, and you're an archangel. I hope he'll wear as well as Roger.'

Cynthia looked grave. 'That was a very silly affair,' she said. 'We were two as unsuitable people' —

'It has ended, and that's enough. Besides, I've no more time to waste; and there's your smart young man coming here in all haste.'

Mr and Mrs Kirkpatrick sent all manner of congratulations; and Mrs Kirkpatrick, in a private letter, assured Mrs Gibson that her ill-timed confidence about Roger should be considered as quite private. For, as soon as Mr Henderson had made his appearance in Hollingford, she had written a second letter, entreating them not to allude to anything she might have said in her first; which she said was written in such excitement on discovering the real state of her daughter's affections, that she had hardly known what she said, and had exaggerated some things, and misunderstood others: all that she did know now was, that Mr Henderson had just proposed to Cynthia, and was accepted, and that they were as happy as the day was long, and ('excuse the vanity of a mother,') made a most lovely couple. So Mr and Mrs Kirkpatrick wrote back an equally agreeable letter, praising Mr Henderson, admiring Cynthia, and generally congratulatory; insisting into the bargain that the marriage should take place from their house in Hyde Park Street, and that Mr and Mrs Gibson and Molly should all come up and pay them a visit. There was a little postscript at the end. 'Surely you do not mean the famous traveller, Hamley, about whose discoveries all our scientific men are so much excited. You speak of him as a young Hamley, who went to Africa. Answer this question, pray, for Helen is most anxious to know.' This P.S. being in Helen's handwriting. In her exultation at the general success of everything, and desire for sympathy, Mrs Gibson read parts of this letter to Molly; the postscript among the rest. It made a deeper impression on Molly than even the proposed kindness of the visit to London.

There were some family consultations; but the end of them all was that the Kirkpatrick invitation was accepted. There were many small reasons for this, which were openly acknowledged; but there was one general and unspoken wish to have the ceremony performed out of the immediate neighbourhood of the two men whom Cynthia had previously rejected; that was the word now to be applied to her treatment of them. So Molly was ordered and enjoined and entreated to become strong as soon as possible, in order that her health might not prevent her attending the marriage; Mr Gibson himself, though he thought it his duty to damp the excellent anticipations of his wife and her daughter, being not at all averse to the prospect of going to London, and seeing half-a-dozen old friends and many scientific exhibitions, independently of the very fair amount of liking which he had for his host, Mr Kirkpatrick, himself.

CHAPTER 57

Bridal Visits and Adieux

The whole town of Hollingford came to congratulate and inquire into particulars. Some indeed – Mrs Goodenough at the head of this class of malcontents – thought that they were defrauded of their right to a fine show by Cynthia's being married in London. Even Lady Cumnor was moved into action. She who had hardly ever paid calls 'out of her own sphere', who had only once been to see 'Clare' in her own house – she came to congratulate after her fashion. Maria had only just time to run up into the drawing-room one morning, and say –

'Please, ma'am, the great carriage from the Towers is coming up to the gate, and my lady the Countess is sitting inside.' It was but eleven o'clock, and Mrs Gibson would have been indignant at any commoner who had ventured to call at such an untimely hour; but in the case of the Peerage the rules of domestic morality were relaxed.

The family 'stood at arms', as it were, till Lady Cumnor appeared in the drawing-room; and then she had to be settled in the best chair, and the light adjusted before anything like conversation began. She was the first to speak; and Lady Harriet, who had begun a few words to Molly, dropped into silence.

'I have been taking Mary – Lady Cuxhaven – to the railway station on this new line between Birmingham and London,* and I thought I would come on here, and offer you my congratulations. Clare, which is the young lady?' – putting on her glasses, and looking at Cynthia and Molly, who were dressed pretty much alike. 'I did not think it would be amiss to give you a little advice, my dear,' said she, when Cynthia had been properly pointed out to her as bride-elect. 'I have heard a good deal about you; and I am only too glad, for your mother's sake – your mother is a very worthy woman, and did her duty very well, while she was in our family – I am truly rejoiced, I say, to hear that you are going to make so creditable a marriage. I hope it will efface your former errors of conduct – which we will hope were but trivial in reality – and that you will live to be a comfort to your mother – for whom both Lord Cumnor and I entertain a very sincere regard. But you must conduct yourself with discretion in whatever state of life it pleases God to place you, whether married or single. You must reverence your husband, and conform to his opinion in all things. Look up to him as your head, and do nothing without consulting him.' – It was as well that Lord Cumnor was not amongst the audience; or he might have compared precept with practice – 'Keep strict accounts; and remember your station in life. I understand that Mr—', looking about for some help as to the name she had forgotten, 'Henderson – Henderson – is in the law. Although there is a general prejudice against attorneys, I have known two or three who are very respectable men; and I am sure Mr Henderson is one, or your good mother and our old friend Gibson would not have sanctioned the engagement.'

'He's a barrister,' put in Cynthia, unable to restrain herself any longer. 'Barrister-at-law.'

'Ah, yes. Attorney-at-law. Barrister-at-law. I understand without your speaking so loud, my dear. What was I going to say before you interrupted me? When you have been a little in society, you will find that it is reckoned bad manners to interrupt. I had a great deal more to say to you, and you have put it all out of my head. There was something else your father wanted me to ask – what was it, Harriet?'

'I suppose you mean about Mr Hamley?'

'Oh, yes! we are intending to have the house full of Lord Hollingford's friends next month, and Lord Cumnor is particularly anxious to secure Mr Hamley.'

'The Squire?' asked Mrs Gibson, in some surprise. Lady Cumnor bowed slightly, as much as to say, 'If you did not interrupt me, I should explain.'

'The famous traveller – the scientific Mr Hamley, I mean. I imagine he is son to the Squire. Lord Hollingford knows him well; but, when we asked him before, he declined coming, and assigned no reason.'

Had Roger indeed been asked to the Towers and declined? Mrs Gibson could not understand it. Lady Cumnor went on –

'Now, this time we are particularly anxious to secure him, and my son, Lord Hollingford, will not return to England until the very week before the Duke of Atherstone is coming to us. I believe Mr Gibson is very intimate with Mr Hamley; do you think he could induce him to favour us with his company?'

And this from the proud Lady Cumnor; and the object of it Roger Hamley, whom she had all but turned out of her drawing-room two years ago for calling at an untimely hour; and whom Cynthia had turned out of her heart! Mrs Gibson was surprised, and could only murmur out that she was sure Mr Gibson would do all that her ladyship wished.

'Thank you. You know me well enough to be aware that I am not the person, nor is the Towers the house, to go about soliciting guests. But in this instance I bend my head; high rank should always be the first to honour those who have distinguished themselves by art or science.'

'Besides, mamma,' said Lady Harriet, 'papa was saying that the Hamleys have been on their land since before the Conquest; while we only came into the county a century ago; and there is a tale that the first Cumnor began his fortune through selling tobacco in King James's reign.'

If Lady Cumnor did not exactly shift her trumpet and take snuff* there on the spot, she behaved in an equivalent manner. She began a low-toned, but nevertheless authoritative, conversation with Clare about the details of the wedding, which lasted until she thought it fit to go; when she abruptly plucked Lady Harriet up, and carried her off in the very midst of a description she was giving to Cynthia about the delights of Spa, which was to be one of the resting-places of the newly-married couple on their wedding-tour.

Nevertheless, she prepared a handsome present for the bride: a Bible and a Prayer-book bound in velvet with silver-clasps; and also a collection of household account books, at the beginning of which Lady Cumnor wrote down with her own hand the proper weekly allowance of bread, butter, eggs, meat, and groceries per head, with the London prices of the articles; so that the most inexperienced house-keeper might ascertain whether her expenditure exceeded her means, as she expressed herself in the note which she sent with the handsome, dull present.

'If you are driving into Hollingford, Harriet, perhaps you will take these books to Miss Kirkpatrick,' said Lady Cumnor, after she had sealed her note with all the straightness and correctness befitting a countess of her immaculate character. 'I understand they are all going up to London tomorrow for this wedding, in spite of what I said to Clare of the duty of being married in one's own parish-church. She told me at the time that she entirely agreed with me, but that her husband had such a strong wish for a visit to London, that she did not know how she could oppose him consistently with her wifely duty. I advised her to repeat to him my reasons for thinking that they would be ill-advised to have the marriage in town; but I am afraid she has been overruled. That was her one great fault when she lived with us; she was always so yielding, and never knew how to say "No".'

'Mamma!' said Lady Harriet, with a little sly coaxing in her tone, 'do you think you would have been so fond of her, if she had opposed you, and said "No", when you wished her to say "Yes"?'

'To be sure I should, my dear. I like everybody to have an opinion of their own; only, when my opinions are based on thought and experience, which few people have had equal opportunities of acquiring, I think it is but proper deference in others to allow themselves to be convinced. In fact, I think it is only obstinacy which keeps them from acknowledging that they are. I am not a despot, I hope?' she asked, with some anxiety.

'If you are, dear mamma,' said Lady Harriet, kissing the stern uplifted face very fondly, 'I like a despotism better than a republic; and I must be very despotic over my ponies, for it's already getting very late for my drive round by Ash-holt.'

But when she arrived at the Gibsons', she was detained so long there by the state of the family, that she had to give up her going to Ash-holt.

Molly was sitting in the drawing-room, pale and trembling, and keeping herself quiet only by a strong effort. She was the only person there when Lady Harriet entered; the room was all in disorder, strewed with presents and paper, and pasteboard boxes, and half-displayed articles of finery.

'You look like Marius sitting amidst the ruins of Carthage,* my dear! What's the matter? Why have you got on that woe-begone face? This marriage isn't broken off, is it? Though nothing would surprise me where the beautiful Cynthia is concerned.'

'Oh, no! that's all right. But I've caught a fresh cold, and papa says he thinks I had better not go to the wedding.'

'Poor little one! And it's the first visit to London too!'

'Yes. But what I most care for is the not being with Cynthia to the last; and then, papa – '; she stopped, for she could hardly go on without open crying, and she did not want to do that. Then she cleared her voice. 'Papa,' she continued, 'has so looked forward to this holiday, – and seeing – and – and going – oh! I can't tell you where; but he has quite a list of people and sights to be seen – and now he says he should not be comfortable to leave me all alone for more than three days – two for travelling, and one for the wedding.' Just then Mrs Gibson came in, ruffled too after her fashion, though the presence of Lady Harriet was wonderfully smoothing.

'My dear Lady Harriet – how kind of you! Ah, yes, I see this poor unfortunate child has been telling you of her ill-luck; just when everything was going on so beautifully; I'm sure it was that open window at your back, Molly – you know you would persist that it could do you no harm, and now you see the mischief! I'm sure I shan't be able to enjoy myself – and at my only child's wedding too – without you; for I can't think of leaving you without Maria. I would rather sacrifice anything myself than think of you, uncared for, and dismal at home.'

'I'm sure Molly is as sorry as any one,' said Lady Harriet.

'No. I don't think she is,' said Mrs Gibson, with happy disregard of the chronology of events, 'or she would not have sate with her back to an open window the day before yesterday, when I told her not. But it can't be helped now. Papa too – but it is my duty to make the best of everything, and look at the cheerful side of life. I wish I could persuade her to do the same' (turning and addressing Lady Harriet). 'But, you see, it is a great mortification to a girl of her age to lose her first visit to London.'

'It is not that,' began Molly; but Lady Harriet made her a little sign to be silent, while she herself spoke.

'Now, Clare! you and I can manage it all, I think, if you will but help me in a plan I've got in my head. Mr Gibson shall stay as long as ever he can in London; and Molly shall be well cared for, and have some change of air and scene too, which is really what she needs as much as anything, in my poor opinion. I can't spirit her to the wedding and give her a sight of London; but I can carry her off to the Towers, and watch her myself; and send daily bulletins up to London, so that Mr Gibson may feel quite at ease, and stay with you as long as you like. What do you say to it, Clare?'

'Oh, I could not go,' said Molly; 'I should only be a trouble to everybody.'

'Nobody asked you for your opinion, little one. If we wise elders decide that you are to go, you must submit in silence.'

Meanwhile Mrs Gibson was rapidly balancing advantages and disadvantages. Amongst the latter, jealousy came in predominant. Amongst the former – it would sound well; Maria could then accompany Cynthia and herself as 'their maid'; Mr Gibson would stay longer with her, and it was always desirable to have a man at her beck and call in such a place as London; besides that, this identical man was gentlemanly and good-looking, and a favourite with her prosperous brother-in-law. The 'ayes' had it.

'What a charming plan! I cannot think of anything kinder or pleasanter for this poor darling. Only what will Lady Cumnor say? I am modest for my family as much as for myself,' she continued.

'You know mamma's sense of hospitality is never more gratified than when the house is quite full; and papa is just like her. Besides, she is fond of you, and grateful to our good Mr Gibson, and will be fond of you, little one, when she knows you as I do.'

Molly's heart sank within her at the prospect. Except on the one evening of her father's wedding-day, she had never even seen the outside of the Towers since that unlucky day in her childhood, when she had fallen asleep on Clare's bed. She had a dread of the countess, a dislike to her house; only it seemed as if it was a solution to the problem of what to do with her, which had been perplexing every one all the morning, and so evidently that it had caused her much distress. She kept silence, though her lips quivered from time to time. Oh, if the Miss Brownings had not chosen this very time of all others to pay their monthly visit to Miss Hornblower! If she could only have gone there, and lived with them in their quaint, quiet, primitive way, instead of having to listen, without remonstrance, to hearing plans discussed about her, as if she was an inanimate chattel!

'She shall have the south pink room, opening out of mine by one door, you remember; and the dressing-room shall be made into a cosy little sitting-room for her, in case she likes to be by herself. Parkes shall attend upon her, and I'm sure Mr Gibson must know Parkes's powers as a nurse by this time. We shall have all manner of agreeable people in the house to amuse her downstairs; and, when she has got rid of this access of cold, I will drive her out every day, and write daily bulletins, as I said. Pray tell Mr Gibson all that, and let it be considered as settled! I will come for her in the close carriage tomorrow, at eleven. And now, may I see the lovely bride-elect, and give her mamma's present, and my own good wishes?'

So Cynthia came in, and demurely received the very proper present, and the equally coveted congratulations, without testifying any very great delight or gratitude at either; for she was quite quick enough to detect there was no great afflux of affection accompanying either. But, when she heard her mother quickly recapitulating all the details of the plan for Molly, Cynthia's eyes did sparkle with gladness; and, almost to Lady Harriet's surprise, she thanked her as if she had conferred a personal favour upon her. Lady Harriet saw, too, that, in a very quiet way, she had taken Molly's hand, and was holding it all the time, as if loth to think of their approaching separation – somehow, she and Lady Harriet were brought nearer together by this little action than they had ever been before.

Molly had hoped that her father might have raised some obstacles to the project; in this she was disappointed. But she was satisfied when she perceived how he seemed to feel that, by placing her under the care of Lady Harriet and Parkes, he should be relieved from anxiety. And now he spoke of this change of air and scene as being the very thing he had been wishing to secure for her, country-air and absence of excitement as this would be; for the only other place where he could have secured her these advantages, and at the same time sent her as an invalid, was to Hamley Hall; and he dreaded the associations there with the beginning of her present illness.

So Molly was driven off in state the next day, leaving her own home all in confusion with the assemblage of boxes and trunks in the hall, and all the other symptoms of the approaching departure of the family for London and the wedding. All the morning, Cynthia had been with her in her room, attending to the arrangement of Molly's clothes, instructing her what to wear with what, and rejoicing over the pretty smartnesses, which, having been prepared for her as bridesmaid, were now to serve as adornments for her visit to the Towers. Both Molly and Cynthia spoke about

dress as if it were the very object of their lives; for each dreaded
the introduction of more serious subjects; Cynthia more for Molly
than for herself. Only when the carriage was announced, and
Molly was preparing to go downstairs, Cynthia said – 'I'm not
going to thank you, Molly, or to tell you how I love you.'

'Don't,' said Molly, 'I can't bear it.'

'Only you know you are to be my first visitor; and, if you wear
brown ribbons to a green gown, I'll turn you out of the house!'
So they parted. Mr Gibson was there in the hall, to hand Molly
in. He had ridden hard; and was now giving her two or three last
injunctions as to her health.

'Think of us on Thursday,' said he. 'I declare I don't know
which of her three lovers she mayn't summon at the very last
moment to act the part of bridegroom. I'm determined to be
surprised at nothing, and will give her away with a good grace to
whoever comes.'

They drove away; and, until they were out of sight of the house,
Molly had enough to do to keep returning the kisses of the hand
wafted to her by her stepmother out of the drawing-room window, while at the same time her eyes were fixed on a white
handkerchief, fluttering out of the attic from which she herself
had watched Roger's departure nearly two years before. What
changes time had brought!

When Molly arrived at the Towers, she was convoyed into
Lady Cumnor's presence by Lady Harriet. It was a mark of
respect to the lady of the house, which the latter knew that her
mother would expect; but she was anxious to get it over, and take
Molly up into the room which she had been so busy arranging for
her. Lady Cumnor was, however, very kind, if not positively
gracious.

'You are Lady Harriet's visitor, my dear,' said she, 'and I hope
she will take good care of you. If not, come and complain of her
to me.' It was as near an approach to a joke as Lady Cumnor ever
perpetrated, and from it Lady Harriet knew that her mother was
pleased by Molly's manners and appearance.

'Now, here you are in your own kingdom; and into this room I
shan't venture to come without express permission. Here's the
last* new *Quarterly*, and the last new novel, and the last new
essay. Now, my dear, you needn't come down again today, unless
you like it. Parkes shall bring you everything and anything you
want. You must get strong as fast as you can, for all sorts of great

and famous people are coming tomorrow and the next day, and I think you'll like to see them. Suppose for today you only come down to lunch and, if you like it, in the evening. Dinner is such a wearily long meal, if one isn't strong; and you wouldn't miss much, for there's only my cousin Charles in the house now, and he's the personification of sensible silence.'

Molly was only too glad to allow Lady Harriet to decide everything for her. It had begun to rain, and was altogether a gloomy day for August; and there was a small fire of scented wood burning cheerfully in the sitting-room appropriated to her. High up, it commanded a wide and pleasant view over the park, and from it could be seen the spire of Hollingford Church, which gave Molly a pleasant idea of neighbourhood to home. She was left alone, lying on the sofa – books near her, wood cracking and blazing, wafts of wind bringing the beating rain against the window, and so enhancing the sense of indoor comfort by the outdoor contrast. Parkes was unpacking for her. Lady Harriet had introduced Parkes to Molly by saying, 'Now, Molly, this is Mrs Parkes, the only person I am ever afraid of. She scolds me, if I dirty myself with my paints, just as if I was a little child; and she makes me go to bed, when I want to sit up,' – Parkes was smiling grimly all the time – 'so, to get rid of her tyranny, I give her you as victim. Parkes, rule over Miss Gibson with a rod of iron; make her eat and drink, and rest and sleep, and dress as you think wisest and best.'

Parkes had begun to reign by putting Molly on the sofa, and saying, 'If you will give me your keys, Miss, I will unpack your things, and let you know when it is time for me to arrange your hair, preparatory to luncheon.' For, if Lady Harriet used familiar colloquialisms from time to time, she certainly had not learnt it from Parkes, who piqued herself on the correctness of her language.

When Molly went down to lunch, she found 'cousin Charles', with his aunt, Lady Cumnor. He was a certain Sir Charles Morton, the son of Lady Cumnor's only sister: a plain, sandy-haired man of thirty-five or so; immensely rich, very sensible, awkward, and reserved. He had had a chronic attachment, of many years' standing, to his cousin, Lady Harriet, who did not care for him in the least, although it was the marriage very earnestly desired for her by her mother. Lady Harriet was, how-ever, on friendly terms with him, ordered him about, and told him what to do, and what to leave undone, without having even a doubt as to the willingness of his obedience. She had given him his cue about Molly.

'Now, Charles, the girl wants to be interested and amused without having to take any trouble for herself; she's too delicate to be very active either in mind or body. Just look after her when the house gets full, and place her where she can hear and see everything and everybody, without any fuss and responsibility.'

So Sir Charles began this day at luncheon by taking Molly under his quiet protection. He did not say much to her; but what he did say was thoroughly friendly and sympathetic; and Molly began, as he and Lady Harriet intended that she should, to have a kind of pleasant reliance upon him. Then, in the evening, while the rest of the family were at dinner – after Molly's tea and hour of quiet repose, Parkes came and dressed her in some of the new clothes prepared for the Kirkpatrick visit, and did her hair in some new and pretty way, so that, when Molly looked at herself in the cheval-glass, she scarcely knew the elegant reflection to be that of herself. She was fetched down by Lady Harriet into the great, long, formidable drawing-room which, as an interminable place of pacing, had haunted her dreams ever since her childhood. At the further end sat Lady Cumnor at her tapestry-work; the light of fire and candle seemed all concentrated on that one bright part where presently Lady Harriet made tea, and Lord Cumnor went to sleep, and Sir Charles read passages aloud from the *Edinburgh Review* to the three ladies at their work.

When Molly went to bed, she was constrained to admit that staying at the Towers as a visitor was rather pleasant than otherwise; and she tried to reconcile old impressions with new ones, until she fell asleep. There was another comparatively quiet day, before the expected guests began to arrive in the evening. Lady Harriet took Molly a drive in her little pony-carriage; and, for the first time for many weeks, Molly began to feel the delightful spring of returning health; the dance of youthful spirits in the fresh air, cleared by the previous day's rain.

CHAPTER 58

Reviving Hopes and Brightening Prospects

'If you can without fatigue, dear, do come down to dinner today; you'll then see the people one by one as they appear, instead of having to encounter a crowd of strangers. Hollingford will be here too. I hope you'll find it pleasant.'

So Molly made her appearance at dinner that day; and got to know, by sight at least, some of the most distinguished of the visitors at the Towers. The next day was Thursday, Cynthia's wedding-day; bright and fine in the country, whatever it might be in London. And there were several letters from the home-people awaiting Molly, when she came downstairs to the late breakfast. For every day, every hour, she was gaining strength and health; and she was unwilling to continue her invalid habits any longer than was necessary. She looked so much better that Sir Charles noticed it to Lady Harriet; and several of the visitors spoke of her this morning as a very pretty, lady-like, and graceful girl. This was Thursday; on Friday, as Lady Harriet had told her, some visitors from the more immediate neighbourhood were expected to stay over the Sunday; but she had not mentioned their names, and, when Molly went down into the drawingroom before dinner, she was almost startled by perceiving Roger Hamley in the centre of a group of gentlemen, who were all talking together eagerly, and, as it seemed to her, making him the object of their attention. He made a hitch in his conversation, lost the precise meaning of a question addressed to him, answered it rather hastily, and made his way to where Molly was sitting, a little behind Lady Harriet. He had heard that she was staying at the Towers; but he was almost as much surprised by her looks, as she was by his unexpected appearance, for he had only seen her once or twice since his return from Africa, and then in the guise of an invalid. Now, in her pretty evening-dress, with her hair beautifully dressed, her delicate complexion flushed a little with timidity, yet her movements and manners bespeaking quiet ease, Roger hardly recognised her, although he acknowledged her identity. He began to feel that admiring deference which most young men experience, when conversing with a very pretty girl: a sort of desire to obtain her good opinion, in a manner very different to his old familiar friendliness. He was annoyed when Sir Charles, whose especial charge she still was, came up to take her in to dinner. He could not quite understand the smile of mutual intelligence that passed between the two, each being aware of Lady Harriet's plan of sheltering Molly from the necessity of talking, and acting in conformity with her wishes as much as with their own. Roger found himself puzzling, and watching them from time to time during dinner. Again in the evening he sought her out, but found her again preoccupied with one of the young men staying in the house, who had had the advantage of two days of mutual interest, and acquaintance with the daily events, and jokes and anxieties, of the family circle. Molly could not help wishing to break off all this trivial talk and to make room for Roger: she had so much to ask him about everything at the Hall; he was, and had been, such a stranger to them all for these last two months, and more. But, though both wanted to speak to the other more than to any one else in the room, it so happened that everything seemed to conspire to prevent it. Lord Hollingford carried off Roger to the clatter of middle-aged men; he was wanted to give his opinion upon some scientific subject. Mr Ernest Watson, the young man referred to above, kept his place by Molly, as the prettiest girl in the room, and almost dazed her by his never-ceasing flow of clever small talk. She looked so tired and pale at last that the ever-watchful Lady Harriet sent Sir Charles to the rescue; and, after a few words with Lady Harriet, Roger saw Molly quietly leave the room, and a sentence or two which he heard Lady Harriet address to her cousin made him know that it was for the night. Those sentences might bear another interpretation than the obvious one.

'Really, Charles, considering that she is in your charge, I think you might have saved her from the chatter and patter of Mr Watson; I can only stand it when I am in the strongest health.'

Why was Molly in Sir Charles's charge? why? Then Roger remembered many little things that might serve to confirm the fancy he had got into his head; and he went to bed puzzled and annoyed. It seemed to him such an incongruous, hastily-got-up sort of engagement, if engagement it really was. On Saturday they were more fortunate: they had a long *tête-à-tête* in the most public place in the house – on a sofa in the hall where Molly was resting at Lady Harriet's command, before going upstairs after a walk. Roger was passing through, and saw her, and came to her.

Standing before her, and making pretence of playing with the gold fish in a great marble basin close at hand –

'I was very unlucky,' said he. 'I wanted to get near you last night, but it was quite impossible. You were so busy talking to Mr Watson, until Sir Charles Morton came and carried you off – with such an air of authority! Have you known him long?'

Now, this was not at all the manner in which Roger had predetermined that he would speak of Sir Charles to Molly; but the words came out in spite of himself.

'No! not long. I never saw him before I came here – on Tuesday. But Lady Harriet told him to see that I did not get tired, for I wanted to come down; but you know I have not been strong. He is a cousin of Lady Harriet's, and does all she tells him to do.'

'Oh! he's not handsome; but I believe he's a very sensible man.'

'Yes! I should think so. He is so silent, though, that I can hardly judge.'

'He bears a very high character in the county,' said Roger, willing now to give him his full due.

Molly stood up.

'I must go upstairs,' she said; 'I only sate down here for a minute or two, because Lady Harriet bade me.'

'Stop a little longer,' said he. 'This is really the pleasantest place; this basin of water-lilies gives one the idea, if not the sensation, of coolness; besides – it seems so long since I saw you, and I've a message from my father to give you. He is very angry with you.'

'Angry with me!' said Molly in surprise.

'Yes! He heard that you had come here for change of air; and he was offended that you hadn't come to us – to the Hall, instead. He said that you should have remembered old friends!'

Molly took all this quite gravely, and did not at first notice the smile on his face.

'Oh! I am so sorry,' said she. 'But will you please tell him how it all happened? Lady Harriet called the very day when it was settled that I was not to go to'—Cynthia's wedding, she was going to add, but she suddenly stopped short, and, blushing deeply, changed the expression – 'go to London, and she planned it all in a minute, and convinced mamma and papa, and had her own way. There was really no resisting her.'

'I think you will have to tell all this to my father yourself, if you mean to make your peace. Why can you not come on to the Hall when you leave the Towers?'

To go in the cool manner suggested from one house to another, after the manner of a royal progress, was not at all according to Molly's primitive home-keeping notions. She made answer –

'I should like it very much, some time. But I must go home first. They will want me more than ever now' —

Again she felt herself touching on a sore subject, and stopped short. Roger became annoyed at her so constantly conjecturing what he must be feeling on the subject of Cynthia's marriage. With sympathetic perception, she had discerned that the idea must give him pain; and perhaps she also knew that he would dislike to show the pain; but she had not the presence of mind or ready wit to give a skilful turn to the conversation. All this annoyed Roger, he could hardly tell why. He determined to take the metaphorical bull by the horns. Until that was done, his footing with Molly would always be insecure; as it always is between two friends, who mutually avoid a subject to which their thoughts perpetually recur.

'Ah, yes!' said he. 'Of course you must be of double importance, now Miss Kirkpatrick has left you. I saw her marriage in the "Times" yesterday.'

His tone of voice was changed in speaking of her; but her name had been named between them, and that was the great thing to accomplish.

'Still,' he continued, 'I think I must urge my father's claim for a short visit, and all the more, because I can really see the apparent improvement in your health since I came – only yesterday. Besides, Molly,' it was the old familiar Roger of former days who spoke now, 'I think you could help us at home. Aimée is shy and awkward with my father, and he has never taken quite kindly to her – yet I know they would like and value each other, if some one could but bring them together – and it would be such a comfort to me, if this could take place before I have to leave.'

'To leave – are you going away again?'

'Yes. Have you not heard? I didn't complete my engagement. I'm going again in September for six months.'

'I remember. But somehow I fancied – you seemed to have settled down into the old way at the Hall.'

'So my father appears to think. But it is not likely I shall ever make it my home again; and that is partly the reason why I want my father to adopt the notion of Aimée's living with him. Ah, here are all the people coming back from their walk. However, I shall see you again; perhaps this afternoon we may get a little quiet time, for I've a great deal to consult you about.'

They separated then, and Molly went upstairs very happy; very full and warm at her heart; it was so pleasant to have Roger talking to her in this way, like a friend; she had once thought that she could never look upon the great brown-bearded celebrity in the former light of almost brotherly intimacy, but now it was all coming right. There was no opportunity for renewed confidences that afternoon. Molly went a quiet decorous drive as fourth, with two dowagers and one spinster; but it was very pleasant to think that she should see him again at dinner, and again tomorrow. On the Sunday evening, as they all were sitting and loitering on the lawn before dinner, Roger went on with what he had to say about the position of his sister-in-law in his father's house; the mutual bond between the mother and grandfather being the child, who was also, through jealousy, the bone of contention and the severance. There were many details to be given, in order to make Molly quite understand the difficulty of the situations on both sides; and the young man and the girl became absorbed in what they were talking about, and wandered away into the shade of the long avenue. Lady Harriet separated herself from a group and came up to Lord Hollingford, who was sauntering a little apart, and, putting her arm within his with the familiarity of a favourite sister, she said –

'Don't you think that your pattern young man, and my favourite young woman, are finding out each other's good qualities?'

He had not been observing as she had been.

'Whom do you mean?' said he.

'Look along the avenue; who are those?'

'Mr Hamley and – is it not Miss Gibson? I can't quite make out. Oh! if you're letting your fancy run off in that direction, I can tell you it's quite waste of time. Roger Hamley is a man who will soon have a European reputation!'

'That's very possible, and yet it doesn't make any difference in my opinion. Molly Gibson is capable of appreciating him.'

'She is a very pretty, good little country-girl. I don't mean to say anything against her, but'—

'Remember the Charity Ball; you called her "unusually intelligent", after you had danced with her there. But, after all, we're like the genie and the fairy in the "Arabian Nights' Entertainment", who each cried up the merits of the Prince Caramalzaman and the Princess Badoura.'*

'Hamley is not a marrying man.'

'How do you know?'

'I know that he has very little private fortune, and I know that science is not a remunerative profession, if profession it can be called.'

'Oh, if that's all – a hundred things may happen – some one may leave him a fortune – or this tiresome little heir, that nobody wanted, may die.'

'Hush, Harriet, that's the worst of allowing yourself to plan far ahead for the future; you are sure to contemplate the death of some one, and to reckon upon the contingency as affecting events.'

'As if lawyers were not always doing something of the kind!'

'Leave it to those to whom it is necessary. I dislike planning marriages, or looking forward to deaths, about equally.'

'You are getting very prosaic and tiresome, Hollingford!'

'Only getting!' said he, smiling; 'I thought you had always looked upon me as a tiresome, matter-of-fact fellow.'

'Now, if you're going to fish for a compliment, I am gone. Only remember my prophecy, when my vision comes to pass; or make a bet, and whoever wins shall spend the money on a present to Prince Caramalzaman or Princess Badoura, as the case may be.'

Lord Hollingford remembered his sister's words, as he heard Roger say to Molly, when he was leaving the Towers on the following day –

'Then I may tell my father that you will come and pay him a visit next week? You don't know what pleasure it will give him.' He had been on the point of saying 'will give *us*'; but he had an instinct which told him it was as well to consider Molly's promised visit as exclusively made to his father.

The next day Molly went home; she was astonished at herself for being so sorry to leave the Towers, and found it difficult, if not impossible, to reconcile the long-fixed idea of the house, as a place wherein to suffer all a child's tortures of dismay and forlornness, with her new and fresh conception. She had gained health; she had had pleasure; the faint fragrance of a new and unacknowledged hope had stolen into her life. No wonder that Mr Gibson was struck with the improvement in her looks, and Mrs Gibson impressed with her increased grace.

'Ah, Molly,' said she, 'it's really wonderful to see what a little good society will do for a girl. Even a week of association with such people as one meets with at the Towers is, as somebody said of a lady of rank whose name I have forgotten, "a polite education in itself".* There is something quite different about you – a *je ne sçais quoi* – that would tell me at once that you have been mingling with the aristocracy. With all her charms, it was what my darling Cynthia wanted; not that Mr Henderson thought so, for a more devoted lover can hardly be conceived. He absolutely bought her a *parure** of diamonds. I was obliged to say to him that I had studied to preserve her simplicity of taste, and that he must not corrupt her with too much luxury. But I was rather disappointed at their going off without a maid. It was the one blemish in the arrangements – the spot on the sun. Dear Cynthia! when I think of her, I do assure you, Molly, I make it my nightly prayer that I may be able to find you just such another husband. And all this time you have never told me whom you met at the Towers?'

Molly ran over a list of names. Roger Hamley's came last.

'Upon my word! That young man is pushing his way up!'

'The Hamleys are a far older family than the Cumnors,' said Molly, flushing up.

'Now, Molly, I can't have you democratic. Rank is a great distinction. It is quite enough to have dear papa with democratic tendencies. But we won't begin to quarrel. Now that you and I are left alone, we ought to be bosom friends, and I hope we shall be. Roger Hamley did not say much about that unfortunate little Osborne Hamley, I suppose?'

'On the contrary, he says his father dotes on the child; and he seemed very proud of him, himself.'

'I thought the Squire must be getting very much infatuated with something. I dare say the French mother takes care of that. Why! he has scarcely taken any notice of you for this month or more, and before that you were everything.'

It was about six weeks since Cynthia's engagement had become publicly known, and that might have had something to do with the Squire's desertion, Molly thought. But she said –

'The Squire has sent me an invitation to go and stay there next week, if you have no objection, mamma. They seem to want a companion for Mrs Osborne Hamley, who is not very strong.'

'I can hardly tell what to say – I don't like your having to associate with a Frenchwoman of doubtful rank; and I can't bear

the thought of losing my child – my only daughter now. I did ask
Helen Kirkpatrick, but she can't come for some time; and the
house is going to be altered. Papa has consented to build me
another room at last, for Cynthia and Mr Henderson will, of
course, come and see us; we shall have many more visitors, I
expect, and your bedroom will make a capital lumber-room; and
Maria wants a week's holiday. I am always so unwilling to put
any obstacles in the way of any one's pleasure – weakly unwilling,
I believe – but it certainly would be very convenient to have you
out of the house for a few days; so, for once, I will waive my own
wish for your companionship, and plead your cause with papa.'

The Miss Brownings came to call and hear the double batch of
news. Mrs Goodenough had called the very day on which they
had returned from Miss Hornblower's, to tell them the astounding
fact of Molly Gibson having gone on a visit to the Towers: not to
come back at night, but to sleep there; to be there for two or three
days, just as if she was a young lady of quality. So the Miss
Brownings came to hear all the details of the wedding from Mrs
Gibson, and the history of Molly's visit at the Towers as well. But
Mrs Gibson did not like this divided interest, and some of her old
jealousy of Molly's intimacy at the Towers returned.

'Now, Molly,' said Miss Browning, 'let us hear how you
behaved among the great folks. You must not be set up with all
their attention; remember that they pay it to you for your good
father's sake.'

'Molly is, I think, quite aware,' put in Mrs Gibson, in her most
soft and languid tone, 'that she owes her privilege of visiting at
such a house to Lady Cumnor's kind desire to set my mind quite
at liberty at the time of Cynthia's marriage. As soon as ever I had
returned home, Molly came back; indeed, I should not have
thought it right to let her intrude upon their kindness beyond
what was absolutely necessary.'

Molly felt extremely uncomfortable at all this, though perfectly
aware of the entire inaccuracy of the statement.

'Well, but, Molly!' said Miss Browning, 'never mind whether
you went there on your own merits, or your worthy father's
merits, or Mrs Gibson's merits; but tell us what you did when you
were there.'

So Molly began an account of their sayings and doings, which
she could have made far more interesting to Miss Browning and
Miss Phoebe, if she had not been conscious of her stepmother's

critical listening. She had to tell it all with a mental squint; the surest way to spoil a narration. She was also subject to Mrs Gibson's perpetual corrections of little statements which she knew to be facts. But what vexed her most of all was Mrs Gibson's last speech before the Miss Brownings left.

'Molly has fallen into rambling ways with this visit of hers, of which she makes so much, as if nobody had ever been in a great house but herself. She is going to Hamley Hall next week – getting quite dissipated, in fact.'

Yet to Mrs Goodenough, the next caller on the same errand of congratulation, Mrs Gibson's tone was quite different. There had always been a tacit antagonism between the two, and the conversation now ran as follows: –

Mrs Goodenough began,

'Well! Mrs Gibson, I suppose I must wish you joy of Miss Cynthia's marriage; I should condole with some mothers as had lost their daughters; but you're not one of that sort, I reckon.'

Now, as Mrs Gibson was not quite sure to which 'sort' of mothers the greatest credit was to be attached, she found it a little difficult how to frame her reply.

'Dear Cynthia!' she said. 'One can't but rejoice in her happiness! And yet – ' She ended her sentence by sighing.

'Ay. She was a young woman as would always have her followers; for, to tell the truth, she was as pretty a creature as ever I saw in my life. And all the more she needed skilful guidance. I'm sure I, for one, am as glad as can be she's done so well by herself. Folks say Mr Henderson has a handsome private fortune over and above what he makes by the law.'

'There is no fear but that my Cynthia will have everything this world can give!' said Mrs Gibson with dignity.

'Well, well she was always a bit of a favourite of mine; and, as I was saying to my granddaughter there' (for she was accompanied by a young lady, who looked keenly to the prospect of some wedding-cake), 'I was never one of those who ran her down, and called her a flirt and a jilt. I'm glad to hear she's like to be so well off. And now, I suppose, you'll be turning your mind to doing something for Miss Molly there?'

'If you mean by that, doing anything that can, by hastening her marriage, deprive me of the company of one who is like my own child, you are very much mistaken, Mrs Goodenough. And pray remember, I am the last person in the world to match-make.

Cynthia made Mr Henderson's acquaintance at her uncle's in London.'

'Ay! I thought her cousins was very often ill, and needing her nursing, and you were very keen she should be of use. I'm not saying but what it's right in a mother; I'm only putting in a word for Miss Molly.'

'Thank you, Mrs Goodenough,' said Molly, half angry, half laughing; 'when I want to be married, I'll not trouble mamma. I'll look out for myself.'

'Molly is becoming so popular, I hardly know how we shall keep her at home,' said Mrs Gibson. 'I miss her sadly; but, as I said to Mr Gibson, let young people have change, and see a little of the world while they are young. It has been a great advantage to her being at the Towers, while so many clever and distinguished people were there. I can already see a difference in her tone and conversation: an elevation in her choice of subjects. And now she is going to Hamley Hall. I can assure you I feel quite a proud mother, when I see how she is sought after. And my other daughter – my Cynthia – writing such letters from Paris!'

'Things is a deal changed since my days, for sure,' said Mrs Goodenough. 'So, perhaps, I'm no judge. When I was married first, him and me went in a post-chaise to his father's house, a matter of twenty miles off at the outside, and sate down to as good a supper amongst his friends and relations as you'd wish to see. And that was my first wedding jaunt. My second was, when I better knowed my worth as a bride, and thought that now or never I must see London. But I were reckoned a very extravagant sort of a body to go so far, and spend my money, though Jerry had left me uncommon well off. But now young folks go off to Paris, and think nothing of the cost; and it's well if wilful waste don't make woeful want, before they die. But I'm thankful some-what is being done for Miss Molly's chances, as I said afore. It's not quite what I should have liked to have done for my Anna-Maria, though. But times are changed, as I said just now.'

CHAPTER 59

Molly Gibson at Hamley Hall

The conversation ended there for the time. Wedding-cake and wine were brought in, and it was Molly's duty to serve them out. But those last words of Mrs Goodenough's tingled in her ears, and she tried to interpret them to her own satisfaction in any way but the obvious one. And that, too, was destined to be confirmed; for, directly after Mrs Goodenough took her leave, Mrs Gibson desired Molly to carry away the tray to a table close to an open corner window, where the things might be placed in readiness for any future callers; and underneath this open window went the path from the house-door to the road. Molly heard Mrs Goodenough saying to her granddaughter –

'That Mrs Gibson is a deep 'un. There's Mr Roger Hamley as like as not to have the Hall estate, and she sends Molly a-visiting' – and then she passed out of hearing. Molly could have burst out crying, with a full sudden conviction of what Mrs Goodenough had been alluding to: her sense of the impropriety of Molly's going to visit at the Hall when Roger was at home. To be sure, Mrs Goodenough was a commonplace, unrefined woman. Mrs Gibson did not seem to have even noticed the allusion. Mr Gibson took it all as a matter of course, that Molly should go to the Hall as simply now as she had done before. Roger had spoken of it in so straightforward a manner as showed he had no conception of its being an impropriety – this visit – this visit, until now so happy a subject of anticipation. Molly felt as if she could never speak to any one of the idea to which Mrs Goodenough's words had given rise; as if she could never be the first to suggest the notion of impropriety, which pre-supposed what she blushed to think of. Then she tried to comfort herself by reasoning. If it had been forward or indelicate, really improper in the slightest degree, who would have been so ready as her father to put his veto upon it? But reasoning was of no use, after Mrs Goodenough's words had put fancies into Molly's head. The more she bade these fancies begone the more they answered her (as Daniel O'Rourke* did the man in the moon, when he bade Dan get off his seat on the sickle, and go into empty space): 'The more ye ask us, the more we won't stir.' One may smile at a young girl's miseries of this kind; but they are very real and stinging miseries to her. All that Molly could do was to resolve on a single eye to the dear old Squire, and his mental and bodily comforts; to try and heal up any breaches which might have occurred between him and Aimée; and to ignore Roger as much as possible. Good Roger! Kind Roger! Dear Roger! It would be very hard to avoid him as much as was consistent with common politeness; but it would be right to do it; and, when she was with him, she must be as natural as possible, or he might observe some difference; but what was natural? How much ought she to avoid being with him? Would he even notice if she was more chary of his company, more calculating of her words? Alas! the simplicity of their intercourse was spoilt henceforwards! She made laws for herself; she resolved to devote herself to the Squire and to Aimée, and to forget Mrs Goodenough's foolish speeches; but her perfect freedom was gone, and with it half her chance – that is to say, half her chance would have been lost with any strangers who had not known her before; they would probably have thought her stiff and awkward, and apt to say things and then retract them. But she was so different from her usual self that Roger noticed the change in her, as soon as she arrived at the Hall. She had carefully measured out the days of her visit; they were to be exactly the same number as she had spent at the Towers. She feared lest, if she stayed a shorter time, the Squire might be annoyed. Yet how charming the place looked in its early autumnal glow, as she drove up! And there was Roger at the hall-door, waiting to receive her, watching for her coming. And then he retreated, apparently to summon his sister-in-law, who came now timidly forwards in her deep widow's-mourning, holding her boy in her arms as if to protect her shyness; but he struggled down, and ran towards the carriage, eager to greet his friend the coachman, and to obtain a promised ride. Roger did not say much himself; he wanted to make Aimée feel her place as daughter of the house; but she was too timid to speak much. And she only took Molly by the hand and led her into the drawing-room; where, as if by a sudden impulse of gratitude for all the tender nursing she had received during her illness, she put her arms round Molly, and kissed her long and well. And after that they came to be friends.

It was nearly lunch-time, and the Squire always made his appearance at that meal, more for the pleasure of seeing his grandson eat his dinner than for any hunger of his own. Today, Molly quickly saw the whole state of the family affairs. She thought that, even had Roger said nothing about them at the Towers, she should have seen that neither the father nor the daughter-in-law had as yet found the clue to each other's characters, although they had now been living for several months in the same house. Aimée seemed to forget her English in her nervousness, and to watch, with the jealous eyes of a dissatisfied mother, all the proceedings of the Squire towards her little boy. They were not of the wisest kind, it must be owned; the child sipped the strong ale with evident relish, and clamoured for everything which he saw the others enjoying. Aimée could hardly attend to Molly for her anxiety as to what her boy was doing and eating; yet she said nothing. Roger took the end of the table opposite to that at which sat grandfather and grandchild. After the boy's first wants were gratified, the Squire addressed himself to Molly.

'Well! and so you can come here a-visiting, though you have been among the grand folks! I thought you were going to cut us, Miss Molly, when I heard you was gone to the Towers. Couldn't find any other place to stay at, while father and mother were away, but an earl's, eh?'

'They asked me, and I went,' said Molly; 'now you've asked me, and I've come here.'

'I think you might ha' known you'd be always welcome here, without waiting for asking. Why, Molly! I look upon you as a kind of daughter more than Madam there!' dropping his voice a little, and perhaps supposing that the child's babble would drown the signification of his words.

'Nay, you needn't look at me so pitifully; she doesn't follow English readily.'

'I think she does!' said Molly, in a low voice – not looking up, however, for fear of catching another glimpse at Aimée's sudden forlornness of expression and deepened colour. She felt grateful, as if for a personal favour, when she heard Roger speaking to Aimée the moment afterwards in the tender terms of brotherly friendliness; and presently these two were sufficiently engaged in a separate conversation to allow Molly and the Squire to go on talking.

'He's a sturdy chap, isn't he?' said the Squire, stroking the little Roger's curly head. 'And he can puff four puffs at grandpapa's pipe without being sick, can't he?'

'I san't puff any more puffs,' said the boy resolutely. 'Mamma says "No". I san't.'

'That's just like her!' said the Squire, dropping his voice this time, however. 'As if it could do the child any harm!'

Molly made a point of turning the conversation from all personal subjects after this, and kept the Squire talking about the progress of his drainage during the rest of lunch. He offered to take her to see it; and she acceded to the proposal, thinking, meantime, how little she need have anticipated the being thrown too intimately with Roger, who seemed to devote himself to his sister-in-law. But, in the evening, when Aimée had gone upstairs to put her boy to bed, and the Squire was asleep in his easy-chair, a sudden flush of memory brought Mrs Goodenough's words again to her mind. She was virtually *tête-à-tête* with Roger, as she had been dozens of times before; but now she could not help assuming an air of constraint; her eyes did not meet his in the old frank way; she took up a book at a pause in the conversation, and left him puzzled and annoyed at the change in her manner. And so it went on during all the time of her visit. If sometimes she forgot, and let herself go into all her old naturalness, by-and-by she checked herself, and became comparatively cold and reserved. Roger was pained at all this – more pained day after day; more anxious to discover the cause. Aimée, too, silently noticed how different Molly became in Roger's presence. One day she could not help saying to Molly –

'Don't you like Roger? You would, if you only knew how good he is! He is learned, but that is nothing; it is his goodness that one admires and loves.'

'He is very good,' said Molly. 'I have known him long enough to know that.'

'But you don't think him agreeable? He is not like my poor husband, to be sure; and you knew him well, too. Ah! tell me about him once again. When you first knew him? When his mother was alive?'

Molly had grown very fond of Aimée; when the latter was at her ease, she had very charming and attaching ways; but, feeling uneasy in her position in the Squire's house, she was almost repellent to him; and he, too, put on his worst side to her. Roger was most anxious to bring them together, and had several consultations with Molly as to the best means of accomplishing this end. As long as they talked upon this subject, she spoke to him in the quiet sensible manner which she inherited from her father; but, when their discussions on this point were ended, she fell back into her piquant assumption of dignified reserve. It was very difficult for her to maintain this strange manner, especially when once or twice she fancied that it gave him pain; and she would go into her own room and suddenly burst into tears on these occasions, and wish that her visit was ended, and that she was once again in the eventless tranquillity of her own home. Yet presently her fancy changed, and she clung to the swiftly passing hours, as if she would still retain the happiness of each. For, unknown to her, Roger was exerting himself to make her visit pleasant. He was not willing to appear as the instigator of all the little plans for each day, for he felt as if, somehow, he did not hold the same place in her regard as formerly. Still, one day Aimée suggested a nutting expedition – another day they gave little Roger the unheard-of pleasure of tea out-of-doors – there was something else agreeable for a third; and it was Roger who arranged all these simple pleasures – such as he knew Molly would enjoy. But to her he only appeared as the ready forwarder of Aimée's devices. The week was nearly gone, when one morning the Squire found Roger sitting in the old library – with a book before him, it is true, but so deep in thought that he was evidently startled by his father's unexpected entrance.

'I thought I should find thee here, my lad! We'll have the old room done up again before winter; it smells musty enough, and yet I see it's the place for thee! I want thee to go with me round the five-acre. I'm thinking of laying it down in grass. It's time for you to be getting into the fresh air, you look quite woe-begone over books, books, books; there never was a thing like 'em for stealing a man's health out of him!'

So Roger went out with his father, without saying many words till they were at some distance from the house. Then he brought out a sentence with such abruptness, that he repaid his father for the start the latter had given him a quarter of an hour before.

'Father, you remember I'm going out again to the Cape next month! You spoke of doing up the library. If it is for me, I shall be away all the winter.'

'Can't you get off it?' pleaded his father. 'I thought maybe you'd forgotten all about it.'

'Not likely!' said Roger, half-smiling.

'Well, but they might have found another man to finish up your work.'

'No one can finish it but myself. Besides, an engagement is an engagement. When I wrote to Lord Hollingford to tell him I must come home, I promised to go out again for another six months.'

'Ay. I know. And perhaps it will put it out of thy mind. It will always be hard on me to part from thee. But I daresay it's best for you.'

Roger's colour deepened. 'You are alluding to – to Miss Kirkpatrick. Mrs Henderson, I mean. Father, let me tell you once for all, I think that was rather a hasty affair. I'm pretty sure now that we were not suited to each other. I was wretched when I got her letter – at the Cape I mean – but I believe it was for the best.'

'That's right. That's my own boy,' said the Squire, turning round, and shaking hands with his son, with vehemence. 'And now I'll tell you what I heard the other day, when I was at the magistrates' meeting. They were all saying she had jilted Preston.'

'I don't want to hear anything against her; she may have her faults, but I can never forget how I once loved her.'

'Well, well! Perhaps it's right. I was not so bad about it, was I, Roger? Poor Osborne needn't have been so secret with me. I asked your Miss Cynthia out here – and her mother and all – my bark is worse than my bite. For, if I had a wish on earth, it was to see Osborne married as befitted one of an old stock, and he went and chose out this French girl, of no family at all, only a' –

'Never mind what she was; look at what she is! I wonder you are no more taken with her humility and sweetness, father!'

'I don't even call her pretty,' said the Squire uneasily, for he dreaded a repetition of the arguments which Roger had often used, to make him give Aimée her proper due of affection and position. 'Now, your Miss Cynthia was pretty; I will say that for her, the baggage! And to think that when you two lads flew right in your father's face, and picked out girls below you in rank and family, you should neither of you have set your fancies on my little Molly there! I dare say I should ha' been angry enough at the time; but the lassie would ha' found her way to my heart, as never this French lady, nor t' other one could ha' done.'

Roger did not answer.

'I don't see why you mightn't put up for her still. I'm humble enough now, and you're not heir as Osborne was who married a servant-maid. Don't you think you could turn your thoughts upon Molly Gibson, Roger?'

'No!' said Roger shortly. 'It's too late – too late. Don't let us talk any more of my marrying. Isn't this the five-acre field?' And soon he was discussing the relative values of meadow, arable and pasture land with his father, as heartily as if he had never known Molly, or loved Cynthia. But the Squire was not in such good spirits, and went but heavily into the discussion. At the end of it he said, *àpropos de bottes** –

'But don't you think you could like her if you tried, Roger?'

Roger knew perfectly well to what his father was alluding; but for an instant he was on the point of pretending to misunderstand. At length, however, he said, in a low voice –

'I shall never try, father. Don't let us talk any more about it. As I said before, it's too late.'

The Squire was like a child to whom some toy has been refused; from time to time the thought of his disappointment in this matter recurred to his mind; and then he took to blaming Cynthia as the primary cause of Roger's present indifference to womankind.

It so happened that, on Molly's last morning at the Hall, she received her first letter from Cynthia – Mrs Henderson. It was just before breakfast-time; Roger was out of doors, Aimée had not as yet come down; Molly was alone in the dining-room, where the table was already laid. She had just finished reading her letter when the Squire came in, and she immediately and joyfully told him what the morning had brought to her. But when she saw the Squire's face, she could have bitten her tongue out for having named Cynthia's name to him. He looked vexed and depressed.

'I wish I might never hear of her again – I do. She's been the bane of my Roger, that's what she has. I haven't slept half the night, and it's all her fault. Why, there's my boy saying now that he has no heart for ever marrying, poor lad! I wish it had been you, Molly, my lads had taken a fancy for. I told Roger so t'other day, and I said that for all you were beneath what I ever thought to see them marry – well – it's of no use – it's too late, now, as he said. Only never let me hear that baggage's name again, that's all, and no offence to you either, lassie. I know you love the wench; but, if you'll take an old man's word, you're worth a score of her. I wish young men would think so too,' he muttered as he went to the side-table to carve the ham, while Molly poured out the tea – her heart very hot all the time, and effectually silenced for a space.

It was with the greatest difficulty that she could keep tears of mortification from falling. She felt altogether in a wrong position in that house, which had been like a home to her until this last visit. What with Mrs Goodenough's remarks, and now this speech of the Squire's, implying – at least to her susceptible imagination – that his father had proposed her as a wife to Roger, and that she had been rejected – she was more glad than she could express, or even think, that she was going home this very morning. Roger came in from his walk, while she was in this state of feeling. He saw in an instant that something had distressed Molly; and he longed to have the old friendly right of asking her what it was. But she had effectually kept him at too great a distance during the last few days for him to feel at liberty to speak to her in the old straightforward brotherly way; especially now, when he perceived her efforts to conceal her feelings, and the way in which she drank her tea in feverish haste, and accepted bread only to crumble it about her plate, untouched. It was all that he could do to make talk under these circumstances; but he backed up her efforts as well as he could, until Aimée came down, grave and anxious: her boy had not had a good night, and did not seem well; he had fallen into a feverish sleep now, or she could not have left him. Immediately, the whole table was in a ferment. The Squire pushed away his plate, and could eat no more; Roger was trying to extract a detail or a fact out of Aimée, who began to give way to tears. Molly quickly proposed that the carriage, which had been ordered to take her home at eleven, should come round immediately – she had everything ready packed up, she said – and bring back her father at once. By leaving directly, she said, it was probable they might catch him after he had returned from his morning visits in the town, and before he had set off on his more distant round. Her proposal was agreed to, and she went upstairs to put on her things. She came down all ready into the drawing-room, expecting to find Aimée and the Squire there; but during her absence word had been brought to the anxious mother and grandfather that the child had wakened up in a panic, and both had rushed up to their darling. But Roger was in the drawing-room awaiting Molly, with a large bunch of the choicest flowers.

'Look, Molly!' said he, as she was on the point of leaving the room again, on finding him there alone. 'I gathered these flowers for you before breakfast.' He came to meet her reluctant advance.

'Thank you!' said she. 'You are very kind. I am very much obliged to you.'

'Then you must do something for me,' said he, determined not to notice the restraint of her manner, and making the re-arrangement of the flowers which she held as a sort of link between them, so that she could not follow her impulse, and leave the room.

'Tell me – honestly, as I know you will, if you speak at all – haven't I done something to vex you since we were so happy at the Towers together?'

His voice was so kind and true – his manner so winning yet wistful, that Molly would have been thankful to tell him all. She believed that he could have helped her more than any one to understand how she ought to behave rightly; he would have disentangled her fancies – if only he himself had not lain at the very core and centre of all her perplexity and dismay. How could she tell him of Mrs Goodenough's words' troubling her maiden modesty? How could she ever repeat what his father had said that morning, and assure him that she, no more than he, wished that their old friendliness should be troubled by the thought of a nearer relationship?

'No, you never vexed me in my whole life, Roger,' said she, looking straight at him for the first time for many days.

'I believe you, because you say so. I have no right to ask further, Molly. Will you give me back one of those flowers, as a pledge of what you have said?'

'Take whichever you like,' said she, eagerly offering him the whole nosegay to choose from.

'No; you must choose, and you must give it me.'

Just then the Squire came in. Roger would have been glad, if Molly had not gone on so eagerly to ransack the bunch for the choicest flower in his father's presence; but she exclaimed –

'Oh, please, Mr Hamley, do you know which is Roger's favour-ite flower?'

'No. A rose, I dare say. The carriage is at the door, and, Molly my dear, I don't want to hurry you, but'—

'I know. Here, Roger – here is a rose! I will find papa as soon as ever I get home. How is the little boy?'

'I'm afraid it's the beginning of some kind of a fever.'

And the Squire took her to the carriage, talking all the way of the little boy; Roger following, and hardly heeding what he was

doing, in the answer he kept asking himself: 'Too late – or not?
Can she ever forget that my first foolish love was given to one so
different?'

While she, as the carriage rolled away, kept saying to herself –
'We are friends again. I don't believe he will remember what the
dear Squire took it into his head to suggest for many days. It is so
pleasant to be on the old terms again! and what lovely flowers!'

CHAPTER 60

Roger Hamley's Confession

Roger had a great deal to think of, as he turned away from
looking after the carriage as long as it could be seen. The day
before, he had believed that Molly had come to view all the
symptoms of his growing love for her – symptoms which he
thought had been so patent – as disgusting inconstancy to the
inconstant Cynthia; that she had felt that an attachment which
could be so soon transferred to another was not worth having;
and that she had desired to mark all this by her changed treatment
of him, and so to nip it in the bud. But, this morning, her old
sweet, frank manner had returned – in their last interview, at any
rate. He puzzled himself hard to find out what could have
distressed her at breakfast-time. He even went so far as to ask
Robinson whether Miss Gibson had received any letters that
morning; and, when he heard that she had had one, he tried to
believe that the letter was in some way the cause of her sorrow.
So far so good. They were friends again after their unspoken
difference; but that was not enough for Roger. He felt every day
more and more certain that she, and she alone, could make him
happy. He had felt this, and had partly given up all hope, while
his father had been urging upon him the very course he most
desired to take. No need for 'trying' to love her, he said to himself
– that was already done. And yet he was very jealous on her
behalf. Was that love worthy of her which had once been given to
Cynthia? Was not this affair too much a mocking mimicry of the
last – again just on the point of leaving England for a considerable
time – if he followed her now to her own home – in the very
drawing-room where he had once offered to Cynthia? And then,

by a strong resolve, he determined on his course. They were friends now, and he kissed the rose that was her pledge of friendship. If he went to Africa, he ran some deadly chances; he knew better what they were now than he had done when he went before. Until his return he would not even attempt to win more of her love than he already had. But, once safe home again, no weak fancies as to what might or might not be her answer should prevent his running all chances, to gain the woman who was to him the one who excelled all. His was not the poor vanity that thinks more of the possible mortification of a refusal than of the precious jewel of a bride that may be won. Somehow or another, please God to send him back safe, he would put his fate to the touch. And till then he would be patient. He was no longer a boy, to rush at the coveted object; he was a man capable of judging and abiding.

Molly sent her father, as soon as she could find him, to the Hall; and then sate down to the old life in the home drawing-room, where she missed Cynthia's bright presence at every turn. Mrs Gibson was in rather a querulous mood, which fastened itself upon the injury of Cynthia's letter being addressed to Molly, and not to herself.

'Considering all the trouble I had with her *trousseau*, I think she might have written to me.'

'But she did – her first letter was to you, mamma,' said Molly, her real thoughts still intent upon the Hall – upon the sick child – upon Roger, and his begging for the flower.

'Yes, just a first letter, three pages long, with an account of her crossing; while to you she can write about fashions, and how the bonnets are worn in Paris, and all sorts of interesting things. But poor mothers must never expect confidential letters; I have found that out.'

'You may see my letter, mamma,' said Molly, 'there is really nothing in it.'

'And to think of her writing, and crossing*to you who don't value it, while my poor heart is yearning after my lost child! Really, life is somewhat hard to bear at times.'

Then there was silence – for a while.

'Do tell me something about your visit, Molly. Is Roger very heart-broken? Does he talk much about Cynthia?'

'No. He does not mention her often; hardly ever, I think.'

'I never thought he had much feeling. If he had had, he would not have let her go so easily.'

'I don't see how he could help it. When he came to see her after his return, she was already engaged to Mr Henderson – he had come down that very day,' said Molly, with perhaps more heat than the occasion required.

'My poor head!' said Mrs Gibson, putting her hands up to her head. 'One may see you've been stopping with people of robust health, and – excuse my saying it, Molly, of your friends – of unrefined habits: you've got to talk in so loud a voice. But do remember my head, Molly. So Roger has quite forgotten Cynthia, has he? Oh! what inconstant creatures men are! He will be falling in love with some grandee next, mark my words! They are making a pet and a lion of him, and he's just the kind of weak young man to have his head turned by it all, and to propose to some fine lady of rank, who would no more think of marrying him than of marrying her footman.'

'I don't think it is likely,' said Molly stoutly. 'Roger is too sensible for anything of the kind.'

'That's just the fault I've always found with him; sensible and cold-hearted! Now, that's a kind of character which may be very valuable, but which revolts me. Give me warmth of heart, even with a little of that extravagance of feeling which misleads the judgment, and conducts into romance. Poor Mr Kirkpatrick! That was just his character. I used to tell him that his love for me was quite romantic. I think I have told you about his walking five miles in the rain to get me a muffin once when I was ill?'

'Yes!' said Molly. 'It was very kind of him.'

'So imprudent, too! Just what one of your sensible, cold-hearted, commonplace people would never have thought of doing! With his cough and all!'

'I hope he didn't suffer for it?' replied Molly, anxious at any cost to keep off the subject of the Hamleys, upon which she and her stepmother always disagreed, and on which she found it difficult to keep her temper.

'Yes, indeed he did! I don't think he ever got over the cold he caught that day. I wish you had known him, Molly. I sometimes wonder what would have happened, if you had been my real daughter, and Cynthia dear papa's, and Mr Kirkpatrick and your own dear mother had all lived. People talk a good deal about natural affinities. It would have been a question for a philosopher.' She began to think on the impossibilities she had suggested.

'I wonder how the poor little boy is!' said Molly, after a pause, speaking out her thought.

'Poor little child! When one thinks how little his prolonged existence is to be desired, one feels that his death would be a boon.'

'Mamma! what do you mean?' asked Molly, much shocked. 'Why, every one cares for his life as the most precious thing! You have never seen him! He is the bonniest, sweetest little fellow that can be! What do you mean?'

'I should have thought that the Squire would have desired a better-born heir than the offspring of a servant – with all his ideas about descent and blood and family. And I should have thought that it was a little mortifying to Roger – who must naturally have looked upon himself as his brother's heir – to find a little inter-loping child, half-French, half-English, stepping into his shoes!'

'You don't know how fond they are of him – the Squire looks upon him as the apple of his eye.'*

'Molly! Molly! pray don't let me hear you using such vulgar expressions. When shall I teach you true refinement – that refine-ment which consists in never even thinking a vulgar, commonplace thing! Proverbs and idioms are never used by people of education. "Apple of his eye!" I am really shocked.'

'Well, mamma, I'm very sorry; but, after all, what I wanted to say as strongly as I could was, that the Squire loves the little boy as much as his own child; and that Roger – oh! what a shame to think that Roger—' And she suddenly stopped short, as if she were choked.

'I don't wonder at your indignation, my dear!' said Mrs Gibson. 'It is just what I should have felt at your age. But one learns the baseness of human nature with advancing years. I was wrong, though, to undeceive you so early – but, depend upon it, the thought I alluded to has crossed Roger Hamley's mind!'

'All sorts of thoughts cross one's mind – it depends upon whether one gives them harbour and encouragement,' said Molly.

'My dear, if you must have the last word, don't let it be a truism. But let us talk on some more interesting subject. I asked Cynthia to buy me a silk gown in Paris, and I said I would send her word what colour I fixed upon – I think dark blue is the most becoming to my complexion; what do you say?'

Molly agreed, sooner than take the trouble of thinking about the thing at all; she was far too full of her silent review of all the traits in Roger's character which had lately come under her notice, and that gave the lie direct to her stepmother's supposition. Just then, they heard Mr Gibson's step downstairs. But it was some time before he made his entrance into the room where they were sitting.

'How is little Roger?' said Molly eagerly.

'Beginning with scarlet fever, I'm afraid. It's well you left when you did, Molly. You've never had it. We must stop up all intercourse with the Hall for a time. If there's one illness I dread, it is this.'

'But you go and come back to us, papa.'

'Yes. But I always take plenty of precautions. However, no need to talk about risks that lie in the way of one's duty. It is unnecesary risks that we must avoid.'

'Will he have it badly?' asked Molly.

'I can't tell. I shall do my best for the wee laddie.'

Whenever Mr Gibson's feelings were touched, he was apt to recur to the language of his youth. Molly knew now that he was much interested in the case.

For some days there was imminent danger to the little boy; for some weeks there was a more chronic form of illness to contend with; but, when the immediate danger was over and the warm daily interest was past, Molly began to realise that, from the strict quarantine her father evidently thought it necessary to establish between the two houses, she was not likely to see Roger again before his departure for Africa. Oh! if she had but made more of the uncared-for days that she had passed with him at the Hall! Worse than uncared for; days on which she had avoided him; refused to converse freely with him; given him pain by her change of manner; for she had read in his eyes, heard in his voice, that he had been perplexed and pained, and now her imagination dwelt on and exaggerated the expression of his tones and looks.

One evening after dinner, her father said –

'As the country-people say, I've done a stroke of work today. Roger Hamley and I have laid our heads together, and we've made a plan by which Mrs Osborne and her boy will leave the Hall.'

'What did I say the other day, Molly?' said Mrs Gibson, interrupting, and giving Molly a look of extreme intelligence.

'And go into lodgings at Jennings' farm; not four hundred yards from the Park-field gate,' continued Mr Gibson. 'The Squire and his daughter-in-law have got to be much better friends over the little fellow's sick-bed; and I think he sees now how impossible it would be for the mother to leave her child, and go and be happy in France, which has been the notion running in his head all this time. To buy her off, in fact. But that one night, when I was very uncertain whether I could bring him through, they took to crying together, and condoling with each other; and it was just like tearing down a curtain that had been between them; they have been rather friends than otherwise ever since. Still, Roger' – (Molly's cheeks grew warm and her eyes soft and bright; it was such a pleasure to hear his name) – 'and I both agree that his mother knows much better how to manage the boy than his grandfather does. I suppose that was the one good thing she got from that hard-hearted mistress of hers. She certainly has been well trained in the management of children. And it makes her impatient, and annoyed, and unhappy, when she sees the Squire giving the child nuts and ale, and all sorts of silly indulgences, and spoiling him in every possible way. Yet she's a coward, and doesn't speak out her mind. Now, by being in lodgings, and having her own servants – nice pretty rooms they are, too; we went to see them, and Mrs Jennings promises to attend well to Mrs Osborne Hamley, and is very much honoured, and all that sort of thing – not ten minutes' walk from the Hall, too; so that she and the little chap may easily go backwards and forwards as often as they like, and yet she can keep the control over the child's discipline and diet. In short, I think I've done a good day's work,' he continued, stretching himself a little; and then, with a shake, rousing himself, and making ready to go out again, to see a patient who had sent for him in his absence.

'A good day's work!' he repeated to himself as he ran downstairs. 'I don't know when I have been so happy!' For he had not told Molly all that had passed between him and Roger. Roger had begun a fresh subject of conversation, just as Mr Gibson was hastening away from the Hall, after completing the new arrangement for Aimée and her child.

'You know that I set off next Tuesday, Mr Gibson, don't you?' said Roger, a little abruptly.

'Of course. I hope you'll be as successful in all your scientific objects as you were the last time, and have no sorrows awaiting you when you come back.'

'Thank you. Yes. I hope so. You don't think there's any danger of infection now, do you?'

'No! If the disease were to spread through the household, I think we should have had some signs of it before now. One is never sure, remember, with scarlet fever.'

Roger was silent for a minute or two. 'Should you be afraid,' he said at length, 'of seeing me at your house?'

'Thank you; but I think I would rather decline the pleasure of your society there at present. It's only three weeks or a month since the child began. Besides, I shall be over here again before you go. I'm always on my guard against symptoms of dropsy. I have known it supervene.'

'Then I shall not see Molly again!' said Roger, in a tone and with a look of great disappointment.

Mr Gibson turned his keen, observant eyes upon the young man, and looked at him in as penetrating a manner as if he had been beginning with an unknown illness. Then the doctor and the father compressed his lips and gave vent to a long intelligent whistle. 'Whew!' said he.

Roger's bronzed cheeks took a deeper shade.

'You will take a message to her from me, won't you? A message of farewell!' he pleaded.

'Not I. I'm not going to be a message-carrier between any young man and young woman. I'll tell my womenkind I forbade you to come near the house, and that you're sorry to go away without bidding good-bye. That's all I shall say.'

'But you do not disapprove? – I see you guess why. Oh! Mr Gibson, just speak to me one word of what must be in your heart, though you are pretending not to understand why I would give worlds to see Molly again before I go!'

'My dear boy!' said Mr Gibson, more affected than he liked to show, and laying his hand on Roger's shoulder. Then he pulled himself up, and said gravely enough –

'Mind, Molly is not Cynthia. If she were to care for you, she is not one who could transfer her love to the next comer.'

'You mean, not as readily as I have done,' replied Roger. 'I only wish you could know what a different feeling this is from my boyish love for Cynthia.'

'I wasn't thinking of you when I spoke; but, however, as I might have remembered afterwards that you were not a model of constancy, let us hear what you have to say for yourself.'

'Not much. I did love Cynthia very much. Her manners and her beauty bewitched me; but her letters, – short, hurried letters – sometimes showing that she really hadn't taken the trouble to read mine through – I cannot tell you the pain they gave me! Twelve months' solitude, in frequent danger of one's life – face to face with death – sometimes ages a man like many years' experience. Still, I longed for the time when I should see her sweet face again, and hear her speak. Then the letter at the Cape! – and still I hoped. But you know how I found her – when I went to have the interview which I trusted might end in the renewal of our relations – engaged to Mr Henderson. I saw her walking with him in your garden, coquetting with him about a flower, just as she used to do with me. I can see the pitying look in Molly's eyes as she watched me; I can see it now. And I could beat myself for being such a blind fool as to—What must she think of me! how she must despise me, choosing the false Duessa!'*

'Come, come! Cynthia isn't so bad as that. She's a very fascinating, faulty creature.'

'I know! I know! I will never allow any one to say a word against her. If I called her the false Duessa, it was because I wanted to express my sense of the difference between her and Molly as strongly as I could. You must allow for a lover's exaggeration. Besides, all I wanted to say was – Do you think that Molly, after seeing and knowing that I had loved a person so inferior to herself, could ever be brought to listen to me?'

'I don't know. I can't tell. And, even if I could, I wouldn't. Only, if it's any comfort to you, I may say what my experience has taught me. Women are queer, unreasoning creatures, and are just as likely as not to love a man who has been throwing away his affection.'

'Thank you, sir!' said Roger, interrupting him. 'I see you mean to give me encouragement. And I had resolved never to give Molly a hint of what I felt till I returned – and then to try and win her by every means in my power. I determined not to repeat the former scene in the former place – in your drawing-room – however much I might be tempted. And perhaps, after all, she avoided me when she was here last.'

'Now, Roger, I've listened to you long enough. If you've nothing better to do with your time than to talk about my daughter, I have. When you come back, it will be time enough to inquire how far your father would approve of such an engagement.'

'He himself urged it upon me the other day – but then I was in despair – I thought it was too late.'

'And what means you are likely to have of maintaining a wife. I always thought that point was passed too lightly over when you formed your hurried engagement to Cynthia. I'm not mercenary – Molly has some money independently of me – that she by the way knows nothing of – not much; – and I can allow her something. But all these things must be left till your return.'

'Then you sanction my attachment?'

'I don't know what you mean by sanctioning it. I can't help it. I suppose losing one's daughter is a necessary evil. Still' – seeing the disappointed expression on Roger's face – 'it is but fair to you to say, I'd rather give my child – my only child, remember! – to you, than to any man in the world!'

'Thank you!' said Roger, shaking hands with Mr Gibson, almost against the will of the latter. 'And I may see her, just once, before I go?'

'Decidedly not. There I come in as doctor as well as father. No!'

'But you will take a message, at any rate?'

'To my wife and to her conjointly. I will not separate them. I will not in the slightest way be a go-between.'

'Very well,' said Roger. 'Tell them both, as strongly as you can, how I regret your prohibition. I see I must submit. But, if I don't come back, I'll haunt you for having been so cruel.'

'Come, I like that! Give me a wise man of science in love! No one beats him in folly. Good-bye.'

'Good-bye. You will see Molly this afternoon!'

'To be sure. And you will see your father. But I don't heave such portentous sighs at the thought.'

Mr Gibson gave Roger's message to his wife and to Molly, that evening at dinner. It was but what the latter had expected, after all her father had said of the very great danger of infection; but, now that her expectation came in the shape of a final decision, it took away her appetite. She submitted in silence; but her observant father noticed that, after this speech of his, she only played with the food on her plate, and concealed a good deal of it under her knife and fork.

'Lover *versus* father!' thought he, half sadly. 'Lover wins.' And he, too, became indifferent to all that remained of his dinner. Mrs Gibson pattered on; and nobody listened.

The day of Roger's departure came. Molly tried hard to forget it in working away at a cushion she was preparing as a present to Cynthia; people did worsted-work in those days. One, two, three. One, two, three, four, five, six, seven; all wrong: she was thinking of something else, and had to unpick it. It was a rainy day, too; and Mrs Gibson, who had planned to go out and pay some calls, had to stay indoors. This made her restless and fidgety. She kept going backwards and forwards to different windows in the drawing-room, to look at the weather, as if she imagined that, while it rained at one window, it might be fine weather at another. 'Molly – come here! who is that man wrapped up in a cloak – there – near the Park-wall, under the beech-tree – he has been there this half-hour and more, never stirring, and looking at this house all the time! I think it's very suspicious.'

Molly looked, and in an instant recognised Roger under all his wraps. Her first instinct was to draw back. The next to come forwards, and say – 'Why, mamma, it's Roger Hamley! Look now – he's kissing his hand; he's wishing us good-bye in the only way he can!' And she responded to his sign; but she was not sure if he perceived her modest, quiet movement, for Mrs Gibson became immediately so demonstrative that Molly fancied that her eager foolish pantomimic motions must absorb all his attention.

'I call this so attentive of him,' said Mrs Gibson, in the midst of a volley of kisses of her hand. 'Really, it is quite romantic. It reminds me of former days – but he will be too late! I must send him away; it is half-past twelve!' And she took out her watch and held it up, tapping it with her fore-finger, and occupying the very centre of the window. Molly could only peep here and there, dodging now up, now down, now on this side, now on that, of the perpetually-moving arms. She fancied she saw something of a corresponding movement on Roger's part. At length, he went away slowly, slowly, and often looking back, in spite of the tapped watch. Mrs Gibson at last retreated, and Molly quietly moved into her place, to see his figure once more, before the turn of the road hid him from her view. He, too, knew where the last glimpse of Mr Gibson's house was to be obtained, and once more he turned, and his white handkerchief floated in the air. Molly waved hers high up, with eager longing that it should be seen. And then, he was gone! and Molly returned to her worsted-work, happy, glowing, sad, content, and thinking to herself, how sweet is friendship!

When she came to a sense of the present, Mrs Gibson was saying –

'Upon my word, though Roger Hamley has never been a great favourite of mine, this little attention of his has reminded me very forcibly of a very charming young man – a *soupirant*,* as the French would call him – Lieutenant Harper – you must have heard me speak of him, Molly?'

'I think I have!' said Molly absently.

'Well, you remember how devoted he was to me, when I was at Mrs Duncombe's, my first situation, and I only seventeen. And, when the recruiting party was ordered to another town, poor Mr Harper came and stood opposite the school-room window for nearly an hour, and I know it was his doing that the band played 'The girl I left behind me', when they marched out the next day. Poor Mr Harper! It was before I knew dear Mr Kirkpatrick! Dear me! How often my poor heart has had to bleed, in this life of mine! not but what dear papa is a very worthy man, and makes me very happy. He would spoil me, indeed, if I would let him. Still, he is not as rich as Mr Henderson.'

That last sentence contained the germ of Mrs Gibson's present grievance. Having married Cynthia, as her mother put it – taking credit to herself as if she had had the principal part in the achievement – she now became a little envious of her daughter's good fortune in being the wife of a young, handsome, rich, and moderately fashionable man, who lived in London. She naïvely expressed her feelings on this subject to her husband, one day when she was really not feeling quite well, and when consequently her annoyances were much more present to her mind than her sources of happiness.

'It is such a pity!' said she, 'that I was born when I was. I should so have liked to belong to this generation.'

'That's sometimes my own feeling,' said he. 'So many new views seem to be opened in science, that I should like, if it were possible, to live till their reality was ascertained, and one saw what they led to. But I don't suppose that's your reason, my dear, for wishing to be twenty or thirty years younger.'

'No, indeed! And I did not put it in that hard unpleasant way; I only said I should like to belong to this generation. To tell the truth, I was thinking of Cynthia. Without vanity, I believe I was as pretty as she is – when I was a girl, I mean; I had not her dark eyelashes, but then my nose was straighter. And now – look at the difference! I have to live in a little country-town with three servants, and no carriage; and she, with her inferior good looks, will live in Sussex Place,*and keep a man and a brougham, and I don't know what. But the fact is, in this generation there are so many more rich young men than there were when I was a girl.'

'Oh, oh! so that's your reason, is it, my dear? If you had been young now, you might have married somebody as well off as Walter?'

'Yes!' said she. 'I think that was my idea. Of course I should have liked him to be you. I always think, if you had gone to the bar, you might have succeeded better, and lived in London, too. I don't think Cynthia cares much where she lives; yet you see it has come to her.'

'What has – London?'

'Oh, you dear, facetious man! Now, that's just the thing to have captivated a jury. I don't believe Walter will ever be so clever as you are. Yet he can take Cynthia to Paris, and abroad, and everywhere. I only hope all this indulgence won't develop the faults in Cynthia's character. It's a week since we heard from her, and I did write so particularly to ask her for the autumn fashions, before I bought my new bonnet. But riches are a great snare.'

'Be thankful you are spared that temptation, my dear.'

'No, I'm not. Everybody likes to be tempted. And, after all, it's very easy to resist temptation, if one wishes.'

'I don't find it so easy,' said her husband.

'Here's medicine for you, mamma,' said Molly, entering with a letter held up in her hand. 'A letter from Cynthia.'

'Oh, you dear little messenger of good news! There was one of the heathen deities in Mangnall's Questions,* whose office it was to bring news. The letter is dated from Calais. They're coming home! She's bought me a shawl and a bonnet! The dear creature! Always thinking of others before herself; good fortune cannot spoil her. They've a fortnight left of their holiday! Their house is not quite ready; they're coming here. Oh, now, Mr Gibson, we must have the new dinner-service at Watts's I've set my heart on so long! "Home" Cynthia calls this house. I'm sure it has been a home to her, poor darling! I doubt if there is another man in the world who would have treated his step-daughter like dear papa! And, Molly, you must have a new gown.'

'Come, come! Remember, I belong to the last generation,' said Mr Gibson.

'And Cynthia won't mind what I wear,' said Molly, bright with pleasure at the thought of seeing her again.

'No! but Walter will. He has such a quick eye for dress, and I think I rival papa; if he's a good stepfather, I'm a good step-mother, and I could not bear to see my Molly shabby, and not looking her best. I must have a new gown, too. It won't do to look as if we had nothing but the dresses which we wore at the wedding!'

But Molly stood out against the new gown for herself, and urged that, if Cynthia and Walter were to come to visit them often, they had better see them as they really were, in dress, habits, and appointments. When Mr Gibson had left the room, Mrs Gibson softly reproached Molly for her obstinacy.

'You might have allowed me to beg for a new gown for you, Molly, when you knew how much I admired that figured silk at Brown's the other day. And now, of course, I can't be so selfish as to get it for myself, and you to have nothing. You should learn to understand the wishes of other people. Still, on the whole, you are a dear, sweet girl, and I only wish – well, I know what I wish; only, dear papa does not like it to be talked about. And now cover me up close, and let me go to sleep, and dream about my dear Cynthia and my new shawl!'

Concluding Remarks

(By The Editor of the *Cornhill Magazine*)

Here the story is broken off, and it can never be finished. What promised to be the crowning work of a life is a memorial of death. A few days longer, and it would have been a triumphal column, crowned with a capital of festal leaves and flowers; now it is another sort of column – one of those sad white pillars which stand broken in the church-yard.

But if the work is not quite complete, little remains to be added to it, and that little has been distinctly reflected into our minds. We know that Roger Hamley will marry Molly, and that is what we are most concerned about. Indeed, there was little else to tell. Had the writer lived, she would have sent her hero back to Africa forthwith; and those scientific parts of Africa are a long way from Hamley; and there is not much to choose between a long distance and a long time. How many hours are there in twenty-four when you are all alone in a desert place, a thousand miles from the happiness which might be yours to take – if you were there to take it? How many, when from the sources of the Topinambo your heart flies back ten times a day, like a carrier-pigeon, to the one only source of future good for you, and ten times a day returns with its message undelivered? Many more than are counted on the calendar. So Roger found. The days were weeks that separated him from the time when Molly gave him a certain little flower, and months from the time which divorced him from Cynthia, whom he had begun to doubt before he knew for certain that she was never much worth hoping for. And if such were his days, what was the slow procession of actual weeks and months in those remote and solitary places? They were like years of a stay-at-home life, with liberty and leisure to see that nobody was courting Molly meanwhile. The effect of this was, that long before the term of his engagement was ended all that Cynthia had been to him was departed from Roger's mind, and all that Molly was and might be to him filled it full.

He returned; but when he saw Molly again he remembered that to her the time of his absence might not have seemed so long, and was oppressed with the old dread that she would think him fickle. Therefore this young gentleman, so self-reliant and so lucid in scientific matters, found it difficult after all to tell Molly how much he hoped she loved him; and might have blundered if he had not thought of beginning by showing her the flower that was plucked from the nosegay. How charmingly that scene would have been drawn, had Mrs Gaskell lived to depict it, we can only imagine: that it *would* have been charming – especially in what Molly did, and looked, and said – we know.

Roger and Molly are married; and if one of them is happier than the other, it is Molly. Her husband has no need to draw upon the little fortune which is to go to poor Osborne's boy, for he becomes professor at some great scientific institution, and wins his way in the world handsomely. The Squire is almost as happy in this marriage as his son. If any one suffers for it, it is Mr Gibson. But he takes a partner, so as to get a chance of running up to London to stay with Molly for a few days now and then, and 'to get a little rest from Mrs Gibson.' Of what was to happen to Cynthia after her marriage the author was not heard to say much; and, indeed, it does not seem that anything needs to be added. One little anecdote, however, was told of her by Mrs Gaskell, which is very characteristic. One day, when Cynthia and her husband were on a visit to Hollingford, Mr Henderson learned for the first time, through an innocent casual remark of Mr Gibson's, that the famous traveller, Roger Hamley, was known to the family. Cynthia had never happened to mention it. How well that little incident, too, would have been described!

But it is useless to speculate upon what would have been done by the delicate strong hand which can create no more Molly Gibsons – no more Roger Hamleys. We have repeated, in this brief note, all that is known of her designs for the story, which would have been completed in another chapter. There is not so much to regret, then, so far as this novel is concerned; indeed, the regrets of those who knew her are less for the loss of the novelist than of the woman – one of the kindest and wisest of her time. But yet, for her own sake as a novelist alone, her untimely death is a matter for deep regret. It is clear in this novel of *Wives and Daughters*, in the exquisite little story that preceded it, *Cousin Phillis*, and in *Sylvia's Lovers*, that Mrs Gaskell had within these five years started upon a new career with all the freshness of youth, and with a mind which seemed to have put off its clay and to have been born again. But that 'put off its clay' must be taken in a very narrow sense. All minds are tinctured more or less with the 'muddy vesture' in which they are contained; but few minds ever showed less of base earth than Mrs Gaskell's. It was so at all times; but lately even the original slight tincture seemed to disappear. While you read any one of the last three books we have named, you feel yourself caught out of an abominable wicked world, crawling with selfishness and reeking with base passions, into one where there is much weakness, many mistakes, sufferings long and bitter, but where it is possible for people to live calm and wholesome lives; and, what is more, you feel that this is, at least, as real a world as the other. The kindly spirit which thinks no ill looks out of her pages irradiate; and while we read them, we breathe the purer intelligence that prefers to deal with emotions and passions which have a living root in minds within the pale of salvation, and not with those that rot without it. This spirit is more especially declared in *Cousin Phillis* and *Wives and Daughters* – their author's latest works; they seem to show that for her the end of life was not descent amongst the clods of the valley, but ascent into the purer air of the heaven-aspiring hills.

We are saying nothing now of the merely intellectual qualities displayed in these later works. Twenty years to come, that may be thought the more important question of the two; in the presence of her grave we cannot think so; but it is true, all the same, that as mere works of art and observation, these later novels of Mrs Gaskell's are among the finest of our time. There is a scene in *Cousin Phillis* – where Holman, making hay with his men, ends the day with a psalm – which is not excelled as a picture in all modern fiction; and the same may be said of that chapter of this last story in which Roger smokes a pipe with the Squire after the quarrel with Osborne. There is little in either of these scenes, or in a score of others which succeed each other like gems in a cabinet, which the ordinary novel-maker could 'seize'. There is no 'material' for *him* in half-a-dozen farming men singing hymns in a field, or a discontented old gentleman smoking tobacco with his son. Still less could he avail himself of the miseries of a little girl sent to be happy in a fine house full of fine people; but it is just in such things as these that true genius appears brightest and most unapproachable. It is the same with the personages in Mrs

Gaskell's works. Cynthia is one of the most difficult characters which have ever been attempted in our time. Perfect art always obscures the difficulties it overcomes; and it is not till we try to follow the processes by which such a character as the Tito of *Romola* is created, for instance, that we begin to understand what a marvellous piece of work it is. To be sure, Cynthia was not so difficult, nor is it nearly so great a creation as that splendid achievement of art and thought – of the rarest art, of the profoundest thought. But she also belongs to the kind of characters which are conceived only in minds large, clear, harmonious and just, and which can be portrayed fully and without flaw only by hands obedient to the finest motions of the mind. Viewed in this light, Cynthia is a more important piece of work even than Molly, delicately as she is drawn, and true and harmonious as that picture is also. And what we have said of Cynthia may be said with equal truth of Osborne Hamley. The true delineation of a character like that is as fine a test of art as the painting of a foot or a hand, which also seems so easy, and in which perfection is most rare. In this case the work is perfect. Mrs Gaskell has drawn a dozen characters more striking than Osborne since she wrote *Mary Barton*, but not one which shows more exquisite finish.

Another thing we may be permitted to notice, because it has a great and general significance. It may be true that this is not exactly the place for criticism, but since we are writing of Osborne Hamley, we cannot resist pointing out a peculiar instance of the subtler conceptions which underlie all really considerable works. Here are Osborne and Roger, two men who, in every particular that can be seized for description, are totally different creatures. Body and mind, they are quite unlike. They have different tastes; they take different ways: they are men of two sorts which, in the society sense, never 'know' each other; and yet, never did brotherly blood run more manifest than in the veins of those two. To make that manifest without allowing the effort to peep out for a single moment, would be a triumph of art; but it is a 'touch beyond the reach of art' to make their likeness in unlikeness so natural a thing that we no more wonder about it than we wonder at seeing the fruit and the bloom on the same bramble: we have always seen them there together in blackberry season, and do not wonder about it nor think about it at all. Inferior writers, even some writers who are highly accounted, would have revelled in the 'contrast', persuaded that they were doing a fine anatomical dramatic thing by bringing it out at every opportunity. To the author of *Wives and Daughters* this sort of anatomy was mere dislocation. She began by having the people of her story born in the usual way, and not built up like the Frankenstein monster; and thus when Squire Hamley took a wife, it was then provided that his two boys should be as naturally one and diverse as the fruit and the bloom on the bramble. 'It goes without speaking.' These differences are precisely what might have been expected from the union of Squire Hamley with the town-bred, refined, delicate-minded woman whom he married; and the affection of the young men, their kindness (to use the word in its old and new meanings at once) is nothing but a reproduction of those impalpable threads of love which bound the equally diverse father and mother in bonds faster than the ties of blood.

But we will not permit ourselves to write any more in this vein. It is unnecessary to demonstrate to those who know what is and what is not true literature that Mrs Gaskell was gifted with some of the choicest faculties bestowed upon mankind; that these grew into greater strength and ripened into greater beauty in the decline of her days; and that she has gifted us with some of the truest, purest works of fiction in the language. And she was herself what her works show her to have been – a wise, good woman.

Words found in the *Oxford English Dictionary* are not generally given below unless they are used in a special sense. Similarly, dialect words or phrases are only translated if their meaning is not obvious. (*COD* = *Concise Oxford Dictionary*.) I have consulted the editions of *Wives and Daughters* edited by Frank Glover Smith (Penguin, 1969) and Angus Easson (World's Classics, 1987), and have acknowledged any note which derives from either of those sources. I am particularly indebted to Joan Leach, Secretary of the Gaskell Society, for her help with locational and local notes of interest and, as ever, to Dr Jennifer Fellows for her meticulous work on the text and notes, and for her invaluable suggestions.

Chapter 1

p. 3 **rigmarole of childhood**: an accumulating sequence of statements, identified by Easson as from the nursery rhyme 'This is the key of the kingdom'. He rightly stresses its creation of the atmosphere of childhood in these early chapters.

p. 3 **'scomfished'**: spoiled, damaged.

p. 3 **quilling**: material folded into cylindrical shapes.

p. 3 **Hollingford**: based, like Cranford, on Knutsford in Cheshire.

p. 4 **Five-and-forty years ago**: i.e. the beginning of the 1820s, with Molly's childhood approximating to Gaskell's own in chronological terms. While *Wives and Daughters* was being published serially, George Eliot was writing *Felix Holt, the Radical*, which was published in June 1866, and which opens with the words 'Five and thirty years ago . . .'. Both novels stress the impact of change on the past.

p. 4 **the entrance-lodge of a great park, where lived my Lord and Lady Cumnor**: Tatton Park, ten miles in circumference, was the home of the Egerton family (created lords in 1859 and earls in 1887) for over

300 years. Cumnor Towers and the family can be closely identified with Tatton and the Egertons, who were lords of the manor of Knutsford and major property holders. The gateway 'forms a handsome ornament to the town' (J. H. Hanshall, *Itinerary of Cheshire*, 1817).

p. 4 the Reform Bill: the first Reform Act of 1832, the basis for all later political reforms, extended the franchise, removed rotten and pocket boroughs and gave parliamentary representation to new industrial towns such as Birmingham and Manchester.

p. 4 Whig family of Cumnor: Wilbraham Egerton was MP 1812–31, a Tory strongly opposed to reform, but Gaskell cunningly changes the party emphasis, thus avoiding direct identification with the Egertons and focusing on the Hamleys as the traditional Tories.

pp. 4–5 those days before railways: the Stockton-Darlington railway opened in 1825, and over the next twelve years there was major expansion. The Birmingham-London line opened in 1837–8.

p. 5 *sansculottes*: without knee-breeches (French). One of the many extreme groups in the French Revolution, they wore trousers instead of the aristocratic knee-breeches.

p. 5 'industrial': where the pupils were taught day-to-day domestic, practical skills.

p. 5 *de rigueur*: required by custom (French).

p. 6 covey: unobtrusive irony, since a covey is a small flock of birds, especially partridges.

pp. 6–7 *the* doctor of the neighbourhood: Dr Peter Holland, Gaskell's uncle, was paid about £100 each January (Egerton Accounts); although he was apparently not like Mr Gibson in character, there is little doubt that Gaskell's description of Mr Gibson's practice derives from her knowledge of her uncle's professional life.

p. 7 school-scrimmage: a scrimmage is a confused struggle, the term here used in a laid-back, slangy way.

p. 7 singed: refers to the superficial burning-off of hair or bristle.

p. 8 *Drosera rotundifolia*: the common sundew, which grows in wet, drenched areas. Henry Green's *Knutsford: Its Traditions and*

History (1859) mentions rare marsh saxifrage being found in Knutsford moor.

p. 8 in town: i.e. in London, where fashionable families often spent 'the season' (in early summer).

p. 9 bodkin: i.e. between two, wedged tightly because of lack of space.

p. 10 string myself up: brace myself, make the attempt (to do something).

p. 11 artificials: i.e. artificial flowers.

Chapter 2

p. 11 mode cloak: one suitable for the occasion, though note that it looked 'old-fashioned' on Molly.

p. 11 a watched pot never boiling: (cf. *Mary Barton*, ch. 31). Proverbial, meaning that impatience makes things seem longer in happening than they actually take.

p. 11 incommoding: inconveniencing.

p. 12 *perron*: the 'double semi-circle flight of steps' in the preceding sentence.

p. 15 the bows and arrows: archery was a popular sport for girls in the nineteenth century (see George Eliot's *Daniel Deronda* [1876; set 1864–6], ch. 10, which describes an archery meeting.)

p. 16 not quite the thing: not fully recovered.

p. 16 the *Peerage*: a book containing the list of peers, the nobility, and their genealogies; elsewhere referred to as the Red Book.

p. 17 make a piece of work: i.e. don't over-dramatize it.

p. 20 the 'Three Bears': the classic fairy story appears in the miscellany *The Doctor* (1834–47) by Robert Southey (1774–1843), poet laureate, though obviously dating from a much earlier period.

p. 20 the Sleeping Beauty, the Seven Sleepers: the first from the French tale by Charles Perrault. She sleeps for one hundred years before being awakened by the prince who marries her. The second refers to the legend of the seven noble youths of Ephesus who were walled up in a cave during the persecution by the Emperor Decius *c*. AD 250.

p. 21 *Lodge's Portraits*: Edmund Lodge (1756–1839), biographer, best known for his *Portraits of Illustrious Personages* (1821–34).

p. 24 **Ponto's**: i.e. the dog's.

p. 25 *Sir Charles Grandison*: the last of the novels by Samuel Richardson (1689–1761) was published in 1753–4, the eponymous hero being a model of refinement and impeccable behaviour.

p. 25 **concert pitch**: the peak of good manners.

Chapter 3

p. 26 **intelligence**: news.

p. 26 *Che sarà sarà*: What will be, will be (Italian).

p. 27 **muscular Christianity**: strong faith and physical activity combined, health in spirit and body, epitomized by the régime set up by Thomas Arnold at Rugby in the 1830s and exemplified in the writings of Charles Kingsley. Later, Disraeli was to use the phrase in *Endymion* (1880): 'his muscularity was Christian'.

p. 27 **a slight Scotch accent**: Mrs Gaskell's father came from Berwick-on-Tweed; she confers Scottish blood as a sign of distinction on other characters in her fiction.

p. 27 **the Stuarts**: dynasty of English monarchs from 1603 to 1688, interrupted by the English Revolution (1640–60), Charles I being executed in 1649.

p. 28 **Sir Astley**: Sir Astley Cooper (1768–1841), English surgeon who raised the practice and status of his profession from crudity to a science.

p. 28 **consumption**: a wasting disease, pulmonary tuberculosis, the scourge of the nineteenth century.

p. 29 **narrowness of his crape hat-band**: the implication is that there was not enough black on his hat as was appropriate for his mourning or grief.

p. 29 **quizzed her**: teased or mocked her.

p. 31 Miss Eyre: the name suggests a private compliment to Charlotte Brontë (Gaskell's life of her friend was published in 1857), whose *Jane Eyre* (1848) established her reputation.

p. 31 a cross: a mark made instead of a signature, the symbol of illiteracy.

p. 31 'hidden worm i' th' bud': silent suffering which undermines one. Cf. *Twelfth Night*, II. iv. 110–11: 'But let concealment, like a worm i' th' bud,/Feed on her damask cheek.

p. 31 the one crook: i.e. the one person who spoiled things for her.

Chapter 4

p. 34 *bien entendu*: of course.

p. 35 'on which side of the blanket': i.e. whether legitimate or illegitimate.

p. 35 the great continental war: the French were finally defeated at Waterloo in June 1815 by the allies, the victory being credited to the Duke of Wellington and the Prussian General Blucher.

p. 35 black-a-vised: dark-complexioned.

p. 35 thistly dignity: 'thistly' indicates that he was prickly and easily put out, but with a pun on the thistle as the Scottish emblem.

p. 36 the Thirty-nine Articles: the doctrines of the Church of England to which all those taking holy orders must subscribe.

p. 37 a certain Squire Hamley: the Squire and his hall bear some resemblance to the Mainwarings and Over Peover Hall. The Mainwarings were proud of their ancestry, which stretched back to the Norman period. The hall in red brick dates from 1585. In chapter 6 we learn that 'the wooden stocks were close to the gates': the entrance lodge of Over Peover Hall adjoins the Whipping Stocks Inn, formerly called the Mainwaring Arms.

p. 37 the Heptarchy: loose confederation of Anglo-Saxon kingdoms from the fifth to the ninth century AD.

p. 38 been plucked: failed an examination, here with the statement that he did not return to Oxford to re-sit it.

p. 38 either university: Oxford or Cambridge.

p. 40 **Rugby:** Mrs Gaskell's choice is perhaps made with insight – Rugby emerged as a great public school under the headmastership of Thomas Arnold, which lasted from 1828 until 1842.

p. 40 **the lap-dog and the donkey:** from the fable by Aesop (*c.* 570 BC); the donkey, seeking its master's attention and jealous of the caresses given to the dog, is beaten.

Chapter 5

p. 42 **behind his day:** i.e. not up with the current practice.

p. 43 **aloes:** these were thought to have laxative properties.

p. 43 **pomfret cakes:** liquorice sweets for the throat.

p. 43 **laughing . . . in his sleeve:** quietly or slily mocking.

p. 44 **two-and-sixpence:** half-a-crown, eight of these making £1 in pre-decimal currency.

p. 44 **Corbyn's bill:** i.e. the drugs he has supplied to Mr Gibson: 'bill' indicating an itemized list (as in a playbill or a bill of fare).

p. 45 **marks of Cupid's finger:** the phrases, as Easson rightly notes, 'are typical of Elizabethan poetic compliment'.

p. 45 **"Johnson's Dictionary":** the great dictionary published in 1755 by Dr Samuel Johnson (1709–84), the distinguished man of letters.

p. 46 **R. Verecundiae . . . R. Gibson, *Ch.*:** this parody prescription lists an ounce of modesty, an ounce of domestic respect and three grains of silence to be taken three times a day diluted in water. '*Ch.*' is 'chirurgeon' (surgeon).

p. 47 **reckoned without his host:** proverbial, meaning that he would have to think again about the person he was dealing with.

p. 47 *dégagé*: easy, free.

p. 47 **he girded up his loins for the battle:** Biblical, then proberbial, meaning that he prepared himself, got ready.

p. 49 **the Hollingford Cricket Club:** perhaps a contemporary reference rather than an 1820s one. The *Macclesfield Courier* records on 27 July 1861 that Manchester defeated Knutsford at Old Trafford by an innings.

p. 50 King Midas's barber . . .: in Ovid's *Metamorphoses*, Book XI, King Midas wishes to be rid of his wealth, makes his home in the country, praises the music of Pan and speaks slightingly of that of Apollo, who gains his revenge by giving him the ears of an ass. Mr Gibson summarizes the story admirably.

p. 51 Una: in Edmund Spenser's *The Faerie Queene*, Book I, she passes through all dangers unharmed, standing for True Religion. See p. 615 for a linked reference ('the false Duessa') to *The Faerie Queene*.

p. 52 Scylla to Charybdis: see Homer's *Odyssey*, Book XII. The monster and the whirlpool were on either side of a narrow strait, so that ships passing through risked destruction by one in avoiding the other.

p. 52 his one ewe-lamb: see II Samuel 12:3: 'the poor man had nothing, save one little ewe lamb, which . . . lay in his bosom, and was unto him as a daughter'.

p. 54 three old ladies sitting somewhere . . . : the Fates of classical mythology – Clotho, Lachesis, Atropos – thought to control the destiny of mankind.

p. 56 the 'Beggars' Opera': the celebrated, widely popular opera by John Gay (1685–1732) was first performed in 1728.

Chapter 6

p. 57 true clan-tartan: authentic tartan belonging to a real Scottish clan.

p. 57 wooden stocks: a reminder of the village's long history – offenders were placed in the stocks and left in public view, their feet in holes from which they could not remove them. (See note to p. 37 above.)

p. 58 the old red-brick hall: see note to p. 37 above.

p. 60 Mrs Hemans: Felicia Hemans (1793–1835), a popular early nineteenth-century poet, perhaps best remembered now for 'Casabianca', with its famous line 'The boy stood on the burning deck'.

p. 60 as Tennyson's would be in this: Alfred, Lord Tennyson (1809–92) would be at the peak of his popularity in the mid-1860's, having become poet laureate in 1850, following the death of Wordsworth and the impact of his own *In Memoriam* in the same year.

p. 60 wranglers: candidates taking high honours in the mathematical tripos at Cambridge.

p. 60 Chancellor's medals: two were given for outstanding work in classics, and one for English poetry (Easson).

p. 64 cribbage: a card game, common in the period, for two or more players, the score being kept on a board through the use of pegs.

p. 65 the *Morning Chronicle*: founded in 1769, considered unassailable for a long period, it suffered from competition with the *Daily News* and was ultimately absorbed into the *Daily Telegraph* in 1862.

p. 66 Cumnor Charity School: the charity school, known locally as Lady Mary's School, was supported by the ladies of the Egerton family for nearly a hundred years. It taught the girls 'whatever would render them useful in society'.

p. 66 spud: walking-stick with sharp, pointed end.

p. 66 window-tax: a tax on houses according to the number of windows; it was instituted in 1784 and abolished in 1851.

p. 66 Sir Walter Scott's novels: the novels of Scott (1771–1832), from *Waverley* (1814) onwards, took England by storm.

p. 67 'Bride of Lammermoor': published in 1819, it is a tragic love-story involving the heroine Lucy Ashton and the Master of Ravenswood.

p. 68 marrow: like, replica.

p. 68 Natural History at Cambridge: the Natural Science Tripos, set up in 1848 (Easson).

p. 69 King Alfred: 849–99; Anglo-Saxon king of Wessex, but not 'King of all England'.

p. 69 Queene Anne: she reigned 1702–14.

Chapter 7

p. 70 unconsidered trifles: Autolycus, the pedlar in *The Winter's Tale*, refers to himself as 'a snapper-up of unconsidered trifles' (III.iv.24).

p. 71 **a five-pound house:** small, easily managed, and cheap.

p. 75 **Venus herself:** the Roman goddess of love.

Chapter 8

p. 78 **the 'moated grange':** *Measure for Measure*, III.i.255, 'there at the moated grange resides this dejected Mariana'. Tennyson's poem from this, called simply 'Mariana', was published in 1830.

p. 79 *junior optimes:* placed in the third or lowest class in the mathematical tripos.

p. 81 **'from grave to gay, from lively to severe':** from Alexander Pope's (1688–1744) *Essay on Man* (1733–4), IV.380.

p. 81 **hobbledehoyhood:** clumsiness, awkwardness.

p. 82 *Vae victis*!: literally 'woe to the vanquished', attributed to the Roman writer Livy.

p. 83 **The reason why ... full well:** from Thomas Brown's (1663–1704) lines on Dr Fell, 'I do not like thee, Dr Fell/The reason why I cannot tell/But this I know, and know full well ...'

p. 84 **the Gordian knot:** i.e., taking decisive action over something extremely difficult, a reference to Alexander the Great's cutting with his sword of the knot whose undoing would supposedly make him the most powerful man in the world.

p. 85 **Grisi's concert:** Julia Grisi (1811–69), celebrated Italian soprano, performed regularly in London, the Italian composer Bellini creating roles for her.

p. 86 **rigging out:** the cost of buying her clothes.

Chapter 9

p. 90 **the colour ... emotion:** ironic indication that she used rouge to heighten the colour of her complexion.

p. 91 **good-will:** established reputation.

p. 92 **toiling and moiling:** working and drudging.

p. 92 **old Chelsea china:** porcelain made in Chelsea in the eighteenth century was considered to be very fine indeed.

p. 93 **condescension:** graciousness, but without the implication of being patronizing, as now.

p. 96 **'first catch your hare':** proverbial phrase, here meaning how is he (Gibson) to find the right woman, as the next sentence makes clear, though Mrs Kirkpatrick as the 'hare' soon suggests itself to him.

p. 97 *ab extra*: taken from outside.

Chapter 10

p. 99 **winnow . . . corn:** distinguish what is good.

p. 100 **Hyacinth:** as Easson points out, Hyacinth and Cynthia are unconnected in derivation, and Mrs Kirkpatrick's association of them is silly. Hyacinth was by derivation a male name.

p. 104 **a gush of love:** the phrase is echoed in Coleridge's 'The Rhyme of the Ancient Mariner' (1798), line 276.

p. 107 **bag-wigs:** wigs fashionable in the eighteenth century, the black hair being enclosed in an ornamental bag.

p. 108 **wet sling-net:** Roger had been casting the net into ponds or streams or both to get specimens of the wild life.

p. 110 **clue:** Theseus got out of the Cretan labyrinth by marking his way with a ball (or 'clue') of thread. Roger has not yet found the way to help Molly out of her suffering.

p. 115 **the man in the moon with his bundle of faggots:** i.e. carrying the bundle of wood which he has collected, his imprisonment in the moon being a punishment for working on a Sunday. This folklore representation, as Easson points out, derives from the stoning of the Sabbath breaker in Numbers xv.

Chapter 11

p. 121 **bread-and-cheese:** the staple diet of the labouring classes; hence Mrs Gibson's disapproval.

p. 121 **acrostic:** the first letter in each line of a poem forms a word vertically.

p. 123 **parlour-boarder:** a pupil who lives with the mistress of the school – like Harriet Smith in Jane Austen's *Emma*.

p. 126 babes in the wood: the sad story of 'The Children in the Wood' is from *Reliques of Ancient English Poetry* (1765) edited by Thomas Percy. It is a ballad of 160 lines which derives from an old play.

p. 126 pink sentimentalism: emotional self-indulgence.

p. 126 Two is company … trumpery: i.e. Molly feels that she is superfluous, an emphasis made clear as she thinks over recent events.

p. 129 Mentor: he was originally the friend and adviser of Telemachus, son of Odysseus and Penelope in Homer's epic poem, *The Odyssey*. The word has become synonymous with the role of the guide.

p. 129 *en détail* … *en gros*: in particular and in general.

Chapter 12

p. 131 mesmeric: of a hypnotic state produced by the influence, power of suggestion, of another person, the word derived from the practice of the Austrian physician Anton Mesmer (1734–1815).

p. 131 'To make a Roman holiday': Easson identifies this quotation as being from Byron's *Childe Harold*, iv, cxli (1818) and notes that Byron took his oath in the House of Lords on 13 March 1809.

p. 134 'promiscuous': i.e. on the off-chance, casually.

p. 135 her course of true love will run smooth: cf. *A Midsummer Night's Dream*, I.i.134 – 'The course of true love never did run smooth'.

p. 136 curling-time: the nightly ritual of the period – putting one's hair in papers so that it would curl.

p. 136 Like the Caliph in the Eastern story: both Dickens and Gaskell refer to the story some ten years or so earlier in their *Hard Times* (1854) and *North and South* (1855) respectively. Easson found it also in C. R. Maturin's *Melmoth the Wanderer* (1820).

p. 137 backwards: i.e. with her back to the coachman.

Chapter 13

p. 139 Egeria: Italian water-nymph, mistress of Numa, the second king of Rome, to whom she gave advice.

p. 141 **The man recovered of the bite . . .:** 'Elegy on the Death of a mad Dog' (1762), by Oliver Goldsmith (1728–74), lines 31–2.

p. 142 **Cap-paper:** paper protecting against dust.

p. 145 **favour:** resemble.

p. 145 **post-chaise:** carriage with seats for one or two passengers, with the driver on one of the horses which pulled it. Easson points out that 'yellow is traditionally a wedding colour'.

p. 145 **the 12th or the 1st:** beginning of the season for shooting grouse (August) and partridge (September) respectively.

p. 148 **Madame du Barri:** 1741–93; mistress of Louis XV of France; guillotined in 1793.

Chapter 14

p. 150 **bring you out:** i.e. introduce properly into society, a conventional form marking a girl's arrival at young womanhood.

p. 151 **"Lady Bettys":** Betty would be a familiar nickname for Elizabeth: Mrs Kirkpatrick is affecting informality. The reference here is clearly to yarn.

p. 152 **Miss Edgeworth's tales:** Maria Edgeworth (1767–1849), Irish novelist, initially celebrated for *Castle Rackrent* (1800) and a number of tales and children's stories. This is a put-down of Preston's pretensions to gentility. Miss Edgeworth was personally known to the Holland family.

p. 153 **Pecksy and Flapsy:** Lady Harriet is referring to one of Mrs Sarah Trimmer's stories of instruction for children (1786) in which there are two robins with those names (Easson).

p. 153 *ménage*: household.

p. 155 **Mercury:** the messenger of the gods in Roman mythology.

p. 159 **Homeric appetite:** i.e. on the scale of the gods in Greek mythology and epic, hence very large.

p. 159 **Ivanhoe . . . Friar Tuck's guest:** *Ivanhoe*, one of Sir Walter Scott's major successes, was published in 1819. Easson points out that Mrs Gaskell is in error, since his disguised guest was Richard the

Lionheart, who was given very little to eat. Friar Tuck's appetite was enormous.

p. 159 *fioriture*: a musical term denoting the 'improvised decoration of a melody' (*COD*).

p. 159 on the tight-rope: i.e. at top pitch.

p. 159 the ordinary: set meal at a set price in a room where such food was served.

p. 160 Huber: a Swiss naturalist (1750–1831), who may well have influenced Charles Darwin.

p. 161 the "George": coaching inn which still exists in Knutsford and is known under this name, though strictly it is the Royal George. It was renamed from the George and Dragon after Princess Victoria dined there in 1832. Here there were the Assembly Rooms built by the gentry for their own use.

p. 161 forty winks: a nap, as is made clear later.

p. 162 Sunday silk: dress worn on Sundays and on special occasions.

p. 162 Johnson's: based on Joseph Jackson (see *Cranford*, ch. 13), as shown by advertisements in the *Warrington Guardian* for 'congou' tea. Miss Matty consulted Mr Johnson about selling 'congou' tea in Cranford.

Chapter 15

p. 163 'unked': dialect for 'unfamiliar'.

p. 167 of the antique world: cf. *As You Like It*, II.iii.57 – 'O good old man, how well in thee appears/The constant service of the antique world' (Orlando's tribute to Adam's loyalty).

p. 168 ran-tan: onomatopoeic combination to convey the sound of the double knock on the door.

p. 169 as it was ... old woman's: identified by Easson as 'Victuals and drink/Were the chief of her diet', from an old nursery rhyme.

p. 169 receipts: recipes.

p. 169 timbales: dish of mincemeat or fish in pastry.

Chapter 16

p. 171 'musical glasses' of the day: glasses filled with various amounts of water; when tapped (for example with a spoon) they give out different notes. Gaskell is showing the trivial nature of the conversation, as well as its fashionability.

p. 171 run up: i.e. to London.

p. 173 a Russian merchant: a dealer who imported wares of various kinds from Russia.

p. 173 entailed: i.e. already legally left to someone.

p. 175 flys and cars: light horse-drawn carriages.

p. 175 Ashcombe Manor-house: probably based on Ashley hall, which the Egerton family owned from 1842.

Chapter 17

p. 184 last fall of timber: i.e. calculating how much the felling of trees was worth (with regard to the Hamley estate).

p. 186 Whitworth doctors: the Taylor family undertook cures in the eighteenth century, particularly of cancer, though they were without medical training. They practised at Whitworth, Lancashire, and built a considerable reputation; hence the Squire's reference here in his desperation.

p. 190 Major Dugald Dalgetty: camels can go for days without food, being able to store their food. Major Dugald Dalgetty is a character in Sir Walter Scott's *A Legend of Montrose* (1819).

Chapter 18

p. 202 *perdu*: concealed.

Chapter 19

p. 203 the 'Umpire': the London-Liverpool coach which called at the George Inn every day at 12 o'clock.

p. 204 the 'Angel Inn': in King Street, at which coaches called: it was a posting-house, where relays of horses delivered and collected letters, and an excise-office.

p. 206 a Scotch sister, or a sister *à la mode de Bretagne*: any relative of the same sex and approximate age, as distinct from closer relatives like a half-sister or a sister-in-law.

p. 206 Love me not for comely grace . . .: Easson traces this as being set by John Wilbye (1574–1638) as number 12 in his *Second Set of Madrigals* (1609).

p. 207 'being all things to all men': I Corinthians 9:22.

p. 208 The quiet waves closed over her . . . : this echoes Job 7:10.

p. 209 Doughty Street: Dickens's first London house was here (it is now the Dickens House Museum). Easson stresses that as Mr Kirkpatrick became more upwardly mobile he moved westwards to an area of increased status.

p. 210 Only the actions of the just . . .: the much-quoted lines by James Shirley (1596–1666) are from his masque *The Contention of Ajax and Ulysses* (1659).

p. 210 rule-of-three sum: discovering the missing number when you know three of the four; given two in relation to each other, the 'missing' number is one that relates in proportion to the third: e.g. '1 is to 2 as 2 is to? (= 4).

p. 211 *chansons*: songs.

Chapter 20

p. 213 crewels: thin yarn used for embroidery and tapestry.

p. 214 brougham: a closed carriage, indicative of social status.

p. 217 the vanity of human wishes: perhaps a deliberate echo of the title of Dr Johnson's celebrated poem (1749).

p. 218 "kismet": from the Arabic, meaning fate.

p. 220 force-meat: stuffing, seasoning.

Chapter 21

p. 224 *nil admirari*: wonder at nothing.

p. 226 Matlock: the Derbyshire spa much frequented at the time.

p. 226 Queen Charlotte: wife of George III, she died in 1818; her birthday balls were designed to raise funds for the hospital which took her name.

p. 226 your quips and your cranks: an echo of *L'Allegro* ('quips and cranks and wanton wiles') by John Milton (1608–74).

p. 228 vingt-un: the card-game pontoon, in which players try to get cards with a total value of twenty-one points.

p. 228 a silver threepence: a coin in circulation from the accession of Queen Victoria (1837). Gaskell is slightly out here, since we have not arrived at that date in the narrative action.

p. 229 no great shakes: i.e. nothing out of the ordinary.

p. 232 "no blate": i.e. he is not slow to push himself forward, not diffident.

Chapter 22

p. 236 'Have mercy upon me . . .': an echo of Psalm 31:9.

p. 236 nervous: strong, direct.

p. 237 *mauvaise honte*: self-consciousness, false modesty.

p. 240 point-device: impeccably correct.

p. 240 Horse Guards: this clock is in Whitehall, and is celebrated for keeping the correct time. The Horse Guards, like the Life Guards, are crack regiments.

p. 241 'girning': irritable, make a face.

p. 242 "Give me the portion that falleth to me": Luke 15:12 (the parable of the Prodigal Son).

Chapter 23

p. 247 the Temple or Lincoln's Inn: two of the Inns of Court, which those intending to take up a legal career are required to join.

p. 247 In spite of Milton: John Milton (1608–74) was given £10 for *Paradise Lost* when it was published in 1667.

p. 247 a popular writer of sonnets: Easson suggests William Lisle Bowles or Wordsworth. Bearing in mind the date, and the title of Osborne's first sonnet, the latter would appear to be the more likely.

p. 248 'Boney' ... 'Johnny Crapaud': the first is the colloquial abbreviation for Napoleon Buonaparte (1769–1821), emperor of the French; the second is an insulting term for a Frenchman – 'Johnny Toad'.

p. 248 Catholic emancipation: the bill to remove restrictions from Roman Catholics (among other things they could not hold government office or sit in Parliament) was passed in 1829, when the Duke of Wellington was Prime Minister. It had aroused fierce controversy.

p. 248 "Lucy": a further indication that Osborne has Wordsworth in mind, since 'Lucy' is the subject of a number of his poems.

p. 248 *Blackwood* and the *Quarterly*: two celebrated magazines, the first beginning in 1817 and the second in 1809. *Blackwood's Edinburgh Magazine* (known as 'Maga') saw the appearance of *Scenes of Clerical Life* (1857), the first work by Gaskell's great contemporary, George Eliot.

p. 249 Deighton: Cambridge booksellers and publishers.

p. 250 take us to Australia: Gaskell is echoing the contemporary stimulus to emigration, which had increased in her own time as against the fictional time of *Wives and Daughters*.

p. 251 the Prince of Wales being made Regent: this was in 1788, with the onset of madness in George III. The Prince of Wales, later George IV (1820–30), was effectively the centre of political intrigue throughout his regency.

p. 251 White Surrey: named after Richard's III's horse. Richard was defeated by Henry VII at Bosworth Field in 1485, Henry becoming king.

Chapter 24

pp. 253–4 'art of polite conversation': Gaskell's irony is enhanced by the reference to Jonathan Swift's (1667–1745) satire, which was published in 1738 and pillories the trivialities of conversation.

p. 254 comparative osteology: the study of bones.

p. 254 "Prisoner of Chillon": by Lord Byron (1788–1824). Published in 1816, it describes the incarceration of the Genovese politician and minister Bonnivard (1493–1570).

p. 255 Johnnie Gilpin: from a light-hearted popular ballad, published in 1782, by William Cowper (1731–1800).

p. 257 *Tu t'en repentiras, Colin* . . . : the refrain of 'You will regret it Colin, you will regret it, if you take a wife . . .' is superbly ironic in view both of what the reader knows of Osborne and of the fact that it is a French ballad.

p. 257 *mal-àpropos*: underlines the above note and Mrs Gibson's unwitting part in the submerged drama.

p. 259 Kalkbrenner's: Friedrich Kalkbrenner (1785–1849), popular German composer and pianist.

Chapter 25

p. 262 One of the few books: i.e. the *Peerage*, first published by John Burke the genealogist in 1826, and established as an annual record of the aristocracy thereafter. See note to p. 16 above.

p. 262 she never told her woe: an echo of Cesario's (Viola's) 'She never told her love/But let concealment, like a worm i' the bud/Feed on her damask cheek' (*Twelfth Night*, II.iv.109–11).

p. 264 the Blues: a crack regiment, the Royal Horse Guards.

Chapter 26

p. 268 excursion-trains: Gaskell is once again carefully dating her narrative – it was not until the 1840s that holiday trains were introduced, soon becoming popular and widespread.

p. 268 'regardless of their doom': cf. 'Alas, regardless of their doom,/ The little victims play!' – 'Ode on a Distant Prospect of Eton College' (1747), lines 51–2, by Thomas Gray (1716–71).

p. 271 *esprit-forts*: wits.

p. 271 a lovely turban: this would be fashionable evening wear at the time.

p. 274 **figuring away**: dancing.

p. 276 *recherché*: i.e. choice, well-selected.

p. 278 'Monymusk': name of a country-dance tune.

p. 278 *à l'enfant*: dressed in a youthful way.

p. 284 *Règne Animal*: *Animal Kingdom*. Identified by Easson as being by Baron Cuvier the zoologist (1769–1832). It was published in 1817.

p. 284 **three-tailed bashaw**: an extremely high-ranking prince among the Turks, having a standard of three horse-tails borne before him.

p. 285 *Le Siècle de Louis XIV*: *The Age of Louis XIV* (1751), the classic study of the period by Voltaire (see note on p. 300 below).

Chapter 27

pp. 285–6 **'a Katherine Pear on the side that's next the sun'**: traced by Easson to Sir John Suckling's (1609–42) 'A Ballad upon a Wedding'.

p. 287 **M. Geoffroi de St. H.**: Geoffroi de Saint-Hilaire (1772–1844), celebrated zoologist.

p. 287 **mounseer**: i.e. monsieur.

p. 290 **(of Alsace!)**: i.e. they would acquire French spoken with a predominantly German accent; almost an echo of the Squire's own anti-French attitude.

Chapter 28

p. 295 **It was the time of roses . . .**: from Thomas Hood (1799–1845) in 'Ballad: It Was Not in the Winter' (1827).

p. 297 **'Red Book'**: a book carried by ladies for recording the dances allocated to particular partners.

p. 300 **ministered to a mind diseased**: an echo of Macbeth's 'Can'st thou not minister to a mind diseas'd' (V.ii.40).

p. 300 **Voltaire**: 1694–1778; the great French author who embodied the age of enlightenment in France prior to the Revolution.

p. 300 **Alnaschar vision**: the beggar in *The Arabian Nights' Entertain-*

ment who envisages marriage with the Vizier's daughter but whose dreams are shattered by his own clumsiness.

p. 301 **'Old lamps for new':** another *Arabian Nights* reference – Aladdin's wicked uncle offered new lamps for old in an attempt to secure the magic lamp that had brought his nephew wealth, and thus tricked Aladdin's princess wife into giving it to him.

p. 304 **one man may steal . . .:** the implication is that the favoured person can do no wrong, the unfavoured can do no right.

Chapter 29

p. 305 **Bush-fighting:** uncharacteristic military reference which reflects Mrs Gibson's strategy – misguided – with regard to Osborne and Roger and their involvement with Cynthia and Molly.

p. 306 **"her eyes are load-stars":** echoes *A Midsummer Night's Dream*, I.i.183.

p. 307 **paid him for horse-flesh:** i.e. provided him with enough money to enable him to keep a horse.

p. 308 **white swelling:** acute pain in the joints but without inflammation: see Gaskell's *Letters*, ed. Chapple & Pollard, no. 217 (27 October 1854), p. 319 – 'One poor woman lost a boy seven years ago of white swelling in his knee, and F.N. went twice a day to dress it.' (F.N. is Florence Nightingale.)

p. 310 **slinging trot:** easy, relaxed cantering as distinct from a regular pace.

p. 311 **the *Grand Seigneur*:** the Sultan, with the implication that Molly and Cynthia are his harem (of course a perfectly innocent remark).

p. 313 **the strophe and anti-strope in a Greek chorus:** the verse statement followed by the verse response in Greek drama.

p. 315 **"at the foot of the letter":** i.e. literally, from the French *au pied de la lettre*.

p. 315 **a delving Adam than a spinning Eve:** cf. 'When Adam delved, and Eve span/Who was then the gentleman?' (from John Ball's sermon on the outbreak of the Peasants' Revolt in 1381).

p. 316 **three-cornered note:** a note folded so as to make a triangle.

p. 317 *empressement*: eagerness, alacrity.

Chapter 30

p. 318 **'preserve':** see that the game are 'preserved' for the sportsmen.

p. 320 **covers:** undergrowth where the game are 'preserved'.

p. 320 **agait:** being undertaken.

p. 321 **tile-drainage:** specially made tiles for drains to take the water away.

p. 322 **roadster:** a horse used on the roads.

p. 324 **Philip drunk to Philip sober:** reasoning with the reasonable son and not with the unreasonable father.

p. 325 **winked at:** ignored.

Chapter 31

p. 326 **the Hanoverian succession:** i.e. to the English throne, beginning with George I (originally Elector of Hanover) in 1714.

p. 327 **jumped with his humour:** suited him, was agreeable to him personally.

p. 327 **'scatter his enemies':** direct quotation from the second stanza of the British National Anthem – 'O Lord our God arise,/Scatter his [the king's] Enemies'.

p. 328 **made-wines:** i.e. home-made.

p. 328 **birch-wine:** drink made from the sap of the birch tree by tapping it off.

p. 329 **won golden opinions:** another *Macbeth* echo – 'I have bought/ Golden opinions from all sorts of people' (I.vii.32–3).

p. 330 **the world was out of joint:** cf. *Hamlet*, I.v.188 – 'The time is out of joint'.

p. 330 **'a rock of strength, under whose very shadow there is rest':** Isaiah 32:2.

p. 331 'to sport with Amaryllis in the shade . . .': from *Lycidas* (line 68) by John Milton (1608–74).

p. 331 inglorious ease: echoes 'ignoble ease' in Milton's *Paradise Lost*, II. 227.

p. 334 frabbed: put about, worried.

Chapter 32

p. 334 Doctor's Commons: i.e. Doctors of Civil Law, administering courts and holding legal documents such as wills.

p. 335 Gray's Scandinavian Prophetess . . .: from *The Descent of Odin* (1768) by Thomas Gray (1716–71). This is the refrain line (50, 58, 72).

p. 337 *Mea culpa*: the fault is mine, a phrase used in the Roman Catholic confessional and in some Christian prayers.

p. 339 Sterne . . . "Thine own and thy mother's friends forsake not": Mrs Gibson is in fact (mis)quoting Proverbs xxvii.10 and misascribing the quotation to Laurence Sterne (1713–68), author of *Tristram Shandy* and *A Sentimental Journey*. Cf. p. 611 below, where she considers the biblical phrase 'apple of his eye' a vulgar expression.

p. 341 Lilliputian darts: verbal equivalents of the tiny arrows shot at Gulliver by the Lilliputians in *Gulliver's Travels* (1726) by Jonathan Swift.

p. 342 "how sweet is solitude!": the quotation is from *Retirement* (1782) by William Cowper (1731–1800) – 'How sweet, how passing sweet, is solitude!', a sentiment the poet ascribes to the French writer de la Bruyère.

p. 344 the 'Hall of Apollo' . . . Lucullus: the latter was the Roman consul whose servants knew what to provide for his guests according to which room he indicated would be used.

p. 344 the Duke of Bridgewater: 1756–1829; he left £8000 for the best treatise written on the goodness of God as manifested in the creation, though eight authors of treatises eventually shared the bequest.

Chapter 33

p. 350 **traps:** the necessary equipment he would need for the trip, his apparatus etc.

p. 350 **set up:** conceited.

p. 351 **cracking:** talking (here with the implication of 'praising').

p. 353 **seven years, and seven years more:** echoes Genesis 29: 18–30, Jacob's service for Rachel.

Chapter 34

p. 354 **quips and cranks:** from *L'Allegro*, line 27 (see note to p. 226 above).

p. 355 **'her pretty lips with blackberries were all besmeared and dyed':** from the ballad of 'The Children in the Wood' (see note to p. 126 above).

p. 356 **carried on in earth's diurnal course . . .:** an echo of 'A Slumber Did My Spirit Seal', by William Wordsworth (1770–1850) – 'Rolled round in earth's diurnal course/With rocks and stones and trees'.

p. 358 **weeds:** clothes worn in token of mourning.

p. 358 **pendule:** decorative small clock.

p. 361 *au grand sérieux*: literally, seriously.

Chapter 35

p. 364 **aneurism of the aorta:** damage to the main artery of the heart.

Chapter 36

p. 377 **netting:** open-meshed work to produce fancy articles.

p. 379 **countervent:** contradict, oppose.

p. 381 *tapis*: here, subject, matter which is under consideration.

Chapter 37

p. 382 apophysis and epiphysis: the first is a protuberance which forms a continuous part of a bone, the second 'an extremity of long bone which has originated in a centre of ossification distinct from the rest'. (Easson).

p. 386 *Edinburgh*: the *Edinburgh Review*, one of the major reviews of the early nineteenth century, was first published in 1802.

p. 388 *"les absens ont toujours tort"*: the absent are always wrong.

p. 391 the world was out of joint: see note to p. 330 above.

p. 393 Huon: not identified.

p. 394 Aristotle and Pliny: the first (384–322 BC) is the great Greek philosopher, whose knowledge embraced natural history; the second (AD 23–79) wrote an encyclopaedia of natural history which was the major source for such knowledge until the seventeenth century.

p. 395 King Solomon's judgment: see I Kings 3:16–28 for the full version.

Chapter 38

p. 397 rolled calf's head: Easson points out that after the removal of the bones, spices are inserted and the head is simmered.

p. 397 javelin-men: sherriff's men who escorted judges at assizes, the 'javelins' being their spears or pikes.

p. 398 The three black graces: the three professions dressed in black: a parody of the three classical Graces, the beautiful sisters who bestowed beauty and charm.

p. 398 hide ... under a bushel: cf. Matthew 5:15.

p. 398 many a time and oft: an echo of *The Merchant of Venice*, I.iii.101, Shylock's address to Antonio.

p. 398 the rule o' three: see note to p. 210 above.

p. 399 Robespierre and Bonyparte: Robespierre (1758–94), leader of the Terror in Revolutionary France that led to his downfall; Buonaparte, later Napoleon I, emperor of the French, finally defeated by the allies at Waterloo in 1815.

p. 402 **the Academy Exhibition:** held annually, and hence an important social and cultural event; the Royal Academy displayed the work of contemporary artists.

Chapter 39

p. 405 **He threw off his friends . . .:** cf. 'Retaliation', lines 107–8, by Oliver Goldsmith (1730–74), ('threw' should be 'cast', and 'liked' should be 'pleased').

p. 407 **M. de la Palisse est mort . . .:** M. de la Palisse is dead/In losing his life; A quarter of an hour before his death/He was still living'.

p. 409 **'gar auld claes look . . .':** from 'The Cotter's Saturday Night', stanza 5, by Robert Burns (1759–96). The sense is 'make old clothes look nearly as good as new ones'.

p. 411 **Blair's sermons:** the sermons of Hugh Blair (1718–1800), a Scottish preacher, enjoyed a reputation beyond their worth.

p. 416 **Spa:** Belgian health resort.

Chapter 40

p. 420 **Nora Creina:** named after the sweetheart in one of the *Irish Melodies* by Thomas Moore (1779–1852), an immensely popular series (Easson).

p. 421 **elevenpence-halfpenny postage:** in the pre-1840 period, postage was charged according to distance: in 1840 penny postage was introduced for inland letters.

p. 423 **'As tall and as straight as a poplar tree':** identified by Easson as from the comic opera *Rosina* (1782).

p. 423 **phaeton:** open four-wheeled carriage, commonly drawn by two horses.

Chapter 41

p. 426 **frangible:** less common usage for fragile, breakable.

p. 429 **the Geographical Society:** founded in 1830, it later became the Royal Geographical Society.

p. 431 the British Essayists: notably Addison and Steele of *Spectator* fame, but also Dr Johnson's contributions to *The Rambler* and Goldsmith's *The Bee*. The works of these eighteenth-century writers, as Easson notes, were often collected into volume form.

Chapter 42

p. 437 wandering out at her own sweet will: an echo of Wordsworth's sonnet 'Composed upon Westminster Bridge', line 12 – 'The river glideth at her own sweet will.'

p. 437 For youth, but not for crabbed age: cf. Shakespeare's *The Passionate Pilgrim*, xii: 'Crabbed age and youth cannot live together.'

p. 437 macadamized streets: from John McAdam (1756–1836), Scottish inventor and engineer who revolutionized roads by combining crushed stone bound with gravel and raised to improve drainage.

Chapter 43

p. 446 the Worcester Festival: the Three Choirs Festival, still held annually in the cathedral cities of Worcester, Hereford and Gloucester by turn, dates back to the early eighteenth century.

p. 448 pet: temper.

p. 450 *semestre*: half-year course or term.

p. 451 condescended: lowered himself, stooped to.

p. 452 and down will come father and mother and all: deliberately echoing the nursery rhyme 'Rock-a-bye Baby' – 'Down will come baby and cradle and all', with Cynthia so conscious of the repercussions of her past conduct.

Chapter 45

p. 464 the Bang-up: this coach called regularly at the George, and served Liverpool and Birmingham.

p. 465 'protesting too much': echoing *Hamlet* III. ii. 224–5.

p. 465 somebody's sword: i.e. that of Damocles, a fourth-century courtier who praised rulers, only to find that when he attended a royal feast a sword was suspended above his head and that he could have been killed at any moment.

p. 467 **"There's no place like home":** the song (1823) by John Howard Payne (1791–1852) achieved enormous popularity.

p. 467 *'toujours perdrix'*: literally, 'always partridge', with the implication 'always the same', a reference to the deliberate serving of the same dish instead of giving variety to the meal. Easson gives the original anecdote.

p. 468 **"dragging at each remove a lengthening chain":** 'And drags at each remove a lengthening chain' (Goldsmith, *The Traveller* (1764), line 10).

p. 469 **Houbigant:** later, fashionable glove-makers of Regent Street.

Chapter 46

p. 472 **snaring . . . :** the trapping of rabbits, which were not designated as game; the killing of the latter required a licence.

p. 473 *mal-àpropos*: unfortunate, inappropriate.

p. 473 **Book Society:** a subscription group, members paying in to buy books to be circulated among themselves.

p. 476 **'shouldering the crutch, and showing how fields were won':** cf. 'Shouldered his crutch, and showed how fields were won' (Goldsmith, *The Deserted Village* (1770), line 158).

p. 476 **pound-cake:** so called because the recipe uses one pound in weight of each ingredient – currants, sugar, peel, etc.

p. 477 **tickler:** more choosy, fussy.

p. 478 *àpropos de rien*: in respect of nothing.

p. 478 **Molly:** this is the colloquial version of 'Mary', the implication being that Molly is behaving like a servant-girl in her clandestine meetings (Molly would be a common name for a servant).

p. 479 **"More folks know . . .":** proverbial, meaning that people know more about a person than that person supposes.

Chapter 47

p. 485 although she was not the rose ...: i.e. not because of herself, but because of the reputation of her sister.

p. 485 the Highchester Bank broken: echoes the situation in *Cranford*, ch. 13, when Miss Matty loses her money with the collapse of the Town and County Bank.

p. 486 tarradiddles: colloquial euphemism for lies, fibs.

p. 490 *inconséquence*: illogicality.

p. 491 "Satan finds some mischief still for idle tongues to do": from 'Against Idleness and Mischief' by Isaac Watts (1674–1748), celebrated English hymn-writer. Gibson is upset, but typically changes the 'hands' of the original to the gossipy 'tongues' here.

p. 491 quarter-deck march: an expressive way of indicating Gibson's passionate rejection of the gossip – it is as if he is pacing up and down in the confined space on board ship.

Chapter 48

p. 499 moped: depressed.

Chapter 49

p. 501 Lord Cumnor ... with his pockets full of halfpence for the children: a further association with Wilbraham Egerton, who records in his accounts: 'Five shillings in half pence to the schoolchildren.'

p. 502 a notable: an industrious person.

p. 502 blind man's holiday: twilight.

p. 502 fruit-nets: nets to keep the fruit from being eaten by birds.

p. 503 pawky: drily humorous (*COD*).

p. 503 *gaucherie*: awkwardness.

p. 505 the "Beauties of England and Wales": identified by Easson as being published in eighteen volumes (1801–15) and covering the various counties in terms of description, history, topography.

p. 506 'Don Quixote and Sancho Panza': the reference is to *Don*

Quixote by Miguel de Cervantes (1547–1616), the great Spanish novelist. Don Quixote is the comic knight-errant, Sancho Panza his servant; Lady Harriet is comparing herself and Phoebe to them as champions of Molly's innocence.

p. 506 *parler de l'âne* . . .: speak of the ass and one sees its ears – a version of the proverbial saying 'talk of the Devil and he's sure to appear'.

Chapter 50

p. 511 **dividends:** interest on money invested.

p. 513 **'souffre-douleur':** drudge, here running about at the beck and call of Lady Cumnor.

p. 514 **Waterloo House:** in Pall Mall East, where material etc. could be purchased. It was regarded as fashionable, superior.

p. 516 **the typical worm:** i.e. she turns but cannot escape (proverbially the worm turns, that is, rebels).

p. 517 **rub:** problem, trouble, vexation.

Chapter 51

p. 528 **The truth had entered his soul before this:** cf. Psalm 105:18 – 'The iron had entered his soul.'

Chapter 52

p. 533 **the Cape:** the Cape of Good Hope, at the southernmost tip of Africa.

p. 533 **And now he cried aloud with an exceeding bitter cry:** Esau's response to his father, Isaac (Genesis 27:34).

p. 536 **desk:** portable writing-desk which rested on the knees. Trollope used one on trains and ships for writing his fiction, travel books, etc.

Chapter 53

p. 542 *Mémoires de Sully:* duc de Sully (1560–1641), chief minister to Henry IV of France; he restored the French economy. His memoirs were published in 1638.

p. 545 **long lingering look:** another echo of Gray's 'Elegy Written in a Country Churchyard' (1751) ('Nor cast one longing lingering look behind?', line 88).

p. 546 *soupe blanche*: bread dipped in milk.

p. 547 **boots:** the boy appointed to clean the guests' boots and shoes.

p. 548 **choose how far:** who knows how far.

p. 550 **"all the appointed days":** Job 14:14.

Chapter 54

p. 552 **waur:** worse.

p. 555 **had 'taken the turn':** was improving.

p. 556 **a window in his breast:** from Momus, spirit of grumbling in classical mythology, who complained that man should have a window in his breast so that his feelings and thoughts could be seen.

p. 557 **"Oh, call her fair, not pale!":** see S. T. Coleridge (1772–1834), *Christabel* (1816), line 289 – 'Her face, oh call it fair not pale.'

p. 557 **Concerts of Ancient Music:** identified by Easson as a concert organization in London which performed music written prior to the previous twenty years.

p. 557 **'some must watch . . .':** echoes *Hamlet*, III.ii.267–8.

p. 558 **notability:** hard-working domesticity.

p. 561 **a famous form of speech:** a syllogism – a form of reasoning in which a conclusion is drawn from two premises, but the conclusion may be invalid, as here (to be young is not necessarily to be happy).

Chapter 55

p. 564 **Hottentot:** tribe in south-west Africa.

p. 564 **Caesar and Pompey berry much alike:** an early example of the platitude that people of the same race all look alike so that outsiders cannot differentiate them.

Chapter 56

p. 571 'Off with the Old Love, and on with the new': from the song 'It is best to be off with the old love/Before you are on with the new.'

p. 573 budget: pouch.

p. 573 to put his fate to the touch: identified by Easson as by John Graham, Marquis of Montrose (1612–50).

p. 575 *juste milieu*: happy medium, i.e. somewhere between the two extremes (Mr Preston and Roger).

p. 576 the Faithful John of the German story: from the fairy-tale by the Brothers Grimm called 'The Frog King, or Iron Henry'. As Easson points out, Gaskell is confused, 'Faithful John' being the title of another story.

Chapter 57

p. 579 the new line between Birmingham and London: this was opened in 1838, and hence is not within the chronology of the novel.

p. 581 shift her trumpet . . .: i.e. her ear-trumpet; another reference to Goldsmith, (*Retaliation*, line 146) – 'He shifted his trumpet, and only took snuff', the movement enabling him (Sir Joshua Reynolds) to avoid hearing what he didn't want to hear.

p. 582 Marius sitting amid the ruins of Carthage: Gaius Marius (157–86 BC), Roman soldier and consul, fled to Africa after being defeated by his rival consul Sulla, and, arrived at Carthage, associated his own fallen state with that of the city, which had been destroyed in 146 BC.

p. 586 last: latest.

Chapter 58

pp. 593–4 'Arabian Nights' Entertainment . . .': the story of Prince Caramalzaman and Princess Badoura occurs in the *Arabian Night's Entertainment* (variously translated) and occupies nights 178–235.

p. 595 "a polite education in itself": identified by Easson as being by Steele in the *Tatler*, no. 49.

p. 595 *parure*: a set of jewels, ornaments, to be worn together.

Chapter 59

p. 599 Daniel O'Rourke: in the Irish folk-tale he continues to hold his sickle when he throws it up, and so finds himself in the moon. Gaskell uses this also in *North and South*, ch. 28.

p. 605 *àpropos de bottes*: suddenly.

Chapter 60

p. 609 crossing: saving paper by writing first across its width, then from bottom to top, so that the lines of writing cross one another.

p. 611 the apple of his eye: see Deuteronomy 32:10; and cf. p. 339 above.

p. 615 the false Duessa: in Spenser's *The Faerie Queene*, the false Duessa stands for evil and, assuming the appearance of Una (True Religion), for a while corrupts people and deceives the Red-Cross Knight.

p. 618 *soupirant*: wooer.

p. 619 Sussex Place: fashionable part of London, near Regent's Park.

p. 619 Mangnall's Questions: the textbooks by Richmal Mangnall (1769–1820), which employed a question-answer technique and were constantly reprinted and revised. The heathen deity is the winged messenger Mercury.

Angus Easson's collection of reviews and opinions in his *Elizabeth Gaskell: The Critical Heritage* (London: Routledge, 1991) is invaluable for anyone examining the reception of Mrs Gaskell's novels, stories, and biography of Charlotte Brontë by her contemporaries. The first extract below is from Henry James's unsigned critique of *Wives and Daughters* in the *Nation*, 22 February 1866 (*The Critical Heritage*, pp. 463–4):

> We cannot help thinking that in *Wives and Daughters* the late Mrs Gaskell has added to the number of those works of fiction – of which we can not perhaps count more than a score as having been produced in our time – which will outlast the duration of their novelty and continue for years to come to be read and relished for a higher order of merits. Besides being the best of the author's own tales – putting aside *Cranford*, that is, which as a work of quite other pretensions ought not to be weighed against it, and which seems to us manifestly destined in its modest way to become a classic – it is also one of the very best novels of its kind. So delicately, so elaborately, so artistically, so truthfully, and heartily is the story wrought out, that the hours given to its perusal seem like hours actually spent, in the flesh as well as the spirit, among the scenes and people described, in the atmosphere of their motives, feelings, traditions, associations. The gentle skill with which the reader is slowly involved in the tissue of the story; the delicacy of the handwork which has perfected every mesh of the net in which he finds himself ultimately entangled; the lightness of touch which, while he stands all unsuspicious of literary artifice, has stopped every issue into the real world; the admirable, inaudible, invisible exercise of creative power, in short, with which a new and arbitrary world is reared over his heedless head – a world insidiously inclusive of him (such is the *assoupissement* of his critical sense), complete in every particular, from the divine blue of the summer sky to the June-bugs in the roses, from Cynthia Kirkpatrick and her infinite revelations of human

nature to old Mrs Goodenough and her provincial bad grammar –
these marvellous results, we say, are such as to compel the reader's
very warmest admiration, and to make him feel, in his gratitude for
this seeming accession of social and moral knowledge, as if he made
but a poor return to the author, in testifying, no matter how
strongly, to the fact of her genius.

For Mrs Gaskell's genius was so very composite as a quality, it
was so obviously the offspring of her affections, her feelings, her
associations, and (considering that, after all, it *was* genius) was so
little of an intellectual matter, that it seems almost like slighting
these charming facts to talk of them under a collective name,
especially when that name is a term so coarsely and disrespectfully
synthetic as the word genius has grown to be. But genius is of many
kinds, and we are almost tempted to say that that of Mrs Gaskell
strikes us as being little else than a peculiar play of her personal
character. In saying this we wish to be understood as valuing not
her intellect the less, but her character the more. Were we touching
upon her literary character at large, we should say that in her literary
career as a whole she displayed, considering her success, a minimum
of head. Her career was marked by several little literary indiscre-
tions, which show how much writing was a matter of pure feeling
with her. Her *Life of Miss Brontë*, for instance, although a very
readable and delightful book, is one which a woman of strong head
could not possibly have written; for, full as it is of fine qualities, of
affection, of generosity, of sympathy, of imagination, it lacks the
prime requisites of a good biography. It is written with a signal want
of judgment and of critical power; and it has always seemed to us
that it tells the reader considerably more about Mrs Gaskell than
about Miss Brontë. In the tale before us this same want of judgment, as we may still call it in the absence of a better name,
presuming that the term applies to it only as it stands contrasted
with richer gifts, is shown; not in the general management of the
story, nor yet in the details, most of which are as good as perfect,
but in the way in which, as the tale progresses, the author loses
herself in its current very much as we have seen that she causes the
reader to do.

Almost invariably, bearing in mind the subject-matter of the novel
and the ironic modes employed in its presentation, *Wives and
Daughters* was compared to the work of Jane Austen, with *Pride
and Prejudice* in particular providing points of comparison and

contrast. This is from an unsigned review in the *Spectator*, 17 March 1866 (*The Critical Heritage*, pp. 474–5):

> Mrs Gaskell's last book is certainly, *Cranford* excepted, her best; and absolutely her best if we are to consider a larger and more complex design, somewhat less perfectly worked out, higher than a little gem of exquisite workmanship, but depending exclusively for its art on the humour of a delicate memory, skilful at noting the little symptoms by which warm hearts betray the yoke of narrow interests, and at recalling all the quaint customs of country-town society. *Wives and Daughters* is not an exciting story; it is a story the character of which is nearer to that of Miss Austen's tales than to *Mary Barton* or *Ruth*. But there is more depth of character, more value for intensity of feeling in it than in anything which Miss Austen ever wrote, though the execution is much less equal than that great novelist's. The characters of both hero and heroine, for instance, are vague and unimpressive. The sketch of Mr Gibson, the surgeon, is the nearest to Miss Austen's style of drawing, and his dry caustic humour and acute reserve remind one sometimes so closely of Mr Bennett, in *Pride and Prejudice*, that it almost suggests some unconscious lingering of that happy picture in Mrs Gaskell's memory. When the lovers of the two heroines in *Pride and Prejudice* have declared themselves, Mr Bennet drily observes, 'If there are any more young men waiting downstairs for Kitty or Mary, send them up, for I'm quite at leisure;' and after Lydia has married the worthless rascal Wickham, her father remarks to his favourite daughter, Lizzie, 'Wickham is perhaps my favourite, but I think I shall like your husband quite as well as Jane's.' And in this story, when Mr Gibson's step-daughter Cynthia breaks with Roger Hamley, after a previous breaking away from Mr Preston, in order to marry Mr Henderson, a rich barrister, Mr Gibson says to Molly [chapter 57], 'Think of us on Thursday. I declare I don't know which of her three lovers she mayn't summon at the very last moment to act the part of bridegroom. I'm determined to be surprised at nothing, and will give her away with a good grace to whoever comes.' And of Mr Henderson himself he observes [chapter 56], 'I think him perfection. I don't wonder she preferred him to Roger Hamley. Such scents! such gloves! and then his hair and his cravat!' However, Mr Gibson is not another Mr Bennett, but a much less indolent and less selfish man, but he is certainly the character in which Mrs Gaskell's art touches most closely that of the

most delicate artist of the last generation. There is just the same extent of delineation, the same limited degree of insight permitted into the character, in both cases. Miss Austen never went further. She painted with absolute perfection the upper stratum of feeling, and no more. Mrs Gaskell often goes deeper; but into the interior of Mr Gibson's character she never pretends to see further than Miss Austen herself would have seen. Indeed he is the kind of man who does not see further himself, for he habitually pushes aside trains of thought or feeling that are not immediately practical, and so scarcely knows what he himself thinks or feels on any subject, if no purpose is to be answered by distinctly realizing his own state of mind. Mr Gibson is seen, like most of Miss Austen's stronger characters, in but a half-light; for she seldom exhibits more of the natures of any but weak chatterers and fools. Miss Austen herself would scarcely have drawn Mr Gibson better than Mrs Gaskell has done.

Equally inevitably, Gaskell's great contemporary George Eliot is brought into the frame of analogy and evaluation by another reviewer, in an unsigned notice in the *Saturday Review* of 24 March 1866 (*The Critical Heritage*, pp. 482–3):

Compared with the genius of 'George Eliot', Mrs Gaskell's gifts still maintain a character of their own. Between the pathos of the two writers there is just the difference that there is between *Romeo and Juliet* on the one hand, and *Othello* or *Hamlet* on the other. 'George Eliot's' men and women are less like the ordinary men and women of every-day life, and have a more vigorous individuality than Mrs Gaskell's and the firmness with which they are drawn, and the depth of light and shade with which they are coloured, are in harmony with their intrinsic natures. Maggie, in *The Mill on the Floss*, is a character of tragic grandeur, thoroughly human, but most difficult to treat. In the way of wit and humour there is nothing more delightful in all fiction than Mrs Poyser in *Adam Bede*, and the three sisters in *The Mill on the Floss*; and the vigour with which they are painted is extraordinary. Now and then, indeed, 'George Eliot' writes completely in what may be called Mrs Gaskell's manner. Such is her story of the *Sad Fortunes of the Rev. Amos Barton*, who lies in bed 'snoring the snore of the just,' while his wife sits up sleepless with care, and darns the dull and dreary curate's worsted stockings. The last scene in the tale, too, where the heartbroken Amos flings himself upon his wife's newly-made grave in an agony of grief before leaving the scenes of his own past selfish dulness, might have been written by either of these two accomplished painters of the real life of man. This thorough reality is, in truth, the characteristic of them both, and the difference of their novels is nothing but the result of the difference of the ways in which they have looked upon the life around them. In 'George Eliot' it is impossible not to recognise one who feels intensely the mystery of existence, and who, while capable of an exquisite relish for the ludicrous, wherever it presents itself, is at the same time filled with a profound sympathy for every fellow-creature who is struggling onwards through the battle of existence and gazing intently at every glimpse of the unseen. Hence the essentially tragic character of her stories, and the brilliant distinctness with which her men and women stand out almost alive from her canvas. Mrs Gaskell's thoughts, on the other hand, are ever with rich and poor alike, as they pass the routine of ordinary ways, chequered with sunshine and sorrows, not tortured with any unsolved problems of weal or woe, but satisfied to sustain and brighten life with the gentle resources that are at hand to every one who will use them. In both, however, there is the same thorough genuineness and reality both of thought and feeling; in both, everything has been studied from real nature, and nothing from novel-nature. The one fills the reader with thought and sadness, and is intense even in her merriment. The other awakens tranquil sympathies, and reminds one that it is really possible to enjoy the absurdities of one's fellow-creatures without a particle of ill-will. But both alike force upon us the unpleasant reflection that, with all our host of novel-writers, those who can understand and describe humanity as it is, with a due regard to the nature of all true art, are few indeed.

Throughout the twentiety century there has been a steady increase in interest in Gaskell and her work. Around the centenary of her death in 1965, a number of studies were published, while in 1966 *The Letters of Mrs Gaskell*, edited by J. A. V. Chapple and Arthur Pollard, provided fresh insights into the novelist both in her domestic and in her professional capacities. In his own book, *Mrs Gaskell: Novelist and Biographer* (1965), Pollard addresses various aspects of her art, and has this, among other things, to say of *Wives and Daughters* (pp. 226, 228–9):

Because everybody matters all the time, there are a number of lines of interest to be kept constantly in mind, interweaving with each other, forming new patterns, at times puzzling patterns, for the reader to contemplate. As they move towards, across and away from each other, first one line of interest, then another, appears most prominent. Mrs Gaskell is always aware of the way in which the lives of the members of any community impinge upon each other, but this awareness is nowhere else allied with the feeling of depth so fully as it is in *Wives and Daughters*. The lives of the characters are seen here not only to impinge upon, but to interpenetrate, each other.

It has been remarked that Mrs Gaskell here makes a rare incursion into the life of the aristocracy; and descending in the social scale she includes the squire, the professional man, the impoverished but genteel spinsters, and even at one stage briefly enters the labourer's cottage. Hollingford is Knutsford yet again – after Cranford, Duncombe ('Mr Harrison's Confessions'), Barford ('The Squire's Story'), Hamley ('A Dark Night's Work') and Eltham ('Cousin Phillis'). As elsewhere, the day-to-day activities of the little town assume the inflated importance that such events do in such places, but now they are used much more to reveal character than they had been in earlier works.

Nothing much happens. We are not to look for the spectacular in *Wives and Daughters*, but this is not to say that there are no large, public scenes. The book may be said to begin with one, with the garden party for the Hollingford folk at Cumnor Towers, but even this occasion is strictly centred upon the young girl Molly and the fact that she is left behind by the Miss Brownings and falls into the hands of Clare. Much more various in its uses is another public scene, that of the charity ball (chapter XXVI), in which Mrs Gaskell, first of all, conveys the sense of public excitement, not without plenty of humour. The old maids 'aired their old lace and their best dresses' (p. 268); and, as the townspeople wait for the coming of the county-magnates and their parties, 'the aristocratic ozone being absent from the atmosphere, there [is] a flatness about the dancing of all those who considered themselves above the plebeian ranks of the tradespeople' (p. 273). The 'plebeians' wait for the coming of the Duchess of Menteith wearing her famous diamonds:

> In came Lord Cumnor with a fat, middle-aged woman on his arm; she was dressed almost like a girl – in a sprigged muslin, with natural flowers in her hair, but not a vestige of a jewel or a diamond. Yet it must be the duchess; but what was a duchess without diamonds? (p. 277).

But besides the comedy there are the serious implications in the reactions of the other characters – Mrs Gibson's dislike, for example, of Cynthia's dancing with people she considers inferior and her anxiety lest by this Cynthia should miss the opportunity of dancing with the young men staying at the Towers – 'and who could tell to what a dance might lead?' (p. 273); or Preston's anger at Cynthia's disregard of his request for the first dance after nine o'clock. Lesser characters also have their distinctive role – Lady Harriet, often more candid than gracious, but now aware, with an election in the offing, of the need to notice the burgesses; or, almost at the other social extreme, the crabbed Mrs Goodenough uttering her disappointment in the occasion. Even in minor respects such as this Mrs Gaskell shows us the encounter of convention and individuality, responsibility and inclination.

J. G. Sharps's *Mrs Gaskell's Observation and Invention* (Arundel: Linden Press, 1970) is the most comprehensive introduction to Gaskell: it is a source book for scholars and general readers, and it is doubtful whether it will ever be superseded. Here he focuses on Mr Gibson and his historical, professional placing (pp. 483–5):

> In Mr Gibson Mrs Gaskell's earlier fictional doctors find their consummation. His origins almost certainly go back to the author's girlhood, when she accompanied the Knutsford surgeon on his daily rounds. Although Meta Gaskell averred 'No two people could be more unlike than Dr Gibson and Mr Holland', most scholars refer to the writer's uncle as the main source for all her medical men. The historian of the Hollands, for instance, remarks that Knutsford was 'the model of the town in her novels, *Cranford*, and *Wives and Daughters*, and [that] her uncle, Dr Peter Holland, and his family can be recognised among the characters in her stories.' We have mentioned that Mrs Gaskell had other relatives in the profession – for example, her cousin (Henry Holland) and her brother-in-law (Sam Gaskell) – ; but, since *Wives and Daughters* patently looks back to the time of her girlhood, her youthful observations of Peter Holland's practices may reasonably be supposed of greatest importance. Nevertheless it should not be forgotten that in later life Mrs Gaskell used to stay with the Miss Hollands (whose father did not die till 1855): nor that, according to Lady Ritchie, Knutsford people spoke '*of her long country drives with an old friend, a doctor, going his rounds, twenty and thirty miles at a time; of her talk and interest in all the details along the way.*'
>
> Mr Gibson's professional relations with the Cumnors are nicely contrasted with those of his predecessor. Mr Hall was 'received with

friendly condescension'; and he took his meals 'in the housekeeper's room, not *with* the housekeeper, *bien entendu*.' On privileged occasions he was admitted to the ceremony of dinner, there to meet some distinguished medical man who was advising at the Towers (it sounded well to mention such visits to the neighbouring squires). Mr Gibson, on the other hand, having a Scottish accent not a provincial one and possessing a dignified bearing, found a readier access to Cumnor dinners, though he regarded them as professional duties rather than as pleasurable events. This aristocratic recognition of Mr Gibson as a man as well as a surgeon apparently paid handsome dividends as far as his general practice was concerned; hence a low rate of payment seemed justified, it being supplemented by the prestige of attending at the Towers. If the countess took a (slightly unfair) pecuniary advantage from her position with regard to Mr Gibson, his second wife rather enjoyed being made use of – as her ladyship's agent in carrying out small commissions. These, involving as they did bills for flys and cars, scarcely pleased her husband; yet he found the subsequent presents of game no less distasteful, albeit for a different reason.

With the Hamleys Mr Gibson was socially more at ease. Except for the scientific Lord Hollingford, the squire was the man to whom he took most kindly; but there was still that difference in rank which prevented Squire Hamley from viewing with favour any connexion by marriage with the local surgeon.

Mrs Gaskell astutely suggests the cultural isolation to which men like Mr Gibson were prone. If he remarried, he would hardly favour a bride from a farming family, a woman without refinement or education; nor could he, a mere country practitioner, presume to court a squire's daughter. He was little better off in male company; for 'there was no one equal to himself among the men with whom he associated, and this he had felt as a depressing influence, although he never recognised the cause of his depression.' Such isolation made a visit from Mr Kirkpatrick, Q.C., very welcome: from the outset the attraction was mutual.

In her *Elizabeth Gaskell* (Oxford, 1976), Winfred Gérin establishes the connections between Gaskell's own life and her creative conceptions (pp. 280–1):

George Smith had evidently told Mrs Gaskell of a suitable house for sale at East Grinstead which she now deplored not having snatched-up in time. 'Oh! What a fool I was to let the East Grinstead house slip through my fingers!' she cried. From that first mention of her secret purpose in December 1864, throughout the writing of *Wives and Daughters* the following year, the thought never far absent from her mind was the acquisition of the impossible house.

Her great and increasing physical fatigue, and low health and spirits in winter, were reason enough for wishing to live in more congenial surroundings than Manchester, but there may also at this time have entered into her feelings a more positive need, revived by the writing of *Cousin Phillis* and the renewed contacts with Knutsford – a home sickness for the life of the countryside and the pleasant ways she had known in her girlhood. *Wives and Daughters* may in this context be thought of as an escapist novel, a kind of sequel to *Cousin Phillis* in exploring the fuller potential of the theme of rural life, after which Mrs Gaskell was thirsting as after a lost Arcadia.

There is such a sense of pleasure apparent in all her descriptions of the fields and lanes and copses and hedges of Hollingford; such amusement felt in the exchanges of the Miss Brownings and the mischief-making Mrs Goodenough, speaking an English that was antiquated in Queen Anne's day; such zest in the memories of the uncouth medical students eating their huge helpings of pudding; such relish in the doctor's cool and cutting snubs at their expense; such enjoyment of the numberless subterfuges the gossips resorted to in extracting a kernel of slander from an item of news. There is excitement to be found in the daily pageant of life in the principal street, at the draper's, and the library, by leaning out of windows to see what is afoot, by chance encounters, and by observing the carriages, gigs, and country carts as they occasionally stop for an exchange of greetings. One comes to know the inhabitants of Hollingford quite intimately, and over the whole scene, Mrs Gaskell casts a magic golden light. This is not to say that she was not acutely aware of the limitations and follies of such a way of life, and of the ridicule it must provoke. The irony does not escape her but it is muted by her memories and by the essential good nature of the people she describes. There is no real malice, nor wickedness. Mr Preston is a cad, but he is genuinely in love with Cynthia and motivated not by greed but passion.

The residents of Hollingford are more fully realized than their predecessors in Cranford. *Cranford* is the reflection of the world she left on quitting Knutsford to get married; Hollingford is the place of her return, seen with more penetrating eyes, its busy hum heard with more acute ears, and above all absorbed by a mind matured by experience. *Wives and Daughters* is, of course, something more than a panegyric of country life. It is a long-term view, one might almost say a valedictory view, of the author's life and of life in general, particularly as it affected women in relation to every phase of family commitment, as daughter, sister, wife, mother.

It was a subject of topical and absorbing interest to her at the time, as has already been noted, with her daughters passing from girlhood into young womanhood, developing their individual characters and abilities, going their several ways, falling in love, marrying, realizing the potential within themselves. What Mrs Gaskell hoped for them is the measure of the fulfilment she had hoped for herself. It is noteworthy that, while she secured her daughters the best education possible at the time to develop what talents they had – whether for music or painting – in order to promote their own pleasure in life and make intelligent companions of them for their future husbands, she never at any time contemplated careers for them, and by her own hard work and earnings ensured that they did not have to work for a living.

Gaskell's historical certainties and her cultural derivations are admirably conveyed in Angus Easson's *Elizabeth Gaskell* (London: Routledge & Kegan Paul, 1979) (pp. 187–8):

Hollingford is generally held to be another re-creation of the Knutsford of Gaskell's childhood, apparently confirmed by 'Chesterford', its original name in the manuscript, soon disguised as Hollyford, and then fixed as Hollingford. A closer look suggests (in the latter part, at least) that this is rather the Midlands of Warwickshire and schooldays in Stratford – two miles outside Hollingford, Molly can see 'the blue range of the Malverns', while Aimée, travelling to find her husband, takes the Birmingham coach from London. Warwickshire words ('scomfished', 'unked') may further suggest the setting. If establishing the exact location may seem unimportant, this physical separation of Knutsford and Hollingford serves to stress that Gaskell is not evoking, however skilfully, a single place she knows, but is creating time and place, even if at the back of it there may be experience and reminiscences of her own. To use scenes and even a period of time which she has lived through may help her to see and so create, but Hollingford is not Knutsford and Molly Gibson is not the young Elizabeth Stevenson.

The period of the novel is that of Gaskell's youth, certainly; it is set before 'the passing of the Reform Bill' of 1832. There is a fairly easily calculable chronology, from about 1822 when the story opens and Molly is twelve, while the main action, beginning about 1826, occupies just over two years. This sequence is disturbed by Osborne's son, according to his birth-certificate, being born in 183– and nearly two years old at this time. But this is a minor blemish (the age is right for the overall scheme) in the general control of the action. Molly was born roughly in the same year (1810) as Gaskell, so no doubt memory serves in establishing a sense of period through hints, allusions and commentary – we are in the years before Catholic Emancipation (1829) began to be talked of, though Byron is dead (1824). The period setting is not far from the world of George Eliot's *Felix Holt* (1866) and *Middlemarch* (1871–2), both placed about the time of the 1832 Reform Act, and overlaps in part with that of *Vanity Fair* (1848), which runs from about 1813 to 1840. Gaskell, however, is not here concerned with the dynamics of history, though like Thackeray and Eliot she is aware of a world removed from her own in customs and costumes. Other references remind us of our own new age, since we are reading of days before railways, before Muscular Christianity, when memories are still fresh of the French Revolution and the Regency crisis, while real figures such as Sir Astley Cooper the surgeon and the biologist Geoffroi-St Hilaire appear briefly. Eliot offers a quasi-scientific analysis of the pressure of circumstance upon individuals; Thackeray, the portrayal of manners. Gaskell differs from both, since her past, of which she insistently makes us aware, has two functions: to allow the action to be completed and contemplated from the satisfaction of distance which shows the whole; and to take advantage of sympathies for an age which while past hovers yet in the memory of many readers and so charges events with our own feelings for childhood and youth.

The culture that was Gaskell's, the accumulation of a lifetime, is fully in evidence, even though often in no more than muttered fragments or faint whispers, so that the novel is often an echoing grove. She was confident enough to write quotations from memory, so that James Shirley's 'Only the actions of the just/Smell sweet and blossom in the dust' came as 'The sainted memory of the just/Smells sweet and blossoms in the dust' before being corrected in proof. Yet clearly she possessed Shirley's verses, as she possessed Shakespeare ('smiling at grief' or Lady Cumnor looking like Lady Macbeth in black velvet), calling up such things at will from the store; falling into half-quotations (as she sometimes indicates an intensification of language by enclosing it in inverted commas to give it the status of quotation) and this mosaic colours the work. If Lady Cumnor and Lady Macbeth are no more than momentarily alike, yet a childhood song, long before copied out into one of those manuscript music books, will come at need and sound ironically as Cynthia sings 'Tu t'en repentiras, Colin ... si tu prends une femme', 'such a pretty, playful little warning to young men', as Mrs Gibson calls it, blissfully unaware that the listening Osborne is already married and to a French girl.

Patsy Stoneman's *Elizabeth Gaskell* (Brighton: Harvester Press, 1987) contains some fine analysis which involves gender, behaviour and speech (pp. 196–7):

> Over-rigorous propriety, on the other hand, requires a 'lying' refusal of attention even where care exists. Molly, brought up as a companion to her father, regulates her friendship with Roger by habits of care and attention in which gender is irrelevant. Her dealings with Mr Preston are also so entirely formulated by the matter in hand that she 'was as unconscious that he was a young man, and she a young woman, as if she had been a pure angel of heaven'. But before her final visit to Roger at Hamley Hall (Ch. 59), Mrs Goodenough's hints force on her a shameful consciousness which spoils 'the simplicity of their intercourse' and prevents her from treating Roger with more than 'common politeness'. Her 'constraint' and 'reserve' prevent her even from seeking his advice; 'she believed that he could have helped her more than anyone to understand how she ought to behave ... if only he himself had not lain at the very core and centre of all her perplexity and dismay'. Thus 'propriety' shuts her out from moral advice, just as 'surveillance' prevents Cynthia from disentangling herself from Mr Preston. Roger in turn is 'perplexed and pained' by a withdrawal of attention which he interprets as an absence of care.
>
> The painstaking detail of the conversations in *Wives and Daughters* supports a general plea for the power of speech in establishing a more open and rational intercourse between the sexes, in which the arts of pleasing shall not masquerade as love, and propriety shall not exclude care. It is disappointing that Molly allows Roger to take the initiative in their final *éclaircissement*, which leaves her 'red as a rose'. Nevertheless his simple question and her direct reply suggest a potential for communication and trust which is a significant advance on the secrets and silence of their parents, and in this context the

novel's evasion of explicitly sexual consciousness is less of a fault than it might appear. Molly's 'innocence' is not the dangerous ignorance of Ruth, unable to distinguish Bellingham's 'attentions' from love, and her ability to affirm friendship for a man saves her from the crippling shame of Margaret Hale and Cousin Phillis. When the author makes a motherly little joke at her expense, as she waves goodbye to Roger and thinks 'how sweet is friendship!', her innocence seems an endearing aspect of her youth, but the refusal of sexual shame is also the basis of womanly strength.

Finally, Jenny Uglow's *Elizabeth Gaskell: A Habit of Stories* (London: Faber & Faber, 1993) is a comprehensive biographical and critical study which firmly evaluates its subject's claims to greatness: here is some consideration of the nature of the society Gaskell is describing in her final novel (pp. 586–7):

> *Wives and Daughters* is also, for instance, a study of the power-shifts in British society: of the rise of aggressive middlemen like Preston, the emergence of a scientifically led intelligentsia, the resurgence of the legal and financial establishment of the south. The industrial capitalists of the north, who dominated *Mary Barton* and *North and South*, are notably absent here, a recognition, perhaps, that by the 1860s economic power was again based firmly in the south. As in the 1820s aspiring eyes and empty purses looked not to Drumble but to London. And one could see the novel too as an interesting example of the limits of mid-Victorian thinking about race (even among committed abolitionists) in the patronizing stereotypes and music-hall jokes applied by Mr Gibson to the African peoples Roger encounters on his expedition.
>
> Gaskell is aware that the society she describes is founded upon exploitation and empire, but she depicts a world seen through the eyes of characters whose horizons are national and local. Within these horizons, and within their houses, she dramatizes their struggles for power and for control of the resources – material and emotional – on which their lives depend. Her deeper interest, however, is in an underlying battle of values, of self-interest and self-sacrifice.
>
> If we pick out a particular thread, that of money, we can see how it weaves into all the other strands, the psychological drama, the analysis of class, of the role of women, of altruism and egotism, truth and lies. Money had always been a force in Gaskell's novels, but *Wives and Daughters* could almost have been written on bank-notes (and in a way it was, for each sheet went to pay for the Lawn

and her own move south). Notes of all denominations flutter through these pages, tokens of paternal or husbandly provision. Even small sums are significant: the price of tea is a bond between the Misses Browning and Lady Harriet. The stakes at *vingt-et-un* cause much debate – should they be 3d or 6d? Molly has no turn for gambling: Cynthia stakes high and is 'at one time very rich', but ends in debt to Molly, claiming to have forgotten her purse.

The coinage has more than face value. Molly does not care if she wins at cards: she is wretched because Cynthia has 'won' Roger's attention. Cynthia cannot pay because she is saving to buy off Preston. (Eventually she repays him with interest, carefully calculated at five per cent.) Everything that matters most has a price: Cynthia's beauty, Osborne's love poems, Squire Hamley's beloved trees and the drainage works which represent his emotional investment in his land. Land is entailed, lives are insured; we are at the start of an actuarial age. The competing moralities here are neatly represented by Mrs Gibson and her husband. What is the point, she says, of visiting a patient who is dying anyway: 'Does he expect a legacy, or anything of that kind?' Mr Gibson, on the other hand, may joke to his apprentices about the motto 'kill or cure' that it would not do to 'make away with profitable patients' who pay two-and-sixpence a visit. 'But you go every morning, sir, before breakfast,' says the puzzled Mr Wynne, 'to see old Nancy Grant, and you've ordered her this medicine, sir, which is about the most costly in Corbyn's bill?'

This conflict of self-interest and altruism in relation to money finds a different expression in the contrast between Mrs Gibson and Mrs Hamley, where it forms part of a critique of the role and expectations of women. Before she marries, when she is staying at the Towers, Clare admires a muslin-dressed looking-glass (a perfect image), and laments that for a schoolteacher this highly desirable object is so hard to maintain:

> 'Now here, money is like the air they breathe. No one even asks or knows how much the washing costs, or what pink ribbon is a yard. Ah! it would be different if they had to earn every penny as I have! They would have to calculate, like me, how to get the most pleasure out of it. I wonder if I am to go on all my life toiling and moiling for money? It's not natural. Marriage is the natural thing; then the husband has all that kind of dirty work to do, and his wife sits in the drawing-room like a lady.' (Ch. 9)

Even so marriage does not stop her counting and calculating (or, more often, miscalculating).

Biography and Criticism

Elizabeth Gaskell has been the subject of scholarly and critical interest in some depth since the centenary of her death in 1965. The following is a selection which reflects that interest, with brief evaluative comments, together with one or two earlier studies which have some importance for the general reader.

George F. Payne, *Mrs Gaskell and Knutsford* (Manchester: Clarkson & Griffiths, 1905). Locations, history and other identifications. Interesting photographs.

A. Stanton Whitfield, *Mrs Gaskell: Her Life and Work* (London: Routledge, 1929). Somewhat diffuse, but with useful insights.

A. B. Hopkins, *Elizabeth Gaskell: Her Life and Work* (London: John Lehmann, 1952). Intelligent appraisal before the positive interest picked up pace; well researched and documented.

J. G. Sharps, *Mrs Gaskell's Observation and Invention: A Study of Her Non-Biographic Works* (Arundell: Linden Press, 1970). A must for the Gaskell enthusiast. Introductions to each of the works, with biographical and critical information, meticulously researched: a mass of detail which makes it the complete companion to Gaskell studies.

Arthur Pollard, *Mrs Gaskell: Novelist and Biographer* (Manchester: Manchester University Press, 1965). Good general evaluation.

Angus Easson, *Elizabeth Gaskell* (London: Routledge & Kegan Paul, 1979). Wide-ranging critical investigation, particularly good on the shorter works and on *Wives and Daughters*.

Patsy Stoneman, *Elizabeth Gaskell*, (Brighton: Key Woman Writers Series, Harvester Press, 1987). Provocative and stimulating feminist investigation.

Jenny Uglow, *Elizabeth Gaskell: A Habit of Stories* (London: Faber & Faber, 1993). The fullest life and most complete critical evaluation to date.

Angus Easson (ed.), *Elizabeth Gaskell: The Critical Heritage* (London:

Routledge, 1991). A selection of contemporary reviews and opinions, but also a very useful extension of these in the form of further comments up to 1910.

Letters

J. A. V. Chapple and A. Pollard (eds), *The Letters of Mrs Gaskell* (Manchester: Manchester University Press, 1966). The best possible introduction to the author, showing her primarily in her domestic situation with her family worries and concerns, but also revealing her in positive relation to her writings.

J. A. V. Chapple and J. G. Sharps (eds), *Elizabeth Gaskell: A Portrait in Letters* (Manchester: Manchester University Press, 1980). As above; stimulating, delightful.

The Gaskell Society (founded 1985) holds conferences, produces a *Newsletter* and the *Gaskell Society Journal*, and is a friendly and active organization which promotes the writer and her background.

TEXT SUMMARY

Note: the number printed in brackets before a chapter number refers to the part (monthly) publication of the novel in the *Cornhill Magazine* (August 1864–January 1866).

(I) Chapter I: The Dawn of a Gala Day
Introducing Molly Gibson – her excitement at the prospect of going to Cumnor Towers – how she came to be invited – the Cumnors – the presence of 'Clare' – the Misses Browning – the preparations for the visit.

Chapter 2: A Novice amongst the Great Folk
The journey to the Towers – description there – Molly overheated – falls asleep in park – Clare brings her food and wine – she hardly touches it – rests – misses the carriage – upset at prospect of not going home – Mr Gibson arrives to collect her – Molly's devotion to him.

Chapter 3: Molly Gibson's Childhood
Retrospect on Mr Gibson's coming to Hollingford – his marriage – death of his wife – Molly's love for him – the 'apprentices' – Miss Eyre and Betty – their roles in Molly's upbringing.

(II) Chapter 4: Mr Gibson's Neighbours
Lord Hollingford – scientific interests – Mr Gibson's interests too – his relations with the vicar – Squire Hamley and family – focus on Mr Coxe and Mr Wynne.

Chapter 5: Calf-Love
Mr Gibson intercepts Coxe's love-letter to Molly – responds with a witty if cruel reply – interviews Coxe – dismisses Bethia – arranges for Molly to stay with the Hamleys – Molly resistant.

Chapter 6: A Visit to the Hamleys
Molly does not wish to leave her father – she is kindly received by Mrs Hamley – responds, learns much of the sons, particularly Osborne – Squire Hamley unthinkingly reveals that Mr Gibson was expected to

marry again after his wife's death – Molly broods – further detail on Osborne's prospects.

(III) *Chapter 7: Foreshadows of Love Perils*
Mr Gibson's domestic problems – Miss Eyre goes – he decides to request that Molly stays on with the Hamleys – they agree, though Squire Hamley feels she would be a temptation to his sons – Osborne's return is conveniently delayed.

Chapter 8: Drifting into Danger
News of Osborne's poor examination result – Molly initially blames Roger for bringing the bad news – meanwhile Mr Gibson 'drifts' towards Mrs Kirkpatrick – the latter invited to the Towers – first mention of Lord Cumnor's land-agent, Preston.

Chapter 9: The Widower and the Widow
Mrs Kirkpatrick at the Towers – Lady Cumnor sends for Mr Gibson – Lord Hollingford asks Mr Gibson if he has thought of remarrying – Mr Gibson sees Mrs Kirkpatrick – the latter comes across a sentence when she is reading Lord Cumnor's letter aloud to Lady Cumnor which suggests the possibility of Mr Gibson marrying her.

(IV) *Chapter 10: A Crisis*
Mr Gibson proposes – Lady Cumnor reveals Lord Cumnor's innuendo – Mr Gibson goes to Hamley to tell Molly – the latter is stricken – Roger's kindness to her – Mrs Hamley too – Molly gets an invitation to the Towers.

Chapter 11: Making Friendship
Mrs Kirkpatrick intent on quick marriage – self-interestedly pleasant to Molly – the latter inquisitive about Cynthia – Molly introduced to Lady Cumnor – stands up to her – Molly suffering because she feels her father does not want her at home – Roger again kind to her.

(V) *Chapter 12: Preparing for the Wedding*
Mrs Kirkpatrick still intent on early marriage – Mr Gibson's generosity to her – confides to the Misses Browning his fears for Molly – tells them of his coming marriage – they are put out that Molly is to go to the Hamleys.

Chapter 13: Molly Gibson's New Friends
Roger misses Molly when she is away – she visits the Misses Browning – anger between her and the elder sister – Mrs Kirkpatrick shows

Molly the home improvements – she and her father stay at Preston's the night before the wedding – Preston reveals that he knows Cynthia.

Chapter 14: Molly Finds Herself Patronised
The wedding – Molly and Lady Harriet – the latter's dislike of Preston – Molly visited by Roger – invited again to Hamley – the arrival of Osborne – Lady Harriet visits the Misses Browning.

(VI) Chapter 15: The New Mamma
Molly back home – welcomes her father and stepmother – Molly waits up for her father after his visit to a patient – Betty to be replaced, cook leaves, domestic autocracy of Mrs Gibson – Mr Coxe departs.

Chapter 16: The Bride at Home
Roger and Osborne call on Mrs Gibson – Molly and Roger continue friends – Mrs Gibson jealous of Lady Harriet's attention to Molly and the Misses Browning – Squire Hamley comes to get Molly – Osborne has failed to secure a Fellowship – Mrs Gibson holds on to Molly, angers the Squire – Molly resistant, rebellious.

Chapter 17: Trouble at Hamley Hall
Molly arrives at Hamley – Mrs Hamley obviously ill – disappointment over Osborne – his debts – Molly a comfort – anxiety of the Squire – Mr Gibson examines Mrs Hamley – Roger and Osborne to return home – Molly leaves – another disagreement with Mrs Gibson.

(VII) Chapter 18: Mr Osborne's Secret
Decline of Mrs Hamley – Roger upset, Osborne still absent – Molly in attendance – Mr Gibson's compassion – arrival of Osborne – the Squire's irritation with him – Molly inadvertently learns that Osborne is secretly married.

Chapter 19: Cynthia's Arrival
Molly goes home – Cynthia – beautiful, takes to Molly – news of Mrs Hamley's death – Molly greatly upset – Cynthia reveals her incapacity to 'care much for anyone', edgy about mention of Preston – Molly yearning for the Hamleys.

Chapter 20: Mrs Gibson's Visitors
Preston calls – enquires after Cynthia – she arrives – Preston reveals that Roger Hamley is a Senior Wrangler – asserts that the Squire has mismanaged the Hamley estate – Cynthia in opposition to Preston – later Osborne calls – Mrs Gibson much impressed – begins matchmaking.

(VIII) *Chapter 21: The Half-Sisters*
Molly pondering on Osborne's secret – her interest in Roger – the
Easter ball – Roger meets Cynthia – is very taken with her – still kind
to Molly – post-ball conversation – Mrs Gibson put out by mention of
Preston – Roger confides to Molly his feelings for Cynthia.

Chapter 22: The Old Squire's Troubles
The Squire's suffering – his confrontation with Osborne – they are
beset by debts – the family atmosphere penetrates to the servants.

Chapter 23: Osborne Hamley Reviews His Position
Osborne broods on his needs – his poems about Aimée – his father's
dislike of the French – Osborne asks Roger to help him get the poems
published – Roger talks to their father – a relief for them both.

(IX) *Chapter 24: Mrs Gibson's Little Dinner*
The dinner party – Mrs Gibson's favouring Osborne – her unknowing
blunders *re* Osborne's secret – Molly's playing – the interactions of the
evening.

Chapter 25: Hollingford in a Bustle
The preparations for the charity ball – Cynthia resistant to their having
Preston as a guest – Lady Harriet's visit – Mrs Gibson goes to the
Towers – does not enjoy it but says that she has on her return – flowers
arrive for Cynthia from Preston – he sends her a note with them – her
resentment and Molly's on her behalf.

Chapter 26: A Charity Ball
Cynthia admired – gossip at the ball – the dancing – Preston's black
mood – Mrs Gibson's snobbery – Preston talks to Molly – the party
from the Towers arrives very late – Lady Harriet seeks out Molly –
meets Mrs Goodenough – Cynthia and Preston in strained interaction
– Molly learns of Lord Hollingford's respect for Roger – after the ball
Cynthia is abstracted.

(X) *Chapter 27: Father and Sons*
Hollingford calls at Hamley to see Roger – misses him but leaves
message inviting him to meet a French scientist – the Squire objects –
Roger decides not to go – retrospect on Aimée – the Squire urges Roger
to keep his appointment at the Towers.

Chapter 28: Rivalry
Mrs Gibson with Osborne, who missed the ball – much on the flowers,
Preston's nosegay – Mrs Gibson suggests a picnic in the woods – hopes

Osborne will take to Cynthia – meanwhile Roger obviously loves her –
she is languid – Roger concerned – that concern oppresses Molly
somewhat – Cynthia improves – Roger visits, Mrs Gibson snubs him –
Molly sensitive on his account – warms to Cynthia for her rejection of
her mother's insensitivity.

Chapter 29: Bush-Fighting
Osborne's appraisal of Molly's prettiness – Mr Gibson's domestic
clear-sightedness – he meets Osborne, suspects illness, invites him to
lunch – Cynthia and Molly in interaction with him – mention of
Preston – he is to succeed Sheepshanks as land-agent – Cynthia
obviously upset by this – Osborne reveals that Rober too has returned
– Osborne is invited by Mrs Gibson, who pets him.

(XI) Chapter 30: Old Ways and New Ways
Preston settles in – encounter with the Squire – the row – infringement
of boundaries – Roger calm and dignified – the Squire enraged – but
goes back to see his dying tenant.

Chapter 31: A Passive Coquette
Preston's reaction of disgust against the Squire and Roger – the change
from life with Sheepshanks – sociability of Preston – his pursuit of
Cynthia – the latter always the centre of Roger's feelings too – Roger
raises money for his father – the Squire still determinedly anti-French.

Chapter 32: Coming Events
News of Osborne's child – details of his marriage – Roger bent on
getting money – goes to London – meanwhile Lady Harriet visits Mrs
Gibson – the latter makes sure Molly is not at home – Lady Harriet
reveals the legacy to Lord Hollingford and that the latter intends to
approach Roger *re* a scientific voyage – Mr Gibson delighted by news
– Molly aware that she will miss Roger.

(XII) Chapter 33: Brightening Prospects
Mr Gibson rides to Hamley – Squire proud of Roger – gives Mr Gibson
details – Roger raises money on life insurance – some feeling between
them over Osborne and his motives – Roger's preparations to go.

Chapter 34: A Lover's Mistake
Molly returns from her walk – Roger is with Cynthia – Molly goes to
her room – when she goes downstairs she learns that Roger and
Cynthia are engaged – it must remain a secret – Roger says goodbye –
brotherly to Molly – the latter suffers – her interaction with Cynthia
does not convince her that Cynthia loves Roger.

Chapter 35: The Mother's Manoeuvre

Mr Gibson is told of the engagement – Mrs Gibson reveals that she has eavesdropped over Osborne's health – Mr Gibson is furious – the domestic row follows – Mr Gibson realizes his impotence against his wife's insensitivity – Cynthia tells him of the secrecy of her engagement – Mr Gibson tells the Squire – he is angry in his turn – he comes round somewhat and wishes to meet Cynthia.

Chapter 36: Domestic Diplomacy

Mr Gibson gives news of the Squire's invitation – further domestic argument – Mrs Gibson eventually decides to go – Molly later gives her father an account of the visit – he questions her about Osborne – she relieves his anxiety.

(XIII) Chapter 37: A Fluke, and What Came of It

The return of Mr Coxe – he switches his love to the fascinating Cynthia – is rejected – Cynthia confesses that she cannot help flirting – confides in Molly that she may never marry Roger – Molly is upset – Cynthia wants to escape from Preston – meanwhile the domestic compromise of the Gibsons is apparent – Molly's health declines – news of Roger having fever – Molly prays for him – Cynthia little concerned.

Chapter 38: Mr Kirkpatrick, Q.C.

Molly ponders Cynthia's dislike of Preston – visit of Mr Kirkpatrick – gossip about this – brief history of Mr Kirkpatrick – he is very taken with Cynthia – invites her to visit his family in London – Mrs Gibson affronted at not being invited herself – Cynthia worried about money – Mr Gibson gives her a present of some so that she can go.

Chapter 39: Secret Thoughts Ooze Out

Cynthia decides to go – talk about Osborne looking ill – Cynthia sends the Squire notes – Squire does not like Mrs Gibson – tells Osborne of Roger's attachment – Osborne asserts his independence – goes to see Cynthia – she resents the breaking of her secret again – Mrs Gibson angling to go to London.

Chapter 40: Molly Gibson Breathes Freely

Cynthia nearly confides in Molly – the latter delighted that Mrs Gibson is to go – feels it is like old times with her father – the Misses Browning gossip to Molly about Preston – later they come to believe that Molly is in love with him.

(XIV) *Chapter 41: Gathering Clouds*

Mrs Gibson's news from London – Molly in doubt that Cynthia loves Roger – Cynthia returns from London – not interested in Roger's work in Africa – the Misses Browning hint to Mrs Gibson of Molly's involvement – Molly and Mrs Gibson argue – Cynthia comes to take Molly's part – tells Molly later not to mention her in connection with Preston.

Chapter 42: The Storm Bursts

Molly goes for a drive with her father – walks back home – sees Preston and Cynthia holding hands – Cynthia begs her to come to her – Preston claims that Cynthia promised to marry him – Cynthia hysterical – considers herself not engaged to Preston or to Roger – but admits she gave Preston her promise when she was very young – she owes him £20, which he will not take – he leaves, Molly is quiet – at night, Molly goes to Cynthia.

Chapter 43: Cynthia's Confession

Cynthia confides – the story as above – her promising that she will marry Preston when she is 20 – the money he loaned her – Mrs Gibson also involved with Preston – Cynthia has written Preston love-letters – criticized her mother in them – Molly determines to get the letters and to make Preston take the money.

Chapter 44: Molly Gibson to the Rescue

A visit from the ailing Helen Kirkpatrick is mooted – the meeting between Molly and Preston is planned – they argue when they meet – Preston wants to know to whom Cynthia is engaged – Molly refuses to tell him – threatens to tell Lady Harriet – they are interrupted by Mr Sheepshanks – Molly returns to Cynthia.

Chapter 45: Confidences

Cynthia again invited to the Kirkpatricks – Molly reads Roger's letter to Cynthia – the latter gets her letters returned from Preston – Molly left with her stepmother – learns of Mr Henderson's attentions to Cynthia – Molly alone when a very ill Osborne calls – he confides in her about Aimée and the child.

(XV) *Chapter 46: Hollingford Gossips*

Miss Phoebe Browning appears – Osborne leaves – Molly prepares to go out with Miss Phoebe – takes Cynthia's note to give to Preston – he is conveniently in the bookshop when they enter – Molly is seen by Mrs Goodenough giving him the letter – the latter spreads the news –

other sightings of the pair are repeated – Mrs Goodenough defends Molly.

Chapter 47: Scandal and Its Victims
Mr Gibson goes to see Osborne – letters from London – gossip about Molly and Preston in Hollingford – the Misses Browning talk of Molly – Miss Browning determines to act – goes to see Mrs Dawes – hears her account – tells Mr Gibson when he calls on them – he is greatly disturbed but naturally will ask Molly about it.

Chapter 48: An Innocent Culprit
Mr Gibson taxes Molly over Preston – Molly, aware of Cynthia's secret, asserts her own integrity – Mr Gibson recurs to the rumours – he trusts Molly though – Mrs Gibson continues to speculate about Mr Henderson.

Chapter 49: Molly Gibson Finds a Champion
Lord Cumnor reports the rumour *re* Molly and Preston – Lady Harriet rightly suspects that Cynthia is more likely to be involved – calls on the Misses Browning – rightly deduces the real situation – has complete faith in Molly – Lady Harriet demands the truth from Preston – he concedes it, despite his humiliation.

Chapter 50: Cynthia at Bay
Mrs Gibson recovers from 'flu – Cynthia reveals that she has refused Mr Henderson – Mrs Gibson appalled – she visits the Towers – Lady Cumnor reveals the Preston affair – Mrs Gibson defensive – Lady Harriet faces her with the truth *re* Cynthia – Mrs Gibson taxes Cynthia on her return – Mr Gibson likewise talks to Cynthia – the latter greatly upset, injured by his tone – Cynthia shuts Molly out.

(XVI) Chapter 51: 'Troubles Never Come Alone'
Cynthia says all is over between herself and Roger – sticks to her position – dramatic news of Osborne's death – Molly insists on going to the Squire – the uncontrollable grief of the Squire – Mr Gibson's compassion and control.

Chapter 52: Squire Hamley's Sorrow
Molly questions her father about Osborne's illness – tells him of the marriage – the Squire breaks down – Molly tells him of Osborne's wife – the Squire longs for Molly to stay and for Roger – he does not know that Cynthia has given up Roger – her letter is as yet unopened – Molly returns to Hamley.

Chapter 53: *Unlooked-for Arrivals*
Molly helps and comforts the Squire – Mr Gibson tells Molly that Aimée must be told of Osborne's death – the letter is written – Aimée is already on her way – arrives, collapses – the Squire feeds the child – Molly worried about Aimée.

Chapter 54: *Molly Gibson's Worth Is Discovered*
Mr Gibson gives Aimée and the child his attention – insists that Molly goes to bed – Cynthia once more on a visit to the Kirkpatricks – Molly herself begins to feel ill – her father takes her home – Lady Harriet writes to Cynthia to tell her the real state of affairs – Cynthia comes home – Molly begins to improve – the Squire visits her regularly.

(XVII) *Chapter 55: An Absent Lover Returns*
The return of Roger – Molly anxious for news of him – Roger putting things to rights – still upset over Cynthia – he visits Molly – is his usual kind self – reveals that Aimée is still weak – Cynthia returns – Molly urges her to see Roger.

Chapter 56: *'Off with the Old Love, and on with the New'*
Mr Henderson to pay a visit – Mrs Gibson delighted – Roger rides over – hears voices – asks Molly about Mr Henderson – leaves before seeing Cynthia – the latter has accepted Mr Henderson on her own terms – the marriage to take place in London – further recognition of Roger's achievements.

Chapter 57: *Bridal Visits and Adieux*
Lady Cumnor visits – further mention of Roger's scientific distinction – his being invited to the Cumnors – Lady Harriet calls – Molly not well enough to go to Cynthia's wedding – Lady Harriet invites her to the Towers – farewell to Cynthia – Molly taken under the protection of Sir Charles.

Chapter 58: *Reviving Hopes and Brightening Prospects*
Molly sees Roger at the Towers – other guests are attracted to her – Roger finally gets to talk to her – reveals that the old Squire misses her – Roger gets over Cynthia's marriage – Molly goes home – has promised to visit Hamley – sees the Misses Browning and Mrs Goodenough – Mrs Gibson proud of Cynthia's marriage.

Chapter 59: *Molly Gibson at Hamley Hall*
Molly overhears Mrs Goodenough saying that Mrs Gibson is sending her to Hamley so that she may attract Roger – interaction between the Squire, Aimée and the boy – Molly fond of Aimée – the latter notices

her feelings for Roger – Roger explains that Cynthia's decision was all for the best – the Squire critical of Aimée – suggests to Roger that he might marry Molly – Molly beset by the Squire's wishes – completely reconciled to Roger.

(XVIII) *Chapter 60: Roger Hamley's Confession*

Roger's loving feelings – Molly tells Mrs Gibson of the Squire's love for his grandson – Mrs Gibson's snobbery – the boy has scarlet fever – Mr Gibson arranges for Aimée and the boy to take up residence near to the Squire – Roger confides in Mr Gibson about his feelings for Molly – the latter indicates his support for Roger – Roger takes his romantic farewell – interaction between Molly, her father and step-mother – ('*HERE the story is broken off*' – later, Roger and Molly are married – rounding-off – (*the rest is critical commentary*).